DATE DUE			
May 16 '77 R			

THE GRAND TRADITION

Seventy Years of Singing on Record

Elisabeth Schwarzkopf

J. B. STEANE

The Grand Tradition

Seventy Years of Singing on Record

CHARLES SCRIBNER'S SONS
NEW YORK

Contents

Part II DECLINE AND SURVIVAL
The Electrical 78 1925–1950

Part III RENAISSANCE
The Long-Playing Record 1950–1970

Acknowledgments for permission to reproduce photographs are due as follows:
Bayreuther Festspiele Bayreuth for no. 87; Chicago Lyric Opera for no. 131; Decca Records for nos. 85, 92, 120, 122, 123, 128, 133; EMI Records for nos. 89, 90, 104, 106, 108, 109, 113, 114, 117, 119, 125, 132, 134, 137; Harold Rosenthal Collection for nos. 37, 48, 91, 100, 107, 108, 131; Houston Rogers for nos. 88, 99; RCA Records for nos. 80, 112, 135, 136; Pathé Marconi for no. 129; San Francisco Light Works for no. 126; Stuart-Liff Collection for nos. 1–6, 8, 9, 11–35, 38, 39, 42–7, 49–70, 72–9, 81, 82, 86, 93–7, 101–3, 105, 111, 115, 116, 118, 121, 124, 127, 130, 138; Stuart-Liff Collection and Anthony Crickmay for no. 36; Toshiba Industries and Walter Legge for the Frontispiece.

To Edward Greenfield
and the memory of John Dodd

List of Illustrations

The roles of the singers have been identified wherever it was possible to do so with certainty.

Preface

SOME books are easier to write than to stop writing. In this instance, it has been hard at every stage to draw the line that says 'Thus far' when each month brings a glut of new reasons for never drawing it. Records are published in ever greater numbers, always (it seems) presenting the musical score with greater completeness than ever before; older singers produce their second or even third version of the opera or song-cycle most closely associated with their name; younger ones appear in a recording that for the first time shows their true worth, and thus upsets the chapter in which they had received a passing mention. Nor is the past a closed book. One might suppose that whatever is coming to light of some great singer long dead has now come, but a new collection of previously unpublished material is suddenly announced. One assumes that another great singer not dead but long retired has run his course as far as the gramophone is concerned; but no, an enterprising pirate has captured a pre-war broadcast, and of course it is said to be the singer's best work on record. There is nothing for it but to echo the beleaguered historian of the siege of Rhodes and cry 'Mon siège est fait'.

But time dictates its own terms. A few years ago this book could hardly have been attempted, for the material was not available, and in a few years' time it will again, in its present form, be unwritable. At present we can look back over nearly three-quarters of a century, and find that the survey divides naturally and aptly into three periods. But already the last period, the shortest in years, is the longest in pages. Very soon the output of long-playing records will be unmanageable and so enormous in relation to the first fifty years, that the period of 78s may seem a kind of pre-history. It will be unfortunate, I think, if this happens. An artist who has left no more than a dozen records on 78 may have as much to teach about singing as another who has recorded several miles of track on LP. And while the general standard of music-making has no doubt risen a great deal during the century, I do not believe that there are more singers of genius before us in the 1970s than there were forty years earlier, or seventy.

That we can survey these seventy years at all, or with anything like completeness, has only recently become possible. Before the days of LP, the rare records were to be found in a fair number of widely scattered collections. Some generous and enterprising collectors made re-pressings available in the later days of 78s, and the record companies themselves would sometimes start up a 'heritage' or 'archive' series. But the vast majority of old records would still be obtainable only on the second-hand dealers' lists, in short supply and often at prohibitive cost. Nowadays there are still some important gaps, but a large proportion of worthwhile material on 78s has found its way at one time or another on to LP. For the first time, it has become possible with quite modest means to assemble enough into a single collection for the necessary jobs of co-ordination and comparison to be feasible.

Ideally, while engaged in such a task as this, one should hear everything, dismiss nothing, and compare everything with at least something else. It is a great relief to know that this cannot be done. But readers will no doubt understand that much more has been heard than is noted in these pages, and that, wishing to be inclusive, I have had to be selective. I would like, however, to forestall the objection of a reader who looks up his favourite singer, searches for his favourite record and, not spotting it in the place of honour which is its due, exclaims 'Oh, but he hasn't mentioned so-and-so! How is it possible not to mention so-and-so?' First, it may be that the missing record is indeed mentioned but in a different part of the book; second, it may be that another record appeared to me to illustrate the particular point about the singer even better than that one. On the other hand, one has to admit, it is quite possible that I may never have heard so-and-so, or even of it. But that too is part of the thesis: the richness of the field. Records, unlike writers and their readers, are in fact quite inexhaustible.

I would like to stress that I am not attempting to offer a *history* of singing on record. That would have to be done very differently, with much stricter attention to chronology, with greater inclusiveness and much more sheer listing. The book is a critical survey, and examples are given as steps in an argued presentation. I have tried to be precise in reference, choosing a particular record and if possible a particular moment in it to illustrate a representative point about the singer, who will himself have his representative place in a larger context. On the other hand, I have not worked with any *a priori* thesis. There is no dark scheme, for instance, behind the choice of material for comparisons. I have made comparisons in a deliberately non-systematic way, partly for that very reason, using the records that have been at hand at the time so that the juxtapositions will less often be the already familiar ones that invite a stock response both in oneself and in the reader. The purpose of the comparisons is never to establish 'the best version' (or 'the best buy'), but to throw into relief a quality of the artist under consideration.

It remains to thank some of the many people who have given me help. The most pervasive debt is to the enterprise of collectors and enthusiasts who have issued transfers of rare records onto LP; also to those whose published research has provided so much of the necessary knowledge about the existence of recordings, their date, origin and so forth. Some of these are mentioned in the bibliography, but special gratitude is due to Mr James Dennis, editor of *The Record Collector*, and to his contributors over the years. To Mr Dennis also many thanks for permission to reprint from articles of my own, published originally in his magazine. Among the enterprising collectors referred to earlier is Mr S. J. Gray, who has also lent me tapes and provided me with an introduction to Mr Vivian Liff. The great Stuart-Liff photograph collection was thus put at my disposal, and so was a lot of Mr Liff's time and energy: I am extremely grateful to him. Also to Mr Harold Rosenthal for further help with photographs, and to Decca,[1] EMI and RCA Victor for assistance generously given. Among other individuals and institutions I must mention Dr A. H. Marshall, Mr P. V. Winston, Mr James Lyons of the *American Record Guide*, the BBC Record Library, the Coventry City Record Library and the editor and staff of *The Gramophone*. Mr Malcolm Walker, assistant editor, has also most kindly read the first proofs. Finally, the dedicatees. The late John Dodd was a friend in the earliest days of record collecting, and his enthusiasm for the projected book was a great source of inspiration to go ahead and write it. Mr Edward Greenfield provided the rest, by encouragement and example and by giving me ready access to his comprehensive collection of LPs. Possibly it should be said in fairness to Mr Greenfield that he is not to be held responsible for any errors of fact or judgment in the text; indeed, at the present time he has hardly seen the book. Without him, there would quite probably be no book to be seen.

[1] Decca recordings are issued in the USA on the London Label, and HMV (EMI) on Angel.

Introduction

Singers and Records

EDISON hit on a good word, proud but unpretentious, when he called his new cylinders 'records'. The term has the dignity of simplicity, also that of association with history: we call historical documents records. In spite of which we are still curiously reluctant to regard records as historical documents.

Perhaps that is not so surprising after all. The gramophone is a recent invention, not a century old, and the use of records as a source of history is obviously open to abuses; but then, so are most other sources of history.

This present book is primarily concerned with what the gramophone can tell us about the history of singing in the last hundred years – for that is virtually the span of time involved. The first records discussed here were made by singers who were active in the 1870s and 1880s; the last were made in 1970 by artists who will presumably be prominent in their sphere for a good time to come. So what kind of historical evidence can the gramophone provide? Can it, for example, tell us of a Golden Age of Singing? And if so, is it to be found in the very earliest of our recordings? And in what respect are they particularly golden? Or does the gramophone, on the contrary, suggest that these Carusos, Melbas, Galli-Curcis and so forth, were merely songbirds for the despised canary-fancier; 'golden voices' without musicianship or dramatic sensibility? Does it show that modern singers tend to have more intellect and less sheer voice than the great ones of the past? Or more technique and less personality? Does it show change at all?

Certainly it ought to, for the last hundred years have seen vast alterations in most respects, and the role of the singer has not failed to change with the times. 'There are no stars except in the skies', said Toscanini to Geraldine Farrar, who had made an unavailing claim for the old order in rehearsal at the Metropolitan. He himself was intent upon making the singer serve in a collaborative artistic enterprise firmly under the conductor's direction; and this is one of the changes that time has brought about. In a restricted kind of way, 'stars' still appear in the opera houses and concert halls today: every so often they are allowed a solo recital on record or at the Festival or

Carnegie Hall, and their photographs are familiar from the covers of the record magazines or from the boxes, sleeves and booklets accompanying their recordings. But there is little for them to compare with what once was. When Emma Calvé visited Honolulu around the turn of the century, her boat was greeted by hundreds of balloons with her picture attached to them, blown out from the harbour and floating over the city (or so she says!); a bust of her in the role of Santuzza stood in Windsor Castle (does it still?); a band of officers and cadets drew her troika in St. Petersburg; three hundred cowboys ('fine, strapping fellows') were waiting for her at the station in Houston. No opera singer in our time has known this kind of attention and acclaim; and Calvé was one of perhaps a dozen singers who in her day were treated with such colourful fuss by royal personages, heads of states, newspapers, critics, cowboys and general public alike. Nowadays, a Sutherland or a Nilsson comes and goes; an audience cheers, and reviews are written; but the Heads of States are as unlikely to know or care about it as the general public, and the newspapers are interested in a prima donna only if she has tantrums or falls victim to one of the gruesome hazards of operatic production.

With this change of outward status has gone a change in real power. Not to go to rehearsals if one could help it, was Patti's advice to aspiring Queens of Song ('They tire you too much nowadays with these ordeals', said Marietta Alboni, who attributed her preservation to abstinence in this respect). That is not representative, yet not unsymptomatic either. Once arrived at rehearsal, the stars could exercise their power in other ways. 'He is too young and inexperienced to sing with me', was Melba's verdict at a stunningly successful rehearsal for Titta Ruffo in 1903; so the management had to cancel the brilliant new baritone's appearance, and Covent Garden audiences lost the chance of hearing him ever again. This too is not entirely representative (though not untypical of Dame Nellie), yet we find that even as late as 1935 Conchita Supervia could write to the management of the Royal Opera and virtually cast the operas in which she was to sing. Her letters were brisk and business-like, and her suggestions were all accepted; again we find it surprising. But it was nothing to the committee of prima donnas, their husbands and mothers, who ruled the roost when Gatti-Casazza became director of the Metropolitan Opera House in 1908:

'Now what opera, Mr Gatti, are you going to give on Monday?'
I would suggest, mildly, *Rigoletto.*
'But *Rigoletto* has been done'.
'That's true, but not in the same subscription'.
'Who will be the Duke – Caruso?'
'He's not free that night,' the director replies, 'what about Bonci?'
The cross-examiners seem dubious.
At another time the director suggests that the opera be *La Bohème.* 'Who will be Mimi?' demands the husband of one prima donna. In the same

moment the mother of the other makes the same request, for in effect it is a request. The director must then decide who will be Mimi with the interested parties in front of him, saying nothing, but demanding what they conceive to be justice in every look and gesture.[1]

These stories, however well authenticated, remain in the realm of opera house gossip, but they still tell an essential truth. And although there are no doubt some fine and fascinating stories circulating in our opera houses today, the balance of power has shifted: managers, producers and conductors have occupied the ground which the singers have lost.

Following upon this, the singers have found themselves with added responsibilities, a different kind of challenge, and a new dignity. Nowadays, like other musicians, they must be able to read a difficult score. Of course we know that new scores always were difficult: Melba threw *Madama Butterfly* across the room declaring it was impossible, and at the French première of *Rigoletto* the critics said 'Il n'y a pas de mélodie'. But the habit of suggesting by analogy is in this instance facile and misleading: modern works are difficult to an extent that no new music has been in comparison with that of its immediate past. Subtleties of every kind, melodic, harmonic, rhythmic, interpretative, confront a professional singer, presenting problems with which an amateur could not begin to cope. A few years ago Mr Peter Dawson would sing songs in a repertoire ranging from Handel to Vaughan Williams, and an amateur with a sturdy voice and a good ear could attempt it all himself with reasonable success. But today's reigning Peter is Pears. He, as we know, has a way of moving from one phrase or one note to another as though it were the most natural, the most easy, and indeed the only right way conceivable. But let an amateur start out in confidence that he can do it too, and he will soon find himself a note or so down here and half a bar behind there; and though his 'artistry' may seem to him to make up for a lot (for Pears' vowel sounds and his colouring are not hard to imitate), no professional conductor would put up with him for five minutes. There is in fact an astonishing supply of professional singers able to meet these difficulties, just as the academies are producing immensely accomplished musicians of every sort. But there it is: essentially, the singer now is 'just' a musician. He plays his part, like the first clarinet; must be as efficient, and must not expect much more fuss made over him. The loss in popular glamour has been compensated by an increase in professional respect. Not that the demarcation lines should get overthickened: the old singers, as far as one can generalise, were true artists, serious, able and conscientious, and modern singers are not without their foibles, temperament and taste for the limelight. But the status of the great singer has nevertheless changed, in these fifty years or so, from 'star' to musician.

Change usually brings loss as well as gain, and here the gramophone is

---

[1] G. Gatti-Casazza: *Memories of the Opera*, p. 15–16.

invaluable, not only as historian, but also as the partial preserver of something precious which would formerly have been lost for ever. But that word 'partial' brings us back to the original enquiry. How reliable are records as 'historical documents'? How far is the essential and true Caruso preserved for us? Or, to weight the question more heavily (for Caruso was generally recognised as being exceptionally fortunate in the fidelity of his recordings), how far do those early sopranos, whose voices sound to the casual listener so curiously disembodied, 'survive' on records? Is the Melba of her recordings anything like the Melba heard in the great opera houses?

The distortions of 'pre-electrical' recording (that is, the 'acoustic' process prevalent until electrical recording was established in 1925) affect the singer's tone, intonation and artistic freedom. The frequency range was limited so that a voice would be shorn of the full richness of its harmonics. In some ways this could be flattering, giving that sort of ethereal effect we hear from a voice singing off-stage in the theatre (every opera-goer knows the disappointment of discovering that his Manrico for the evening is a coarse-toned brute though he had seemed well enough in the wings as he sang 'Deserto sulla terra', and that many Madama Butterflys are never the same woman again after making the arduous ascent, off-stage, to Pinkerton's love-nest on its nine-hundred-and-ninety-nine year lease). The loss was greater than any gain, however, for a voice remarkable for its purity of tone, as Melba's was, would be reduced to something pipelike when the harmonics were cut; a contralto whose voice was naturally rich would sound plummy as the edge was blunted; a bass would seem hollow or wooden when the qualities that made for a rich depth were removed. Tenors generally came off best; the characteristic tenor's sound is bright-edged, and the voice is well in the middle of the gramophone's frequency range.

The recordings, then, did not do the singers justice. On the other hand, they are by no means as bad and unreliable in their reproduction of sheer tone as is often thought; and frequently, when they are contemptuously dismissed, it is something other than the original record which merits the contempt. It may be the machine on which the record is played; it may be the individual copy; or the LP transfer.

The machine first. In the early days, several singers were indifferent or even hostile to their own recordings. They heard them played back on the primitive gramophones, knew that they were not hearing their true selves, and passed the records for publication only as being better than nothing, or as something incidental and unimportant in their career, or simply as a source of income. The American soprano Emma Eames was one of those who originally had little time either for her own records or for the gramophone itself. But in 1939, Desmond Shawe-Taylor visited her, she being then an old lady, very grand and still rather formidable, and played for her a record made in about 1905 of Pol Plançon. Plançon was a bass, and his voice was not readily captured by the acoustic process, but the reproduction was good, and 'He might be in the room!' was the exclamation of his old contemporary. And as we listen to these records properly reproduced, all sorts of things that we had thought lost forever in sheer completeness of sound begin to reappear: even the elusive sibilants, even the latent quality of splendour which makes us begin to hear Melba's recordings as newly credible and impressive.

The copy or the nature of the record itself can also affect what we hear and how we judge. Wear on the particular copy is obvious enough and, however annoying, does not present a problem. Wear on the matrix is more insidious; the matrices of popular recordings deteriorated, so that, for example, many of the later pressings of records by Caruso have a nagging hardness and show a loss in richness and beauty. One also finds that in some years certain companies used an inferior shellac, and so the voice has to fight its way through a turgid hiss of surface noise that all but overwhelms it.

More harmful still are the vagaries of the people who make up transfers of these old 78s. Many are marvellously well done, and of course many of the worst earn our gratitude by the sheer virtue of their having made generally available in some form, however imperfect, material which otherwise one might not have been able to hear at all. But distortions are frequent and serious. Some falsify the singer's tone by 'improving' the sound, adding an echo-chamber and cutting upper frequencies so as to eliminate surface-hiss. More often the trouble is a matter of carelessness or ignorance in getting the speeds right. As everyone knows, playing-speed determines pitch, and a change in pitch affects the intrinsic character of the sound: if a '33' is played at 78 it twitters like an aviary, and a reading by T. S. Eliot sounds like something by Minnie Mouse. It was not until late 1927 that speed became standardised at 78 revolutions per minute, and even then there were many exceptions. So if a record was made to be played at, shall we say, 74 rpm, and the people responsible for an LP transfer assume that the speed is 78, it will come out about half a tone higher than it should; the voice will then sound thinner than its true self, the vibrato will become more rapid and fluttery, and the vowel sounds will become whiter and more open. If the opposite happens and the pitch is too low, then the voice takes on a sluggish quality, its vibrato becomes slower, more of a flap than a flutter, and the vowels close in, stodgily rounded.

It may seem from this that such effects would be obvious and the mistakes easy to prevent, but this is not so. One wonders, for example, how many older record collectors who have long possessed and known on 78s Martinelli's record of the Improvviso from *Andrea Chénier* realise that it plays a semitone high; and that the same is true of Elisabeth Schumann's record of 'Deh, vieni non tardar' from *Le Nozze di Figaro*. Both of these were made electrically when playing-speed was supposed to have been standardised, so that one takes its correctness on trust. Both have also been transferred to LP, the first on Camden, the second on HMV's *Great*

Recordings of the Century series. The second corrects the fault; the first does not.

The distortions, in fact, are less than obvious; but they are real and damaging in a way comparable to that in which reproductions of a painting can distort the colours of the original. The owner of the reproduction becomes accustomed to his colours, and his knowledge of the painting is falsified. With singers on record, the damage is rather greater, because with each new issue a few more casual listeners will have judged and condemned, or shrugged and dismissed. When people say 'Oh, those old records, they're not worth wasting time on', one can nowadays nearly always trace the remark to some badly edited LP transfers.

With good reproduction, then, these old records will generally give a very adequate idea of a singer's voice: often much more than that, for they can be quite astonishingly vivid and immediate. But whether we can judge the singers as artists is another question. Conditions in the recording studios were not conducive to a studied and serious interpretation of the music or to intensity in the dramatic portrayal. Emma Eames described how she felt about it, in a broadcast given in 1939:

> To a sensitive person the conditions were unnerving. We had to sing carefully into the very centre of a horn to the accompaniment of an orchestra which invariably sounded out of tune, owing to the fact that metal horns were substituted for the wooden sounding-boxes of the violins. In the case of a brilliant and vibrant voice like mine, as one approached the climax, or high note, the climax was turned into an anti-climax for fear of a blast, so-called; one was gently drawn back from the horn, so that instead of a ringing high note one sounded as though one had suddenly retired into the next room. The process enervated me, as I felt that with even the most satisfactory results, my voice would be diminished and deformed, and the cross vibrations eliminated completely.

If the music was a duet or a concerted piece there would be the sort of competition described by Gerald Moore:

> The charging and pushing that went on made me marvel that they had any breath left for singing. Victory usually went to avoirdupois, a welter being no match for a heavy-weight. (*Am I Too Loud?*, p. 61).

There was none of the minutely painstaking preparation, rehearsal, discussion and so forth that goes into a modern recording. Moreover, one mistake meant that the whole thing had to be done again, or passed for publication warts and all. There were several great artists (Marcella Sembrich was another) who never really got used to this, or felt able to sing with anything approaching the dramatic conviction of their stage performances. The remarkable fact is that so much life is there. It is hard to think of a gayer record than the Patter Duet from *Don Pasquale* recorded by de Luca and Corradetti in 1907, or a more vivid enactment of tragedy than Tamagno's records of Otello's death made in 1903. Usually the singers of those days put heart and soul into what they were doing; but it should never be suggested that the facts of a successful career can in any way be altered by a singer's relative failure to come to terms with the new medium. So this must be a history with a caution. And the caution has still to be exercised when we have left the pre-electrical era of recording and move into more recent times. As long as records were made on 78s, there must still have been a sense of pressure, not necessarily fully conscious, in the knowledge that the piece must be finished, or an agreed ending-point reached, within about four minutes. Often when going back to 78s and recognising that here is some glorious singing, one is nevertheless cheated of the fullest pleasure by a sense of hurry, sometimes because the tempo is faster than we usually find today, and sometimes because there is not sufficient expansiveness within the given tempo. Whether this difference was one of style or of conditions of recording is debatable; but, interestingly, the gramophone itself provides useful evidence. Stage performances by many of the famous artists of the inter-war years exist on records usually with a private circulation though well-known to collectors. One can therefore compare performances; and thus, for example, Elisabeth Rethberg's singing of the Ave Maria in *Otello* (timing from the first sung note to the last) took three minutes thirty seconds in the studio, four minutes and twenty-five seconds in performance at the Metropolitan on 12 February 1938; Lawrence Tibbett's record of Boccanegra's Council Chamber Scene (starting 'Plebe, patrizi' and finishing at the end of the great concerted passage) takes four minutes fifty seconds, while his stage performance took five minutes twenty-five seconds in 1939, the same year as the studio recording. It is not true, as one might think, that performances will always go more slowly in the theatre than in the studio (apart, that is, from the business of moving around on stage – but the examples given here are 'static'). If we compare modern examples, stage and studio performances are usually about the same in their timing: thus Callas singing the two verses of 'Casta diva' took five minutes, twenty-five seconds at Covent Garden on 8 November 1952, exactly the same in the studio recording made in 1954 (5·18 in the 1960 recording); and Joan Sutherland exactly five and a half minutes for 'Bel raggio' both in a performance of *Semiramide* at La Scala on 19 December 1962, and in the complete recording on Decca. So again we must beware of concluding that the singers and the period itself were limited in their feeling for a piece of music because their studio recording of it lacks the expansiveness which we have now come to expect.

All of these are cautions against adverse judgment. When we come to the records of our own time, the principal caution has to be exercised in the other direction. If 78s present part-truth because they are so defective, LPs are suspect witnesses simply because they are so very nearly perfect. So many 'takes' may be made during a recording session that all the grosser imperfections of note-values, intonation, and tone itself can be eliminated in the final product. There is nothing insincere, immoral or inartistic about this, as some people think: it represents a genuine collaboration of many people intent upon producing as fine an artistic achievement as possible. But it does remove the gramophone record one degree further from historical truth – if that resides essentially in the singer's live performances, whether in the opera house, concert hall or recording studio.[1]

With these qualifications duly acknowledged (and one or two others, for not all the important singers of the century were extensively recorded), it can safely be claimed that the gramophone does in fact tell a great deal of the historical truth about the development of this art within this period. One last point remains. Singers are 'on record' only when the records are heard; and hearing introduces the listener, a third and highly subjective element.

Can criticism and discussion be satisfactory and useful when tastes differ so widely and people hear singers so differently? Of course, a musical performance involves much that can be observed and checked objectively. If one artist sings a run in a single breath while another takes three breaths over it, then that is a fact, not an opinion; similarly, if one of them sings distinctly and exclusively the notes that are written, while the other is indistinct and inexact, then these are facts which a scientific instrument could record. There are probably few people who would then object if one proceeded to the kind of value judgment involved in calling the first performance 'clean' and the second 'untidy', or quite simply (other things being equal) 'good' and 'bad'. But suppose the records in question are performances of 'Il mio tesoro' from *Don Giovanni*, the first by McCormack, the second by Gigli; one may then meet with the objection 'Oh, but I like Gigli's voice better than McCormack's, so naturally I would prefer his record'. It might be thought that one then reaches a full-stop, and that all critical discussion is doomed to futility, ultimately retreating to the subjective and unarguable checkmate-position of 'I like it', 'I do not'.

It is true that this may be the end of the game, but the end can still be profitably deferred if even the slightest concession is made to particularity. If, for instance, instead of the blank 'I like . . .', the remark goes 'Gigli's voice is so much warmer than McCormack's'. 'Warm' is a fairly vague, subjective critical term, but at any rate one can begin to engage in discussion. 'Yes, but is that very latin warmth of tone suited to this music?', one might ask, and one might go on to ask something further about the latin temperament that informs the style. Gigli's admirer may stick to his guns and his preferences, but the discussion will not have been futile because both disputants are likely to have learnt something about singing and about the music itself by making the comparisons and giving their feelings some

---

[1] As against this, the tendency in recent years has been to record in longer stretches. An example is noted by Edward Greenfield (*Joan Sutherland*, 1972, p. 34). Three separate sessions were scheduled for recording the Mad Scene in the recent *Lucia di Lammermoor*, but Sutherland and Bonynge insisted on the need for continuity, and in fact the whole thing was done in a single session.

kind of critical articulation. Of course tastes differ, but they can meet in discussion, and through comparisons. Comparisons make standards; and that they can be made so readily and widely is another of the unique values of the gramophone.

But the total value of the gramophone to the lover of singing lies in this and much besides. When all the limitations mentioned earlier have been allowed full weight, the marvellous fact is still there: that we can hear Caruso; that Chaliapin is not just the legend he would otherwise have been; Elisabeth Schumann is still a living presence in the musical world; Maria Callas seems to have retired from the operatic scene but we can still hear her. These are distinctive artists whom it would be a loss to miss; and as one comes to listen to the whole range of recordings from 1900 to the present time one realises how few are the singers who have left nothing personal and valuable behind them in their records. The field is immensely rich.

The chapters which follow survey this field in its three main stages of development: the pre-electrical period of recording from 1900 to 1925, the electrical 78 from 1925 to about 1950, and the age of the long-playing record up to 1970. Some of the strands are drawn together in an appendix devoted to detailed comparisons, and the final chapter will attempt to assess the gains and losses which our century has brought to this highly cultivated, specialised and civilised way of singing that we have called the grand tradition.

Part I

The Golden Legend

Pre-Electrical Recording 1900–1925

1. The Old Order: Nineteenth-Century Echoes
Adelina Patti   Francesco Tamagno
Lilli Lehmann

In 1900 the gramophone was a toy, in 1902 a musical experiment, in 1904 an established medium. The seal was then to be put upon its success two years later when the record-makers and their equipment were admitted to Craig-y-Nos Castle in Wales and the Company would announce that they had history for sale. For nearly half a century, Adelina Patti had reigned, as the record catalogue would claim, 'undisputed queen of song': a few years more and the famous voice would be stilled forever. But now, through the workings of the new machine, it could be heard by the twentieth century as by the nineteenth, and indeed for all time to come. A new vista had opened.

A festive flourish was natural and fully justified, though when the first excitement was over and the records settled down to become (or so it was unrealistically assumed) a permanent part of the HMV Historic Catalogue, then eyebrows would come to be raised and ears to be puzzled by the actual sounds that the queen of song appeared to have made. The present writer has a vivid memory of an angry woman returning two records to the local shop from which she had recently bought them. The records were frauds, she said, terrible and hopeless. There on the counter they lay, surveyed by the mild-eyed shopkeeper. Money changed hands for the second time without much argument and the records stayed on the counter where for the first time one very young record collector gazed at the pink labels that were Patti's special preserve. I played 'Comin' through the Rye' and 'Robin Adair' on the shop's gramophone, thought the angry woman well justified in demanding the return of her twenty-five shillings, and dismissed Patti and the Historic Catalogue as snare and delusion, nothing more.

At times one still veers between laughter and rage at Patti's records. The quaint half-spoken, questioning expression of 'Gin a body kiss a body' in that same 'Comin' through the Rye' still seems comical; and one smiles a little more maliciously when the hectic speed she uses for the second-half of the *Don Giovanni* aria, 'Batti, batti', involves her in a flurry of snatched breaths and scrambled or missing notes. One feels that her professionalism, if nothing else, should have warned her that at sixty-two her surviving mastery might best be displayed within limits. We look askance at the youngster who attempts 'Casta diva' at her very first recital; perhaps it is best simply to turn a deaf ear to the prima donna who offers it again in her sixties. But Patti's record exists and we are eager to hear it. How sad, then, to find nearly all the phrases broken (the breath between 'casta' and 'diva' is typical), light aspirates used, and some of the written fioriture simplified as for a novice. How maddening then to turn from this great test-piece to 'The Last Rose of Summer' and find what might have been a likeable record marred by the singer's scooping approach to the note on 'rose' and by her overloud assault upon every similar note in the song. It is not, as is often said, the condition of her voice that so often spoils these records, nor is it the primitive technique of recording. It is rather that certain features of Patti's style at this date simply were not musical.

If that were the whole truth about the records it would be wise to bury them, and let the great singer's reputation rest on the facts of her career. She had been before the public since 1859, when she had sung, in that first season, fourteen leading roles. This in itself speaks for her musicianship, while there survive countless testimonials to the beauty of her voice and the wonder of her technique. But the records have many beauties in spite of their faults, and so engage a critical attention.

Good reproduction makes a great difference. The enraged woman in the record shop was probably disappointed not so much with the style of the singing she heard as with the sheer unsatisfactoriness of the sound. Modern equipment reveals quite passably clear recording, that catches not only a still remarkable voice but also a strong and vivid personality. But whether one is playing from originals or from LP transfers the problem of speed raises difficult problems. Nobody seems to know for certain about the keys which Patti used in those days for the songs and arias she recorded, but it is important not to take what one is hearing for granted. It seems most likely, for instance, that that record of 'Batti, batti' was made in the key half-a-tone lower than the F major in which it is printed. It certainly sounds more comfortable there; and if the angry purchaser had tried 'Comin' through the rye' in A instead of B flat, she would have heard a brightly energetic voice instead of a thin and strident one, and she might have kept the record and even come to value it.

For there is much to enjoy. There is, in the first place, a most beautiful and distinctive tone to be heard in the middle register. One comes to love it as one plays a series of Patti's records, or, to choose a single instance, as one plays the song from *Mignon*, 'Connais-tu le pays?'. Some exquisite phrases in this bring us close to the sound that charmed so many audiences for so many years. At the line 'Où la brise est plus douce et l'oiseau plus léger' she uses the lightest of tones that still has the glow of a gentle warmth. In the last phrase – 'C'est là que je voudrais vivre' – this soft, perfectly supported sound is allowed freedom to linger; one can, for a few bars, hear the famous voice without flaw. Of course there are faults here too, but what one recognises above all in this record is how imaginative an artist she could be. The point emerges again in some comparisons on p. 577: among the six versions of 'Ah, non credea mirarti' compared there, Patti's is by

1. Adelina Patti

far the nearest to that of Callas in its variety and plasticity of tone. In 'Connais-tu le pays?' her distinction becomes very clear if we compare the well-sung but far more stolid performances by Sembrich, Fremstad and Farrar. Patti's smiling tone at 'l'oiseau plus léger', her warmer colouring of 'Hélas, que ne puis-je te suivre', the deeper emotion of 'aimer et mourir', and the return to a wistful tenderness for the ending of the song – all this presents a genuine imaginativeness and involvement. It also provides a lesson in the valuable art of moulding a verse.

If students of singing have gone back to Patti's records, however, it has probably been in search of other lessons: in how to produce runs of dazzling brilliance, for instance. At sixty-two Patti had not this to offer, though I fancy a singer is likely to recognise certain accomplishments in even and rapid scale-work that the less expert listener accepts unthinkingly. But one feature of her technique that cannot fail to impress is the trill: it was of unrivalled grace and delicacy. 'Pur dicesti', a song by the early eighteenth-century composer Antonio Lotti, is the best record to sample for this. Patti's trill was perhaps the most finely grained of all, and it came naturally as a part of the main flow of tone, not as a specially added ornament. 'Pur dicesti' is not a perfect record, but certain features of it come as near to perfection as any we know.

At its best it has a warm delicacy, an easy grace, that we might wish Patti had preserved throughout her records. But then she would not have been herself, and we, as posterity, would know only a kind of prettiness in her art. The records as a whole preserve a more vital spirit than this. The Jewel Song from *Faust*, with all its signs of age and occasional scoops, is alive with excitement. 'Comin' through the Rye' has a genuine open-air feeling about its energy and boldness. Best of all, the Spanish song 'La Calasera' brings all this vigour and zest vividly before us. There is not only an unmistakeable smile with the voice, and a proud Spanish toss of the head at the end of the verses, but a remarkable display of strength, in the cries and the full-voiced high notes.

These records of Patti, then, do not exactly present us with the nightingale and rose of Gautier's poem about her (the 'Etoile aux éclairs d'or de l'art cécilien'), any more than they can preserve the voice that caused such a sensation nearly half a century earlier. But they do show a warm and vigorous woman whose voice and technique still allowed her to sing beautifully; whose style and critical sense at this stage often prevented her from doing so; and who nevertheless was an imaginative artist, one of the most lively and individual singers on record.

Patti's phonographic remains, for all their limitations, have a demonstrable distinction. Hearing, we can believe. Not all the famous singers of her period survive on wax as well as she has done. She, after all, gave her name to an age: the sixties, seventies and eighties of the nineteenth century in vocal history were the Age of Patti. It is fair to expect something interesting even at her advanced years. But the nineties were the Age of de Reszke, and we might reasonably expect still more from the protagonists of this vaunted period, if only because they were a few vital years younger. Of Jean de Reszke himself, alas, we have very little. There are some Mapleson cylinders in which he can be faintly heard through the din, still going strong (and musical) at the end of the first act of *Siegfried*, and fervently combining with the brilliant-sounding Lucienne Bréval in Act IV of *L'Africaine*. He was just over fifty when these stage performances were given.[1] Then in 1905 came the famous visit to the Fonotipia studios in Paris, and the recording of 'O Souverain, o juge' from *Le Cid* and 'Salut, tombeau' from *Roméo et Juliette*. Famous and frustrating fact to collectors, for the records appear never to have been issued; presumably de Reszke did not pass them for publication. 'If such were indeed the case,' Roland Gelatt remarks (*The Fabulous Phonograph*, p. 91), 'he showed a keener regard for the verdict of posterity than many of his confrères'. More than did, for instance, his brother Edouard, who allowed the issue of three records in the Columbia Grand Opera series of 1903. This was not a good year for him. Critics remarked that he was sounding tired in this his last season at the Metropolitan, and his tone colour is certainly dull in the recordings. There is no vibrancy, and in that respect he makes an interesting comparison with his contemporary Pol Plançon. Plançon too has a 'clean' tone with hardly any vibrato: yet there is still a lustre, a life and resonance that make de Reszke sound ungainly and charmless. In the aria 'Infelice' from *Ernani* de Reszke uses a lack-lustre tone, and going with this the drooping portamentos are doubly depressing (but then this was the year he sang in the Metropolitan *Ernani* revival and caused W. J. Henderson to note that '"Infelice" was particularly unhappy'). There are elegances, it is true, and, as with some of Patti's records, a feature of de Reszke's technique that will impress the most sceptical is his trill. He demonstrates it twice in the Drinking Song from *Martha*, and it is a beauty: slow it down on the turntable and there it is, exact and even, a remarkable grace in so hefty and seemingly unlovely a voice. Still, in most ways his records remain in the armoury of those who say with G. B. Shaw: 'Let us hear no more of a golden age of bel canto. We sing much better than our grandfathers.'

Perhaps de Reszke felt inhibited by the strange business of recording: no audience, but only this impersonal, or possibly hostile-looking horn put there to sing into. Certainly the accounts of vivid characterisation on the stage forbid any belief that the stolidity of his *Martha* record is representative (I see P. G. Hurst in *The Golden Age Recorded* calls it 'excellent', adding that it is sung 'without exaggeration', where I should say it was sung without expression). Similarly with another of the famous singers of this period,

---

[1] A detailed analysis is made in *The Recordings of Jean de Reszke*, by John Stratton (*Recorded Sound*, 27, 1967). Interestingly, he concludes that de Reszke was 'before all else a declamatory singer'. Instancing the first Lohengrin cylinder, he says: 'He sings as if every note counted for something: that in nothing were any of the notes there just for filler. I have a strong impression that it was this attitude that was the main source of his genius as a singer.'

Victor Maurel. One reads contemporary accounts of his Iago, particularly of his way of singing 'Era la notte', and listens in vain to find anything correspondingly impressive in the recordings he made of it (see p. 586). Here is a pleasant, well-controlled baritone, producing a genuine *mezza voce* for the words of Cassio's dream: but as a portrait of evil it does not exist. 'His art was intellectual, reflective, analytical, subtle, even hypnotically masterful at times', wrote W. J. Henderson. What a pity, then, that with this 'subtle, intellectual power' he should have chosen such wretched stuff to sing as de Lara's 'Rondel de l'adieu' (recorded twice). Some of these notably unintellectual songs, such as Tosti's 'Ninon' and a swaggering affair called 'Mandolinata', do reveal at any rate a singer of character. And Don Giovanni's Serenade shows a well-preserved, virile voice and an aristocratic finish to the style (if he does get the time wrong at one point). Even in this record, though, it is difficult to connect what we hear with the account of his live performance as given by Calvé: 'a marvel of lightness and grace', she calls it. What are we to conclude: a marked discrepancy between these singers' recordings and their characterisations in the theatre, or a standard of performance much lower than ours? The former perhaps, for there is one record by Maurel which does show him unmistakeably as a singer-actor of marvellous resourcefulness; and this record had a studio audience. In a Fonotopia disc of 1907, the first Falstaff of all sings 'Quand' ero paggio' three times, cheered on by a claque whose own vocal resources range from what James Joyce calls the bass-barreltone to a falsettist who in a delirium of enthusiasm cries 'bis' after everyone else has finished. At the first performance of *Falstaff* Maurel was forty-four and at the height of his powers; now he was nearly sixty, and a great career was virtually over. He still had a voice, though it is sometimes out of focus, but what impresses most is the buoyancy ('ero sottile, sottile, sottile' bounces gaily on its podgy toes) and the colourful vocal acting. It is a delightful memento.

But the gramophone in its infancy was continually offering surprising commentary on contemporary criticisms. Of Patti we might have expected a sort of superficial prettiness: what we find is an imaginative interpreter, an accomplished technician with a warm middle voice and a remarkable, sometimes disconcerting fund of energy. Of Maurel we might have expected a subtle intellectual art with limited vocal powers: what we find is a pleasing voice, capable of sturdiness and softness, but (with the exception of the *Falstaff* record) providing little of interest in the interpretations. When we turn to Maurel's famous associate in the original cast of *Otello* another surprise awaits. References to Francesco Tamagno nearly always concern the great power and metallic ring of his voice, and often some kind of limiting comment goes with this. Sir Henry Wood found little to please him in Tamagno's Otello once the 'Esultate' was over; 'magnificent screaming' was Shaw's way of putting it. But what the records show, in addition to the great voice, is a reflective, plastic style in which, as P. G. Hurst says, 'a strain of tenderness is never far away', and which never departed from the musical line or degenerated to shouting. There is also a certain nobility, inherent in a sincere, and probably very simple devotion to a high calling.

Certainly the records leave no doubt about the surviving splendour of voice: any one of them will demonstrate it, either of the excerpts from *William Tell* for example. 'O muto asil' is among the most taxing of arias; the long, hard climb on the words 'egli non m'ode più', the great octave leaps to the high B flat, the final demands of a strenuous cadenza, all to be confronted in the context of a lyrical, yet passionate gentleness. Tamagno meets all these demands. He also sings the piece that follows, Arnoldo's call to arms, with an incredible display of sheer voice. It is probably transposed down half-a-tone; the singing is hardly less wonderful even so. The three highest notes are brilliantly taken, but almost more remarkable is the fullness of the As and Gs. Tamagno was one of the very few singers who could preserve an open, uncovered voice from top to bottom, and survive. It was a seamless voice, wonderfully even in production over a two-octave range. But while the 'Corriam' is what one would expect of him, the 'O muto asil' is something else. The opening phrase and its later repetition are taken softly, the quiet high G coming easily, the tone having still the life of a young voice. One might wonder whether it is fair to the older singer to take down the superb and very lyrical record made by Martinelli in his prime and play this alongside his. There need be no fears, however, for the poetry and lyricism of Tamagno's performance survive the comparison unharmed. His breath will not serve him to phrase broadly, but any loss there is compensated by the warmth and sweetness which so increase the expressiveness of this immensely powerful voice. ·

The poetic quality of 'O muto asil' is typical. The *Hérodiade* solos are also particularly good: 'Quand nos jours' has a severe nobility about it, and 'Adieu, vains objets' is subtly shaded, with an art constantly alive to the developing emotions of the piece. Comparison nearly always serves to enforce this. The aria 'Sopra Bertha' from Meyerbeer's *Le Prophète* as recorded by eminent tenors of the next generation has nothing of Tamagno's stylistic distinction: Mario Gillion and Francesco Vignas both had fine voices and healthy top notes, but Gillion's is an undisciplined tone and Vignas is somehow stiffly heroic, lacking tenderness. Or in the air 'Re del ciel' from the same opera, where in the ringing performance by Carlo Albani and the strong but refined one by Jaques Urlus is there anything to match the bold *marcato* style which gives such fervour and power to Tamagno's cadenza? A further comparison with Martinelli suggests itself when we come to the record of Samson's call to his fellow captives, 'Arrêtez, o mes frères' (or 'Figli miei, v'arrestate' in Tamagno's version). Martinelli is all fire; by comparison, Tamagno is very gentle. Martinelli sings with a Toscanini-like forward drive on the music; Tamagno holds it back, relishing each phrase with feeling and deliberation. There is much to be said for both: the pulse and cohesion of the music are better felt in the later record, but Tamagno's, with its own kind of fire, registers impressively as a religious cry, a call to a serious act of worship.

Most interest in Tamagno's records will centre on the three excerpts from *Otello*, the great role which he sang at the opera's first performance in 1887. He was especially famous for the way his voice rang out in the fearsome twelve bars in which Otello has to establish himself on his arrival in Act I. The records (two performances were published) are certainly impressive, though the phrasing is not broad as one understands it to have been in his great days, and intonation is sometimes faulty. Distinction lies in the tone, the emotion and the expansiveness. Compare it with two Otellos of more recent times, Mario del Monaco and Jon Vickers. Both sing with a safer, more closed tone: Tamagno sings his high A ('dopo l'armi') with the kind of openness that most tenors would find risky on an F sharp, and the effect is exactly to give that full authoritative exultancy that is wanted. Vickers doesn't sound exultant at all: the relatively dull vowels are one cause. Del Monaco sings with more urgency but, either of his own accord or in submission to his conductor Karajan, takes the short solo too quickly for it to make much impact. Here is a problem of interpretation, for Verdi left no indication of tempo.[1] Perhaps, then, it should be taken in strict time, or as near to the minim beat of the storm music as possible. Or perhaps it should be read as free melodic declamation, virtually in the hands of the singer, who after all has a task almost beyond mortal man if he is to make an impression after the house has rung to the fortissimo of chorus and orchestra in the opening pages (one has known members of the audience to take quite eminent Otellos at their first entrance for some anonymous messenger). The second of these alternatives is certainly the more attractive both to singer and audience, though the first might be exciting rhythmically. Can it be assumed, however, that in Tamagno's records we have something definitive: that this (the free, expansive way) was how it was done in Verdi's lifetime and how he wanted it done? Doubtful, I think. Much more doubtful when we come to consider 'Ora e per sempre addio' from Act II, which Tamagno takes very slowly indeed. The marking in the score is *Allegro assai ritenuto*, presumably meaning that while the passage is to be regarded as basically a quick one, there is to be no sense of hurry. Tamagno has reversed the emphasis; his direction would read *andante assai vigoroso*. Various writers have assumed that Tamagno's treatment must have had Verdi's blessing and that in the records we have a vital historical document

[1] In the booklet issued with his recording of *Otello*, Sir John Barbirolli writes on the subject of speeds in the opera; and what he says might seem to support the historical authenticity of Tamagno's tempo in this solo. Barbirolli's father played in the first performances of *Otello* and he told how Verdi was particularly insistent on the *assai ritenuto* of 'Ora e per sempre addio'. He would illustrate the point by singing the passage at Verdi's speed. But the tempo Barbirolli himself adopts is still notably faster (crotchet = c. 80) than Tamagno's, while Toscanini, who can also claim some first-hand authority, takes it even faster than the marking in the score (at crotchet = c. 100).

concerning the authentic performance of this music. But Verdi was not at the recording session. Tamagno could have it all his own way; and he had a liking for slow speeds. Moreover, the published score does bear a metronome marking (crotchet = 88), which Tamagno's recording (the ten-inch one) revises drastically (crotchet = 66, with numerous rallentandos).

No, if the records are historically important it is in their own right. They are artistic and devoted performances by a singer of exceptional gifts; one whose timbre was peculiarly suited to Otello's music, which was very probably written with his voice in mind. We may well wonder if anyone has ever made Otello's 'O gloria!' ring out with quite such fullness; whether the cry 'Ah morta, morta, morta' has ever had quite that intensity, agonised on the second 'morta', lingering emptily on the third; and many are the notes and phrases in everything that he recorded which come back to us in memory as bearing irreplaceably the stamp of his vocal character. This is the sign of a great artist, and it gives Tamagno quite as secure a niche in musical history as any attempt to present his Otello records to posterity as part of the last will and testament of the great composer.

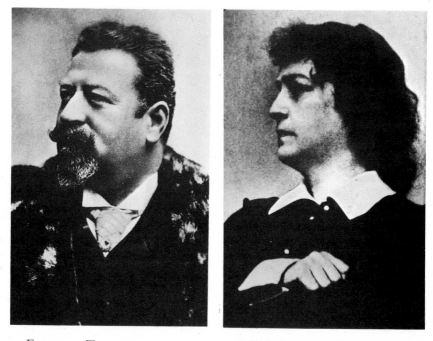

2. Francesco Tamagno   3. Lilli Lehmann as Leonore
                                          in *Fidelio*

His records are interesting in another connection. The reality of the 'golden age' is debatable: 'we sing much better than our grandfathers' was Shaw's verdict. Perhaps; but if we try to think of an Italian tenor born in this century who can match Tamagno in his combination of strength and gentleness, simplicity and imagination, we are left wondering. If we then turn to the records of Lilli Lehmann, another of our grandfather's singers and one of a very different school, the question mark thickens.

Lehmann was the great Brünnhilde and Isolde of her age. Unfortunately she recorded only one excerpt from the Wagner operas, an ardent but rather laboured version of 'Du bist der Lenz' from *Die Walküre*; but we can hear and judge her in a wide variety of music by other composers, music in which we might expect to hear a Sutherland or a Ponselle, never a Flagstad or Varnay. Constanze's arias from *Die Entführung aus dem Serail*, for example, present formidable demands for rapid scale work, agile leaps, and sustained brilliance above the stave. On later 78s the best-known recordings of 'Martern aller Arten' were by lighter voices such as Hempel, Ivogün, Ginster, Korjus and Berger; on LP we look to Rothenberger, Stader or Dobbs. If Birgit Nilsson were to do it, that would be in the Lehmann tradition; and the piece needs something of the heroic shine and challenge that a Brünnhilde voice can bring to it. Lehmann's is one of the most marvellous of early records. It meets every technical demand, and has power and majesty beyond comparison. The other aria, 'Ach, ich liebte', flawed as it is by excessive portamento, is nevertheless in some ways still more remarkable: for as well as the Wagnerian sonority, the daring and complete success of the runs, and the easy dealing with a cruel tessitura, there is some lovely soft singing, with a sweetness of tone that is again rare in a voice of such regal power. The arias, it should be added, were recorded in 1907. Lehmann made her debut in 1865, and the year when most of her records were made was her sixtieth.

In the *Entführung* solos, Lehmann's age is rarely apparent. In other records one knows well that a great career must be nearly over. The *Don Giovanni* records of 1905 show her with one bad patch in a wonderfully well-preserved voice; but it is distressing to hear, and it exposes what must have been a flaw in her method. The affected notes are those from middle G to the B flat above, the worst point coming at the break after the chest register which she carried rather fiercely to middle F sharp. It involves her in some embarrassing moments during Donna Anna's narrative, and accounts for the painfully hard work she has to do at the arpeggios, 'vendetta ti chiedo' (bars 56 to 59) in the aria 'Or sai chi l'onore' which follows. There are also faults that are not due to age. Her very polished, aristocratic way of beginning a note softly and then swelling it sometimes seems mannered: not in the *Don Giovanni* record where it is finely used on the long top As, but in the aria from *Les Huguenots* ('O beau pays', or 'O glücklich Land'), for example, where in combination with an unsmiling character it becomes rather irritatingly academic. Then in a deeply felt, meditative performance of 'Ah! fors' è lui' from *La Traviata* she ignores the rests in the opening phrases; and it cannot be said that what seems to be offered as a trill is acceptable as one. More obtrusive is a particular kind of 'scoop': not the carelessness or sentimentality of many singers, but a sort of regal seizure of power. Rather in the manner of the objectionable queens in *Alice*, it seems to say 'Here comes the diva to do what she wants with you'. There is a good parody of the style by Elisabeth Schwarzkopf as the Prima Donna in *Ariadne auf Naxos*.

Excesses of regality are not greatly surprising. By the beginning of the twentieth century, Lehmann was much the honoured doyenne, involved in grandeur as a teacher whose past was already legendary in the annals of opera, and whose occasional personal appearances were awesome events. Her very genuine, firmly-based authority remains. It is grounded in the technical mastery evident in such contrasted arias as 'Porgi amor' (or 'Heil'ge Quelle') from *Le Nozze di Figaro* and 'Sempre libera' from *La Traviata*. In the first we hear a finely poised tone, sustaining the long phrases with firmness and warmth; in the second, scrupulously precise scale-work, a brilliant glow on the voice, and apparently unlimited energy. In everything there was stature. Donna Anna's 'Or sai chi l'onore' and the recitative 'Don Ottavio, son morta' have been noted as flawed; but the faults are like the damaged front of a great cathedral. Again it is instructive to compare two singers on LP. Suzanne Danco, the Donna Anna of a Decca set conducted by Josef Krips, provides a good instance of what until recently was the modern style of performance. She sings exactly what is written, no more and no less. There are no appoggiaturas in either scena or aria, and the tempo is strict throughout both. Nor is there any portamento. Intonation is exemplary, and every note, high or low, is sung without fuss or apparent difficulty. The final effect is of a musical machine whose efficiency earns gratitude. The voice has its attractiveness, and no doubt the record is more agreeable work-a-day listening than Lehmann's. But Lehmann's is titanic: her Donna Anna is tragic where Danco's is no more than business-like. The expressiveness is not subtle, yet it ranges from a towering desperation in 'O Dei', through a gentler tone in 'Torcermi e piegarmi' (I suppose, suggesting shame in the memory), to a fine, sad diminuendo on 'col dargli morte'. Danco's is a drama on much smaller scale. Going from that to Birgit Nilsson, whose voice is comparable to Lehmann's, we find a more vivid seriousness and greater variety. But in this record (the RCA set under Leinsdorf) Nilsson's seems to my ears at times an uneven, gusty production, and the dramatic stature is smaller: emotion pitched at the level of a complaint, where Lehmann is Juno-like in anger and certainty. 'Quegli è il carnefice' resounds as the essence of operatic grandeur, and the sweep and intensity of the whole performance remain unequalled.

Lehmann's records are among those that largely match the impression given by contemporary writers. 'Aristocratic elegance of finish . . . a full-toned dramatic soprano immense in volume and resonance . . . of the heroic mould': these were among W. J. Henderson's terms of description. Guarded, sober young Shaw, denying her greatness, admitted her excellence: 'She acts intelligently, sings effectively and in tune, and is attractive enough, attaining in all these respects a degree of excellence that makes it impossible to call her commonplace'. It still is that.

One swallow does not make a summer, and Patti, Tamagno and Lehmann are not a golden age in themselves, though with the reputations (rather than the records) of Maurel and the de Reszke brothers the count begins to add up. There were of course many others. The Viennese contralto Marianne Brandt made three records at the age of sixty-three, one of them Fidès' lament from *Le Prophète*: a noble performance, the voice rich and steady over its great range, the touch of authority again unmistakeable. The Italian baritone Giuseppe Kaschmann, recording in his fifties, shows mastery of the grand style, fluently decorative, commanding and spirited, in 'O dei verdi anni miei' from *Ernani*. Jean Lassalle, a few years older, achieves a magical tenderness and range of feeling in his 'Promesse de mon avenir' from Massenet's *Roi de Lahor*, and even makes the same composer's 'Pensèes d'automne' an attractive song. Sir Charles Santley was of an earlier generation still. He sang his first public solo on Christmas Day, 1848, and made his first record in 1903, his seventieth year. His 'Non più andrai' (*Le Nozze di Figaro*) is even and steady, cheerful and brisk, with a skilful interpolated scale passage down to a low G that seems to me a very pleasant and acceptable embellishment; and his 'Simon the Cellarer' provides a splendid example of an early singer managing to put a song over on records with the vividness of a concert performance. Sir Henry Wood wrote of Santley: he 'had the strongest rhythmic sense of any vocalist I ever accompanied. The technique of his Handelian vocalisation was clarity itself, and the phenomenal compass of his voice, from the low bass E flat to the top baritone G, was brilliantly even throughout' (*My Life of Music*, ch. xvii). Sir Henry's final sentence on the subject may serve as an antitext to Shaw's assertion that we sing much better than our grandfathers. 'Oh where has fled the art of singing today?' It is the familiar cry of the old; but it came from a musician with at least as much right to pronounce as GBS.

All the singers so far considered were of the old guard. The infancy of the gramophone found nearly all of them in retirement. What we hear on records gives us a valuable idea of how they sounded in their great days, but it has about the same relation to truth as an echo has to the sound which produces it: what is remarkable is that the echo should afford so much evidence of mastery and character. There comes now a generation of artists who were in their prime at the turn of the century. Recording brings them much more realistically before us, and it is from the records of these singers that we can best begin to judge what earlier writers meant when they spoke of a golden age of singing.

2. The Golden Age: Five Great Singers
Nellie Melba   Ernestine Schumann-Heink
Fernando de Lucia   Mattia Battistini
Pol Plançon

BEAUTY of tone, mastery of technique, devotion to the art, and authority of style. These should surely be features common to the great singers of any age that one might want to call golden.

If anybody had them all, in the right proportions and in high degree, it was the French bass Pol Plançon. What a golden age singer should be, he was. It was he who came nearest to giving W. J. Henderson second thoughts when he delivered himself of the weighty maxim, 'There has never been a faultless singer'. 'Even Plançon,' he went on to say, 'had some faults' though he was 'one of the greatest masters of vocal technique that ever trod the stage'. Records bear this out. They are not perfect, but the art they preserve has a completeness and distinction that at any rate *suggest* the ideal; and that is rare enough.

His technical mastery is most joyfully displayed in a song from Ambroise Thomas' comic opera, *Le Caïd*, in which a drum-major sings of his triumphs, amatory and military. One half of the song is sentimental, the other jaunty – a florid first-cousin of 'The Man that broke the bank at Monte Carlo'. Plançon made four records of it between 1902 and 1907, and the last one is best of all. It has one oddly stiff downward arpeggio: otherwise perfection. The legato is virtually incomparable, for not only does he command the long phrase and the even line, but he also displays a tone which, while full-blooded and sonorous, is as near to being without the disturbance of vibrato as any healthy voice can be. To hear him in the first section of this piece, or in so much more of the music he sang, is like passing the hand over a piece of finely grained, highly polished mahogany. Then, marvellously, this dark, smooth richness of tone begins to glow and dazzle, as the fast section brings scales, roulades and trills. The swagger of the music finds an answering humour in the singer, while its technical demands are met with the joyous assurance of one who has mastered every exercise in the book and never stopped practising. This is golden-age singing right enough.

Thomas' drum-major song is pleasant light entertainment but not much more; as with most of his contemporaries, Plançon's records include what seems to us a large proportion of second-rate music. When the music deepens, however, so does his art. Thus, King Philip's scene and aria in *Don Carlo* shows Plançon as an imaginative interpreter, feeling the music and the drama in a way that makes an interesting and worthy comparison with a great Philip of later times, Boris Christoff. For many of us in the nineteen fifties and sixties, Christoff's has been the classic performance. It is hard to hear the music in one's mind without at the same time hearing his voice in it and recalling his style. We probably approach a comparison between him and Plançon conceding little more than that the early singer might have some superiority in tone; so that it is not surprising to find Plançon more scrupulously voicing the group of notes marked *allargando* written for the word 'languenti'. What one probably does not expect is that in the comparison it is Plançon who moulds the phrases with the greater imaginativeness and the more varied tones. Both singers are fine in the 'bloc' contrasts they make; and there is a wonderfully indrawn feeling about Christoff's performance as well as the tragic depth that a great Boris Godunov must be able to bring. But for a live, affectionate handling of the music phrase by phrase I would go first to Plançon; for a finely nourished, scrupulously exercised tone too.

After this serious and majestic record it is interesting to hear Mephistopheles' Song of the Flea from Berlioz' *Damnation of Faust*. Here the large, deep voice frisks with the ease of a practised buffo. Compare Gérard Souzay, who has the advantage of a lighter, baritone voice and who has been one of the most able technicians of his time. It is the bass who achieves a thoroughly clean definition of tone; and it is the bass who copes, as the more 'athletic' singer, with the difficult pairs of quavers in each verse. Souzay caricatures vigorously, souring his voice a little to suggest devilry, but again it is the older singer who strikes one as having an inner sense of fun, communicated in the sprightly variety of his performance, always alive in words and rhythm, and always scrupulous in the production of the voice.

One turns repeatedly to this word 'scrupulous' when thinking of Plançon. Going with the recognition of this feature is a sense that here is an aristocratic singer, not only in style and technique but also in quality of tone. He never permitted himself the popular appeal of a loose vibrancy: all the sonority of his voice was contained within a precisely defined line. In his later recordings we occasionally lose some of the excitements of operatic singing because of this: he will not risk the free, open sound on high notes that we would ideally like to hear. But it is a small price to pay for what is so distinctively preserved. Once into their fifties, few singers ask less.

By contrast, a cautious husbandry of resources played little evident part in the declining years of Mattia Battistini, the great baritone of this period. He sang with an energy and attack that seem almost reckless, yet his voice survived to record some particularly taxing arias in his sixty-eighth year, and in all he was before the public for nearly half a century. With him it is the lower part of the voice that craves indulgence. It is not troublesome on his

4. Pol Plançon   5. Mattia Battistini

earliest records, the Warsaw series of 1903, made when he was forty-seven;
but as time went on, notes from middle E downwards were apt to be colourless and sometimes constricted. Perhaps it was to help free the tone in this
difficult register that he often used a downward portamento in approaching
the lower notes; the effect is not pleasant, however, and I find that it mars
the sound-picture of his singing that one carries in one's mind. Going back
to the records is inevitably to marvel afresh at the beauty of voice and live-
ness of style: one of the greatest of singers, this, with a kind of mastery
possessed by no other baritone on records. Still, certain criticisms have to
be made; and one has also to note that both the strengths and limitations of
Battistini's records are not exactly those conventionally associated with a
singer who is so frequently described as the master of *bel canto*.

'*Bel canto*' is perhaps the vaguest term in the musical glossary, and the
most pretentiously used. Its primary connotation is probably an even flow
of beautiful, unforced tone. Smoothness is thought of as one of the great
virtues, and with this conception, in the general musician's mind (not that
of the specialist-enthusiast) goes a kind of critical 'placing', which feels that
while such smoothness may have the beauty of a cloudless summer day or
of a face that is placidly perfect and regular, it is elsewhere that one turns
for depth and expressiveness in music. Baritones whom I would think of as
fulfilling these expectations of *bel canto* are Mario Ancona, Giuseppe de
Luca and, among modern singers, Robert Merrill. But Battistini's art was

very different. It is rare to hear him sing a passage in which some note or sequence of notes is not marked by a special kind of emphatic treatment; rare too to find him providing that easy kind of listening that one expects of de Luca or Merrill. Sometimes this brings real disappointments. For example, he recorded the Love Duet from *Pagliacci*, music that one would not readily associate with him but which gives splendid opportunities to a lyric baritone with a high, resonant voice and some elegance of style. The composer has marked it *cantabile con garbo*; that is, in a smooth singing style with grace, manner, bearing. So it would seem to be just the piece for Battistini. But in fact he punches the music, forces the climaxes, ignores directions like *sempre a mezza voce, voluttuosamente*, and produces a version quite remote from the composer's declared intentions. In a performance recorded on LP (on the Philips label, with Richard Tucker as Canio) the part is sung by Clifford Harvuot, pleasant and competent, though not, I would think, a particularly distinguished baritone. But there is no doubt that his style here is far better than Battistini's: he is much more smooth and unforced, much more recognisably singing in what one thinks of as the *bel canto* tradition.

It might seem from this as though Battistini were, unexpectedly, a precursor of those Italians whom we shall later criticise for developing an over-emphatic and emotional style, destructive of true legato. And perhaps there is a partial truth in this, but it is one that has to be very decisively qualified. For there was an underlying discipline in Battistini's production that must have involved initially a cultivation of the very finest legato. The variety was always achieved within the boundaries of a tone that he never allowed to spread: his voice is perhaps the steadiest, least throaty and best defined of any baritone on record. With this superbly economical definition of tone he could 'bind' his phrases with the utmost evenness. It was his virtuoso's command over the instrument that led him to mark his performances with an almost reckless variety of dynamics. There is a rococo luxuriance about his style, but the technique which enabled him to develop it was formed by classical disciplines.

Perhaps this underlying 'classical' quality is most clearly heard in the early records: in, for example, 'No, non plorar' from Rubinstein's *The Demon*, or the aria from Act I of *Eugen Onegin*. But it is present in almost everything he did, from a full-voiced aria like Macbeth's 'Pietà, rispetto, amore', sung with superbly bold characterisation and absolute control, to an easy-going song like Tosti's 'Ideale', its soft tone gentle and warm, its crescendos finely graded. Then there is the astounding facility in florid music, incomparably brilliant, for example, in the triplets and scale passages of the cabaletta, 'Bel sogno beato', in *I Puritani*. This virtuosity is a feature of the last records as of the first: the cadenza of 'Urna fatale' (*La Forza del Destino*), recorded when Battistini was sixty-eight, has the same fleet sureness as that immensely (and outrageously) energetic, high-speed 'Largo al factotum' of 1903. The firmness and focus remained impressive too: it is an eloquent testimony to the completeness of his training and the soundness of his basic method.

This would be distinction enough. But the final reason for valuing Battistini has to do with interpretation and personality. The point is illustrated in the note on Germont's aria in *La Traviata* (p. 583): Battistini and Gobbi are by far the most *interesting* interpreters in this set of comparisons, and Battistini has all the plasticity of style that the score (as opposed to our conventional idea of the aria) clearly requires. But almost any number of comparisons can be made to enforce the point. For example, a particularly fine recording of 'Vien Leonora' from Donizetti's *La Favorita* was made just after the Second World War by Paolo Silveri. His voice was then at its most beautiful, and his style was disciplined and musical. Yet one can listen to him in one's sleep; and by comparison with Battistini it is almost as though Silveri were (very beautifully) singing in his sleep too. Battistini pleads insistently instead of nominally; he voices passion with bared teeth; his flourish on the words 'per corona' challenges attention regally and boldly like the spreading of a peacock's tail; a most exquisitely indrawn, soft tone on the final repetition of 'mai del don si pentirà' adds an irresistible intimacy to the appeal. This is to break down into a few analysable characteristics the complex quality that we call magnetism. No question at all from contemporary accounts that Battistini possessed it, and any doubts as to whether the gramophone records support such accounts are stilled as soon as one starts to make comparisons. For example, there is a commonplace song called 'Mia sposa sarà la mia bandiera': commonplace, at least, when sung by Battistini's contemporary Mario Ancona or (in his very different way) Titta Ruffo, both exceptionally fine baritones. But what a difference when one comes to Battistini himself. He woos at one moment, velvety and sad, then at another the proud, full chest swells to give heart and soul to the song's declaration. Possibly he is overplaying, but how such a style compels attention. This kind of command is pre-eminently what the so-called golden age had to offer in its great singers. Pasquale Amato, Lawrence Tibbett and Tito Gobbi were other baritones whose records have something of this strongly individual intensity and subtlety; and it must be added that they all had a way of characterising *evil* that Battistini seems to have lacked. Yet I doubt whether even these masters of expression possessed quite that ability Battistini had to hold an audience in his spell with an art that was at once powerful and delicate. This is the singer as magician, and Battistini (as Aldous Huxley once said of Tennyson) knew his magician's business.

The Victorian Poet Laureate, going about his business in 'Aylmer's Field', that remarkable poem of his old age, made his own peculiar magic in the lines about a feeling that

> Lay hidden as the music of the moon
> Sleeps in the plain eggs of the nightingale.

It is an image that sometimes comes to mind as one listens to these old records while following a score. There lie the notes, and there in print are a few words now and again telling the singer how the thing should be done. The gramophone plays and one observes how notes and words are for the most part dutifully translated into sound, or how they are sometimes ignored or distorted. But just occasionally a singer, without imposing on the music, warms them to life in a way that is particularly creative: and then the print begins to glow as the 'plain eggs' might begin to sing.

This is true above all of the tenor, Fernando de Lucia. Born in 1860 (some give 1861), four years later than Battistini, he now strikes us as being of a very similar school. It was a school that exercised a singer till he had a technique that made him feel lord of creation and then allowed him the freedom to exploit his good or bad taste to the full. This was a perilous system but at least it made life interesting. Nowadays our musical expectations are both more secure and more narrow: we have no reason to fear performances so bad that a composer would not know his own music, yet we have almost as little to hope for any so good that they will stay in the mind as something irreplaceably individual and marvellous. Thus, to take a personal example and one closely associated with de Lucia, I have seen many good performances of *Il Barbiere di Siviglia* and yet cherish memories of none. Probe into this a little further and I realise that nearly all have come alive with the arrival of Don Basilio when the plot thickens and the comedy broadens. Never has the music for the other principals, charming and sparkling as it is, exercised any real magic over the audience. And never have the singers been allowed (or perhaps even sought) those freedoms by which the magician's business can be done. The story on records is the same. Almaviva's two serenades in Act I of *Il Barbiere* have been well recorded by generations of able tenors but in my experience only one Almaviva haunts the memory. It is nonsense to say that we no longer have tenors with the *technique* to perform such very exacting music: in Valletti, Benelli, Pavarotti and Alva this generation has four very good ones. What is lost is essentially an interpretative power.

De Lucia had a wonderful feeling for this music. He seems to have known exactly when to linger, when to soften, when to add an ornament, when to join one phrase to another. In the second song, 'Se il mio nome', the embellishments are exquisite (at one point – the repetition of the words 'che a nome vi chiamo' – wooing so irresistibly that one feels, yes, it must have been just then that Rosina finally decided to get out of bed and come to the window!). His ornamentation of the second verse is exceptionally bold, both in its departure from the written line and in the demand it makes upon the performer (it involves, for instance, a downward glissando of an octave and a fifth). Yet so naturally and easily is it done that one never feels this is flashy or out of place: never anything but a charm and a pleasure in having the music 'held'. This beauty of a moment 'held' is one of the great features of de Lucia's singing. Desmond Shawe-Taylor (*Opera*, July 1955) has noted a delightful example, the holding of the word 'beato' in the 'Obbligato' duet from *L'Elisir d'Amore*. He adds: 'When the Scala Company brought *L'Elisir d'Amore* to London in 1950, Tagliavini and Tajo made very little effect with this delightful duet because they took it quite straight, without those hesitations and playful touches which are the life and soul of such music'. This is typical. The solos from *Mignon*, *Pêcheurs de Perles*, *Rigoletto* and *Traviata* all have some point in de Lucia's recordings where a freedom is boldly and beautifully exercised. There comes a point in all of them where the moment is captured and held, an effect of suspension where we can savour the experience as *present*, not (as we generally meet it) as a point where the music drama moves from past to future. No doubt this kind of treatment can destroy an operatic performance if it is applied too often or in music where it is inappropriate. If de Lucia sang the whole role of Lohengrin in the lingering style he applies rather poetically to the Farewell, both drama and music would lose cohesion and the audience would not go home till morning. But in certain kinds of music it is precisely this treatment that makes the drama real. I have certainly never felt the dramatic reality of Alfredo's emotions in 'Dei miei bollenti spiriti' (see comparisons on p. 581) as vividly as through de Lucia's very personal realisation of the song. Conversely, in music where the demand is for a forward movement, as in the *Pagliacci* solos, one rarely catches de Lucia holding things back.

The *Pagliacci* records bring us to another fact about this extraordinary singer. He had a delicacy and flexibility unequalled among tenors on record, yet his voice was very powerful and his repertoire included roles in which later generations would expect to hear a Caruso, a Pertile or a del Monaco; and none of these would be likely to turn up in *Il Barbiere di Siviglia* or *La Sonnambula*. The strength of his voice is very evident in the *Barbiere* records themselves, and the *effect* of power is greater still, because he had a remarkable ability to intensify the tone in a long steady crescendo or to reduce it so that one has a sense of deep and finely drawn perspectives. His record of 'Vesti la giubba' in *Pagliacci*, then, is not remarkable simply in that it shows a lyric tenor with a strong metallic ring to the voice: that is clear enough as one studies any of his records. What is especially delightful is that the exercise of power brings no loss of refinement. The drama of the situation finds expression in the colouring of tone and in the oddly crowing laughter, holding the pitch of the high A in 'sei tu forse un uom'. But this is a Canio with some tragic dignity: the slow pace and quiet opening of the arioso were no doubt among the features which made P. G. Hurst (in *The Age of de Reszke* and again in *The Golden Age Recorded*) recall de Lucia's as an incomparable performance in the theatre. He brought an aristocratic touch to this, and indeed to still more unlikely music. He treats 'O sole mio', for instance, as though it were something exquisite from the age of pastorals. The full-throated abandon of Caruso and Gigli is probably what the song calls for, but de Lucia's record is a musical delight and a singing lesson in itself.

One limitation this record shares with several others is that the phrasing lacks breadth. This may be found more of a check on enjoyment than the features most commonly cited for criticism – liberties taken with the score, and the quick vibrato of the voice. This vibrato is certainly very marked in the earlier recordings; later it became less prominent. Whether it decreased with age I do not know; this does happen with certain voices. On the other hand it is certainly true that the early recording process was particularly sensitive to this kind of quick flutter, and that with many singers it threw a natural characteristic into undue prominence. The explanation often lies, however, quite simply in the playing-speed of the records. If the record is playing too fast, the vibrato becomes a parody of itself, and going with the thinned tone and unnatural vowels the voice appears to bleat and nag. Many LP transfers have been carelessly produced in this respect, and no doubt de Lucia's reputation has suffered accordingly.

For the phrasing, it is true that de Lucia sometimes takes a breath that modern singers would try to avoid. Yet paradoxically the flow of his singing is a feature that memory retains as one of his most remarkable characteristics. A marvellous example of this is the duet from Act III of *Pêcheurs de Perles* (sung in Italian as 'Non hai compreso'). If one follows the score and de Lucia's breathing, there is no very remarkable span, yet so smooth is the production, with such fine instrumental 'bowing' of the line, that one has the impression of completely unbroken melody. It all comes back to the exact and disciplined matching of technique and imaginativeness. For all the romanticism of these free interpretations, his singing was essentially schooled and patrician. One measure of his aristocratic standing among Italian tenors is provided by Stradella's air 'Pietà, Signore', recorded in later times by Caruso, Gigli and Corelli. All sing with glorious tone and all are relatively crude in their style. This was the aria sung in 1921 at Caruso's funeral, and de Lucia, thirteen years Caruso's senior, was the singer. It must have been a strange and moving reminder of the old school in which Caruso himself had been brought up and from which he developed a style so different.

'The old school', however, was not an exclusively Italian preserve. De Lucia and Battistini appear as the twin 'glories of Italy', but Plançon was a French product, and for women singers of this period who match these in distinction we have to look to Germany, Australia and Eastern Europe. Sembrich, Krusceniski, Neshdanova and Boronat were among the great singers of the time but they will have their place in later chapters. Lilli Lehmann, a soprano of astonishing power, flexibility and grandeur, has been discussed already. Matching her in these qualities, and adding a warmth and tenderness entirely her own, was the contralto Ernestine Schumann-Heink. And there remains that most paradoxical of great singers, Nellie Melba.

Schumann-Heink, like Lehmann, came to be thought of, in opera at least, as primarily a singer of Wagnerian roles. At the Metropolitan she was

6. Fernando de Lucia.　　　　7. Ernestine Schumann-Heink

famous for her Brangäne, Waltraute and Erda, a part that she sang in *Das Rheingold* at the age of seventy-one. But again like Lehmann, she was out-standingly well-schooled in florid work, and some of her solos have a brilliance and boldness probably unequalled by any other contralto on record. She was also typical of her time in recording a good deal of music that our age generally ranks as insignificant, though at least one of these songs is a charmer, and in it the singer is at her most accomplished. This is a piece by Arditi, a Bolero called 'La Gitana'. Schumann-Heink recorded it three times, the last time rather regrettably in 1929, but first for the Columbia Grand Opera series of 1903 (one verse only, but very good, catching the richness of the lower voice particularly well) and then again for Victor in 1907, a record that surely ought to be prescribed study for all modern contraltos, aspiring or professing. Here one has tone that is deep and rich but not plummy; power and authority which are exercised with feather-weight delicacy. The scale-work is marvellously rapid, precise and even; there is also a fine trill and a remarkable range. With this goes a live feeling for rhythm and tone-shading, and a charm and generosity that one comes to recognise as characteristic. What more can one ask? Worthier music, some might answer. Yet good tunes are not in such very plentiful supply after all, and Arditi has written his with grace and vigour.

When we turn to the records of operatic arias which call for the same virtuosity, the quality of the music itself is probably not all that much higher.

The Drinking Song ('Il segreto per essere felice') from Donizetti's *Lucrezia Borgia*, for instance, is a lively likeable tune; Fidès' Prison Scene from *Le Prophète* has a certain grandeur of conception; and the aria 'Partò' from *La Clemenza di Tito* is supple and workmanlike. None of them, not even the Mozart, is exactly great music; and yet there is a greatness about Schumann-Heink's records of all three. All three have a marvellous technical assurance: the long trill and bold intervals of the Brindisi, the fearsome leaps and long runs of the Meyerbeer, the clarity of the fast triplets over a big range in the Mozart. Even so, more than a technique is put before us in these virtuoso pieces, and ultimately it is for their strong individuality and true musical feeling that we return to the records.

Schumann-Heink was a singer whose whole person seemed to be involved in the music she was singing. One sees a face behind the song, and a strikingly different one as the songs change in mood and meaning. This is much rarer than one might think. Many famous singers, noted for their interpretations as for their voices, rarely manage in their recordings to suggest an expressive face, a changing, responsive human being behind the sound, but Schumann-Heink is always vivid and fully human. Her smile leading back to the tune in the *Lucrezia Borgia* Brindisi; her frown at the beginning of the Meyerbeer; her tenderness in the unaccompanied words 'guardami, guardami' from the Mozart aria – one *sees* these as facial expressions, as surely as one hears the notes. When such intensity of emotion bears on feeble music it can admittedly be almost embarrassing: a song called 'The Cry of Rachel', poor stuff by any standards, is sung with just the same concentrated imagination and sincerity as Schubert's 'Erlkönig'. But her record of that too is a wonderful piece of dramatic projection. She tells the story with intense vividness: the description of the Erlking 'mit Kron und Schweif' is boyishly awestruck, the weird blandishments have a cunning smile, and the 'ich liebe dich' becomes suddenly frightening and grasping. Then the face changes entirely as the voice lightens for another of Schubert's best-known songs, 'Die Forelle' (a fine record, with, for once, the welcome concession of a piano accompaniment instead of the usual wretched orchestra).

But Schumann-Heink does not strike one as being given to a sort of calculated dramatisation; much more to an expressiveness which was felt through the music. One can sense this in the way she shapes almost any musical phrase. One example would be Dalila's 'Printemps qui commence' (sung in German) where there is an exquisite care for the score in every line. Or what may come more readily to hand, the famous old duet from *Trovatore* 'Ai nostri monti', sung with Caruso. The whole thing is beautifully alive in feeling, and particularly admirable is her way with the chromatic phrase 'Tu canterai sul tuo liuto', coloured with more varied shading than I can remember in other performances. Indeed, taking two other versions down from the shelves, one from the past (Caruso's other partner, Louise Homer) and one from the present (Rosalind Elias singing in a complete recording with Richard Tucker), one finds no more than a routine saunter through the overfamiliar pages, and very dull they sound. Yet a look at the score shows that Verdi has left his singers with no excuse for this sort of dullness, for he has marked the phrases suggestively, and his directions all point to Schumann-Heink's way of singing them. She has had the imagination to see what the composer wanted, and the conscientiousness to attend in detail to the score. The result is a much strengthened piece of music. We then bless the composer afresh, and also the singers who have so understandingly represented him.

This is precisely the kind of artist whom posterity is likely to sift out and hold in renewed esteem. Not that Schumann-Heink was in any narrow sense a connoisseur's singer in her own day. Like John McCormack she had the popular touch and in America she even became something of a national figure – if we are to believe W. J. Henderson 'the soldiers and sailors called her Mother Schumann'. Still more remarkable, then, that she retained so completely the esteem of musicians and critics. It is not surprising, however, when we think of that extraordinary final paragraph in her operatic career, the Metropolitan appearance as Erda in 1932 and the recording made of Waltraute's Narrative from *Götterdämmerung* three years earlier at the age of sixty-eight. Her voice runs into trouble in one of the more declamatory phrases near the start, and the higher and most strenuous passage is omitted, but it is still a wonderful record, unforgettable in the tenderness of phrases such as 'dann noch einmal, zum letzten Mal, lächelte ewig der Gott' and 'er gedachte, Brünnhilde, dein'. And the pleasure a wider public took in her is just as clear when one turns to lighter music: to that charming song of Delibes', 'Bonjour, Suzon', or to the joyfully lilting Austrian song, 'I und mei Bua' (one high note sharp here, the rest bliss). There is the same devotion in these as in the Wagner: the same resourcefulness of colouring and the same application of a highly developed technique. Above all, the sense of a complete and valuable human being.

With the records of all these old singers, then – Patti, Tamagno, Lehmann, Plançon, Battistini, de Lucia, Schumann-Heink – the appeal has been not simply in the fine voices and masterly technique but in an interpretative strength and some quality of character that one can value in itself as one might the face in a fine portrait. The remaining singer to be discussed here is something of an exception, for not much interpretative distinction can be claimed for the records of Nellie Melba. Nor does her singing convey, to this listener at any rate, any particularly valuable or moving human quality except one – that of energy. But 'Energy is eternal delight' says William Blake, and I certainly find a perpetual and increasing delight in Melba's records. None of the five great singers discussed here has been more unhesitatingly chosen for inclusion: and that is merely one of the paradoxical things about her.

In Peter Dawson's autobiography (*Fifty Years of Singing*, 1951, p. 138) we learn that they used to refer to Melba as 'Madam sweet and low' – the voice was sweet but the language was low. Her singing itself often evokes an oddly similar sense of contrasts. Sometimes the disparate elements are acceptable, even endearing. A song she particularly made her own was another tuneful piece of Arditi's, called 'Se saran rose' (it came to be known as 'the Melba waltz', though, as Andrew Porter points out, it was dedicated to Patti). In this she sings with great spirit, doing wonders throughout, and drawing on that vast fund of energy. But the mental picture it conjures up varies strangely: sometimes it is of a fairylike being, a Juliet at her first ball, and then suddenly it becomes a knees-up-mother-Brown pearly-queen, enjoying herself with all the rough abandon of a cockney mum out for a day's spree at the seaside. Never mind that; the high spirits are infectious and the singing is wonderful. What is regrettable is that this same kind of strong-willed assertion comes forward to seize hold of the notes on less appropriate occasions. She takes by assault the first note of 'Caro nome', and this, of all things, must be tender, with a gentle kind of wonder. Then in the Willow Song from *Otello*, where the call is again for delicacy, she has a very ugly way of doing the octave leap on 'cantiamo': the high note is approached swoopingly and emerges with a chesty fullness that is completely out of character. This habit of taking emphatically loud notes from below was most marked in the region of the upper F and F sharp. Elena Gerhardt comments on Melba's production of certain notes and finds an interesting word for it: 'how common it sounded when she forced her lower notes up to F and even G from the chest register' (*Recital*, p. 139). Melba knew what she was doing and said that she understood her own voice. But that is not exactly what is in question: it is more a question of taste. So one is back to the paradox. The voice takes one to the elysian fields with a purity of tone that is incomparable, then down to earth one comes, as some ungracious seizure of a note cries aloud for the self-discipline that a more sensitive musicianship would have brought with it.

But when this is said – along with all the other points about limited repertoire and a lack of emotional depth – there remain certain important respects in which Melba is the best of all recorded singers. Hers was the purest and firmest of voices, the most perfect scale, the most exact trill. The pinpoint definition of her notes made accurate intonation an absolute necessity, and all contemporary accounts mention this as one of her outstanding characteristics. And so it is on her records if they are well reproduced, although the occasional faults are mercilessly exposed when such a voice as hers is shorn of its natural harmonics by the old recording process. Moreover, it was a voice that projected brilliantly, and this too is clear from the records. W. J. Henderson, an invaluable chronicler of these old singers, wrote about Melba's voice: 'There is one quality which it had and which may be comprehended even by those who did not hear her; it had splendor. The tones glowed with a starlike brilliance. They flamed with a white flame. And they possessed a remarkable force which the famous singer always used with continence. She gave the impression of singing well within her limits' (*The Art of Singing*, p. 420). Henderson was writing just after Melba's death, and perhaps the distance of years had lent enchantment. But that her singing in its great days had the splendour he describes is not just an article of faith, for the gramophone can demonstrate it.

Henderson was no doubt looking back to the eighteen-nineties, and we have to remember that when Melba came to make commercial recordings the first half of her career was practically over. The 1904 series, nevertheless, catches her in her prime and marvellous records they are. One could point to many individual beauties: the leap to the high C in Ophelia's phrase 'et l'alouette . . . planait dans l'air', the veiled tone at 'misterioso' in 'Ah! fors' è lui', the perfect arpeggio at the beginning of the passage from Lucia's Mad Scene. But the real merit lies in the sound of her voice and the habitually free and even production of it. This continued to be true to a quite remarkable degree ten years later, when, well over fifty, she was still making records of dazzling assurance and tonal beauty. The long preservation of her voice is itself a testimonial to the excellence of her production, though I do not, for myself, find the records made at her Covent Garden Farewell Performance in 1926 as impressive vocally as is often claimed (the 'Donde lieta' is good, but there are some gruesome moments in the unpublished material). On the other hand, two solos recorded in the studios at the end of the same year are remarkably fine. The pleasant 'Clair de lune' by Szulc is sung with grace and a still beautiful tone; and a bold performance of 'Swing low, sweet Chariot' makes an unexpectedly moving 'encore' song at the end of her recording career.

That career dates back even beyond 1904, for on 11 March 1901, Colonel Mapleson set up his recording machine in the prompter's box of the Metropolitan Opera House and put onto a cylinder some few minutes of Melba's singing in the evening's performance. This was of *Les Huguenots*, then a popular production, for in it the management would offer a 'Night of Seven Stars' usually with Melba in the role of Queen Marguérite. The cylinder has become something of a legend, and there are certainly exciting sounds on it, though I think Desmond Shawe-Taylor exaggerates when he says 'not a semiquaver, even in the most rapid upward arpeggios, is out of place'. Slowing the turntable from 33 to 16 r.p.m. I can still hear the upward arpeggios only as a general impression, and in some places the semiquavers are definitely *not* all there – on the word 'chants', for instance, where she reduces eight of them to four. But it is true that the voice 'flashes out with amazing brilliance and strength'; the cadenza is especially vivid, with its bold *marcato* As and Bs and the superb trill that follows them. Here one really does glimpse the splendour that Henderson wrote of. Yet, after all, it is there in so many of the later records, if one plays them on a good gramophone. A perpetual marvel to me is the recording of 'Depuis le jour' from *Louise*, made in 1913. The cleanness of tone and intervals has never been matched, and the voice does exactly 'glow with a starlike brilliance'. Nor should one need anything more than the record of 1907, made with

Caruso, to hear for oneself the sound that thrilled Mary Garden when she heard Melba sing in *Bohème*: 'The way Melba sang that high C was the strangest and weirdest thing I have ever experienced in my life. The note came floating over the auditorium of Covent Garden ... I have never heard anything like it in my life, not from any other singer, ever' (*Mary Garden's Story*, p. 91).

8. Nellie Melba as Queen Marguérite in *Les Huguenots*

Perhaps critics were right who in such moments found her only *coldly* perfect. Frances Alda, also a Marchesi pupil, says in her autobiography 'there was something rigid in Melba, glorious as her voice was'; one can feel the truth of that. And yet it is not right to place her as a sort of singing machine. In certain records she shows true musical sensitivity: examples are two songs of Bemberg, 'Chant Hindou' and 'Sur le lac', or Debussy's 'En sourdine'. In others there is a touch of emotion that might be, so to speak, imported for the occasion but is nevertheless there as part of the performance: phrases such as 'e manderò il portiere' in Mimì's farewell, or the 'unico raggio' in the Act II duet from *Traviata*. And always there is this energy: pushing forward with an almost aggressive vitality in the Jewel Song from *Faust* or in Juliet's 'Je veux vivre' (no starry-eyed dreamer, this one, but a young woman full of life and eager for more). All of these qualities, I find, combine to produce an emotional effect, however little the singer herself may have been experiencing it. There is no very apparent reason, for instance, why one should not remain perfectly dry-eyed throughout a second-rate piece like 'John Anderson, my jo', for the setting she uses is not at all a good one. Yet I find the record affecting, and certainly not because of any eloquent or subtle emotion on Melba's part. It is rather because such heavenly sounds as she produces towards the end of the song are as near to perfection as one can come, and there is always something moving about an earthly encounter with a heavenly perfection.

So Melba's records are in a way the crowning glory of the age called golden. For all their faults and limitations they present a marvellous singer. It would be a mistake, however, to think of them as typical of their period. Melba was not a representative singer. Because she continued, year after year, to provide the implausible spectacle of a fifty-or-sixty-year-old Mimì, because she never was remarkable as an actress or an expressive musician, it is sometimes thought that one can say 'Look at Melba' and imagine one has effectively indicted a whole era. But while her strengths were typical of her time in their kind, her limitations do not appear to have been widely shared by her colleagues. For a judgment on the 'golden age' the other four singers provide a much fairer basis. Of course, it is also true that these were singers of an excellence that by definition is untypical, but individual genius generally has its basis in a high degree of cultivation among the general practitioners, and the excellence of these few suggests a high standard among the many.

That standard flourished, nevertheless, only in certain fields. Accomplishment in florid music and the cultivation of a true legato seem to have been the dominant technical interests; while a personal command over the musical material, with the performer as at least an equal partner, was the prevalent aesthetic assumption. We turn now to a new generation of singers, whose interests and assumptions were rather different. They brought with them new kinds of excellence and a new 'age' of opera. Whether it was less 'golden' or more is another matter.

3. New Times, New Gods: The Changing Opera
Enrico Caruso   Titta Ruffo

AT the turn of the century the greatest names in opera were still Patti and the de Reszkes. Melba, Sembrich and Calvé held the stage, and more than the stage; for the diva of the opera house was in those days fêted and acclaimed as a very grand and glamorous creature indeed. Distinguished elders like Lehmann and Maurel could lay down the law in regal style, and Battistini, the king of baritones, travelled round Europe like a prince.

But the future did not lie with them. The last days of the nineteenth century had brought together two men, a tenor and a conductor, who in their different ways were to influence the singing of opera more than any other performing musicians then alive; and on one of the first evenings of the new century they were both facing the same difficult audience at La Scala, Milan, during what looked like being a thoroughly unsuccessful performance of *L'Elisir d'Amore*. The impresario, Gatti-Casazza, then Director of La Scala, tells the tale. The audience had been bored and restive through the first two scenes and the atmosphere was frigidly hostile. The author then slips into the dramatic present:

> Now it is Caruso's turn. Who that heard him would not remember? Calm and conscious that at this point will be decided the fate of the performance, he modulated the reply 'Chiedi, al rio perchè gemente' with a voice, a sentiment and an art which no word could ever adequately describe. He melted the cuirasse of ice with which the public had invested itself, little by little capturing his audience, subjugating it, conquering it, leading it captive. Caruso had not finished that last note of the cadenza when an explosion, a tempest of cheers, of applause and of enthusiasm on the part of the entire public saluted the youthful conqueror. So uproariously and imperatively did the house demand a repetition, that Toscanini, notwithstanding his aversion, was compelled to grant it . . .
> 'Una furtiva lagrima' interrupted at every phrase by exclamations of admiration, has to be repeated by Caruso and the public almost insists upon its being sung a third time. The curtain falls for the last time. Toscanini comes on the stage. We are all thrilled with emotion and happiness – viva Donizetti! Toscanini, radiant, as he was going before the curtain with the artists to thank the public embraced Caruso and said to me: Per Dio! se questo Napoletano continua a cantare cosi, fara parlare di se il mondo intero. (*Memories of the Opera*, p. 108)

In 1900 Caruso was still establishing himself as a reputable tenor in Italy, but Toscanini had already become a power in the land. It was Toscanini who brought into the mainstream of Italian opera the principles generally accepted in Germany and Austria, that opera was a musical form, like the symphony, and that what the composer had written is what should be performed: no cuts in Wagner, no encores in Verdi – and no whimsical exhibitionism on the part of the singers. Opera was really 'opus' in Toscanini's view: a single work, a unity and not a string of loosely connected bits and pieces. In this he was reflecting the changing course of composition. The prime influence was Wagner's, but Italian composers too were evolving a concept of opera in which each Act was bound up as a musical and dramatic entity, with the recitative more interesting and musical than it had been and the set pieces less separate. In *Otello* it was just as impossible, or at any rate as unseemly, for a soloist to come to the footlights, sing his big numbers to the audience and be encored, as in *Götterdämmerung*. Yet this meant a change in operatic manners and it did not come all at once. Gatti-Casazza's account of the performance of *L'Elisir d'Amore* at La Scala, where the audience made itself felt so positively and where the whole house ends rejoicing in beauty and throwing 'good behaviour' to the winds, is very like E. M. Forster's description in *Where Angels Fear to Tread* of a provincial *Lucia di Lammermoor*: 'Philip had grasped the principle of opera in Italy,' he says, 'that it aims not at illusion but at entertainment, and he did not want this great family gathering to turn into a prayer meeting.' Toscanini did not want that either but he did want the family to behave itself, on both sides of the curtain. Audiences must not interrupt; singers must not show off. When the audience at La Scala demanded an encore of the tenor Giovanni Zenatello in the middle of *Un Ballo in Maschera* Toscanini left the house and resigned his post. He then in 1908 went to New York where for seven years he brought to the Metropolitan the musical standards and disciplines that he had embodied in Milan. He again worked with Giulio Gatti-Casazza as Director of the company, and again he found himself with the tenor who had promised so well in 1900.

Caruso's rise to fame in the intervening years had been spectacular, and fortunately it coincided with that of the gramophone: Caruso and the gramophone were almost twin institutions in the early twentieth century and each increased the popularity of the other. His voice and temperament suited the new machine admirably, and, more important, suited the new music too. The exciting ring of such full-bodied tone and the uninhibited involvement of a passionate nature produced an ideal instrument for the Italian style of music-drama now being created by Puccini and his contemporaries. Moreover, as his tones darkened, especially in the lower part of the voice, he came to have just the kind of weight and authority to give to Verdi and the other nineteenth century composers the dramatic reinterpretation that the new century wanted from them. He may not have always looked plausible in his operatic roles, but he always sounded it (and though

Toscanini had inaugurated the Age of the Conductor, the Age of the Producer was still to come).

So Caruso came to stand for the opera singer in the new century as no other single artist could have done. Moreover, as time went by, his own style changed, leaving the nineteenth century further behind, and making both gains and losses in the process. We can trace the changes in the records that Caruso made over a period of nearly twenty years, the voice growing steadily more powerful, dark and rich in the lower notes, more fiercely ringing in the upper ones. In style he never ceased to be basically a lyrical singer, with the line well 'bound' and the tone always in focus, whatever the emotional or musical pressure; but he allowed himself more use of the aspirate and of devices for emphasis, and he cared less for minutiae of phrasing and of light and shade.

'Una furtiva lagrima' itself provides one example of the changes. He made four recordings of it, all between 1902 and 1911. It is in the version of 1904 that we can perhaps come nearest to hearing the Caruso of that performance at La Scala. Here he was allowed to record the aria on two sides, one for each verse, so there was no worry about time, and he could feel free to expand as in a stage performance (though whether Toscanini would have allowed this kind of expansion is questionable, for Caruso sings here with something like the free style of de Lucia). In this recording, the word 'invidiar' in the first verse is ornamented, and 'cor sentir' in the second; the end of the first verse is spread, and so is the cadenza at the end of the aria; he makes a superbly memorable phrase out of 'i miei sospir confondere ai suoi, ai suoi sospir', beautifully softened and most expressively shaded; and the long crescendo leading into 'M'ama' is another triumph of control and resource. All this is the work of the best of tenors. Now, unfortunately for simplicity of statement, comparisons with the other versions do not quite tell the story one might expect. One might expect the earliest record, possibly the Zonophone of 1902, to be the lightest and most lyrical, and the 1911 to be the least. But in fact the Zonophone is sung with a surprising amount of dramatic emphasis (very unlike the G & T record made at much the same time), and the Victor recording of 1911 is still very lyrical and gentle. What it had lost are some of the refinements of the 1904 version, and these have been shorn, not I think so as to get the whole aria on a twelve-inch side (it goes with room to spare), but because by this time such refinements seemed old-fashioned. They belonged to the world where opera was largely a collection of separate pieces, where everything could stop while the singer 'held' this moment or that. Caruso could no doubt have 'held' as many moments as he liked, and have held up hundreds of operatic performances in the process; but he was a good colleague, and he moved with the times.

That there was a loss is clear if we turn from the early records to the later ones and back again over a number of examples. In 1904, but not in the version of later years, Caruso began 'Recondita armonia' softly (as

9. Enrico Caruso as Raoul in *Les Huguenots*.

marked in the score but very rarely observed) and, more remarkable still, he ended 'Celeste Aida' softly.[1] In the 1906 version of 'M'apparì' from *Martha* there is much broad and imaginative phrasing, but by 1917 his singing was more conventional in style and the long phrases were broken up. It is also true that in the recordings of his last years there is often a sense of prodigious effort. Ordinary listeners who do not like Caruso often say 'Oh, he sounds as though he's bursting a blood vessel'. The remark is irritating, but it has its basis of truth in that Caruso *gave* so much. He was always, right to the end, capable of singing gently and softly, but when the climaxes came it was as though he were constitutionally incapable of witholding any part of the voice and energy he had in him. So of course his records do not make restful listening. In the solo 'Rachel, quand du Seigneur' from *La Juive* one is aware of what sounds like very painful breathing: *La Juive* was the last opera Caruso added to his repertoire, and the record was made in September 1920, only three months before the illness that was to prove fatal. But there is something the matter with a listener who cannot respond to such magnificence because of the dis-ease.

Or perhaps such a dissenting listener should be allowed a loophole. For another possibility is that he is hearing the record on one of these very inadequate LP transfers that have become so common over the last twenty years. Caruso has suffered more than any other singer from this kind of injustice (and, of course, in the early 'thirties he underwent another misfortune at the hands of Progress, for about thirty of his best-known solos were doctored: a 'symphony orchestra' was added, surface-noise disappeared and part of his voice disappeared with it). The hard, constricted tone that many LPs present is immediately exposed as a distortion if one is able to hear a good original on a good machine. In default of that, listeners would do well to wait until they can be sure of a long-playing record that adequately catches the luscious, full-bodied voice that is certainly there on the 78s.

The earliest records are so rare that few collectors could now afford or obtain them. Fortunately these have been well transferred in the first volumes of the complete Caruso recordings projected by the Olympus Company, and a fair selection was given in the reliable *Great Recordings of the Century* series. So that one can hear convincingly the fresh voice of the young Caruso and note what a very authoritative style he had even at that time. Throughout his career, Caruso (like Gigli) put much of the best of himself into those Italian songs that look so bad on paper and sound so well when the right singer sings them. Thus one of the finest of the 1902 Zonophone records is a song called 'Un bacio ancora', sung with wonderful suppleness of line and a rare combination of sweetness and power. That and the next years brought gloriously free and resourceful performances of the Siciliana from *Cavalleria Rusticana*, unapproachable in their warmth of tone. The 1902 series also included the famous recording of 'Vesti la giubba' which was said to have decided the impresario Heinrich Conried to bring

[1] 'Celeste Aida', 1902, first matrix only.

Caruso to the Metropolitan.[1] In 1906 began the specially labelled records of distinguished partnerships like the inaugural one with Antonio Scotti in a dignified but deeply felt performance of 'Solenne in quest'ora' from *La Forza del Destino*. From then on till 1920 most of Caruso's repertoire found some representation in the catalogues. Not all, for in 1910 he sang in the first American performances of Gluck's *Armide*, and excerpts from this were obviously not thought to be a paying proposition. More surprisingly, nothing was recorded by any of the principals from Puccini's *La Fanciulla del West* which had its highly publicised world-première at the Metropolitan in the same year. To compensate, there were two priceless records from *Otello*, an opera Caruso studied but never sang on the stage. 'Ora e per sempre addio', with the passage just before it, is given with exactly the right balance of lyricism and declamation, and the Oath Duet ('Sì pel ciel') with Titta Ruffo is one of the most exciting of records. For all the excitements of his singing and the animal vitality that went with it, there remained, moreover, a remarkable dignity inherent in the voice and style, so that it is quite wrong to think of Caruso as a barnstorming player, tearing a passion to tatters and incapable of such tragic depths as the role of Otello requires. This dignity is felt in surprising places: in two war-horses from *Trovatore* for example, where in the 'Di quella pira' every note is scrupulously cared for, and where in 'Mal reggendo', instead of the customary quivering and thumping, we hear the solo moulded with natural good taste as well as incomparable natural resources. His gaiety was as vivid as his seriousness and sadness. Many of the songs illustrate it: a charmingly light-hearted and light-voiced Florentine song called 'Pimpinella', or the war song 'Over There' recorded in English and French with a huge voice and a spirit to match.

But when all is said, Caruso's records with very few exceptions are marvellous and moving from the first in the series to the last, and his two-hundred-and-fifty-odd sides are the richest legacy we have from these early days of the gramophone. Toscanini is reported to have said of him that he was at his best when he first came to the Metropolitan and that he declined steadily from that time on. But another remark which may perhaps be quoted against Toscanini's is attributed to the veteran small-part singer at the Met, Angelo Bada. Caruso *became himself* more and more, he said, and none of his performances were so much the full and true Caruso as those of his last seasons. Anyway, as long as he was alive, so his old colleague put it, there was no one to touch him.

If one singer existed in those days who could measure up to him in sheer opulence of sound it must have been his partner in the duet from *Otello*, Titta Ruffo. In the years of their greatest fame Caruso and Ruffo sang together on the stage very rarely, (they were in performances of *Pagliacci*

---

[1] An apocryphal story, for the engagement dated back to 1901 (see Kolodin: *The Story of the Metropolitan Opera*, p. 185).

at Buenos Aires and Montevideo) and met at only one recording session, in 1914. As well as the *Otello* duet they recorded 'Enzo Grimaldo' from *La Gioconda* but this remained tantalisingly unpublished. Five years younger than Caruso, Ruffo was very much his counterpart among baritones. He too suited the trend of operatic development, with a darkly dramatic voice and a magnificence of sound that could produce a thrill matching the broad emotional appeal of the new verismo operas. His singing has still less repose about it than Caruso's, and he sometimes 'pressurised' the tone in a way that Caruso never did, so that its vibrancy would become an emotional quiver of sound around a tonal centre. I personally find that three or four records are enough at one stretch, though at the same time the voice is one of those that creates an appetite for more. One returns to him as to some favourite food for a full-bodied satisfaction that nothing else can quite offer. Expectations are sometimes disappointed: instead of the open sound we want, a half-closed vowel frustrates the fullness that we know lies in reserve. But that rich reserve is what still calls us back, permanently addicted, hoping to hear the most glorious sounds that a baritone voice can produce, and always, somewhere or other in the three or four records we allow ourselves, hearing them.

Perhaps the most addictive record of all is the unaccompanied solo from *Africana*, 'All'erta, marinar'; and this principally for the last few bars of it. It is a kind of *locus classicus* in singing, for sounds of this quality are always in our minds as the ideal that neither the opera house nor the gramophone seems ever quite to bring before us. I have certainly never heard that kind of magnificence in live performances or elsewhere on records – the only baritone whom I think of as having given anything at all comparable in the theatre is Giangiacomo Guelfi in the late 'fifties. Ruffo's tones have a magnificently full body and an even resonance, and the power of them is quite exceptional. In this way his record of Iago's Creed from *Otello* and his part in the duet with Caruso are incomparably fine.

Nor was he any mere volume-monger. 'Adamastor, re dell' aque profonde', another solo from *Africana*, shows him changing the colouration of his voice with startling effectiveness. The dark tones have conveyed a defiant menace, almost a snarl of power in their thrust and edge, and the laughter is open-mouthed and vivid. Then, like the sudden change of an actor's face or a dancer's position, comes a new voice underlining a new figure in the music and bringing out its full pictorial vigour. He was a master of vocal colour, shading in a way that often brings to mind Tito Gobbi, so much the great colourist of later times. The veiled and shaded sound of some phrases in the records from Thomas' *Hamlet* could almost be mistaken for Gobbi, especially in the brooding 'Essere o non essere' and the minor middle section of the Brindisi. Perhaps comparison between the two is most striking in *Rigoletto*. Ruffo was a great Rigoletto in his time, but not entirely fortune's favourite when he came to make records of it. Whereas Gobbi has left a complete performance on records, Ruffo has only a few

10. Titta Ruffo in *Hamlet*

excerpts. Whereas Gobbi has a stimulating and musical Gilda in Maria
Callas, Ruffo had for three of his five duets Maria Galvany, a Spanish soprano
who most notably on records could sound like a whistling kettle on a high
E flat. Added to this, he found himself with an unusually depressing pre-
electrical orchestra and with small-part soloists who could well have been

recruited from it. So all that survives in any very listenable form is the final duet, well sung with the exquisite Graziella Pareto, and the 'Pari siamo' from Act I. This, happily, is a splendid record and shows just how sensitive the lion among baritones could be. Rigoletto's monologue is as good a test of an opera singer's imagination as any. It calls for the flexibility of mood and the expressiveness of word-painting that are so much more the province of a specialist in Lieder, and it is not surprising that German baritones like Hüsch and Schmitt-Walter should have made excellent records of it. Italians do not have this kind of ability quite so much 'in the blood', though at least there is likely to be a freedom from inhibitions or artificiality in the broader dramatic effects. Ruffo and Gobbi both go far beyond this, combining the Latin timbre of their voices with genuine insight into the music-drama. Each has his own perceptions and character, but if for a moment we allow ourselves a competitive comparison between two such great singers we shall find that Ruffo is quite Gobbi's equal as an interpreter. The bitter self-pity, the imitation of the Duke's voice (an effete *tenore di grazia* in this version), the uneasy look into the future and the impulsive dismissal, all these are vivid points in his performance. More eloquent still is the suddenly veiled, indrawn and extremely beautiful tone at the important phrase 'Il retaggio d'ogni uom m'è tolto, il pianto': it is well done in Gobbi's record but one catches the breath in Ruffo's. Then when it comes to a phrase marked *tutta forza*, or to the long high G of 'follia', Ruffo can turn his enormous power to artistic purpose because he has held the full voice in reserve for those particular moments.

He was, then, a genuine artist. His use of this huge voice, too, was often fine in its preservation of a true legato: in 'Pari siamo' one finds that so many baritones aspirate the descending quavers in the E major phrase, 'Ma in altr'uom quì mi cangio', but Ruffo's line is faultlessly smooth. Where his style did lead to trouble was in the extent he allowed, perhaps even encouraged, his tones to spread under pressure. The extreme vibrancy was a form of emotional expression, but it was no doubt a reason for his relatively early deterioration. The few electrical records made in 1929 carry more than a hint of what once was, but there is much unsteadiness and loss of brilliance. Nor was the influence of such vast power as both he and Caruso exhibited an entirely good one upon younger singers. A passage in Kolodin's *Story of the Metropolitan Opera House* (p. 278) shows W. J. Henderson, beginning perhaps to get a little old and crotchety by this time, nevertheless putting his finger on a truth that was to become more evident as the next twenty years went by:

The success of Ruffo and the excited talk about him prompted Henderson to an article entitled 'Get Rich Quick Singing' on December 3 (1929) which shows rather clearly what, in his opinion, had brought the golden age of the nineties to an end. The urge to make a big sound (Caruso was the model for the tenors, Ruffo for the baritones) had made for 'hurried preparations for short careers'. Nor did the house demand such power. 'There was not a spot . . . where the moderato of Sembrich or the finest spun mezza voce of Bonci could not be heard'. But that kind of mastery takes time and singers are impatient. The outcome, in Henderson's view, was that 'only a few singers are provided with a real vocal technic, and even some of these sacrifice their voices to . . . big tone. The others go to pieces anyhow in a few brief seasons . . . most become teachers of that which they never knew, namely the art of bel canto'.

All this is not an accusation to be hurled against Ruffo or Caruso personally: an artist cannot be judged by his imitators. But records, both in writing and on shellac, suggest there was a substantial truth in the critic's diagnosis.

Ruffo, as it happens, would probably have been the first to agree with him. In his last years in retirement at Florence he was asked (by Edward J. Smith) why he did not teach. The answer must be unique:

'I never knew how to sing', he said simply, 'that is why my voice went by the time I was fifty. I have no right to capitalise on my former name and reputation and try to teach youngsters something I never knew how to do myself.' (From a sleeve note of TAP.T.309.)

4. Good Deeds in a Naughty World: Lyricism Resistant
Lucrezia Bori   Alma Gluck
John McCormack   Alessandro Bonci
Giuseppe de Luca

RUFFO had a rival among the students at Rome and later in the opera houses of the world. This was Giuseppe de Luca, who competed in the only possible way, by developing the classic virtues of a smooth style and a compact production; and if you can keep your voice while all around are losing theirs, that is also some consolation for not setting the ear-drums buzzing and the chandeliers a-rattle. De Luca had other compensations too for it was he who as a young man was chosen to sing in various important premières, including that of *Madama Butterfly* in 1904; and at the other end of the business it was Ruffo who retired from the international scene in middle age while de Luca sang on and on, making his final appearance at the Metropolitan in the 1945–6 season and his last records only a short time before his death in 1950. 'De Luca was the mouse. He could do so,' was Ruffo's reported comment. 'But Ruffo was the lion,' he added, 'and the lion can roar no more'.

Certainly there is nothing very mousy about de Luca's voice on records. He holds his own with some formidable duettists, Caruso among them, and had a remarkable power to intensify his tone to the point where it glowed into a brilliant ring. But his great strengths were the perfect placement of a beautiful voice, and an unfailingly musical and sensitive use of it through a long career. The velvet of his round, warm tones was matched by the smoothness of his style. He never shouted and never forced, never broke the line with an aspirate or a rough joining of registers; and, once his debut at La Scala was over (as Alberich, of all things, in *Das Rheingold*), he always sang what was within his voice. In these respects he was and is a model for any young singer, and with the long preservation of his voice he brought to many performances a reminder of what the golden age was supposed to stand for – though in fact he probably embodied the ideal of perfect smoothness more consistently than any of the earlier 'golden age' singers on record.

Like Ruffo he was an admired Rigoletto, and his records from the opera have a merit all their own, for no one, I believe, has made certain lyrical passages sound so beautiful. The duet 'Piangi, fanciulla' is one example: the opening phrases, rounded and gentle yet glowing with a fine resonance, set a standard that should be central study for his successors. In 'Cortigiani, vil razza' the same kind of beauty marks the final section, the broad D flat melody starting 'Miei signori'. The value that a study of de Luca might have for a modern singer is clear if one listens to such a performance as that of Ettore Bastianini in a complete recording under Gavazzeni. He too was essentially a lyric baritone, clear-voiced rather than dark and dramatic; but there the likeness must end, for when we play his record of this passage it is to find the line broken by aspirates, the phrases innocent of any kind of shaping, and no change of tone even when the score marks a pianissimo. Return to de Luca and we hear every musical requirement perfectly met: the rise and fall of the phrase 'Miei signori, pietade' is a lesson in itself. How characteristic too is that final touch of graciousness and care in the perfect rounding of the last note, the firm long holding of it and the finely controlled *diminuendo*. All this is the work of a master-singer.

One sometimes feels that when the melodic line is sensitively and beautifully sung, as it is here, the dramatic force of such music will speak for itself. In this particular section of the solo I think that is true, though in the whole scene and aria it is not. For many opera goers in mid-century the music is almost bound to bring to mind the performances of Tito Gobbi, and he is, after all, incomparable in the vividness of his characterisation: the venom in 'più nojoso voi siete', the variety and expressiveness of the 'la ra's, the tragic irony of 'avrò dunque sognato'. There is richness and subtlety here that range beyond any brief analysis, and the pathos of it remains moving, not as a calculated piece of art but as true feeling. To this I would say that, among early baritones, Pasquale Amato has some intensity and imaginativeness corresponding; but de Luca has not. His performance is by no means undramatic. There is emotion and much authority. His reading of the character may be valid in a way different from Gobbi's, for this Rigoletto maintains a dignity and status in his pleading and does not grovel. This is so with most of the dramatic side of de Luca's work on records. There is a certain nobility in his manner, and his singing commands attention by virtue of this manner as well as by its intrinsic beauty. But his Rigoletto, Amonasro, Rodrigo and Germont père all sound very alike, and just what their emotions are at any particular time it would usually be hard for the uninitiated to say.

He was, however, one of those rather rare artists who manage to convey a sense of humour on records. We must regret that his Figaro or Malatesta could not have been recorded complete, for they would surely have been among the best. The few excerpts from *Don Pasquale* show him as something like the ideal Malatesta, singing 'Bella siccome un angelo' really '*siccome un angelo*', giving sparkling encouragement to Lucrezia Bori, his Norina in the duet from Act I, and enjoying himself tremendously with Feruccio Corradetti in the Patter Duet – one of those early Fonotipias where there is no sense of studio constriction and where the singers play up to each other with

11. Giuseppe de Luca

infectious enthusiasm. Another irresistible touch of humour comes from the very end of his career, a jubilee recital given at the New York Town Hall in 1947, recorded privately and then issued by the ASCO company. No doubt the recital itself was a great success, though, as with most of these affairs, recording brings a chilly touch of the-morning-after into a place where all was affection and high spirits. Where the record becomes captivating is with the encores, of which my own favourite, as it seems to have been the audience's, is an absurd song called 'Marietta', sung in a peculiarly endearing kind of English, with charm, lightness and fun, and very properly provoking an uproar at the end. There is also, among the encore songs, a 'Ninna nanna', so exquisitely tender that you can feel the audience holding their breath and sitting back contented at the finish. And then, finally, another humorous piece, called 'Serenata gelata', where by the end of the evening the seventy-year-old singer has almost sung himself back to youth, and the whole hall has become one great family party.

But de Luca will be a posthumously welcome and, one hopes, influential singer for many years yet. His records are a rich store: the beautifully fashioned 'Eri tu', the touchingly vivid monologue of Michonnet in *Adriana Lecouvreur* (a part de Luca created in 1902), the ringing yet elegant 'Sei vendicata' from *Dinorah*, the delicacy of Pasquini's song 'Susurate intorno a Clori', the sunshine of the Neapolitan songs 'Oi luna' and 'Nutate e sentimento'. These and so many more are touchstones for any lover of singing, and in their time as in ours they have presented an excellence that is central to the continuing tradition.

As Caruso was Ruffo's counterpart among tenors, so de Luca's was Alessandro Bonci. Audiences, critics and singers themselves seemed to agree that 'delicacy, refinement, grace and elegance' were the words for him, though Henderson noted that he was evidently too good for the Italians of New York: 'the exquisite vocal art of Bonci is wasted on his compatriots. He cannot make sound enough to please them. They would rather hear the reverberations of Mr Zenatello's hard unsympathetic tones, because they are bigger and more brilliant' (*The New York Sun*, 20 December 1908). Now this much has to be put by way of historical statement, because when we come to Bonci's gramophone records some major qualifications have to be made. For while de Luca, with whom we began by comparing him, is one of the most reliable recording artists, Bonci is one of the least.

In *Le Grandi Voci* Rodolfo Celletti begins his discussion of Bonci by saying that his records are 'generally disappointing'. He has a long list of criticisms, including colourless expression, artificial diction, a tendency to drag, inflections 'un po' belante' ('bleating'), a certain awkwardness ('fissità') in the voice between middle and upper registers, and a bad habit of attacking high notes with an acciaccatura. To this I would add that his intonation is troublesome, his vibrato pronounced, and that his diminuendos are sometimes achieved only with a little break in the filament. So poor Bonci seems to have collected a formidable array of black marks, and it may be wondered what can possibly redeem so many faults. The answers are that the virtues are also very great, that the vices are not always present in a record at all, and that in some ten or twelve records at least we can well believe that here is the finest lyric tenor of the century.

The most famous of them is of 'A te, o cara' from *I Puritani*. It is usually said (almost as a point of honour) that Bonci sings this in the original key of D major and that the record therefore boasts a high C sharp and various other wonders on the way. I used to believe this and, while marvelling greatly at the celebrated note as well as the beauties of style, I found the vibrato so marked that pleasure in the voice itself was virtually cancelled. But of course the voice one hears as 'A te, o cara' plays in D is a parody of itself when playing half-a-tone lower. The transposition is normal and arguably an improvement, for D flat generally registers as a more relaxing key, the sort one thinks of as right for Chopin nocturnes and so for Bellini arias of this kind. It would be better, then, for admirers of Bonci to surrender the high note and preserve the voice from the disrepute it will certainly run into if many more LP transfers give us this aria in all the pride of its original key. Played at the slower speed it is one of the classics of the gramophone. The treatment is poetic, relishing the long phrases, making magic in the tradition of the old school, for this is how de Lucia might have handled the aria though he would have sung with a less mellow, less intrinsically beautiful voice. An example of Bonci's finesse is the phrase 'fra la gioia l'esultar' with its finely controlled *diminuendo* on the high A flat and its graceful rounding of the first verse. When the high C comes, it is taken 'out of the air': no climb upwards, no exhibitionist's bellow. As the scale moves downwards the phrase is seen as a whole, and meltingly sung. At the end of the solo comes one of those tiny flaws in the thread of sound as it is being softened for the very last notes: it is a pity and it is characteristic. Still, a small flaw indeed in so fine a performance.

'Spirto gentil' from *La Favorita* is a companion piece to this one, and is outstanding in much the same way. The voice has an easy, sweet flow, but still enough body and substance not to be insipid. 'Una furtiva lagrima' and 'Cercherò lontana terra' from *Don Pasquale* also show the full ringing tone that this most delicate of voices could produce. Such music was his natural element, but outside it he also has some fine and instructive singing to offer. A passionate performance of 'Ah, non mi ridestar' ('Pourquoi me réveiller' from *Werther*) shows, for instance how to sing *marcato* on the words 'della tristezza' without disrupting the line; he also sings out a bold *marcato* in the last bars of Gounod's 'Ave Maria', making unexpectedly strong music out of it. Another felicity in the solo from *Werther* is the treatment of the high note in each verse; always a difficulty, this, where French tenors, even Clément and Thill, can sound none too happy. Bonci takes both of the notes cleanly and with an easy ring, and the second he joins to the following phrase by means of a well-executed portamento. This is one kind of pleasure his records afford; and another, more valuable perhaps, in the way that de

Luca's records were timely reminders of a classic style, is the example that he sets in the unforced voicing of what was then the new music. The air 'Mai più, Zazà' from Leoncavallo's opera was recorded some years later in a fiery and memorable way by Martinelli; but to play Bonci's performance to ears that have grown accustomed to that other sound, so strenuous in style and keen-edged in tone, is almost to lay balm on a sore place. There is a basic difference of approach here: almost the difference between thrust and caress. Bonci intensifies a well-rounded tone rather as de Luca does. He sings with strength and feeling but also with a kindly flow of easy sound, such as one might hope to hear from a good tenor singing, say, Alfredo's 'Un dì felice' in *Traviata*. In other words, the more emphatically emotional music of the verismo school is treated with a classic grace, and sounds all the better for it. It is a record that makes wholesome study – except for one note.

And, alas, there is so often an 'except for' to be added to the praise of records by Bonci. In this instance, it is an unusual failure of taste: he sings an unwritten high note at the end, breaking the mood of the piece, seeming to play for applause in a rather cheap way, and yet taking it none too comfortably, with an uneven vibrato. The composer was there in person at the piano, so the arrangement must have had his blessing – may even have been his suggestion. That makes it none the less a blemish, though not a typical one. The recurrent weakness of Bonci's singing on record is its undependable intonation. This is most persistent as a sharpness in the notes around the lower A flat (the record of 'Salve dimora' from *Faust* illustrates it). Often in these old recordings one is inclined to give him the benefit of the doubt and ascribe vagaries of intonation to faults in the recording or pressing, but one also meets it in duet (for instance, 'Del tempio al limitar' with Magini-Coletti) where the other singer is perfectly well in tune. Again it is particularly regrettable when the record has been a good one until the last note; yet the last note in several of them leaves one dissatisfied. 'Fra poco a me' from *Lucia di Lammermoor* is an example here: almost a model performance until the last note which goes well sharp of D. So while the annals of opera suggest that Bonci must have been all but the finest of lyric tenors, the gramophone gives this only fitful support. At their best his records are a delight; but far more dependable in a similar repertoire are those of de Lucia, Tito Schipa and John McCormack. And to that list we should perhaps add the modern lyric tenors Ugo Benelli and Luciano Pavarotti.

Certainly McCormack's placing in the front rank is as assured as that of any of these tenors. And during the first two or three decades of the century he too, like Bonci and de Luca, could be held up as a shining example of technical accomplishment and stylistic grace. He was rather younger than the other singers we have been discussing (born in 1884, eleven years after Caruso, fourteen after Bonci), but he belonged to the operatic world of Caruso's period, and he went about his singing in the traditional way. He

12. Alessandro Bonci   13. John McCormack

cultivated a finely poised tone, compact and pointed, yet also in those days sweet and ingratiating. His scale was even, rapid and perfectly distinct: a match for Melba among tenors. His breath control enabled him to sing the most difficult runs in Handel and Mozart, and he is one of the few tenors to demonstrate on records (though briefly) a trill. He was no actor, and the stage was not his natural home. Even so, some of his operatic records show a greater command and generosity of emotion than have been achieved by many a noted and full-time operatic artist since his day, and in his own fields he later became one of the most expressive singers of the century.

Like de Luca and Bonci, McCormack gave several performances on record of music that is often belted out by singers with greater power and more fiery emotions. The pleasure lies in hearing how a sound technique, a good voice and a musical style will be quite sufficient, even giving the piece a new and probably much more likeable character. So when McCormack sings Puccini there is no huffing and puffing, no 'be-he-lle-he forme' in 'E lucevan le stelle' and only the most tenderly continent of addresses to Mimì in 'O soave fanciulla'. Then in the duet for Enzo and Barnaba in *La Gioconda*, with the baritone Sammarco singing at his impressive double forte in a style of voice usage that no one would want to call continent, McCormack maintains possibly the most beautifully smooth line and focused tone ever heard in these ardent and arduous pages. Nor is this purity of style achieved at the expense of the drama: his 'infamia' bites excitingly, and his 'maladetto' is as convincing as the noisiest of them.

Still, it is in the gentler lyrical music of the earlier nineteenth century that we would expect to meet McCormack at his best, and in many records the expectations are fulfilled. In Bonci's own territory he does a particularly fine version of the aria from *La Favorita*, 'Spirto gentil'. Less imaginative and supple than Bonci, he can still set the Italian an example in phrasing and breath control. The first four phrases are taken on a single breath, so that the melody floats smoothly and beautifully as it should (for an example of how it should not go, hear the stolid but otherwise admirable French tenor, Emile Scaremberg, who breathes after each of the phrases - most singers do something in between). In the solo 'Bella figlia dell'amore' at the beginning of the Quartet in *Rigoletto* we can compare him with Caruso. The Caruso of 1908 sang with McCormack's grace and his own incomparable richness, but by 1917 it was a different story, and here the style has grown far more strenuous and emphatic. Turning back from this to the purer legato and easier production of McCormack is to register another victory for the old school and what one likes to think of as *bel canto*. Not that McCormack is always true to the ideal. His record of 'Una furtiva lagrima' has not quite the purity and poise of Schipa's, any more than it has the inspiration or the tonal resources of Caruso's 1904 recording. But it is by any standards a fine piece of singing: the tone round in body, precise in definition, the handling of the line warm and idiomatic, the cadenza brilliant and sonorous. If he had recorded nothing beyond these pieces, within the normal range of the Italian lyric tenor, he would still have earned his place in the chapter.

But this aria of Donizetti's was coupled on McCormack's record with one by Mozart, and in this he demonstrates distinction of a rarer kind. His 'Il mio tesoro' from *Don Giovanni* is one of the most famous records of the pre-electrical period and has become a key-illustration in any talk about standards in singing. In that role it is produced for discussion in the last part of this book (see pp. 561–2); for the present it will be enough to say that McCormack copes with this most testing of arias in a way that no one matched on records for over half-a-century. How sad that he recorded nothing else from the Mozart operas: he might have done a beautiful version of Fernando's 'Un' aura amorosa', but nobody appears to have thought much of *Così fan tutte* in those days. We do at least have an elegant performance of 'Ridente la calma', and there are one or two arias of Handel that help to satisfy the appetite so frustratingly whetted. 'Come, my beloved' from *Atalanta* is one of the best of all his records: the shining tone, the magical octave leap to the high A on a perfectly supported *mezza voce*, all, down to the graceful rounding of the last note, are a delight. Then there is that almost legendary record (when was it last seen on a dealer's list?) of 'Oh sleep, why dost thou leave me' with its delicious short trill, and the long, long run on the word 'wandering' which is said later in life to have provoked from the tenor the admiring cry 'By God, it can't be done'. To sigh for what might have been is all very unavailing, we know, but how surprising it is that a British company should not have recorded such an outstanding Handelian in some solos from the oratorios. Or, if it comes to that, what about so many other things – Gerontius, for example? One would imagine him to have been ideal; but imagination is all that is allowed us.

An especially interesting extension to our knowledge of McCormack's art is provided by the dozen or so of Lieder that he recorded. Desmond Shawe-Taylor (in notes on the collection of classical songs and arias in the *Great Recordings of the Century* series) says that 'his repertory of serious music became vast and the brief classical groups with which he used to begin his regular recitals only touched the fringe of it'. Records show that he could be very good indeed (but see the notes on 'Anacreons Grab' p. 606 and on Brahms' 'Die Mainacht' p. 602). The bitterness of 'Die Liebe hat gelogen' (Schubert) is made boldly vivid, while Brahms' 'In Waldeseinsamkeit' is beautifully still and tender. With its fine control and the miraculous use of the head-voice at the ending, the song shows how perfectly McCormack's technique and artistic insight were suited. It is so in Wolf's 'Auch kleine Dinge': the indrawn feeling (though there is never any 'whisper-singing') is perfectly expressed by the voice in that most delicate phrase, 'Und düftet doch so lieblich'. In two of Wolf's most deeply felt songs, 'Herr, was trägt der Boden hier' and 'Ganymed', McCormack achieves some of his most profoundly expressive singing. 'Ganymed' becomes marvellous about half way through (though for many listeners his is the definitive performance from start to finish). At the words 'Du kühlst den brennender Durst meines Busens' there comes a new rapt and passionate feeling, answering the new character of figuration in the music, and it is at this point that McCormack's singing acquires greatness. Then in the long final phrase, the voice, as Shawe-Taylor puts it, 'floats upward and out of sight . . . in a manner of which this singer alone held the secret'.

It was, after all, a remarkable thing that an Irishman brought up at this time to sing Italian opera should have developed the special love for Hugo Wolf that McCormack had. But then, from his first dealings with Irish songs, he knew more than most Italians about the power of the word in singing. Italian songs express joy and misery, but songs about Irish emigrants and so forth tell stories: you have to get the words across and your voice has to respond in its tones to the stories you are telling. McCormack's experiences with opera probably taught him much less about this side of singing, for it is rare to hear the manner that was most personal to him in his operatic recordings – his singing of 'Ganymed' has more in common with 'Kathleen Mavourneen' than with the Finale of *Lucia di Lammermoor*. It was, of course, in such songs as that one that McCormack exploited most frequently the 'secrets' of his expressiveness (a way, for example, of suddenly taking the edge out of his voice for a warmly emotional phrase – suddenly that pointed economical tone which was normal usage in his singing would swell not so much in volume as in breadth, and it would express a warmth and full-heartedness that was far more emotionally charged by virtue of the contrast). Sometimes the tunes and words of these songs were extremely feeble, and one would wonder what anybody could ever find in such stuff. But then no doubt many people must despise the ones I happen to like, so it does not do to be too contemptuous. I like, for example, 'Off to Philadelphia', and love the comic self-pity that McCormack so expertly caught:

> But my heart is sad and weary;
> How can she be Mrs Leary,
> When I'm off to Philadelphia in the morning?

'The Star of the County Down' is another beauty, and it should be noted that in all these Irish songs there is no 'quaint' Leprechaun charm; McCormack was rarely meretricious in his singing. In such a 'sentimental' English song as 'I'll walk beside you' he would sing quite simply, enunciating clearly and letting the song carry its own kind of truthfulness. He had Gerald Moore to accompany him instead of the glossy, inflated orchestras that no doubt he could have commanded, and that is another sign of grace. Of course, in his later years, and certainly during early wartime when he recorded that song, his voice was not an instrument of great beauty. On many of the records made after about 1930 it seems somewhat hard and unsteady, while the thin 'ee' sounds begin to grate. He had also developed two bad habits, one of taking notes from a little below (a mannerism distinct from the portamento), and the other of 'closing' a syllable prematurely. Instead of giving full length to the note on its vowel sound, he would close it in with the consonant (as in 'Where'er you walk', where 'fan' and 'shall' nearly always have these shortened vowels). The nasal sound that was sometimes complained of does not seem to me to be very troublesome on records. Anyway, few of these criticisms, or any others, can be brought against those numerous pre-electrical records where he sang simple, unaffected songs for a popular audience, with the native good taste he brought to opera and Lieder. 'Ben Bolt' ('Oh do you remember the school, Ben Bolt, and the master so kind and so true . . .') is a model of its kind. We have nothing corresponding nowadays, no 'serious' singer of international standing who has also a place in popular culture; and both that culture and the art of singing itself are the poorer for it.

At least McCormack in his Irishry had some shapely and amusing songs to enliven his repertory of 'pops'. When an American counterpart (like Richard Crooks a little later) tried to use his own national material for similar purposes, he had much poorer resources to draw on. Similarly, Alma Gluck, a delightful soprano who enjoyed great popularity with a widely ranging audience in America, involved herself in a recording career weighed down by such square and maudlin numbers as 'Oh that we two were maying' and 'Carry me back to old Virginny' (the company sold more than a million copies of that one). Still, as McCormack had his Mozart, so Gluck had her Rameau, and some of the 'pop' songs are not too bad either. Of those, my own favourite (in the face of no very great competition) is a waltz called 'Carmena'. It has a nice period flavour (pre-First World War, Gertie Millar performing at Daly's etc.), and like so many of these not very exalted party-pieces it seems to have a succession of tunes that might float a modern musical for a few profitable seasons at least. In it we hear some very accomplished singing: a delicate yet ample tone, a good range, an even chromatic scale, much personal attractiveness, and a clean, athletic way with bold intervals that calls to mind several illustrious and more widely honoured names. That of Marcella Sembrich, for example; and (with the wisdom of hindsight) it is not so surprising to find that Gluck was in fact a pupil of that great singer. She had the rather unusual humility to go to her for lessons in Berlin in 1913 when she herself was already well-established with the public and critics of New York (after a performance of Flotow's *Alessandro Stradella* Henderson wrote of her 'beauty of tone that is valuable beyond price'). Presumably Gluck learnt to obtain brilliance out of a voice that was round-toned rather than Italianate and also relatively small from the past mistress of that art. Perhaps it was also because of this exposure at second hand to the Lamperti school that Gluck sometimes reminds us of the 'floating' type of German soprano, like Selma Kurz. This dreamy, 'pressureless' manner is heard in Loewe's 'Canzonetta', as the brilliant attack characteristic of Sembrich is heard in a Tuscan folk song called 'Colomba' or in the waltz song just mentioned.

Generally I suppose one would go to records of Alma Gluck for the voice and style rather than the repertoire, yet she recorded some out-of-the-way music, and she knew very much more. An unaccompanied song from *The Tsar's Bride* (Rimsky-Korsakov) has high notes of exquisite purity. Two 'Folk Songs of Little Russia' are alternately gentle and spirited; sung in Russian too, for she was an accomplished linguist (though some of the strange diphthongs in her English are not reassuring on the point). A lovely performance of 'Come, beloved' from Handel's *Atalanta* reminds us again of her similarities with McCormack (it was there in some aspects of style and technique too, for she could hold a long soft high note to beautiful effect – in Coleridge-Taylor's song called 'Dawn', for instance – as McCormack does so marvellously at the end of 'Ah, Moon of my Delight'). Her pianissimo is most delightfully heard in the English song 'Have you seen but a white lily blow' or in Hahn's 'L'heure exquise', where there is a purity of tone and technique that makes comparison with Melba the natural one. There is also, it must be added, a graciousness of manner that can only evoke a supplementary contrast. Perhaps best of all is the aria 'Rossignols amoureux' from Rameau's *Hippolyte et Aricie*: just the sort of music that the great golden age singers leave most conspicuously alone, yet requiring the assurance of technique and beauty of voice that were supposed to be theirs. Gluck's record, with its clear placing and pure flutelike ease, did something to fill a notable gap in the old catalogues.

These records go further than those of most of Gluck's contemporaries towards that perfection which is so very elusive in singing as in all things else. But she was not without her faults: an occasional trouble over intonation or with the tone on lower notes; more regularly a slightly 'syllabic' style, perhaps deriving from a feature of technique, for it was rarely her habit to 'grow' on a note, rather the reverse. This is no more than a tendency, generally not disturbing at all. What is more limiting is that though the interpretations have their light and shade and a face behind them, sad or happy as the case may be, they do not often go much further than that. If one compares her with, say, Ninon Vallin, who was herself by no means a Callas or Muzio in expressiveness, it is usually to find Vallin more interesting. In 'Le bonheur est chose légère', a charming song by Saint-Saëns, it is Vallin who gives the virtuoso performance as well as the more imaginative interpretation. In the Shepherd Lehl's song from Rimski-Korsakov's *Snow Maiden*, we hear pleasant singing from Gluck, but far more sense of what the music can do in Vallin's performance. And if one were to extend the comparison to include Lucrezia Bori, who also recorded a song from this opera, it would be to find that both Gluck and Vallin tend to retreat into the background as such an exceptionally individual vocal personality comes more vividly into focus. But these were all fine and valuable sopranos, and Gluck's singing is capable of giving pleasure now as it did when one of her least interesting records was selling in its thousands. She also provided a reminder in her time that good singing need not be loud singing, and that a good soprano does not necessarily imply anything very much 'in alt', or a top C fit to rouse the dead.

14. Alma Gluck   15. Lucrezia Bori

Something similar might be said about Lucrezia Bori herself. If the reference to her just now were taken to suggest some tremendous prima donna eclipsing all around her by implicit assertions of grandeur it would be very unfortunate, for the truth is almost the reverse of this. I daresay first impressions of her records have often been rather like first reactions to her singing at the Metropolitan. 'Pallid and infantile' was Henry Krehbiel's verdict at the first interval in *Manon*, the opera of her debut in 1912. During the remaining acts, however, the critic came to change his mind, as did the New York public with him; and Bori remained for the next twenty-three years as one of the most admired artists in the company.

A sense of something slender and fragile, perhaps sentimental, even girlishly winsome, may still come first, but one does not have to stay with her records very long to find also a force of character that is womanly rather than girlish, and a depth and dignity which do not easily go hand in hand with the sentimental. Her gaiety too has a genuine presence, with its source in an unforced vitality. Charm there is in plenty, but I think that while we begin by liking a charming frailty in Bori, we end by admiring strength.

The combination of strength and charm is impressive in the records from *La Traviata*. Her performance of the great solo in Act I stays firmly in the memory after many more opulent and showy ones have vanished. Her sympathy with the text never goes to sleep; every phrase is felt, the wonder of 'è strano', the quickening glimpse of a different life in 'essere amato amando', the suppressed excitement of 'Ah! fors'è lui' (the purpose of those rests imaginatively understood). The purely vocal graces are also those of a most accomplished singer. Rapid and brilliant fioritura serves an artistic purpose in this music, and Bori's singing of 'o gioia' has the assurance of a virtuoso. She uses an exquisite piano tone (particularly lovely in the echoed 'delizia al core' of the cadenza), and, although one does not feel this to be a voice remarkable for its size, there is plenty of perspective, so that the climaxes always tell. Notes which sopranos tend to sing awkwardly in this aria are the A flats near the beginning (at 'solinga ne tumulti', for instance), but these Bori negotiates without apparent difficulty. Where she is less happy is in the 'Sempre libera', the tessitura lying uncomfortably high. In the theatre her voice found greater freedom, and her singing of 'Sempre libera' on the stage has been called electrifying. But the dry Victor studio gave no help, and her high notes sound rather as I imagine those of Victoria de los Angeles would if recorded under similar conditions. In two excerpts from the last Act, luckily, the gramophone has caught the beauty of sound as well as the vivid dramatic projection. 'Addio del passato' with the recitative included before it achieves exactly the right balance between the musical and the dramatic. Bori's tone and her sense of line are delightful in themselves; the gradations of volume too are most finely judged (anything approaching full tone allowed only for the short passage in A major, the phrases that wear a kind of hectic flush after the gentler pathos of the earlier bars in major key, playing with sad unfulfilment round the third of the scale). In 'Parigi, o cara', from a little further on in the Act, the same magic is worked by a fine control of these gradations and by very beautifully judged portamenti. It is sad that we have to be content with so few records of Bori in the opera, but they are sufficient to show us one of the great singers of this role, possibly the best of all in her due proportioning of depth and delicacy, charm and pathos.

One stage performance of Bori's, her Mélisande, has been preserved for us on a private record, but the sound is very dim indeed. Excerpts from Deems Taylor's *Peter Ibbetson*, produced at the Metropolitan in 1934 for the last time, tell us little, and some broadcast selections from *Manon* are embarrassingly produced in a bad English translation. But the gramophone affords precious glimpses of her performances in many roles: of her Zerlina there is a 'Vedrai, carino', tender in manner, delicately precise in tone (another example of good Mozart from the bad old days); of her Butterfly and Louise the inevitable single selection, both done with the appeal one would expect, together with a power that one might not. Her Mimì was evidently as fine as her Violetta, and again such very personal inflections imprint themselves on the mind, so that many of the key phrases in Mimì's part ('il perchè non so', 'vivo sola soletta', 'ma quando vien lo sgelo', 'come bello e morbide') will always, for one who knows her records, sound in Bori's voice.

Like so many memorable voices, it was an odd one. There was a spot of acidity in the mixture, a little squeeze of lemon juice, which could sometimes simply be sour, yet generally added piquancy. The change of register around the low F was marked, and one occasionally notices a rather strange characteristic, as though the chest voice were being used as a springboard for a higher note – though this generally achieved an emotional effect, as it does just before 'Adieu, notre petite table' in the excerpt from *Manon*. Sometimes the high notes were a little pinched, and at least one top C (at the end of the otherwise delightful duet from *Don Pasquale*) may fairly be described as excruciating. Her pronunciation was as individual as her voice – most of the vowels very open and the 'e' sound (as in 'sincera') shaded to 'ee'. Listeners might also wonder how such a thread of sound, as it often seems, carried in a large opera house. They may find interesting, therefore, the experiences related by a correspondent in *The Record Collector* (X.1) who tells how, because of the gramophone records, he had been prejudiced against Bori until he heard her first, in 1927. The opera was *Bohème* and, says the writer, 'before the first act was over I was entirely captivated by this exquisite and patrician singer. Bori's voice stirred and moved me to an extent that her recordings had not in any way prepared me'. He mentions that at about the same period he also heard Galli-Curci, and noted that the sound of her voice, in *La Traviata*, was exactly as he had expected it to be from his knowledge of her singing for the gramophone. He returns to say more about Bori and then compares the two sopranos:

What astonished me about Bori's voice was not its clarity, precision, and security (all qualities evident in her best recordings), but its power and beauty. The beauty of tone (seeming to come from the whole body rather than merely from the throat, as in all great voices – though the edginess of her voice was still apparent) can be only partially heard in her recordings; but the power and dramatic impact of her voice are not truly discernible at all. Galli-Curci's recording of 'Sempre libera' is superior to Bori's in beauty of tone and ease of execution, but in actual performance Bori's singing of this aria was electrifying whereas Galli-Curci's was merely adequate and charming. (In the purely lyrical passages of *Traviata*—such as 'Dite alla giovine'—Galli-Curci was celestial). Bori's 'lack of ease in the exacting fioritura' of 'Sempre libera' is exaggerated in her recording and the exhilarating vitality and power are minimized.

When this writer describes the feeling he had about Bori's records he says 'her voice sounded to me (as I remember these records and even as I now play them) light, brittle and metallic. The steel was there, but there was no velvet; and the steel, while finely tempered, was like a thin, bright rapier'. 'Only those who heard her', he concludes, '. . . can fully understand why in our time, she was in a class apart.' Such clearly described personal impressions, checking the effect of records against the live performance, are always valuable, but I think the records would in themselves lead one to these same adjectives ('exquisite and patrician') and to the same conclusion ('in a class apart'). Or if she is to be classified at all, it must be in the company of the continent, lyrical stylists whom we have been discussing. She came upon the scene, as Roberto Celletti remarks (*Le Grandi Voci*, p. 92), at a time when the trend was towards a violent, declamatory style among women singers as among men (Celletti instances Carelli and Burzio, both of whom portrayed even Mimì in a 'dramatic' manner). Bori led away from this towards grace and refinement. 'So shines a good deed in a naughty world', says Shakespeare's Portia. At any rate, viewing the teens and twenties of this century in retrospect, we can see that it was the elegant lyricism of these singers which kept the central torches of the tradition alight, though no doubt others were shining with more spectacular brilliance at the time.

5. Coloratura: The Soprano as Virtuoso
Marcella Sembrich   Luisa Tetrazzini
Amelita Galli-Curci   Frieda Hempel
Selma Kurz   Margarethe Siems

No event arouses so much excitement in the opera house and so little in the musical world outside as the entrance upon the scene of a really outstanding coloratura soprano. She will arrive by way of *Lucia di Lammermoor*. The Mad Scene will be applauded for twenty minutes by the gallery and a good five by the rest of the house. But serious musicians in the city will be attending a concert elsewhere, and when they hear about the success of the new madame and her Donizetti they will still have little interest in the tickets that may be available for subsequent performances. Just possibly the opera of the debut might be *Il Barbiere di Siviglia*, and, if it were happening in the early years of this century, the aria written for Rosina's Lesson Scene would be followed by 'Home sweet home' or 'The Last Rose of Summer' and assorted songs about birds. The serious musician would still prefer his concert, and only if the programme there presented one of the virtuoso pianists in some flamboyant transcriptions or inane 'paraphrases' might he reflect that he could not have done worse if he had gone to the opera after all. The cult of the keyboard virtuoso was indeed rather like that of the coloratura soprano. More and more marvellous technique was devoted to sillier and sillier ends, so that as a pianist made it his life's ambition to play the left hand of the 'Revolutionary' Study in octaves, so a soprano might spend hours of her time practising scales, arpeggios and trills in public, and following her tame flautist higher and higher in imitation of one 'birdling' or another.

The decline of interest in this kind of soprano later in the century could be quite sufficiently explained by the surfeit everybody had had during the first decades (though, as we shall see, there were other causes, and their effect upon singing was for a while unfortunate). Certainly we hear among the early singers a far more cultivated facility in florid work than has been a general feature of the musical scene since those days. Moreover, among the most successful practitioners was usually something which could have a valid claim on the attention of a musician. Even so, there was plenty that could only crave his indulgence.

The soprano-virtuoso who probably commanded the greatest respect was Marcella Sembrich. She sang Susanna, Zerlina and the Queen of Night as well as the customary consumptives, sleep-walkers and so forth, and on retiring from opera continued a series of song recitals that became noted events in New York, lasting until 1917, her sixtieth year. She also played the piano and violin 'excellently', according to Henderson (and Liszt), and 'could have made a creditable career with both' (*The Art of Singing*, p. 464). To Henderson she was, in fact, the singer most beloved of all, and his essay on her, published shortly after her death in 1935, is one of the most precise and convincing appreciations of a singer ever written. We really need to have that article in hand as we listen to her records, for the impression they give is sometimes rather different.

For example, Henderson speaks of the emotional appeal of her singing and the magic she exercised 'in purely lyric music embodying tender pathos'. Records give little indication of this. As we listen carefully, there is a tenderness in 'Qui la voce', and perhaps it is not fanciful to detect an elegiac tone in her singing of Gilda's line in the Quartet from *Rigoletto*; but this is not a quality that the records would normally have brought to our attention. Again, we learn from the critic that she 'bubbled over with the comedy of Rosina', and there is a photograph (the one that became a trade mark for Marcella cigars) that suggests a lively portrayal. But it cannot be said that her one record from *Il Barbiere di Siviglia* 'bubbles over with comedy', any more than her record of the Mad Scene would suggest that she 'vitalised every phrase of Lucia's'. Nor do the records of 'Wohin' and 'Der Nussbaum' reveal a great Lieder singer ('the greatest . . . among women ever heard in New York'), or the solo and duet from *Le Nozze di Figaro* a very good Mozartian ('Within the memory of this generation there was no other Mozart singer like her'). On the other hand, what the records do show is a virtuoso of astonishing brilliance in fast scale passages (cf. Henderson: 'There have been more astonishing singers than Sembrich') and a corresponding brilliance and fullness of tone in the upper voice that one would imagine to have rung through the house as a most exciting sound (though in fact it seems that Melba was thought of as possessing some kind of exciting 'star' quality that Sembrich did not).

These anomalies are bewildering. It is commonly said that Sembrich's was a difficult voice to record and that her records do not do her justice. We can believe this and yet continue to ask questions. We can readily believe, for example, that the impersonality of recording accounts for a lack of humour in her performance of 'Una voce poco fa'. We can also understand that the very full-voiced, round and forward sound of notes about the high F sharp should have hit upon a vulnerable place in the recording apparatus and tended to 'blast', while the lower part of the voice, sweet-toned and flute-like, should have suffered in this primitive recording process by the loss of harmonics. But what is really disturbing in the records is something which must surely be a basic effect of her method of voice production. Very often, an outstanding and marvellous characteristic of Sembrich's singing is the absolute purity of a held high note; perfectly round and even, so that one feels it could be drawn, as a regular, unflawed column or tube. But sometimes the column wavers, uneven vibrations appear as a flutter upsetting the firmness, and there are many examples of this on the records. The 1903 Columbias have it: in the *Traviata* and *Ernani* arias the flutter is so marked that one would swear that the records were playing high, yet the pitch is correct and transposition seems unlikely. Then, the often brilliant 'Bel raggio' of 1908 begins with a strangely infirm tone, and the quaver in the voice is particularly marked on the first high note.

One is also very much aware of method as one listens to Sembrich, and yet in these recordings the method seems to bring curious technical limitations. One such feature is the absence of growth on a note. Of course she makes effective crescendo on a held note when she wants to, but her general practice (one hears it also in Alma Gluck, her pupil) is to hold a note as an organ pipe does, or, if anything, to make the moment of striking the loudest point. This is what limits the pleasure of her singing in the Letter Duet, 'Che soave zeffiretto', from *Le Nozze di Figaro*. It is tonally quite beautiful, but there is a kind of stiffness that is at odds with the flow of the music – it needs playing as on a violin, not as the Stopped Diapason of an organ without Swell pedal. Again, as we listen to the first section of 'Casta diva' through all the surface noise of an unfiltered 78, it is with just a faint awareness that this is not the legato of one's dreams; but hear it with the scratch reduced and the voice exposed, as is nowadays possible, and the imperfect flow, the separateness of notes within the phrase, is really quite marked. One feels, listening to these records, that the old recording process, for all its shortcomings, is revealing weaknesses that the magic of the singer's own presence would very largely cover.

There is, then, a quite exceptional interest in the recordings of 1919, discovered in 1968 by the late William Seltsam and issued on a long-playing disc by the International Record Collectors' Club. The first sound of the record, the opening of a song called 'Ouvre tes yeux bleus' by Massenet, is electrifying: immense in its purity and boldness. The next song ends with a brilliant high C, in the next there are some lovely soft tones, in the next an astonishing vigour of attack . . . and so forth. One could wish for better songs, and age is apparent in the lower part of the voice, which has lost its edge. But then, the singer was sixty-one years old, and she had worked her voice hard over a career which went back beyond the opening of the Metropolitan Opera House in 1883 (she had sung there as Lucia di Lammermoor in the very first performance of all). The art of the concert singer is well exercised in the story-telling of 'Pretty Polly Oliver', and throughout both recording sessions hardly a note is out of tune. There were, incidentally, two sessions: six songs recorded in one, five in the other: two good days' work for anybody.

Such preservation of voice is of course one of the best proofs of a sound method. The difference of impression that these late recordings create may have several reasons: she may have been overworking during those early years of the century and have benefited from semi-retirement; the recording process had itself improved; and she was making the records unofficially, for her own pleasure and for distribution among friends. But in other ways they confirm the enthusiasm which the earlier records promote in spite of their faults. For, if there were disadvantages in Sembrich's method (and hearing these late records one begins to doubt it), there were also plenty of gains.

She combined mellowness and brilliance, and is virtually unique among coloraturas in doing so. The typical Latin high soprano (Tetrazzini, dal Monte, Pagliughi) is bright-toned but has edge rather than roundness. The typical German (Siems, Kurz, Ivogün) floats charmingly but lacks punch, especially on high notes. Perhaps Galli-Curci and Sutherland at their best have had the virtues of both types, but if one then compares their florid work with Sembrich's there is still something relaxed and easy-going about it: however lovely in tone and marvellous in accomplishment it has not quite that daring athleticism, the boldness of stride and speed of strike that Sembrich had. 'Parla', a waltz-song (yet another) by Arditi, brings all three sopranos together and shows them to have much in common. There is not a shrill note from any, there is much delicacy from all, and in spite of the delicacy all make an impression of brilliance. Sutherland lilts beguilingly with a portamento she must surely have learnt from Galli-Curci, and Galli-Curci has her own individuality, a smiling gracefulness and unfussy exactness that make the record one of her most charming. Sembrich sings the opening tune with skilful phrasing and nuance, but her distinction lies most essentially in the quality of attack. When Sutherland sings a wide interval in this, the high note is arrived at, perhaps ever so little, by a slide from below. When Sembrich leaps an octave, it is with the absolute precision and easy vigour of an athlete in prime condition. If we then go on to the decorations and cadenzas of 'Una voce poco fa' and 'Bel raggio' we hear the most intricate vocal knots tied and untied with dazzling skill: a transcription would look almost outrageously unsingable. With that rounded, vibrant tone there is an exhilaration that no other singer offers in the same degree.

Two 'freak' additions to the catalogue of Sembrich's recordings help in their strange ways to make more vivid this exhilaration as it must have been conveyed in live performances. One is a cylinder, recorded by Gianni Bettini in 1900 and transferred on to disc sixty-five years later, having meanwhile been discovered in the loft of a hotel in New Zealand. In this, Sembrich sings an arrangement of 'Voices of Spring', where in spite of the odd acoustic (as though recorded in a nearby bathroom with singer and piano under water) we hear a clear, fresh voice, without a suspicion of the 'hooting' that some listeners find in her commercial recordings. There is also a full-bodied tone, untroubled by the anxieties of later studio days when the fear of 'blasting' must often have inhibited singers from giving their best. Then, more precious still, there are a few moments from her actual stage performances at the Metropolitan, recorded among the Mapleson cylinders. Best of these are the 'Rataplan' chorus from *La Fille du Régiment* where we hear Sembrich, neat, light, and clear, ride high above the whole company; and a part of 'Sempre libera' from *La Traviata* with runs of just that electrifying brilliance that the records lead us to hope for. Perhaps added to the list should be one of the unpublished songs that has now found its way on to LP, Reynaldo Hahn's 'Si mes vers avaient des ailes'. This is beautifully sung, and especially interesting because it shows more persuasively than her other records how good a concert singer she could be. Here, the middle voice is heard to be a sound, firm instrument, and we also hear her using it as a violin and not an organ pipe, moulding the phrases with the care and imagination that Henderson says were habitually hers. Still, the outstanding feature of Sembrich's records remains their brilliance in fioritura: the tone shining, yet with the kindly brightness of candlelight, the sheer agility and accuracy incomparably assured. So the gramophone presents another paradox: that to this most musical of virtuosi we come essentially for the virtuosity. Other singers, far less musical, have left more of purely musical interest behind them.

16. Marcella Sembrich

17. Luisa Tetrazzini

Among these, however, is not Luisa Tetrazzini. Her gramophone repertory was much the same as Sembrich's, with a few extra mad scenes and
bird songs thrown in.

While about Sembrich, her methods, her excellences and faults, there is
always something that raises questions, with Tetrazzini everything is clear
as daylight. Perfectly clear, if we listen to her at her best, in 'Ah non giunge'
for example, are the reasons why we should value her records. Like Sembrich and Melba she is an invigorating singer, bold, full of spirit and energy.
Unlike them, she did most of her recording around the age of forty instead
of fifty (born in 1871, she was thirteen years younger than Sembrich, ten
younger than Melba), so there was a healthy glow on the tone which with
its bright, keen edge took with comparative readiness to the gramophone,
notoriously inadequate as it was for recording the soprano voice. She had
the bright tone of a Bach trumpet. There was also something of a dramatic
soprano's fullness in her voice from about the upper F to B flat: it seems an
odd comparison, but if I cast around asking whom these upper notes remind
me of, the only answer that comes is Birgit Nilsson. Nilsson is much louder,
but the kind of sound, clean, bright and strong, is oddly similar. Percy Pitt,
conductor of many seasons at Covent Garden, used to say that Tetrazzini
could have been a dramatic soprano herself, though it must surely have been
these upper notes that made him think so, for the voice as a whole was too
imperfectly equalised. Still, in 'Ah non giunge', a record typical of Tetrazzini
at her best, we have the coloratura soprano *in excelsis*. Here is this shining,
brilliantly projected tone in its sprightliest form, taking the runs, trills and
staccatos in sheer joy, singing with just that easy vitality that the spring of
the music requires.

Especially remarkable was the accuracy of her staccato. It graces many
of her records; the solo from *Crispino e la Comare*, for instance, a jolly piece
called 'Io non sono più l'Annetta', superbly sung by Tetrazzini as it is in a
modern recording by Joan Sutherland. Or, in more familiar music, we hear
it to good advantage in the cabaletta of Leonora's aria 'Tacea la notte'
from Act I of *Il Trovatore*. These are the pages where most sopranos who
undertake the part find themselves far from home. Renata Tebaldi, after a
lovely performance of the aria in the complete recording, is suddenly out of
her element, and, although she gets by, conscientiously doing her best with
trills and staccatos, we feel that the voice is an unwieldy instrument for this
music. With Tetrazzini the position is reversed. Her aria has had nothing
(apart from its top notes) to commend it: there has been some short-
breathed phrasing, and in the middle voice an undernourished tone. But the
'Di tale amor' is a sparkler, voice and technique meeting the demands with
rare assurance – and indeed exceeding them in the end, for after a full-
voiced trill there comes a triumphantly held E flat in alt, and very exciting
and proper too in this context.

In this performance the bright effectiveness of accurate staccato work
plays a big part. But (for here we have to note some faults) it could have

made a more distinguished performance still if only the famous singer had spent half an hour or so taking a careful look at the score. Several more staccatos are specified there, so are several rests, and the music is all the better when they are observed. But really scrupulous care over this sort of detail was not her habit (in the matter of rests, for example, she ignores those in the opening bars of 'Caro nome' where they are so essential to the character and mood of the piece). Nor was she always thorough in those passages which called specially for her own kind of skill: a second listening to some of the scale work does not discover the proverbial row of perfectly matched pearls, excellent though much of it is. 'I had to practise very much when I began my study – when I was sixteen', she told Harriette Brower; 'but now I do not have to spend much time on scales and exercises; they pretty well go of themselves' (*Vocal Mastery*, p. 73). It is an engaging remark and to use it in evidence against her is a little ungallant: but the records do carry a suggestion that things were going 'pretty well of themselves' and that the learning and practising of earlier days were excessively relied on.

Her records are strangely variable. Sometimes it seems that there was hardly any voice at all in the middle and lower registers, and yet in other records (as in a very uncharming 'Voi che sapete') it sounds sturdy and quite adequate. Sometimes one feels she has not the slightest interest in interpretation, yet her *Traviata* records are genuinely dramatic, and in 'Una voce poco fa' she gives not only a glorious display of virtuosity but also a vivid characterisation, snapping out a crisp 'ma', singing her 'amorosa' with nice suggestiveness, and 'prima di cedere' with cunning. She varied a good deal from one recording session to another. London 1912 found her in a hurry: 'down to work and get it over' seems to have been the policy out of which came hearty but otherwise expressionless arias from *La Sonnambula* ('Come per me'), *Les Huguenots* and *I Puritani* (a 'Vien, diletto' without the specified *estasi*, *sotto voce* or *incalzando*, just an energetic 'sing'). Sometimes one version of an aria would be distinctly better than another: 'Io son Titania' was better in 1908 than in 1911, 'O luce di quest' anima' better in 1910 than 1914. It is interesting too to hear the Zonophone recordings made around 1904. The Mad Scene from *Lucia di Lammermoor* has some delightful embellishments shorn in other versions, and the voice produces none of those odder sounds that would later intrude almost comically from time to time.

But Tetrazzini remains. She is another who suggests an ideal and some-times fulfils it. The suggestion itself is a great contribution to singing. We know, through her, how certain kinds of music can sound, and it is the better part of her voice that we hear singing these when we listen inside our own heads. She is also a tonic. For after listening to the more enervating beauties of the German coloraturas and the drooping loveliness of some of our own contemporaries, we feel how refreshing a little simple, forthright liveliness would be; and then it is time to look out a good Tetrazzini.

Of course it is very rare to find anything enervating or even moderately relaxing among the high sopranos of Latin countries. One of those who does provide a gentle tone, free from any hardness and yet still having the firmness that one values in the Italians, is Graziella Pareto. Spanish born and a good generation younger than Tetrazzini, she recorded with a youthful freshness and much charm. The firmness of her middle voice is well heard in 'Siccome un dì' from *Pêcheurs de Perles*, and the fluency of her fioritura in 'Ah, non giunge' from *La Sonnambula*. There is delicacy of style and warmth of feeling: a lovely performance, for instance, in 'Dite alla giovine' (*La Traviata*) with the baritone Mattio Dragoni. A good deal of personal charm is also present in some very delightful Spanish songs, simply and tastefully sung, reminding one, as her records often do, of the limpid and affectionate style of Galli-Curci. Beecham speaks of her in *A Mingled Chime*: she had 'a voice of exquisite beauty, haunting pathos and flawless purity' he says, and he adds that her Violetta in *La Traviata* was the most attractive in his recollection.

Galli-Curci was Pareto's near contemporary (both singers born in the eighteen-eighties), and she, after all, is the gentlest of the Latin sopranos: the only one (perhaps with Pareto) who will float a dreamily lingering phrase as Germans like Kurz and Dux will do. She also had a tone-quality that one would not expect to have originated north of the Alps, a certain warm challenge in its girlishness, so that she is a singer who combines several kinds of appeal. The appeal is most essentially that of herself, however; not a matter of the characteristics of this school or that, but of a delightful individual. She is one of those whose voices on record come to arouse a personal affection – I think of Bori, Schumann and de los Angeles as other sopranos who have this power. She is also one whose records are continually prompting a fresh recognition. That is: however much one thinks one knows and loves them, there is always likely to come some moment, perhaps during the first record of Galli-Curci in an evening's listening, where one exclaims 'What a singer!' as though hearing her for the first time.

If one were indeed hearing her for the first time, the dominant impression would be of a light voice certainly, very pure and clear, used with spirit as well as charm, yet without any hint of a prima donna's assertiveness. The strong projection of Melba and the brilliant ring of Tetrazzini's upper notes might be missed, but one could not listen to much of Galli-Curci without recognising a more winning graciousness than the one singer possessed, and a more equalised voice than the other. For she was not one of those coloraturas who only begin to be useful in the top octave of their voices, and her scale was perfectly even over more than a two-octave range. A correspondent to *The Record Collector* quoted a few pages back (p. 64) wrote of the special beauty in the opera house of her singing of lyrical passages such as 'Dite alla giovine' in *La Traviata*. Records confirm this: 'Comme autrefois' (*Pêcheurs de Perles*), Grieg's 'Chanson Solveig', or the Spanish song 'La Paloma' are excellent in their evenness of line and in the firmness of the middle voice. Above the stave she was never shrill: there was no hardness or tremolo under pressure, and with the finest control she could swell a long-held high note till it would ring powerfully and then diminish again to silence. Her breath control and the ease with which she could pass over the whole instrument of her voice are evident in Adolphe Adam's pleasant variations 'Ah, vous dirai-je, maman', the last variation before the cadenza having beautifully clear arpeggios sung in series on a single breath. The musical content of the piece is slight, yet it would be a very austere listener who could not find some delight in sounds of such rare delicacy. Galli-Curci's virtuosity had an instinctive refinement and so gives a genuine musical pleasure. She was a true virtuoso none the less, though there is rather a habit of speaking condescendingly about her, as if those who know what a scale and a trill should sound like know that hers were somehow inferior. It is true that her trills occasionally disappoint (lazy, for example, in the *Trovatore* arias): a curious feature of some of them (the end of the Polonaise from *I Puritani* provides an example) is that she will trill on the note itself and the note below, not the note above. But these are exceptions: generally her fioritura is wonderfully accomplished, and in runs it is rare to find a semiquaver out of place.

All of this, however, must be taken to apply essentially to her pre-electrical records, for Galli-Curci suffered for fifteen years from a throat ailment, and although eventually, in 1935, the tumour was removed it had affected her singing over a long period, causing a noticeable deterioration in the records made in the late 'twenties. The occasional flatness audible in certain of the pre-electrical records became more frequent. The upper F was a note particularly apt to flatten. It sometimes does so even in the 'Un bel dì' of 1922, and regularly in the electrical recording of 'Parigi, o cara'. Some of these later records are still very beautiful, however. There is a Cantata of Scarlatti, a lovely and unusual piece; a sparkling and delightful display of virtuosity in some variations by Proch; and a performance of 'D'amor sull'ali rosee' from *Il Trovatore*, most graceful and haunting if rather faster than we usually hear it nowadays. Even such a record as the 'Parigi, o cara' mentioned above has much beauty (quite apart from having Tito Schipa at his most exquisite). But there is no question that by and large she is heard at her best in the earlier recordings.

As to the records of her prime, they too have their limitations. As with some other excellent artists, there is a certain sameness about her records. She is not a great colourist with the voice, and if one compares, say, her record of 'O Luce di quest'anima' (*Linda di Chamounix*) with Joan Sutherland's, I think it is to find her outshone both in brilliance of fioritura and in interest of dynamics. But enough remains, and to spare. She had her own way with music and quite often it is unforgettable. Who could know her record of Lakmé's Bell Song without always hearing in his mind her voice so dreamily magical in the opening vocalise; or the 'Obéissons' from Massenet's *Manon* without hearing her winning and individual inflections in the melody, crowned by a dazzling success in those passages where only

18. Amelita Galli-Curci as Violetta in *La Traviata*

a soprano of her particular accomplishments can perform the music comfortably. Nor, for all the dreaminess of her singing (and a way of making language sound like the murmur of a distant brook), was she lacking in sprightliness and a sense of comedy. All her many gifts are present in a delicious performance of 'Una voce poco fa'. But then, it was this (the pre-electrical version) that introduced the present writer to the pleasures of old records so perhaps it is not surprising that he still finds it the best of all.

Better even than the recording by Frieda Hempel, though that is one of this excellent singer's best, and a fascinating interpretation. Hempel, singing in German, brings quite a different kind of temperament and musical intelligence to bear, presenting a Rosina who schemes languidly and at her leisure. She dreams up her plots and floats them on high, letting them circle round or trail away in little wisps of sound, fine and airy as a piece of muslin. The will-power behind these unhurried meditations is felt in the upward movement of staccatos, and by the end we have no more doubts about the dominance of this easy-going machiavel from Leipzig than about that of the most fearsome of mediterranean vixens. The voice too is at its most beautiful, warm and clear, equally at home on the stave and above it.

Hempel could be a most captivating singer, and her technical equipment was exceptional. Her repertoire was varied, including Elsa in *Lohengrin* and Eva in *Die Meistersinger* as well as the usual range of lyric and coloratura parts in French and Italian opera. She was also, with Margarethe Siems, the first of the Marschallins, and in a rather dimly recorded performance of the Monologue we hear her, reflective and fresh-voiced in the music, not deep perhaps, but achieving the right balance of seriousness and lightness and making an impression in the phrases ('so viel geheim', 'da liegt der ganze Unterschied') which most test the artist's sensibility. She had a long career as a concert singer too, and just enough remains on records to show how delightful much of her recital work must have been (from the classical aria, such as 'Oh had I Jubal's lyre', which might have opened the programme, to 'The Blue Danube' or 'Wine, Women and Song' which might have closed it). Above all, she was a devoted Mozart singer, one of the best of her time.

Her recorded Mozart has many attractions. 'Deh vieni, non tardar' is well-phrased, sung in a clean style likely to suit modern tastes better than most of the performances of those days, even if it does have what was then the usual cadenza added at the end. With 'Voi che sapete' one can go further and say that it has virtues that most modern performances lack: the exquisitely lightened phrases act as a leaven most urgently needed in such stodgy singing as we generally hear. When she turns to meet the great challenge of 'Non mi dir' (Donna Anna's aria in Act II of *Don Giovanni*) her success lies not only in the broad phrasing of the opening lines and in the fluent runs of the last section, but also in her warmth and imagination, responsive to the music as it briefly takes on a minor tonality, then most delicately leading back to the opening theme. She was not one of the great interpreters of the century; she had not the individuality and intensity that have marked a Calvé, a Muzio or a Callas. But she was no mere warbler, and at least one of the Mozart records shows her to be capable of a genuine depth. This is the first aria of the Queen of Night in *Die Zauberflöte*, 'Zum Leiden', sung here in Italian. In the first, minor section, the Queen is singing in the very tones of her daughter. The music has the family likeness: Pamina in grief also expresses herself in G minor, begins with a similar descending phrase, and in both arias the sting of sadness makes itself felt through the flattened A. Hempel's performance is the one, above all others, that makes the likeness clear, gives some intensity to the meaning of the words, and shows an interpretative grasp of the music's character. The portamento, old-fashioned even when used as mildly as this, is here something better than a gratuitous 'warming' of the 'dispassionate' Mozart; it is one of the means to an interpretative end, and here it seems to me to be musically quite acceptable. Another means is the delicate play of light and shade, with a most beautiful close in the soft melancholy phrase 'la madre, la madre non bastò'. Then, of course, the allegro springs up with an additional vigour and sturdiness made possible through contrast.

In the more famous second aria, 'Die Hölle Rache', Hempel is less admirable. Her record has many excellences but at two of the most testing moments she fails to set the standard. One point is the staccato passage with the high F's, prepared for by a snatched breath which most singers nowadays manage without. The other shortcoming is that the triplets are not really triplets at all: instead of three even quavers, Hempel sings in effect a dotted quaver, semiquaver and quaver. This is easier to do, but one feels that such virtuosos who go out of their way to make difficulties for themselves in their elaborations of second-rate music should at least prove their musical usefulness by giving an expert performance when their skills are called upon in an undoubted masterpiece. But there it is: all of these great singers are disappointing in some ways and Hempel is no exception. Such points of detail run through many records. From Italian opera, for instance, there is the Page's first song, 'Volta la terra', in *Un Ballo in Maschera*. Staccatos are marked frequently and are obviously important. Singers of the role in modern recordings observe them. There is Eugenia Ratti in a Columbia set, Sylvia Stahlman on Decca. The first of these is rather too bright and needly in tone, the second is not bright enough. Neither of them is a singer of Hempel's standing; yet both do the staccatos scrupulously and ably, while Hempel is content with one every now and again.

Still, such defects are incidental, and for the most part we are happy to enjoy a lovely voice used with rare skill. The skill itself, isolated from any other kind of interest, is exhibited in arias from Auber's *Muette de Portici* and Isouard's *Das Lotterielos* (humorously entitled 'Nein, ich singe nicht'). Better, because more inventive and not so long, are the Adam variations 'Ah vous dirai-je, maman', even more brilliant than in Galli-Curci's record. A dazzling concoction this, with its arpeggios in staccato to the top of the range, followed by scales still more impressive, then the tune given in altissimo, then trills and downward scales and still more to come. Complementary to these accomplishments was her development of a true legato and a firm, even tone throughout the range. A lyrical aria such as 'Mi chiamano Mimì' or a simple song like 'Ben Bolt' finds her drawing a clean, fresh line, singing with heart and without sentimentality. 'It is hard to think of a brilliant soprano, apart from Sembrich, who has so much artistic intelligence, temperament, warmth and strength of feeling as Frieda Hempel', said *The New York Times*. The last fifty years have no doubt added a few names that might come to mind, but the list is short and Hempel's place in it is still assured.

So is that of three comparable German sopranos, Selma Kurz, Margarethe Siems and Maria Ivogün, for this was an unusually good period in the production of such singers. Ivogün, born in 1891, is discussed in a later chapter. Kurz and Siems, though not so very much older (Kurz was born in 1874, Siems in 1879), sound to modern ears to be singers of an earlier generation altogether: Hempel and Ivogün register as moderns by comparison. Yet all four have much in common when compared with the Italians and Spaniards. They flute sweetly and dreamily, and though they leave the composer behind quite as often as the others, one feels they do so as musicians. They too will sing the customary birdsongs, and they will exhibit trills and scales without any feeling that this is holding up the show, which no doubt should be moving forward to the next significant development of the music drama. But at least their embellishments are inventive, their cadenzas shaded in response to a sense of beauty rather than a will to excitement. Moreover, their technical accomplishments were certainly as remarkable as those of their Latin contemporaries or perhaps on balance more remarkable still. And for some few moments, every now and again, they work a special magic, delightful in kind and precious in quality.

Kurz is both a prototype and archetype. She was the first soprano heard on records (as early as 1900) to have that kind of tone we call 'creamy' or 'floating': among lyric-dramatic sopranos, Bettendorf, Lemnitz, Milanov, Stich-Randall and Rysanek were related to her in this. At her best, she achieved to perfection that kind of relaxed, 'floating' beauty we hear in Lemnitz's 'Leise, leise' or Milanov's 'D'amor sull'ali rosee'. 'Maria Wiegenlied', recorded when she was nearly fifty, is a fine example. Her singing here is wonderful in its poise. It is like a piece of delicate china, while the music itself is Christmas marzipan, made in a nineteenth century German kitchen to an age-old recipe. Singer and song are well-matched in a charm that, by its tenderness and simplicity, goes just a little beyond that of a pretty ornament.

But perhaps only a little, and this is suggestive of Kurz's limitations. We do not, on record, hear her sing with passion; she does not express grief[1] in her singing, and joy is usually confined to the limits of a serene, almost

---

[1] But note the expressiveness of her face in the photograph (p. 80).

19. Frieda Hempel

20. Selma Kurz as Violetta in *La Traviata*

meditative happiness. Beyond these boundaries lies trouble. Gay Rosalinda throwing caution to the winds in the Czardas of *Die Fledermaus* tempts her to a fuller tone and faster tempo than are wise, and the last section becomes an absurdly fussy scramble. An incisive tone is lacking, as in the duets from *Rigoletto* and *Il Trovatore*, recorded with the young and excellent Heinrich Schlusnus. These are passages requiring a firm, strong line as well as some tragic nobility, and they do not really find either.

On the other hand, where the pathos is of a milder sort, as in 'Qui la voce', Kurz will sing feelingly; and where, as in this aria, she is under no pressure, she will produce a defined, even tone on the stave as well as above it. On a good gramophone, with plenty of top and due care about playing-speed, this emerges as a fine performance, though unless these conditions are fulfilled its merits will become apparent only in the florid work. And there is certainly no denying the distinction of this. The scales are superb: light as a feather and perfectly even. The decorations are exquisite, and are crowned by the famous trill which glitters with a hundred winking lights for fifteen seconds or so while we hold our breath in admiration. Perhaps this sounds like the pure trapeze-artist among singers caught at last, and it might do so even more when one adds that sometimes, with Kurz, one feels that the aria exists for the cadenza. Rather remarkably, the truth is that it is in these cadenzas that she most clearly registers as an expressive artist. As an actor makes his body talk in mime, so Kurz talks, unaccompanied, in free passages of vocalise. So it is when the aria from *Don Pasquale* or the song 'La Villanelle' stops briefly while Kurz sings an interpolated passage on her own. In principle such a practice sounds indefensible; in these instances it is delightful and genuinely expressive.

If a singer's taste comes into question, it may be instructive to see what happens when he or she turns to Mozart. As a Mozartian, Kurz is certainly not impeccable. By too much portamento she will sometimes create a nineteenth century cosiness, draining the energy and obscuring the clarity. 'Voi che sapete' is sentimentalised in this way. But at other times she is almost ideal. There is nothing sentimental about her singing of 'L'amerò sarò costante': simply an exceptionally beautiful voice that in its purity and fineness of grain goes with a refinement of style and technique to make the perfect instrument for this music. This is an essentially lyrical aria, severely testing in its own way yet not demanding the most dazzling exhibitions of coloratura. Where rapid passage-work and decorative brilliance are required, as in the allegro of the Queen of Night's first aria, she comes into her own afresh. The scales are done with superb exactness, and with a sweetness of tone that is unrivalled. She does not, it is true, convey a sense of awesome will-power, or, in the first section, a sense of sympathy that strikes imaginative depths. At her characteristic best, in fact, she offers 'mere beauty'; and a subtle compound with ugliness will sometimes produce more memorable and moving art. In default of that, 'mere beauty' is no bad thing to contribute to the world's pleasures.

At least there is nothing 'mere' about Margarethe Siems, the last of the sopranos to be considered in this section. She was many things, and all of them on the grand scale: immensely interesting, accomplished and versatile, and (in case it should be concluded that she was 'merely' perfect), sometimes rather shockingly out-of-tune.

Siems is probably the soprano, as de Lucia is the tenor, who brings before us most vividly the singer's world of earlier times. With a technique that is continually amazing, she will take the music boldly into her own hands, 'holding' a moment, embellishing a phrase, interpreting with genuine devotion, yet with a freedom that for any modern singer would be unthinkable. Some most exquisite things are done. There is a record of 'O beau pays' ('O glücklich Land') from *Les Huguenots*, where the dreamy nostalgia is captured to perfection, the singer's virtuosity being essentially at the service of an expressive art: like Kurz, she will make a cadenza talk. She could achieve a very haunting kind of echo effect (it is used most imaginatively in this record and in the opening of the Bell Song from *Lakmé*); and what would normally be showpieces, like the perfect descending chromatic scale and the long, long trill at the end of the aria, here have meaning,

21. Margarethe Siems

preserving the dreamlike quality of the idyll. Or to take another piece of operatic nostalgia, Aida's 'O patria mia', very different in its demands on the singer, we again find Siems giving an imaginative, dramatic reading of the music and an admirable demonstration of technical mastery at the same time. She is one of the very few singers – Elisabeth Rethberg and Leontyne Price are others – who have recorded the top C softly, without breaking the phrase on the ascending notes. In a different style again, there is Frau Fluth's aria in *Die lustige Weiber von Windsor*. Here Siems is gay and charming, not with the verve of Lotte Lehmann it is true, but with a fine artful suavity of her own; and her florid work is quite fantastic. Anybody who needs a little encouragement in his belief that things are not what they were might enjoy comparing Siems' record of this (or Lotte Schöne's for that matter) with the performance of Ruth-Margret Pütz in the complete set on HMV.

But it will not do to use Siems as a stick to beat the modern singer with, for some telling retorts would come all too easily. One may defend many of the liberties taken with the score, but some of them remain questionable, and a few are deplorable. How one regrets, for instance, the high C suddenly introduced, on the word 'mio', into the recitative before 'Ah! fors'è lui'; even more so as it is attacked (in a way common to several of these German sopranos) from just slightly above centre. Then again, it may be that these long trills and pianissimo high-notes have a kind of magic when they are heard on a few rare records by a singer long dead, but if they were normal practice and heard as a regular feature in record after record by (say) a modern singer like Anna Moffo, then the charm might begin to wear thin (and it would not be the excellent Miss Moffo's fault). But Siems' main trouble is undependable intonation. Sometimes what appears to be the singer's mistake will be a distortion caused by recording or a fault in the pressing. This is likely to be so when the pitch wavers, for her voice was perfectly firm and steady. But recurrent sharpness is another matter. An example occurs in her record of 'Die letzte Rose' ('The Last Rose of Summer'), where in the first verse the high note at the end of the third line (in English 'no rosebud is nigh') floats above its proper pitch. This does not happen at the corresponding place in the second verse, and the probability is that it would if it were due to a mechanical fault. Such troubles as this will occur perhaps only once or twice in a record, but they prevent one having quite that confidence in the master-vocalist that so much else in her singing certainly encourages. The beauties of her voice and style offer more than abundant compensation for the occasional lapses, and her records are still among the wonders of the world of singing. Anyone who has not gone a little out of his way to appreciate their quality has missed a marvellous piece of work on his travels.

So much, then, for the great virtuosi. Like their counterparts among the pianists, they provide many genuine musical pleasures in spite of much that is mere show. Certainly there was an astonishing concentration of them in these early years of the century, and there were, of course, many others

apart from the six discussed here, whose accomplishments were by subsequent standards very remarkable indeed. Among the Germans were
Hermine Bosetti, brilliantly able in such music as the allegro of the Queen of
Night's first aria though not very satisfactory in the second; Hedwig
Francillo-Kaufmann, who like Bosetti sings Zerbinetta's aria in *Ariadne
auf Naxos* in its original key of E major; and Irene Abendroth, whose
scale-work was of unparalleled lightness and agility. A lyric soprano also
skilled in coloratura was Claire Dux, heard at her loveliest in an aria from
Mozart's *La Finta Gardiniera*. Still more satisfying on records was Berta
Kiurina, often a most beautiful singer, excellent in purely lyrical music like
Liù's solos in Act III of *Turandot* or in the florid cabaletta of 'Casta diva'.

The characteristic German sound, largely shared by these singers, is
sweet rather than penetrative, relaxed rather than energetic. Their Latin
equivalents were also highly-skilled technicians, and they provided a more
challenging liveliness if less pure pleasantness and comfort. Typical
southerners in this respect were Maria Galvany, Elvira de Hidalgo and
Maria Barrientos, whose combined penetrative qualities sound fit to shatter
the Crystal Palace. Galvany had a pleasant middle voice, and her facility
in rapid staccato was extraordinary, rivalled in later times only by the
Brazilian, Sofia del Campo, a charming and highly accomplished singer.
An astonishing showpiece of Galvany's is the song 'L'Incantatrice' (Arditi
again); another is a barely recognisable version of 'Die Hölle Rache'. De
Hidalgo (a teacher of Callas) sings with fine Spanish temperament and a
fascinatingly lusty chest-voice: a good example is the 'Carceleras' from
Las Hijas de Zebedeo. Barrientos had the distinction of being the first to
record Falla's *Seven Popular Songs*; with the composer at the piano, the performance has some historical interest, but the singing is not attractive.
More characteristically she was heard in Bell and Shadow songs, with the
amazingly fluent technique most fully demonstrated in 'Già fra la danza',
a piece of nonsense from *Fra Diavolo* and for coloratura fanciers only. A
curious feature of her scale work was the change of vowel: 'ahooah,
ahooah' and so on.

But all of these were genuine virtuoso singers, and in this respect the
standard of the times was extremely impressive. The virtuosity was international, and it was not confined to the soprano voice. Among mezzos,
Eugenia Mantelli, rich and powerful (her parts included Brünnhilde!),
demonstrates her prowess in 'Non più mesta', from *La Cenerentola*; and
Guerrini Fabbri, with a deeper contralto timbre, likewise shows how the
roulades in Rossini can be done with a true legato (it is interesting to compare these early singers with corresponding modern records by mezzos
like Berganza and Dominguez). There were also the Russians (Boronat,
Neshdanova, Lipkowska, Bronskaya), and the French (Calvé, Arral,
Bréjean-Silver, Ritter-Ciampi). From Belgium came the exquisite Alice
Verlet, a soprano with a legato that is perhaps as flawless as any on record,
and her scale work is also marvellously even and fluent: the Queen's aria,

'O beau pays', from *Les Huguenots* shows both these characteristics, as well as the sure poise of delicately placed high notes. Also, in the 'twenties, there came from Australia a singer of unusual sweetness and purity, Evelyn Scotney: her career was soon over, but she made some delightful records, including a particularly lovely 'Caro nome' and some Strauss waltzes that are delicate and beguiling in the manner of Ivogün or Lotte Schöne (and by no means inferior). American singers like Eames, Farrar and Garden, essentially lyric sopranos, also developed skill in fioritura, while the specialists, such as Mabel Garrison, Ellen Beach Yaw and Lucy Marsh, were as brilliant as most of their European contemporaries, and often (like Scotney) rather more pleasant to listen to.

Altogether, these singers, mostly born in the 'seventies and 'eighties of the previous century, form a most remarkable school. But even here the dialectic of history plays its tricks, and abundance in one age promotes scarcity in the next. With the plentiful supply of scales, trills and arpeggios, the virtuoso school came to lose its fascination, and musicians began to feel that, like the butter, on a famous occasion, it was getting in the works and stopping the clock. By way of retort, as on that occasion too, its admirers could at least protest, mildly and ruefully, that it was the *best* butter.

6. Approach to Wagner:
Questions of Balance
Emmy Destinn Johanna Gadski
Jacques Urlus Hermann Jadlowker

GOVERNING the changes in opera during the nineteenth century was a growing demand for realism. This forbad such stylisations as the repeated iteration of a single phrase or sentence, and so the dramatic and naturalistic qualities of the libretto became more important. The syllables of a word were to be allowed the natural relative lengths they had in speech, and the words themselves were to be pointed expressively by the music, which would thus intensify the drama. Orchestral commentary on the stage action could provide additional interest, and as the symphony orchestra was now capable of so many subtleties of tone-colour, it should be exploited to the full.

These were some of the underlying principles, and they were associated above all with the name of Wagner. The true causes of change no doubt lay deep in the history of European culture, and involved much more than an individual of genius (Wagner was seen as a revolutionary figure, but the style of operatic composition which was evolving in the long and very different career of Verdi took much the same direction). For singers, the effects were of vast importance, and, because Wagner was so generally held to be the terminative point in the new developments, his operas came to be thought of as specialised territory, requiring powers which singers trained for the traditional repertory would probably not possess; making little use, moreover, of the skills that up to then had been most assiduously cultivated. Wagner had nothing very much to offer the coloratura soprano, for example, or the *tenore di grazia*. The whole of *The Ring* contains not a single scale or roulade, and to an average singer of the late nineteenth century much of it must have seemed more like speech than song.

So it is not strange that some of the early attempts on Wagner should have been unsatisfactory to composer and singer alike. The surprising thing is that singers adapted themselves as readily as they did. As the later and more formidable operas came to be known outside Germany, so all sorts of unlikely people began to grapple with the scores: stalwarts of the Italian wing like Scotti and de Luca were cast as Sachs and Alberich, Tetrazzini, at the special request of royalty, learnt 'the sublime airs of the tragic Isolde', as she tells us, and Caruso himself ventured a solitary Lohengrin at Buenos Aires in 1901. Older generations had also faced up to the new demands. Lilli Lehmann, accomplished singer of Mozart, Bellini and Verdi, became a great Brünnhilde and Isolde. Before her, Emma Albani, famous for her Handel as for her *Traviata*, even risked the wrath of society and the Press in 1884 by singing her Senta and Elsa in German (instead of Italian). *Lohengrin* in particular attracted the attention of singers like Melba and Eames, de Lucia and Battistini, who otherwise had little to do with Wagner. The de Reszke brothers had appeared together in this opera long before Jean was persuaded, as he was in 1896, to undertake the labours of Tristan, with Siegfried following in the next year. In all of these instances, Wagner was given by singers trained in the traditional Italian operas: smoothness of line, beauty of tone and elegance of technical accomplishment were among their attributes, and the presentation of Wagner's operas benefited accordingly. But it was not always so.

The dreaded word 'Sprechgesang' looms large in critiques of many early performances. Singers who slipped into the style thus characterised would, it was said, rap out the words at whatever expense to the tone, and make explosive sounds unpleasing to the ear, ruinous to the voice, and completely destructive of traditional legato. The 'Bayreuth bark' came to be complained of, bitterly by G. B. Shaw for example, and by Wagner himself, who is said to have constantly urged his interpreters to sing in the Italian manner. The experience of hearing Wagner's music truly *sung*, as it was in the eighteen-nineties when Jean de Reszke and Lilli Lehmann headed the cast, was a new joy on both sides of the Atlantic, and the commentaries of Shaw and Henderson leave no doubt that the relief from unmusical vocalism was heartfelt. The gramophone, unfortunately in one sense, does not act quite convincingly as historian to support this. If *Sprechgesang* was so common in Wagnerian singing, one might expect it to have found its way rather more obviously onto records. And there is indeed plenty of bad Wagner among these early records. Only it is not usually bad in just that way.

Rather, it is a matter of stodgy, charmless singing, sometimes strained, sometimes unsteady. The tenors provide the most obvious examples. Two of the old guard survived to make records at the very beginning of the century, and both surely afford minimal pleasure. Ernest Marie Hubert van Dyck sang Parsifal at Bayreuth in 1888 and earned a great reputation over the next fifteen years or so. His records are few and copies are rare, but one can hardly wish them otherwise, for the style has little to commend it and the voice is not in good condition (and this at no great age – he was forty-two in 1903, the year of his first recordings). Van Dyck was a tenor reputedly of the *Sprechgesang* school, and in this is usually contrasted with the other notable relic of early days, Hermann Winkelmann, who in 1878 was Hamburg's first Siegmund and Siegfried, London's first Walther and Tristan in 1882, and the first Parsifal of all, at Bayreuth later that year. He is said to have preserved a lyrical style, and his records are sometimes recommended as demonstrations of 'the authentic way of interpreting the Master's music'. Too bad for the Master in that case, for his solos from *Tannhäuser*, *Lohengrin* and *Die Meistersinger* are choppy in their phrasing, unmusical in their hard-hitting *marcato* style, and quite without lyrical impulse. The G & T records were made in 1905, when Winkelmann was fifty-six. He still had a strong, pointed and usually steady voice, but there it ends.

Of a younger generation were Jacques Urlus (born 1867), Erik Schmedes (1868), Heinrich Knote and Karl Burrian (1870) and Leo Slezak (1873). Schmedes, another exponent of *Sprechgesang*, was much admired in Vienna, though rather less in London and New York. His records were numerous and nasty: he obviously meant what he was singing, but his tone is unsteady and tired, even in records made as early as 1904. Still more numerous, however, were the recordings of Leo Slezak, who was the most popular of German tenors in the first decades of this century. From 1901 to 1931 he made nearly four hundred records, including eleven versions of the Prize Song from *Die Meistersinger* and of 'Celeste Aida', nine of 'Ah, fuyez, douce image' from *Manon*, and a mere seven of the Triumph Song in *Le Prophète*. It seems sad to have to admit to finding only a small proportion of this great output enjoyable, perhaps the smallest proportion of all surviving as valuable in the Wagner which was certainly one of his specialities. He sang Lohengrin, Tannhäuser and Walther with much success, but the records are generally unattractive. One of his great possessions was a velvety, admirably controlled *mezza voce*, and this does distinguish passages like the opening of the 'Romerzählung' in *Tannhäuser* or of Lohengrin's Narration and Farewell. But his tone becomes unsteady under pressure, and it is rare to find him singing this music with interpretative insight or poetry of spirit. Yet there was a genuine greatness about him. One catches it in his *Otello* records, or in the Lieder that he recorded, sometimes meltingly, for Polydor in 1928. He is probably at his most pleasing on record when the half-voice can be used throughout: a really miraculous example here is the air 'Viens, gentille dame' from Boïeldieu's *La Dame Blanche*, which passes as a pleasant, undistinguished tune when sung in routine style by so able and likeable a tenor as Alessandro Ziliani, but is sheer magic when done by Slezak. Even so, all these 'Celeste Aidas' and 'Prize Songs', along with so much that he recorded from the standard repertoire of the heroic tenor, have little to preserve them from time's neglect, though the mere fact of their plentiful existence is touching testimony to a long and worthy career.

The three other Wagnerian tenors, Burrian,[1] Knote and Urlus, included the heaviest parts in their repertoire, and the voices of the last two survived the ordeals of wear and tear remarkably well. Moreover, their reputations as preserved by the gramophone also survive impressively. Knote made

---

[1] Burrian was one of the most honoured and important singers to have come from Czechoslovakia, but his records are frequently disappointing. He wrote in verse on the subject (the lines are translated in *The Record Collector*, XVIII, 7):

firm-voiced, forward recordings for G & T in 1906 (among his first was an artistically moulded performance of 'Am stillen Herd') and probably his best records of all by the electrical process in 1930, when he was sixty years old. There is marvellous energy in these, getting stronger and stronger throughout the Prize Song, so that it gains through its vigour a substitute for the subtler kind of poetry that he lacked. Jacques Urlus, almost forgotten today except perhaps in the Netherlands, must have been one of the best singers the century has known. His voice was powerful, evenly produced throughout its range, sonorous and full-bodied in tone. Everything he did was musical, and his versatility was exceptional: he was the Evangelist of Mengelberg's annual performances of the *St. Matthew Passion*, famous for his singing of Mahler's *Das Lied von der Erde*, as well as being the indispensable Heldentenor of so many presentations of *Tristan* and *The Ring*. He preserved his voice wonderfully well. One can hear a little evidence of ageing when the Edison records are placed side by side with the G & Ts, but on their own they would pass as the performances of a man in his thirties: in fact, he was getting on for fifty-five. Even the very last records, made in 1927 at the age of sixty, are impressive in the quality of voice as of artistry, and that most arduous of solos, Lohengrin's 'In fernem Land', displays an admirable combination of power and refinement.

The record companies of those days interested themselves very little in Bach and not at all in Mahler, so the full range of Urlus' achievements is unrepresented. We do, however, have two arias from *Die Zauberflöte*, elegant and interesting, though the music really makes no call for a voice of this size. There is also an impressive record of Schubert's *Allmacht*, which does benefit from such resources of power, as does Florestan's aria in *Fidelio*, where every phrase is beautifully shaped, and the whole thing deeply, imaginatively felt. In French opera, there is a 'Flower Song' that rises to a soft high B flat; and a version of 'Rachel, quand du Seigneur' from *La Juive* which, though less passionate and exciting than Caruso's, gives unfailing musical pleasure by its smoothness and the careful grading of tone. Among the excerpts from Italian opera, his record of Otello's death is outstanding. The soft-voiced, sad-toned opening, the ring of 'O Ehre' ('O gloria'), the dark baritonal sound of 'Otello fu', proclaim an ideal Otello voice. The drama of the piece too is beautifully captured: 'noch einmal' ('un bacio ancora') full of yearning and passion, and no additional death-noises to spoil the dignity of this genuinely noble portrayal.

When we come to Urlus' Wagner it is to recognise what one had probably not believed before – that Melchior had a great predecessor in this century.

My voice was not of glassy stone,
  Though that's what the gramophone captured.
Today and forever 'twill sound dull:
  It's difficult to can one's soul.

It is also said that he recorded on a couch, drinking beer. The Czech songs and *Dalibor* aria are recommended.

Urlus does not have quite the romantic and passionate manner of Melchior (on records), and his high notes do not ring with a comparable shine and exhilaration. But his vocalism is almost perfect in preserving a scrupulously musical appeal. The G & T *Rienzi* aria is a superb example of the full resonant voice and the fine legato. In Lohengrin's Narration we have the pleasure of hearing phrases that are so often explosively treated, voiced as perfectly musical progressions. In 'Winterstürme' (*Die Walküre*) we have the confidence that is inspired by a *continent* style: this singer has more power to draw on, and all in good time we shall hear it. In Siegfried's Narration from *Götterdämmerung* ('Mime heiss ein mürrisches Zweig') we hear how intelligently he could characterise his music, with incisive diction, a sense of fun, and a rare sweetness in reserve for the phrases of the wood-bird's song. This is all the work of a singer who deserves honour: he certainly repays attention.

The list of Wagnerian tenors flourishing in these early years of the century is not complete yet: there are Johannes Sembach, vigorous yet lyrical in such testing music as Siegfried's Forging Song, and (most interesting of all) Hermann Jadlowker. Jadlowker is a phenomenon: a Wagnerian

22. Jacques Urlus as Siegmund in *Die Walküre*

23. Hermann Jadlowker as Gerald in *Lakmé*

coloratura tenor. Trained as a Cantor in the Synagogue, he brought to operatic music the flexibility acquired in this art, and yet still had a big enough voice to sing such roles as Lohengrin and Parsifal. He is remarkable in another way too; for one is likely to come upon a whole series of records that present him as a charmless, even ungainly singer, whereas it becomes quite clear from others that he was exceptionally musical and sensitive, as well as being one of the most accomplished tenors of his century. In sheer flexibility of voice he ranks with de Lucia (and he too was a tenor with a big voice, a Canio and Lohengrin as well as an Almaviva). His 'Ecco ridente' from *Il Barbiere di Siviglia* (sung in German) has probably the finest of all tenor trills, as well as the best lubricated of runs: a feeling, too, that the line might flower any moment with an extra cadenza or a trill. With this goes an admirable legato: the tone well-nourished and smooth, able to soften and sweeten. It is not the sort of voice one associates with Mozart, yet here also his singing achieves real distinction: the 'Il mio tesoro' has supple, well-articulated runs, so too the difficult arias from *Die Entführung*. His expressive range included gaiety, well heard in the jolly solo from *Alessandro Stradella*, with its brilliant cadenza and fine *diminuendo*. And for depth of feeling we have his recording of Florestan's great solo in *Fidelio*, the opening sentences movingly enunciated, though the last section is a little constrained. In the lyrical pages of Italian opera we find him meditative and well inside the dramatic situation: his is a beautifully softened and shaded version of 'Dei miei bollenti spiriti' from *La Traviata*. And in 'Ah si, ben mio' from *Il Trovatore* he is able to supply the trills. Some of the Wagner, too, is pleasing (he is a convincingly romantic Lohengrin in 'Atmest du nicht'). Yet on the whole, the Wagner records present the least attractive aspect of his art, stolid in tone and interpretation, clipped in the phrasing of Lohengrin's Narration, dull in the passage from *Parsifal* recorded with Paul Knüpfer, and solidly and unringingly loud in the long solo from *Tannhäuser*.

Grace in Wagner is generally wanting also in the basses and baritones of the period. The great German baritone of the nineteen-tens and twenties was Josef Schwarz, and Wagner did not feature very prominently in his repertoire: he seems to be exceptional in the beauty of his singing, the ancestor of a notable generation of German baritones, Schlusnus, Hüsch and Janssen chief among them. It is a distinctively German voice: his Prologue to *Pagliacci* has none of the Italian's rich vibrancy, though the tone is strong and resonant and the upper range brilliant. Like Schlusnus, who was in fact only eight years his junior, he maintained an exemplary legato, fine, for instance, in such basic Italian test-pieces as 'Il balen' and 'Eri tu'. These, too, are done with the interpretative interest one more confidently expects from a German, as well as remarkable fluency in the cadenza. His work extended to songs and oratorio (a fine version of 'It is enough' from *Elijah* in spite of a ghastly cello solo accompanying), and it is rare to find a disappointing record.

Less engaging, both in voice and interpretation, is Leopold Demuth. Here again, however, one knows he was an invaluable artist in the opera house and concert hall, and the firm, virile tone is still impressive on records. He could also mould his phrases with imagination and fervour in some surprising selections, such as the 'Resta immobile' from *William Tell*. Two Pauls, Knüpfer and Bender, are again somewhat stolid in many of their recordings, though with Knüpfer one always admires the powerful, sturdy voice, and its freedom in the upper register. Remarkably too he sings his *Nozze di Figaro* arias with lightness and humour, and in King Philip's aria from *Don Carlo* he shows the fineness of his legato and the flexibility of this large, dark voice. In Wagner one hears him clearly as ancestor of Gottlob Frick, a firm, sonorous King Mark, a formidable Hagen. By comparison, I find it very difficult to enjoy Bender's records of the same excerpts. Something curiously closed-in about the vowel sounds and unvibrant in the tone diminishes the appeal of this singer; and, greatly admired as he was for his interpretations, there seems little difference here between characters. His Osmin sounds more schoolmaster than keeper of the harem; his pompous pedagogue of a Basilio is better (singing the Slander Song, it appears, in the original key); and surprisingly vivid, and open-mouthed, is his Gounod-Mephistopheles. Wilhelm Hesch, the third notable bass of this period, and a genuine basso-profundo, reverses this list, his Mephistopheles being a bourgeois beer-barrel (in 'Le veau d'or'), but his Osmin presenting itself as something like the ideal. His splendidly full-bodied low notes help, but there is also a sense of fun and a good deal of technical expertise. His too was a fine legato as he shows in Sarastro's arias from *Die Zauberflöte*. His main limitation in fact seems to be a certain tightness in the upper part of his range, and this affects the success of his best-known Wagnerian record, 'Das schöne Fest' from *Die Meistersinger*. He sounds a plausible, good-hearted Pogner, but the tessitura is unmistakeably trying, and the style remains pedestrian.

The greatest historical interest probably attaches to the few and rare records of Anton van Rooy, supreme as Wotan in the years around the turn of the century. With a voice of immense power and strikingly dark, rich quality, he is often referred to as a spectacular example of a great singer succumbing to the *Sprechgesang* style, and shortening his career drastically as a consequence. Again the gramophone fails to provide conclusive evidence. In the Dutchman's 'Nur eine Hoffnung' there is some explosive declamation, and there are also some heavily attacked high notes which certainly sound unpleasant as recorded (but then, early recording processes were hardly likely to cope very well with the kind of challenge van Rooy provided). On the other hand, an excellent legato marks his *Tannhäuser* records, and at times his singing has that kind of old-fashioned gentlemanly finish that recalls the stylishness of a Plançon. More important, the two records in which his Wotan survives show an unmistakeably distinguished portrayal. The passage from Wotan's Farewell in *Die Walküre* is remarkable for authority of attack, cello-like smoothness, and bold, eloquent breadth in 'freier als ich, der Gott' at the end. Still better is his 'Abendlich strahlt' from the last pages of *Das Rheingold*. This reveals the voice magnificently: less honeyed than Friedrich Schorr, but dark and of rock-like firmness, the control impressive throughout a wide range. The nearest sound to this that we in mid-century have heard is probably the massive bass of Gottlob Frick; but he, of course, has been the great Hagen and Gurnemanz of our time, rather than the Sachs and Wotan. And perhaps this comparison may suggest a reason for van Rooy's early decline. His voice on records is more bass than baritone, and the tessitura of the great bass-baritone parts may well have been unduly tiring. Frick's is a still deeper voice, but there must have been times when conductors, producers and critics have wondered whether he might not be a marvellous Sachs or Wotan. Whether or no, he has remained with the bass roles proper, and so could still sing superbly in his late fifties, while the international career of van Rooy, for all his nobility of voice and style, was over before he was forty.

More surprising, as we turn now to the sopranos, was the relatively early decline of Emmy Destinn. During the first quarter of the century she was generally the most honoured of lyric sopranos in Germany, England and the United States; and her repertoire covered a wide range of operas, French, German, Italian, Russian and Czech, as well as including Wagner's Elsa, Senta and Elisabeth. Yet by 1921 when she was only forty-three her career was over. It had been interrupted by the war which had brought her some grievous personal troubles (she had, for one thing, become devoted to the Algerian-French baritone Dinh Gilly who was interned as an alien in Prague, and she herself was later arrested there). Perhaps we should also remember the very early age at which she made her debut – she was only nineteen, and only twenty-three when she sang the demanding role of Senta at Bayreuth. Still, it appears that she returned to Covent Garden in magnificent voice for the first post-war season (P. G. Hurst recalls her singing with Martinelli of the duets in *Un Ballo in Maschera* as one of the most exciting things in his long and well-stocked memory); and one might then have confidently wished her a continuing reign, happy and glorious, to last another ten years or so.

Her records are not often recommended as satisfactory mementoes. This is readily understandable, for while the best of them leave no doubts about her greatness, there are also plenty of passages where the sound is far from pleasing and the style undistinguished. Very unusually among the famous singers of this period, her middle voice recorded with something approaching a wobble. At a good forte there is no soprano on record with a firmer tone than Destinn, and her high notes, whether loud or soft, were always perfectly steady. But the middle voice, especially at a mezzo forte, had a distinct beat, which recording picked up and probably exaggerated, for I have never seen a review of live performances which criticised her for unsteadiness. Yet the gramophone cannot record something that is not there, and it may have caught more sensitively than the ears of her listeners a characteristic which was to play its part in the deterioration during her early forties. One hears it in most of the records made after about 1912.

There are other limitations, not so much matters of voice as of style and interpretation. She favoured a broad portamento in slow music, and it is hard for modern listeners to accommodate themselves to this. The first bars of 'Vissi d'arte' provide an example, and the airs 'Leise, leise' and 'Und ob die Wolke' from *Der Freischütz* become thickly sentimental with so indulgent a treatment. A flatness in pitch can also be troublesome, even when one makes a mental note that this may be a deliberate colouration, acceptable and even attractive in live performance but beyond the power of the old recording processes to reproduce. When taking a high note softly, Destinn could produce a pure, almost ghostlike 'column' of sound, which would float easily in the great opera houses, and remain to haunt the memory long afterwards. On records, even played with maximum 'top', these notes will often come out simply as empty of resonance and as ever-so-slightly flat. An example is the last note, a high A, in the generally fine Columbia recording of 'O patria mia'. I am sure it would be magical in the opera house, but the actual sound one hears on record is both slightly immature and slightly below pitch. Then if we try her in 'Ach, ich fühl's', Pamina's aria from *Die Zauberflöte*, we have to observe that the soft notes, which may be lovely in themselves, are really too unlike the voice at its normal mezzo forte, and that the tone then is rather thick and stolid for this music. The runs are hefty progressions, each note *marcato*, and the upward scales are hurried. There are some good things, but the final effect is ungainly, making one wonder yet again about the standards of the age commonly called golden.

Where, then, lies Destinn's greatness? Well, first one might play a record to dispel any doubts as to whether it exists. The finale of *Madama Butterfly* will settle that question: a gloriously firm, full, strong and shining sound Destinn's voice makes here, the individual timbre of it intensely memorable, and the urgent emotion of the piece deeply felt without being overplayed. One senses, even in the box-like recording acoustic of those times, the thrust of her voice, the exciting, unconstricted projection of it into a great auditorium. Less unrestrainedly enjoyable but equally impressive (and in a rarer fashion) are the two excerpts from *Salome* recorded in 1907. The passage starting 'Dein Haar ist grässlich' is a genuine *tour de force*, especially when one thinks how fearsome this music must have seemed when it first appeared. Destinn has complete mastery of the score; she sings with a virtuoso's assurance and a true musician's accuracy. Moreover, although writers have denied this, she gives every sign of having grasped the meaning of score and libretto imaginatively and without inhibitions: *aussere sich* is the direction Strauss provides, almost impossible to fulfil, one would think, when recording an extract in cold blood, yet Destinn is successful in this as in everything else here – including the phrase 'Lass mich ihn küssen deinen Mund', vividly prurient and indrawn in its enunciation.

She was also accomplished in the graces which many of her successors neglected. The aria from *Robert le Diable* ('Eh' ich die Normandie verlassen' in Destinn's German version) demands the fleetness of what we now think of as the 'coloratura soprano'; and it gets it. The 'D'amor sull'ali rosee' from *Il Trovatore* has the distinction of excellent trills, a fine cadenza, some high notes taken with marvellous softness and accuracy, a stunning high D flat, and some interesting phrasing. Even so, it remains a very extrovert performance, rarely relaxing, rarely attempting or achieving subtlety. Modern singers could learn much from it in matters of tone and technique, but no doubt Destinn might have learnt from them in the matter of interpretation.

In Wagner she shows a similar balance: much beauty of sound, some genuine urgency and feeling; not very much, however, that is subtly characterised. Isolde's Liebestod, for instance, is warm in tone and feeling, has a confident sense of direction, and is splendidly exact in the placing of the high notes; Senta's Ballad rings out with energy, and has some beautifully softened passages. Both are exceptionally good performances; yet neither has quite that final touch of inner fire and imagination to make greatness. More satisfying, perhaps, is her Elsa. Throughout the Love Duet she is continually giving delight with pure-voiced soft singing, tenderness and finesse (thrown into high relief by the dreadful sounds made by her Lohengrin, Ernst Kraus). Best of all is the fragment of Elsa's Dream ('Einsam in trüben Tagen'): absolutely lovely record, the girlish, fresh voice having a bright clarity reminding one of the young Ljuba Welitsch. In such forthright, fine-toned singing she set a standard which still seems central; with just enough that is personal and distinctive to inspire some of the affection which she commanded so liberally in the great years of her career.

With the word 'just' italicised and doubly underlined the same could be said of one of the greatest of Wagnerians, Olive Fremstad. In America especially, her singing of Brünnhilde, Isolde and Kundry evoked the warmest response of all; nobody wrote of her without acknowledging some spark of divine fire. But though Columbia's recording studios did not quite extinguish it, they damped the flame to a point where only the faithful and the patient would find it. A casual listener will hear in her records a pleasantly steady soprano voice, with something of a mezzo quality, capable of considerable power and some delicacy. A little less casual, and he will be impressed by the breadth and command of her Battle Cry from *Die Walküre*, noting how in her other recording from that opera, Sieglinde's 'Du bist der Lenz', she could sing with an 'inner' humanity, as in the phrase 'Freundlos war mir das Nahe'. This entrance to a private world of emotions, outside the scope of the conventional prima donna, is achieved more impressively in her 'Vissi d'arte' from *Tosca*; while her distinction as a vocalist is evident in that most difficult phrase 'le voce delle cose' from the Love Duet in Act I of the opera (it seems hardly possible that a Brünnhilde should be able to manage this with such lightness and precision). Then for a vivid glimpse of the grandeur and energy of her portrayals there is an inspired record of 'O don fatale' from *Don Carlo*. So putting together the best features of the best records (for there are some faults in all of them) we can recognise a true greatness. Perhaps the record that illustrates it most completely is 'Dich teure Halle', Elisabeth's Greeting from *Tannhäuser*. The size and warm heroic quality are clear, also the spirit and exuberance. But what suggests the presence of a great singing-actress is her marvellous softening of the middle section, the dream, which becomes more and more indrawn till it achieves a perfect stillness in the line 'Aus mir entfloh der Frieden'. This is something: a precious souvenir. But it is maddeningly little when one thinks that here was an artist perhaps comparable in stature to Maria Callas, and that those many insights, moments of exultation and irreplaceable individuality are beyond recall.

24. Emmy Destinn as Aida

25. Johanna
Gadski as
Brünnhilde

A Wagnerian soprano for whom the gramophone did much better service was Johanna Gadski. In the written annals of opera she goes down as a worthy singer if not a very exciting one; holding her own in illustrious international casts at the Metropolitan from 1900 to 1917, yet rarely gaining outstanding personal acclaim. Critics speak of a fine voice and a good technique, but Henderson, for instance, denied her 'the creative imagination of an interpreter'. Perhaps a homely appearance and a certain lack of personal magnetism about her stage characterisations account for this rating, for when one cannot see but can only hear, there is a very notable interpretative distinction about her work; a highly individual timbre, too, capable of heroic brilliance and an exquisite fragility also.

She made nearly a hundred records (compared with Fremstad's fifteen) and, considering the power and vibrancy of her voice, was kindly treated by the old processes. She sang out with no sense of constriction: Liebestod, Immolation and Battle Cry, all emerge with a formidable ring and fullness in the high notes, and it is not hard, with modern reproduction, to imagine this voice sailing out splendidly in the vastness of a great theatre. The stamp of authority is unmistakeable, and her right to it derives impressively from a sure grasp of the score. Like Destinn's, her *Salome* record ('Jokanaan, ich bin verliebt') shows a mastery of difficult music. Her performance of Brünnhilde's 'Fliegt Heim, ihr Raben', from the end of *Götterdämmerung*, is also marvellous in the assurance of attack and the combination of accuracy with energy – and all of it whizzing along at a daunting tempo so as to be sure of fitting it onto the 78 side. Other of her Wagner records reveal a more complete artist still. Brünnhilde's great cry from Act II of *Götterdämmerung* ('Betrug!') illustrates the intensity and grandeur of her interpretation (and this is the word to which records keep bringing us back – 'the creative imagination of an interpreter'). The plea, 'War es so schmählich' from Act III of *Die Walküre* illustrates the pathos and tenderness which she could also command. This is eloquent in its way with the words (irresistibly human in the inflections of 'O sag Vater, sieh' mir ins Auge'): it also leads one to another fact about Gadski's records – that they quickly establish themselves as vivid and valuable in the memory.

She is memorable, moreover, in a wider range of music. A most beautifully shaded performance of Pamina's aria 'Ach, ich fühl's' from *Die Zauberflöte* marks her out immediately from the stormy sisterhood of Wagnerian trumpeters. She is movingly tender and young in sound, and magically light on the difficult high B flats: this is one of the great pieces of singing on early records. Some of her Lieder have a similar delicate magic, wholly unexpected either from the Gadski of Henderson's rather lukewarm description or indeed from any Brünnhilde at all (it is certainly not easy to think of another who has left comparable records). 'Auf Flügeln des Gesanges' shows her feeling for rubato and portamento, never overdoing either, yet using both more freely than a modern singer would be likely to; and the Strauss 'Ständchen' (its unfocused last note a single blemish) shows her enchanting and intimate as an Elisabeth Schumann or Irmgard Seefried in her 'drum leise mein Mädchen', sensitively darkening the tone too for the third verse ('hier dämmert's geheimnisvoll'). This delicacy she could also bring to bear in Italian opera, and in places where singers born to this music were relatively stolid. In the arias from *Un Ballo in Maschera* she is vividly dramatic (again one does not feel them to be essentially studio performances), and is plastic in her moulding of the phrases: the music never goes to sleep with her. Her Aida too haunts the memory in its quietness. 'O patria mia' has a real sense of longing and inwardness; and the plea to Amneris (a towering performance here by Louise Homer) is touchingly frail and heartfelt.

She was not without faults. Her Bavarian origin is betrayed in some curious Italian vowels. 'Misayrayray', she sings in *Un Ballo*, 'piayta' in *Aida*. She is occasionally syllabic and lumpy, and sometimes rather colourless in the middle register. More troublesome, a quick vibrato will flutter unevenly every now and then so that one does not have the feeling of absolute security that Flagstad could give. Because of the vibrato, it becomes particularly important that Gadski's records should not be played above the correct pitch (at the time of writing, there is only one Gadski LP on the market, a Belcantodisc, and this, though it gives an excellent selection of her records, has most of them reproduced a semitone too high and so inevitably exaggerates the vibrato). With so many strengths, however, she can carry a few weaknesses. She remains the best Brünnhilde on pre-electrical records,[1] one of the most sensitive and musical singers of her day, and a continuing pleasure half-a-century later.

What then of Wagnerian singing in these early years? Evidence on records is very incomplete, and tells no certain tale. We find, I think, a higher proportion of plodding ungainliness then than now, more choppy phrasing, less attention to detail and less understanding of the need for light and shade. The singers were not grossly inaccurate, but one finds them careless over the precise length of notes and occasionally getting intervals wrong (an octave for a sixth and that sort of thing). Wagner's insistent advice to look after the little notes (the big ones would take care of themselves) was apparently being heeded, but, against this, one sometimes senses a stiff literalism, as though singers were doing their duty by the music rather than feeling and understanding it.

On the credit side, there are the recordings of Gadski and Urlus, which stand perfectly well with the Leider or Nilsson, Melchior or Windgassen

---

[1] A challenge to this comes at the end of the period from Gertrude Kappel who in 1924 recorded the Immolation Scene with strong heroic tone and style. In this she lives up to the reputation of her stage performances, belied by slovenly recordings of the Countess's arias from *Le Nozze di Figaro* in 1911. At the very beginning of the period, Sophie Sedlmair claims attention, showing some grandeur in Elisabeth's greeting and some vitality in the Champagne Song from *Die Fledermaus*, but often indulging in too much portamento. Rather more interesting and sensitive is Bertha Morena, particularly in excerpts from *Lohengrin*.

of later generations. There are certain individual records, gems in their own way, which suggest a fine range of Wagnerian singing that at best we today would be hard put to match. Schumann-Heink's *Rienzi* aria or the superb record by Edyth Walker, Journet in Hagen's Watch, de Luca, Renaud or Stracciari in the baritone solos from *Tannhäuser*, are examples. Destinn, Fremstad, Knote and Sembach are others who clearly knew how to sing Wagner: records tell us this as well as their reputations. Italians like Amelia Pinto, and the tenors Borgatti and Ferrari-Fontana, give performances that are lyrical and full of conviction. The Russian tenor Sobinoff, and the Frenchmen Dalmorès and Scaremberg, all recorded excellent *Lohengrin* solos. And, evidence of a different kind, the Mapleson cylinders tell in their extraordinary fashion of performances in the Metropolitan at the beginning of the century powerfully and accurately sung: among the attractions, an all-star and apparently well-disciplined troup of Valkyries, and a *Siegfried* Brünnhilde with a brilliantly precise top C.

This was Lillian Nordica, and mention of her brings us back to the grey truth about this chapter of the gramophone's history. She was one of the great heroic sopranos of the last hundred years, yet all that the Columbia recording company issued of her Wagner was an Isolde's Liebestod, hurried and uncomfortable, a useless memento. And this is how it so often was. Either the recording conditions impeded the artist or the powerful voice terrified the recorders. Either the pressure of a four-minute limit drove everyone forward at a feverish speed or the extract lost its dramatic life by being torn out of context. In any case, the accompaniment would be a parody of a Wagnerian orchestra and the balance with the soloist would be hopelessly wrong. These were the regular trials of recording in those days, but for obvious reasons Wagner suffered more than most. Sometimes the results were just dreary. Knüpfer and Jadlowker in part of the Good Friday music from *Parsifal* might have sounded well in a modern recording, but they made a singularly depressing record in 1911. Sometimes the combination of inadequacies produced a real horror. My own favourite among the horrors is the daunting 'Entweihte Götter' from *Lohengrin* blasted forth by Margaret Matzenauer (a glorious voice and an invaluable musician, but a most unlistenable record). Sometimes they were disastrous enough to be comical. An early version of the Quintet from *Die Meistersinger* goes awry when the Sachs (Journet) enters a beat early. He sticks to his idea of the thing, and the others go their quite different way, 'getting together at the end' as amateur piano duettists say happily to each other. The final irony is that the record was issued with a photograph of the artists smiling approvingly as they supposedly listen to the play-back.

So the record companies had made a beginning with Wagner, but not much more. Singers, too, had not long emerged from the first phase of a relationship that had a long development ahead. They had to work out a new scheme of balances in their art: lyricism balanced with declamation, verbal significance with vocal purity, power with quality, drama with music.

The problems were not new in essence, but Wagner raised them to a degree where they made a special challenge. Recording, too, had its balancing problems. How could you record Wagner unless you had a full orchestra and could make it sound like one? In a monumental answer to that question, Albert Coates conducted a generous set of records representing the British National Opera Company's *Ring* in English. It had the excellent Florence Austral and Tudor Davies in the cast, and it had a real orchestra. A fairer balance was achieved by placing the soloists further back than usual. Yet all was not well: one seemed often to get the worst of both worlds. The violins were still barely recognisable, and the voices lost much in brilliance. Clarence Whitehill, who sings Wotan's Farewell, was an outstanding artist. One can tell it from his record of the 'Confutatis' from Verdi's *Requiem*; but not, alas, from the *Walküre* excerpt, where he is too remote, too much a part of that dim and dismal orchestra. No, a beginning had been made. But to learn how Wagner could be sung, the record public in general had to wait for the advent of electrical recording and the great days of Leider, Melchior, Schorr and Flagstad – as, to hear Wagner truly *performed* they have had to wait for the age of LP, of Solti, Kempe and Karajan.

7. Eastern Europe: A Cultural Exchange
*Olimpia Boronat   Antonina Neshdanova
Dmitri Smirnoff   Feodor Chaliapin
Leff Sibiriakoff*

THE concept of opera as music-drama is nowadays accepted nearly everywhere, and the composer who consciously and conspicuously fathered the
idea was certainly Wagner. But among singers, the one who did most to
emphasise the dramatic side of opera was not a Wagnerian, not a German
at all, nor a dealer in Italian verismo. He was born in the poorest quarter of
Kazaan, and grew into a man of gigantic stature with a sonorous bass voice
and a passion for theatre and music; an acute observer of his fellow men,
moreover, and a vivid human being, intense in his sympathies and devotion.
After a few years of starving and shivering, he joined a provincial opera
company and so started on one of the great and spectacular careers of
operatic history. This of course was Feodor Chaliapin, who with Caruso
and Ruffo represented most powerfully the new age in singing. Like them,
he found that the traditional *bel canto* was only a starting point for his
purposes, and like them he developed expressiveness in singing so intensively that smoothness and elegance of decoration were sometimes
sacrificed. But he could also sing with great beauty of tone and line; and
just as with the Italians this has sometimes been obscured in memory because
they were so powerful and so emotional, so with Chaliapin it has been
overshadowed by the fact that he was probably the greatest actor-singer the
operatic stage has known.

One of the great pleasures of his recordings is certainly the sheer beauty
of sound. If anybody goes to his records of *Boris Godunov*, for instance,
expecting a lot of declamatory old-style 'drama', with, as Henderson put it,
'some fleeting moments of tolerable singing', he is in for a surprise. The
Monologue exhibits a pure and disciplined style: the notes have their full
value, the phrases are well-bound, and there is no unwarranted *Sprechgesang*. The Death Scene (especially fine in the version recorded from a
Covent Garden performance in 1928) is a masterpiece of dramatic resource
and command, but what impresses afresh with every hearing is the tonal
beauty of the quiet passages, the Prayer being incomparably haunting in
its warm and sustained pianissimo. Chaliapin must have put his voice

26. Feodor Chaliapin as Mefistofele (Boito)

through some considerable stresses during his long career (the dramatic repertoire and the determination to give his utmost on all occasions might well have joined forces to terminate his singing-life in middle age); but in fact the records show hardly any evidence of ageing in the voice at all. His tone never spread; there was never even the hint of wobble, but always a perfectly defined sound, the vibrations regular, the sheer volume somewhat diminished but the resonance and sonority still warm and healthy as in his prime. Some of the famous *Boris* records were made in 1931, when he was fifty-eight; and two years later he was still in marvellous form recording the attractive but demanding songs Jacques Ibert wrote for the film of *Don Quixote* (Chaliapin played in this to the Sancho of George Robey). The survival proves the method: there were defects and oddities in Chaliapin's style, but his basic production was as sturdily sound as that of the most schooled exponents of celebrated methods.

His defects included a very peculiar characteristic, and one that might seem to involve a basic technical fault: for, instead of the intrusive 'h', an intrusive 'w' is brought in to help him through the runs. 'Vieni, la mia vende-we-we-wetta' is the sound we hear in the first line of the air from *Lucrezia Borgia*. The little six-note groups of 'Le Veau d'or' from *Faust*, or the triplets in Mephistopheles' Serenade provide other examples. It was a habit that grew on him, found a good deal more commonly in the later records than in the pre-electricals; and it is certainly rare to hear him singing a run in anything like the conventional way. The mannerism is different in kind, however, from the use of an easing aspirate. With an 'h' the singer breathes out and if this is habitual the tone itself becomes breathy. That is one danger: the other is that it will simply but disastrously interrupt the flow of sound. Chaliapin's odd 'wubber' is no delight to the ear (it must be one of the few mannerisms of great singers not to have found its imitators), but it does not affect the tone-production. And, though it is impossible to make a hard-and-fast distinction in this kind of thing, I would register it as a fault of style rather than of technique (no doubt, however, if he had been more interested in singing runs perfectly, he would have developed a technique that forbad the use of such a stylistic device).

But his primary and dominating interest in music was that it provided a means of creating characters and expressing emotions. The strength and range of his characterisations are perfectly apparent on records as one turns from his tragic Boris Godunov to the roistering Varlaam, or from the craftily poisonous Don Basilio (his Slander Song must have been the devil to accompany but is a supremely effective performance) to the yearning mood of the love song in Rachmaninoff's *Aleko*. Or, to take a single record, there is the song of Khan Khontchak in *Prince Igor*, in which Chaliapin also sings the few phrases of the captive Igor himself. The indrawn, greyly-coloured character of these phrases is most imaginatively played off against the rough bonhomie of the Khan. If one is inclined to think that such a piece of contrasting characterisation is elementary, it only needs a few comparisons to show how rare Chaliapin's gift was – and is. An inter-war record by Khaidanoff, and one on LP by Christoff both emerge as surprisingly pedestrian. The first has another singer to take Igor's part, but it is done quite without character; and Christoff, who sings it himself, achieves little of the poignancy provided by Chaliapin. Similarly in the portrayal of Khontchak: Khaidanoff's is a light-weight characterisation; and Christoff's, fearsomely authoritative, is nevertheless a smaller person, less interesting, less varied. Chaliapin presents the rough masculinity, jovial, insinuating, cajoling and affectionate by turns, yet strong and formidable throughout.

His work in the recording studios was crowned by the 1931 version of Boris' Monologue ('I have attained the highest Power') and the 'Clock Scene' which follows the Tsar's interview with Shuisky. Of course, the score itself is so powerful that it is hardly possible for an artist who is anything of an interpreter to be ineffective in it. But the greatness of the opportunities means that once a truly exceptional artist has given himself to the part with his whole being, and finds that it fits as though made for him, then we may hope for one of the great experiences of a lifetime. So it was with Chaliapin's Boris; and it must remain a marvel that after singing the role for so many years he still sounds so spontaneous in it, for the Monologue is deeply felt as by a man newly in love with the score. It is also a wonder that he could project such a vivid dramatisation in a piece torn from the rest of the opera, and with no audience to play to or receive inspiration from. Yet it is incomparably vivid. In the Clock Scene we can almost see the gesture of the man loosening the robes at his neck; we see the troubled brow, the growing horror, possession and desperation; and the limp weariness as his fever dies away.

In this and so much more he was the great exponent in the west of a culture essentially Russian. Not that he was ever the archetypal Russian *profundo*. He was a genuine bass, and not at a loss for low notes (there is a respectable bottom D at the end of his not so very respectable record of 'Der Tod und das Mädchen' – coupled, however, with a fine if Russified 'Doppelgänger'); but his voice was shaded towards the bass-baritone, and the cavernous deeps were never open to him, as they were, for instance, to his contemporary Leff Sibiriakoff. But the national character of his singing, nevertheless, was unmistakeable, and the Russian songs he recorded are as valuable and distinctive as the operatic repertory. There is 'Dubinushka', the labour song that he defied respectable authority to sing for a working-class audience in 1905 (see his *Man and Mask*, (1932), chs. vi and vii). And, towards the end of his life, a marvellous session with Russian chorus and balalaika players in Paris yielded a hauntingly sad song called 'Down the Volga' complementary to that gayest, most infectious of all his records, 'Down the Petersky'.

But this distinctively Russian quality was less evident in most of the Russian singers whose records and reputations reached western ears. Among the tenors, the finest voice was probably that of Leonid Sobinoff:

his tone was bright but warm, his legato was admirable and he sang with spirit and tenderness. An attractive record is Lesko's Serenade from *May Night*, and surprisingly interesting is the sensitive, feelingly-shaded performance of Lohengrin's Farewell. But 'surprising' it is, for Sobinoff generally registers as a dependable and pleasing artist, but not a very interesting one; and in this he can be contrasted with the other internationally-known Russian tenor of the period, Dmitri Smirnoff. Smirnoff's singing has not quite the easy reliability of Sobinoff's; his voice was less full-bodied, perhaps a little disconcerting in the openness of some vowel sounds and in its light flicker of vibrato. He was, however, a supremely interesting artist, creative in his handling of the music he sang and often breathtakingly beautiful in matters of nuance and phrasing. He had also the distinction of preserving a fully-flavoured Russian character while showing a most imaginative feeling for the ways and means of the western tradition.

Most essentially Russian is a solo from Moussorgsky's *Sorochinsky Fair*, sung, oddly enough, in French, as 'Pourquoi mon triste coeur'. The music itself has a grey, melancholy beauty, the first phrases anticipating the opening bassoon figure in Stravinsky's 'Rite of Spring'. The sense of desolation and tender longing has its perfect expression in Smirnoff's record, and, in spite of the French language, the singer's nationality is never in any more question than that of the music. We hear in this mostly unaccompanied solo a lovely play of tones, with many delicate shadings and mouldings; a marvellous evenness over the voice in all its variety, and the magical rounding-off of a high B flat, taken softly and then so gradually distanced that one can hardly say when it is out of hearing. This is one of the finest of all these old records. Scarcely less fine as singing (and certainly no less Russian) is a version of 'The Song of the Volga Boatmen' made as an electrical recording around 1926 when Smirnoff's international career was near its end. The full resources of the singer are used here: the reiterated high A's hammered out for five bars thrillingly with the full voice, and an exquisite *diminuendo* to pianissimo on the final note. His way of singing the famous four notes on the word 'euchnyem' is to give the second syllable a subdued *sforzando* corresponding to a tug on the ropes as the boatmen heave. At first, the word is murmured wearily, almost between closed lips, sometimes it is given with a kind of sombre energy, later sighed. None of these features, moreover, emerges as mere 'effect': there is restraint as well as feeling, order as well as variety, and, over all, the technical control of an exceptionally accomplished singer.

His technical accomplishments enabled him to sing Almaviva's second song, 'Se il mio nome' from *Il Barbiere di Siviglia*, with all de Lucia's embellishments and some of his own. His breath control was remarkable enough for him to bind the phrases in 'Spirto gentil' (*La Favorita*) while still taking the song at the relaxed tempo that is right for it. Technique seconds musical feeling, and his record of des Grieux's 'Ah, fuyez, douce image' from *Manon* (sung in Italian as 'Ah, dispar, vision') is surpassingly

27. Dmitri Smirnoff as Dmitri in *Boris Godunov*

fine in the imaginativeness of its phrasing. This is a tender performance, reflective and poetic. Memory suggests Lucien Muratore's record as the most comparable; when one comes to play it, however, it is to be delighted by tone, tempo and personality – everything, in fact, but the phrasing, which is pedestrian. Here Smirnoff provides a revelation – and one which extends in application well beyond that particular piece of music.

In a somewhat similar way, ears are opened to new possibilities by the records of Olympia Boronat, a lyric soprano of rare accomplishment, delicacy and authority.

Not that there is anything notably Russian about her. She was Italian by birth and Russian by adoption: a favourite singer of the Tsar, we are told, and certainly in high esteem among the great record collectors. Her recording of 'Qui la voce' in *Puritani*, says P. G. Hurst (*Golden Age Recorded*, p. 63) 'will remain a classic example of the true way to sing Bellini when the ability to do so is present'. There is remarkable unanimity among critics on this point, and one suspects oneself of being deliberately or subconsciously 'contrary' in questioning the judgment. But, really, *is* this 'the true way to sing Bellini', or, more specifically, to sing this aria? With a big breath in the first phrase, and another in the second? And is 'bel canto' (for it is as a supreme example of this that the record is usually offered) served by such emphatic treatment as is given to the word 'soave' in the first phrase, or by the little exclamatory, half-sobbing inflections that come later? And did Bellini really want the verb and its object, let alone the notes of his phrase, put asunder by the 'lunga pausa' (for breath) that we hear in 'ah, rendetemi la speme'? There are lovely things in this record, and it has much to teach modern singers: but it also contains too many demonstrations of how *not* to sing the music for it to be regarded as the classic and 'true way'. Boronat's claim on our regard has to be defined in different terms.

Like Smirnoff, she is always interesting and personal. Her 'Sempre libera' has a brilliant projection of spirit as well as voice and her 'Caro nome', superb in its technical facility, is a constant delight in the beauty of phrasing and the delicacy of its shading. In 'Tutte le feste', also from *Rigoletto*, there is an almost Callas-like imaginativeness in the inflections of 'Ciel, dammi coraggio', and everything she does here is meaningful. She takes her own time, pulls back and urges forward when she wants to, as no modern singer would, but the effect is to make far better musical sense than the dutifully literal performances that have succeeded Boronat's in the record catalogues. In her singing, as in de Lucia's, we have to listen with a love of sound: willing to linger with this note and that, not always fidgeting to move on to the next thing, and certainly not just perfunctorily passing the time. She was a singer with whom we are always aware of quality.

Boronat does ask for the co-operation of her listener, however: I would never play one of her records for the first time to someone unfamiliar with them and be confident that it was going to be enjoyed. With Antonina Neshdanova I would have every confidence. Probably no soprano is more readily enjoyable on pre-electrical records. Her voice sounds fresh and young, clear and firm, her technique is always admirable, often dazzling, and she sings with heart and intelligence. Hers is an exquisite record of 'O beau pays', the first part of the Queen's great solo in *Les Huguenots*; her manner is affectionate and smiling, and one feels less aware of method than in the more famous German versions. She seems in fact a splendidly un-selfconscious singer, with none of the narcissism of the conventional prima donna. Yet all the accomplishments are there: the vocalise in the middle of this solo is superb as a virtuoso-piece, and her trill is a beauty. She had the fine middle-voice of a lyric soprano, a Mimì or an Elsa perhaps, yet we find her singing the Queen of Night, with excellent staccatos and no fuss about the notes in alt. When she does turn to lyric roles, as in Elsa's Song to the Breezes, we hear the keen edge and admire the steady sustaining power of the voice. In Russian music she will sometimes produce a genuinely dramatic quality, as she does in the aria from *The Tsar's Bride*, or in Tamara's Romance from *The Demon*; yet she can also sing with the softest, most lulling *mezza voce*, as she does in Tchaikowsky's Cradle Song. In arias from *Ivan Susanin* and *Russlan and Ludmilla* the unity of the voice is another impressive feature: these are arias with an extensive range, and there is never any suspicion of a break between registers. One of the loveliest of all sopranos in this early period of the gramophone, she seems also to approximate more nearly than others to the mythical condition of the singer without faults.

But when we come to look around a little more widely, it is clear that there was a vastly impressive richness of quality in the opera houses of Moscow and St. Petersburg in these years. Some of the best singing in Europe was to be heard there, and that in all voices, from high soprano to basso profundo. Among the sopranos, Marie Michailova, Lydia Lipkowska and Marie Kouznetsoff are well worth seeking out; Kouznetsoff in particular had a fine, individual style, boldly dramatic in an aria from Tchaikowsky's *Enchantress* and delicately poetic in Juliet's waltz song, 'Je veux vivre'. Of a rarer distinction is Medea Mei-Figner, shading her beautiful voice with imagination and feeling, as in Lisa's aria from *The Queen of Spades*. She and the contralto Eugenia Zbruyeva are quite exceptionally strong in the dramatic effect of their singing, Zbruyeva magnificently commanding in a song by Grechaninoff called 'Death' where the powerful low register has ample scope and where the fine projection of her strong-edged voice is amongst the most formidable on record. And what remarkable tenors the Russians had. Smirnoff and Sobinoff are well-known to us, and they are themselves a remarkable pair. But there were also Leff Klementieff, round-toned and free-throated, Alexander Davidoff, a singer of much grace and personal magnetism, and, perhaps most impressive of all, Ivan Erschoff. His was a sturdy, ringing, heroic voice as we hear in an excerpt from *Tannhäuser*, but, more than that, he could wield this powerful instrument with grace and elegance. We hear the variety of his singing, the

28. Antonina Neshdanova

brilliance and imaginativeness of it, in some marvellous singing of solos from Meyerbeer's *Le Prophète*. An eminent baritone was George Baklanoff, dark-toned and vibrant, well-suited to such a music as Iago's Creed in *Otello*. And, apart from Chaliapin, pre-eminent among the basses were Vladimir Kastorsky (who gives perhaps the most instrumental and imaginatively shaped performance on record of Gremin's aria in *Eugen Onegin*), and the cavernous Leff Sibiriakoff.

Sibiriakoff made some astonishing records. His voice is one of the most evenly produced and most opulent in quality of all recorded basses. The depth is sumptuous (a song which exploits it more than most is one called 'The Execution', rather a jolly melody too, despite the very Russian title); but what impresses still more is the ease and resonance of the high notes (none of that tightness or dryness that one often finds apparently inseparable from freedom and fullness in the low register). Moreover, his legato is exemplary: the song mentioned above provides a fine example, but it is a feature of everything he does. Unfortunately, his interpretations do not have the same distinction. He recorded the Monologue of Boris Godunov, and, though his instrumental style in this much-abused music is fine, there is really very little expression and no sense of inner tension. The point usually becomes more inescapable as one makes comparisons: for example, there is a recording of *Khovanshchina* on LP in which the bass, Dushan Popovich, sings Shaklovity's Aria in Act III with nothing of Sibiriakoff's glory of tone, but there is more variety and more sense of a compassionate sorrow in his performance. Still, Sibiriakoff makes a superb sound, and, as one returns to him, it is to wonder whether it has ever been quite matched since his day.

All this adds up to a genuine school, and a very fine one: at once a part of the western tradition and an extension of it.

A footnote for the opera at Warsaw. Here too there was great singing to be heard in the early years of this century. Some of the famous Italians became established favourites there, Battistini and the tenor Anselmi among them; and a few Polish singers made distinguished reputations abroad. The de Reszkes were Polish by birth and Marcella Sembrich was originally Praxede Marcelline Kochanska. They had one exceptionally fine bass in Adamo Didur, who could sing Italian arias like the 'Infelice' from *Ernani* with the finest caressing smoothness, and whose record of the Drinking Song from *Der Freischütz* shows a marvellous fund of energy as well as astonishing virtuosity in the florid passages. He had one of the most sonorous voices on records, preserving its richness at both extremes of the compass. He was also a master of characterisation, so that in the 1908 recording of 'La Calunnia' his Don Basilio, smiling and menacing, is like a portrait that leaps out of its frame. The arrival of electrical recording in mid-twenties found him with loosened control, but in his prime he was one of the few great bass singers of the century. None of the other Polish singers we have to mention can claim quite such distinction as this, though they were memorable artists. The baritone Mossakowski, subtly dramatic and resourceful in 'Pari siamo', the lyric soprano Bandrowska Turska, who has one sitting up in a most exciting aria from *Kröl Roger*, the coloratura Ada Sari, floating her way with great charm and accomplishment in the solos of Lucia di Lammermoor: these were among the early Polish singers whose records repay attention. It is a field which few western collectors have exploited, and, as with the lesser-known Russians, the records are hard to come by. Recent LP transfers have shown that there is more worthwhile material than most people suspected, and it may well be that we are still underestimating the achievements of these opera centres in Eastern Europe before war and revolution came to usher in the new age.

8. France: Years of Plenty
Emma Calvé   Edmond Clément
Leon Escalaïs   Maurice Renaud
Marcel Journet

FROM Italy, the ideals of voice, temperament and facility; from Germany, musicianship; from France, elegance. The formulation is just about as true as claims concerning national qualities usually are, and, of course, in discussing them one speedily faces so many exceptions that the generalisations begin to fade and blur almost to extinction. National characteristics exist all the same, and in singing, as in most things else, the French have made a distinctive contribution.

Elegance is certainly one of its features. Perhaps the most exemplary figure is the Grand Old Man of a century of singers, Lucien Fugère. Fugère made his debut in 1874 and sang in the first performances of about twenty French operas in the late nineteenth century. He performed Verdi's Falstaff in the year of its French 'creation' by Victor Maurel, his exact contemporary. He was still at the Opéra Comique in 1927 and made most of his gramophone records in 1928 and 1930, by which time he was eighty-two years old. Old age is not usually immaculate. With singers, the refinements are often shed in the fifties: an incontinent spread of tone, an assertive loudness in place of resonance, a way of sliding up to notes that becomes habitual and easy, like slipping in a pair of false teeth, these are some of the sad relaxings of standards we observe as our favourite singers grow old. But Fugère remained elegant and trim. His runs were lithe and supple, his movements spanning broad intervals still assured and precise. His tone, never luscious (in the latter half of his singing life, at any rate), now dried but remained firm and well-placed. We should not talk of him in a you-are-old-father-William fashion, however, for his value is not that of an agile old grandfather, wonderful for his age; it lies in the elegance which survived in him, a relic of earlier times. All his arts are present in an excerpt from *Le Maître de Chapelle* by Ferdinando Paër. The florid work has the aristocratic command of Plançon; the cadenza is graceful, the *mezza voce* charming. Moreover, the technical ease, with which he passes over the old, well-tempered instrument is complemented by a genuine stage-trouper's command of changing moods – an astonishing procession of them. This record, or the nimbly sung arrangement of Couperin's little keyboard piece 'Le Tambourin', are lessons for the actor-singer: all have the grace of thorough professionalism, and the energy and forthright projection which guard elegance from preciosity.

Much the same might be said of Hippolyte Belhomme, a superb bass, and a contemporary of Plançon; but one would have to add that this singer had also one of the best voices to be heard on record. Well-rounded, resonant and ample, it was absolutely seamless, produced evenly and easily over a wide range, as we hear in one of Plançon's favourite solos, the 'Vallons de l'Helvétie' from *Le Chalet*. Something which Plançon rarely offers is a good strong, resonating fortissimo, and this we find in a second solo from the same work, this one called 'Dans le service d'Autriche'. There is also a brilliant cadenza, for Belhomme is past master of the florid style, and can turn a trill with the neatness of a coloratura soprano – he does so in music whose title suggests further mysteries, 'Air de Falstaff' from Ambroise Thomas' *Le songe d'une nuit d'Eté*. In this we catch a fine swagger, but generally speaking there is not a great deal of character in Belhomme's interpretations, and this is a main limitation to the value of his work: another is the nature of the repertoire itself, for much of it is very dull music. But for aspiring basses there can be few better models than Hippolyte Belhomme.

But the France which produced a Fugère, Belhomme and Plançon was well-stocked with singers of skill and refinement, many of them with excellent voices, some gaining international reputations. France was always fortunate, at least up to the Second World War, in having plenty of good tenors. In these early years there were Charles Rousselière, Emil Scaremberg, Augustarello Affre, Léon Beyle and Léon Campagnola, all gifted singers whose voices took well to recording. Lucien Muratore, Charles Dalmorès and Paul Franz, tenors widely admired outside their own country, make a trio still more distinguished. Franz was a genuine Heldentenor, with the fullness and power that the heaviest Wagnerian roles demand and with far more lyrical grace than most of their exponents can command. His voice in its prime is heard in ardent but finely poised solos from *Lohengrin* or in a ringing performance of 'Celeste Aida' (interesting also because it ends in the way Verdi suggested as an alternative to the pianissimo high B flat – the only version to do this, as far as I know, till Richard Tucker came along armed with a letter from Verdi and sang it so in a 1949 broadcast, later issued as a recording). Despite strenuous demands upon it, the voice is recognisably itself, unforced, lyrical and strong, with broad, well-bounded phrases in some electrical recordings made twenty-five years later, his 'Prize Song' from *Die Meistersinger* giving a still impressive example of his singing of Wagner.

A subtler stylist, Dalmorès had rather less than Franz's resonant fullness. His too was an heroic voice, though a Lohengrin rather than a Tristan, and, as recorded, not rejoicing very freely in the high notes. His aristocratic singing of 'Ah, si, ben mio', with its beautifully turned trill, is famous (the trill rationed to a single appearance though it is required twice); but, as with so many of these singers, it is some less than first-rate operatic music that best records his quality, and an air ('Ouvrez-vous') from Massenet's *Grisélidis* shows him colouring his tone with variety and creative feeling. To a still greater extent, a live sense of style marks the records of the third of these tenors, Muratore. His voice was warm and almost Italianate, but he sang with fastidious taste and a way with words that is essentially French. The Provençal song 'O Magali' provides a winning example of his natural, unselfconscious grace, his easy flowing tone modulated to a delicious softness or intensified at will to a full-bodied ringing sound. His imaginative way of moulding phrases, using just the right amount of caressing porta-mento, is heard in Ossian's Song, 'Pourquoi me réveiller', from *Werther*, lovely, for instance, in its rounding of the first verse and its opening of the second. Muratore was something of a matinée-idol in his great days,[1] but, without this information, we would know from his records that he carried himself with style: he wore his voice like a finely-tailored coat, warm of texture, elegant of cut, and very French.

But the tenors who remain to be discussed have probably more to offer the present-day listener even than these. Léon Escalaïs was the archtype of the heroic tenor and Edmond Clément of the lyric, and David Devries is essentially *sui generis*. Escalaïs' records, made in 1905 and 1906, are famous among collectors for the brilliance of sound: no question of a dim likeness darkly penetrating the old wax every now and then, but an almost startling face-to-face encounter with a singer of astonishing power. His high notes (for those interested in such unfashionable things) were among the most brilliant recorded: the aria labelled 'Je veux entendre' from *Jérusalem* ('La mia letizia' from *I Lombardi*) is a prize example, its top C sharps taken with almost incredible ease and boldness. But Escalaïs was more than a singer with a loud voice and stentorian high notes, as this same record shows very well. Like Plançon, Fugère and other masters of the graceful style, he was a product of the nineteenth century (his Paris debut was made in 1883), and the evenness of production, the seamless voice, perfectly steady, the readiness of the instrument to execute an embellishment gracefully, or to drop to a sweet-toned softness, all are impressively heard in the Verdi aria. Perhaps finer still is the 'Sicilienne' from Meyerbeer's *Robert le Diable*. The first part of this is a rollicking martial piece, and one wonders why 'Sicilienne', but the jogging six-eight of the second half provides the answer and also an opportunity for the singer to show his command of contrasting styles. Escalaïs does more than this. He shows how, with the voice of an Otello or, one would think, a Tristan, it may still be possible to sing runs with a full voice, perfect cleanness and agility; how such ringing strength

---

[1] Which did not extend into the period of electrical recording, for his songs on Pathé are sung as dully as they were written.

may still be moderated to take a high note *mezza voce*; how an heroic tenor may be able to trill on a long note and make a crescendo on it too. He had his limitations: the *Otello* monologue (sounding all wrong in French and accompanied by a remorselessly clonking pianist) is not the great record one looks forward to, and his reading of 'Asile héréditaire' ('O muto asil' from *William Tell*) is not poetic like Tamagno's. But in an impressive series of performances, Escalaïs has left us some of the most exciting of tenor recordings and has demonstrated one important lesson: that the heroic tenor can move with as much ease and grace as the coloratura soprano. It lies in the training, and in the conception of an ideal elegance to be kept in view.

Such a conception must be a good deal more vivid to a modern singer if he has heard the records of Edmond Clément and David Devries, alike in this even though they are tenors of quite different schools, Clément very French in the cut of his voice, Devries much more Italianate in the vibrato, which is not unlike the sort we hear in records of de Lucia. In fact there is much to remind us of de Lucia in Devries' singing, not least in the exceptional flexibility of his 'Ecco ridente' from *Il Barbiere di Siviglia*. The versions are independent, Devries singing ornamentations that are said to have been traditionally in use at the Paris Opéra; they also involve an accomplishment that I believe we do not hear in de Lucia, a genuine trill. Technical limitations are shown up badly by 'Il mio tesoro', however: the

29. Léon Escalaïs

30. Edmond Clément as Don José in *Carmen*

long held F natural is not steady, later on there is a bad case of fading on the note; as for the long run in the middle, he takes four breaths over it, which is practically a record. The limitations are not just technical, either, for in the last part of the solo we find him leaving the vocal line to sing some extra high notes with the accompaniment. The procedure might possibly find a defender; not here, however. Yet in his native French music he shows all the charm and taste which one would have expected to produce good Mozart. Arias from *Werther*, *Mignon* and *Manon* have much delicacy, and a rapt, lingering, personal style that imprints itself upon the memory. His *mezza voce* was also a thing of wonder: it allows him to rank among that very small handful of tenors who take the high note in the Flower Song from *Carmen* as Bizet wrote it. Most of these skills and charms are present in what is probably his most famous record, the 'Rêverie de Georges Brown' from *La Dame Blanche*. The style is imaginative and the technique miraculous.

Edmond Clément, many years his senior, is the cleanest of singers. His tone is a pure, firm sound, no judder of vibrato disturbing it, no fattening or muddying through any kind of throatiness. The style matches: even and elegant, unemphatic and scrupulous. If all this suggests a cold perfection (and it is certainly true that there are other singers, Muratore, for instance, who have a warmer, more imaginative art to offer), then one should sample the songs recorded with piano accompaniment at a single session in 1911. The 'Chanson Lorraine' with its innumerable verses and risk of monotony finds him splendidly resourceful: gay and sad by turns, always a singer with a face. A charming and fast-moving song by Bemberg, 'La Neige', is exemplary in achieving clarity of enunciation with the minimum sacrifice of tone, and the eighteenth century 'Bergère légère' contains a delightful example of that important art of leading into a melody so that it shall captivate and persuade the listener, as it were, to sing with the singer in his own mind. That Clément had some dramatic intensity beyond charm is clear from his *Werther* record ('Pourquoi me réveiller') where the second verse glows with added impulse and declamatory force. But essentially he charms, and not so much by a Tauberesque exercise of personality as by sheer quality of voice and intelligence of usage. A notable series of duets with Geraldine Farrar includes an intelligently studied version of the 'Lontano, lontano' from Boito's *Mefistofele*: notable too as an example of the way in which singers of those times still projected their soft singing, whereas today there is a kind of microphone technique, happily used in the recording studios, frustratingly imported (as it often is) into the opera house. He also recorded with that formidably sonorous bass, Marcel Journet, and (perhaps having more than his fair share of the recording horn) was not overcome. One of their duets is a long, rather jolly piece from *Robert le Diable*. Again Clément shows the way: the square, hearty music is treated with elegance and becomes acceptable. Smooth, unaspirated runs, the added grace of an occasional trill, the dash of a well-executed arpeggio: the record provides a model of pure, tasteful and unaffected style, and we must not be surprised that it was from the France of this period that such a model should have come.

What these French tenors were among most of their counterparts abroad was Maurice Renaud among baritones. 'The handsomest Don Giovanni ever seen in this town . . . a consummate skill in make-up and most artistic taste in costume . . . endeavoured to fit every movement and gesture into the music so that everything should have a meaning': thus W. J. Henderson of the *New York Sun* writing on Renaud's death in 1933. The gramophone cannot preserve this, and in fact it preserves only twenty-one arias and songs by Renaud, most of them recorded two or three times: only a tiny portion of the singer's repertoire. Even so we are left in no doubt that here was an artist of the front rank. The beauty of voice ('of moderate power', Henderson says, admonishing his volume-mongering readers) is immediately impressive, and so is its finely-judged instrumental usage: so that the Air of the Evening Star in *Tannhäuser* ('O douce étoile' in Renaud's version) has an aristocratic finish and something of the lightness of air, which it lacks in most German performances. In his records of 'Vien, Leonora' from *La Favorita* the melancholy is most beautifully caught, and the purity of style and tastefulness of decoration are exquisitely of the old school. His singing was not flamboyant and it might be possible to think of him as a 'central' singer, almost too correct and admirable to be interesting. A few comparisons suggest how wrong that would be. A record unlikely to be admired today is the *Don Giovanni* Serenade. It is rather slow, more like a nineteenth century love-song, and towards the end of the verses there is a suggestion of hot passion that we are certainly not used to hearing nowadays. Perhaps it is all wrong but it is at any rate interesting, and might just raise the question whether the pretty little marionette's piece which it has tended to become is the essential Mozart after all. And Renaud does not have to be arguably unsound to be interesting. His 'Vision fugitive' from Massenet's *Hérodiade* is so beautifully sung that it may escape attention how intense the feeling is; but again comparison helps. A record of the aria was made not long after Renaud's by Edouard Rouard, a fine and popular French baritone of the period: it is a good piece of singing, but to follow it with Renaud is not only to hear the exceptional beauty of voice but also to realise how imaginatively Renaud captures the 'vision'. There is a rapt excitement about his performance, a surrender to the music as well as a very complete grasp of its character, in sum and in details – the exaltation of the phrase 'dans une même ivresse', for instance, and its softened, 'inner'-voiced repetition. It is noteworthy, however, that both baritones, as did all the great singers who recorded it in those days, made magic of the note leading back into the melody of the opening. Renaud was indeed one of a school, but it was a good one, and his excellence in it is all the more remarkable therefore.

If the gramophone preserved only a fraction of Renaud's art, it could do

31. Maurice Renaud

still less for the most famous of singing-actresses, Emma Calvé. Men's voices recorded better than women's, and Calvé's voice was of a kind particularly difficult for the old processes to reproduce: it was a 'pure' voice, as Melba, Sembrich and Eames were pure, and had not the Italian vibrancy that could withstand the frequency-cut. Of her essential spirit, the records preserve less than do her autobiographies – marvellous documents, these, written from a full heart and a full life, and, perhaps significantly, not mentioning gramophone records even when commenting on mementoes of her triumphs or lamenting the passing into mere hearsay of an artist's glory. But the records have their greatness. The beauty and accomplishment of her singing are manifest in a pleasant traditional song called 'Ma Lisette'. The phrases are all finely sustained, but the crowning glory is two soft high notes of astonishing quality, the first an A, the second a D, taken from its lower octave and held perfectly clear and steady: and what modern Carmen, one wonders, could do that! For Carmen was, of course, the role with which Calvé came to be firmly identified in the public mind. The records give us little more than a glimpse of this famous impersonation, perhaps the most vivid being afforded by the duet 'Là-bas dans la montagne', with Dalmorès stylishly shaping José's music. The record begins with the last bars of the Flower Song, and Calvé's first phrases brood darkly, intuitively moving towards Carmen's next step. This, the incitement to desert and follow her to the mountains, is taken much more slowly than we usually hear it (perhaps it was the normal speed in those days, for Geraldine Farrar's record goes at a similar tempo). The effect (it comes particularly from slowing the first four notes of the main phrases) is to make a much more seductive thing out of the otherwise innocent melody. It becomes dreamily hypnotic, and this, too, is the character that Calvé's record so very vividly confirms in the last phrases: her 'si tu m'aimes' in the last solo bars is so coloured that for one or two seconds the effect is visual: we see eyes, mouth and body, and for a moment hold ourselves as still as poor José under the spell. But generally the singing-actress has to be represented by what can only be heard; and in some ways the ears are most satisfied by the records made at a time of life when she might well have had nothing very impressive to offer the auditory senses at all. She left the Victor company in 1916 and some time later, at about the age of sixty, made a few records for Pathé. These catch the edge and body of her voice remarkably well, so that, although she is plainly taxed by the climax of the aria, her record of Fanny's Air from *Sappho* is a most lovely and persuasive one: the beauty of voice and the tender expressiveness are both touching. Her epitaph for the gramophone was still to be recorded, by her own voice reading and speaking, even singing a few notes, two days (we are told) before her death, in 1942. For this, 'touching' would be a poor term. 'Good taste' is flouted, and 'elegance' is not in question; but one *is* made thankfully aware that behind these qualities in French art and character there are also reserves of feeling and greatness. So Calvé survives.

32. Emma Calvé as Carmen

33. Marcel Journet as Klingsor in *Parsifal*

And so, with a little less lustre but still plenty of merit, do many others from the French operatic scene in the early years of this century. Among the sopranos Aïno Ackté (Finnish by birth), Georgette Bréjean-Silver, Lucette Korsoff, Alice Verlet and Geneviève Vix; the mezzos Bressler-Gianoli, Marie Delna and the sumptuous-voiced Gerville-Réache; the tenors already listed; the baritones Charles Gilibert and Dinh Gilly (a dark characterful voice and some memorable records); the basses Jean-François Delmas, Juste Nivette and later Léon Rothier: all deserve more than a mention. Then there were Blanche Arral, giving perhaps the most French and spirited of *Faust* Jewel Songs, and Louise Edvina, the French-Canadian soprano hauntingly imaginative in 'Depuis le jour'. After the First World War Gabrielle Ritter-Ciampi, a most accomplished lyric-coloratura soprano, came to the fore. She brought character, taste and a radiant voice to her Mozart, while her record of 'Sweet bird that shun'st the noise of folly' from Handel's *Il Penseroso* is one of the finest of its kind. The French are not often thought of as Handelians, but another excellent performance is Armand Crabbé's of 'Oh ruddier than the cherry' from *Acis and Galatea*, sprightly and wicked in its characterisation, faultless in its placing of the rapid semi-quavers. He was an able technician and a versatile artist, and his record (in French) of 'Largo al factotum' is one of the few performances of that over-familiar song that actually make one feel like laughing with the busy barber instead of switching him off.

Crabbé had one of those very French voices, a baritone shaded to tenor (as the basses are sometimes shaded to baritone, and the sopranos to something almost needle-sharp and sword-bright compared with their anglo-saxon or teutonic sisters). An example of the high bass is Marcel Journet, certainly one of the best singers of his period. When the electrical recording process came in the mid-twenties, Journet was still singing at La Scala and the Paris Opéra, though by 1927 he was sixty. The records made at this stage of his career show him in fine form in the extensive upper register, but less full-bodied below, and certainly less firm-toned than formerly. This has to be said, because if the complete set of *Faust*, made about this time, were taken to show his Mephistopheles at its best he would be much underrated. Its best is to be found in the solos and concerted items (with Caruso, Farrar and others) made about 1910: a splendid version of the Serenade, for instance, demonstrates the arts of combining a polished style with meaty Mephistophelean characterisation – and it also boasts a genuine trill. So does a pleasant aria, 'Dans un délire extrême' from Nicolo's *Joconde*; but here Journet is most elegantly of the school of Plançon and Belhomme, handling the melody with superb style and skill. He had a great range and great fluency of technique (Ezio Pinza, who heard him when he himself was a young, aspiring basso, wrote 'I never heard anyone go from high notes to low ones with the ease and sonority of the middle-aged Journet'). On records we hear this in an air, 'Dans le service', from *Le Chalet*, where the big voice is managed with vivacity as well as splendour.

He had an enormous operatic repertoire, including many of the great Wagnerian parts. His recordings of Wotan's Farewell and Sach's Monologue were made electrically, when his voice was past its best; but a superb performance of Hagen's Watch from *Götterdämmerung* shows him firm as a rock, and projecting a dark bass voice menacingly and magnificently.

And so the account of French achievements could go on, for it is necessarily incomplete. No mention yet, for instance, has been made of Félia Litvinne, a famous soprano of the late nineteenth and early twentieth centuries, an Isolde and Brünnhilde, Donna Anna and Tosca, Marguérite and Gilda. Her records show power, skill, sensitivity and a fine voice, though one has to listen with a sympathetic ear to some rather 'difficult' recordings (rewarding, however, in the richly elegiac 'Pleurez, mes yeux' from *Le Cid*, or in Isolde's Liebestod, an expressive and individual performance of this). But her claim to a place at the end of the chapter derives not only from her distinguished career and recognisable excellence on disc, but also to a sentence she wrote in her autobiography, dear to record collectors. The voice that was once so beautiful, she says, is now stilled. But 'J'ai quelques disques très beaux. Je dis toujours, en touchant le gramophone, "Ci gît Félia Litvinne"'. She was one of the few to realise the importance of these old recordings, and one of the many to add to it.

If those numerous French singers had joined her, put all their records on top of that gramophone, touched it and said 'Here lies the glory of French singing', they would not have been far wrong. Other good French singers, perhaps two or three great ones, were to follow. But in the other periods of recording that we have to consider in this book there is never to be such richness as in these early years. These were the times of plenty. There is much that the gramophone left uncaught; but it tells enough to make us sure about that.

9. America: Talent and Training
Emma Eames Geraldine Farrar
Frances Alda

IN New York as in Paris, the first decades of this century and the last of the nineteenth were years of incomparable abundance in the provision of operatic singing. Not much of it, however, was done by the natives; for the day of the American singer was still to come.

Certainly America welcomed the great ones of Europe with open arms. Phineas Barnum gave the American public its first taste when he introduced Jenny Lind in 1850. Her appearance, said the *New York Herald*, was thought 'as significant an event as the appearance of Dante, Tasso, Raphael, Shakespeare, Goethe, Thorwaldsen or Michael Angelo . . . she has changed all men's ideas of music as much as Bacon's inductive system revolutionised philosophy'. A mere singer has probably never had so exalted a place in the cultural hierarchy since. Still, the arrivals, close on Jenny Lind's heels, of Mario and Grisi, Sontag and Alboni were also considered events of major public interest; then, before the 'fifties were out, a new goddess of song emerged, in the person of a sixteen year old girl called Adelina Patti. And to the extent that she had been brought up in New York from the age of two, Patti was an American. Sometimes an all-American (or Canadian) star was born: Sybil Sanderson of Sacramento, California, went to Paris and became the first Thaïs in Massenet's opera; Marie Louise Lajeunesse from Chambly near Montreal went to Milan and became Emma Albani. In 1883 the Metropolitan opened, in 1906 Hammerstein's Manhattan Company began competition, and in 1909 New York was said to be 'opera mad': in five months (from November 1909 to the beginning of April 1910) approximately three-hundred performances of opera took place in the city. But the role of the American singer was still, in general, a subordinate one.

There were exceptions. Lillian Norton of Farmington, Maine, appeared with the Metropolitan Company in 1891 and sang there, one of the most valuable artists in a great period, until 1909. She was the genuine 'Yankee Diva' – but 'Norton' had to become 'Nordica', and she also had to reach New York by way of Milan, St. Petersburg and London. In Milan she had lessons; in the other cities she sang major roles in great opera houses. At home in America it was virtually impossible to obtain experience in opera, and many considered that it was necessary to go to Europe for instruction too. There were, in fact, some good teachers in America: Nordica is a case in point, for she went to Italy as an accomplished technician, and we gather that she learnt there principally matters of pronunciation and repertoire. But Albani was a Lamperti pupil in Italy; Farrar, years later, went to Lilli Lehmann in Germany; and hosts of American girls seem to have made the pilgrimage to Paris to be put through their paces by Mathilde Marchesi and thus become a second Melba or Calvé, both of whom she had taught.

One of these American Marchesi pupils was an outstanding singer, who returned to make an illustrious name in her own country. More fortunate in recording, however, was a soprano from New Zealand, also to be discussed here, as her subsequent career and life were so essentially American: this was Frances Alda, whose records make easy listening where Emma Eames' do not. Eames had that sort of timbre that seems to have been most difficult to record. Alda, eighteen years younger, sounds less round, more vibrant, fresher voiced though probably less purely beautiful. Both were highly accomplished, recognisably assured in the face of technical difficulties, in the way that Melba appears supremely confident and capable, though with Eames the confidence seems sometimes to have been daunted by the conditions under which she had to record (see p. 9). 'The process enervated me, as I felt that with even the most satisfactory results, my voice would be diminished and deformed, and the cross vibrations eliminated completely'. So she said during a broadcast in 1939, not the least interesting feature of the remark being the reference to the fairly subtle matter of what she calls 'cross vibrations'.

Eames was aware of technical and stylistic problems, and critical of her own shortcomings, as she heard them, much as one understands Elisabeth Schwarzkopf to be among modern singers. 'One day', said Eames, 'I realised that I had fallen into the habit, so dear to Jean de Reszke and Caruso, who abused it to a fault, of using too often a portamento effect. I went home and got out all my scores, and went through them, eliminating every portamento except those that were absolutely indispensable'. This was possibly one cause of her being thought a cold artist, the description which has always dogged her reputation though it fits the records hardly at all. The records are, on the contrary, full of feeling – and all too often (it must be added) of portamento. Perhaps the finest of all is of Schubert's 'Gretchen am Spinnrade' (see comparisons p. 593), and the use of portamento is one of its most remarkable features. Tosti's 'Dopo' is also intensely conceived; and 'warm' is exactly the term that comes to mind to describe its tone and feeling. It has also a good example of those 'cross vibrations' that recording did manage to catch: the elegiac tone of the opening with its dark shading, and then the ending deliberately and beautifully drained of colour and vibrancy. Joy was also within her scope. Bemberg's 'Chanson des Baisers' is the sort of song for which one nowadays feels that apologies have to be made, yet it waltzes away happily with a well-and-truly committed melody and good, vigorous intervals. Eames is superb in it. Her fioriture have the expertise of Melba, her voice retains its customary warmth but rings more brightly than in most records, and she has an enchanting way of leading back into the waltz tune. Some of her records lack lustre; several have quite specific faults (in the 'Ave Maria' from *Otello* she does not observe the markings over 'prega per noi', and she holds the final A flat for only four beats instead of six, and so forth). But enough that is fine remains of her voice and art to make her a valuable 'terminal', another 'archetype': a certain grandeur, a roundness that extends right to the high A's and B's where others thin out and become piercing, a flexibility and assurance probably finer than any lyric-dramatic soprano (and she was a Sieglinde and Elsa, as well as Aida and Donna Anna) since her time. Above all there was spaciousness in her singing: a grand sweep that made Gounod's 'Ave Maria' imposing, and a matriarchal authority that made 'Dixie' positively regal. Her voice also needed space to do it justice, and all too often less than justice was done. Still, at worst, it was by no means as 'diminished and deformed' as its owner feared, and at best it glows with a rare individuality and warmth.

More and less can be said of Frances Alda. She does not exactly rank in the mind as an archetype. One does not often think 'Ah, how Alda might have sung that' as one does Eames or Destinn, Ponselle or Muzio, Callas or de los Angeles. Yet she is probably the most consistently satisfying lyric soprano on pre-electrical records. Her voice took to recording better than most. It is vibrant but without the marked vibrato that so many of the Italians had, and without their tendency to abrupt changes of register. More sensitive and interesting than Farrar, fuller in voice and easier above the stave than Bori (on records), less given to excessive portamento and (again on records) steadier than Destinn in the middle voice, she emerges as a singer valuable beyond what the facts of her career, distinguished as it was, might suggest.

The full, impressive measure of her excellence can be taken from her own favourite record, the aria 'Ah, dunque, ei m'amera' from Catalani's *Lorelei*. The voice is fresh and full-bodied, and one senses immediately the warmth and intelligence of its direction. The technical accomplishments are outstanding: the cleanness of difficult leaps (one to a full-voiced high C, another to a soft high A from the D a twelfth below), the fineness of the trills, the firmness of sustaining power. She was a good, sensitive stylist, warming the phrases of Micaëla's song in *Carmen*, in a way that is always live with feeling, never sentimental. That she just misses greatness as a singer is, perhaps, inescapable when one comes to compare her singing of (say) the aria 'Ebben, ne andrò' from *La Wally* with Muzio's record, or 'Elle a fui' from *Les Contes d'Hoffmann* with Bori's. Alda is lovely in both, yet the first comes just short of tragic depth, and the second lacks the passionate fragility in which Bori is so right and so touching: in neither

34. Emma Eames as Valentine in *Les Huguenots*

35. Frances Alda as Manon

record is the imagination such a fully creative, individual thing as it is with the other singers. Yet if Alda misses this standard of greatness it is by a hair's breadth, and in many cases comparisons turn in her favour over precisely such matters of sensitivity and interest. Elisabeth Rethberg, for instance, puts up a sturdy performance singing out with fine tone in the trio 'Qual volutà trascorrere' from *I Lombardi*, but Alda's singing of this is far more imaginative: she caresses the phrases, using fine gradations of tone to mould them, and holds the full voice in reserve for climaxes. In this and many another record she has left some exquisite contributions to the collector's library.

The great contribution of her rather more famous contemporary and rival, Geraldine Farrar, was a simple matter: she would sing broad upward intervals with the most bracing vitality and precision. If a young soprano with Mimì, Butterfly and Marguérite in her repertoire wants to set herself a standard in this particular matter, then it is to Farrar she should apply. Mimì's duet with Marcel in Act III of *La Bohème* is a model in this respect. We are always hearing the high notes in this approached from below, even if by ever such a little, but how doubly thrilling is the effect when they are taken with the perfect cleanness of Farrar's attack here. The placing of notes in Butterfly's entrance music ('Ancora un passo') is also surpassingly pure and accurate in Farrar's version; and in the final trio from *Faust* she can teach the whole soprano race, from Melba to Sutherland. As an interpreter, too, she has left her mark. Her Butterfly survives on records in a fragmentary state, but sufficiently complete and vivid for us to recognise an admirable portrayal. Phrases like 'chiamerà Butterfly' from 'Un bel dì' charm the memory with their delicacy, and the unforced power and passion of 'O a me, sceso dal trono' in the last pages of the opera are intensely moving. Her Carmen also survives well. The voice was not especially interesting in the lower part of its range, and a Carmen needs some colour and richness that Farrar did not have. But her 'Séguédille' is distinctively realised, and again phrases fix themselves in one's mind ('J'emmènerai mon amoureux', 'Qui veut m'aimer? Je l'aimerai!', 'Je pense à certain officier', and the first reprise of 'Près des ramparts'). Still, generally speaking, Farrar is not remarkable for the subtlety or individuality of inflections; nor would she seem outstanding among the vast ranks of musicianly singers for any great musical imaginativeness. She is, in most of her records, a pleasing, straightforward singer with a healthy voice and an assured manner. In a few, she attains a genuine musical and dramatic distinction. But nearly always there is to be heard, at one point or another, this one feature which will suddenly lift the heart and tighten one's sense of standards. And just occasionally in the opera house, as one hears a young lyric soprano take a note with unwonted ease, freshness and accuracy, one is fleetingly visited by the ghost of an old record, and searching in the darkness to fix the recollection, remembers Geraldine Farrar.

Farrar also reminds us of bygone public interest in the opera singer as a

36. Geraldine Farrar as Manon

beauty and 'personality'. She herself, vastly appreciated by the Kaiser during her time in Germany, became the centre of much fan-club adoration at home. The glamour of the opera house was potent in those days, and beautiful and striking women were drawn there as they were later drawn into films: Lina Cavalieri, Louise Edvina, and not long after these Maria Jeritza, like Farrar, were among them. Oddly, celebrated beauties seem to be no longer with us, and nor do the well-rounded Tetrazzinis (or Carusos for that matter): yet the New Yorkers of these years relished both. In particular they took to their hearts a remarkable woman, born in Scotland, trained in America and France, famous as the first Mélisande, and the conqueror of its composer. This was Mary Garden, who said of herself 'It is by an art quite different from that of other opera singers that I have found my way, and I want to be judged not alone by my singing or my acting or my stage appearance, but by these combined into one art that is entirely different from the rest'.[1] The written records of her successes are impressive enough, and the special judgment for which she appeals cannot be arrived at from gramophone records. These do dispel one legend, however. It is sometimes said that her voice was 'nothing special', but it clearly was an unusually fine instrument. Her *Traviata* record (the Act I aria in French) shows not only a warm and lovely tone, but also great flexibility. The voice was well-preserved as late as 1929, though it had lost some top notes. A record of the Card Scene from *Carmen* made at this time shows too her ability to act with the voice: a fine and unusual sadness marks this performance, inevitable fate given sighing acceptance. The legendary record made with Debussy's accompaniment, the short solo 'Mes longs cheveux' from Act II of *Pelléas et Mélisande*, is clean, tender and virginal, not notably subtle, however. But, as she herself would best have known, the complete Mary Garden was (even more than with most singers) outside the power of the gramophone to present.

These four sopranos make an impressive quartet, and others were Suzanne Adams and Bessie Abott (Marchesi pupils), Alice Neilsen, Marie Rappold and Pauline Donalda, who also made records of which some think highly. The other voices, however, are of less account. Riccardo Martin and Orville Harrold, tenors, Herbert Witherspoon and Reinald Werrenrath, baritones, Sophie Braslau and Florence Wickham, contraltos: all did good work without leaving notable recordings. David Bispham was a much-respected bass-baritone, and some of his records explain why (an agreeably lightened 'Hark, hark, the lark', for instance). Others (like the punched-out and charmless 'Il balen') merely pose that question. Louise Homer, the contralto, is the other American of this generation whose records are still impressive. The page's song 'Nobil signor' from *Les Huguenots*, though unsmiling and stolid, shows her brilliance in florid work,

---

[1] From an interview of 1907, quoted by J. F. Cone in *The Manhattan Opera Company*, p. 134.

and one record after another brings the power, definition and wide range of her voice most vividly before us. Sometimes her vowels are dull and she sings as though with a mouth too closed. Sometimes one feels that this is a majestic sound but that characterisation and variety are lacking. Occasionally she breaks free of these limitations and gives us (for instance) a fearsome witch in an extract from *Hansel and Gretel*. But for sheer voice she has few equals, and because of its strong edge and sharp focus her voice took exceptionally well to recording under pre-electrical conditions. Passages like Amneris' 'Alla pompa', where a sumptuous tone and grand style are called for, ring out superbly in Homer's records. By and large, she is the most satisfyingly recorded contralto of the period.

But she too was trained in Paris, and came to the Metropolitan via opera in Vichy, Brussels and London. Until American singers could get their training at home – and could believe that this training was not somehow inferior – they would be at a marked disadvantage. And until some local centres sprang up throughout the country there could be no future for anything that might with any justice be called American opera.

10. Italy: Bel Canto Con Forza
Celestina Boninsegna   Salomea Krusceniski
Giuseppe Anselmi   Riccardo Stracciari
Pasquale Amato

'Bel Canto means simply beautiful singing . . . Because these magic words are in the Italian tongue does not mean that they apply to something only possessed by Italians . . . In fact, I consider American voices, in general, better trained than those of Italy, Germany or France. The Italian, in particular, has very little knowledge of the scientific side; he usually sings by intuition'.

That, at least, was one man's opinion: a baritone and a teacher (American), Herbert Witherspoon, giving an interview to Harriette Brower for her book *Vocal Mastery* published in 1917. No one, looking at the list of singers coming from the countries mentioned, is likely to take his assessment of the comparative virtues very seriously. Yet the shots he aims at the land of song itself do not fall so entirely wide of the mark when one considers the ways in which Italian singing was changing during these early years of the century. The development of Caruso's style illustrates it; the career of Titta Ruffo points the way more significantly still. More power, more passion, more excitement, more realism: these were the trends, both in the taste of the public and in the kind of opera composers were writing. Singers responded, and the results, good and bad, can all be sampled on records.

The best sampling-ground, if one is looking for representative products, is the output of the Fonotipia Company. Here are many hundreds of performances, recorded with care over the musical preparation and over the technical procedure. Most are by famous Italian singers of the day, and many are extremely good. But playing a typical dozen or so in succession may not yield quite the joy anticipated, and after a time nerves begin to protest if only because tried by so much brilliance and vitality. But they also have other, less effete reasons for protesting, and these relate directly to the kind of training Italian singers were receiving in those days.

The sopranos emerge worst. If a well-produced voice should be a well-equalised one, without a sharp break between registers; if it should be steady, without wobble or obtrusive flutter-vibrato; if it should not be shrill at the top and white in the lower half of the range: then there was hardly a well-produced voice among them. If a good stylist should phrase broadly, keep a smooth line, show a respect for the score by following its instructions (and these seem to be not unreasonable conditions): then there was hardly a good stylist either. What these sopranos did have was, in the first place, a splendid facility in florid work (though they were quite capable of simply missing out a difficulty of the composer's own invention), and, secondly, a generous fund of emotion and temperament. Most had strong voices; some had partially beautiful ones. Some of them began their careers at a ridiculously early age; many declined or retired at about the age of forty; none it seems was still singing regularly in public at fifty.

Vibrato was a marked characteristic. Gemma Bellincioni, Esther Mazzoleni, Rosina Storchio and Amelia Pinto were all considerable artists, and it is possible that the old recording exaggerated the vibrato, but there it is, an insistent feature, in the face of which one makes strong demands for compensation. Storchio, the first Madame Butterfly, sings with live character, excellent runs, a good trill, and a voice that is sensitively modulated: in arias from *Don Pasquale*, *Linda di Chamounix* and *Fra Diavolo* she gives pretty and accomplished performances. Pinto, an Italian Isolde, shrill and squally in her aria from *Die Meistersinger*, rings out with some feeling and body in 'Il va venir' from *La Juive*. Mazzoleni sings with intensity and an expressive line in 'Teneri figli' from Act II of *Norma*. Her vibrato was probably the most insistent of all, but at least it was regular. Bellincioni had that worst kind, the vibrato that flutters unevenly: the sustained note on 'giurato' in 'Voi lo sapete' and the last note of the *Fedora* aria are two examples out of many. She, certainly, was an interesting singer. Verdi is said to have admired her Traviata; and the second half of 'Ah! fors' è lui', with its lingering style, its decorations, and the extended cadenza that is brilliant yet reflective, has a genuine beauty. But one can hardly believe the composer enjoyed hearing his rhythms and note-values so loosely treated as in the first half. And could Boito, one wonders, have approved of her way with 'L'altra notte' in *Mefistofele*, the runs and arpeggios done very brilliantly at lunatic speed (the aria can, presumably, be looked at as another Mad Scene)? And can there be any excuse for breaking the very first phrase ('L'altra notte infondo (breath) al mare') as she does?

Similar enquiries present themselves as one listens to records of four other famous sopranos of these years. Emma Carelli, Regina Pacini, Eugenia Burzio and Tina Poli-Randaccio flutter less but hardly make easier listening. Carelli is spirited and, in her records from Giordano's *Siberia*, sings well in loud and soft passages: but her basic tone is unsteady, and there is a marked break between registers. This was true also of Burzio and Poli-Randaccio. The latter, a powerful lyric-dramatic soprano, sounds curiously light on records: an imaginative singer (appealing in such passages as Aida's 'Pietà ti prenda'), but shrill on high notes and hard in the chest register. Burzio *means* everything she sings: there is great fervour and dramatic intensity. But it is achieved at the expense of the vocal line, and often by such means as a little preliminary cry or gulp (Pacini does this too) before the note. This happens in an eloquently desperate version of 'Madre, pietosa vergine' (*La Forza del Destino*), at times fine, at others almost hysterically overplayed. Again, one sees her duet from Act IV of *Il Trovatore* singled out by a connoisseur-collector for praise, yet the 'Mira d'acerbe' is rough and the 'Vivra! contende' a scramble of slurred semiquavers and inexact note-values.

More congenial to most listeners nowadays are Giannina Russ and Celestina Boninsegna, though they are recognisably of the same school. On records, Russ establishes herself as the best stylist among these sopranos, and Boninsegna as the singer with the most pleasing voice. Both recorded 'Casta diva', as testing a piece of nineteenth century opera as any, and it is interesting to see how they measure up to its demands, Russ with delicacy and an 'inner' feeling, Boninsegna with forthright, outgoing tone, warmth and fullness but little subtlety. In the opening phrases both draw a firm line, in that they keep the tone at even volume instead of inflecting it in the swell-box style that Joan Sutherland adopts; and whereas Sutherland glides up to notes rather like a film in slow motion, the old Italians are direct and unmannered. All this is credit to them. But their legato is not exemplary; both will often use a light aspirate to help them along, and sometimes (in the 1909 Columbia recording) Boninsegna's change of registers brings her down with a bump on the key-note, while Russ's tendency – it is no more than that – to vibrato will sometimes disturb the evenness of her line. When it comes to fioriture both are very good, though while Russ does the descending chromatic scale towards the end excellently as written, Boninsegna substitutes an easier and less effective cadenza of her own. Neither appears to use the original key of G, as Sutherland is able to do, much to the music's advantage.

Russ is an excellent artist in the delicacy of nuance and the beauty of some very fine-drawn soft singing, doubly effective in a voice of such considerable power. Her Violetta survives affectingly in excerpts, gentle and sensitive in 'Addio del passato', the phrasing interesting, the difficult top A's taken softly. In music like Aida's 'Ritorna vincitor', with its demands for a heavier voice, she shows the exciting quality and fullness that she had at command, and, alone among these sopranos, she preserved a unified tone, without a sharp division of registers.

Boninsegna had a very distinct chest register, which she could take with magnificent power up to the low F sharp (as in an exciting performance of 'Suicidio' from *La Gioconda*), and, perhaps as a result, a slightly weakened part of the voice just above it. Nevertheless, it was a voice of such exceptional beauty and often used with such sincere feeling that she wins an assured place for herself in the line of great singers. She shared fully in the accomplishments of her time. If her singing of the aria 'Casta diva' leaves something to be desired, the cabaletta, 'Ah! bello a me', which follows, is brilliant both in the warm, forward tone and in the verve and precision of the runs. Better still is the finale of *Norma* (Deh non voleri), sung with smoothness and restraint, the voice in marvellous condition and the style exemplary. The high B is splendidly integrated here into the phrase and into the main body of the voice. This is not always so with Boninsegna's high notes: for example, she makes very obvious preparation for the high C in Aida's 'O patria mia', and in 'Ma dall'arido stella' from *Un Ballo in Maschera*. That record should, one feels, have been among the best of her achievements, but it is a rather prosaic account of this dramatic music. Yet she *could* capture drama in her recordings. She does so in 'Condotta ell'era in ceppi' from *Il Trovatore*: a fascinating record this, for the music exploits the deep notes of a contralto's voice, and Boninsegna fills the low-lying bars at the end of the piece with a fine baleful expressiveness. Fine too is the tragic colouring of her three recordings of 'Pace, pace, mio dio' from *La Forza del Destino*. In the first version, the G & T of 1907, there is a deep marking of the 'profondo il mio soffrir'; in the Columbia, two years later, a sighed 'ahimè languir'; in the Edison of about 1910 a magnificent power and resourcefulness in the high ending. All are impressive, and they show an artist with whom music would change and grow. There are some who do the same thing with their music at every performance, but one can feel Boninsegna responding as a live woman, and this is not the least attractive feature of her many fine recordings.

But though this school of Italian sopranos had its merits, it seems to belong firmly to the past, and probably not many modern listeners will be sorry. The representative voice of the Italian soprano in more recent years has been Tebaldi's, a voice without shrillness, vibrato, or break between registers. Some of the excitements and accomplishments of the early school may be lacking too: it seems that we cannot have everything, though among the dramatic sopranos singing in Italy during these early years there was one who came near to combining the virtues of all the schools. This, perhaps significantly, was not an Italian. Salomea Krusceniski, a Polish soprano, became one of the most admired singers at La Scala and provides an interesting comparison with the native breed. She comes in for some critical (as well as enthusiastic) comments in *Le Grandi Voci*, where Rodolfo Celletti describes her as having a voice more penetrating than powerful, and as being inadequately represented by her records which he says do less than justice to the qualities as an interpreter, on which her reputation in the theatre was founded. But perhaps this is an example of the different ways in which Latins and 'Anglo-Saxons' hear the same sounds. Her voice comes to me as an altogether welcome relief from the penetrative sound of the Italians; and the prime impression made by the records themselves is of a dramatic, imaginative singer, a vocal actress with Muzio and Callas as her most eminent successors. She also strikes one as being a 'modern' singer: that is, credible as a good modern singer who happened to have recorded pre-electrically; part of a continuing tradition.

Her recordings, it is true, have some of the freedoms of their period. Her

37. Celestina Boninsegna

38. Salomea Krusceniski as Salome

39. Pasquale Amato as Barnaba in *La Gioconda*

40. Giuseppe Anselmi

'Vissi d'arte' is an urgent, forward-pressing performance, rather wilful in its *rubato* and choppy in its phrasing. Far happier and more characteristic is the *rubato* of 'L'altra notte' (*Mefistofele*), especially the 1903 version which has only one verse. Her voicing, in this and the later Fonotipia record, of the phrases 'l'aura fredda . . . anima mia' again calls Muzio to mind, and the pulling-back of the tempo at such points intensifies the emotion without distorting the musical sense. Her singing is often exquisite in pure vocalism: the scales and arpeggios of the Mancenillier Scene in *L'Africaine* are smooth, accurate and easy, and the legato of a beautifully spacious version of 'Ritorna vincitor' is unflawed. But above all she registers as a sensitive creative interpreter and a thorough musician. Of her Salome and Elektra nothing remains, but there is a warmly sympathetic recording of Brünnhilde's 'War es so schmählich' from *Die Walküre*. She is distinguished among Italy's sopranos in one further point: she was still singing in her mid-fifties, and even made some records by the electrical process in 1927. These are of Ukrainian folk songs, the voice still firm and, in the middle register, still beautiful; moreover, through the voice shines the character, intense in feeling, strong in projection.

There is no doubt, however, that Italy was still rich with fine voices and, indeed, sterling artists. One has only to list the baritones: an astonishing array, compared with the provision we are used to at present. Of the old guard, Battistini and Kaschmann have been discussed; of those emerging at the beginning of the century, de Luca and Ruffo. These alone are enough to distinguish their generations. But there remain Ancona and Magini-Coletti, Scotti and Sammarco, Amato and Stracciari – and more still.

Mario Ancona is worth remembering, for the production of his voice is so easy and free-throated, the tone so full-bodied and even, that he affords an enjoyment rarer than one fancies. All the great baritones have recorded 'Eri tu' from *Un Ballo in Maschera*, and in it most of them have left some mark of their particular kind of excellence. Ancona's special excellence is the impeccable placing of a well-nourished and essentially homogeneous tone. He is a 'central' baritone, warm-voiced and unexaggerated; not a subtle colourist, yet not a cold singer either. The 'Eri tu' lacks something in variety, but a finely shaded and vigorously dramatised record of Valentine's Death in *Faust* shows how the old Italian school could convey emotion unaided by the high-pressured quiveringly passionate manner to which their successors were becoming more and more addicted. And sometimes their contemporaries too: for Antonio Magini-Coletti, able and admirable singer as he was, and five years Ancona's senior, is often less than scrupulous in the preservation of a true legato. The section of Rigoletto's 'Cortigiani, vil razza' starting 'Miei signori' has not the unaspirated smoothness of a de Luca. Yet what a fine performance this is, with its rich, easy resonance and authoritative style. He was one of those, too, who can act with the voice. In an extract from *Falstaff*, starting with the lute song and finishing with 'Quand'ero paggio', we hear a convincingly *fat* Falstaff voice; and his sense of fun presents the whole scene with vivid gaiety and enjoyment. One would never imagine that these records, or most of Ancona's, were made by a man of fifty or more. The voices are full of sap, as well as being firm and resonant, and easy from top to bottom of the big range. Time is kinder to baritone voices than to tenors and sopranos, but there are few whose records show less sign of their fifty years than these two stalwarts of the nineteenth century.

Their mettle is proved again when they are confronted by demands for agility. Ancona in the cadenza of 'A tanto amor' (*La Favorita*), Magini-Coletti in the runs of 'Dunque io son' (*Barbiere di Siviglia*, with Regina Pinkert as a marvellously fluent if somewhat fluttery Rosina), Giuseppe Campanari, another veteran and a virtuoso Figaro, in 'Largo al factotum': these show a degree of accomplishment rarely cultivated by baritones since their day. On records, Antonio Scotti, too, is perhaps most impressive in his dealings with occasional florid passages: he is splendidly deft and accurate with the sequence of fast-moving quavers in the duet 'Vado, corro' from *Don Pasquale*, or in the scales and roulades of 'Come paride' from *L'Elisir d'Amore*. But Scotti was widely acclaimed as a singer-actor and not much of his distinction here emerges on record. His Scarpia looks marvellous in photographs, and has been impressively described, but his single commercial recording from the opera (the solo from Act II) is poor: indeed one hardly hears it as a Scarpia voice at all.

He and Mario Sammarco are the two baritones of the time whose careers were notably more distinguished than their records. Sometimes, of course, the reverse happens; and it may be that records are relatively flattering to Riccardo Stracciari. He made less of an impression on the American public than did Scotti and Sammarco, yet from his records one would judge him to have been a better singer. His voice blooms but does not spread; he has brilliant high notes but does not disappear from view below the middle of the bass stave. His legato is good, his runs are excellent, and his interpretations live. An oddity that became more noticeable as years went by was a kind of squeeze or even squirt, given to notes usually at medium volume in the middle register. If the word was 'usanza' (as in the Prologue to *Pagliacci*), then it might come out as something like 'usuanza', opening up on the second syllable as though by widening a more than half-closed mouth. At such moments one is also aware of Stracciari as a singer with a throat (cf. the axiom 'Per l'Italiano non esiste la gola'); and this is itself strange, for most of the time he impresses one as among the freest, least throaty of baritones.

These misgivings hardly arise in the early records. He did some particularly fine work in arias from the early operas of Verdi: two beauties from *Nabucco* ('Chi mi togli' and 'Dio ti giuda'), 'In braccio alle dovizie' from *I Vespri Siciliani* (recorded with some similar characteristics years later by Heinrich Schlusnus), and 'O vecchio cor' from *I due Foscari*. These are some of the gems of the Fonotipia catalogue. The last-named of them particularly is a model in the purity of legato, with the *marcato* notes still beautifully integrated into the line, the *fioritura* a graceful and genuine flowering of the melodic phrase. Beginning with a velvety *mezza voce* and an inner feeling rare among these singers, he treats the aria like a painter with the finest sense of light and shade, and entirely without exaggeration. His voice production was at this time absolutely unconstricted, and its excellence is confirmed by his long survival as a singer of the front rank. Born in 1875, he continued to be a prolific recorder after the electrical process came in in 1926, and was still singing publicly in 1936. The electrical recordings include complete performances of *Il Barbiere di Siviglia* and *Rigoletto*, as well as some Neapolitan songs, with Stracciari in superb voice. The music is not 'good', but to some listeners (myself among them) irresistible none the less, when sung like this; and pieces like 'Sto pensanno a Maria' and 'Luntenanza' by de Curtis (surely the High Master of this school) are perfectly designed to bring out the best in an Italian singer's voice and temperament. Stracciari's records of these things, like Caruso's and Gigli's, are full of warm feeling and rich sound; we come very close to the singer's happiest and best self through them.

Stracciari made records to which one says at different times 'Fair', 'Good', 'Splendid', 'Excellent'. But there is also the cry of 'Great', and in my experience only one of the baritones now under discussion provokes that. This is Pasquale Amato. He had a voice which could be unpleasant, and which was certainly far from suiting all kinds of music equally well. In the Fonotipias, recorded before his success in America, his vibrato and the keen-edged tone make a fierce impression; and later on he could still sound very unlovely, the voice too hard and dark for parts like Germont père in *La Traviata*, powerful yet not opulent when in the company of Caruso and Tetrazzini for the Sextet in *Lucia di Lammermoor*. Nor was he one of those whose voices survived into advanced middle age: two or three years younger than de Luca and Stracciari, he did not, like them, make records by the electrical process, and contemporary accounts suggest that this was as well. But between 1911 and 1915 when he was under contract to the Victor Company he recorded many of the best-known baritone arias in Italian opera in such a way as to prompt the cry which greets only a rare excellence.

His was exactly the right voice for Verdi's Iago. The 'Credo' opens with a biting intensity, and Amato also had a fine way of veiling this thrustful tone so that the last section, with its hymn-like chords and its gaunt silences, is painted darkly by the voice, the repetition of 'e poi' filling the emptiness only as a hollow brooding echo. This colouring of tone, or rather the sense of an artist working both in colours and in shapes, is also felt in 'Eri tu', which requires so much more in the way of pure singing than the 'Credo'. He is responsive to every call for light and shade, yet preserves a fine legato and never fusses the phrases. More than this, he *grieves*: taking a few performances that come to hand, those by Ancona, Stracciari, de Luca, Tibbett

41. Riccardo Stracciari as Rigoletto

and MacNeil, all of them finely sung, one finds that none has come into possession of its emotions as Amato has. In fact the one comparison that can be safely made in this respect is with Tito Gobbi who has certainly entered the drama and the music and, like Amato, presents us vividly with an expressive *face* and a realisation of the suffering mind behind it. With Amato it is sometimes as though all the art and sensibility have been brought to a focal point as intensely as a thinker's concentration bears down upon the frown between his brows. It is in this way that one feels the concentration of his 'Cortigiani, vil razza'. The individual strengths are analysable (the bitter attack of the rolled 'r' in 'razza', the effectiveness of 'io piango', so much greater because the break in the voice seems to come in spite of the will to control it, the *diminuendo* on 'tu taci' as hope vanishes and only the sighed 'ahimè' is left), but behind all of this is a sensibility entirely absorbed by the composer's material. Again Gobbi is a comparable artist. One point at which Amato leaves even him behind (and no doubt one could find places where Gobbi has the advantage) is in a particular way of handling certain phrases, as though they were indeed susceptible to touch. Examples occur in the Prologue to *Pagliacci*. The phrase 'Un nido di memorie . . . cantava un giorno' is given tenderly by Gobbi: but with the most exquisite use of portamento and half-shades it is as though Amato actually takes the nest in his hands, holding it with an appreciation of its fragility, and with an affectionate reverence for the life it contains. Can a modern singer ever quite do this? It is most unlikely unless he knows from long experience that the conductor will follow him; and of course the modern singer's experience is generally that he must follow the conductor, who is nearly always concerned with cohesion and impulse, so little with the possible beauties of this moment and that.

One further note on Amato: he also recorded one of the best versions of Figaro's 'Largo al factotum', perhaps the best of all. His vitality evidently extended to a rich comic sense. A 'posh' voice for reminding us that he is a barber of quality, a sly, veiled tone for the ladies and gallants who call on his diplomatic skills, a leery smile for the one, a most delightfully natural chuckle as he thinks of the other, a fine collection of cracked toothless old voices for the summoning 'Figaro's: and with these, exactly the right feeling for Rossinian crescendo. It is a most vivid piece of comic singing, and a fine testimony to the range of Amato's skills as an actor-singer.

In the gaiety of this record by Amato there is a kind of charm; as there is in Stracciari's Italian songs, de Luca's easy smoothness, and Battistini's princely boldness of style. Yet charm is not really a notable feature of Italian singing. The French, Austrians and Spaniards have it, and sometimes in a chubby way (as with Gigli) Italians have it also. But comparisons are revealing as ever. The aria 'Promesse de mon avenir' from Massenet's *Roi de Lahore* was a favourite with Italian baritones as with the French, and many of them recorded it. Playing some of these at random – de Luca, Scotti, Giuseppe Pacini, and the brilliantly resonant and fresh-voiced

Eugenio Giraldoni (he was the first Scarpia) – one finds much to admire in all. But then play two Frenchmen, the veteran Lassalle and his successor Renaud, and one finds a quality that all along one has vaguely missed in the Italians' records: it is that kind of elegant, cultured handling that brings *charm* to it. It is not simply that this is the advantage Frenchmen must have in French music, for a possibly finer, more charming performance still is given by Emilio de Gogorza, the Spaniard brought up in America. And what a stylist he was! Whether in 'Where'er you walk' or 'John Peel', or the popular Spanish songs he did so well (including famous performances of 'La Paloma'), or operatic arias like this one, he sings with a combination of dignity, vitality and imagination that makes charm. By some subtle chemistry the elements are differently mixed in the Italians, and this elusive quality in fact eludes them.

At least the basses might claim exemption from this stricture, as charm is a quality they so rarely have the opportunity of exercising. Vittorio Arimondi, Oreste Luppi and Francesco Navarrini were the most prominent Italian basses in this period of recording, and one of them at least comes as near as any singer to having that kind of elegance we associate with the French bass Plançon. This was Navarrini, who sings 'Vi ravviso' from *La Sonnambula* with exceptional beauty of tone and style: steady and supple, full-bodied yet smooth and gentle. He made few records but in those few there is hardly a flaw.

Not many of the tenors can have this said of them. The list of names is long, and so is the catalogue of their records. Edoardo Garbin, Giuseppe Anselmi and Giovanni Zenatello in particular were prolific recorders, and so after all were de Lucia, Caruso and Bonci whom we have discussed in previous chapters. These and their many gifted contemporaries make a remarkable school: marvellous voices all of them, and often individual and creative stylists. Even so, with all of them, alas, there are arias, phrases, individual notes that one might wish otherwise, and as one listens to a random choice of the Fonotipias made by the three first mentioned one again has to question the direction of Italian singing. Was there in these first years of the twentieth century anything that one can properly call a golden age in Italian singing? If so we should surely find a rich legacy in these tenor recordings, for tenors are an Italian speciality, the primitive gramophone took to them well, and there were a great many of them.

Let us go back a generation and look briefly at a contemporary of Tamagno, Francesco Marconi, born in 1853. Most of his records were made when he was fifty-five, and we know from later artists that purity of style tends to be less fastidiously preserved as a singer gets on in years. So, with Marconi, we hear an occasional aspirate, for instance in the broad phrases of the 'Ingemisco' from Verdi's *Requiem*. But the even emission of tone is very little affected: everything is in focus, and he sings with a fine aristocratic finish as well as plenty of fervour. He can work a special kind of musical delight, as in the first verse of 'Cielo e mar' (*La Gioconda*), rounded off with an elegant turn in the last 'o sogni d'or'. Better still is the grace and charm of 'Tu che a Dio' from *Lucia di Lammermoor*, the voice beautifully even from top to bottom, the drama powerfully enacted but never at the expense of tone and lyricism. Here, I think, is some evidence of the Italian tradition in lyric-dramatic singing as the nineteenth century knew it: a few valuable records to go with the dozen or so by Tamagno and the many by de Lucia, to point to an excellence that existed for the early twentieth century to draw on if it wished.

We can feel this nineteenth century tradition present in the singing of both Garbin and Anselmi. Both were important artists in their time, but the curious colouration of Garbin's voice, sometimes apparently lustreless, sometimes overbrilliant, makes him an 'interesting' singer rather than an attractive one. Anselmi, on the other hand, has one of the most likeable tenor voices on record. It is most beautifully warm and sweet-toned in the middle register, rounder in quality than de Lucia, more heroic than Bonci, less strenuous in usage than Caruso. He also possessed great personal magnetism ('il tenore delle donne' says Eugenio Gara in *Le Grandi Voci*), and this too is projected in the recordings: he will spin a phrase, hold it out, almost offering it visually, so that attention is drawn to the singer as a person, and the emotions become vivid and immediate in the process. He is, then, another of those singers (Battistini is perhaps the prime example) who exercise a command over essentially lyrical material, creating dramatic effect by musical means, but assuming an interpretative authority beyond anything permitted a singer nowadays. So compare his recording of 'Quando le sere' from *Luisa Miller* with a recent one (in the complete performance of the opera) by Carlo Bergonzi, whose sense of style usually distinguishes him among modern tenors. Bergonzi sings with well-placed tone and generally a good legato (though, like Anselmi himself, he aspirates the dotted notes in the 'mi tradìa' phrases). But keeping strict time, he leaves us in possession of *nothing* – or nothing that matters. Extend the comparison a little to include another by Bergonzi (to make sure that his interpretation might not have been quite different with a different conductor), one by del Monaco, and one by Richard Tucker; and then play a sequence of records from the '78' period, say, Schipa, Pertile and Bonci. I found myself surprised at the sheer dullness of the moderns: Bergonzi is no more imaginative in his recital record than in the set; del Monaco is remarkably smooth but communicates no feeling; Tucker does project an interesting and valid interpretation (noting the direction *appassionatissimo*, he makes it an angry aria rather than a sad one), but there is no *piano* singing and no charm. All of the older singers have greater virtues here: Schipa poised, economical and elegant (though he avoids some of the low notes), Bonci the smoothest and sweetest-voiced of them all, Pertile quite breathtakingly 'inner' and alive. Yet Anselmi still makes one listen afresh. More than all the others he makes a pleasant piece momentarily exquisite. He can draw out the phrases in exactly the right proportions (hear that first high phrase 'lo sguardo inamorato', the leading note spun out and held over to join the highest note, taken softly); and he can feel this in the way that probably only a singer can do. It is a part of a singer's art, and one that conductors have now largely usurped. Anselmi is his own conductor; and with that kind of singer in that kind of music, the perilous procedure is vindicated. The later, musicianly and disciplined singers have had their wings clipped; the music pleases, but the magic has gone.

Anselmi preserves the magic in several other fine performances, many of them in the sort of music (the Siciliana from *Cavalleria Rusticana*, Ossian's Song in *Werther*, 'Amor ti vieta' in *Fedora*, for instance) that generally takes some hard knocks in the stress and forward drive of later, more turbulent tenors. But there are also plenty of records in which one can see taste and technique far less happily exercised. The aspiring has been mentioned, but in places where it is only a venial sin. In 'Ecco ridente' from *Il Barbiere di Siviglia* it is a maddening characteristic, for so much of the passage work is marvellous in its dexterity and smoothness, and obviously with a little more trouble everything could have been superb. Again, in the much-praised Handel record, a light-footed florid aria 'Va godendo' from *Xerxes*, not all the semi-quavers are distinct and even, and yet the performance is so *near* to being a brilliant demonstration of what should be golden-age standards. Then, while so many of the embellishments that Anselmi introduces into nineteenth century music are delightful and well-judged, there are some that are inexcusable: for example, the addition of a high C to the last high phrase ('in un sogno supremo') of 'Giunto sul passo' in *Mefistofele*. And that record brings us to the most troublesome fault, an uncertainty of intonation. Sometimes this must surely be due to recording, or to a badly centred 'swinging' copy. But it occurs too often to be entirely explained in this way. Anselmi had a voice, style and technique that place him in the front rank; yet one can never hear a record of his for the first time and be confident that it will not have some feature that just as surely takes him out of it.

The uncertainties over Zenatello must be put another way. Here it is that, in my experience, one can play half-a-dozen records and really find nothing to recommend him to the care of posterity. He obviously had a strong voice and plenty of energy, so that he was a useful man to have in an opera company. But there is often nothing more than that, and then, when one does come upon something individual in his singing, it is as likely as not to be an unpleasantness, whether of style or tone or production of vowel sound. And yet, just as one is about to cast him into outer darkness, there comes a record where one says 'And yet, after all it *was* a remarkable voice', and then perhaps one where one suddenly realises that he is really singing most beautifully. A striking example comes from Puccini's *Manon Lescaut*: the appeal, 'Guardate, pazzo son', which des Grieux sings despairingly in Act III. It is so often torn to shreds with hysterical over-emphasis, yet Zenatello opens with a fine legato and shows a sure feeling for the flexibility of tempo that the passage requires: this is the work of a genuine artist. More important, he was a famous Otello (he sang the role more than 500 times), and some of the records show him as a great one. The finest is probably a performance of the Monologue, 'Dio, mi potevi scagliar', recorded for Fonotipia in 1908. There is also a Victor recording of this, made electrically in 1928; but though the fifty-two-year-old tenor sings the piece with love and still a good deal of voice, the tempo is too quick for the dark brooding mood of the first half, and there are far more departures from the note in declamation. The Fonotipia record, however, is a performance both passionate and scrupulous, showing what magnificent body the voice had in its prime, and how artistically he could use it in music that suited him.

Two other dramatic tenors of this period also leave a vivid and valuable impression. Both recorded extracts from *Otello* and it is interesting to compare them. Bernardo de Muro had probably the most heroically ringing voice after Tamagno, and he is superb in the 'Ora e per sempre addio': firm and brilliant, both in the testing high passages and in the still more important middle voice (the last 'è questo il fin' is magnificently full-bodied and broad). The other tenor, Carlo Albani, recorded the same passage, and what we find here is a remarkable contrast, considering the two were singing at much the same time. Albani harks back to the nineteenth century: in the vibrato (regular and controlled, as with de Lucia), in the lyricism brought to this declamatory music, and, more interestingly, in the rhythmic freedom. The passage immediately before the 'Ora e per sempre' is taken not so much as angry denunciation, but as lament. Again, it is singing that would not be permitted these days, yet it is a genuine interpretation, and there is true imaginative involvement in the loathing of 'l'orrendi baci di Cassio': de Muro, much nearer to the moderns, incisive and accurate, has nothing of this imaginativeness to offer. In several other fine records, solos from *Don Carlo* and *La Gioconda* (but hear also the 'Or son sei mesi' from *La Fanciulla del West* as an example of rhythmic freedom which has become mere looseness and which must have been a conductor's nightmare), Albani shows himself one of the last Italian tenors distinctively of the old school. De Muro too had many of its virtues, and one has only to hear his records from *Andrea Chénier* or Mascagni's *Isabeau* to know that here is a tenor of very great merit: powerful and brilliant, yet capable of a veiled softness, fiery and yet dignified.

So two cheers (but rousing ones) for the tenors. They all had weaknesses, and their records have all sorts of faults that the musical and recording disciplines of later times would have done much to correct. But these were vintage years; and, in their fund of talent, the decades immediately following were to be only a little less richly endowed.

Perhaps then we can leave this period of recorded singing in Italy, counting the blessings and dismissing the blemishes as part of the spotty youth or adolescence of the gramophone. Italy, in the years we have been discussing, produced Tetrazzini, Boninsegna, Caruso, Bonci, Anselmi, Amato, Scotti, Ruffo, and so many others: does not this in itself speak of a golden age of Italian singing? In a sense it does, for these were outstanding singers and the list is far from complete. But let us put it another way: there is not one of these singers listed above (unless it is Caruso) whose recordings do not show major faults, whether of inaccuracy, or unsure intonation, or bad joining of registers, or excessive vibrato, or lack of restraint. And one has this saddening observation to make about Italian singing: that one can never quite rely on it. If, for instance, one were to leave a musical friend with a random pile of twenty or thirty Fonotipias, one could never be sure that among the glories there would not also be a kind of recurrent careless-ness about musical detail which would simply evoke the comment 'Thank God for Progress'. My own belief is that, as with many debates on the reality of progress, it is a matter of swings and roundabouts: we have gained in accuracy but lost in inspiration, ironed out faults but dampened excite-ment. The body of recordings from these times is a valuable legacy, but far more uneven in quality than its advocates will usually admit.

More regrettable, however, are the signs pointing the way ahead for Italian singing. We can tell very clearly from the records of earlier singers like de Lucia and Battistini what the great contribution of Italy has been. It lay in a highly cultivated virtuosity in florid work for one thing. And this was still a feature of the singing of those not entirely satisfactory sopranos we have discussed in this chapter: they were all good on scale work and divisions. But we can also see that composers were gradually asking for these skills less and less, and that singers were being required instead to cultivate great volume and dramatic power. We can also see how the passionate declamation of so much of this music was likely to tempt singers away from the legato style which had been Italy's other great contribution. The signs are there in many of the singers under present discussion, and later we are to see more of this sad process of disintegration.

But the next chapter belongs to a new section of our survey. For the new phase in singing coincides with a new era in the history of the gramophone. By mid-twenties most of the great singers of the early years – Caruso, Melba, Destinn and so forth – were dead or in retirement or well past their prime. And at about the same time a remarkable new generation of German singers – Lotte Lehmann, Elisabeth Schumann, Friedrich Schorr and their con-temporaries – were coming to the fore. They were fortunate, for their prime was captured by a new recording process, which came upon the record-buying public in 1925. Sound was now recorded electrically, and this meant among other things that the gramophone had a wider frequency range to exploit. An orchestra could now be recorded convincingly, and so a whole new area of music was opened up. Opera, particularly Italian opera, and particularly Italians singing it, had been the mainstay of the pre-electrical recording era. After 1925 it was no longer at the centre; and, with some shining exceptions, it no longer deserved to be.

Part II

Decline and Survival
The Electrical 78 1925–1950

11. Decline:
New Talents and Lost Discipline
Lily Pons Aureliano Pertile

CARUSO, Melba, Battistini, Plançon . . . such names from the gramophone's first period remain great ones, potent even when they represent little as direct musical experience to the critic who invokes them or to readers who are none the less impressed. Tetrazzini, Galli-Curci, Ruffo, Chaliapin . . . the list seems endless, and the status of these singers somehow larger than life. Despite all their unevenness, some hundreds of pre-electrical records remain in impressive existence, to be valued by a posterity which must count itself lucky to be able to hear these famous voices at all. The strange and often lovely sounds have their intrinsic worth seconded by the romantic appeals of rarity and age, and there are always likely to be specialists, curio-seekers and antiquarians to feel the fascination of collecting original copies, its excitements and frustrations promoting a genuine relish for what is heard beneath the expensive sizzles and bumps.

But the electrical 78, which we turn to now, possesses no comparable romantic appeal, and at this present stage has very much the appearance of an in-between period. This applies to vocal records especially, for in the thirties and forties of this century the recording companies interested themselves most valuably in instrumentalists and conductors. Casals, Schnabel, Horowitz, Toscanini . . . these are the names that have the kind of authority we associate with the great singers of earlier days. And for part of this time, singing was an art in decline. If we try to think of great singers who came to prominence in the nineteen-thirties, it is not easy to get beyond Flagstad and Björling. There is much that is wonderful on electrical 78s, but most of it comes from singers who were well launched on their careers by the early twenties, or from some at the other end of the period, whose recording careers belong more properly to the age of LP. In between is a sag, weighed down by a good deal that deserves the oblivion into which it will no doubt fall.

Plenty remains to be enjoyed, but we will look first at the nature of this decline. The art of two singers may illustrate some of its main features. Both were very famous; brilliant performers who gave much pleasure over long careers. But the faults are important ones, and are fairly symptomatic of their times. In an earlier age, and perhaps in ours, singers as gifted as Pons and Pertile might have performed very differently; as it is, their recordings leave us only a flawed distinction to admire, and some lost disciplines to sigh for.

That Lily Pons should be chosen for some adverse comment may be more readily acceptable in England than in America, where she has had as much success as any singer in recent times. English music critics have always been rather critical of her, sometimes, one suspects, because she was popular and pretty and went into films – formidable drawbacks. She did not sing in England very often, but Metropolitan audiences in New York heard performances of *Lucia di Lammermoor* (for example) where their enthusiasm seems to have matched the applause for Joan Sutherland in our own time. We can hear for ourselves the applause on one of the many off-the-air recordings that we shall be discussing. Privately published but achieving a wide circulation among collectors, these records have deficiencies of many kinds, but they do offer a fascinating glimpse of famous singers at their work in the theatre, many of them caught very vividly and valuably indeed. There are excerpts from a performance of *Lucia di Lammermoor* at the Metropolitan, with the audience responding rapturously in the first Act, and ecstatically in mid-Mad Scene. Lily Pons' high notes are no doubt a principal cause; they seem invariably to be well taken and well sustained, with what I assume to be an F in *alt* ringing out full and true at the end of 'Ardon gl'incensi' (transposed up). Some of the fioriture are good too: the upward scales are distinct, and there is some accurate arpeggio work, powerful and rather brilliant. The trills are poor: loose and sketchy, or hardly there at all. Interpretation can hardly be said to be in evidence either: 'Regnava nel silenzio', the solo at the fountain, is inexpressive, and the Mad Scene is treated conventionally as pretty music. As far as one can judge tone, it is sweet, but while there is evident beauty in the high notes, the voice sounds shallow and even tremulous on the stave. Very occasionally, the intonation is suspect. These records are (we have to keep reminding ourselves) very imperfect technically, and it would be unfair to judge on them alone. But the general impression they give is not at all contradicted by the commercial records.

Some of these are quite beautiful, and they show what a delightful singer she could be. There is the 'Caro nome' of 1931, sung with a tenderness and absorption with which she seems rarely to be credited. We also hear in this record a very lovely voice, floating gently up to the high G sharp, where in this aria so many sopranos grow hard. Perhaps more surprisingly, she achieves a rare beauty in 'Ach, ich fühl's', Pamina's aria from *Die Zauberflöte*, sung in French as 'Ah, je le sais'. Here is reflective, sensitive singing, and we have the pleasure of hearing the high passages taken well within the compass of the voice. Yet even in this some of the faults begin to obtrude. The fluting runs are very lightly feathered with aspirates, so that the legato is not quite true, and the tone, often fine, is sometimes slightly tremulous. It has not the firm placing heard, for example, in the recordings of this aria by Janowitz, Seefried, Rethberg, or (a voice closer to Pons in range and lightness) Lotte Schöne.

42. Lily Pons

These characteristics became more marked as the years went by, so that by 1941 when she made some promising records from *La Fille du Régiment*, her runs and embellishments, though still remarkable, are nearly all aspirated, and the middle voice has lost much in definition and character. The slow aria 'Il faut partir' suffers from this, and it is typical of all that music, basic to the repertoire, where a firm, even and well-focused cantilena is required. If one then turns up some of her first records, for instance the *Lakmé* solos made for Odeon in 1929, the loss is clear. These are appealing performances, for they show the voice with all its freshness and promise, and more of a French quality – sufficient 'bite' to give a firm definition, even when confined to notes on the stave. But this is already just what is wanting when, two years later, she came to record the relatively simple 'Tutte le feste' from *Rigoletto*. Nor, to take up a different point, did the artistic imagination develop to compensate in some way: several successive recordings of Lakmé's Bell Song make no more than a pretty show-piece of it. She also recorded some songs by Handel, Pergolesi and other seventeenth- and eighteenth-century composers, but whatever she might have felt about them we shall never know, for it remains uncommunicated. The runs are aspirated, almost as a point of honour, and there is no mincing it that they sound very bad, as does the frequent scooping approach to high notes (as in 'Se tu m'ami'). Occasionally there would come, in the midst of these unsatisfactory recordings, something that was enjoyable and creditable. Milhaud's difficult Ronsard songs, written for Pons, I believe, and first sung by her, are a fine example. They served to remind, at the time, that here was a still lovely voice and an exceptional talent; and for us at this later date they remain a pleasant memento of a remarkable career.

But it is a far cry from the palmy days of the 'coloratura' soprano as discussed in earlier pages. The 'coloratura' was now becoming a specialised performer of whom only certain things were expected. She was to sing in only a small number of operatic roles. Once Lily Pons' international career had begun, her operatic repertoire consisted of little more than ten roles, and her opposite number in Italy, Toti dal Monte, was similarly restricted. The prime qualification, moreover, was the ability to sing sweetly and with agility above the stave; what she did *on* it was considered less important, though perhaps three-quarters of the music lay within a normal soprano's compass. Nor was much dramatic insight expected: Pons is said to have given well-acted performances in the theatre, but it is rare on records to hear her tone carrying any emotional depth or dramatic suppleness. With this delimiting of the 'coloratura''s province went a change in the technique acquired. Because a firm *cantilena* was not the focus of attention, there was less incentive to cultivate it. Yet this is the basis of singing in the European tradition, and a deficiency here goes with the sort of short-cut to flexibility in fioritura of which the aspirate is the clearest example. This in turn is likely to affect the tone itself, encouraging breathiness and withdrawing from the singer the power to draw a poised, economical line of sound.

The tastes of the public and the interests of the composers were largely responsible for this. The ability to sing florid music meant less to Wagner, Puccini and Debussy than did most other vocal gifts. Verdi himself became less decorative and more insistent upon volume in his writing for the voice as he developed in maturity as a composer. Public taste caught up with the composers in the early decades of this century, and the effects upon singing were extremely harmful. The kind of accomplishment needed for passing gracefully and rapidly from one note to another over a wide range had been one of the essentials of European singing. This was one of the basic disciplines that came to be lightly regarded, but even more important in the tradition has been the cultivation of a true legato. By the thirties of this century, the first of these abilities had been relegated to a 'fringe' activity in music: in the style developed and typified by Aureliano Pertile, the other singer to be discussed here, the second almost disappeared.

As an example, we may take the short solo, 'Mal reggendo', part of the duet between Manrico and Azucena in Act II of *Il Trovatore*. Manrico was one of Pertile's chief roles, and he recorded a complete performance of the opera in 1930. As Verdi wrote it, the melody is clear-cut, well-balanced, elegant yet spirited, and it mounts to a natural, effective climax. This is how it sounds when Jussi Björling or Placido Domingo sings it, or, best of all, Caruso (who has realised that the story he is telling is no occasion for swaggering). But Pertile seems unwilling to allow even single notes, let alone phrases, to tell their own tale. They must be pushed and squeezed, pummelled and wrenched. The score says *cantabile*, but the very first note is given a quivering kind of vibrato, and during the first sixteen bars aspirates break the flow eight times, while individual notes are emphasised *sforzando*, and three take leave of their proper pitch altogether for declamatory emphasis. In this kind of treatment, the whole basis of Italian singing is destroyed.

Going with this over-strenuous style is an exceedingly bright, edgy tone, the brilliance of which has been gained partly at the expense of the natural vowel sound. Even on an 'ah' or 'oh' he rarely produces a sound of comfortable openness or roundness. But comfort was not the object: excitement was. And so the whole voice was set a-quiver with passion, passion that expressed itself in *sforzandos* and immensely powerful crescendos, while the pitch would sharpen and the basic production lose its steadiness. Playing a series of his electrical recordings, made around 1930, one becomes so used to this quivering tone as the norm that it hardly registers as wobble. Yet if one comes to an electrical recording of this period (say to 'Donna non vidi mai' from *Manon Lescaut*) after listening to some of his pre-electricals it is inescapable. The aspirates are now no mere technical convenience, but an expressive stylistic device to blow the gusty passion in every eye, as he does with many a palpitation, many a sob, in the aria 'Una furtiva lagrima', formerly thought of as an elegant solo, to be sung with all the arts of what was called *bel canto*.

Pertile is all the more remarkable as a symptom of his times, when one knows that he was an intelligent, conscientious artist, a favourite of Toscanini, vastly admired by Serafin, a singer in whom there was a genuine greatness. Many considered him the supreme tenor of his time, and some of his records show why. He could sing with warmth, lyricism and subtlety as his 1926 Fonotipias show. Later on, when he had developed more disturbingly the style described above, he was still able to sing beautifully, as he does in solos from *Lohengrin*. These have real imaginative power, restraint, poetry and beauty of line; as has, for instance, his singing of 'Celeste Aida' in the recording of the complete opera. The opening is almost murmured; the phrasing is broad; there are no aspirates, but on the contrary every grace in the diminuendos and the observation of Verdi's *sempre dolcissimo* marking at the words 'Il tuo bel cielo'. It is rare too to hear a Pertile recording that does not open the ears to some new feature of the music. His earlier record of the Improvviso in *Andrea Chénier* is thoughtfully conceived as a series of long-drawn, carefully controlled crescendos, and we feel the presence, in character, of both the romantic poet in Chénier and the bitter, declamatory rebel. Even Leoncavallo's 'Mattinata' is worth having: the faults are there clearly enough (it's like water boiling over, frothy at the surface), but his tenderness at the beginning of the refrain ('Mette anche tu') building up to the climax is a lovely and imaginative touch. There are many surprises among his records: on one side of a 10″ 78 'Come un bel di' (*Andrea Chénier*'s 'E lucevan le stelle') is sung with coarse style and unpleasing tone, while on the other is a solo from *Adriana Lecouvreur*, 'La dolcissima effigie', with the voice in its full glory and a personal stamp on the interpretation which makes this the version one will always hear going on inside one's own head in the future. Then, at the very end of his recording career (June 1942), there are some excerpts from *Otello*, unsteady of voice and often crudely overt in emotion, yet having intensely memorable moments – the quiet, very inward singing of 'Ma, o pianto, o duol' in the Monologue, the dignity and deliberation that mark his duet, 'Dio ti giocondi', with Desdemona. Perhaps more surprising still, is his recording of 'Quando le sere' from *Luisa Miller*. Apart from some explosive emotionalism towards the end, this is a wonderful piece of singing: an indrawn, rapt quality, beautifully moulded phrases and a true legato kept for most of the time.

And no doubt he could have kept it for the whole time had he wanted. But a true legato does not palpitate, so it would not do. For Pertile was born into the Italy that was taking the verismo composers to its heart. By the turn of the century there existed a ready enough liking for them, but the real emotional grasping, the full response, came later. As these composers throbbed with stormy, romantic passion, so the singer's voice must palpitate and set the senses aflame. Pertile was caught up in this moment, and his art suffered. There was also a gain, of course: the passion always impresses as real, never imposed, and the intercourse between passions and musical

sensibility produces singing that is always alive and characterful. But the
cost was excessive, and Italian singing paid dearly.

43. Aureliano Pertile as Lohengrin

12. Italy: A Handful of Exceptions
Toti dal Monte   Hina Spani
Tito Schipa   Beniamino Gigli
Renato Zanelli

IN a book of provocative essays published in 1932 and called *Around Music*, Kaikhosru Sorabji writes: 'Italy . . . for a long time past has ceased to be the land of great singers, but for a handful of rare exceptions . . . The great old art of true and beautiful singing has been replaced by a repulsive emotion pumping, and a noisy voluminousness of tone . . . The fact is, that Italians as singers are living in the past . . . Où sont les neiges d'antan? Certainly not in Italy'. In this chapter we shall discuss five singers (two of them South American but making a large part of their careers in Italy) who might claim to be among the exceptions to these strictures, and even these are hardly untouched by the inauspicious conditions of the time.

Even Sorabji's own favourite, Toti dal Monte ('whose art has a jewel-like delicacy and fineness that must be heard to be believed'), is not immune. Her admirer describes her tone as 'bright, clear, firm, clean, pure and steady', and it is good to learn that these were the predominant impressions made by her voice when heard in the theatre, for on records one hears these qualities, certainly, but in combination with others that are less beautiful. A hardness in the upper register, even a certain sense of discomfort there from time to time, makes one flinch somewhat as a high note looms ahead. Sometimes this turns out to be quite needless, the high note being a beauty and no trouble at all, but on other occasions the rather hard, pinched quality emerges piercingly, prepared by an extra-long breath or a laborious portamento. The very open vowel sounds do not fall easily on our ears, and it must also be said that for the most part the expected trills do not fall kindly or otherwise, for generally speaking they are not there at all. She has certain classic qualities even so, and picking a careful way through her records one comes to recognise a personality, a style and beauty that become valuable possessions.

The process by which one comes to value her singing more highly as time goes by is illustrated in the notes on 'Ah, non credea mirarti' from *La Sonnambula* (p. 577). Her unfussy purity of line and shining definition of voice act as touchstones when we come to fix standards for a certain kind of excellence. On the other hand, she is not good in the cadenza, and if one's introduction to dal Monte as 'coloratura soprano' derives from this rather pedestrian, effortful piece of florid work one is unlikely to come back for more. But then we find her records from *La Fille du Régiment*, and hear the brilliant arpeggios at the start of 'Chacun le sait' (sung in Italian as 'Lo dice ognun') and the fluent downward scale over two octaves. Or with the voice at its freshest and most youthful, a 'Caro nome' made in 1925 shows her technical accomplishment (agile and even scale-work, precision in staccato) seconded by a sweet tone and tender manner. She is also brilliant in the upper notes, in the high B and C sharp, for example, which first alternate and then give way to a D sharp which is not a mere peck at the note, but a firm yet delicate musical sound. 'Una voce poco fa' (*Il Barbiere di Siviglia*), on the other side of the record, also offers some outstanding virtuosity and the pleasing characterisation of a Rosina who is playful but not too arch.

For dal Monte was not shallow in her dealings with either music or drama. Those who heard it speak of the emotional force of her Lucia di Lammermoor, and we can sense this as we play her recording of the Mad Scene and come to the phrase 'alfin son tua, alfin sei mia'. More recent singers like Callas and Sutherland are always thought of as exploiting the depths of the passage and people sometimes write as though nobody in living memory had done this before; as far as I know, it was dal Monte's intensification of the simple lines that first showed the way on records.

A better demonstration of her strong imagination and personality comes from the lyric-dramatic repertoire and is found in the one complete opera that she recorded, *Madama Butterfly* made with Gigli in 1939. The child-like voice that she uses takes on depth and warmth as the opera develops, but from the start it was accompanied by a humour, resilience and plasticity that guarded against sentimentality or mere prettiness. Hers is not a Butterfly that makes comfortable, luscious listening, and in several important places the writing calls for fuller, rounder tones than she seems able to give (the arrival, the love duet, the solo just before her death, are high-spots of the work but not of dal Monte's performance). Where she is marvellous is in something that is quite central to the tragic force of the opera, however; that is, that the trust and joy which are so childlike should come to maturity by such a very bitter experience of reality. The child of fifteen whom dal Monte's pure and high-pitched voice makes so real is still physically present when the character has achieved a maturity to stand with such generous nobility before the woman to whom she has lost. Those are the general lines of the characterisation. In detail, the performance has certain moments that are possibly more touching than in any other recorded interpretation of the part, especially in Act II around the Letter Duet. The devotion with which she greets the letter ('on my lips'), the appreciation of the Consul's kindness ('you're the best man that ever existed') registering as so much more heartfelt because of its discreetness and restraint, and the anguished incredulity at the very notion that she could conceivably have forgotten:

all these gain depth by contrast with the childlike gaiety and energy of mimicry as she tells of the wonders of American justice. She rises then to a genuine tragic intensity in the following passage where Sharpless forces upon her the recognition of a cruel possibility. And then in turn, she makes us look out with her onto the harbour where the man-of-war has been sighted, so vividly does she seem to see it herself.

All this is the work of a great artist, and there is a certain rightness in the role that reveals it. Even in this role, with its relatively moderate tessitura, we sometimes feel the high notes to be hard work, and we are also aware that the voice has thinned and hardened somewhat since the earlier series of recordings. In his autobiography (*The Gigli Memoirs*, p. 211), Gigli suggests why this happened at a comparatively early age. Dal Monte's impresarios, he says, were determined that she was to be a coloratura soprano, and so it was in such parts as Rosina, Lucia and Gilda that she most often appeared. But he himself remembered her at the beginning of her career as a lyric soprano of singular charm, and he suggests that it was to lyrical roles that her voice was best suited. The records tend to support this, as well as demonstrating that, if a mistake was made, at least it was a natural one. Her facility in florid work was certainly exceptional, especially for those times; and her upward range extended to (and no doubt beyond) a solid, vigorously sustained top E flat. But we can hear even from the very early records that her production changed somewhere around a high A, with a tendency to hardness, which over-use obviously could aggravate. So it was; and the result can be heard at its least delightful in 'Ah! fors' è lui' (*La Traviata*) where the tone sounds pinched and the upper notes appear to be taken with difficulty – it is hard to believe that one is listening to a great singer at all. Nor do the *Mignon* and *Linda di Chamounix* arias have that ease above the stave which is expected of singers who specialise in such pieces. In some ways, the most charming of dal Monte's singing is to be found in a modest pre-electrical record where we can hear the young voice of a lyric soprano, as Gigli heard it all those years ago. This has 'Deh, vieni, non tardar' (*Le Nozze di Figaro*) on one side and 'Selva opaca' (*William Tell*) on the other. The *Gramophone* critic of those days was not at all happy about it: she pulled the rhythm about, regarded it as a vehicle, and took unwarrantable liberties, he said. Perhaps we are a little less academic about Mozart today; I rather hope that a modern reviewer would note the 'liberties' and fall in love with them – they so obviously come from a singer who is loving the music. The other aria has the same freshness of sound, and again a fine legato and some lovely shading and phrasing. In these and other records one hears some affinity with the limpid quality of Galli-Curci. But comparison brings out the firm, positive nature of dal Monte's vocal character. 'A nightingale singing in its sleep' was Philip Hope-Wallace's phrase for Galli-Curci; 'a nightingale totidalmonted somewhere in the distance' was a phrase memorable for its neologism in a novel by Richard Aldington. But Mr Aldington's nightingale must have been singing during waking hours; for dal Monte's voice was bracing and alert – it was like sunshine on clear water. The records probably give a very incomplete picture, for no doubt this brightness of timbre needs an opera house to shine in. Yet heard in opera-house perspective, the records preserve a good deal; having known them, one would not be without.

No such aural adjustment is needed on behalf of the second of the singers to be discussed in this chapter. This is the South American soprano, Hina Spani, who made her debut at the Scala, Milan, in 1915 and sang a great deal in Italy over the next twenty years. Her voice seems to carry its own opera house with it: intensely dramatic in timbre, rising excitingly to the high notes, and coupled with an authority that at once commands attention, this is the kind of sound that great theatres are made for. Yet its owner has declared that she prefers song to opera, and that the 'expressive power' of the Lied is to her the greatest source of satisfaction. This is quoted in a valuable article and discography in *The Record Collector* (vol. 9, no. 4). As part of their preparations, the authors interviewed Spani and were immensely impressed by the breadth of her musicianship, as well as her energy and strength of will: 'Moussorgsky, Stravinsky, Prokoviev, Schubert, Schumann and Strauss . . . she knows them all, and has never stopped adding to her study and re-study of them'. This may explain some of the appeal of her operatic records, for one feels an intelligence at work, responsive to changing moods and the sense of words, in the way that is habitual with so many German singers and so few Italians (notable too that it is her first teacher, in Buenos Aires, whom she credits with her introduction to a worthwhile repertoire of songs). Something of this suppleness of taste can be sensed in the many-shaded tones of her Verdi and Puccini; and, although she made some charming records of songs (lively in 'Se Florindo è fedele', intense in Trindelli's 'Primavera'), it is in the standard operatic repertoire that she will be remembered.

Her own favourite recording is said to be that of 'D'amor sull'ali rosee' from Act IV of *Il Trovatore*. Fine as it is, there are things that Verdi asks for which Spani does not give. Her performance is an exciting one, certainly. She brings to the opening bars a subdued lilt and buoyancy answering to the motion of wings in the night air, which Leonora has just invoked, and to the new hopefulness which overcomes the fear she has also expressed in the recitative. But this aria does need a good trill, and her substitute offering is not satisfactory. Nor does she observe Verdi's marking of *dolce* over the first high B flat, or, in the great phrases of the climax, the fact that it is the note before the highest in the curve that is marked for accentuation (the lovely effect of this is conveyed well by Eva Turner, who then detracts from it by a laborious portamento from F to B flat in the alternative version of the text, whereas Spani sings a powerful and exciting high D flat, which one always wants to hear in this aria). Better than this, and perhaps the supreme example of her work on record, is the aria 'Ma dall'arido stella divulsa' from *Un Ballo in Maschera*. Her subtlety and warmth, the excellent legato, her firm yet gentle taking of the difficult, unprepared high note towards the end, and the heavenly pianissimo of what follows: everything here answers to the demands that the composer makes. The resources are impressive: at one extreme, a dramatic steely tension for the 'mezza notte' section, then a gloriously soft tone and broad, generous legato for the great lyrical phrases, 'Deh, mi reggi, m'aita, o Signor'.

When such grandeur and charm are brought to Puccini, Spani's distinction becomes (for her own period at least) almost unique. Moreover, these qualities are combined with a southern warmth and the ability to hold a sense of tragedy within the tone of the voice. Her record of Tosca's 'Vissi d'arte' is one of the very best, combining the stylistic and technical purity of a Rethberg with the emotional intensity of a Muzio.

Of course, she is not without faults. In the 'Vissi d'arte' one would like to hear the descending notes of the climax sustained longer and allowed a *diminuendo*. There are also occasional intrusions or uncertainties of vibrato and (very occasionally) intonation. The first very slightly affects the lovely *Manon Lescaut* record, and the second is again just slightly troublesome in her affecting farewell in Massenet's *Manon*. But only about forty sides exist to remember Spani by, and it would be a poor critical sense that prevented their enjoyment. The two *Lohengrin* solos have a depth of tone and feeling, a delicious feeling for shading and the moulding of phrases, a thousand delicacies: 'infinite riches in a little room', and no doubt representative of the work she did throughout a busy career in which she sang over seventy operatic roles. She was an artist of great distinction and made what on the whole is the most satisfying series of soprano records to come out of Italy in the inter-war years.

Perhaps before turning to two great Italian tenors of the period, we should note the distinguished work of another South American artist singing in Italy at this time. Renato Zanelli, born in Chile in 1892, had two careers: the first as a baritone taking him for a time to the Metropolitan, and the second as a heroic tenor. This career was centred in Italy (his tenor debut taking place at Naples in 1924) and no doubt would have continued with success for many years longer but for his death from cancer in 1935. His records are not numerous, but they are valuable in the way that Spani's are; both as a baritone and a tenor he sang with a rare sense of style, a dramatic quality inherent in the tone, and a musical dignity pervading most of his work.

'Most' but not all. His recording of the Final Scene in *Carmen* is interesting in that it so clearly shows the kind of influence exerted by the Italy of those years. The Carmen with him is Giannina Pederzini, none too steady and rather shrill on top but bristling with temperament, and Zanelli too sings with very overt passion and overloads the last phrases with sobs. The Don José characterised here is desperate with self-abasement and self-pity. These things enter also, though to a lesser degree, into the scene of Otello's death, where again the sobbing diminishes the dignity of a performance which in

44. Toti dal Monte as Rosina in *Il Barbiere di Siviglia*

45. Hina Spani

46. Tito Schipa

47. Beniamino Gigli

many ways is a great one. His Otello is represented on records by five extracts, deeply impressive and in some respects unmatched. Limitations still have to be noted: an 'Esultate' which seems rather dully edged, a Love Duet without distinction of phrasing, and a declamatory passage (just before the 'Ora e per sempre addio') where the upper notes sound forced.

At other points he is ideal. The gentle tone, well-rounded but strong, suits the opening of the Love Duet to perfection; a honeyed voice it seems, a touch of Piccaver or Domingo about it, very unlike the Otellos of Zenatello or Martinelli. The richness of his middle-voice brings an unusual beauty to the opening bars of the Death Scene, 'Niun mi tema'; authority, deep feeling and a wide range of dynamics help to make the interpretation a moving one. But the great record is the 'Dio, mi potevi scagliar'. It is here rather than in the death scene that Zanelli's afflicted Otello attains full tragic status, for the dignity of restraint intensifies the emotion. As the unison strings lead deeper and deeper into darkness, the voice must seem to come from the innermost soul of the man; Zanelli's declamation has an inner, haunted quality, and the mellow, richly sombre voice paints in tones that match the orchestral colouration. He leaves the reciting note, but in doing so remains sensitive to the anguished harmonies accompanying the voice, and as he moves into the second part of the solo it is with a warmth and gentleness that he will intensify with a finely preserved legato up to the first climax, and from which he can make fully effective the disruption into exclamatory violence which follows.

No doubt the mellowness of voice owes something to his earlier years as a baritone. On the other hand, and speaking personally, I think it unlikely that I would recognise the records that he made when a baritone as being by the same singer. If it did so happen, then it might be due to some point in his artistry rather than to a similarity of voice. The declamation of Otello's Monologue might just possibly come to mind as one hears him declame those words, usually sung but written as speech, in the Prologue to *Pagliacci* (they come just after the opening, 'Poichè in iscena ancor le antiche maschere', and the direction is translated in the English score as 'speaking to the violoncello'). Certainly one would feel that the young singer of this record had an assured future ahead, and as the high notes are exceptionally brilliant, it might occur to one that the future could lie with the tenor repertoire. Anyhow, this record, with its vigour and resonance, its broad phrasing, and (more remarkable) its smile, is certainly one of the best of Prologues, and the other baritone records all afford the pleasures of a fine natural voice and a tasteful style. Music that might well seem banal or merely dull becomes newly delightful. A popular song like 'O primavera' is sung with a lilting charm, its melody affectionately moulded, and even 'La Spagnola' ('Stretti, stretti, nell'estasi d'amor' – it is the song Aldous Huxley generally quotes when he wants to suggest Italian bad taste) acquires some elegance without loss of vitality. No doubt Zanelli will be remembered principally for his Otello. Charm and lightness of touch are not common

48. Renato Zanelli as Otello

among the great singers of that role; and this too is one of his distinctions.

But for charm and lightness of touch among tenors in Italy one did not have to look far at this time. Any prize, then, now or formerly, would be divided equally between two contemporaries, Beniamino Gigli and Tito Schipa. And if songs like the two mentioned above were likely to help singers to these qualities, then it must be said that both of them got plenty of practice. Such songs can be delightful, but some kind of musical puritan-ism (perhaps) tells one that they have to be earned. They are encore pieces rather than the main stuff of a recital. Yet with Schipa in particular they gained a dominance in his recorded repertoire that eventually excluded practically everything else.

Schipa's name nowadays is generally quoted as though synonymous with elegance and a fastidious taste. But he is at once an expression and a victim of Italian musical life in his own and earlier periods. Going back for a moment to the South American soprano, Hina Spani, we have to reflect that if she had gone on recording later in her career it would have been, no doubt, to offer a variety of songs by worthwhile composers; even as it was, she left us songs by Brahms, Scarlatti, Pergolesi and Granados. Schipa, with his vastly larger output, has only three of Scarlatti's and a Schubert 'Ave Maria' and 'Serenade'. The list of songs recorded by him in 1942, 1951 and 1955 (these, according to the only discography I have seen, were the years in which he had recording sessions) contains nothing but Italian café music of the sort he had recorded in abundance already. Times have changed. A tenor who has been something of a counterpart to Schipa in more recent years is Cesare Valletti, who was indeed a pupil of Schipa; unlike his master, he has been able to record sensitive and enterprising recitals of German, French and Italian songs, putting his Italianate lyricism and beauty of tone to the service of worthy music. Schipa was lucky to have escaped the bad ways of singing in which many of his age were being brought up; but, with all the refinement of his style, he did not greatly broaden the musical horizons that Italy could offer a young man in his time.

Still, who knows what we would have lost as well as gained if he had done so. A young Tito Schipa brought up on Bach and Handel, Debussy and Hugo Wolf, might well have looked down a sensitive nose at mere Neapo-litan songs, and perhaps at Bellini and Donizetti too; and then, of course, he would not have been Schipa at all, but somebody else, famous perhaps for his collaboration with Respighi or Pizzetti like Pears with Britten or Bernac with Poulenc. As it was, he was brought up to the strains of 'Santa Lucia' and *Rigoletto*, and we have a delightful artist within that kind of repertoire.

As far as records give evidence, it is largely pious self-deception to sigh for the Mozart and Handel he did not record. When he did turn to the 'art song', the results were not really very happy: Scarlatti's 'Le violette', for example, has some lightness and character, but too many notes are taken from below, and the singing does not smile. His Mozart is represented by the two arias of Ottavio in *Don Giovanni*, and, among the (published) private recordings, part of a live performance given at St. Louis in 1941. His 'Il mio tesoro' is really something of an embarrassment: he takes it slowly so there is less difficulty about making the notes clear, and in a way that is to his credit (better than Gigli's slithery performance), but the runs are stiff-jointed, and in the live performance he muffs the start of the long run, missing the first notes entirely. There are points to admire (the incisive, utterly personal tone, for instance), but this 'respectable' part of his repertoire yields little joy, whereas the cafe songs have zest, grace and charm abounding. There is one called 'Chi se nne scorda occhiù'. Its composer was one Barthelmy, and the sight of its score would probably freeze the blood in a well-brought-up musician's veins. A preposterous and joyful piece, a sort of Edwardian music-hall song set against the Spaccanapoli or Via Roma instead of the Old Kent Road, it makes an irresistible record. Exquisite nuance, point, imagination, life: the qualities stream forth, all summed up in the last refrain, sung at first pianissimo, on an apparently endless breath (he could still do this in 1953 when he was last heard in London); then there is an all-together-now one-more-time round of the rumbustious old tune, given with a resonance that is never raucous or over-ripe but shining and pointed. Such plebeian gusto and patrician grace make a strange mixture, and a magical one.

Signor Barthelmy also wrote a song called 'Pesca d'amore' (some of the most beautifully poised of soft singing is to be heard in the last bars of Schipa's earlier recording). Tosti, in a vein that seems remote from 'the home life of our own dear Queen' whose music master he became, wrote one called 'Marechiare' (Schipa sings it with incomparable verve and feeling for nuance). With more refinement there is Donaudy's 'O del mio amato ben' (not quite the thing of sighs and loveliness that Claudia Muzio makes of it, but full of character); and with a good deal less there are the works of Bixio whose saxophones and syncopations are very much of the thirties, the Cole Porter of the Italian films in which Schipa himself appeared. In their unrespectable way, all these are a joy, and if for some reason they had to be lost from one's collection they would leave a black gap where once was sunshine. One could better spare much better music.

A main part of the enjoyment of these records comes from the recognition of a character: his voice is like the sort of face you never forget or a person who, met once, seems to have been a lifelong friend. And the character is one whom most listeners have come to know first through opera. Here three great qualities come to mind. One is a simple, well-founded purity of method. His record of 'Una furtiva lagrima' (*L'Elisir d'Amore*) illustrates it. It is not an exciting performance of the aria (he does not, for instance, phrase over at the modulation into major key, and his cadenza is relatively tame), but it is gratefully heard partly because it avoids everything that cheapens so many, and partly because it shades and varies the sound only within the limits of an even, 'unpressurised' tone – and in this, he is the exact opposite of his contemporary, Aureliano Pertile. The second quality is imagination: an un-pedestrian, creative way with the music he sang. The point is clear as one compares his earlier record of 'Sogno soave e casto', the short aria from Act I of *Don Pasquale* with other versions (noting, however, that even his own performance in the complete recording of the opera is not up to the separate record). The sound floats, airy and luminous as the dream he sings of, kept airborne by a very individual way of phrasing-over. It is only a creative artist who can come by this sort of rightness – or who can see through, for instance, to the magical possibilities of that phrase, 'sei pur bella', in the Cherry Duet from *L'Amico Fritz* where the listener suddenly holds his breath before this fine-spun delicate thread of sound.

This record also illustrates the third quality: a passionate intensity, rare in a lyric tenor, where grace and elegance will often seem to preclude depth of emotion and strength of character. But Schipa had some of the fire that one associates with a *spinto* like Martinelli. It is present, in the unusual company of a perfect lyricism, in his first record of 'Pourquoi me reveiller?' from *Werther* (also when we hear it in a partially preserved public performance of the opera, given in Italian, in 1934, where a close relationship with a demonstrative audience can also be sensed). It is there too in the last scene from *La Bohème* where the spoken words are given with strength and passion quite different from the chubby plaintiveness of Gigli's enunciation, or from the gawky ineffectiveness of many others. There is always something patrician in Schipa's art. The technical discipline, the grace and the timbre itself provide a dignity that distinguishes him among his contemporaries; and the passion, so far from cheapening, strengthens the impression. It never quite deserts him, even when accompanying Bixio's saxophones or taking to the streets and the cafés with Signor Barthelmy; and in his operatic work it is an invariable distinction. Whatever the record, delight and admiration are rarely absent for long.

Both more and less can be said about the other great lyric tenor of those times, Beniamino Gigli. 'Patrician', 'dignity', 'discipline': these are not so likely to be the appropriate terms. Yet Gigli's singing (the voice itself, but the style too) conveys a warmth, a vivid, central humanity that is perhaps the most engaging among all the singers of this period.

It depends, of course, what the music is; but we will first take him at his best, in the operas of Puccini. He recorded the roles of Rodolfo, Cavaradossi and Pinkerton in complete performances. Possibly they are not very easily distinguishable as characters: Pinkerton chuckling over his 'easy-going gospel' might be Cavaradossi chaffing Tosca 'before the good Madonna' or Rodolfo pleased that the candles are out so that they can go searching in the darkness. But the personality is so vivid it hardly matters; the music and drama guide it sufficiently, and the personality in turn lights up each episode with its individuality and energy. In *La Bohème*, for instance, Gigli's way of making the voice act is alive from the infectious smile of his first phrase to the unaffected (and affecting) weeping in the last bars of the opera. His gaiety is always a joy: probably more real than that of any other tenor on records apart from Caruso himself. We hear Rodolfo's 'Nei cieli bigi' as a joke (the Bohemians rub their hands and stamp their feet to keep warm, but the chimneys of Paris seem to be kept busy enough), and it is this cheerful spirit, rather than the sacrificial verse-drama, that warms the bohemians' attic for us. The delicate passage at Mimì's first arrival is also beautifully done. A breathed 'Ed ora come faccio? ... così ... che viso d'ammalata', a tender 'segga vicino al fuoco', a smiling 'che bella bambina': all lovely touches. 'Buona sera' is sung lightly, still under the spell of this new-felt beauty. Turn to Act III, and the range of emotional responsiveness is evident. For the grumbling complaints about Mimì to his friend Marcel ('Mimì è una civetta') he uses sneering, mean vowels, opening out to a new seriousness and dropping the play-acting (to himself as to Marcel) at 'Ebbene no'. In this and the other Puccini recordings there are many such phrases and passages that stay with one as incomparably vivid (one more example – Lt. B. F. Pinkerton, surveying his rice-paper house with chubby amusement, affectionately patting his 'shining light of brokers' on the back, shrugging with a wrily self-deprecating, genially permissive smile as he answers square old Sharpless about what the hell he thinks he's doing). With these goes the most beautiful tenor voice of the period, and perhaps of the century.

In any session at home with the gramophone, the first Gigli of the evening is always a surprise: so often one has forgotten by just how large a degree it surpasses the others in sheer easy beauty of sound. To stay with the recording of *La Bohème* a little longer, the passage mentioned above, starting 'Ebbene no' in Act III, brings the characteristic roundness and resonance of the middle-voice before us. The shining sound of it and its clear projection are impressive also in the music where Rodolfo is heard as one voice among many. In the concerted music of Act II, Gigli's voice is not remarkable for its size and power, but the clear focus and bright tone make it carry without effort. He is steady too, where most of his colleagues in the cast are in the grip of vibrato or wobble, the Musetta having both. Privately recorded stage performances reinforce the impression. There is, for example, a recording of *La Traviata* at Covent Garden in 1939. The first impression is of a very light tenor indeed: his Brindisi a delicate, shy piece of singing, and even in the ensembles of Act III he has the confidence to sing *mezza voce* – for confidence is also involved in the 'shy' singing of the first Act. When he opens out and uses the full voice in the denunciations of Violetta (Act III) we hear the sound ring powerfully, but essentially he gains our attention by other means – principally by the sheer beauty of voice and the magnetism of personality.

This (and the *Bohème* recording) was after he had been singing for a quarter of a century: his longevity as a singer was exceptional. Many in England will remember his concerts of 1952 when he was sixty-two years old. There was an Albert Hall recital in that year where by half-way through the arduous programme it did seem to be the very same voice that we knew on the old records; and the very last encore (it was a jaunty Neapolitan song called 'Quanno a fammena vo') could have been (or so it seemed) the very performance recorded in the first days of the electrical recording process, in 1925. Two or three years later the same could not be said, and the final Carnegie Hall recital of 1955, though it was attended by an enthusiastic audience, is a rather sad event to hear on record. Records are often cruel: they can fail to convey a beauty of tone that makes a singer delightful to listen to even when he is guilty of faults in breathing, intonation and style, all of which they reveal. So Gigli's records cease to be very pleasing at a date (perhaps about 1945) when he was still giving wonderful performances. Nevertheless, the survival of so much for so long still remains something of a miracle.

If at the time this survival seemed less astonishing, it is probably because Gigli's voice always sounded as though it had years of life ahead. One never felt – as with, say, the records made towards the end of Fleta's short career and towards the beginning of Martinelli's long one – that this was marvellous but it couldn't last. The ease was always remarkable. The voice seemed always in good health, never running to wobble or dryness, hardly ever losing pitch (I would have said never, but for the *Traviata* recording mentioned above: the intonation in Act I is sometimes quite bad, and though one might have been inclined to put it down to the vagaries of the private recording, we see from Harold Rosenthal's history of Covent Garden that Gigli was criticised for 'some flat singing' in his *Traviata* that season). With his characteristic excellences in mind, it is not surprising that authorities like the teacher Herbert Caesari should have seen Gigli as the culmination of the great Italian tradition.

Yet there are many who would say that this needs a good deal of qualification. Gigli was never a 'connoisseur's singer', and he did indeed have some serious faults. At his best in Puccini and Neapolitan songs, he was out of his element in Mozart and the 'arie antiche', airs by seventeenth and eighteenth century composers. His performances as Ottavio in *Don Giovanni* were often praised by the critics, but his records of the two arias are notoriously sloppy, the descending runs in 'Il mio tesoro' being, as one critic has put it, like coming downstairs on a tea-tray instead of the usual way (I have also seen the record in the sales list of a second-hand dealer, marked 'Great!'). In the classical Italian songs, which he recorded mostly after the war, his style is equally remote from anything most listeners nowadays will want to hear in such music. It is a pity, for they are all sung with love. Caccini's 'Amarilli', for example, done with an even-toned half-voice and with conscientious devotion, is still wrong from start to finish according to most modern ideas of how it should be sung. The way of lifting to notes from below, the invariable aspirating of runs or of any two notes that share the same syllable, the croony sliding and pouty pathos: all seem alien and wanting in taste. Such singing has its defenders who will say that those who find fault with Gigli's performance of such pieces are applying German standards, while Gigli is singing in 'the classic Italian style'. So much the worse for the classic Italian style in that case. But of course, Caccini and his fellows said nothing in favour of sliding and aspirating, and the standards by which these things are criticised are not 'German' but musical. This is not the classic Italian style in fact, but the inter-war Italian style. Gigli, like many of the singers discussed in these chapters, fell a victim to the bad habits of his period.

If these had not intruded into the tenor's basic repertoire of nineteenth century opera it would matter less. Gigli had the ideal voice for quite a lot of operatic music that, on record at least, gets something less than ideal treatment. The Finale of *Lucia di Lammermoor* begins beautifully; the singing is gentle but firm, the music flows, and the passion is musically contained as the voice begins to swell and the style to become more emphatic. This is the aria 'Tu che a dio spiegasti l'ali'. But an earlier passage from the scene has been marked by some bad aspirating and interruption of line, and the scene ends with a puffy, self-pitying pathos that is embarrassingly abject. These originate as faults of taste, but the taste leads the technique, and the sentimentality of style has some connection with what became a distinctive flaw in the technical business of his singing. As he got older, he began to sing in two voices; the honeyed *mezza voce* which was always a wonderful part of his voice became a sort of indulgence, and something distinct from the main body of the voice. The 'separateness' can be heard as long ago as 1931 in the very beautiful record of 'Je crois entendre encore' from *Les Pêcheurs de Perles* (sung in Italian as 'Mi par d'udir ancora'). Beautiful as it is, it can cloy, this sweet, luscious, almost bodiless tone which, though not a falsetto, is near enough to it for that word to come to mind. But it evidently produced the kind of effect he wanted, and it added in later years to the ease of performance as, no doubt, did the aspirating. But both are likely to register with us as limitations of technique as well as of taste.

But perhaps it is ungrateful to speak of limitations in the face of so much plenty. The fifty-odd sides of pre-electrical recording are themselves a rich legacy, showing his voice at its freshest. The Improvviso, 'Un dì all'azzuro spazio' from *Andrea Chénier* is a superb piece of singing: the tone incomparably beautiful, a scrupulous line maintained, and a passionate declamatory style when required. This was made in 1922, and by 1941, when the complete recording of *Andrea Chénier* was made, he had gained expressiveness and lost remarkably little in voice. The two records make an impressive frame to enclose the best years of his singing.

The best of all were probably issued between 1925 and 1930. Even here, the voice of criticism still nags. 'M'appa-hari', he very predictably goes; and one senses that he was not the most selfless of artists in ensemble (an unyielding forte throughout sextet, quartet and trios recorded at this time forced everybody else into competition or into relative obscurity). The Earl of Harewood in *Opera* (vol. 3, no. 2) makes another criticism. Mentioning the Gigli–de Luca duets of 1927, he writes: 'De Luca is superb, but I cannot bear Gigli's lacrymose singing in *Forza*'. 'Cannot bear' puts it strongly, so one takes down the record ('Solenne in quest'ora') and tests one's own powers of endurance. Certainly, emotion breaks the line at the words 'al cor mio', and there is a little (for Gigli, very little) aspirating. Yet the placing is firm, the intervals are clean, there are no sobs, the emotion is warm (and after all the man does believe himself to be dying). And in the meantime one has the most beautiful tenor voice then in creation. I find I can bear it. As I can when in one Neapolitan song after another he puts heart and soul into the unsophisticated music, catching the sadness or the gaiety: 'Maria Mari', Tosti's 'La Serenata', Mascagni's short song 'Stornelli marini', the essential Gigli is in these almost more than in his Verdi. Yet who ever sang 'La donna è mobile' as winningly, its second verse so playful and rhythmical (and exactly as he sang it in the opera house, as we find from another of the private recordings)? There he is in his element. He would not be in his element, one would say, in *Otello*; but again private recordings bring us the unexpected, with two excerpts, the 'Esultate' sung to welcoming cheers from the audience, and the Monologue of Act III, both done with unforced resonance, understanding and even nobility.

One can, in fact, well understand the teacher's view that here was a singer with an absolutely central position in the tradition and history of the Italian voice. To us at this later date he still presents a kind of norm from which his contemporaries and rivals were brilliant deviates. He was born in the middle of a nine-year-period that was extraordinarily productive of good-to-great Italian tenors. Martinelli and Pertile (born in the same year in the same small town), Francesco Merli, Schipa, Gigli, Lauri-Volpi: the list is formidable without being at all complete. But today the members of the general public who have heard of Gigli probably begin to compare with the number who have *not* heard of any of the others. Popularity and merit can be quite disproportionate, we know, but with the popular entertainer, as with 'serious' genius, the sheer extent of the fame suggests this kind of centrality: an artist somewhere at the heart of the kind of experience his art represents.

'We have at last found THE TENOR': so, we are told, said the adjudicators of the Parma competition which Gigli won in 1914. That is it: for better or worse, he is THE TENOR, a position inherited from Caruso and without subsequent heir.

13. Around Italy: A Second Harvest
Lina Pagliughi Giannina Arangi-Lombardi
Magda Olivero Giacomo Lauri-Volpi
Mariano Stabile Tancredi Pasero

WE have discussed six singers (including Pertile in the first chapter and the two South Americans in the last) who sang with distinction in Italy, and whose records show to us considerable artists, still valuable and vivid, whatever else. In this chapter we will take a more general view of the Italian scene, harvesting what seems worthwhile.

It will be a sad day when Italians, having ploughed the field and scattered the good seed, are unable to reap a few good tenors. The generation that had grown to maturity just before the First World War was particularly well-favoured. Even so, the opera houses still felt able to welcome several foreign tenors, notably three Spaniards, Miguel Fleta, Hipolito Lazaro and Antonio Cortis. The last of these is discussed in a later chapter, but perhaps we should look at the others now, to compare with the native breed. On the whole, they make the Italians look remarkably well-behaved.

Fleta enters musical history principally as the tenor to sing Calaf in the first performance of *Turandot*, and he made gramophone history when his record of a song called 'Ay ay ay' became a best-seller. Neither of these claims to fame concerns us very much here, for he recorded nothing from *Turandot*, and 'Ay ay ay' is not worth listening to. He was, however, a frequently astonishing singer. At his best, he is one of the most poetic of tenors. It is so in his solos from *Lohengrin* (as with Pertile, the music seems to appeal to the latin imagination, which finds a poem where the Germans see only prose); in 'Che gelida manina', where his manner dreams (after all, Rodolfo is a poet) and woos, letting the first high note fade to nothing and lead deliciously into the next phrase; or in 'O paradiso' from *L'Africana*. But here we come to one of the troubles. His opening of the aria is heavenly – a beautifully floated, honeyed tone, an elegant lead from the recitative to the aria's first phrase, and a rapt vision conveyed with imagination. But soon under pressure a wobble begins to be troublesome, and the last part of the record is by no means such a joy as the first. The soft veiled tone and the fine control he has over it have little in common with the hard-driven but (presumably) disobedient full voice. Turn to Jussi Björling's record for comparison, and one finds a much greater over-all unity of voice, and indeed a magnificent piece of singing, though he still misses the rapt quality and something of the flowing lyricism that Fleta captured. In his native Spanish music he could capture still more. With great personal magnetism, a sort of Spanish Tauber, he sings with an exotic kind of brilliance: superb, for instance, in the Jota from Chapi's *La Bruja*, where the chorus shouts what sound like encouragements and appreciations until overwhelmed by the orchestra. But as he loved to have an audience eating from his hand, so he found that the fare they loved best included all sorts of bad habits. He would hold a high note, letting the music stay where it is, while the audience would hold its breath; he would soften it so they could see it change colour, hear it vibrate, and watch it disappear into silence. 'E lucevan le stelle' from *Tosca* provides an example; and in it we can also hear how he would sob his heart out and give a fine demonstration of the hysterics if this too seemed in order (in one record he does, and in another, not). He also developed a wobble, a kind of yo-yo effect, on some of these held notes: pronounced enough to have a fascination of its own, but nobody would call it well-mannered singing.

But the listener who thinks Fleta's hysterical conclusion of 'E lucevan le stelle' to be the best demonstration piece for this kind of singing should hear Lazaro's. This is twice punctuated by a shriek of bloodcurdling character. The only comparable sound on record, as far as I know, was made by Darrell Fancourt ecstatically contemplating his object all sublime. The shrieks come as the climax of an emotional outpouring in which the singer has several times shaken himself badly off the tonal centre of the note he is supposed to be singing, the prime example being on the words 'e muoio disperato'. There is also a neglect of legato (the ascending phrase comes out as 'le be-helle-he forme' and so forth), but a great care for the dying away of long held notes, an effect which is in itself quite beautiful. So we have another paradox, that in this extravagant stylist there is an artist, and one who would sometimes give the performance of a great singer. The voice itself sounds powerfully resonant and its upward range was extensive. He could modulate the tone to a velvety softness, and he had the stamina to sustain some extremely taxing music. 'One of the greatest recordings of all time' was Rodolfo Celletti's verdict on the duet from Act II of Mascagni's *Il Piccolo Marat*, and the critic goes on in considerable detail to show why. With a simple song before him, Lazaro could relax, forget about competing with Caruso, and sing simply for pleasure: there is one called 'El Huesped del Sevillano', where the brass band plays something very like 'I do like to be beside the seaside' *alla marcia*, and where Lazaro exercises the singer's magic as he goes pianissimo into the second tune of each verse. And yet so much is so bad, and even when good of its kind the admiration it provokes is most frequently an athletic rather than a musical sensation. The fiercely piercing high notes, always taken if at all possible on an 'eh' sound to make them still more penetrative, do not redeem (for example) a recording of 'Di quella pira' where the semiquavers are smudged, the phrases choppy and several notes taken untidily from below. And how typical that when the verse is over, the orchestra should play on and on through the passage which soloist and chorus should be singing so that Lazaro can reappear at the very end to hurl a final and annihilating high C out of the blue.

Return now to the Italians, and we see them as models of restraint and tastefulness. The lyric tenors, with Schipa at their head, numbered Dino Borgioli, Alessandro Ziliani and Franco Perulli in their ranks. The latter sings gracefully in a duet from *Linda di Chamounix* with Lina Pagliughi, and one would like to hear more of him. Ziliani sings with fresh voice in *La Traviata* (to the Violetta of Anna Rosza) and imaginatively in a long duet from Zandonai's *Francesca da Rimini* with Gina Cigna. Borgioli, good in Rossini as in parts like Cavaradossi and the Duke of Mantua, was a distinguished musician whose records are surprisingly rare. His tone sometimes sounds a little hard and thin, but one comes to realise how scrupulous and stylish an artist he was as soon as one begins to make comparisons. In 'Questa o quella', for example, there is a lot of life about di Stefano's recording, but Borgioli has far more elegance and a better legato. Then, Pizzetti's song 'I Pastori' is evocatively sung by Cesare Valletti, but Borgioli has more charm; and where Valletti certainly brings the intimacy of an experienced Lieder singer into the ending, Borgioli achieves some imaginative scene-painting, and his pianissimo is magical.

The lyric-dramatic tenors included Gigli, Pertile and Martinelli (who sang rarely in Italy once he was established at the Metropolitan, New York), Francesco Merli, Giuseppe Taccani and Giacomo Lauri-Volpi.

Merli's powerful, vibrant tone and his live temperament were what the Italians call 'phonogenic', and he was employed in several complete opera recordings as well as making a good series of solo records. The *Manon Lescaut* arias show his qualities well: passionate but controlled, a tenor with fine high notes and a full-bodied sonority throughout the voice. This suggests *Otello*, and his records made with Claudia Muzio of the duets from the first and third Acts make a worthy memento of a role that came to be very much his own in Italy during the thirties. A little tremulous at the start of the Love Duet, and something less than intense in the denunciation of Act III ('a hollow and terrible voice', the score directs), he nevertheless encompasses both the lyrical and declamatory parts of the music, and gives us the rather uncommon pleasure of hearing an Otello whose voice is in full bloom.

Whereas Merli seems to have been relatively immune from the over-emotionalism, forcing and loss of focus common in this period, we see a fine tenor succumb to these things in Taccani. His recording of 'Un dì all'azzuro spazio' (*Andrea Chénier*) begins well, but the firm voice quivers at the emotional climaxes, regaining quality for some quieter passages, and then indulging to the end in a declamatory style without restraint or proper definition. The 'Di quella pira' is not unlike Lazaro's: popping up with a sudden top C of comical magnificence at the end, having given no attention to such matters (clearly marked and clearly meant in the score) as a softening of the voice at the change from major key to minor. We see how the style in singing and in composition went together in an extract from Mascagni's *Guglielmo Ratcliff* ('Quando fanciulla'). Taccani has the right voice for it, but the tone spreads, the aspirates intrude, the emotion begins to pump and eventually voice and music become one in hysterical stridency. Yet another extract from the opera ('Ombra esecrata') leaves one with much admiration for the command and the brilliant high notes, while other records, like the duet from Act IV of *La Forza del Destino* with Pasquale Amato, show what a very good singer he could be, phrasing well and sustaining quite a fine legato. There seems to be no accounting for the differences of standard. In an acoustic record of 'Vesti la giubba' the tone spreads and the style is over-emphatic. Yet in the electrically recorded final scene from *Carmen*, so often an invitation to extravagances of barn-storming and grovelling, he is not only well-defined and rich in tone, but also restrained and dignified. Born in 1885 and still singing in 1940, Taccani disappeared from the view of record collectors around the mid-twenties. He was perhaps a typical tenor of the period, and that goes for the richness of his gifts, as well as the ways in which he used them.

The rich endowment of the period itself is in no doubt. After all this talk of tenors, we have still not discussed the one who in Italy itself most successfully challenged the notion of Gigli as IL TENORE. This was Giacomo Lauri-Volpi, a remarkable singer and a colourful character. In his long, contentious life he has become the most articulate of singers (the author of five books), watching over the Italian scene, and surviving long enough to have had the melancholy honour of composing obituaries for many of his former colleagues. Between him and Gigli, the rivalry was keen and comic. At the Metropolitan, we gather, he was allowed an extra ten cents so that it could be said his salary was higher than Gigli's. Rosenthal's *Two Centuries of Opera at Covent Garden* quotes Geoffrey Toye's telegram from Italy, where he was trying to engage the services of at least one of the tenors in 1934: 'Gigli indignantly refuses, and Volpi will never recover from insult of my offer. Returning London immediately'. But however the opera houses clamoured for both singers, the recording companies of Victor and HMV were seriously interested in only one of them, so that today where Gigli has his hundreds, Lauri-Volpi has only his tens, and when it comes down to recordings of a proper standard we have very few in which to hear the true excellence of a highly individual artist.

A series of recordings for Fonotipia marked the beginning of his career, and four complete operas for Cetra the end. Perhaps one should qualify that and mention one of the strangest recordings in existence. This is a private issue on the EJS label, comprising parts of a late broadcast, some songs in church, and some talk and bits of singing in his home. Remarkable features here include people talking through much of the singing, a motor-bike apparently starting off during one of the items, and a method of accompaniment on the piano where the right hand plays a kind of doodle of alternating notes at the interval of a third and the left fills in more or less by chance. As is usually the case, it is nice to know that he could still sing so late in life,[1] but records of tenors in advanced age are generally to be seen and not heard. I daresay that for most listeners this would hold of most of the records he made after about 1940. Perhaps the 'Cielo e mar' and 'Non piangere, Liù' made about that time are sufficiently impressive (it is still a voice and a half) but the style involves aspirating and sliding, and the voice is really good only at extremes of loud and soft. Nor are the earliest records very creditable. Many are spoilt by bad intonation: some like the lament of Federico (*L'Arlesiana*) are consistently sharp, others, like 'Che gelida manina' and 'Ah, non mi ridestar' (*Werther*), rise disconcertingly every now and again. There is no mistaking the distinction of timbre and often that of style (among the best are 'Giunto sul passo' from *Mefistofele* and 'Una vergine' from *La Favorita*, though that one too lacks the charm and interest of the style which, say, Miguel Fleta brought to it). But there is a limit to the pleasures of a magnificent sound that can never be relied on to stay in tune.

The distance between these recordings and his best self is clear when one plays the earlier and later versions of 'Un dì all'azzuro spazio' (Andrea Chénier's 'Improvviso' and the solo which repeatedly provides golden opportunities and a fair test for these tenors). The electrical version is superb, beautifully graded, completely in tune, thrilling in its resonance. An interesting second comparison is one with Franco Corelli, the tenor who in the post-war generation most resembles him. Corelli gives an exceptionally fine performance in his complete recording of the opera, but he misses one interpretative point: it is the change to something new and personal which one should feel as the poet turns to Maddalena with the words 'sull'occhio vostro', and here Lauri-Volpi introduces just the right note of tenderness. For he became a sensitive and imaginative interpreter, both of the drama and the musical line. A good example of the former comes at the end of Act III of *Aida*. Radamès is confronted with the nightmare recognition of his own ruin as the Ethiopian king reveals his presence, and his declamation here is vividly dramatised. It is followed by the heroic phrase 'Sacerdote, io resto a te' sung on a massive span of breath without a hint of shouting but with lyricism intensified. The musical imagination enriches some of the best of all tenor records. It is, for example, marvellous to find that with the power and heroic quality of a Radamès in *Aida* he should be able to sing Bellini with something near the grace of the earlier tenors like

[1] And even later than this. *Opera*, June 1972 has a headline *Lauri-Volpi sings again*, and tells how the 79 year old tenor sang 'Nessun dorma' at the Liceo, Barcelona, leaving 'the audience bewildered at the miracle by which he seems to have made time stand still for him'.

49. Giacomo Lauri-Volpi
(photograph inscribed to the
soprano, Margaret Sheridan)

Bonci and de Lucia. Perhaps his electrical recording of 'A te, o cara' (*I Puritani*) is almost too much of a good thing, with the comings and goings of crescendo and decrescendo bringing light and shade and a sensation like driving past trees against sunshine. But it was a marvellous way of moulding and caressing that he had. Put these into a solo like 'E lucevan le stelle', and one has a very near-perfect poetry; he softens on the high A with wonderful control, spreads the phrases deliciously, lingering on the grace notes, and bringing a shining power and resonance to the climax. It is a few records like this that earn and assure his place on posterity's shelves.

The commercial recordings of this period (around 1930) are supplemented by one private transcription from a live performance. This is of two excerpts from a performance of *Aida* given at Covent Garden in 1936, the Triumphal Scene and the duet with Amneris (the Swedish mezzo, Gertrude Wettergren) in Act IV. One wonders how much his closeness to the microphone in the commercial recordings exaggerated the vibrato, but it seems not to have done so to any marked extent. I would swear to it that the Pharaoh of the performance was Robert Easton though his name does not appear on the label. His very pronounced flicker-vibrato (and a feature of a very fine voice too) is answered almost exactly by Lauri-Volpi's in the opening exchanges. Two other things are clear from the recording. One is that Lauri-Volpi was not the most disciplined of singers; or at any rate, he is not at one with the conductor in the duet. The other is that it really was one of the very exciting voices of the century. His solos are quite personal and irreplaceable in tone (though again Corelli comes to mind), and he cleaves through the ensemble with unstrained power. One can quite see why at the Metropolitan they thought it worthwhile to pay all that and ten cents too.

The decade 1885 to 1895 that was so productive of tenors matches the previous decade in its provision of baritones (Stracciari, de Luca, Amato, Ruffo, Danise, Magini-Coletti). But the Italian tenors who flourished in the inter-war years grew up with baritones who are much less vividly remembered through their records. In the Ruffo tradition was Apollo Granforte. His Iago, Tonio, Scarpia and di Luna are preserved in complete recordings and they are clearly the work of a seasoned and authoritative artist. The Iago, especially, has imaginative strength as well as the tonal opulence appropriate to one so named. The Credo has phrases like 'vile son nato' enunciated with bitterness, and the 'e poi' held long and very quietly, peering steadily into the unseeable. There are also some fine solo recordings made in opera-house perspective, as from seats well away from the stage and with the orchestra given due prominence. The Prologue to *Pagliacci* is recorded in this way, showing an ample, warm voice with an effective edge and superb high notes. Yet the complete operas also show him as tending to spread under pressure, and in such passages as the finale to the Convent Scene in *Il Trovatore* with Pertile all puff and push, Granforte joins in unpleasing competition forfeiting his steadiness and focus. His, however, impresses most as a voice among the heavier dramatic baritones of this period. Giovanni Inghilleri was another who enjoyed considerable success at the time. The Amonasro of HMV's *Aida* recorded in 1928, he survived long enough as a singer to take part in one of the first fully successful operas on LP, the *La Bohème* of 1952 with Tebaldi and Güden as Mimì and Musetta. Benvenuto Franci also reappeared after the war, though not, as far as I know, on records. He sang with a quick vibrato and a voice that could be exciting, as it is in 'O sommo Carlo' from *Ernani*. Little that he recorded lodges in the mind for its interpretative insight, and on the high notes his vibrato becomes disproportionate. To northerners especially, Cesare Formichi's less vibrant tone may be more congenial, though instead of a vibrato I think one hears every now and then a slight unsteadiness that threatens to become wobble. It is there very slightly in 'Cortigiani, vil razza', well sung though not very interestingly phrased or individual as vocal acting. He is probably at his best in a strong, clear-cut version of 'Nemico della patria' from *Andrea Chénier*.

The lyric baritones include Poli, Urbano and Galeffi. Alfro Poli was a pleasant rather than distinguished Malatesta to Ernesto Badini's characterful Don Pasquale, and a warm-voiced, good-natured Marcel in Gigli's *La Bohème*. With an outstandingly beautiful voice and the ability to sing a true legato, Galeffi had the talents to become one of the best baritones on record, but his taste (or that of the period) led to undue exhibitionism on high notes and the sort of overt emotionalism which spoils, for example, the opening of his 'Dio possente', Valentine's air in *Faust*. He was an interesting singer, however, vivid and personal in the Prologue to *Pagliacci* and showing his finest qualities in arias from *Nabucco*. His long career (seventeen seasons at the Scala) contrasts with the short one of Umberto Urbano, who, in the mid nineteen-twenties, made a series of records remarkable for their pure lyricism and the beauty of tone. Arias like those from Leoncavallo's *Zazà* that one associates with Ruffo's exciting but uneven singing reappear as flowing instrumental melodies, the voice resonant but firmly defined, the style warm but continent. He could command the style and technique to sing the baritone arias from *La Favorita* in the tradition of Battistini: the fioriture are fluent and even, and there is a certain appropriate regality of manner. A little more variety would not come amiss, yet he is not without interpretative skill: the dream-voice in Iago's 'Era la notte' shows it, or the middle section of Hamlet's 'Brindisi', the expression made severe and the voice shaded towards bass as the music modulates to a minor key. All of these are delightful performances and add a distinction to the baritone recordings of this period.

But their greatest ornament should be the very much more famous talent of Mariano Stabile. The Earl of Harewood has written so appreciatively of this, 'the greatest stylist amongst contemporary Italian singers' (*Opera*, May 1956) that it would probably be best simply to quote him, for I personally find myself less impressed. Lord Harewood speaks of his voice as 'a firm, athletic instrument' and of the intensity of his performance as founded upon 'the expressiveness of an unbroken but constantly moulded line'. With this goes 'a startling ability to make use of words'. Among the records he considers Figaro's 'Aprite un po' quegli occhi' to be the finest version of all available at that date, and the excerpts from *Falstaff* to be vivid souvenirs, rich in detail, of 'one of the greatest performances of our time in one of the greatest roles'.

Perhaps one may be forgiven for assuming the role of devil's advocate for a paragraph. I find 'firm' a surprising word to use about the voice. It is hard to use any word other than 'wobble' for the kind of tonal unsteadiness that mars the *Falstaff* records. In 1942, when they were made, Stabile was fifty-four and a veteran, and of course one takes that into account. But a recording from 1936 has more recently become available to collectors (Act I of a broadcast from the Salzburg Festival conducted by Toscanini), and in this too the sound is loose: the beginning of the Honour monologue in particular has a wobble not much less pronounced than in the studio performance six years later. Back in the nineteen-twenties the voice was firm, certainly, but it still seems to me to be dry and undernourished. To sample the *Figaro* again, I listen to the other solos, 'Se vuol ballare' and 'Non più andrai', and admire the liveliness and the clear diction. A personality emerges, but not, to my ears, an engaging one: there seems little warmth and, in 'Se vuol ballare', little sense of fun (Figaro has serious matters in hand, but his mode of expression can still be humorous). What, too, can one say of the stylist who in 'Non più andrai' imposes an *allargando* every time the third line of the rondo tune comes round?

To return to the *Falstaff*, it does start with the disadvantage (as Lord Harewood says) that Stabile was 'fat neither physically nor vocally'. The voice is not just 'not fat' – it is lean. All the more of an artistic triumph, perhaps, that he could characterise this tun of man so successfully. And certainly there is a vividness of characterisation about the recordings, some of it gained by the rather dangerous process of gruffing-up the voice, as he does very effectively when turning to the thieves who prate of honour ('L'onore! ladri!' – the crescendo on the first syllable of 'ladri' culminates in a gruff-voiced menace on the second syllable vivid as a fist shaken in the face). There are some nice light touches: the complacent acceptance of Mistress Quickly's compliments, the panache of his duet with Ford (Ford being finely sung in the 1942 recording by Alfro Poli). Best of all is the monologue from Act III. For one thing, he seems to be recorded rather closer to the microphone, and the quieter music allows a deeper quality to settle into the timbre of the voice. His denunciation of the wicked world has a fine depth of self-righteous disgust, and the prolonged syllables of self-examination ('impinguo troppo' – 'I've got too fat') has the quite different depth of inner confession. The great artist is there on records after all, though I wonder whether a new generation that has not been captivated (as Lord Harewood has been) by Stabile on the stage will ever hear the records in quite the same way. I myself saw him once, in the *Don Pasquale* of 1948, and remember what I thought was a sparkling actor and a poor singer. But then, he was quite old and I was quite young.

Age, at any rate into the fifties where we follow him on records, seems to have had little effect upon the remaining male singer whom we must discuss: the basso, Tancredi Pasero. Born in 1893, only eight months after his great contemporary Ezio Pinza, Pasero based his career in his native land, and it is probably true that outside Italy his records have not won the recognition they deserve. Like Lauri-Volpi and Franci, he had a rapid vibrato that is inescapable on the records, just that degree more pronounced than Pinza's rather better 'integrated' vibrancy; and on disc his characterisations do not impress with comparable vividness. He does not sound satanic in the Serenade of Gounod's Mephistopheles (in spite of some low laughter), and as Boito's Mefistofele it is only in 'Son lo spirito', not in 'Ecco il mondo', that he sounds really dangerous. In the 'Catalogue Song' from *Don Giovanni* his Leporello seems a very decent fellow, dignified and rather serious-minded; if Sarastro ever sang *allegro* he might sound like this. His Don Basilio, however, was a real character, and (an impressive addition to the Italian repertoire) his Boris Godunov suffers and frets with striking conviction.

His Boris was surely the ancestor of Nicolai Ghiaurov's: well acted no doubt, but essentially distinguished by its lyrical qualities and by the beauty of voice. Pasero's voice always impresses by its richness and also the even-

50. Mariano Stabile as Falstaff   51. Tancredi Pasero as Orazio in
Gli Orazi

ness of its quality from top to bottom of the wide range. The upward range includes Boris' high G flats taken with a fine, sustained resonance. Downwards, we can judge from Sarastro's first aria in *Die Zauberflöte* (sung in Italian as 'Qui sdegno'). In the low phrases, where many a genuine bass will become gruff, forced or unsteady, he maintains an easy, smooth production. With this go a sonority and a healthy glow, wonderfully impressive in the old *Barbiere di Siviglia* with Stracciari, and the kind of legato that a melody like Bellini's 'Vi ravviso' (*La Sonnambula*) calls for, and generally in vain. A tasteful singer, he does not allow Philip II any extravagance of emotion, but sings the great solo ('Ella giammai m'amo') with feeling and dignity. If singing of this kind had been representative of Italy between the wars there would be no cause for concern.

And perhaps, as one begins to line up the ladies for review, it might appear that concern is really quite unnecessary. Lina Pagliughi, Giannina Arangi-Lombardi, Rosetta Pampanini, Mafalda Favero, Gina Cigna, Maria Caniglia; it is a fair array of soprano talent, and to it has to be added the still resounding name of Toti dal Monte. The mezzos were headed by Irene Minghini-Cattaneo and Ebe Stignani; two more singers of undoubted merit. So are we perhaps mistaken in seeing Italian singing as an art in decline during those years?

Leaving Stignani for a later chapter, let us hear Minghini-Cattaneo before turning to the sopranos. It was a fine strong voice, possibly a little like Fiorenza Cossotto in our own time, more mezzo than contralto and particularly free and resonant in the upper register (she did have some soprano roles in her repertoire, including Isolde and Elsa). The low register nevertheless brought a powerful chest voice into play, and it is heard impressively in the duet 'L'amo come il fulgor del creato' from *La Gioconda*. Full-bodied and passionate, she leads into this melody with a certain grandeur, which also marks her singing of Amneris' great scene in the last Act of *Aida*. Her outburst against the priests is a really fine piece of dramatic work, and the solo is crowned with a ringing high A at the conclusion. She was yet another singer with a fairly insistent vibrato, but the vibrations are rapid and even and there is an inherently dramatic quality in the voice to which this no doubt contributed. Her runs are fluent, and the legato line, if sometimes a little stiff, is not disturbed by much over-emphasis. In fact, one of the limitations is that she does very little by way of shading. Azucena's 'Condotta all'era in ceppi' goes by, without attention to the subtler markings in the score, and the cabaletta of 'O mio Fernando' (*La Favorita*) makes less impression than it should because the singing of the air itself has been too strong and outgoing to secure a sense of contrast or development. There are times too (the early records of Verdi's *Requiem* have examples) when the breath control appears to be inadequate to the span of the music. She made good records, but not great ones; and that, after all, is the story of the present chapter (nor, I think, would Stignani's presence in it affect that summary, for her records do not make the impression of greatness that her stage performances would often leave).

By the outbreak of war, the sopranos most prominent in Italian opera were probably Pagliughi in the coloratura repertoire, Caniglia in the lyric-dramatic and Cigna in the dramatic-heroic roles. Caniglia and Cigna seem particularly representative figures. Both are heard at their best in two solos from Cilea's *Adriana Lecouvreur*, Cigna covering the tender, very emotional phrases with a shimmer of delicate ardour, Caniglia's sumptuous lower register enriching them with a deeper lustre. Both singers manage the demands for pianissimo; both have a feeling for the *morbidezza*. Both records, I have to admit, came to me personally as some surprise, so either they are better than most by these singers, or I have been simply accepting the relatively low critical rating they tend to receive in this country. Both points have something in them, the truth, as is so often the case, lying somewhere in the middle. Caniglia we know from early days, when she stepped into the Gigli *Tosca*, deputising for and surely improving on the indisposed Iva Pacetti. Much was gratefully heard, especially the richness of the lower register, but too often the style was gusty, the focus imprecise. Even here she was not really happy with some of the high notes, a characteristic that became more noticeable when she had to take them softly as in Verdi's *Requiem*. By 1943, and the recording of *Un Ballo in Maschera*, she was liable to flatten on top notes and become unsteady under pressure. The whole performance was a matter of now-good-now-bad. In some of the live performances recorded privately in the late 1930s we recognise the beauty of her voice as heard in a great building, and the sincerity of her portrayals: her Violetta at Covent Garden in 1939 is deeply felt and often well sung, and while the Desdemona she sang to Martinelli's Otello at the Metropolitan in 1938 lacks polish it has much beauty of tone.

There are 'live' recordings of Gina Cigna also, including an impressive one of her debut at the Metropolitan as Aida in 1937. It was a scene of great enthusiasm for the new soprano, and we can well understand the ovation after 'O patria mia', sung expressively (Panizza, the conductor, very much with his singers rather than urging them all the time to get on with it), with an ample, tenderly modulated voice and strong emotion that is not over-played. There is much fine singing throughout the opera (in 'Là tra foreste vergine' and the final duet especially), and sometimes a phrase with a rare kind of majesty about it. Some critics complained of vibrato, but it is only occasionally troublesome in the recording, mostly on a few high notes. Nothing should detract now from the evident triumph of that performance, and of others like it. But then one recalls that this is the soprano who only a few years later would be singing so unpleasingly in duets with Cloë Elmo, where the tight vibrato has disappeared and a wobble taken its place. Unsteadiness is intrusive too, if less pervasive, in the complete *Turandot* recorded just before the war. Listening to the Riddle Scene one is not able to enjoy anything comparable to the compact power of Eva Turner in the 1937 recording or of Birgit Nilsson on LP. In the lyrical pages following, though there is no question that this is a true Turandot voice, it is difficult to relish what should be a feast of sound when there is such unsteadiness appearing in alternation with phrases of great splendour. Nor does her Norma have the grace which the role demands just as it does power and dramatic intensity (and these she certainly had). I prefer to go back and hear her on those early Columbia recordings, where there is vibrato but no wobble, and where an aria like Gioconda's 'Suicidio', and Verdi too ('Madre, pietosa vergine' for instance), were sung with a voice just enjoying its first success in a great opera house, and at that time fully worthy of its traditions.

Going back to that year, 1929, when Cigna made her first recording, the sopranos whose status corresponded to that of Cigna and Caniglia about ten years later were Arangi-Lombardi and Carmen Melis; and I think that even in the lapse of a decade one can see a decrease in the completeness of technical preparation and in standards of basic, reliable accomplishment. We can hear Carmen Melis on records over a twenty-year period. The first recordings, of 1907, show the twenty-two-year-old singer with a voice at once fresh and mature; and the electrical recordings made around 1926 have a finely preserved, healthy resonance as well as a genuine refinement of style. Her Tosca, recorded complete in 1929, is well known for its glowing tone and generous feeling. Less well-known are the imaginative records from Massenet's *Manon*, at once luscious and delicate, and a version of 'Depuis le jour' from *Louise* sung fervently but with the high As beautifully lightened, and some lovely personal touches in the final phrases. Occasionally there comes a rather squally tone (on the high B in the 'Depuis le jour', for instance); sometimes, as in 'Ancora un passo' (*Madama Butterfly*), the phrasing is a little too clipped. Nothing that I have been able to hear properly tests her accomplishment in florid work. She nevertheless seems to have been the best lyric soprano to be heard regularly in Italy until the advent of her own pupil, Renata Tebaldi.

The technical accomplishments of her contemporary, Arangi-Lombardi, are well demonstrated on record. And again there does not seem to be anything corresponding a decade or so later. Indeed, the sopranos who have distinguished themselves in subsequent recordings which can compare with Arangi-Lombardi's in *Lucrezia Borgia* have not been Italian at all, but the Greek Callas, the Turk Gencer, the Spaniard Caballé. Arangi-Lombardi is less imaginative than these, but her legato is sound, her tone incisive, her high notes exciting, her triplets, trills and passage work well-schooled. She has some of the Italian characteristics that find less of a welcome further north: as recorded, we sometimes hear an abrupt change of register, a certain hardness on top notes, an occasional intrusion of vibrato. But her Aida is recorded to show a very beautifully rounded middle-voice; and as she plays her scene in the second Act to the strong, vivid Amneris of Maria Capuana (we can see her bearing down on her rival at 'Si, tu l'ami' so vivid is the confrontation), we realise that tucked away in these old, constricted complete recordings of opera on 78s there are performances of great distinction as well as much that is best forgotten.

These old opera recordings included also the Gilda and Lucia di Lammermoor of Lina Pagliughi. This famous coloratura, proclaimed by Tetrazzini as her true successor, recorded also on LP, and there are critics who count her *Sonnambula* as still their favourite. The tone by then was thin and without the brilliance of earlier years, and though the characterisation had appropriate sweetness and pathos its appeal is a frail one. The bright, firm tones of the young Pagliughi on 78s may also have a limited appeal, but here at least is what one has the right to expect of such a voice – clarity, steadiness and agility. Comparing her version of 'Bel raggio', the famous test-piece from Rossini's *Semiramide*, with that of her great predecessor, one notes an assurance and command in the earlier singer where Pagliughi is merely pretty. And comparing her recording of the *Figaro* aria, 'Deh vieni, non tardar', with dal Monte's mentioned in the last chapter, one finds less to trouble the literalists, but also less personality and imagination. Occasionally she resorts to aspirates, and forfeits the purity of legato. Yet a fine legato line and warmth of emotion are just what do distinguish an aria, very beautifully sung, from Giordano's little-known opera, *Il re*; and the Lucia di Lammermoor also is genuinely felt. Required to choose a single record, I would probably ask for her arias from *La Gazza Ladra*. Infrequently heard, these are good, clean-cut melodies, and the limpid voice and smiling manner match them engagingly.

And there were, of course, other sopranos in these years – Rosetta Pampanini, good as Butterfly and Mimì, Mafalda Favero, remembered most widely as Tito Schipa's fresh-voiced partner in the duet from *L'Amico Fritz* . . . The list could be prolonged, but not very usefully. One soprano is still to be mentioned, and for various reasons she is in a class of her own. This is Magda Olivero, whose career began in 1933, seemed to have finished in 1941, began afresh under remarkable circumstances in 1950 and for all I know may not be finished in 1971.[1]

She was the slave-girl, Liù, in the first complete recording of *Turandot*, made just pre-war, with Cigna in the name-part. We used to hear Liù's arias sung by Olivero coming over the radio quite often, and though I have never possessed the records I can hear them very clearly in my mind. She had this quality of making something special and therefore memorable out of whatever she sang. The fragile, tender wooing manner of her performance in *Turandot* was beautifully suited to such roles as Violetta and Mimì, and through the enterprise of some private collectors much of her singing in these operas has been preserved from live performances given in 1967 in Amsterdam. One is reminded every now and then that this is not a young singer – accepting 1913 as the date of her birth, she was then fifty-four – but an exquisite tenderness and charm still tell of youth.

The first Act of *La Bohème* impresses with that fragile charm one associates primarily with Lucrezia Bori. All is gracious, and wherever one likes to taste the flavour of this performance ('buona sera . . . vivo sola soletta . . . ma quando vien lo sgelo . . . vi sarò vicina . . . amor') it is of a rare and delightful quality. Act II of *La Traviata* is similarly delicate in voice and strong in emotion. The strength is again not just a matter of overall impression but of vividly realised detail. The farewells to Germont include the sort of emotional break-down relished by the Victorians, and perhaps it is excessive; yet the last Act is presented with touching restraint and the 'Addio del passato' is exquisite.

Olivero returned to the operatic stage in *Adriana Lecouvreur* at the personal request of its then aged composer, and to the gramophone in Giordano's *Fedora*. A queenly performance, this, tremendous in authority and grandeur as well as the tenderness that one expects of her. Her voice still shines, and the breath still supports the broad, sweeping phrases of a score written for singers in their prime. In the first of the solos, 'O grandi occhi lucenti', she has some wonderfully controlled pianissimo phrases at the end, and comparing her with Giannina Russ, who made some of the earliest recordings from the opera, one hears Olivero take the soft high note on 'O' (in 'O schiette labbra') cleanly where the earlier singer scoops it. But this is a performance which is always commanding attention and admiration. The

[1] In fact, November, 1971, brought no less an event than her New York debut, described in *Opera* (February, 1972) as dividing the city: the 'full-blooded *verismo* style' seemed to some to be 'just too much to take', while to others the recital was one of the most exciting in memory.

timid self-defence of the last Act, the bold scorn of the first: the superb pride of the answer to the question 'Did he have enemies?' – 'Lui! Giusto cielo! E chi?': she has a way of acting with the voice that suggests Callas, no less. Of course, this was 1969, and Callas was there, on record, to be learnt from. But hardly in 1951 when she recorded a passage from Act II of *La Traviata* ('Amami, Alfredo') where her intensity brings the same comparison to mind; and not at all in 1940 when her recording of the great solo from the first Act set a standard which pointed right forward to the new age of the gramophone and the period that, in grand opera, is still thought of as the age of Callas.

In this singer, Italy had an aristocrat of the operatic stage. The land of song had also a considerable number of artists who could keep the traditions alive. But these artists were much needed, for from the earliest times of the gramophone there was much in Italian development inimical to the art of song for which the country had so long been famous. Beautiful voices, true legato, cultivated agility: these were the essentials. The first was still in abundant supply; the others were ever less apparent. Such, at least, appears to be the evidence of the gramophone.

52. Magda Olivero as Adriana Lecouvreur

14. Germany and Austria: Keepers of the Seal
Maria Ivogün Meta Seinemeyer
Sigrid Onegin Richard Tauber
Heinrich Schlusnus

THE Parlophone-Odeon catalogue of pre-war days was full of 'routine' German performances. They did not look particularly exciting, and relatively few collectors bothered to find out how they sounded. Decca-Polydor also recruited very largely from the German opera houses, and again they looked less attractive than the celebrity-laden catalogues of HMV with their emphasis upon the Italian wing and their traditional monopoly of the acknowledged kings and queens of song. HMV themselves had a special German catalogue containing a large number of records by German singers, but on the whole it was left uninvestigated and we went on buying Gigli and Galli-Curci and such Germans who, like Elisabeth Schumann, were plentifully represented in the general catalogue.

Yet the standard of technical accomplishment among these singers, many of them little known at that time outside their own country, was far more consistent than that of their Italian counterparts; and so we might have guessed, for, testifying to the world in general of the excellence of German singing, there were about ten singers internationally famous, and all coming into prominence within little more than a decade.

One might perhaps have taken it for granted that German singers might display a more cultivated musicianship than Italians; that they might show more feeling for words and a more intellectual interest in interpretation. On the other hand, it would not have come entirely as a surprise to find them barking out noisy declamation, and opposing the *bel canto* of Italy as inexpressive and effete. The 'literary' music of Wagner and Wolf, and even the earlier composers of Lieder, could well have influenced singers to reverse the traditional priorities, legato being sacrificed to expressiveness, beauty to volume or to an arty and pallid intimacy, while vocal agility was relegated as a thing of the past, the pre-requisite of an art now recognised as alien and superficial. Yet as one makes comparisons it is to realise repeatedly that the Italians were sacrificing traditions while the Germans were respecting them. If one wants to hear the full mastery of fioritura by a soprano around the year 1930 one goes to Maria Ivogün and Lotte Schöne.

For a contralto with full technical mastery, Sigrid Onegin, the Swedish singer who learnt and worked very largely in Germany; for a baritone to sing Verdi with the traditional smoothness and grace of the best part of the Italian school, Schlusnus or Schmitt-Walter. They, and so many more, gladden the ear with a flow of evenly, musically produced sound, and they are not to be found aspiring and quivering, breaking phrases and hogging the high notes. It is they who were the true 'keepers of the seal of Italian melody' in this period.

Some of the loveliest of soprano records were made by Ivogün and Schöne. Both had light voices, sweet-toned but firm; they also had marvellous technical control, keeping the tone even and well-defined while on the stave, and moving over the whole instrument with the easy, joyful command of the virtuoso. With this went a refinement of style, fresh and delightful as the voices themselves.

Ivogün is one of the most accomplished singers on record. Probably at the height of her powers around 1930, she made a few recordings for HMV by the electrical process, and these gained a much wider circulation than the more numerous pre-electrical selections. She is also a link between the earliest times of the gramophone and our own age, for her art looks back to singers like Abendroth, Siems and Kurz, virtuosos of the remoter past, and her pupils include Rita Streich and Elisabeth Schwarzkopf, the former continuing the tradition in Ivogün's own repertoire, the latter probably embodying the standards of a true golden age most fully of all. Schwarzkopf has described how she went to Ivogün at a difficult time in her development as a singer. Ivogün took the voice and built it up afresh note by note. The results can be heard in many hours of singing by the pupil on LP, while the teacher's own art is represented by a small number of short recordings, primitive and unflattering by our standards, but also rare and precious.

At least she recorded enough for us to hear a representative recital, the music ranging from Handel to Richard Strauss, with some of the other Strauss thrown in for encores. The Handel would be 'Sweet bird that shun'st the noise of folly' from *Il Penseroso*, a favourite piece with Selma Kurz and Melba. Ivogün warms the music gently (as Melba does not), without letting it languish over-sweetly into sleepiness (as Kurz tends to do). When one thinks the aria is over, there comes some of the loveliest singing: a pencil-thin wisp of sound in alt, and not a silly twitter (for there are those who think the noise of folly and the exercises of a coloratura soprano to be nearly synonymous) but a tone free of the throat and floating above normal human confines, which is what the song is about. It and the light, even-voiced scale-work that follows are all charmingly appropriate.

After Handel, Mozart; and more to choose from here. Both arias of the Queen of Night in *Die Zauberflöte* are well done, her fresh, firm tone making the first part of 'O zittre nicht' as satisfying as the wonderfully even and accurate execution of the allegro. In 'Martern aller Arten' from *Die Ent-*

führung the same technical brilliance is combined with an authoritative manner that compensates for any lack of weight.

Some Italian arias might follow: a nimble, air-borne 'Ah, non giunge' *(La Sonnambula)* or a brilliantly ornamented version of 'Una voce poco fa' *(Il Barbiere di Siviglia)*. Her recording of Gilda's 'Caro nome' is probably the best of all versions on 78s. In England, older opera goers still remember her appearances at Covent Garden in this role in 1927 as something of a revelation, where the character was a girl, not a prima donna, and where the aria was dreamily, meditatively treated, not as a show-piece for the star. Her record is a fine memento, the music taken at a relaxed tempo, the phrases beautifully joined, the high notes floated so that those towards the end seem to be conjured out of the air. The decorations are delicate, the trills so airy and natural that one can almost accept the upward arpeggios which, like many of her contemporaries, she interpolated at the conclusion. It is an intelligently conceived performance, with its dreamy beginning echoed at the end, when the phrases are taken up again, and contrasted with a slightly quicker middle-section in which the repeated jumps of a sixth are done with youthful buoyancy and a very mature technical assurance.

Her most famous record is of Zerbinetta's solo in *Ariadne auf Naxos*. This has such a reputation as the classic and incomparable version that it is perhaps worth testing by some comparisons. Let us take six records, two from each period: Rita Streich and Reri Grist on LP (other good versions by Roberta Peters and Sylvia Geszty), Adele Kern and Ivogün herself on electrical 78s (Erna Berger and Alda Noni should be mentioned as recording in live performances), and Francillo-Kaufmann and Hermine Bosetti on pre-electricals. Great interest attaches to the two last named as they recorded an earlier version, very rarely to be heard since those days. Its main differences are that it does not modulate to D major at 'So war es mit Pagliazzo', so that all that follows is sung in E flat, a semitone higher, this being followed by an extended passage of quite different material with a very high tessitura indeed. What Bosetti is doing I cannot quite make out, for the LP transfer on which this extremely rare record can be heard comes out not in D major, nor yet E flat but in F! Most other items on the recital are in a high key too, and, while one cannot believe that the lady transposed up as a matter of course, the adjustments are not entirely satisfactory either. There is of course much to wonder at in both these early records, but I don't subscribe to the idea that the very fact of their existence shows how degenerate and inferior we have become since those days. The fact is that though they sing at these dizzy heights, they do not add to our musical pleasure by doing so. Bosetti sings without a note of consolation in her tone (and the solo is after all a sermon, its purpose being to console and reconcile). Francillo-Kaufmann, with a voice that sounds rather heavier than the other Zerbinettas heard here, is not very expressive either; but there are also some sketchy scales and some trills that are sketchier still, among other work that is much more admirable. The final E flat is not a note one wants to hear twice, and on the whole it is a relief to leave the early version and return to the usual one in Adele Kern's recording. This is much more expressive, and she manages to get the complete solo on to two sides of the 78 record without hurrying unduly (Bosetti has some curious hurrying *rubato* effects). She is clean-cut, fine on her scales, staccatos and trills, and in manner not unlike Reri Grist who sings in a modern recording under Karl Böhm. If there is any decline to be observed so far in the comparisons it is in the quality of Grist's trills compared with Kern's, also perhaps in the tendency she has to use a very light aspirate in her runs. But just as it is a relief to turn to these two singers after the first two, so a new pleasure comes into the listening with the recordings by Streich and Ivogün. The first distinction is one that they share: Zerbinetta becomes a tender human being. They also are both quite exceptionally accomplished singers, able not merely to meet the difficulties but to do so with delicacy and a beautiful lyricism. Where their ways diverge, and where I personally find Streich's the better performance is in the accuracy of reading and the greater ease she has in the very top part of the voice. Ivogün has a slight tendency to 'wisk' some of the high notes, she cuts one of the runs in two, misses some rests that are obviously meant to be there; there are just a few things of this kind, none gross, but adding up to make the performance something less than the absolute ideal that it very nearly is. I have an idea too that the trill on the high D is sometimes held up for wonder, but am afraid that I can't really hear it as a trill at all; she has a go at it, as does Adele Kern, but it seems much more sensible to do as Streich does and give the note its full tonal value rather than attempting what cannot be done.[1]

The record would still be a brilliant part of this imaginary recital. Ivogün has a charming lightness of touch; the staccato sparkles and is scattered like stars; the fearsome intervals are taken with an ease that seems almost reckless.

But the encores may be the best part of all. Her set of four folk-songs might seem the obvious choice, but charming as they are they are somewhat pale once one knows Schwarzkopf's performances of them, 'Gzätsli' especially with its too tame prettiness and faintly suspect intonation. No, for the encores we should go back to the pre-electricals and to almost any of the waltz songs she recorded: perhaps 'Il bacio' with its smiling pliancy, 'Liebesfreud' where the melody is wooed so beguilingly, or 'O schöner Mai' with its joyful agility and gloriously direct ascents on high. Perhaps we might end (for this is one of those recitals where encore-time spreads itself indefinitely) with both recordings of 'An der schönen blauen Donau': the pre-electrical fresh-voiced and sprightly, the later HMV version more

[1] That it *can* be done is demonstrated by the accomplished Maria Gerhardt, in an Odeon recording of 1924.

dreamy and luxurious in its phrasing-over. All sorts of wonders are performed in these records; and always the trills, scales, arpeggios and the rest of the traditional equipment seem to be there as the appropriate musical ways of lifting the heart and voicing the gaiety. Perhaps it is superficial music. At least it corresponds to the kind of pleasure we feel on a sunny morning with a free day ahead: a 'light' emotion, but a keen one, and not half as common as it ought to be.

If we now give less space to Lotte Schöne it is because so many of the same things would have to be said. Her voice on records is not unlike Ivogün's; the style has similar charm and the technique is almost equally impressive. She too captures happiness. The Viennese lilt is there just as one wants to hear it in her record from *Die Fledermaus* ('Mein Herr, was dächten Sie') and puts in a captivating appearance half-way through Despina's 'Una donna a quindici anni' from *Così fan tutte*. With a vivacity and grace not unlike that of Elisabeth Schumann, she might have been the ideal singer of Schubert's 'Der Hirt auf dem Felsen' but this is one of the rare disappointments among her records. The first section is repeated but the whole of the middle section omitted, and the last part becomes a scramble. The success of another near-triumph, Mistress Ford's solo in *Die lustige Weiber von Windsor*, is also limited. The singing is superb: with lovely purity over the extensive range, admirable facility, and again a charming Viennese touch in the 'Frohsinn und Laune' tune; but she rarely points the satire or lets the fun have its open laughter as Lotte Lehmann does.

Yet she could be an imaginative interpreter, as we find in some of her records from opera and in most of her Lieder. A good deal of hitherto unpublished Lieder was released in the year 1971, as a tribute to the singer celebrating her eightieth birthday. As expected, songs like Schumann's 'Nussbaum' and 'Mondnacht' are sung with all delicacy and lightness, and two songs of Brahms, 'Wie Melodien' and 'Das Mädchen spricht' have just the fresh-voiced warmth and clarity they need. There are also songs by Hugo Wolf, calling for more detailed pointing, and in these too Schöne gives fine performances. Oddly, it is not so much the humour of 'Mein Liebster ist so klein' that brings the best from her but the more sober mood and darker colouring of 'Trau nicht der Liebe', sung with the most beautiful diminuendos at the end of the phrases and with many delicate touches. But she is clearly the sort of singer who can establish contact with an audience: we feel it in the way she tells a story with face as well as voice in Wolf's 'Elfenlied', as well as some of the Christmas songs included in this album.

In her operatic recordings are three arias that pre-eminently show her quality as a lyric soprano. The Farewell from Massenet's *Manon* conveys emotion and urgency affectingly; Liù's 'Signore, ascolta' from *Turandot* remains the classic performance, touching as a characterisation, the last bars floated with heavenly lightness and perfect control; and I doubt whether anybody has recorded a finer performance of Pamina's aria, 'Ach, ich fühl's' from *Die Zauberflöte*.

The perfect voice for that music was probably that of Tiana Lemnitz, and certainly her recording is a fine piece of singing, the tone floating softly yet richly, the musical sensitivity always evident. If anything it is rather too beautiful: so etherial and disembodied a loveliness that it registers as an angelic utterance rather than a human one, and the suffering girl disappears. The principal disappointment of her Pamina as recorded under Beecham in 1937 is due, however, to the rather tremulous sound that limits satisfaction on several of her records. One would also like to hear her less inclined to take notes from below. These faults are a great pity for in so many ways she is one of the loveliest of sopranos. Her recording of the Countess' first aria, 'Porgi amor', from *Le Nozze di Figaro*, for example, becomes a thing of great beauty, but the opening is troubled by this same lack of a firm core; just as in Desdemona's music, where she is sometimes incomparably fine (the last bars of the 'Ave Maria', or the phrase 'Amen risponda' in the Love Duet are examples), there are unfocused regions where something dangerously like a wobble begins to threaten. It may be that the microphone exaggerates these characteristics, for she continued to sing in public another twenty years after these records were made and the reputation of her singing has only increased. We should also note that in 1937 she was already forty and had been singing professionally for at least thirteen years.

Thus it is to the pre-war rather than the later recordings that one tends to go for the full enjoyment of this most comforting of soprano voices. There are exceptions, most eminent among them very probably the *Trovatore* aria, 'D'amor sull' ali rosee'. This meets the technical challenges (the trills are excellent, the runs absolutely even) and, more important, brings the ideal instrument to the music (the sort of tone we were later to hear from Zinka Milanov). She also catches the mood: the rapt feeling of the aria itself, and the more anxious tenseness of the recitative. For Lemnitz was also a live interpreter. In some ways I still find her recordings of the 'Wesendonck' Lieder the most satisfying: after playing Christa Ludwig's performance conducted by Klemperer, one returns to Lemnitz singing with piano accompaniment, whether on 78 or the rather looser-voiced version on LP, and finds so much more intimacy and charm, so much more, for instance, that lifts 'Der Engel' from the earth and floats it heavenwards. One tends to forget too, with the vivid memories of her soft, floated tones uppermost in the mind, that she was a singer of the Wagnerian lyric roles, and that she could fill an opera house with a full-bodied, satisfyingly carrying tone when occasion demanded. This we hear in Elisabeth's Greeting from *Tannhäuser*, her first recording, made in 1934, and one of her best. Still, it is in different music that we most value her: in the tender, gentle phrases of Wolf's 'Wiegenlied im Sommer', and most of all in the two quiet and slow arias from *Der Freischütz*. It is in these that Lemnitz is a really great singer. The warm voice is supported by apparently inexhaustible breath, and there is a wonderful rightness in the lightening of voice at upward curves in the melody. Stillness and depth are caught in an almost holy purity of tone, which can shine and swell to a sound of considerable power, or reduce itself to the gentlest pianissimo without thinning the actual texture. This is *echt* Lemnitz, and a recording amongst the finest examples of a kind of singing that endears itself most readily to most listeners.

Of this kind of singing, another notable exponent was Emmy Bettendorf. She had a similarly warm, gentle tone and a comparable repertoire, but her operatic career in Germany was less exalted, and there was no Covent Garden or offer from the Metropolitan for her. Her records, at least one hundred and twenty strong, were issued on cheap labels, and for years were found on every page of the Parlophone-Odeon catalogue, looking like so much bread-and-butter and exciting little interest. Now they are gone, and we begin to listen afresh.

One needs to hear only a few phrases from the beginning of any record to recognise the beauty of voice. Perhaps after a little more listening one has also to note a certain sameness. How lovely the sounds she makes in Schubert's 'Heidenröslein', but at what a slow jog-trotting tempo; and has one ever heard a performance of 'Who is Sylvia?' at once so beautiful and so phlegmatic. In a nearly complete recording of *Frauenliebe und Leben* how tenderly she sings the comfortable E flat major melody of 'Du Ring an meinem Finger', but how she fails to capture the happiness of 'Er der herrlichste von allen' or the excitement of 'Ich kann's nicht fassen'. We almost conclude by putting her on her own in the more specialist class of the Wiegenlieder singer.

Yet there is a good full body to the voice, and she can use it to make effective contrasts, as in Senta's Ballad from *Der fliegende Holländer*, and the vivacity we have missed in the Lieder records is there in the Sachs-Eva duet from Act II of *Die Meistersinger*, her Sachs being the characterful Alfred Jerger. One of the most enchanting of all her records is also one of the happiest in mood, Waldteufel's 'Barcarolle', a piece with one tune after another, all of them graceful and captivating. Bettendorf was not a flawless singer (like Lemnitz she would often take notes from below, and unlike her would sometimes sing sharp), but she deserves a brighter place in gramophone history than the appearance of so many stodgy Parlophone black labels might suggest.

On those black labels were also about seventy records by one of the least stodgy singers in Europe, Meta Seinemeyer. This soprano had a remarkable personal following in Germany and an international public that would no doubt have multiplied rapidly had it not been for her death in 1929 at the age of thirty-four. At Berlin and Dresden, Seinemeyer nights were occasions. She was a versatile artist, deeply musical, and her voice had a way of moving its hearers by the very sound of it. Those who heard her frequently,

53. Maria Ivogün as Frau Fluth in
Die Lustige Weiber von Windsor

54. Meta Seinemeyer as Marguerite
in *Faust*

55. Sigrid Onegin

will often say that the emotional effect of her voice was quite extraordinary, and that records suggest only a part of it. Still, few lovers of singing will hear a Seinemeyer for the first time without experiencing something of the thrill that occurs rarely but unfailingly when one comes freshly upon the records of a great singer.

In England, the record that must have afforded most collectors that pleasant shiver of recognition is an arrangement of Liszt's third 'Liebestraum', coupled with a song by Rubinstein called 'Die Nacht'. The titles are not promising, but one has the sense of a singer giving her whole self to the song which in these circumstances sounds almost noble. A youthful freshness combines with the mature, dramatic richness of voice, and the emotional involvement, present in whatever she recorded, is always governed by taste and intelligence.

Most of her records are of nineteenth-century opera, but there are also a few songs, including 'Gretchen am Spinnrade' and 'Die junge Nonne', beautifully sung though with unpleasing orchestral accompaniments. She also recorded 'Dove sono', the Countess' aria from Act III of *Le Nozze di Figaro*, complete with the recitative. Hearing the young soprano from New Zealand, Kiri te Kanawa, who won as great an ovation as one has known at Covent Garden after she had sung this aria at the first performance in December 1971, it was Seinemeyer's record that came most vividly to mind, and perhaps the emotional effect here was comparable. The legato is perfect, the style aristocratic, the tone at its loveliest. Responsive to the changes of mood, Seinemeyer brings a radiance to the last section, a good trill too, and the difficult high As are finely poised. Her other extension to the basic nineteenth-century repertoire is less happy, through no fault of hers. She recorded in some excerpts from *Der Rosenkavalier* where the sound twitters with uncharacteristic shrillness. The label defines the playing speed as the customary 78 revolutions per minute, but at that speed the records run a good semitone high. Played correctly they turn out to be good performances, with Seinemeyer's opening phrases of the trio being particularly full-voiced and beautiful; but they may have done her reputation no good, for second-hand copies are frequently found and the fault in them is quite likely not to have been ascribed to its true cause.

A wrong playing-speed affects Seinemeyer's voice more seriously than most, for she had that kind of vibrato which becomes absurd if its already quick pulse is increased or if the basic tone-colour is artificially lightened, the tonal centre of the voice screwed up to something higher and thinner than its normal self. Her vibrato is perfectly regular, part of the resonance of a healthy voice, but when placed close to the microphone it can be obtrusive. It is so in the duet and trio from the last Act of *Faust*. On the other hand, when we hear her in truer conditions, as in the 'Vissi d'arte' from *Tosca*, it has all but disappeared. It then seems that Seinemeyer's voice is making a perfect 'column' of sound. Firm and economical, everything is transformed into pure, precisely directed tone, creating a kind of glamour which, like Spani's voice, has exactly the quality to fill the great soprano roles in Verdi.

Among her best records are arias from the operas of Verdi's middle period, which her contemporaries generally left under-represented in the old catalogues. Seinemeyer's is the only recording made in this period of 'Tu che le vanità', the great solo of Elisabeth de Valois in *Don Carlo*, and it is possibly the best of all. In 'Madre, pietosa vergine' *(La Forza del Destino)* and 'Ma dall'arido stella divulsa' *(Un Ballo in Maschera)* there is a similar warmth and bloom upon the voice; the interpretations are convincing and sensitive, while the style has a personal authority strengthened by close fidelity to the score. Her recording of the Willow Song from *Otello*, made pre-electrically, is another beautiful piece of singing, though, maddeningly, it ends before the great cry of farewell in which one would so like to hear this tense and dramatic tone. The other excerpt from *Otello* is the Love Duet, where Seinemeyer sings with splendid breadth and delicacy, while her partner, Tino Pattiera, chops his phrases, hurries the music along wilfully, makes a quivery start, bellows a normally quiet phrase such as 'la tua pietà', and yet manages to provide a fine and velvety *piano* for the still more important phrase, 'un bacio ancora' towards the end.

Pattiera was a puzzling singer, at least in the way he recorded. Since he sang with Seinemeyer on many triumphant occasions at Dresden and since the record company paired him resolutely with her in a series of duets (which, for the most part, he spoils), we should perhaps say a little more about him straightaway. The voice itself was of an unusual type, more Italian in its vibrancy than most tenors from other countries (he was Dalmatian by birth, with some Italian blood on his father's side), he still had a way of covering the tone that is very unItalian, and he rarely achieved that kind of flow that seems to be second nature to the latins. He is probably at his best in some solos from *Pagliacci*, vividly dramatised, exciting in the way he builds the climax to 'Un tal gioco', and quite beautiful in the soft phrases at the start of 'Vesti la giubba'. But he had a frustrating way of clipping his phrases, of not letting the vowel have its full value, of underlining notes by taking them from below, and of producing a rich sound that was spoilt by some kind of throatiness or constriction. One can hear it quite often as a really fine voice, and sometimes (as in duets from *Trovatore* with a stylish mezzo called Anka Vorvat) he will phrase with unexpected breadth. But generally speaking, the duets by him and Seinemeyer present us with some lovely soprano singing and a tenor who can be marvellous but is not.

Probably the most consistently satisfactory of their duets is the one from Act II of *Andrea Chénier*, and it is coupled with the end of the first Act in *La Bohème*, affording a glimpse of Seinemeyer's Mimì. When she sings 'vi sarò vicina' (but in German) it becomes a movingly profound declaration, and this feeling of depth in the character, the vocal timbre and the emotion pervades her recordings from *Madama Butterfly* too. But among the

Puccini heroines it is Tosca with whom we most associate this kind of dramatic authority, and Seinemeyer's 'Vissi d'arte' is certainly one of her finest performances. The definition of tone, breadth of phrasing, cleanness and smoothness of line, along with the rich, passionate ring of the voice all mark out unmistakeably one of the great lyric sopranos of our century.

If her name does not come as readily to the mind as it might, no doubt the tragedy of her early death is partly responsible, but almost certainly the fact that she did not record for HMV is another reason. There were many singers who remain as relatively provincial in the record collector's map because they did not arrive in the biographical section of the HMV catalogue in the pre-war years. That, together with a steady contract at the Metropolitan, New York, seemed to be the essential guarantee of an exalted status, and perhaps four times out of five the judgment was just and the map well made. Yet among sopranos other than those yet discussed there was the very charming Gitta Alpar, well heard in 'Voi che sapete', still better in 'Charmant oiseau', less acceptably in the Act I solo from *La Traviata* where she is too given to self-pity. There was Adele Kern, another light soprano, equally accomplished and more tasteful, excellent, as we have said, in Zerbinetta's solo from *Ariadne auf Naxos*, delicate in her Mozart, brilliantly accomplished in her Page's aria from *Les Huguenots* which she makes to sound as though written by Johann Strauss. There was also the excellent Luise Helletsgruber, better known in England through her association with Glyndebourne, though her roles in the Glyndebourne recordings of *Così fan tutte* and *Don Giovanni* do not represent her at her best. That best is heard in a variety of operatic arias recorded a few years earlier on the Parlophone label, vital and interesting enough to call Lotte Lehmann to mind. There is much of Lehmann's way with words and character in her singing of Micaëla's song in *Carmen*, and in the impulsive excitement of her 'King of Thule' changing into the Jewel Song in *Faust*. Entirely herself, she gives one of the most satisfying accounts on record of Liù's solos in *Turandot*: singing in German, she uses the language to make meaning press in on us while still preserving the lyricism, bringing out their special quality, full of human feeling but tender like some vulnerable animal, sensitive to the touch.

But a contract with the right recording firm was not enough always to win lasting public favour, even when a fine voice and great fame in the European opera houses went with it. This was proved by Maria Nemeth, the Hungarian soprano and one of the most exciting singers in the nineteen-twenties. An early Turandot, she had the right cold glitter to the voice, a certain steely determination when she comes to the climactic passage of the great solo, and superbly cleaving high notes. But she was a soprano of that rare kind, the lyric-dramatic who was also skilled in florid work. Thus her recording of 'Ach, ich liebte' from *Die Entführung aus dem Serail* is impressive in its technical control, and doubly so when placed next to the 'Ocean' aria from *Oberon*, where there is a clear brilliance of tone and energy that

reminds one of Ljuba Welitsch. Like Welitsch too, there is an individual
personality projected, and she has a way with well-known arias (such as
'Pace, pace, mio dio' from *La Forza del Destino*) that is all her own, born,
one feels, of an individual response rather than a study of other people's
conventions. Even so, all this (together with the lush tune of Goldmark's
Queen of Sheba solo, where the voice soars high above the chorus) did not
make an enduring place for Maria Nemeth in our catalogues. Perhaps the
cold glitter of the tone seemed too needle-sharp; perhaps the lower notes
were felt to be too weak and shallow; perhaps the energy took on a shrewish
force at times. Whatever the reason, the impressive series of records made
by Nemeth in the late twenties disappeared from view in the thirties, and
are now collectors' pieces of some rarity.

Another Maria, a still more famous Turandot, and a soprano still more
beloved of the Viennese, was Jeritza. She too made records that enjoyed a
shorter life in the catalogues than might have been expected in view of her
great fame and popularity. But the explanation here is fairly simple: they
are not really very good records, and they certainly do not represent at all
adequately the phenomenon that everybody recognised in Jeritza when she
sang on the stage. She was, for one thing, an exceptionally beautiful
woman and famous for her temperament as she was for her preference for
singing Tosca's 'Vissi d'arte' while lying on the floor. But she must also
have been a remarkable musician (creating many highly demanding roles,
such as that of the Empress in *Die Frau ohne Schatten*), and of this side of her
career very little is represented on records. Her recording of 'Es gibt ein
Reich' from *Ariadne auf Naxos* suggests something of her distinction
(she has an exquisite way of taking the 'Hermes' phrase, for instance),
but it also shows her as insufficiently accurate over note-values. More
surprising is it that so little character comes over in her records from the
more standard repertoire. The only exotic feature of her *Carmen* solos is
the French pronunciation; the only interest of her 'Vissi d'arte' is that it is
so very unremarkable. Just occasionally something is felt: Brünnhilde's
plea, 'War es so schmählich?', from *Die Walküre*, has much more presence
and intelligence. And, hearing the rather boxed-in, unflattering recordings
played on good modern equipment, one can recognise a powerful, pure
and steady voice: a finely unified tone, for instance, in the 'Adieux, forêts'
from Tchaikowsky's *Joan of Arc*. But records do not match reputation, and
by 1939 the English catalogue retained only one of them.

A soprano whose records did stay the course, and gained great popularity
during the thirties, was Miliza Korjus, and one who surely should have
gained more was Ria Ginster. The repertoire of each had a certain amount in
common. Both, for example, recorded that notable test-piece, 'Martern
aller Arten' from *Die Entführung*: both fluent in the scale passages, with
Korjus clean and decisive in style, certainly more dramatic, Ginster introducing a very lovely pianissimo. That pianissimo was lovely enough to
win its way into the affections of many more than those who bought her

records, one imagines: especially as in a recording which coupled lullabies by Schubert, Brahms and Reger, exquisite in the delicacy of inflections and the poise of tone. But Korjus was the one for the sales, partly no doubt because of an enchanting appearance in a film about Johann Strauss. It always used to seem to me that her high notes made the old gramophone rattle more than anybody else's, and I still hear the very highest as something of a squeak. But there are some good records, and until very recently she was still making them, for a recording company founded by herself and her husband. Among the best of the pre-war issues were the Prayer from *Lakmé* and an aria from *The Tsar's Bride* by Rimski-Korsakov, both of them lyric rather than 'coloratura' pieces.

Just how far one's map of the inter-war musical scene was made by the HMV record catalogue, by the status implied by the 'celebrity' red label, and by the ultimate accolade of inclusion in the biographical section at the end of the catalogue is suggested most of all by the contraltos. Asked to name inter-war contraltos one produces the three O's. Offers, Olczewska and Onegin: there they were, secure in their celebrity, red-labelled and biographically-noted. Alas, it is not possible now to hear Maartje Offers, the Dutch contralto, as the distinguished singer she was generally known to be. Records present a kindly voice, pleasant and ample in the upper regions, but not well supported by the breath which often seemed to be in short supply. Maria Olczewska also begins to fade from the top rank to which she once belonged. The creamy tone and beautifully floated high notes still give pleasure, the intelligence too; but so often one wishes for a firmer basis, a less matronly colouring, especially in her Octavian, the role by which she is most commonly remembered on records. An interesting extension to our knowledge of her singing comes through one of the private recordings made in the very earliest days of such things, in 1934. The opera was *Lohengrin* and the cast also included Rethberg, Melchior and Gustav Schutzendorf, an unsteady and unpleasing Telramund. Olczewska's duet with Rethberg in the second Act is extremely fine, and it is fascinating to hear her warm, smooth tone ringing out into the house in the Accusation Scene. Through the primitive recording, it still sounds a very unbiting kind of tone, but one is left in no doubt about the power behind it and its clear projection into the auditorium.

And one can have very few doubts either about the greatness of the third 'O', Sigrid Onegin. Even so she survives the changes and chances of taste and time with certain qualifications: very occasionally her intonation gives trouble, rather more frequently she sings with more use of portamento than most modern listeners will want to hear, and, probably the most frustrating limitation, she seems reluctant to let the tone ring out full, strong and vibrant. For examples of each of these: the second half of Brahms' *Alto Rhapsody* is productive of much wincing in listeners with a sensitive awareness of pitch; the aria 'Che farò senza Euridice' from Gluck's *Orfeo* indulges the taste for grand sweeping curves which in those days were often thought necessary to warm the classical composers out of their chilly formality; and the climax of 'O don fatale' from *Don Carlo* is constricted both in tempo and volume, the single disappointment of a classic performance.

The greatness, however, can hardly be missed. In the *Don Carlo* aria we hear just that velvety richness that the middle section ('O mia regina') enjoys otherwise only in our dreams. This was a most sumptuous voice, deep port-wine in colouring, and the smoothest velvet to the sense of touch. Erda's warning ('Weiche, Wotan') from *Das Rheingold* shows the quality well, and, although here too there is quite a lot of portamento, it also makes it quite clear that she could move from note to note with the accuracy of a keyboard instrument when she wanted to. In another Wagnerian warning, that of Brangäne from Act II of *Tristan und Isolde* it is another kind of instrument that comes to mind, a cello perhaps, or even a horn: an instrument where the notes are sustained with absolute steadiness, blending into the orchestration so that, even on a pre-electrical recording, we feel the fulfilment of Wagner's intentions in a way that modern recordings and performances have by no means made over-familiar. Attention to mood and meaning is not wanting either: in the *Rheingold* excerpt an ominous tone broods with a sense of the mystery moving through the orchestral harmonies in the earth and air around her, and her Lieder records, if not subtle in an intellectual, analytical way, are heartfelt and responsive, especially in the 'warmer' composers like Schumann and Brahms.

But so far this might still, in kind if not in quality, be almost any contralto; it might even suggest the rather plummy, old-fashioned type of contralto who has gone out of business lately without being too much missed. One corrective to this, as in the case of Dame Clara herself, is the Brindisi from *Lucrezia Borgia*: it displays a frisky sense of rhythm, a challenging flourish about the style, a strong, firm metal within the velvet, and a quite extraordinary flexibility. The technical equipment included a trill of the finest grain, exercised at great length complete with crescendo in this solo, and heard as a delicate and charming embellishment in a great many of her records. The song called 'Jeunes fillettes', for example, has a high trill taken pianissimo, and it introduces us to another of Onegin's skills, for it ends with the voice passing over the octave from middle to high A with perfect control and with the evenness of an instrument that has always been kept in prime condition. For a full demonstration of her mastery one goes either to the aria 'O prêtres de Baal' from *Le Prophète* or to a Chopin Impromptu that was specially arranged for her—and of course preferably to both. In the Meyerbeer aria there is a wealth of material for admiration: the fairy-like lightness of triplets, scales and trills in combination with the deep colouring, and also her imaginative handling of the music, the phrases moulded affectionately and with an intensity that has tragic depth to it. The Impromptu in A flat is a vocalise mostly sung to the word 'vieni'.

The delicate, intricate tracery of the first melody has the sure suppleness of a virtuoso of the violin, while the *sostenuto* of the middle section in minor key is the work of a Casals. The lightness of the many high B flats, the fullness of the low G, with trills and lithe chromatic runs: all are the work of one of the most accomplished technicians on record. And it would not be rash to suggest that among recorded contraltos hers is *the* most beautiful voice.

Two contraltos of this period who also reward efforts to seek them out are Emmi Leisner and Karen Branzell. Leisner was another true contralto, deep toned and rich, steady and powerful. She sang the usual roles in Wagner, and is most commonly remembered in this country by a recording of the Fricka-Wotan scene in Act II of *Die Walküre*. The middle register is gorgeous but the characterisation rather mild. Even so, one believes in her Fricka more readily than her Carmen or Dalila as recorded in excerpt. In the Final Scene from *Carmen*, sung in German, her partner is Helge Roswaenge, who is always personal and interesting, but on the whole he is singing to a voice, not to a Carmen. Her later records, made in 1933, show a voice that never betrays the age of its owner (she was 48), but also a style that does not seem to have developed in character or subtlety, and in the arias of Bach and Handel recorded in 1926 and 1928 the lovely voice is supported by dreadful orchestras and heard often as though coming through a mouth that is more than half-closed. There is no feeling of this kind with Branzell. Born in the same city (Stockholm) and the same year (1891) as Onegin, she too had a major part of her early career and her training in Germany, later joining the Metropolitan, New York, and staying there till 1946. It is in one of the stage performances there, recorded privately in 1937, that we hear her most impressively. Singing Ortrud's duets with Telramund and Elsa in Act II of *Lohengrin* she is able to show the fullness and ring of her voice when placed side by side with Kirsten Flagstad who is at the top of her form. In the studio some years earlier she had sung to the very different, very tender, Elsa of Emmy Bettendorf, and some few years earlier still she made a few pre-electrical records which stand comparison with Onegin herself. In the lament 'Ah, mon fils' from *Le Prophète*, Onegin is possibly more imaginative, but Branzell is both noble and gentle in feeling and does not use the somewhat embarrassing downward portamento for pathos as Onegin does. There is no doubt that Onegin will always be the greater wonder among these singers, but Branzell's firm edge and clean style will still be gratefully heard.

Branzell was another singer who recorded for the lesser companies and whose reputation among record collectors hardly caught up with her merit. But the habit of thinking of the Great Tradition as being embodied in the HMV catalogue is most inveterate when it comes to tenors. If we play the 'who-was-the-greatest?' game with a group of suitable people discussing tenors between the two world wars, the ring is first cleared for the celebrated contest Gigli v. Martinelli (or if we are in Italy it is Gigli v.

Pertile). Pleasant things and unpleasant are then said about Melchior, Lauri-Volpi and Schipa. Somebody would remember that McCormack was still active. Somebody else, English and anti-noise, might suggest that Heddle Nash was 'pretty good', and the more austere contributor, musical and anti-opera, could add that Karl Erb was 'very fine'. But they might converse loud and long and all at once without mentioning Richard Tauber, who has as strong a claim as any. There are two bad reasons for this omission, and one good one: he recorded for Parlophone-Odeon (the others for HMV), he was very popular and he sang quite a lot of rubbish. He also sang plenty of good light music as well as plenty of Mozart and Schubert and a wide range of opera, German, French and Italian. Indeed, his repertoire on records is the broadest of all the tenors under hypothetical discussion, and to whatever he sang he brought a more consistent combination of tonal warmth, charm, individuality, live feeling and musicianship than any of them.

Let us hear him afresh, first of all in some of the usual operatic stock-in-trade. For example, there are the two famous arias from *Tosca* about which we may think nothing new can be found under the sun. But there is the fact that 'Recondita armonia' is in 6–8 time, and that this can give it a lilt and buoyancy that will express the exaltation of an enthusiastic and happy lover. And in the other aria, the still more famous 'E lucevan le stelle', Tauber sings the opening phrases with an 'inner' tenderness very rare among his contemporaries, genuinely catching the tones of a man lost in reflection. Everything that he does is interesting and personal: there always seems to be some new insight into what the music can do. This newness never strikes one as cerebrated; there is no impression of a deliberate search for novelty, but on the contrary of a spontaneity that comes from a true absorption in the music he is singing. Yet no calculated effect could be more exact. His early recording of Don José's Flower Song in *Carmen* has precisely the right degree of unity and contrast, and it grows stage by stage to its climax. When the climax comes it is as Bizet directed, and that is rare indeed: Tauber floats the high B flat with a most beautifully gentle head-voice that emerges naturally from the main stream of tone (the recording of 1946 is different and much less satisfactory, but he was still singing the high phrase softly as late as 1939 as a private recording of part of a broadcast from Holland shows). He was a great technician, capable of many bold and even dazzling effects, but the essential thing about his technique was not the felicity of individual effects but the basic soundness of legato. His tone was splendidly steady, so that when he varied it or used it passionately there was no danger of notes getting out of focus, wobbling or losing pitch. In all of this he is the opposite of the Italian, Aureliano Pertile, yet Pertile's virtues are Tauber's too. We have a similar sense of possession and exaltation, and nowhere more than in this aria from *Carmen* where the control is also so perfect. The tender opening, the passionate caressing of the phrases, the darkening of voice in the middle

56. Richard Tauber as Antonio in *Don Juans letztes Abenteuer*

section, the sense that he is always singing *to* someone: all adds up to the most persuasive and poetic account of the aria.

His is also the most poetic recording of the Prize Song from *Die Meistersinger*. He catches the rapt, intoxicated mood, making the voice glow with restrained inner excitement. The other solo he recorded from this opera, 'Am stillen Herd', is also sung smilingly with a charming *mezza voce* for the opening, and an elegantly executed turn on the word 'hell'. He did not possess quite the power and stamina for major Wagnerian roles in the theatre but his few records are welcome as fresh air in those frequently charmless regions. In German opera, his stage roles included Max in *Der Freischütz* (a fine record of 'Durch die Wälder' made late in his career, and a still finer one among the privately recorded broadcasts of 1937), Bacchus in *Ariadne auf Naxos*, Florestan in *Fidelio* (no recording from either of these, unfortunately), Tamino and Don Ottavio. As a Mozart singer he won particular respect, and his career came to an honourable and indeed heroic end with a performance of *Don Giovanni* at Covent Garden in 1947. Part of this is on a private recording: an excerpt from the duet with Donna Anna (Maria Cebotari sounding unsteady and shallow in tone), 'Dalla sua pace' very finely sung, and 'Il mio tesoro' up to a few bars before the end. The last page of that notoriously difficult aria is sung with tremendous verve, and the semiquaver run has fine accuracy and bravura. For much that has gone before, his breath is insufficient; but of course he was a mortally sick man, and when he left the opera house it was to go to the hospital which he was never to leave—those records are in fact a moving testimonial to the endurance of mind, body and technique. Apart from the *Giovanni* arias recorded in 1939, his Mozart can also be remembered in the recording of arias from *Die Zauberflöte* and *Die Entführung* made a year earlier, and both of them especially delightful in the tender enthusiasm of their opening phrases. He was far bolder in Mozart than most tenors, using contrasted tone and volume, spreading the phrases freely yet tastefully, always alive, never dull.

This charm, authority and imagination, and especially his feeling for the lilt and joy of music, made him supreme in light opera. Perhaps *Les Contes d'Hoffmann* does not quite come into that category (certainly Hoffmann himself is by no means a light singing role), but the two solos which Tauber recorded provide fine examples of these qualities. In the aria from Act II his singing is blissfully warm and lyrical, with a pianissimo second verse that has the listener holding his breath in case the spell should be broken. In 'The Legend of Kleinsack' (the other solo) one also feels how the gaiety seems to come spontaneously out of the man. This feeling is present too in the famous concerted excerpt from *Die Fledermaus* with Lotte Lehmann, Branzell and others. Going at a fast tempo, the sway and charm of the 'Dui-du' passage are nevertheless marvellously infectious, and Tauber makes magic out of his solos. Nor should we shake our heads too censoriously over the devotion of this talent to lesser music. Tauber's association with Lehar provided him with the role he acted seven hundred times (a conservative estimate according to one American sleeve-note, which claims three thousand): that of the Prince Sou-Chong who sings 'Dein ist mein ganzes Herz' (or 'You are my heart's delight') in *Das Land des Lächelns*. A song almost equally inseparable from Tauber is 'Wien, du Stadt meiner Träume', the Opus 1, Number 1 of Dr. Rudolf Sieczinski, and of this too he made some irresistible recordings. Throughout the Second World War he recorded, month after month, popular ballads like 'I'll walk beside you' and 'Bless this house', often with glossy, inflated accompaniments. Perhaps we wish he had offered songs by Richard Strauss, or some more Mozart, but no doubt he kept the home fires burning much better as it was.

He did record songs by 'serious' composers, and often extremely well. In Schumann's 'Mondnacht', for instance, he shades very beautifully, and his record of 'Die Nussbaum' is remarkable for the whispering, sleepy *mezza voce* of the ending. The songs he recorded from *Der Winterreise* are not helped by the rather eccentric piano playing (as in 'Wasserfluth'), but his performances serve to remind us for once that the poet is a romantic and a lover. His pre-electrical record of 'Der Lindenbaum' is particularly welcome. A story is told, a real person is recognised. The branches of the linden-tree speak wooingly and we feel their magic: 'hier find'st du deine Ruh' they say, and we believe them. The tempo is gently eased at the right places, the tone is lightened in a way that exactly fulfils Richard Capell's demands for 'the dreamy quality of the finest mezza voce' in this song (it should be 'forbidden ground', he thinks, to anybody without the quality). There is a sense of drama, not overplayed, and the last phrase of the song is pure magic. Every Tauberlied a Zauberlied, as Irving Kolodin puts it.

Yet time has been a little unkind to Tauber. Because he did so well by Lehar and Johann Strauss, not to mention May Brahe and Oley Speakes, he came almost to be forgotten as a singer of great music. But his 'discography' (a vast document, numbering well over seven hundred recordings) contains an impressive array of arias, Lieder and duets, nearly all of them offering some musical pleasure and insight, quite apart from the rich and individual timbre of his voice. They contain faults, of course: the exaggerated Viennese 'ei' sound can become tiresome, the distortion of other vowels too; occasionally the originality of his readings leads him astray. Nevertheless, the consistency of Tauber's records is as remarkable as their distinction. There are few tenors who have left a better legacy.

One thing he was not: 'inimitable' is the word constantly tagged to his name, yet his marked personal style invited imitation, and, on records, there are at least two excellent tenors who could often be mistaken for him. They were probably not imitating consciously, for both were fine singers in their own right; but in repertoire, style and timbre there was a close resemblance. To Herbert Groh went Tauber's parts in operetta, and to Marcel Wittrisch his operatic roles (and of course there was much interchanging). Groh had a light, easy lyric tenor which recorded very pleasantly. He sang what was in his voice and did it with impeccable control and polish. His duets with Emmy Bettendorf (especially the Garden Scene from *Faust*) are models of lyrical singing, and there is hardly a better record of its kind than his 'Komm' in die Gondol' from *Ein Nacht in Venedig*. Wittrisch had much of this grace, as we hear in one of Tauber's own favourite operatic arias, 'Adieu, Mignon' (though, following Wittrisch's excellent recording with Tauber's performance in one of the 1937 broadcasts is again to marvel at the magician—just that extra degree of imagination and immediacy of communication that make an almost unfair amount of difference). With an exciting voice, capable of ringing out powerfully and rising to fearsome heights, Wittrisch makes a particularly strong impression in the Raoul–Marguérite duet from *Les Huguenots*. He sings with Margarethe Teschemacher, and together they draw a fine line of sound in the long, languorous phrases, complete with high D flat for the tenor. It is one of the most thrilling of operatic records, the very essence of nineteenth-century grand opera.

There are other tenors it would be a pity to forget (Joseph Schmidt, a prolific recording artist and a great favourite until the Nazi persecution; Rudolf Gerlach-Rusnak, a little of whose strange voice goes quite far enough, I find, though he possessed unusual flexibility and a trill) and two more who are certainly unforgettable (and there are also the Wagnerians, who will be discussed in a later chapter).

Helge Roswaenge is the first of these, remembered in England chiefly for his singing of Tamino in the pre-war recording of *Die Zauberflöte* under Sir Thomas Beecham. But this is unfortunate, for he was badly miscast. An ungainly Tamino, he was a splendid Florestan or Canio, and many of his records leave no doubt that he ranks among the best heroic tenors of the century. In the solo (Arrigo's aria) and duet from *I Vespri Siciliani* he displays a fiery energy and clear-cut tone. The brilliant resonance of his top notes, the evenness of his production at this time, and his emotional responsiveness to the surge of melody make these particularly exciting records. Nor was he without finesse and a sense of style that would sometimes serve him perfectly well in Mozart: he gives a smiling and affectionate account, for example, of 'Un' aura amorosa' from *Così fan tutte*. The depth of feeling of which he was capable is clear in his singing of Florestan's great solo in *Fidelio*: he holds back at the modulations in the last section so as to contain the excitement, and when release finally comes it is as from unbearably accumulated emotion. He could still sing it movingly when he was over sixty, with voice finely preserved as a recorded concert in 1959 shows, and we read of audiences cheering him for twenty minutes on end when he was well into his sixties. But essentially we should remember him from some marvellous recordings made on 78s before the war, when, for example, he could give the strenuous virtuoso performance asked of Weber's hero in *Oberon*. Or if one wants a really joyous display of vocal athleticism, the song from *Postillon von Longjumeau*, its velvety tones alternating with the ringing full voice, the gaiety, the grace, and, not least, the two superb high D's. He is one of those singers whose acquaintance becomes a greater pleasure as time goes by.

Possibly this is less true of the other tenor to be discussed here. Yet the devotion of the Viennese audience to Alfred Piccaver, English born and of Spanish lineage, reared in America and trained in Italy, lasted over a period of thirty years and is no doubt alive still among those who remember him. Knowing him only through his records, one may begin with admiration (the beautiful voice, the steady production, the delectable legato), but very soon irritations begin to accumulate. For example, his vowel sounds are curious: sometimes oddly closed-up, or nasal, or sideways-sounding. This dampens the ardour, which is further affected by a casualness and sometimes even an inaccuracy in the style and reading. He is sometimes wilful with tempo and note-values, and the liberties are not generally well-judged. This is so in the electrical recording of 'Ah si, ben mio' from *Il Trovatore*, where there is also a lack of tonal variety and of resonant life in the high notes. It is rare to feel that he is interpreting or experiencing the music keenly: Pinkerton's farewell in the last Act of *Madama Butterfly* has breadth and smoothness and a sort of generalised emotion, but a comparison with Tauber's record shows how much is missing. Tauber responds with a live musicianship, and his legato, while being quite as pure as Piccaver's, is much more supple and interesting. Andrew Porter, as usual, finds the right word for his style: 'It is slack-muscled'. He goes on to look up what Puccini had to say on the subject (Piccaver was singing Puccini's *Manon*) and finds that he too had a word, *squadrato*, 'square'. This is in the course of a review in *The Gramophone* of a Piccaver recital on LP, a record which left the critic with little desire to hear more of the singer.

But of course there is more to be heard. The records on that particular recital were made in the early nineteen-thirties, and they are probably his worst. He began recording in 1912, and the records made then are probably the best. One listens to him in 'Parmi veder le lagrime' *(Rigoletto)* and realises one has never heard a true legato in the music before; or in 'Ah, lève-toi, soleil' *(Roméo et Juliette*, sung in German) and realises how effortful most tenors sound by comparison. His singing in these is both elegant and expressive, handling the melodies tenderly, and producing his voice with an openness of sound that one misses more and more as one follows him through the years. The 1914 series also brought fine things, including some more from French opera: the *Mignon* arias exquisitely sung, and the Invocation from *Werther* ideally, dreamily poetic. Fire and passion are rare with him, but the early version of 'Ch'ella mi creda libera' *(La Fanciulla del West)* has something very close to both. Perhaps most impressive of all is his singing of the 'Ingemisco' from Verdi's *Requiem*. Taken slowly, the phrases beautifully moulded, the tone varied, gentle in the right places yet fervent too—it has all the virtues. He goes straight to the G in the word 'supplicanti' where a slovenly portamento so often intervenes; he sings the broad phrase 'Qui Mariam exaudisti' affectionately and without aspirates; the diminuendos at 'parce deus' and 'spem dedisti' are observed and are exceedingly beautiful. All this is the work of a genuinely distinguished singer. There is plenty to remember, as well as a certain amount to forget, among Piccaver's recordings.

The perfect legato that Piccaver offered at his best was habitual with another singer who enjoyed great popularity and a long career in Germany and Austria. If Battistini had a successor, that man was Heinrich Schlusnus, and again we observe that it is a German who upholds an Italian tradition. With that kind of economical, well-defined baritone voice, he was easy in the high register, less happy in the lower, always firm and smooth, and without any suspicion of unsteadiness. While his singing is not as exciting as some of Battistini's, it compensates by being unmannered and unforced. And again like Battistini, the long preservation of his voice showed the soundness of his production.

In August 1951 he recorded Mahler's *Lieder eines fahrenden Gesellen*: he was then sixty-three, and it was in the following year that he died. He is placed very close to the microphone, and one cannot be sure how much sheer power there is in the voice. But one can inspect its texture; and it invites such inspection because it is perfect. There are no lumps and wrinkles; everything is smooth and unpressurised. Equally impressive is the energy of the third song, 'Ich hab ein glühend Messer', where the voice takes on a sharper edge. He also catches the autumnal feeling in the cycle, murmuring the last phrases of the final song touchingly, after a most lyrical and sweet-toned performance: a moving farewell to the public and the recording studios, and a timely reminder of what singing really means.

On the same record were a number of songs by Strauss, Brahms and Schubert, recorded a year earlier. In these too it is unthinkable that we are listening to a singer in his sixties, so very firm and beautiful is the voice. 'Der Atlas', for example, is not a song one readily associates with so very lyrical a singer, but how welcome that lyricism is: he intensifies the tone until it has true heroic ring, yet there is never an uneven vibration. The beauty of his soft singing is heard well in the end of 'Der Jüngling an der Quelle', and the grace and warm feeling in his style make an extremely lovely record out of 'Nachtstück'. Even so, the interpretations seem to me to be general rather than precise and specific. He does not focus attention upon meaning. For example, I listen to the other song in the Schubert group, 'An schwager Kronos', without a copy of the music or the words: I cannot remember what the song is about, and he does not make me wonder. There are many beauties among his Lieder, it is true. Two songs of Wolf that enjoyed much popularity through his recording (second-hand copies turn up frequently) are 'Verschwiegene Liebe' and 'Er ist's': the first is smiling and magically controlled in the soft high phrases, and the second is light and agile, a short and joyful end-of-recital piece. I think that if I was a singing teacher, I would send my baritones to records of

Schlusnus more often than to the records of any other singer; but it would not be for the interest of the interpretations.

Sometimes, however, the relative simplicity of style is a strength. A reissue of the *Tannhäuser* recording in which he sang Wolfram appeared some few years ago at the same time as another performance in which the part was sung by Dietrich Fischer-Dieskau, and the two versions of 'O du, mein holder Abendstern' made an interesting comparison. Fischer-Dieskau introduced much subtlety and a wide variety of dynamics, perhaps with the feeling (this is what it imparted) that there must be life in the limp, velvet-cushioned old melody if one could only bring it out. But it all seemed misdirected effort, and to return to Schlusnus was to find the ears unexpectedly satisfied by a grace and firmness that needed nothing more. Moreover, it was the old voice that sounded finely, evenly grained, while the younger one emerged in the comparison as of a rougher texture altogether.

But comparisons will nearly always favour Schlusnus in that respect. If one wants, for instance, to hear how Rigoletto's monologue, 'Pari siamo', can be beautiful to listen to as well as dramatic, then again one goes to an early recording (in Italian) by Schlusnus. There is plenty of spirit and a good deal of attention to crescendo and diminuendo markings, but all is done on the primary principle that the voice is a musical instrument and that it must be used with respect for its beauty. This is so in much Italian music where one is quite accustomed to a barnstorming style, and an overspilling, vibrating tone. The duet from Act IV of *Il Trovatore*, with Frida Leider, has di Luna's music finely pointed, sonorous and energetic, but never over-pressed or throaty. His weakness certainly lay in the lower part of the voice: it is slightly comical in Strauss' 'Zueignung' to hear the high note taken with such freedom to be followed by an almost unvoiced low one at the end of the phrase. And stylistically he shared the general liking at that time for more portamento than is in favour today. But he represents a very high point of achievement in this history of singing, and particularly of German singing: a measure of the response, perhaps, to Wagner's demand half-a-century earlier for singers trained in the lyrical style that was then thought of as essentially Italian.

57. Heinrich Schlusnus as Di Luna in *Il Trovatore*

15. Lieder: More than Singing
Elisabeth Schumann   Lotte Lehmann
Elena Gerhardt   Karl Erb
Herbert Janssen   Gerhard Hüsch
Alexander Kipnis

THE flourishing condition of singing in Germany during this period becomes still more impressive when one reflects that two important groups of German singers remain to be discussed. One is the Wagnerians, who belong to the next chapter; and the other is the Lieder singers. Of course, the categories were not mutually exclusive, as this might suggest. Several of the singers already mentioned had an extensive repertoire of song as well as opera, and most of the Lieder specialists were themselves famous opera singers too. Schlusnus, the great baritone discussed at the conclusion of the last chapter, devoted a large part of his career to song-recitals; but, as we noted at the time, the art of Lieder singing (and perhaps on records particularly) requires a very special gift for interpretation and vivid presentation. Fine as his song recordings are, they do not leave one thinking about the song, they do not point towards specific musical and literary meaning, and only to a limited extent do they establish personal contact or create a vivid impression of the singer's own personality. A certain part of the Lieder singer's province is left vacant, and to fill it we turn to others.

To Gerhard Hüsch, for example. Hüsch may not have possessed a voice with quite the individuality and distinction of Schlusnus, but it was a good one, produced with absolute steadiness, and serviceable over a large range. He brought some of the gifts of a Lieder singer to his operatic performances too: to the bland, snakelike 'Era la notte' from *Otello*, the subtly shaded, vividly projected 'Pari siamo' from *Rigoletto*. His singing of Papageno in *Die Zauberflöte*, recorded in the complete opera conducted by Beecham, and also represented by three excerpts in some splendid recordings made a few years earlier for Parlophone–Odeon, is sprightly and resourceful without being in the least arch or facetious. He also sang with a fine legato, so that gentle music like Wolfram's 'Blick' ich umher' from *Tannhäuser* or the 'Berceuse' from *Mignon* finds in him something like the ideal singer, for along with much loveliness of sound goes the tenderly imaginative touch of an artist who has mastered the problems of communication in the more intimate conditions of the song-recital.

Yet it shows just how much concentration is needed for great Lieder singing when one becomes aware that an opera singer as full of character and insight as this does still not impress as having sounded the depths of his Schubert and Wolf. What he does and does not do are represented well in a record that couples two of Schubert's best-known songs, 'Der Musensohn' and 'Der Wanderer'. The first is precise and lively, full of variety and charm, and the second is extremely well vocalised. But 'Der Wanderer' is a profound song, and not merely a pleasant one. When Fischer-Dieskau sings it it encompasses a world of experience, and his echoing of the words 'Immer wo?' is long-drawn, breathed from the innermost feelings, the tragic ghost of a hope. Nothing like this is communicated by Hüsch, though the singing is beautiful and often sensitive. Perhaps in a single song the limitations are not too insistent; but in among the sustained profundity of *Die Winterreise* they become inescapable. As Hüsch is singing, one can often hear the agonised colouring of other performances running simultaneously in one's head (I am thinking of such songs as 'Der greise Kopf' or 'Letzte Hoffnung'), but little more than a pleasant seriousness can be heard coming from the gramophone.

We go to Hüsch's Lieder records essentially for two reasons. One is that when charm and grace are wanted he is perfect. He sings 'Auf dem grünen Balkon' exquisitely, with a smiling lightness, pointing the words with grace and humour, and not overplaying. Or he is again at his best in another song by Wolf, his setting of Goethe's 'Epiphanias', the strange poem about the comical Magi who liked eating and drinking but not paying the bill: Hüsch changes his voice and his face vividly for the pompous large King and the grotesque little one. The other reason for his continuing value is that he is always an extremely good singer: in the even production of fine tone and in the negotiating of technical difficulties he can give lessons to most. He will always delight the musical ear. But he rarely haunts the memory, so like Schubert's Wanderer we have to look further. 'Immer wo?' indeed.

A rich and rare voice was Herbert Janssen's. Of itself it carried a depth of feeling, a dramatic, very individual character, extending this baritone's possibilities beyond Hüsch's lighter emotional range. In his own time he was the singer best fitted for Wolf's 'Harfenspielerlieder', the painful, neurotic chromaticism of which seemed morbid even to Delius, when he heard Janssen's recordings played to him by Elgar on a visit to Grez-sur-Loing. There was an unusual velvety cover to the tone: a quality that was doubly remarkable in that he was able to combine carrying-power with this kind of softness. His method of production had its drawbacks, for there was also a gentle vibrato which every now and then combined with the soft tone to queer the pitch. In a passage of close intervals one is not always in absolute certainty about the note. For example, the first phrase of 'Der Doppelgänger' is all on one note, yet Janssen rises sufficiently on the second word of the phrase ('Still ist die Nacht') to send one to the score to check.

Then, although he apparently kept his voice to the end of his life, in early seventies, records do seem to me to show a quite marked decline during the nineteen-forties (I find it difficult to recognise in the Pizarro of Toscanini's *Fidelio* or in the Jokanaan of Welitsch's Metropolitan *Salome* the singer whose earlier records I have loved so much). Of course, he was then in his fifties and he had in those later years been persuaded to sing Wotan in *Die Walküre* and Sachs in *Die Meistersinger*, both of them heavy roles for his voice. On the other hand, there is no doubt at all about the rare kind of distinction which Janssen enjoys among singers on record—he is one of those who inspires affection, for his voice and style were highly personal and unusually beautiful.

To hear him at his best we could well go to the roles in Wagner which he made so very much his own during the best years of his career. His Wolfram was greatly admired and we can hear why in a recording from the Bayreuth Festival of 1930. His Gunther and Kurwenal have a similar beauty of tone apparent in the private recordings from Covent Garden performances, but most valuable of all these is the one which preserves with striking vividness his singing of the Dutchman in a performance of *Der fliegende Holländer* with Kirsten Flagstad in 1937. One can hardly think that 'Wie aus der Ferne', the aria from Act II, has ever been so beautifully sung as it is here. The *mezza voce*, soft-grained and perfectly firm in the unaccompanied passage, clothes the final phrase with a glory of quietness, warmth and richness; and indeed the whole aria is most beautifully shaped. Sometimes, in more strenuous passages, the voice submerges, but nothing tempts him into an explosive style, or into the way, rather more common nowadays, of hitting the note as it were over the head. In the first aria, 'Die Frist ist um', he builds to an intense climax, and one can judge the stamina, the toughness which preserved this voice as a refined and beautiful instrument, in the ringing tones which he can still produce at the end of this exceptionally demanding first Act. There is plenty of emotion in this portrayal too, but it is conveyed by essentially musical means, the play of the ringing virile tone to express the external authority that the man must have, alternating with the entirely personal soft tones which are so appropriate to the haunted, indrawn character in his loneliness.

Here again the intelligence of a Lieder singer is brought to opera, along with a warm, finely disciplined Italianate lyricism: it is the best of combinations. And of course when we come to the Lieder records themselves, it is to find much in which he is excellent. For present purposes let us take two songs by Schumann and one by Wolf. The familiar Janssen is present in Schumann's 'Die Lotosblume': the softness of voice is ideal, so too the finely judged, very gradual growth in tone to the still gentle climax at the words 'und zittert'. The tenderness of this and the eloquent enthusiasm of the song with which it is coupled on the 78 disc, 'Widmung', show something of the expressive range he could command. It is notable too how in this song, where the modulations have a special poignancy, the singer colours his tone in sympathy with the changing harmonies. Wolf asks for this kind of subtlety with more insistence than Schumann, and the short song 'Denk' es, o Seele' shows how sensitive Janssen's response could be. 'There's a fir-tree growing somewhere', says the poet, 'a rose-tree too. Already it is fated that they will adorn your grave—think of that, o soul'. Janssen's quiet singing always has reserves of depth in it, so the transitions of mood that the song demands can be made naturally. In the second verse, the impulse of music and poem grows, and the tone hardens as the possibility ('vielleicht, vielleicht') of death grows into certainty, while the horses' hooves glisten and clatter, drawing the poet's body to his funeral. A sharply edged but full-bodied tone can shoot out of the customary velvet, and with it grows conviction of the singer's personal involvement. There are limits to Janssen's art (the comparison discussed on p. 563 illustrates them), but as with Gérard Souzay, his nearest counterpart among later singers of Lieder, the fact of a beautiful voice and a smooth line does not preclude depth and insight. They are plentifully present in his many records.

Hüsch and Janssen were useful singers to have on hand when early in the nineteen-thirties HMV began to record the songs of Hugo Wolf extensively and systematically. A pearl of possibly still greater price was one of the small number of great basses on record, Alexander Kipnis.

Kipnis was a miracle among singers. The voice itself was grandly sonorous, flowing like some great river over its easy two-octave compass. The taste with which it was used rarely seemed to falter, and the directing musicianship led it into Mozart and Wagner, Moussorgsky and Debussy, Verdi and Rossini, Schubert, Brahms and Wolf, all with fine results. For a sample of what his voice could do we might take one of his best-known records, Osmin's song, 'Wer ein Liebchen hat gefunden', from *Die Ent-führung* where the extremes of a bass's range touch. Down to the cavernous depths we go: low B flat, A, G. Then straight to the high D, which with Kipnis sounds as easy as though it lay in the centre of his voice. It is perfectly placed, and, coming after the full-voiced low G, light as a feather: it is a matter of unceasing wonder how this bottomless immensity can 'roar you as gently as any sucking dove' and combine so wonderfully delicacy and might. Perfect legato is offset by the bite and menace of diction (suitable to the character concerned) in verses two and three. When such opulence, depth and nobility as we hear in Sarastro's solos from *Die Zauberflöte* are put to work at a comic presto, we might expect something to be lost (either the tone or the comedy), but in Doctor Bartolo's Vengeance Aria in *Le Nozze di Figaro* we have another wonder, for Kipnis performs his patter with the neatness of a D'Oyly Carte Major-General, characterising with enjoyment, not losing true singing-tone yet going at high speed, using a semi-staccato style where appropriate, contrasting the lightest of touches with the deep magnificence that one always knows to be there in reserve. This Bartolo is also a distinctive piece of vocal acting, like his Sarastro, Boris Godunov or Baron Ochs, whom we glimpse for

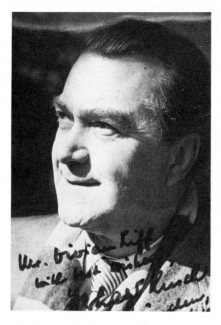

58. Gerhard Hüsch   59. Herbert Janssen as Escamillo in
                                     Carmen

60. Alexander Kipnis as King Mark
    in *Tristan und Isolde*

one vivid passage at the end of Act II: a full-blooded, fat, complacent relish, to which the fine manners of voice and style give a proper aristocratic polish.

He was also distinguished in what he sang of Italian opera. His recording of Fiesco's 'Il lacerato spirito' from *Simon Boccanegra* has a superbly dignified sonority, and the great aria of Philip II in *Don Carlo* is treated in an unusual way, with a bitter, rather snarling manner instead of the introspective melancholy of most performances. Kipnis in Wagner is well represented by the early recording of Wotan's Farewell discussed in some comparisons on p. 584 but there are also private recordings of live performances given at the Metropolitan in the early nineteen-forties. One of them presents him as surely the best of all King Marks, in *Tristan und Isolde* under Erich Leinsdorf. The spirit of the whole performance (Leinsdorf's, one would imagine) is get-on-with-it-and-no-nonsense, and just occasionally Kipnis is a little explosive or given to snarling the vowels rather too much; but his tone and legato, and especially his singing of the last phrases of the long solo, still seem incomparably fine.

With all this, we tend to forget that he is a Russian singer, and the recorded reminders are not, on the whole, particularly attractive parts of his output. Some Russian songs made in 1939 show the voice still in its prime, but a little after this the studio recordings began to emphasise a roughness in the vibrancy, a looser texture, and growing tendencies to aspirate disturbingly and occasionally to sing very slightly below the note. Much better than the studio recordings from *Boris Godunov* made about 1946 are the privately reproduced excerpts from a Metropolitan performance of 1943. This is powerfully voiced, with some exquisite moments of pianissimo singing. The excellence of legato makes acceptable and doubly effective the freely pitched declamation. His is the kind of Boris somewhat out of favour at present, where Petrov and Ghiaurov, for example, win high marks for the restraint of their style and their reducing of the declamatory element as far as possible. But something is lost in that toned-down, 'normalised' way of doing it; Kipnis *sounds* like an Eisenstein film, and something very dramatic, and very Russian, is gained.

But not even with him have we come upon a perfect singer. Turning to the Lieder records, we meet, among the many beauties, a few that are less happy. 'Heidenröslein' finds him aspirating freely, and indulging in too much portamento. It is, on the other hand, marvellous that the voice could be lightened sufficiently to cope with the song in the way he does; as is true also of 'Wie glänzt der helle Mond' by Wolf. This was one of Elisabeth Schumann's songs. She would sing it in concerts after the war when her voice was a slender thread, that in this song would shine out as pure silver, like the moon in the poem. Hers was the right kind of voice, and many buyers of the Wolf Society album in which the song was included must have been mildly astonished that it was given not to one of the sopranos (Lemnitz might have been ideal), nor even to one of the baritones, but to the basso profundo. Kipnis does wonders, but he cannot quite prevent his voice from making those tiny breaks at the end of words, a faintly audible, split-second explosion of sound that slightly but perceptably weakens the spell and makes one concerned for the singer. Yet later, the last, whimsically mystic phrases of the song gain from the richness and depth of the bass voice, while the very last notes are most beautifully lightened and shaded.

Many of his recordings of Wolf are entirely excellent. Three short Eichendorff poems go together on one side of a record: there is 'Der Musikant', smooth but rhythmical and jaunty, then 'Der Soldat' with its pleasantly snarling curl of the lip at the thought of the marrying-type of woman, and finally 'Der Schreckenberger', a thumbnail character-sketch, vivid as, say, Chaliapin presenting Prince Galitsky. Contrasted with these is 'Sterb' ich so hüllt in Blumen meine Glieder'. The lulling, gently syncopated music transforms the poet's rather sickly Liebestod into a deeper wooing of easeful death, and Kipnis' singing, with its flow of soft, rich sound, catches the repose and affection as well as the dark undertones: and with miraculous gentleness in the last lines of the song.

To better purpose still, this dark sympathetic voice was employed by the Brahms Song Society to record the *Vier ernste Gesänge*. In post-war years the work has been recorded perhaps as finely by the Chinese bass, Yi-Kwei Sze (finely, that is, in terms of beautiful tone combined with generally sensitive singing), and it scarcely comes as a surprise to learn that this bass is himself a great admirer of Kipnis. For Kipnis' performances are as good as a whole course of master-classes. The second song, for instance, opens with a magical gentleness which expands with its natural warmth, dying down like a glowing fire to a *mezza voce* that is still round and rich. In 'O Tod, wie bitter bist du', the range of shading, from bitterness to tenderness, is incomparably moving. In these songs, as in others of the album (there is, for instance, a most winning performance of the 'Ständchen'), the singing has surely just the correct balance, so difficult to achieve, between interpretative word-shading and preservation of a fine voice production.

The question of this balance is a problem very much at the heart of Lieder singing. Everyone knows that what tends to be called 'mere vocal excellence' is not enough. *More than Singing* was the title of a small handbook on Lieder-singing by Lotte Lehmann, and naturally the emphasis in the book is upon interpretation, with the natural gifts and technical ability of the singer taken for granted. But sometimes vocal poverty is overlooked in favour of some other kind of strength: a 'spiritual' strength perhaps, which certainly may be real enough, but may possibly be only a fancied or even a wished-for quality. Everyone likes to feel himself to be a good judge, and recognition of an excellence that calls for special discernment is a gratifying experience. So Lieder singers with beautiful voices have sometimes found it hard to gain acceptance in these narrow ranks.

Victoria de los Angeles, for example, was singing her Schubert and Brahms with feeling and intelligence years before she was admitted to the select company, and it sometimes seemed that, because her voice was so exceptionally beautiful, critics felt there must be something wrong—she could not be a Gerhardt yet. Now Gerhardt had of course created the image of the great Lieder singer during these years, and when we listen to her records, it is not really to the voice, but rather *through* it (and its defects) to the song. She, with her less than steady voice and less than perfect intonation, was a great Lieder singer, and there has followed from this a tendency to place interpretation at the head of the priorities for greatness in the field, and beautiful tone at the bottom. Singers then take it that what they must do is to get down to the text, underline things in their score, pop out this significant word with consonants a-clatter, and breathe out that one in a grey whisper. Colouring the tone will often mean taking the harmonics out of the voice and sitting on the flat side of the note. And all this interferes with the production of beautiful sound. None of the singers so far studied allowed much to interfere with the beauty of their tone: possibly this is, after all, a limitation of their art. The balance is extremely fine, and finally personal taste is the arbiter for each individual. But it is notable that of all the singers discussed in this chapter, the two singers most exclusively connected with Lieder—Elena Gerhardt and Karl Erb—come much more closely than the others to satisfying a taste which places beauty of tone (or at any rate a conventional beauty) low among the priorities.

Karl Erb had made operatic records for Odeon in the pre-electric period, including some duets with his wife, Maria Ivogün. His part in these is not generally found attractive: the voice seems bloodless, and, though musicianship is evident, the style is not graceful. But years later, when he was well on towards sixty, there came a series of Lieder records among the finest of all.

It was an extraordinary voice and hard to compare: one can hear a suggestion of it in the latest Lieder records of Ernst Häfliger, and perhaps more often in Peter Pears (or Pears as he sings the Evangelists of the Bach Passions or Peter Grimes' 'Now the Great Bear'). Presumably Thomas Mann had his voice in mind when he describes the soloist's work in the fictitious first performance of Leverkühn-Faustus' *The Apocalypse*. He says that the singer ('Erbe', performing under 'Klemperer' in '1926') had an almost castrato-like high register whose 'chilly crow' and 'piercing communications' were masterly, and showed that the singer had 'with the greatest intelligence grasped the idea'. Few singers can have been handed down to posterity with this kind of tribute.

The tribute itself suggests that this is not the most comfortable of singers to listen to. On records, his famous account of the Evangelist's music in the *St. Matthew Passion* becomes somewhat trying because of the singing (as opposed to the interpretation); and in a song like Beethoven's 'Adelaide' he lacked the necessary youth and gainliness. Yet in Wolf's 'Nun wandre,

Maria' (discussed also in some comparisons on p. 608) the tone of voice, pained and full of patient tenderness, matches the poignant harmonies perfectly; the loving solicitude and sense of holiness are touching almost to tears. Another of Wolf's Geistliche Lieder, 'Schlafendes Jesuskind', was coupled with this on the old 78, and this too catches the holiness and stillness most beautifully. *Sehr innig* says a direction in the score, and Erb is the perfect interpreter here. He achieves a rare other-worldliness in the last phrases of this song in response to the composer's unusually explicit direction *wie in tiefes Sinnen verloren*. How uncharitable to add that there are two descending passages where he reminds one gently but disconcertingly of one of the old gramophones running down; but it is faintly so, even after a few playings have accustomed one to the effect.

Still, the record is a treasure, as are the two songs of Schumann which were also coupled by Richard Tauber, 'Der Nussbaum' and 'Mondnacht'. In 'Der Nussbaum' Erb is distinguished beyond Tauber in that he tells a story: that is, with the intimacy of communication which a great Lieder singer can establish, he gives us the poem as though all afresh out of himself and newly for our delight at this particular time. He captures the lilt, the sense of a breeze blowing lightly through the song, and also its fragility and delicacy. And he makes incomparable magic out of 'Mondnacht'. At his best in creating just such atmosphere as this song requires, he does it to even more memorable effect in 'Das Fischers Liebesglück' by Schubert. This is an especially haunting song, little of whose wonder is apparent as

61. Karl Erb as Palestrina

one looks casually at the notes on paper. A song of happiness, it is neverthe-less one of an unusual kind. The fisherman sings to his mistress in a minor key, hoping that she may come to the boat where the night mists will surround them so that they may weep and laugh together as the world fades from view. Erb feels the longing in the Liebesglück, the melancholy colours of the painting; and he sings the song in the extraordinarily high key of B minor, producing a still remoteness as the high octaves (B to B) float into the night air.

In all this there are many beauties of voice as well as of interpretation (and the distinction is felt in less lyrical songs, such as Wolf's mordent 'Herz, versage nicht'). In fact, if the voice and its production were less satisfying (and both have some curious features), the joy of the interpreta-tions would be appreciably weakened for this listener if not for others. So it is, I find, with as thoughtful a singer as the baritone Heinrich Reh-kemper, and so it is when we come to the singer generally regarded as the greatest of all in German song. That is Elena Gerhardt, whose records have faults of many kinds.

Unsteadiness is the most obtrusive. This does not seem to be essentially a matter of age, for the recordings of 1939 only magnify a tendency present in the Vocalion pre-electricals of 1923 and 1924 and incipient even in her first records, the famous 1907 series with Arthur Nikisch as accompanist. Intonation also gives trouble. Sometimes the flattening of pitch is effective as tonal colouring (as in the extraordinary sound produced in 'Der Weg-weiser' on the word 'keines', held darkly over its subtly changing harmon-ies); but this is not always so. In 'Auf dem Wasser zu singen', recorded in 1926, the sustained note near the end of each verse is pointlessly flat, until with the crescendo it grows tolerable as the voice spreads. This cannot be ascribed to the cutting of upper frequencies inevitable in recording on early 78s, as perhaps can some of the apparent flatness on the pre-electrical Vocalions.

The earliest records only rarely suffer from faulty intonation, but with them we come upon other weaknesses. The phrasing is often short-winded, as in 'Du bist die Ruh' and 'An die Musik'. Gerhardt evidently wanted to breathe and did so; it is as simple as that. But few modern singers would record these songs if their technique did not allow them to phrase more broadly. Possibly this is not a matter of technique but of style, for it may be that she saw no reason why the phrases should not be broken. But if we come to matters of style this would be one criticism and there would then be others. An excessive use of portamento limits enjoy-ment: not only the slow curve, but also a habit of wisking up to notes from below. Examples of both occur in Wolf's 'Und willst du deinen Liebsten sterben sehen?'. In the 1939 recording she had renounced the long drooping portamento on the word 'Fäden' which was a feature of the 1907 version, but she retained the others and added an ungainly attack on the word 'ungezählt' and at 'Lass von den Schultern'. And surely the slow tempo of both performances tends to sentimentalise the song: it loses coherence and becomes a rather sickly lingering affair, with its lush arpeggios and limp structure. Elisabeth Schumann moves it forward and the song gains. Sentimentality is, admittedly, very rare in Gerhardt. Schubert's 'Wiegenlied' might have lent itself, but her tone and feeling are warm without over-indulgence. Another feature of the singing is exposed here, however, and this is the habit of aspirating, which forces itself upon our notice both in this song and in 'Ellens zweiter Gesang' on the other side of the record.

All of these are basic faults, and it is a measure of Gerhardt's greatness that so many of her records survive in spite of them. Playing half-a-dozen songs in sequence, one is drawn to her, perhaps in the first place, by the range of her art, the extent to which a quite different mood is captured in each of the songs. Begin, say, with the record of 'Der Wegweiser' already mentioned, with its stern expression as the face is set towards that path whence, as the lyric says, no traveller returns. Then, with another Schubert song, 'Das Fischermädchen' the face and voice-colour have changed to a lighter, happier character, still modulating softly and subtly at the words 'und mancher schöne Perle in seiner Tiefe ruht' to suggest mystery and depth. From this to 'Wohin?' where she uses a magically light voice, securing just the right kind of live rhythmic emphasis. This deepens into tenderness, warming the opening phrases of Wolf's 'Verborgenheit' on the reverse side of the record: one also feels how every tone of the voice is being utilised in the fine gradation of sound. We might try then the 'Wiegenlied' of Richard Strauss recorded with Nikisch in 1911: there is probably too much portamento, but, to off-set it, the lovely effect of a disembodied floating sound, very tender and opening out as from a full heart at 'Diese Welt zum Himmel mir gemacht'. For a contrast within the same series, there is 'Der Freund' by Wolf, a setting of hearty words by Eichendorff (the second half might almost be by Elgar, with Gerhardt as Clara Butt singing it). Lastly we might hear her rollicking through No. 4 of Brahms' *Zigeunerlieder*; or if the back-slapping zest of this is uncongenial, then we can return to Schubert for a bold and spirited 'Fischerweise'.

And she was a bold artist. One of the valuable lessons her records can teach (and one wonders whether Janet Baker knows Gerhardt's records for she herself has this way with her singing) is that a singer, having studied the music with love and care, should then be able to become it, or let it enter and speak through her whole being, not just the voice and the brain. Those first recording sessions contain singing of wonderful stillness: a lesson in not fidgeting. They also show a singer who is not afraid to let herself go, and this is an experience rarely offered by modern Lieder singers. One wonders who today would sing Brahms' 'O liebliche Wangen' with such impulsiveness, daring to open to a sense of *big* emotions (Janet Baker is again the obvious name to throw into the blank silence). There is something curiously old-fashioned about an artist who seems to hold out her arms or clasp them to her heart; but such gestures (and Gerhardt's

62. Elena Gerhardt

singing often seems a warm expression of them) can speak movingly of human feeling when they emerge truthfully and not as theatrical show. In our times, the fear of the theatrical, perhaps a self-distrust that comes with more introspective, analytical habits of thought, seems to prevent a concert singer from allowing the whole self to be involved: voice and brain certainly, face perhaps, but the whole man or woman very rarely. With Gerhardt we sense this total involvement.

She had that kind of integrity which guarantees at least a rightness of approach. Even where her voice was not suited to a song, that basic rightness was still there. She presents 'Auf dem Wasser zu singen' as a song of joy, and although she makes free with the semiquavers this has the happy effect of helping the lilt to be felt. For 'Gretchen am Spinnrade', also recorded in 1926, her voice was too matronly, but her conception of the song is compelling and right, a passionate turbulence speaking boldly, rather than the weaker nostalgia and regret that mark the emotional limits of many performances.

Hers was not, however, an intellectual art, and consequently the rightness is generalised. She will shade the tone appropriately and sensitively, yet not provide many points of local illumination, as Fischer-Dieskau is constantly doing. For example, Gerhardt's recording of 'Die Stadt', made in 1939, might be compared with Fischer-Dieskau's performance on one of his early 78s. From Gerhardt we have a generalised, intuitive feeling for the song, its seriousness, mystery and pain. With the young Fischer-Dieskau, there is this, together with certain particular insights. With him, in a more precise and vivid way than with Gerhardt, we are peering through the mists to catch the first glimpse of the town. With him, we see more clearly the picture implied in the repeated accompanying figure, for he sings his quavers on the phrase 'in meinem Kahn' and the semi-quavers of 'traurigem Takte' with absolute, pointed precision, so that we are made to feel the measured pull of the boat across the water—and of course, the arpeggios in the piano part, and the low chords following them, now make vivid pictorial sense. There are signs of immaturity (the contrast between soft and loud singing is too great), but it is this genius for illuminating a song, a grasp of it localised in imaginative detail, that with his other gifts makes him a greater Lieder singer for the gramophone.

But that last phrase must be stressed. It is unlikely that any singer has achieved a stronger effect then Gerhardt did in many of her concerts. Desmond Shawe-Taylor provides vivid testimony: 'The eight songs which she did record (from *Der Winterreise*) may convey to young listeners something of the excitement of those *Winterreise* evenings which she gave at the Queen's Hall in 1928 and on subsequent occasions. Speaking for myself, I do not remember to have been more strongly affected by any other concert; nor can I recall another performance of Schubert's cycle which, in the controlled intensity of passionate grief, came within measurable distance of hers. It is in these songs, above all, that we remember the strong, often deliberately harsh, chest notes of her mature voice: it seemed as though sorrow and bitterness had etched themselves into the very timbre, so that (among other consequences) one had no impression of the incongruity of a woman's voice in the tragic story of a man's broken heart.' The words come from Mr Shawe-Taylor's postscript to Gerhardt's autobiography, which contains a list of her records and some valuable comments on them. A much-loved singer, she deserves the honour of later generations, even if the records lead us only part of the way to sharing the intense pleasure that her recitals could give.

At any rate there should be no problem for posterity in the charms of Elisabeth Schumann. Her voice was fresh as spring, the personality warm as a summer's day, and both are likely to be as perennially welcome.

My own introduction to Schumann came through her record of the Quintet from *Die Meistersinger*, and there could not have been a happier one. 'Selig wie die Sonne': the radiance of her tone is the perfect expression of these opening words. She caresses and shades with incomparable warmth and delicacy: one would never believe that this had been a particularly tiresome recording session, with one of the artists making the same mistake until after seven attempts Schumann had said that the next take would have to be the last. The happiness of spirit and tone seemed always perfectly matched. Her records of Adèle's songs in *Die Fledermaus* are brimful of life, and the gaiety is infectious. She was not one of those light sopranos who offer arch prettiness; she presents an energetic human being with a spontaneous sense of fun. Similarly in the waltz song 'Sei nicht böse' from Zeller's operetta *Der Obersteiger*, Schumann captivates by her knowledge of just when to lighten and slow down, apparently quite uncontrived and unselfconscious. This joyfulness is at home in great music as in light: the old records of Bach's B minor Mass, plodding and stolid as they often were, began to shine and breathe more freely when the solo soprano part brought Schumann's summery tone into the performance.

She was famous for her Mozart, and much of it is certainly delightful. The air 'L'amerò sarò costante' from *Il Rè Pastore* is one of the best: fresh-voiced and affectionate, the trills scrupulous, the legato satisfying. The runs are less than perfect; both Ivogün and Dux, among early singers, were more fleet and more sure. There were in fact limitations to Schumann's technique (an example is given in some comparisons on p. 572). The style too is not always so very ideal. The 'Alleluia' from *Exsultate Jubilate* is enthusiastic but untidy, and even 'Deh vieni, non tardar', one of her favourite arias, and very beautifully recorded, leaves something unsatisfied, perhaps because her liveliness of temperament intervenes and will not let the melody float serenely in the evening air and cast its own spell. An interesting comparison here can be made with the plain and magical performance Irmgard Seefried gave of the aria on 78 (contrasted with a later version in which she is much more artful and much less lovely).

A similar qualification might be made about the success of her other most famous role in opera, that of Sophie in *Der Rosenkavalier*. Much in her recording of this is enchanting as one expects it to be, and this Sophie is a credible girl and not a sugar-plum fairy in crinoline. But there are times when the notes could, with gain, be read rather more literally; and here we come to the mannerisms which grew more pronounced as the years went by. One is the swoop or scoop: a thing distinct from the usual portamento of the early singers on record if only because it is quite unsentimental. The other is a habit of leaving a faint trail of sound behind when the phrase or note is over, like the smoke after the snuffing of a candle. Whatever its origins, this is much in keeping with the vocal character, part of its airiness and delicacy, so that one comes to accept it quite readily. And so, with a few misgivings, does one accept most of the swoops. The redeeming feature is that it is not an enervated droop, but on the contrary derives from the singer's vitality: in an early record, the 'Nightingale Song', for instance, complete with the celebrated Schumann whistle, it seems irresistibly involved in the gusto and vigour of the performance.

But Schumann's great contribution to the gramophone is her Lieder. She had the gift of unfolding a scene as if it were present before her eyes, and of telling a tale as if she were turning the pages of a story-book. So in 'Die Forelle' she takes us freshly into the song: the feeling at the beginning is that she has a lot to tell us about and that it has happened just half-an-hour ago. Indignation, half-humorous, grows, and the story ends with a rather frail, very feminine voice, as though deprecating the heartless business of trout-fishing altogether. In 'Heidenröslein' not only has she the ideal freshness and clarity, but also a joy in the narrative where other pleasant-voiced singers make a nice nothing of it: Schumann sees and knows that 'wilde Knabe', that when the rose takes its revenge ('und stach's') the action provokes a little frown which also becomes part of the voice. Yet all is done without undue pointing or mannerism. Brahms' 'Vergebliches Ständchen' is another example of this skill in story-telling, or dramatising. For the luckless serenader she produces a rousing, devil-may-care voice, commanding that the door be undone ('öffne mir, mein Kind') in full conviction that a fellow whose passion has brought him out on such a night ought to have right of way. For the girl, she has a tiny, little-miss voice, and the whole thing is done with a fine sense of fun.

Schumann's liveliness was free from pertness, and one never felt her art charming but shallow. The serenity she brings to 'Du bist die Ruh' is quite as profound as the tragic or stormy emotions required by the heavier songs which she rarely undertook. She shades and moulds her phrases so delicately that we might almost overlook the fullness and womanly warmth of feeling. But she has reserves of seriousness, and the words 'o fühl' es ganz' can draw on feelings that are as substantial as the voice is airy. Some of Richard Strauss' songs show this as well as does her greatly loved Schubert. Hers is exactly the voice and character for Strauss' 'Morgen', a difficult song in several respects. For one thing, the last line has to be supported softly and on a long breath. Then the opening phrase ('Und morgen wird die Sonne wieder scheinen') must seem to emerge from the piano part, as though that long-drawn melody has been the singer's thoughts and the lips have merely opened to sing to herself what is still quite inner. In this, Lotte Lehmann (for instance) was too forthright, while at the other extreme too dreamy a loveliness can sugar the song to sickliness (so it tends to be with Emmy Bettendorf—reminding us that she was Ivor Novello's favourite singer on record, and this his favourite record of her!). Somewhere between these versions, Schumann is ideal, very personal and

63. Elisabeth Schumann

tender, yet with a radiance of tone and personality that can relish the 'sonnen-atmenden Erde': never a soporific, even at its most delicate.

When her Schubert records were collected for LP, Peter Heyworth, a critic not given to saying extravagant things about singers, wrote of it as his 'record of the year (or of the decade for that matter)'. Radiance, gaiety of heart, lack of artifice: these were some of the terms he used. They are qualities of character; and ultimately I suppose it is because we feel ourselves in contact with an enchanting person that we value the records so highly. The other singer of this period to impart such a feeling in any really comparable way on records was Lotte Lehmann.

Again we sense a valuable person, immensely alive, strong and intelligent as well as warm, tender and charming—perhaps after all as complete a human being as we come to know through records of great singers. Again, in human terms, and in a way hard to analyse, Lehmann's art has an additional value in its centrality. It is as though Schumann's singing has all the qualities and colours of sunlight, while Lehmann's moves further to the centre of the spectrum, which we feel obscurely to be right at the heart of human experience. So Lotte Lehmann's human completeness puts the seal upon her greatness as a singer, for she also had the beauty of tone and strength of technique without which this human quality could not have become an artistic fact.

She could reach great depths of seriousness and intensity. Her recording of *Dichterliebe* with Bruno Walter at the piano is exceptionally urgent. The work is understood as a cycle, not a collection, and moves to its climax in the last four songs, themselves containing a fine variety of emotions, but all sung with that forward-moving intensity that might almost suggest the inspiration not so much of her accompanist as of Toscanini. In 'Ich hab' im Traum geweinet' there is no resorting to the deathly tempo and flattened tone nowadays in favour, but it is none the less an experience recollected with disturbing vividness, the biting force of the singer's tone matching the grinding harmonies which accompany the poet's awakening. In 'Allnächtlich im Traume' the dream has seemed to become a kindly one, and the singer's face and tone have changed with it. The line 'Du sagst mir heimlich ein leises Wort' is breathed with an affectionate intimacy; and the phrase 'zu deinen süssen Füssen' is both uninhibited and unsentimental. The swing and energy of the next song, 'Aus alten Märchen', are caught joyously, and the last section ('Ach könnt' ich dorthin kommen') is given out forthrightly like a students' song, growing gently reflective in the last lines. Then in the final song, the strength of music and sentiment is captured with inexhaustible zest and inner seriousness modulating to the moving, personal tones which lead to the piano postlude and the ending of the cycle.

These are songs that often seem not to be recognised as a challenge to the more serious depths of a singer's feelings. If we wanted to test such qualities we might go to Schubert before Schumann, to 'Die junge Nonne' or 'Der Doppelgänger', for instance, and we find Lehmann superb in both. It is interesting to compare her record of 'Die junge Nonne' with Kathleen Ferrier's. Ferrier's voice is extremely beautiful, and the performance is moving in its sincerity. But with Lehmann the song lives twice as long, covering the process by which this serenity is attained. She traces the progression: from the turbulence of night and the old self which it represents, to the gentle motion of peacefulness and the rapt spirit of a very simple girl who can sing her Alleluias with quiet fervour and radiant submission. To play the beginning and ending of the record is to hear a vocal tone that has changed as completely as the girl's life.

Lehmann could sing fiercely, as she does in the opening of this song ('es leuchtet der Blitz'), or in the tortured climaxes of 'Der Doppelgänger', and in the predatory menace of the Erl-king's promise to seize by force. We can then follow her through every shade of emotion, through the devout, aspiring mood of Wolf's 'Zur Ruh', through the whole range of woman's life and love as caught in Schumann's song-cycle, to the high spirits and playfulness of Schubert's 'Die Männer sind méchant' or Beethoven's 'Der Kuss', in which she was superb. Her gaiety was incomparable. Among the operatic records it is most infectious in the solos from *Die Fledermaus*; among the Lieder, with its delicate happiness, Schumann's 'Aufträge', a song that suited her splendidly, confiding and impulsive in her earlier recording of it, slightly more flexible and strong in the later one.

It would be a pity if the Lieder records made after about 1935 for American companies were to eclipse the less readily accessible series made on

Odeon. There are many gems among these, some of them even preferable to the later and better recorded versions. For instance, the 1941 recording of Wagner's 'Schmerzen' is very fine in its exaltation, but the early record wins one afresh with the glory of the voice, and also with the loveliness of contrasting tone at the words 'Ach, wie sollte ich da klagen', that delicious modulation which clearly (and often vainly) calls on the singer to respond with a new colouring. Later in her career, Lehmann seems to have found it difficult to produce a softened tone such as is wanted at this point, or as is demanded in Schumann's 'Der Nussbaum'. The later version of this does indeed produce a magical pianissimo in the ending of the song, but gener- ally the tone is not light enough, so that the continuous exchange of phrases light as air between pianist and singer is lost. In the old record we have the airiness, a smiling lilt, and a most beautifully wistful, tender tone at the phrase 'wusste ach! selber nicht was'.

One cannot have everything in the same singer. Lehmann gives us so many of the pleasures a singer can afford, and in a way it is a condition of her strength that she does not often resort to the relaxed, dreamy softness used in 'Der Nussbaum'. Her vocal character is very unlike that of Lemnitz or Bettendorf. Because of this, Schubert's 'Ave Maria' loses its untroubled, floating loveliness, but gains a strength by becoming a prayer with intensity in its pleading. In some music there is a greater loss. Wolf's 'Auch kleine Dinge' is much too strongly voiced for the fragility of both sound and sense. Pamina's 'Ach, ich fühl's' from *Die Zauberflöte* catches the passionate, suffering woman, but loses the classical beauty of a more statuesque sadness. It also has to be granted that she cannot really meet the technical demands of this music, largely because of problems concerning the supply of breath. Lehmann was very conscious of this difficulty and she generally managed her phrasing cleverly. The later recording of *Frauenliebe und Leben* illustrates the care taken to broaden the phrasing. In the first song, the phrase 'Schwebt sein Bild mir vor' is broken in the early version, but not in the later one, made when the singer was well into her fifties. And in the difficult song, 'Süsser Freund, du blickest mich verwundert an', several of the phrases are taken in a single breath where formerly they were rather nervously divided in two. The tendency to breathe often and audibly remained; but whatever the deficiencies of her breathing, it at least did her the great service of keeping her tone steady and healthy right to the very end of her singing days, when she was over sixty.

It was a strenuous career too, lasting from 1910 to 1951, involving opera- tic work through most of the years, much of it in weighty roles in Wagner and Strauss. She was able to a remarkable extent to sing opera with the intimacy of a Lieder singer, giving out a glorious stream of voice, yet attending imaginatively to the enunciation and colouring of the text. Strangely, she is sometimes described as a patiently made Lieder singer rather than a born one, but there surely never was an operatic artist with more of the natural feeling for the ways in which a phrase can be made

Lotte Lehmann
als Octavian
in „Der Rosenkavalier."

64. Lotte Lehmann as Octavian in *Der Rosenkavalier*

meaningful and vivid, through the detailed, imaginative care for words.

It was this, together with the apt womanly fullness of her voice, and great beauty of presence, that made her the great Marschallin of her time. The abridged version of *Der Rosenkavalier* on HMV preserves a valuable part of the famous portrayal; all the same, the limitations of a recording job imperfectly conceived and carried out detract from the pleasure, especially to a later generation. I have to confess also to a great disappointment in the private recording of a complete performance at the Metropolitan in December 1937. Enjoyment is almost impossible because of the quality of recording (many of these off-the-air recordings are extremely clear and exciting in their immediacy, but this is not one of them). Then, the conducting, by Arthur Bodansky, rushes the music along at a maniac rate, and the rest of the cast is far from ideal (Thorborg quite powerful but womanish and none too steady as Octavian, List as a very wobbly Ochs, and the miscast Friedrich Schorr at first singing beautifully as Faninal, but then unable to cope successfully with the tessitura—it is a role marked for 'high baritone'). Lehmann wisks a lot of the notes, taking the first note of a phrase, or perhaps the highest note within the phrase, from below, and giving far too much in a kind of speech-sing, with an awkward passage in the voice around B or C which seems to break into the unity of tone. Listening and recreating, one can hear fine things from time to time—the opening ('Du bist mein Bub'), the smiled 'Jeder Ding hat seine Zeit', the tender but unmawkish farewell to Octavian, and the passionate end of the first Act (though she cannot take the 'silberne Rose' softly or lingeringly enough to make magic). Personally, the record on which I prefer to hear Lehmann's Marschallin is the earliest she made, a single excerpt ('Die Zeit die ist ein sonderbar Ding') as recorded on Odeon: her warmth and sensitivity are there, and with them one has the essential characterisation.

Going through the operatic records of the twenties and thirties, one can enjoy a wonderful range of music, from Mozart to Strauss. Her Mozart was not classic but it was always alive. In Weber, the *Oberon* aria does not find her equipped with Flagstad's trumpet tone, but it is so full of joy, excitement and boldness that one does not feel the lack. Her Puccini records are also excellent—not the *Turandot* excerpts, though they are interesting collector's pieces, but the 'Vissi d'arte' sung with glorious tone and intense feeling, and Mimì's first solo, full of intelligent, charming touches and all in radiant voice. But it is the sense of a complete woman involved, and a full dramatic realisation of the role, that gives Lehmann's performances their ultimate distinction. Possibly most remarkable of all is the intimacy of her Wagnerian singing. The Sieglinde of *Die Walküre* is recorded in a magnificent performance with Lauritz Melchior, under Bruno Walter. And among the private recordings, this one a real treasure, is the second Act as sung at San Francisco in 1936, where Lehmann's Sieglinde has a tremendous, wide-eyed, terrified intensity that makes her outstandingly memorable among a cast that included Flagstad, Melchior and Schorr! The glow of her tone and the clear, ardent expressiveness of it all are still unmatched. And in the 'Liebestod': has one ever heard an Isolde who so tenderly mirrors the smile she sees in the dead face, or who rises quite so humanly to the great climaxes?

The art of Lieder singing has really taken root when it can flourish on such intimidating heights of heroic drama as this. It requires a remarkably complete artist to bring such unlike forces together; and it is not surprising that Lotte Lehmann should have been the one among our singers pre-eminently to do it.

16. Wagner: The Triumph of Lyricism
Frida Leider   Lauritz Melchior
Friedrich Schorr

THE smile, the dramatic intake of breath, the imaginative care for words: these qualities that Lotte Lehmann brought to Wagner were rarely to be met with in any group of singers, and in the Wagnerians themselves perhaps least of all. They point ahead in fact to modern times, to the vivid and intimate singing of Wagner that has been most highly developed in the recordings conducted by Karajan. But in the inter-war years, greatness among the Wagnerians lay principally in another direction. It lay essentially in the application of sound vocal method to music which so often had tempted singers to a non-lyrical, explosive or merely wooden style. The immense value of the records by Leider, Flagstad, Melchior and Schorr is that they are all *sung*: smoothness, steadiness, sonority, control, they are all present as probably in no generation of Wagnerian singers before or since. These singers were far from giving shallow interpretations, but the distinctive merit of their work as examples to later times (as well as being an unfailing source of pleasure in themselves) lies essentially in the sheer beauty of sound.

There were of course many other singers apart from those four. Among the sopranos, Elisabeth Ohms and Göta Ljungberg: Ohms with a rich, intensely dramatic voice, just occasionally flattening, is heard well in 'Schmerzen', one of the Wesendonck Lieder, and in a duet from *Der fliegende Holländer*; while Ljungberg, shining and clear-edged, though with a vibrato that some will find obtrusive, remains exciting in the final scene from *Salome*, which was her most famous part. Fine heroic sopranos were Helene Wildbrunn and Germaine Lubin. Lubin, principal dramatic soprano at Paris for twenty-five years, has a French edge to the voice, which shines with the sort of brilliance that one can hear, through the boxy recording acoustic, as an exciting one in the theatre. She sometimes indulges in excessive portamento, as in 'Ewig war ich' from *Siegfried*, and her style, which fits her well for an imaginatively varied performance of Schubert's 'Erlkönig' is quite unsuitable for Bach, as we find in a bad record of 'My heart ever faithful'. She was, however, the sort of Brünnhilde who was also a good Tosca: her 'Vissi d'arte' begins warmly and quietly and grows in urgency towards a finely controlled climax. Best of all probably is the solo 'Salut, splendeurs' from Ernest Reyer's *Sigurd*: this is big, romantic music and her singing has some majesty, and, in this one record, a richness of tone that momentarily brings Ponselle to mind. She (Ponselle) comes to mind more frequently as one listens to Wildbrunn. Starting her career as a contralto, Wildbrunn has a remarkably rich, creamy voice that sounds quite exceptionally beautiful in some of her records. The 'Abscheulicher' from *Fidelio* is distinguished by a softly veiled quality in the meditative passages, as well as by great accomplishment in the phrases which so often find out the weaknesses of a good soprano's technique. The interpretation is general rather than specific, and yet she habitually sings with feeling. Isolde's Liebestod is tender and passionate, and the solo from *Siegfried*, 'Ewig war ich', which Lubin also recorded, has a great deal of personal appeal, as well as very cleanly taken intervals. Above all, she sang scrupulously: no wisking or wobbling, no lapse from lyrical standards even in the most strenuous passages in Brünnhilde's Immolation. Although her recordings belong to the late pre-electrical period, she is essentially representative of the generation we are discussing, unfailingly musical and a delight to the ear.

The period was by no means badly off for Wagnerian sopranos when one considers that we have still not mentioned: Florence Austral, Eva Turner (Eva, Elisabeth & Elsa, Sieglinde, Isolde and Brünnhilde were all in her repertoire though she recorded not a note of any), Marta Fuchs, Elsa Alsen, Maria Müller and Nanny Larsen-Todsen. Some of these are discussed later: all very notable artists. Among the men, too, were several worth remembering. The 1936 *Lohengrin* at Bayreuth was remarkable for the singing of Franz Völker as the protagonist, and his many solo records in a wide variety of music show him phrasing carefully and preserving a fine lyrical style and a steady voice. Max Lorenz, a true Heldentenor, did not always do that. The private recording of *Der fliegende Holländer* at Covent Garden, already mentioned on account of Janssen's fine performance, has Lorenz in 1937 singing in a gusty, over-declamatory style, and with a tone that has apparently lost its steadiness. This may have been a bad period, for he went on singing many years after that, and certainly his earliest records show what fine material he offered at the start of his career (two solos from *Die Meistersinger* show how he was able to tone down a voice of remarkable power). Rudolf Laubenthal, the tenor of many recorded excerpts, sounds dry and rather stiff, though at least he is steady. The British Wagnerians, Tudor Davies and Walter Widdop, are often excellent. On the other hand, the basses do not emerge at all well on record. Ivar Andresen, Emanuel List, Emil Schipper: they have impressive weight, but there is not much to cherish in their records. In Wilhelm Rode, I find less still: a much-praised Wotan and Sachs, records suggest that his voice was right for neither of these roles. Lugubrious and effortful, he hoists himself to the unresonant high notes of Wotan's cries to Erda in Act III of *Siegfried*, and in the lyrical pages of the Farewell in *Die Walküre* there is a downward pull affecting pitch as well as quality of voice. Much better is Rudolf Bockelmann, a powerful and authoritative artist. But as Wotan and Sachs, there really survives only one singer from this period, Friedrich Schorr. And in fact, as we look over the whole field of Wagnerian singing in this period, all but four or five begin to recede, and these remain vivid, to be shelved with the classics and enjoyed with the living.

For the rest of this chapter we shall confine attention to three of them. All have a classic status that is well-defined, and not only in the Wagnerian repertoire which was so much their prime concern.

All of them sang a fair variety of music. Frida Leider, for instance, made a fine recording of 'Ah, si la liberté' from Gluck's *Armide*: firm, broad, unfussy singing. Her Donna Anna is represented by two records of the aria 'Or sai chi l'onore', the second being a famous version, thrilling in its command of the grand manner, disconcerting to modern ears in its portamento and freedom with tempo, features which are rather interestingly absent from the fine pre-electrical recording made for Polydor. In Italian opera she is best represented by a rare and surprising record, Princess Eboli's 'O don fatale' from *Don Carlo*: again there is that kind of operatic glamour in the voice which we hear in Meta Seinmeyer and Hina Spani, carrying authority and commanding a certain excited intensity. There are limitations. For instance, she has a tendency to hurry, in particular a way of hurrying over tied notes (as in the climax of the *Ariadne auf Naxos* aria, or in the Duets from Act IV of *Trovatore* with Schlusnus). Then, making comparisons of some versions of Beethoven's 'Ah, Perfido' (Nilsson, Callas, Crespin and Leider) one admires the tone and the legato in Leider (by comparison with the more recent singers), but where towards the end of the aria there comes a passage of severe technical difficulty it is no use looking to Leider to give these modern madames a lesson. In fact they all manage very well though one feels that there is some final degree of mastery that might be found elsewhere; not in Leider, however, for she simply omits the passage. Nor does her interpretation gain the vividness it could from use of contrasts: and she does not lash out or make any dramatic impression comparable to Crespin and Callas in their recordings.

Later in her career, she recorded a selection of songs by Schumann and Schubert. This was in 1943, when she had, as she says, made a special study of the German song-writers; but again one realises how elusive is success in these fields. Skilfully and conscientiously, she lightens the powerful voice; and every now and then there comes a particularly felicitous phrase, as at the end of 'Der Nussbaum'. But the success of even that song is limited by her fondness for scooping and whisking, and, more important, as one listens to the sequence of recordings, one finds little of that sense of changing personality from one song to the next, the sense of a changing face, or a really live feeling for words, that are so essential in this art.

Perhaps the extent of her attainments here might have been foretold by the Wagner records. Again it is wonderful to hear how she could scale the voice down, using an economical tone, shining and finely pointed, fully resonant and never as it were running to fat. But it is rare to hear her bringing the words to life. Kundry's narrative, 'Ich sah' das Kind', in *Parsifal* is an exception. Here the face does change: beautifully tender in phrases like 'gebettet sanft auf weichen Moosen', strong and heroic at 'den Waffen fern, der Manner Kampf und Wuthen', then movingly gentle and hushed at the end, 'und—Herzeleide—starb'. This only gives an outline: the whole performance is very much alive to the text. But in Isolde's Liebestod, which was on the other side of the 78, we have very little sense of specific meaning; and Brünnhilde's Immolation in *Götterdämmerung*, superb (like the Liebestod) in tone and line and the sheer thrill of the voice, hardly presents itself as an interpretation. This comes as a surprise, for everyone who saw her in these roles testifies to the intensity of her involvement in them, and her power too of involving the audience. Yet the point about the records holds: there is no darkening, or sense of a mystery at 'Alles ward mir nun frei', no really inner feeling at 'Ruhe, ruhe, du Gott'. If one compares her contemporary, Nanny Larsen-Todsen, one hears the exact antithesis of Leider in the big, thick, rather cloying tone; but there is certainly a far more vivid response to the words and the changing moods (much more sense of grief, for instance, at the 'Oh ihr, die Eide ewige Hüter' passage).

That Leider survives as a great singer on records (and that the Immolation Scene survives as an example of great singing) is due to her voice. But perhaps that is an over-simplification, for in a way the marvellously dramatic and authoritative quality of the voice is the most essential part of 'interpretation': to sense and cultivate just the right kind of instrument is itself an interpretative act. Certainly it is Leider's tone that I personally want to hear, rather than any of the other great singers, in this music. Warmer than Nilsson's, more glamorous (less motherly perhaps) than Flagstad's or Wildebrunn's, it has the perfect character, existing at that rarely achieved point where the heroic has not become inhuman, and where the human does not undermine tragic dignity. We hear it probably best of all in one of these private recordings that one hopes will one day gain a wider circulation. Furtwängler conducted two performances of *Götterdämmerung* at Covent Garden in 1938, and in one of them Leider was the Brünnhilde. Act II (Scene Three to the end) is on record, and it does seem to preserve one of the best of opera nights. Melchior and Janssen were in the cast and in marvellous voice. Wilhelm Schirp was the Hagen, and though we read that he was criticised in the press, his powerful firm voice sounds mightily imposing on the record. But above all there is Leider. The intensity of her singing is unmistakeable at the great moments (the cries of 'Betrug!' for example), but she is also a singer with presence, and one is aware of it, majestic and human, throughout.

65. Frida Leider

Leider was an adored singer, and especially with Covent Garden audiences in her prime; and while in a way she was unfortunate to be eclipsed in popular regard by Kirtsen Flagstad in the mid-thirties, in another sense it worked well for her, because her reputation became the property of connoisseurs and increased as she herself retired from view. The other two singers to be discussed here, Melchior and Schorr, seem, by comparison, to have been rather taken for granted. They were busy singers, virtually indispensable and to many audiences practically inevitable. There is nothing like this for dulling recognition; but younger generations will find it hard to believe that they have heard a pair of singers to match them.

Both were artists with a wider repertoire than we tend to remember. Schorr sings the bass solos in the old recording of Bach's *Mass in B Minor*. In 'Et in spiritum sanctum' he does not quite catch the serenity, but the 'Quoniam' is excellent. Every semiquaver is in place, there is even a short trill, and the velvet covering to this powerful voice and the perfection of legato have a rich and dignified effect. Most of the time, he sings at a sonorous, easy mezzo forte, keeping the full voice in reserve for the second 'tu solus altissimus' section. He similarly 'builds' and gives a studied, varied reading of the solos he recorded from *Elijah* (marvellous, for instance, the clean, full-voiced taking of the high E flat at the second 'Herr Gott Abrahams'), but beyond that the hardly analysable quality of sincerity impresses lovingly through the noble voice. Nor was he limited to a solemn nobility. In Pizarro's 'Ha, welch' ein Augenblick' *(Fidelio)* he communicates a sense of the hard-driving energy of an evil will-power, even if there is none of the cold, peculiarly teutonic sadism of Fischer-Dieskau's performance, with its more steely tone and the clipped, aggressive hardness of the 'ck' sounds. Schorr's voice always seems one of the most benevolent on records, and so his characterisation of the farmer in Haydn's *The Seasons* sowing the seed and whistling as he follows the plough has a fine straightforward manliness. Compare his singing of the aria 'Schon eilet froh der Ackersmann' with two modern performances, and one finds in Schorr a more scrupulous legato than in either Martti Talvela or John Shirley-Quirk. But the comparison does not end there, for where Talvela's performance loses by being placed against Schorr's (the runs are aspirated, the *tessitura* seems high for him, and there is a general suggestion of old Osmin come from his seraglio), Shirley-Quirk's is strengthened. Where his runs are not legato it is by choice and not need: a keyboard player would use a semi-staccato touch and the rhythmic life of the piece is made more vivid. There is generally more bite and vigour, a feeling that this 'impatient husbandman' really enjoys his ploughing and sowing. But of course, along with Shirley-Quirk is the rhythmic sense of Colin Davis, and one again reflects on the luck of the modern singer and the conditions in which he records. In 1931 the conductor was Barbirolli and the orchestra the London Symphony, but there is nothing to suggest that any imagination went into the accompaniment.

But at least the accompaniments here were 'respectable', which is more than could be said of some of his early song recordings. There is a classic version of 'Der Lindenbaum' with embellishments that seem to include a celeste and a wind-machine, and one verse missing. Yet some of the Lieder records are extremely fine. 'Prometheus' recorded for the Hugo Wolf Society is impressive, and there is an interesting version of 'Die beiden Grenadiere', beautifully coloured, taken slowly and with the triplets dragged like a wounded leg. Schorr's main contribution to recorded Lieder, however, was in the Schumann *Liederkreis*, op. 39. Several markings in the score are ignored, and one knows, too, that this is not the voice of a singer in his prime. Still, he catches the changing play of emotions and achieves some intimacy of expression: 'Die Stille' is a fine example, and 'Zwielicht' finds him with exactly the right voice to colour this rich twilight oil-painting. But the great beauty of these records lies in the tone and its production: here is a warmth, very appropriate for Schumann, a sense of great power in reserve, and a quietness that never degenerates into that rather woolly or yawning sound that is often to be heard when basses with powerful voices turn to such music. And though the gentle flicker of vibrato is present, an integral part of the voice as it was in his youth, there is never a hint of wobble.

Still, it is in Wagner, and particularly as Sachs and Wotan, that Schorr is most himself and most irreplaceable. Again the private recordings of live performances in the opera house supplement the studio recordings, but these were mostly made when Schorr was slightly past his best as a singer, and when the high Es and Fs had to be taken carefully. Even so, they are glorious performances: a *Siegfried* of 1937 showing him in great form, the voice fully resonant, the quiet singing incomparable in its control and beauty of tone, the authority and sense of presence quite personal and unmistakeable. But these recordings simply confirm what we know. We know from the standard HMV recordings, for example, that his Sachs was a wonderfully warm-hearted characterisation. Memory tends to retain most vividly the quieter passages: his gentle, rich-voiced and evocative opening of the 'Fliedermonolog', or the phrases preceding the Quintet where Sachs christens the Prize Song ('die selige Morgen-traum'), or the emotion felt as he addresses the crowd in the last scene ('Euch macht ihr's leicht'), deeply touched by their homage, the depth of the tone and the nobility of line showing just why Sachs is in this position of trusted, paternal authority.

Then playing the records again, one realises what a wonderful sense of perspective the voice affords. So that in the address just mentioned, the velvety sound of the opening, conveying with an innerness the personal truth of the man, can modulate quickly into a fine, vigorous, extroverted sound, with all the incisiveness of tone needed to combat the full orchestra-tion. His singing, for all its grandeur, was always alive and responsive to small changes of feeling in the score, as in the passage in Act III, where Walther has just rehearsed his song. The colouring of the first word, 'Freund', is beautifully right; we feel Sachs can only just trust himself to speak in the emotion of the moment. Then it is as though he shakes off the emotion as he gets up from his seat, only to recapture it partly in his rever-ence for the inspiration of Walther's song and the tenderness of his reference to Eva a little later. All this is conveyed in pure singing; and ultimately what makes Schorr so precious among his tribe is the purity of legato, the steadiness of voice and the great technical command he had over it. He was a more interesting interpreter than Leider (as she appears on records, that is) but, as with her, it is the perfectly apt instrument fashioned by voice and technique that constantly draws one back to these old records as establishing something of great rarity and worth.

Not everything is perfect. The Cobbling Song of Act II is forthright and varied, but he tends to feel the 'halla hallahe's as dotted rhythms and this weakens the music's punch; moreover there are times when notes do not sound quite up to pitch. His phrasing is not always as broad as one would ideally like—the one criticism, this, that one could make of his recording of Wotan's Farewell in *Die Walküre*. That is possibly the best excerpt for sampling his Wotan; but his performance throughout the cycle has been extensively recorded and is everywhere impressive. He also performs that peculiar kind of disservice of which all great artists are glorious guilty, for no one who carries in his head Schorr's singing of 'Abendlich strahlt', the opening phrases of Wotan's music as the gods enter Valhalla in *Das Rheingold*, is likely to hear another performance without some yearning to get back to the gramophone and listen again to Friedrich Schorr.

With Melchior it is much the same: the years go by, and records continue to show him the greatest singer of the century in his own field. Again (although his singing had much more subtlety than is generally attributed to him) it is basically a vocal excellence that distinguishes him. That is: a firm, steady emission of tone, exceptionally resonant and powerful, yet capable of a sweetness and grace of which any lyric tenor might be proud.

Even today we have probably not realised how phenomenal Melchior was. One is even tempted to see an odd kind of perversity in the incomplete recognition, for without him we would have a limited notion of how well Wagner's tenor roles can sound. But where Leider and Schorr are venerated, Melchior is merely acknowledged. When the old records of *Die Walküre* under Bruno Walter were reissued on LP, Lotte Lehmann's Sieglinde was justly praised in the highest terms, while Melchior's Siegmund was

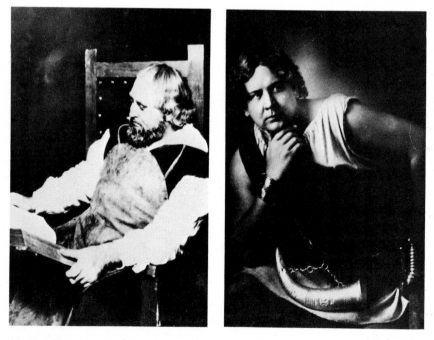

66. Friedrich Schorr as Hans Sachs   67. Lauritz Melchior as Siegfried
    in *Die Meistersinger*

merely (and quite inadequately) accepted. Many of today's senior critics no doubt remember him as a bulky, unromantic figure on the stage, remote from any ideal conception of Tristan or Siegfried; and we know of one critic who after a performance of *Otello* at Covent Garden in the late thirties took himself to the stage door to say boo. Certainly, later in his career the voice lost some of its glow and his interpretations some of their sensitivity. And it is always said that he could be maddeningly and persistently inaccurate: Irving Kolodin mentions the famous remark of one conductor to another on the general unreliability of tenors, adding that at least you knew where you were with Melchior because he always made the *same* mistakes. But we now have a large number of stage performances on records, and so we can hear for ourselves. If the evidence is of any value, I may claim to have followed a good many of these with the score and though deliberately looking for these inaccuracies on Melchior's part have gathered only the most meagre collection. On 1 June 1937 he entered a bar late for the phrase 'du folge willig mir' in *Götterdämmerung*; that is the prize item of a catalogue which otherwise includes a dot here and a quaver there, nothing remotely to justify the remark that all reviewers seem called upon to make that they are 'well aware of his faulty rhythmic sense' and so forth. What does emerge from these recordings with the sharpest clarity is that he was always rhythmically alert; where he is at fault at all it is because he seems to be about to move ahead of the beat, and this is because he has a very live grasp of the energy and rhythmic shape of the phrase in a declamatory passage. Of course it may be objected that these are only a few performances out of the whole of his career; but then it seems that he 'always made the *same* mistakes'. They cannot have it both ways.

I believe that a private recording of Melchior singing *Otello* is in existence: it may even preserve the performance after which my critic-friend booed (Melchior having sung 'ancora un bacio' instead of 'un altro bacio' as his last words, and that being the last straw). But if his recordings made in German in 1927 are anything to go by, it should have been the performance of a lifetime, for the Monologue and Death Scene have rarely been more fully realised than in these. Everything is most deeply felt, yet the emotion is contained, so that, unlike Zanelli's great performance, or McCracken's overplayed one, he feels no need to leave the reciting note to express the tragic force of the words. Then, to suggest a few more comparisons, his voice is in so much better form than was Martinelli's when he came to make his Victor recording—also superb in its way—in 1939. He can rise easily in that strangely difficult final phrase of the recitation, and with sweetened tone to the high G, rounding the passage off softly and rather wistfully in the way that Jon Vickers does. But in this comparison too I find Melchior generally preferable, for there is a greater impression of spontaneity (Vickers, both in his recital record and in the complete opera, goes very slowly giving rather too conscious a sense of deliberation), and there is a more exciting shine on the voice. These are all exceptional performances, but alone among them Melchior's seems to have had less than its critical due. So, it might be added, have his other non-Wagnerian records: a German 'Vesti la giubba', both gentle and powerful, and intensely responsive; a dignified and dramatic version of the duet for Radamès and Amneris in Act IV of *Aida* (with the rich-voiced Margarethe Arndt-Ober, perhaps just past her best); and an 'O Paradiso' *(L'Africana)* in which the lyricism is unflawed and the voice goes from pianissimo to the most ringing double forte with every grade of power in between.

This dates from the early nineteen-twenties when he also recorded some of the great Wagnerian solos for the first time. There is a masterly performance of Lohengrin's Narration, as authoritative as if he had been singing it all his life. Later he would have varied the tone-colour rather more, but his legato was in those days absolutely scrupulous. It seems marvellous enough in the later versions when compared with most other tenors; but whereas (say) the first electrical recording of Siegfried's Forging Song is helped in its vigour by light aspirates (on the word 'blase', for instance, or at 'des Baumes Kohle'), the pre-electrical has every phrase sung with a pure, unbroken smoothness. We realise too, as we hear these records and then the very first he made, when he was a baritone, in 1913, how the baritonal sturdiness never left his voice, though it became most brilliantly and unquestionably a tenor. Incidentally, the baritone records (there is a 'Di Provenza' among them) provide an interesting glimpse of a voice, so to speak, in two minds. One can hear the production change for the lower notes and also feel the pull of the upper end of the voice to gain complete freedom from any kind of baritonal throatiness.

How perfectly the tricky operation of change from baritone to tenor was performed is clear from the long endurance of the voice in spite of the toughest demands upon it. In 1960 he celebrated his seventieth birthday by singing Act I of *Die Walküre*, and that too is on record; it cannot be said that he sounds very comfortable by the time the Love Duet is reached, but before then there are times when one feels that he is *still* the best Siegmund. He never degenerated into wobble, and for long years preserved a youthful shine on the voice, as well as the ability to produce a gentle, velvety tone, almost Tauber-like in its softness. The famous records of the Love Duet from *Tristan und Isolde* with Frida Leider show this *mezza voce* at its finest: the last phrases of the 'sink hernieder' section are given with a perfectly supported pianissimo, and the beauty of his head notes is illustrated in the phrase 'vor deinen Augen süss zerronnen'. His gentleness could also have a wonderfully rapt and exalted character, as in the earlier luxuriating phrase, 'Liebeswonne ihm lacht'. With this exaltation there was often a fine, passionate seductiveness in the inflections: his *Lohengrin* arias (especially 'Höchstes Vertrauen') are examples. And a gentle ecstasy marked his singing of such music as Siegmund's 'Winterstürme', swelling to a gloriously fervent and poetic account of Walther's Prize Song.

In addition he had all the energy and weight to be, vocally at any rate, the ideal Siegfried: never a sort of noisy human lump, but always alive and sensitive in his inflections. His diction, too, was admirable, particularly in passages where the vigour expresses itself through alliteration (though later in his career he came to close the vowel prematurely upon the consonant). Nor has any other tenor been so alive to the emotional sway of this music, the stresses, the passion which can only be fully communicated by controlled crescendos and diminuendos. All of these great merits are to be heard in Siegfried's Narrative and Death, in *Götterdämmerung*, and this, like so much of the work of his two other great contemporaries discussed in this chapter, is certainly among the classics of the gramophone.

17. Splendid Isolationists:
Standards in Britain and France
Florence Austral   Eva Turner
Claire Croiza   Ninon Vallin

DISCUSSING Wagnerian singing in the last chapter, we mentioned the name of Florence Austral. She was a fine singer of a rare kind, yet she sang neither at Bayreuth nor the Metropolitan, and if they knew her name in Italy (pronouncing it 'Owstral') it was because she took part in a highly competitive recording of the final duet in *Aida* with Miguel Fleta. Her career was eminently successful in that wherever she sang she gave great satisfaction and received high critical acclaim. It is also true that the firm tone, the power and unfussy efficiency can be heard on many an old HMV black label; and not so very long ago, some time before her death in 1968, something like justice was done when a collection of her records was published in the *Great Recordings of the Century* series. Even so, one has the suspicion that Fiorenza Strallini or Florenz Stralisch would have done still better on the international scene. And this was generally true for the British singer in these years, the only consolation being that Fleur d'Australie might well have been just as badly off, never being heard of outside France.

Austral's Wagner is most readily heard in Senta's Ballad from *Der fliegende Holländer*. Her electrical recording was for many years a best-seller and was selected as the sole representative of inter-war British singing in the *Fifty Years of Great Operatic Singing* anthology. Warmth and strength of voice, breadth of phrasing and evenness of line in loud singing as in soft, are all to be found in the record. Even so, it is a long way from showing Austral at her best, for which one should go to the final challenge of the Wagnerian soprano, the Immolation Scene from *Götterdämmerung*. There have been more intense and varied performances on record, but none better sung: the voice is glorious, the technique utterly secure, and even the most taxing high notes are taken with pin-point accuracy.

But the best of Austral is not necessarily in her Wagner at all. She had an unusually varied repertoire, including even the Mad Scene from *Lucia di Lammermoor* and 'Sempre libera' from *La Traviata* (and of how many Wagnerian sopranos, before or since, could that be said). These were not recorded, though her impromptu singing of the Forest Bird in *Siegfried* (the soprano engaged had not turned up, so the Brünnhilde stepped in) gives some evidence of how accomplished they are likely to have been. Her singing of Handel, Haydn and Rossini gives more, the latter represented by a fine recording of the 'Inflammatus' from *Stabat Mater* sung with its full complement of trills, turns and top Cs. Then there was some Mozart (a dignified and beautifully sustained 'Porgi amor' from *Le Nozze di Figaro*), Brahms (a generously felt recording of the soprano solo in the *Requiem*—no disembodied comforter, but a voice of warm, substantial humanity, in keeping with the work itself), and Richard Strauss (two songs, both beautifully done). A simple air like 'Killarney', safe and easy in its appeal to an audience, would never draw any sloppiness from her: she takes it at a brisk pace, a song of delight and not of maudlin sentiment, while the bold, open-air cleanness of her attack gives added life to the fresh, well-modulated tone. But it was also a voice to hear soaring high and

68. Florence Austral

clear above full orchestra and chorus, and for this there is a solo called 'The Night is Calm' from Sullivan's *The Golden Legend*. I find this quite irrationally affecting, rather as I do Janet Baker's recording of Elgar's *Sea Pictures*. The music is in fact very Elgarian and beautifully designed for the soprano voice; no soprano voice more beautifully designed for *it*, surely, than Florence Austral's.

She was also fine in Verdi. The various ways of phrasing the broad B major melody in 'Madre, pietosa vergine' *(La Forza del Destino)* can all be heard to great advantage in her recording. In the duet 'Ai nostri monti' *(Il Trovatore)* it appears that, as with the Forest Bird, she was again deputising for an absent singer at the recording session in music she had not sung before. This one would never suppose, for the contralto phrases seem to have grown into the voice and it is all most exquisitely shaded. The record also contains a detail of interpretation so delightful that one wonders why this should be (as far as I know) the only performance that has it. After the chromatic phrase 'tu canterai sul tuo liuto', the tenor enters on a high G, at the same pitch, that is, as the G which the contralto has just sung. The tenor in this recording is Browning Mummery, a clean, business-like singer, who takes up his phrase in a half-voice so that his note merges with Austral's. His descending line sounds like a continuation of hers, until the voices cross and come out in the easy-going harmony of the sixths. There is a musical pleasure here which it is not altogether surprising to find an English performance revealing. For English opera-singing was at this time coming into its own, and benefiting from the un-glamorous soundness of English musical training. So when Austral sings in the duet from Act II of *Aida* with the excellent Edna Thornton as her Amneris and Eugene Goossens conducting, we hear a performance measurably more musical and scrupulous than anything coming out of Italy in these years. The fine voices, the discipline, the avoidance of any sort of cheapness, these were characteristics of the British National Opera Company at its best.

Her partner in many records was Tudor Davies, another of the BNOC stalwarts. Their duet from *Cavalleria Rusticana* is a fine example, for Austral sings so warmly, without any of the hard shrillness often heard in this part, and Davies is as passionate as any Italian. He had the gift, rare among British tenors, of infusing passion into his tone. A genuine *spinto* who also took on roles for a Heldentenor, he was incisive yet (in his recording days) lyrical, turning his voice to most things. He gives a superb account of 'Sound an Alarm' from Handel's *Judas Maccabeus*, sings Tamino's arias in *Die Zauberflöte* with unusually full-blooded relish, and is as clean, vigorous a Siegmund as you could wish to hear. Moreover, he was only one of an unusually hardy generation of British tenors: Walter Widdop, Heddle Nash, Tom Burke, Joseph Hislop, Frank Titterton and Frank Mullings were all singing in the nineteen-twenties. Their modern counterparts are not too easily called to mind, and, as far as the gramophone will let us judge, they also seem to be an improvement on their own predecessors.

Possibly that is unfair; certainly it needs some qualification, and as we have not looked at the first generation of British singers on records perhaps we should do so now. One difficulty is that even in Britain many of the most important records are extremely hard to come by, and they have not been favourite candidates for transfer to LP. Their limitations in terms of real musical value (as opposed to collectors' or historical value) seem to me to be a certain stiffness or even stuffiness of style (softened all too often by a sentimental overuse of portamento) and a repertoire that is over-loaded with poor music. I enjoy (but only mildly) hearing Charles Santley telling of Father O'Flynn, but cannot find anything to like, whether in style, pronunciation, or tone, in his records of 'To Anthea'. The veteran tenor Edward Lloyd also recorded in extreme old age, but though one can admire his clarity and firmness in 'I'll sing thee songs of Araby', his Handel and Gounod make hard listening. Ben Davies, born in 1858, kept his tone firm and well-focused, and style, timbre and repertoire combine to make his records useful 'period documents'. Plunket Greene, the baritone, born in 1865, also retained just enough voice to record, when nearly seventy, clearly enunciated versions of Schubert's 'Organ-grinder' ('Der Leier-mann') and some Irish songs. Sir George Henschel, also in old age, sang, dry of voice but warm of heart, a fair selection of Lieder, accompanied by himself. John Coates, a greatly respected and accomplished musician, left a few records where, again in old age, a sound technique stands him in good stead: continuity and rhythmic life are the prizes gained by his technical feat of taking each verse of Thomas Morley's 'It was a lover and his lass' in just two breaths. Coates who was also a Wagnerian singer, had a kind of refinement that was often lacking in the singers of this period. Among the basses, for instance, there was Watkin-Mills, whose runs in Handel are exceptionally fluent and full-voiced, but whose tone often sounds coarse. Robert Radford, too, sturdy and no doubt invaluable singer as he was, sounds coarse-toned on records. . . . It seems a pity to continue the recitation without more enthusiasm, but on the whole I find it hard to summon.

Two British tenors who as yet remain unmentioned, however, are Gervase Elwes and Walter Hyde, and these, I think, left a valuable legacy of recordings. Hyde, born in 1875 and a pupil of Garcia, is immensely impressive. Lyrical and firm in his Wagner, he made a particularly fine record of Lohengrin's Farewell. No doubt the excellence of his singing here was helped by the fact that he had mastered Handel first. The evenness of tone, the fine sonority of it, and the perfect clarity and fluency in passage-work are all to be heard in solos from *Jephtha*. If one compares the per-formance in a modern recording of the opera where Jephtha is sung by Alexander Young it is rather like placing one of the old Shakespeareans, say Arthur Bourchier or Henry Ainley, side by side with some university actor in the Marlowe Society: the first feeling is that it is a matter of all-voice against all-brain. The modern singer is more varied and subtle in his inflections, the old one seems more sonorous and secure in his use of the voice. For example, Alexander Young allows the syllables of 'Deeper and deeper still' their natural relative weight according to speech-values, whereas with Walter Hyde the two syllables of 'deeper' are sung with exactly the same weight and quality of tone. Hyde is by no means in-expressive, but again it is with the generalised expressiveness of the old actors (he even uses the old actor's 'mi' for 'my' in 'Ah no! heaven heard mi thoughts', like 'mi moneys and mi usances' in Tyrone Power Senior's Shylock). Young makes more of the emotional recoil at 'Horrid thought', and there is more desperation (if less ringing tone) at 'lash me into madness'. In the air, 'Waft her, angels', we find that it is the modern singer who has the broader phrasing: 'Waft her, angels, through the skies' is musically a single phrase, but Hyde breaks it each time with a breath after 'angels'. Again, Young has a sense of the lulling, or 'wafting' motion in the paired notes, where Hyde steps rather than wafts. Nor does the modern singer (any more than the old) spoil his legato with aspirates: he gives, in fact, a highly creditable performance. Yet I feel as I do when comparing Schlusnus with Fischer-Dieskau, that if I had students to bring up it would be to the records of the earlier singer that I would send them, for the evenness and sonority they would find there set the highest standards in the basic ele-ments of any wholesome school of singing.

The student could quite profitably stay with a few of the not very dis-tinguished songs that Walter Hyde also recorded (several of them provide fine examples of the use of the head-voice). But for songs, and a rather better selection of them, the records of Gervase Elwes are worth sampling. His was the first recorded performance of Vaughan Williams' *On Wenlock Edge* (a great deal preferable to the version that followed, by Steuart Wilson), and he also sang some of the pleasant songs of Roger Quilter. The even production and unsentimental style are exemplary, though it is surprising that this fastidious, aristocratic singer should sometimes pro-duce some ugly vowel-sounds, as he does, for instance, in a generally uncomfortable record of Bach's 'Lift up your heads on high'. It is curious, incidentally, to note the rules that seem to apply to singer's pronunciation in those years. The chief one seems to be that the letter r is not there for nothing: it is to be dragged from its obscurity in a word like 'word' or 'heart' and given the rolling it deserves. Another is that the open 'i' or 'y' should be shaded towards 'ay' (as in 'May pretty Jane'), presumably sounding more genteel (this was a feature of Heddle Nash's diction a generation later, and was in notable contrast, I am told, to his pronunciation in normal speech).

So many of these 'period' features are of course most strikingly con-centrated in the singing of Dame Clara Butt. Her repertoire was heavily weighted with songs that were not so much tasteless as boring—though, of course, not to her own audiences. She was in fact pre-eminently the singer of a period, which she represented both with her land-of-hope-

and-glory grandeur and her abide-with-me big-heartedness. If all the statues of old Queen Victoria, standing or sitting in all her Dominions, could have burst into song, it was felt, this is how they should sound. The warm heart introduces many a comforting portamento into 'O rest in the Lord', and eventually brings the kind of half-sob in the voice whose last surviving echo was to be heard when Vera Lynn cheered England up in the dark days of the 1940s. On the whole, I think modern taste still pronounces the verdict 'Excessive', but perhaps less emphatically than it might have done, say, twenty years ago. Clara Butt was singing against a background of the Victorian taste which relished the death of Little Nell and enjoyed being 'broken down' by the May-Queen and Arthur's intolerable address to the fallen Guinevere; compared with which her art may well seem restrained. It was a remarkable emotional force that she could have unleashed at any time, for the maternal warmth took both sexes in its arms, with an unexpectedly frail and very feminine flutter of sound, and then a mighty fie-foh-fum from the cavernous masculine depths. Today, we are at a safer distance from the Victorians; we are less scared by their sentimentality, and possibly more envious of the grandeur of their emotions. Of English singers, we take Janet Baker to our hearts, and she, more than any intervening singer, has dared to open up boldly to large, open-armed emotions. And I sometimes think that in her singing an echo of Clara Butt can be heard, especially in the play of colours making this strong emotional appeal. Modern times also value highly that aspect of Clara Butt's art which seemed to interest her contemporaries least. She sings 'Lusinghe più care' from Handel's *Alessandro* with marvellous agility, while the Brindisi from *Lucrezia Borgia* makes the hair stand on end with its arpeggios and trill, its energy and weird contrasts of height and depth—yet this most marvellous of her records was the one for which she felt constrained to apologise, as she did in a letter published in *The Gramophone* saying that it was issued without her consent. The famous changes of register that made her later records a mimic's dream were not then so apparent; the magnificence of the instrument is overwhelming.

But the wretchedness of repertoire plagues this period very generally. When in later years Clara Butt did record something 'serious' it was bad Dvořák or good (bad) Gounod. When Agnes Nicholls, a soprano of great distinction and the wife of Sir Hamilton Harty, came to record, it would be Liddle's 'How lovely are thy dwellings', very dull stuff indeed. One admires the dash and firmness of attack (as in the fearless, but boxed-up 'Ocean, thou mighty monster'), but I must confess that I do not find affection grows with repeated playings. Any more than it does when I listen to the great Emma Albani D.B.E. Chaminade's 'L'été' on Pathé hints at the great singer: accurate staccatos, fine trills, good runs. But the Handel records are quite simply very bad indeed. I see that P. G. Hurst in *The Golden Age Recorded* refers to her 'magnificent record made in 1904 of Handel's 'Angels ever bright and fair' '. But she breathes in places where both text and music urge that she should not ('take me to (') your rest', and at the end 'take (') me'), she sings 'a-hand' for 'and', and is about as untidy as it is possible to be in moving from one note to another (this also in the Pathé recording of Handel's 'Largo'). The voice itself has a choir-boy purity and certainly does not take well to recording. Memory insists that she was at that time 'very old', and it is quite true that she had been singing for thirty-five years. She was, however, only fifty-two: a bit of the Golden Age that had been better left unrecorded.

A singer who links this early period of the gramophone with the later period of the inter-war years is the Australian bass-baritone, Peter Dawson. With him too, we meet the limitations of a vast repertoire of indifferent music. Not that it is all bad. For instance, on one side of a record there was Maude Valerie White's 'So we'll go no more a-roving', a rather haunting, nostalgic piece, sung by Gervase Elwes, a moving and beautiful example of an old-fashioned gentlemanly style of singing that, as old-timers would say, 'really was singing'; and on the other was 'The Bandolero', written by Leslie Stuart, composer of 'Lily of Laguna', *Floradora*, and 'Soldiers of the Queen', and sung by Peter Dawson. It is full of tunes, swaggering and genteel by turns, and must have been sung in drawing rooms by hundreds of visiting uncles, thumb in watch-pocket, proclaiming themselves gay and gallant outlaws, and hoping to sound like the celebrated singer on the gramophone record. But fairly assuredly they did not succeed, for Dawson was just about the best British baritone or bass within half-a-century, and not only in the 'songs that father sang'. He is splendid in Stanford's sea-songs (though better, I find, in the lyrical, slow-moving songs than in the quick ones). Then, although opera was not his element, any more than was stage villainy, he gives a clear-toned, vigorous account of Iago's Creed in *Otello*, the voice splendidly in focus from top to bottom. More congenial, one imagines, was the Elgarian *nobilmente* of the Lament, 'Oh my warriors', from *Caractacus*. Such sturdy, unforced tone, smoothly produced and clean cut, is always admirable, and in this deeply personal and emotional music very moving to hear. But perhaps the greatest of his claims to a musician's gratitude is some fine singing of Handel. His record of 'Honour and arms' from *Samson* is exemplary. It was Shaw who pointed out what a test-piece this aria is, and he wrote of the absolute evenness and command that Santley had in it, covering a two-octave range without a flaw. If so, Peter Dawson, a pupil of Santley's, was in the master's tradition, for every semiquaver is in place, and the firm sonority of the voice throughout its compass is amply demonstrated. One might compare a recording made in more recent times by Owen Brannigan, a singer with a grand voice and vivid personality. His way of singing the aria can be defended as being in character, for this is the bragging Harapha who should not be allowed too much dignity. But how the music is spoilt by this pummelling of runs and spread of tone. Similarly in 'Oh ruddier than the cherry' from *Acis and Galatea* where the style heaves and puffs so as to present the blustering Polyphemus, Dawson, by contrast, conveys just the right suggestion of caricature in his marvellously accomplished performance of the recitative, and he goes on to sing the aria with liveliness and unpretentious technical mastery that are a joy to hear.

A record of tenor arias by Handel that matches Dawson's in the bass repertoire is a coupling of 'Sound an alarm' from *Judas Maccabeus* and 'Thou shalt break them' from *Messiah*. These were sung by Walter Widdop, a singer with a sturdy, virile voice, useful and often recorded in Wagner, and able to do full justice to the broad, second-empire manner of Gounod in the grand air from *The Queen of Sheba*. Not all of his Handel is beyond criticism, but these two arias are classic. 'Sound an alarm' often brings out the best in a singer (Tudor Davies' record is quite outstanding, and there is another excellent one by Evan Williams, an American tenor who spent the best part of his career in England), and 'Thou shalt break them' can bring out the worst (comparing Widdop with Arthur Jordan, for example, one hears another tenor with a good strong voice and a command of the runs, but a tendency to force and sound ungainly). Widdop sings with marvellous resonance and definition; the breath-control supports the runs, and the style is clean and forthright.

But there was a great deal of Bach and Handel being well sung in England in this period. Far too much to mention, in fact: the modest virtuosity of Elsie Suddaby in 'Rejoice greatly', the gentlemanly, unfussy competence of Keith Falkner in 'Droop not, young lover' or 'How jovial is my laughter', the sonority and evenness of Foster Richardson in 'Honour and Arms', the more flamboyant brilliance of Horace Stevens in 'Why do the Nations' (and what a marvellous record he made of a jaunty piece called 'Sulla poppa' from *Il Prigione di Edinburgh*).

And two other singers, both at their best in the nineteen-thirties, deserve to be remembered by more than a record or two. Heddle Nash was probably the best of English lyric tenors on record. In the operatic repertoire he sings Count Almaviva's arias from *Il Barbiere di Siviglia* with grace and remarkable accomplishment: they will stand comparison with Tito Schipa or anyone else other than de Lucia. The individual timbre of his voice was ideally suited to the Serenade from Bizet's *Jolie Fille de Perth*, and this was probably his most popular record. Records made in the nineteen-forties are kinder to his voice with the warmer acoustic and the fuller frequencies, and the 1944 recordings of arias from *Pêcheurs de Perles* and *La Favorita* show the soft-grained quality of the voice and the poise of his style to perfection. His Handel and Mozart were also fine, but his crowning achievement was certainly in *The Dream of Gerontius*. In this part he immersed himself until the music and his voice were one. He recorded the whole work on late 78s, and it still stands as one of the most worthy achievements of British singing.

The other singer still most vividly associated with British musical life in this period is Isobel Baillie. She was bread-and-butter, day-in-day-out fare for England during the war and for a good many years either side of it. Listening to the records, one can only realise again how fortunate England was. The youthful freshness, with characteristic unfussy precision, can be heard in records made around 1928, including an accomplished version of the Doll's Song from *Les Contes d'Hoffmann* and another of 'Angels ever bright and fair' which is a great deal better than Albani's. The more mature voice, with its warmth and charm of manner, is well captured in the Scottish songs recorded with Gerald Moore. And her value in oratorio is made very clear as one hears her in 'With verdure clad' *(The Creation)* where the scales, trills and turns are those of a thoroughly well-trained singer, and where the voice itself, pure and clear, is at its finest.

But the gramophone does surely record a fairly general and steady improvement in British singing in the first two periods of its history. In opera too there has been a notable advance over the century. The Carl Rosa Company made a start, the Beecham seasons from 1916 to 1920 gave standards a great fillip, the BNOC helped to consólidate between 1922 and 1929, and all was set for the notable accomplishments of Sadlers Wells. But records of the BNOC period also make it clear that there was then a long way to go. Their Wagner remains a great achievement. Their *Faust* with Beecham conducting and Heddle Nash in the title-role is also very presentable (they had a sturdy Valentine in Harold Williams, and a highly individual Mephistopheles in Robert Easton). But *Pagliacci*, recorded in 1927, shows some of the limitations. It is unidiomatic in style, the Nedda (Miriam Licette) with ladylike vowels enunciating the dreadful translation ('For such a passion the whip is the fashion'), and the men's chorus sounds beery in the extreme. Their Canio was that most unlistenable of great singers, Frank Mullings. Great he surely must have been, for contemporary accounts are emphatic about it: a powerful actor with a powerful tenor voice, distinctive and moving in its timbre. But records emphasise faults: the throaty quality, the flatness, the manifest effort involved in not very high notes, the curious way of singing certain vowels. Just sometimes he made a record which is free of these troubles, but so often (as unfortunately in the *Pagliacci* set) his singing distresses the ear, and one is not compensated by any merit other than its patent sincerity.

But a pattern for the future was set in one of these pre-war albums: a special recording of Act IV of *La Bohème* in 1935 under Beecham. This has Dora Labette, who at this stage of her career found it advantageous to become Lisa Perli, singing an exquisite Mimì, Heddle Nash an elegant and high-spirited Rodolfo, John Brownlee a clean and stylish Marcel. The performance was cared for in every detail, and hopefully suggested the shape of things to come.

But another feature of the British singer's life that was still very far from being realised was any likely expectation of a truly international career. In our own time this has come about: the modern British singer thinks more readily in terms of a career that is home-based but widespread, and on the whole, the world is very ready to listen. But before the war, Britain was, like the French, isolationist; the internationalists were exceptional.

There were some, however. Perhaps Britain cannot claim much of a stake in Alfred Piccaver despite his Lincolnshire birth, but there were also Joseph Hislop and Tom Burke, the former a Scottish tenor who made a notable career in Chicago, Milan and Stockholm, the latter a Lancashire lad who trudged twenty miles to hear a tenor called Caruso, decided that that was how he wanted to sing, took himself off for lessons from de Lucia, and sang in most parts of the world with most of the great singers of his time. Burke is not well represented on records, and to remember him I would not choose his operatic excerpts but a song by Tosti, called 'My dreams': it begins with a poised, light, rather thin tone, and towards the end begins to open out, growing till the ears are ringing with it. Hislop is discussed in the section on the Chicago Opera in the next chapter.

Among the women were: Maggie Teyte, who had a new lease of life as a gramophone artist during the war and is discussed in that chapter; Margaret Sheridan, a beautiful Irish woman who became the toast of Milan during the nineteen-twenties, whose records show a fine voice, a passionate temperament, and some faults of style no doubt encouraged by her Italian experiences; Florence Easton, a musicianly soprano with a voice of shining power, singing Brünnhilde and practically everything else at the Metropolitan, making records of imperturbable placidity[1] and splendid tone; and Eva Turner.

Sad to relate, this most famous and honoured of English opera singers was represented in the catalogue by no more than seven arias, six songs (uninteresting ones) and three concerted pieces. Not much, but enough to show later ages what all the fuss was about. The power, brilliant projection and superb top notes were part of it. Also, as in the 'Vissi d'arte' a passionate involvement in the feeling, and, as in 'O patria mia', a fine musical sense for the shading of tone. The excellence of her technique is illustrated in the aria 'D'amor sull'ali rosee' from *Il Trovatore*: her trills are precise and even, her soft high notes well controlled. It was a voice that needed space. In the studio recordings of 1927 the open vowels and the huge volume of sound become a little wearing, though it is impressive to hear at such alarmingly close quarters the fullness of her top A, taken in a way few sopranos could afford to imitate. The 1928 records were made in the resonance of the Central Hall, Westminster; they had Beecham as the conductor; they include the famous solo from *Turandot*; and they still provide the best testimony to Turner's greatness. In the *Turandot* record the ice and steel glitter with incomparable brilliance. However imaginative a Turandot may be, it is no good unless she can stun a great opera house with the power of her top Bs and Cs. Turner is the magnificent answer to

---

[1] There are rumours, however, of an intensely dramatic version of Isolde's Liebestod in existence and possibly to be published one day.

this demand, and the resonance of her top F sharp (that testing, vital note in so much singing) is almost more impressive still. So from one phrase alone—'quel grido e quella morte'—the wonder of this Turandot becomes very apparent.

It is possibly still more evident in recordings from performances at

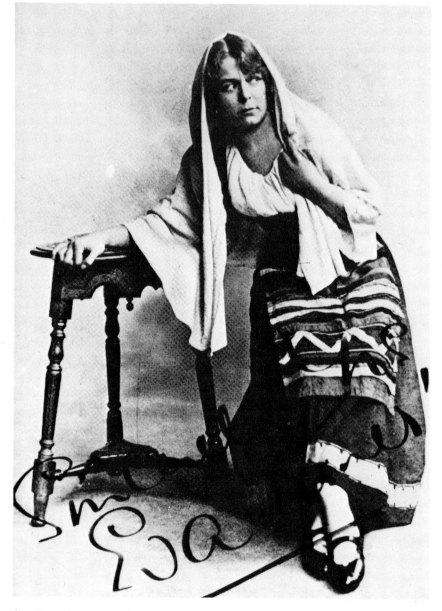

69. Eva Turner as Santuzza in *Cavalleria Rusticana*

Covent Garden in the Coronation Season of 1937. A tiresome legal difficulty has prevented the commercial issue of these, but by devious ways dubbings of a pirated copy have become fairly common in the collectors' world. The Calaf of these performances was Martinelli, so there is further reason for the unusual interest they have aroused. It has to be said that the performance is not all that the heart could desire. The orchestral playing (under Barbirolli) is untidy by modern standards. The chorus sounds fairly lusty, but the Eight Wise Men pronounce their answers to the riddles ('il sangway') in tones neither of Italy nor of China but of stout-hearted customers of *The Nag's Head* across the road. The Liù, Mafalda Favero, sings with fresh, appealing tone but with little finesse, and cries too much. Ping, Pang and Pong can hardly be said to *sing* at all in the little we hear of them. Of Martinelli there is much that one could say: he is sometimes unsatisfying, frequently great, never pedestrian. But Turner is quite magnificent. One can hear the sound in opera-house perspective[1], with the freedom of space around it. Fine in the aria and the riddles, she is at her very best in the 'Figlio del cielo' passage, her top C rising over the chorus strong and clear like a flash of midday sun. Such excitements are no doubt elemental and unsubtle, but they can still be among the most genuine in one's musical experience.

From that same year comes another 'pirated' record, this of broadcasts, including some duets with Dino Borgioli. They show Turner as a severe Mimì and an unyielding Butterfly; they should have sung the *Tosca* duets instead. But she made one more appearance on records. Vaughan Williams, writing his *Serenade to Music* for Sir Henry Wood's jubilee in 1938, kept the character of sixteen British singers in mind and composed a short solo for each of them. None was better suited than Dame Eva, who has a sweeping, powerful line with a high A in its climax. The records were issued in the same year, giving, along with a first hearing of the work, a last brief glimpse of a famous singer. It also provides a pleasant final opportunity to salute the singers who gave such good and honest value in British musical life during the period we have been discussing. The sixteen were: Stiles Allen, Isobel Baillie, Elsie Suddaby, Eva Turner; Margaret Balfour, Muriel Brunskill, Astra Desmond, Mary Jarred; Parry Jones, Heddle Nash, Frank Titterton, Walter Widdop; Roy Henderson, Harold Williams, Norman Allin, Robert Easton. A comparable list in 1971 might go: Heather Harper, Gwyneth

---

[1] Perhaps a personal reminiscence may be permitted. I heard Eva Turner only once, after the war, and in *Turandot*. I knew the 1928 recording, had been thrilled by it in fact, but, like the friend I was with, had not enjoyed the recent broadcast performance in which the great voice seemed unsteady. We were prepared to be disappointed again, expecting power, wobble and wear on the surface. The silence before 'In questa reggia' seemed very tense. The voice we then heard was quite astonishingly beautiful. Of course the power was impressive, but what delighted and frankly surprised us was the beauty of tone. Of the many singers I have heard in this role since then, several have seemed comparable in power, none (except possibly Nilsson in 1967) in beauty.

Jones, Margaret Price, Amy Shuard; Janet Baker, Yvonne Minton, Josephine Veasey, Helen Watts; Stuart Burrows, Charles Craig, Richard Lewis, Peter Pears; Peter Glossop, John Shirley-Quirk, Michael Langdon, David Ward (Geraint Evans is not there, but neither was Dennis Noble). Decline or progress?

French singers have also been inclined to stay at home. In earlier times, with Calvé, Maurel, Plançon, Renaud, Clément and others, France had her glories as well as Italy, but the inter-war years found their successors less widely appreciated. In the thirties, the only French singer to enjoy steady success at the Metropolitan was Lily Pons, while at Covent Garden several came and went without making much impression. One could, however, make out a good case, record by record, for suggesting that the standard of singing among the residents in that first period was quite comparable to that of the exports; and in this middle period too, there appears to have been quite a lot of good singing going on in France without the rest of the world knowing too much about it.

There were, for instance, some extremely good tenors. Apart from the Belgian, Fernand Ansseau, who enjoyed considerable success abroad (see p. 275), there were André d'Arkor, Gaston Micheletti, Josef Roga-chewsky, Georges Thill, Cesare Vezzani and Miguel Villabella. As the names suggest, not all were very French. Thill was Parisian born and bred, but otherwise they were a motley collection of Corsicans, Belgians and emigrés from east and south. They all sang in Paris during the same years, and all had merit. I think d'Arkor probably surprises one most often, while Thill's steady competence is so reliable that he ceases to surprise one at all, until the time comes for comparisons and one realises that 'competence' is an ungrateful word. With a strong, well-placed voice (he was a pupil of de Lucia), he covered a wide repertoire, including much that his more glamorous contemporaries would not touch. He was that rare creature, an operatic tenor who could sing Bach. There is an excellent record of arias from two cantatas, highly accomplished in the technique they display, and sung with a face: that is, a vividness of expression, like happiness or sorrow on the human face, communicated by the voice. Collectors have been known to dismiss his records as very good and very dull, but there is nothing dull about this, or about the efficiency and poise with which he sings the aria 'Bannis la crainte' from Gluck's *Alceste*. His evenness is itself a delight, and (almost as rare) so is the cleanness of his style.

But it is to D'Arkor that we go for the sudden, ringing high note, or for the special *mezza voce*. Both are strikingly present in two solos he recorded from *La Dame Blanche* by Boïeldieu. The energy of 'Ah, quel plaisir' is seconded by a sense of humour and by a bright-edged but full-bodied tone; and in 'Viens, gentille dame' this melts into a gentle, even lyricism that is still virile, with scale passages gracefully sung, triplets clearly articulated, and the high D flats bold and unforced. These are fine records and he made many more. The voice is very unItalian in that it rings out with a minimum of vibrato; one sometimes finds oneself wishing for more juice, less rigidity, in the tone-quality. And in a graceful trifle like the Aubade from *Le Roi d'Ys* he does not exert a romantic, personal charm, as, say, the more recent French tenor, Alain Vanzo, does in his recording. Yet this too is an admirable record in so many other ways: the voice firmly placed, the head-voice well-controlled, a sense of musicianly taste directing the expression.

Some of the Italianate thrill less characteristic of the northern voice is there in Cesare Vezzani. He sang Faust in the complete recording of Gounod's opera (Journet as Mephistopheles), but the brilliant ring of this voice is probably heard best in Corentin's Air from *Dinorah*: a very exciting sound, this. Then, for a greater degree of personal charm in lyrical singing, there is Josef Rogachewsky. An admirable des Grieux in Massenet's *Manon*, he sings with remarkable sweetness of tone, moulding the phrases well in 'Je crois entendre encore' *(Pêcheurs de Perles)*, singing some Russian lullabies in his native language with affection and a magical use of the head-voice. Another lyric tenor who sang principally in France was the Spaniard Miguel Villabella, his voice less honeyed than Rogachewsky's, but light and clear, very free of the throat, and easy on high notes. He is at his best in the duet 'E il sol dell'anima' from *Rigoletto*. His partner in this is Eidé Norena who also sings Juliette to the Romeo of Gaston Micheletti in two excellent records. Micheletti, a Corsican, like Vezzani, had an attractively individual timbre, plenty of body to the voice and an elegant style: all heard in his much more famous excerpts from *Carmen* with Conchita Supervia.

Among the baritones two are outstanding, Arthur Endrèze in opera,[1] Charles Panzéra in song. Panzéra made a special contribution to the gramophone in his recording of the songs of Duparc, the tone always beautiful, and the style tasteful; and his personal, affectionate singing of Schumann's *Dichterliebe*, to the idiosyncratic accompaniment of Alfred Cortot, still appeals as a live presentation even though it doesn't quite sound the depths of the poet's unhappiness. In opera, his fastidious taste sometimes inhibited characterisation: he makes Leporello sing his Catalogue Song with the breeding of an aristocrat and the fine manners of the salon. Another quite remarkable baritone, who did have considerable dramatic ability as well as a charming way with songs, was Robert Couzinou. His is not a rich voice, but his art is resourceful and the effect is always full of character—whether in the lightness of the Queen Mab song in *Roméo et Juliette* or in the commanding declamation of 'Salomé, demande au pri-

---

[1] Endrèze, born in America, came to France in 1922, studied with Jean de Reszke, and had a distinguished career at the Paris Opera. His style has much of the taste and elegance which mark French singing at its best.

sonnier' in *Hérodiade*. Best of all is his charming way with a curious little waltz song called 'Le temps des cérises', its melody something like 'Cockles and mussels' crossed with the tune that Jeanne Moreau sang in *Jules et Jim*: Couzinou's control of a semi-parlando style and the admirable mezza voce of his singing make cafe-music magic.

To make magic out of unlikely material was also an ability well developed in the bass, Vanni Marcoux, who had a special weakness for the sentimental songs of Paul Delmet. But this singer is also one of the least sentimental and self-indulgent. Famous for his portrayal of Don Quixote in Massenet's opera, he provides a fine example in his records of the death scene, an object-lesson in the effectiveness of moderation. Unlike Chaliapin (the comparison between his record and Vanni Marcoux's is made in detail by Desmond Shawe-Taylor, *Opera*, March 1963), he sings everything, down to the last words, and yet the emotion is touching and the drama vivid. He had a rather marvellous way of suggesting tears in the voice with only the minimum of disturbance to the vocal line: we find it in a most beautifully sung record of the father's lullaby in *Louise* and again at one point in the solo from the Coronation Scene in *Boris Godunov*. But the other surprising thing about Vanni Marcoux (and together with the eminently civilised style it puts certain limitations upon his acceptability as a Boris) is that he sounds so very little like a bass. The timbre is remarkably clear and free of the throat, but in the manner of so many French singers it sounds high even when well down on the bass stave. Because of this brightness, the voice presents much younger character than most basses, and it is hard to hear (for instance) a King Philip in the almost tenorial voice that sings the first phrases of the great solo in *Don Carlo*. And yet right from those first words, it is quite clear that here is an artist. The clarity of his enunciation, the sensitive moulding of the phrases, the unbroken legato, and not least the distinctiveness of that high-sounding, brightly-projected voice, together suggest a singer who through his records alone can become a vivid and valuable presence, as he was through the years of his long and honourable career.

As we turn to the women singers, two mezzos still make a strong impression: Alice Raveau, the Orfeo of the first, nearly-complete recording of Gluck's opera, and Germaine Cernay, a very beautiful singer, firm and stylish, though perhaps a little too mature in sound for Mignon and not quite voluptuous enough for Dalila. The sopranos are led in sheer power by Germaine Lubin, discussed in the chapter on Wagnerian singing, and in delicacy by the Swedish singer, Eidé Norena, whose long career at the Opéra in Paris dates from 1928. As a matter of fact, not everything she does is quite as elegant as one is sometimes led to believe: there is a very wayward version of the aria from Act I of *Traviata*, and the tone can sound shallow, as in Stradella's 'Pietà, Signore', with something gauche about the style, as in Gounod's Serenade. Yet much is limpid, sensitive and charming. Her solos from *La Bohème* have engaging wistfulness; she captures a certain fairy-tale melancholy in the short Norwegian song called 'Sne'; and there is exquisite detail in her recording of Liszt's 'O quand je dors'.

Norena's success in France had no doubt something to do with the bright clarity of voice which is so much a characteristic of the native French soprano. This is something of a special taste, which the gramophone rarely helps one to acquire, for a voice which is brilliant in the theatre can often be piercing on records. This I find true of Fanny Heldy and Claire Clairbert, both admired singers in their time. A good coloratura, however, was Leila ben Sedira: very pretty and accomplished in solos from *Lakmé* and *Les Contes d'Hoffmann*. And an exception to most criticisms is Ninon Vallin.

She is one of the best sopranos in our period. For one thing, her voice was absolutely firm: there was never a singer less under suspicion of wobble. She sang with pure tone and even line, having all the virtues of French sound (the bright projection, the unabashed, unsleepy vitality), with none of the drawbacks (that shallow, tweety sound that has one up from one's chair to turn down the treble control). She was also a prolific gramophone artist, making, as far as I know, never a bad record.

Among the most appealing are Jacqueline's air from *Fortunio* and the charming song 'Le bonheur est chose légère' from *Le Timbre d'Argent* by Saint-Saëns. In both of these we admire her lightness and delicacy of style as well as the easy security of the high notes. In the third song of the shepherdess Lehl in *Snegoroutchka* she achieves also a vividness of characterisation; one sees the girl pouting very charmingly, though there is nothing arch or mannered in the performance. In other records we can see more of the depth and command of tragic feeling that was within her range: there is a fine version of 'L'altra notte' from Boito's *Mefistofele* and her Tosca suggests something of the temperament which made her a famous exponent of the role. Carmen was another of her parts, exploiting the unusually strong lower half of her voice. It is an impressive experience to play, one after the other, her high-voiced, gently floating performance of Duparc's 'Chanson triste', and then the three solos from Falla's *L'Amour Sorcier*. With a *tessitura* to suit a contralto rather than a lyric soprano, these find her in great form, singing with firm and trenchant tone, with the authentic challenge and pride of a Spaniard.

It might sound from this account as though Vallin's singing had all the best qualities of all the best lyric sopranos on record, but it would be unfair to her to suggest quite that. In 'Depuis le jour' one still has to go to Melba or Caballé to hear the phrase 'je crois rêver' magically pure and quiet; or to Callas or Edvina to hear 'je tremble délicieusement' imaginative and inner in its enunciation. Then, in the Letter Scene from *Werther*, though Vallin is alive to the changing emotions, there is little of the intimacy and personal magnetism of Lotte Lehmann or of the subtlety of colouring by which Callas chills the atmosphere in the reading of the winter letter (one could almost put out a hand to catch the snowflakes). In the lullaby from Falla's *Seven Popular Songs*, she hardly achieves a genuine piano, and can offer neither the rich and soothing tone of Victoria de los Angeles nor the haunting *mormorato* effect of Supervia's record. That is to say, she does not quite present the memory with those individual colourings and inflections which it loves to store away. But how useful some of her secure vocalism would be to several of those who do.

There remains one more singer to discuss here, and possibly the most French of all. What Ninon Vallin was to the French opera house, Claire Croiza was to French song. She was, in the first place, a remarkably secure vocalist. Her own interest and practice appear to have emphasised inter-pretation and enunciation above all things ('In singing, one may prefer either the sound or the word. No sound however beautiful will ever give me personally the joy that I get from a beautifully enunciated vowel'—the words are quoted in Martin Cooper's finely written sleeve-note to a recent issue of her records). But she could afford this emphasis, for the technical foundation of her art was evidently secure. We hear her mezzo-soprano rise easily into the air, confident of its wings: there is never a tremor, never any awkwardness of changing registers. But it is still for her ability to present the music with the utmost sensitivity that she remains so valuable a singer.

French song is a world of its own. Listening to such a programme as Croiza's recital presents, one feels that not for nothing has the concept of 'commitment' become important in French literature: a bit more 'commit-ment' would not come amiss in the five songs by Roussel, for instance. And even in Fauré and Debussy, recognising and loving Croiza's delicacy which is so exactly right for the music, one sometimes wonders if the emotional range could be increased, the form hardened, the 'commitment' strengthened, by other treatment. In search of an answer, I compare Croiza's singing of Fauré's 'Soir' with a recent recording by Janet Baker, and her version of 'Le jet d'eau' (Debussy) with Maggie Teyte's. In both cases I think at first that the other singers have found this additional strength, and after repeated playings I return to Croiza. In the Fauré song, Baker (accompanied by Gerald Moore) sings a little faster and helps us towards a sense of form; she also moulds the phrases and at one import-ant point phrases more intelligently so that the verb and its (inverted) subject are not divided. And yet Croiza, lingering a little more, captures the 'something dying' which seems to be at the heart of the oddly ambigu-ous poem ('uncommitted' between rapture and pity). Then in the Debussy song, Maggie Teyte makes a stronger, more interesting start: 'Tes beaux yeux sont las, pauvre amante' is more clearly addressed, and has some feeling of weighted tiredness in the stressed syllables. But Croiza then introduces a greater variety of expression into this song, which, with its three verses and refrain to each, needs this kind of responsiveness. The second verse swells in tone and intensity as the soul rises in flight; then as it rests and the impulse flags there comes a delicious change of tone. In the third verse there is a similar growth of exaltation and quietness following: and in all of these, Croiza's recording has a sensitivity to which there is nothing corresponding in the other.

In all these songs there is rare delicacy of voice and sensibility. We feel in 'L'invitation au voyage' a tender incitement, where the 'luxe' and 'volupté' of the poem are translated into the most disciplined of passions and the most crystalline of tones. 'Croiza's art', writes Martin Cooper, embodied 'the emotional ideal of a whole generation'. Of the finest part of that generation, one needs to add, reflecting also that it is a lucky generation whose ideals can be embodied by a singer of such refinement.

18. Old Worlds and New:
Chicago and the Elevating Influence
Claudia Muzio   Dusolina Giannini
Conchita Supervia   Marian Anderson
Richard Crooks

CROSSING the Atlantic in this survey, we still remain very largely in Europe. There were a few American singers who made a name for themselves both at home and abroad, but on the whole the names we shall be dealing with still tend to end in 'ini' or 'elli', 'berg' or 'borg'. When the native American triumphed, everybody was very happy and very surprised, and so great was the pleasure of experiencing a happy surprise that there was as yet very little systematic provision for the training of American singers throughout the country or for the formation of American companies which would give them the experience they needed before moving into the world of international opera at the Metropolitan. Meanwhile the Europeans were still arriving, and tending to stay. For though it was very grand and highly desirable to sing at the Scala, at Bayreuth and Vienna, Paris and Covent Garden, nothing stamped 'Success' upon a career quite so finally and firmly as a regular contract and star-billing at the Metropolitan, New York. And of course with applause at the Golden Horseshoe would come another seal of success, a red one, with the blessing of the Victor recording company upon it.

So most of the best European singers went to America, and most of the best singers in America were Europeans. No doubt all hoped to reach New York, but some stuck at Chicago, one of the more wholesome distinctions of that city being the enviable casts assembled there during the nineteen-twenties and thirties for the season of Grand Opera. Several great singers spent some of their best years here, and among them were some who never were promoted to New York and the Met. Others made their only American operatic appearances there, rare occasions and subsequently collectors' pieces of note. Such were the appearances of the most unmistakeable and individual of all European singers in this period, Conchita Supervia. She made her debut at Chicago as Charlotte in *Werther* in 1915 and later appearances included an engagement in 1932 to sing Carmen. But New York never heard her in opera, and her American reputation belongs to the southern hemisphere rather than the northern. And there seems a certain justice or rightness about that. It is always a little surprising to recall how England took Supervia to its heart, and how she in turn chose to settle there. But England was still part of Europe and its economy, culture and way of life were still its own, and distinct from America's. Supervia's voice and art tell of something essentially untouched by industrialism; they have their roots in the popular culture of latin Europe, and centuries of European civilisation have refined and tamed what is still as near to being a wild growth as is possible in any cultivated singer. It might be fitting if we say a goodbye to Europe (in geographical terms) by way of this delightful artist, representative of so much, and yet so entirely individual.

It is, of course, difficult to be 'entirely individual' without also being in some way controversial. There are some extraordinary people who say they cannot listen to Supervia—she rattles. Pronounced as the rattle of ice in a glass, or dice in a box (I think the phrases have lodged in my mind from appreciative reviews by Philip Hope-Wallace), the famous vibrato is a perfectly regular flicker of sound, that could be a fierce and powerful presence, or it might lie in repose, almost extinct though always likely to revive. On records it is the most immediately obvious characteristic; in the opera house or concert hall one gathers it took its place among the other features. A great admirer of Supervia who swore never to buy her records told me how he heard her in a concert, was duly captivated, called in a record shop, chose and played over one of her records; but he didn't buy it for, he said, it simply was not the voice he had heard (a voice which he described as absolutely free of the throat, seeming to be directed from a point perhaps ten feet above the singer herself). I remember that I did later persuade him to give the records another chance, and played from a French LP a transfer of the song 'Hay in mi jardin'. The record met with a cry of surprise and pleasure, and apparently instant recognition of what memory had preserved. Now, in a technical sense, this was a 'bad' transfer, not absolutely clean-cut, and with about as much 'top', I should think, as we obtained from the gramophones in 78 days. We followed this with the same song on a 'better' transfer, the words clearer, the voice more sharply defined, the vibrato more prominent: and my friend did not want to hear. It seems in this instance to be the 'bad' transfer that told the truth: the 'truth', that is, about how the voice sounded in the spaces of the opera house or concert hall rather than in the recording studio.

Still, it is the recorded voice that remains with us, and for many listeners it is still incomparably exciting, whether the 'truth' or not. This same song, 'Hay in mi jardin', for example, is a miracle of colouring. From the finest thread of silver to a crimson of contralto richness, all the shades of possible tones are exploited with a delicacy and a beguiling lilt that works a quite personal sort of magic. She does not always transform apparently un-distinguished material into something as delightful as this. No amount of art could make sufferable such songs as 'La rosa oriental', and one only

70. Conchita Supervia; an early photograph

wishes the singer had evidently not thought otherwise. But among these inauspicious looking Spanish songs there are some gems, such as the one called 'Lo frare' by a Catalan composer, Juan Manen. This tells how a timid little peasant met a great big friar, who presently revealed himself as a robber. The poor man begs not to be robbed, and makes no secret of his fear—not of the friar, but of his wife, who will give him a terrible time when he returns home. The music is charming in itself, but Supervia has a wonderful gift of story-telling. The narrative is tender and a little wistful, the voice for the peasant is plaintive and wistful, and for the 'friar' a deep basso. This projection of character makes delightful a great variety of songs. There are, for instance, the *Canzoncine*, seven short songs for children by Gennai, with an introduction to each spoken in a lilting, musical voice, and with a smile and liveliness that are an immediate presence in the room. Then there is a group of English songs, in which of course one is won over immediately by the pronunciation, but which are marvellous for their characterisation and a rare sense of fragility and womanly tenderness. In 'Oh no, John' the maiden who stands 'on yonder hill' has a marvellously varied range of negatives: very posh, one of them (as though trained to say 'no' in an expensive finishing school), very feminine another, very gay the last. Then the wooer, imperious and imperative in 'she must answer yes or no', asks whether madame is content 'to live single all her life', clearly with eyebrows alternately raised and depressed at the monstrosity of such an absurd notion. In others, 'When I bring coloured toys', for instance, there is, it seems, a love for the language, the very words and images, all evoking a tender and delicate response (as does the humour of 'A lesson with the fan', conveying its 'delicate suggestion' with the charm of a face that is never inert, always changing and alive). Contrasting with these, are several songs where a latin sexual challenge is well to the fore. The point is clear, as one compares recordings of the Spanish song 'Clavelitos' by Supervia and Victoria de los Angeles. The later singer has every charm of tone and humour, but Supervia adds something less maidenly, rattling out the boast of the carnation girl with superb chesty power: 'la esencia, presencia y potencia que uste vera en mi'. The words need no translation as Supervia sings them.

The comparison with Victoria de los Angeles is a natural one, and it is no matter of a contest which one of the singers must lose. Their performances of Falla's *Seven Popular Songs* make an interesting study. Each has the virtues of the other (de los Angeles is not tame and Supervia is not coarse), but the emphasis is quite different. The songs bring together the traditions of European art song and the rhythms and cadences of Spanish folk music. De los Angeles' performances are very much those of the civilised Spaniard well-trained in the wider European tradition; Supervia's has a voice and manner in which centuries of the fiercer Spanish temperament speak out. Her variety is immense: there is an almost uncomfortable aliveness. De los Angeles allows rather more relaxation, though she is impressively intense and steely in the last song, 'Polo'. Where she is better than Supervia is in the *con grazia* of the 'Seguidilla murciana', its finer neatness possibly helped by the study of French song. And she is certainly more accurate on the staccato and the dotted, three-note figures. Yet when it comes to the ending of that song, with its menacing 'nadie la toma', one feels how lightweight the emotion is by comparison with Supervia's forcefulness: it is almost like play compared with reality. In the *Tonadillas*, the set of short pieces by Granados, I rather prefer de los Angeles to Supervia: the grace and refinement, and the creamy beauty of tone seem altogether more apt. But in the Falla, my own preference lies with the earlier singer, so great and varied her vitality, and so overwhelmingly strong her way with the last of the songs, which is the climax of the cycle: the mouthed bitterness of 'Guarda una pena en mi pecho', and the fierce rise of the chest-voice in the penultimate 'Ay'.

In opera and operetta Supervia is also very much a matter of personal taste. The charm of her stage presence comes over vividly in the records from Lehar's *Frasquita*. But its famous Serenade, meltingly sung by the tenor, Louis Arnault, turns out to be by far the best number, the rest

71. Conchita Supervia

tending to provoke a musical puritanism without having made the indulgence seem particularly enjoyable. Puccini and Strauss do at least offer returns, especially with the kind of smiling seductiveness Supervia gives to her record of Musetta's song (transposed down a tone), and the southern urgency she introduces into the Presentation Scene from *Der Rosenkavalier*. Childlike in *Mignon*, boyish in *Hansel and Gretel*, she is also the most characterful of Cherubinos: I have never heard singing of 'Non so più' to match hers in mobility and vividness of expression. More familiar is her singing of the heroines of Rossinian comedy. These too are nicely spiced with character, and the fioritura is rapid though eased by a very light aspirate. Personally I find a little goes a long way, but that is a comment on the music rather more than the singing.

Carmen is a different matter. 'Kittenish' was a term applied to her stage performances, but it hardly describes the records. The range and depth of this portrayal are on a grand scale; most others seem pale, dwarfish creatures after this. Nothing dwarfish about Callas, Price or Marilyn Horne, of course, and it must be admitted that Carmen is one of those roles in which it is difficult to make little impression; but there is something quite special about Supervia in it. Again there is a marked contrast with Victoria de los Angeles, who also presents an exceptional Carmen, one who wins us with smiles, warmth and musicianship, and with a charm that if 'bohemian' at all is at least of the aristocracy of gypsies. So pervasive is the charm in fact that when she sings 'prends garde à toi' it is not easy to take her very seriously. Supervia is by no means without tenderness ('je pourrais bien aimer') or tragic dignity ('encore la mort'). But she also has the kind of predatory menace in the tone, a sparkle and a hard, teasing sexuality that are all part of the role. Above all, she remains. That is, she fills the memory with certain preciously vivid and individual ways of doing things. So many of Carmen's phrases have her 'way' stamped on them in the mind of anyone who knows her records ('je t'aime', 'il t'attient', 'mon amoureux —il est au diable', 'je l'aimerai', 'je pense qu'il n'est pas defendu de penser', 'vraiment trop bête', 'voyons, que j'essaie'): the list is endless. Other singers have a similar gift: Chaliapin, Martinelli, Gobbi, Callas, for example. None of these singers offers straightforward 'beauty' any more than Supervia does; but their records are priceless possessions none the less.

When we look at the operatic scene in North America during the twenties and thirties we find one soprano who pre-eminently offers the kind of highly charged, characterful singing shared by these singers listed above. This was Claudia Muzio, an Italian who had particularly close associations with the Americas, north and south, and who sang regularly, for many of her best years, in Chicago. She was probably the most imaginative soprano to be heard in the Italian repertoire between Krusceniski and Callas; she commanded the most impressive tragic dignity and the greatest depth of feeling. In his book called *L'Equivoco*, the tenor Lauri-Volpi writes of Muzio 'singing with that unique voice of hers made of tears and sighs and

72. Claudia Muzio

restrained interior fire'. And certainly the mere tone of the voice came, like
Callas's (or perhaps like Sarah Bernhardt's, for sometimes the inflections
seem to be in that tradition) to convey a warmth of suffering and sympathy
that was beyond the expressive range of others.

The later years at Chicago, perhaps around 1930, were probably her
best, and these are precisely the years in which she did not record. Her
career as a gramophone artist was an unusual one. In 1911, probably
at the age of twenty-one (there is some difference of opinion about the
date of her birth) she published one aria and one duet for HMV in Milan;
from 1917 to 1918 she recorded plentifully for Pathé and in the early
nineteen-twenties for Edison. Between 1924 and 1934 there is virtually a
ten-year gap, and then came the series made by the Columbia Company in
Italy, for which she is best known. She was not at that time in good health
or in very happy circumstances, and in 1936 she died. The missing period
would seem to be the very one in which her interpretations had matured
while her voice was still in prime condition. The early records lack the

intensity and creativeness of her later years, and in the famous Columbias one is aware from time to time of physical limitations—just occasionally a slight flatness or uneasiness on high notes, sometimes a failure of sheer volume to enforce a climax or of breath to sustain a broad phrase. Examples of these things occur in the duet, 'Dio ti giocondi', from Act III of *Otello*, yet the record remains a fine one in many details: the tenderness of its greeting, the urgency of the disavowal, with Muzio shading her voice from a light and beautifully floating tone to the dark chest voice of 'parola orrenda'. Even in this late record the voice itself is often of the utmost loveliness (its weaknesses appear only under pressure as in the taxing 'prime lagrime' phrase) and always very steady. Indeed, as one replays Muzio's records, both of the early and late periods, the sharp differentiation between them begins to blur: the first record of all ('Si, mi chiamano Mimì' where the 'face' changes from smiling to seriousness at 'ma quando vien lo sgelo', and where charm and pathos are touchingly present) is clearly that of an interpretative artist, and the very last ones still haunt the memory with the sheer beauty of sound.

The essential Muzio, voice and spirit, one comes to know best through her most famous record, the 'Addio del passato' from *La Traviata*. The music has been so absorbed as dramatic expression that every shade of changing emotion has intense meaning to the singer and in turn receives the stamp of her own humanity—and no one who knows the record well can hear Verdi's music in his head without hearing Muzio's voice also. The air is preceded by the reading of father Germont's letter ('Teneste la promessa') dark and full-voiced, deeply moved, lifting the pitch for the word 'curatevi', allowing all to be overshadowed by the knowledge which comes tragically forward in the words 'è tardi'. The sense of actuality (the glance in the mirror, the hope, just permitted then suppressed, as the doctor's assurances are recalled), every moment is incomparably vivid. In the aria itself we feel the restrained fullness of emotion which will out when the music turns from minor to major and its chequered accompanying figure broadens as the heart swells with its sense of devotion and loss. Much is due to the singer's grasp of the rhythmic disturbance which underlies this placid-looking music; and to her emotional (perhaps even physical) involvement, which experiences the exhaustion of a sick woman, as her emotional stress or the demands of the notes themselves becomes too great for comfort. There is a perfect wedding of all the elements here.

On the same day (6 June 1935) she made a wonderful record of Margherita's aria, 'L'altra notte', from *Mefistofele*. This too is 'essential Muzio', and provides a fine example of the voice 'made of tears and sighs' which Lauri-Volpi described. She achieves a strangely mournful, tragic intonation on the last notes of these short phrases ('L'aura fresca . . . anima mia . . .') letting them trail away into a sigh carrying worlds of unhappiness with it. The record also provides a measure of the change in Muzio's singing, as there is an early version that we can compare with it. By no means superficial, the 1922 recording is much less personal and deeply felt, though by way of compensation we hear a voice of great sweetness, free and full on the high notes, evenly produced, and very accomplished in the fioriture.

The early records open one's ears to many features of Muzio's singing, especially to the excellence of her technique. It is true that she had no trill, and that in the later records she sometimes uses a light aspirate. But her legato was remarkably pure in her prime, and she was well schooled in scale and arpeggio work: one notes the rapid accuracy of her cadenza in 'D'amor sull'ali rosee' in *Il Trovatore*, which makes a striking contrast with the simplified and rather pedestrian performance of Tebaldi in the complete recording. Difficult intervals were boldly and cleanly taken. The loud singing was rich and full-blooded, the soft passages were exquisitely delicate. Two examples of music that makes formidable demands upon the singer are the arias 'Se vano' from *I Lombardi* and 'Dove son?' from Catalani's *Loreley*; Muzio gives virtuoso performances of both. Turning from these to some songs that are among her last recordings, one realises what a very complete singer she was. For a song called 'Colombetta' by Buzzi-Peccia her gaiety becomes as real as the more familiar tragedy in her voice, and for Delibes' 'Bonjour, Suzon' there is an affectionate, and infectious, smile and half-laugh. Donaudy's 'O del mio amato ben' is lovely and deeply moving without mawkishness: she encompassed the extremes of elaboration and simplicity, and was great in both.

One tail-piece to Muzio's legacy for the gramophone is the existence of the ghost of a shadow of her performance in an actual stage production. The San Francisco War Memorial Opera House opened on 15 October 1932, with a performance of *Tosca*. The broadcast of Act I was privately recorded, and the Tosca was Muzio. Through much crackling, fluctuating volume and varying pitch we hear enough to make us bless the private recorder. We hear the delicacy of her 'Non sei contento?' and 'Tornalo a dir' in the Love Duet (Dino Borgioli, the Cavaradossi, singing well), her perfect lightness and accuracy in the difficult phrase 'le voci delle cose', the lingering yet rhythmical way she had with 'Dilla ancora la parola', and the exquisite voicing of 'Ma falle gli occhi neri'. But where we fully realise that this is Claudia Muzio is after Tosca's second entry, where her opening of the elegiac passage 'Ed io venivo a lui tutta dogliosa' is of the utmost beauty, and where her last words, 'Egli vede ch'io piango', leave no doubt that this is one of the greatest of singing-actresses, of whom we are now lucky enough to catch a precious glimpse.

But Chicago had a fine array of 'first ladies' in those years. They had Galli-Curci, who would sing in casts with Tito Schipa and Titta Ruffo, enough in themselves to make many a present-day collector willing to take his chances in the city of Al Capone and Bugs Moran if he had the option. There was also Rosa Raisa, the creator of Puccini's Turandot in Milan, and a singer of striking presence and with a most beautiful voice. She was under-employed by the recording companies, but sings with warmth and skill in the solo mentioned just now in connection with Muzio, 'L'altra notte' from *Mefistofele* (her husband, incidentally, was Giacomo Rimini, whose over-ripe baritone gives limited pleasure in the first complete recording of *Falstaff*).

At this present date, however, the most enviable feature of performances in Chicago is that there was a very good chance one would hear a more than tolerable tenor. On the roster during this period were Schipa, Muratore, Ansseau, Hislop, Burke, Cortis and Hackett, all at their best (also for a brief time there arose one of those apparent anachronisms of casting when Alessandro Bonci gave some of his last stage performances there). These were exceptionally gifted singers, Hackett being the least familiar to English audiences, and yet clearly the possessor of a voice which would be heard widely and eagerly if it were about today. He was a firm-voiced lyric tenor, best suited to music like Romeo's 'Ah, lève-toi, soleil', but capable of a sturdy rendering of 'O paradiso' *(L'Africana)*. A couple of items such as these serve to represent him well enough perhaps, though he was sufficient of a singer to be compared (and by W. J. Henderson) to Bonci himself.

If, as we go through this tenorial college, we claim more on behalf of Joseph Hislop, it is possibly because we have been brought up on his records, but also no doubt because of a finer style and a rather richer, less stolid individuality, as preserved on records. He is a singer for whose ways and means one comes to have much affection, partly through the inter-action of opera and song. I suppose it is in Scottish songs and really rather third-rate English 'ballads' that his art gains its most personal expression, but these also profit from the sense that a full operatic voice is lying in reserve, and that a free fervour, not learnt in concert hall or drawing room, is also available. He had a tender and restrained way with these simple songs, varying his tone from a clear, incisive ring to a gentle *mezza voce*, veiled and floated with fine control. The 'Herding Song' and 'Eriskay love lilt', or 'My love is like a red, red rose' and 'Mary', are records full of art and charm. His record of 'Turn ye to me' lacks the purity of McCormack's singing, but it has more feeling for atmosphere and for the half-lit melancholy of the song. Enjoyable too are his solos from Lehar's *Frederica*, and (even), if one can accept this kind of nineteen-twentyish 'ballad' that nobody now dare sing, Eric Coates' 'I heard you singing'.

When we turn back to his operatic records, it may be with slight disappointment. Sometimes he sang as though determined to show that a Scotsman had as much red blood in him as any Neapolitan: the *Pagliacci* solos are almost embarrassingly dramatic in what one might call their externals, for there is not the real Italian intensity, or quite the authentic cutting edge to the voice. Yet he could pitch the emotion exactly right, as he does in a fine version of the *Lucia di Lammermoor* arias, or in 'Ella mi fu rapita' from Act III of *Rigoletto*. There is a fine snarl of disappointment in the opening phrase, and plenty of intensity in the declamation. The style of 'Parmi veder le lagrime', the aria following, also shows a mastery of *rubato*, in spite of a particularly unresponsive orchestra. But the two faults which limit a confident enjoyment of Hislop's records are a slight occasional flatness and what sounds dangerously like the beginnings of a wobble. These are not gross in degree, but are bound to be troublesome in kind. They are both faintly present in the excerpts from *Faust* recorded from a live performance at Covent Garden in 1928. They are an impressive memento nevertheless, especially as one listens to him holding his line with elegance and control, competing with Chaliapin (the Mephistopheles) in his own way rather than Chaliapin's. He had come a long way since the days when on one of its depressing dark green labels the Zonophone Company offered 'All hail, thou dwelling' sung by Mr. J. Hislop in English. Still, in some ways the sound of that old record, with its promise and fresh lyrical evenness, is more moving than all those products of the international career it heralded.

As Hislop was the only British tenor of his generation to achieve quite this kind of celebrity and be well represented on records, so was Fernand Ansseau the only Belgian. His was a more robust voice, a useful Samson and Lohengrin, though like Hislop he could modulate it well, giving a smooth, sweet-toned account of the Dream Song from *Manon*, and discreetly accompanying Micaëla's melodies in the duets from *Carmen*. In declamation he was vibrant and still musical, the shine on his voice being more vivid in the electrical recordings; he made some good pre-electricals, but generally speaking, the later process showed his voice as a livelier and freer instrument than it had formerly sounded. One would occasionally like a little more imagination, and easier production of certain high notes and certain vowels. But he was a tenor both virile and sensitive, and such records as Romeo's 'Salut, tombeau' or the 'Adieu, donc, vains objets' from *Hérodiade* have an unquestionable distinction.

Perhaps the prime favourite among these tenors in Chicago seems to have been the Spaniard, Antonio Cortis. He sang there from 1924 to 1932, and in these years made some of the finest tenor recordings in existence. One of the best is also the only one that is commonly found in second-hand dealers' lists: Calaf's solos in *Turandot*, almost ideal performances in the richness of tone and live responsiveness of style. His voice had something of the honeyed quality of Tauber or Piccaver; also a very Latin sound with more of a thrusting edge, and a temperament behind it that, for right or wrong, was passionate and spontaneous, always (again like Tauber) feeling the music as something through which his very individual self could find expression. He could throw a veil over his tone in a way rarely practised by Italian tenors, and his voice kept its fullness in the lower part of its range, where so many Italians become thin or inadequate. But then, he was a Spaniard and this does account for some of his attractiveness: for the suppleness, perhaps, and the peculiar kind of command and elegance. It also reminds us that he was a compatriot and contemporary of Miguel

Fleta, at least one of whose faults he shared. This was a tendency to overplay the emotion of the piece: too lacrymose in Werther's Invocation, too barnstorming in the Oath Duet from *Otello*, and grotesquely free with the score in 'Or son sei mesi' from Act II of *La Fanciulla del West*. Still, his worst exaggerations are mild enough compared with Fleta's or Lazaro's, and generally he registers as one of the more aristocratic of tenors. None of his work is perfunctory. The individuality is there in style as in timbre: in his way of taking the first four phrases of 'La donna è mobile' in one breath, of ending the first verse of 'Questa o quella' with a *diminuendo* and a quick, elegant turn, or the quiet ending he gives to the recitative before 'Parmi veder le lagrime'. He darkens the tone eloquently for melancholy, and (what is rarer) can produce lightness and humour, as in Rinuccio's song about Florence ('Avete torto') in *Gianni Schicchi*. But his masterpiece of the recording studios was certainly his performance of the two arias from Giordano's *Le Cena delle Beffe*. 'Mi svesti', from Act II, is given with thrilling breadth and resonance, while 'Ahi, che tormento', the bitter outburst of the tricked weakling painter and poet, in Act I, is one of the most vivid pieces of vocal characterisation on record.

So much, then, for the kind of soloist whose quality gave the Chicago opera its distinction. Contemporary accounts (or indeed present-day standards by most reports) do not suggest other kinds of distinction, of production or ensemble for instance. On the other hand, one could see a great many operas in one season, and the quality of the solo singing was likely to be high: for one thing, the payment was good. Moreover, there was, along with the mink and diamonds and social one-up-ness, a genuine enthusiasm for opera, and a belief in its value. Probably few would go as far as Oscar Hammerstein who had declared 'Grand opera is, I truly believe, the most elevating influence upon modern society, after religion', but they might echo his feeling that 'it lifts one so out of the sordid affairs of life'. The citizens of Chicago in the classic years of the bootleggers had plenty of sordid affairs to be lifted out of, and it is pleasant to reflect that for some three months or so every year they were subjected to the 'most elevating influence' ('after religion').

But we return to the fact that in the casts of any American opera centre that prided itself on getting the best (whether New York, Chicago, or Philadelphia or San Francisco) native talent did not figure very impressively. The contrast with the German or Italian opera houses, or of course with Paris, is very marked. No doubt a good deal of talent had gone untrained, and one source of recruitment, which has in more recent years yielded abundantly, was closed because of race. In Marian Anderson, Roland Hayes and Paul Robeson, America had three negro singers of great ability, but only Anderson ever sang at the Metropolitan, and that after an honoured international career of twenty-seven years.

Paul Robeson had a long list of recordings available in the pre-war English catalogues, as in the American, and the deep, rich voice could be heard in spirituals and popular songs as well as famous items from musicals like *Chu Chin Chow* and *Show Boat*. These are pleasant enough, and some of the spirituals are moving and memorable (I think of 'Water Boy' as an example), but one would have liked an extension of the repertoire in these years of his prime. Perversely, I find that with Roland Hayes, where the recorded repertoire is extremely varied and interesting, it is to the spirituals that I return with most pleasure. He recorded in many languages and knew his Debussy and Berlioz as he did Schubert and Wolf. He explored back to Monteverdi and beyond, to Machaut and the Middle Ages. A song that he made very much his own is 'L'amour de moi', labelled 'A French Chanson of the 13th Century'; I doubt whether the experts would say quite that about what we hear on the record, but it is an agreeable melody smilingly sung. The small runs or groups of notes are articulated clearly but with the help of light aspirates, and although his French pronunciation has always been (no doubt justly) praised, he shares with most of his contemporaries the failure to sing a pure vowel in such a word as 'rêve'. This figures rather prominently on the other side of the record, which has the Dream Song from *Manon* sung with generally very careful enunciation but with a tone that, as recorded here, sounds rather dry until it modulates into the head-voice. This he always used to beautiful effect: even in late recordings when he was nearer seventy than sixty the *mezza voce* was unfailingly lovely. So it is in the spirituals in which again he displays great art, whether in the plaintive cry of 'Were you there when they crucified my Lord?' or the dancing, pianissimo refrain of 'Plenty good room'. Most haunting of all in that group is 'You hear the lambs a-crying', a yearning, troubled expression in the singing, and great beauty of tone.

With Marian Anderson, too, one returns to the spirituals especially if trying to recapture on records something of the special character of her recitals. 'He's got the whole world in his hands' was always a wonderful example of a singer's power to hold an audience; wonderful too for the contrasting tones, strong and hard for 'the lying man, the gambling man, the crap-shooting man', warm and melting for 'the little bitsa baby'. She recorded a great many of them, and several of them more than once; again I'm inclined to go back to the 78s to hear the voice at its richest and freshest, as, for instance, in 'I can't stay away' with its bold style and the magical pianissimo of its repeated refrain. Then there were some that showed the deep lower part of the voice that was so gorgeous in the freer, more relaxed kind of production she used for these songs: 'Tramping' is an example here. It was notable in recitals, and is clear on records too, how her voice changed in the second half of the programme, settling down to the negro songs. It became a warmer, more richly beautiful instrument; but the change also impressed upon one just how much art was involved in creating the voice she used for her Schubert, Brahms and Sibelius. On records, where we can turn backwards and forwards from one kind of song to another at will, the variety of her singing, and the conscious direction of the voice are still more impressive. One feature of the change is the appearance and disappearance of vibrato. The art-songs have a distinctively European fast vibrato, and a more sharply edged tone to go with it: it is there, for instance, in 'Långsamt som kvällskyn', one of the Sibelius songs which became a cherished part of her repertoire. In other recordings the vibrato is there for a time, and then is lost as she settles into the song or as the tone grows in fullness, as in Brahms' 'Die Mainacht'. Her performance of this on 78 is extremely fine: the breath-control is admirable, and the song makes great demands upon it. She grades and shades her tone with much skill, and captures too the kind of yearning happiness-in-melancholy which often proves elusive. She used her imagination and her ability to act with the voice, so that Schubert's 'Der Tod und das Mädchen' brings before us the frightened face of the girl and the other-worldly soothing of Death. This, together with the range of the voice, makes us realise afresh what an operatic artist she might have been. The Schubert song takes her down to a fine unforced low D, and in other recordings she sounds sufficiently comfortable above the stave to suggest that the great Verdi mezzo-soprano roles would have been within her powers. The best-selling solos from *Samson et Dalila* are always newly impressive, and the less familiar Farewell of Tchaikowsky's Joan of Arc shows still more strikingly the inherently dramatic nature of the voice. In several of the operatic arias she recorded ('Mon coeur s'ouvre' and 'O don fatale' for instance) we feel the style is closer to oratorio singing than to operatic, but then, a dramatic style is not acquired without stage experience, and that was denied her. One of the greatest of American singers, she was finally invited to sing at the great national opera house in 1955 a month from her fifty-third birthday. The opera was *Un Ballo in Maschera*, the role Ulrica; she also made some recordings of the music, with which, of course, the voice could not cope in the way it would have done, say, ten years earlier. It is to the recordings of that period, or earlier still, that we return to hear the gorgeous voice and the inimitable artist in finest form.

Not all American artists had to wait as long as she did. Among the mezzos and contraltos were Gladys Swarthout, now remembered best for her part in Toscanini's recording of Berlioz' *Romeo and Juliet*, Marion Telva, also associated with Toscanini in the privately recorded *Missa Solemnis* and famous for her duets with Rosa Ponselle, and Katheryn Meisle, the alto soloist in Koussevitzky's version of the *St. Matthew Passion* and heard as a warm-voiced singer in some of the private off-the-air recordings from the Metropolitan. The soprano Marion Talley 'made' the Metropolitan at the age of twenty, appearing as Gilda, no less. The voice was pretty, as we hear in her few records, but the appearance was premature and it marked the high-point of her whole career. With more solid merit, which her fame as a film-star and 'personality' should not obscure, Grace Moore made her Metropolitan debut at the age of twenty-seven. Her commercial recordings show a healthy voice, but more interesting are the stage performances of *Louise* and *Manon* recorded privately. The *Manon* of 1940 is not very satisfactory as a recording, catching and surely exaggerating a marked disparity between the power of her voice in the medium register and in the notes just above the stave, which seem almost uncomfortably full and resonant. She sings with feeling, though not with great character; certainly not with the character or the freshness and facility of her performance in 1932, a few passages from which exist (Gigli recognisable as an excited des Grieux) showing how in those days she would include the scale passage right up to the high D at the end of 'Obéissons'.

In the 1940 *Manon* Grace Moore was playing to the excellent des Grieux of Richard Crooks. Here too was a curious phenomenon, for Crooks, who was probably the best lyric tenor America has produced, enjoyed a considerable European reputation a good ten years before his engagement at the Metropolitan. His operatic recordings made in Germany in the late twenties must surely have excited some interest at home, for here is a tenor who has the resonant thrust, the gentleness and the passion, for the Siciliana in *Cavalleria Rusticana* as well as the stamina for the taxing solos in *Lohengrin* and *Die Meistersinger*. More remarkable still, he is one of those few tenors who discover the poetry in the Prize Song: he makes a charming love-song of it, with several personal touches and lightenings to give a lift to the melody. The sound basis of his singing is also evident, for in Lohengrin's Narration where singers will often break the phrase or lose the precise focus of tone, Crooks preserves a fine legato, and keeps the full expansiveness of voice in reserve for the last page. The Metropolitan audience and critics did at any rate realise that here was a tenor to be proud of, when he made his debut in 1933 (he is said to have received thirty-seven curtain calls). This was as Massenet's des Grieux, and again the private recording helps us to appreciate his singing better than do the two arias recorded in an unresonant studio. The Dream Song is sweeter toned and less nasal than the studio recording suggests, and in 'Ah, fuyez, douce image' it is marvellous to hear the open production of his high notes and the full perspective of the voice. He was also a singer with some romantic credibility; an American, too, who could bring a touch of French lightness, making magical effect at 'Nous vivrons à Paris'. With this went the technical skill to sing 'Il mio tesoro', not with the facility of McCormack and of several modern singers, and not, it must be said, with sufficient variety of interpretation, but steering himself carefully through the semi-quavers and making them all distinct. He also recorded *Die schöne Müllerin* and some arias from oratorios by Handel and Mendelssohn; also of course a great deal of Stephen Foster and other popular music, for which he became most widely known. Most that he did had its distinction: if one compares, for instance, the song 'If I am dreaming' from *The Dubarry* with the recording by Heddle Nash it is to recognise that extra touch of imaginativeness in Crooks that makes all the difference. He could sometimes be surprisingly square: there is a charmless, over-emphatic recording of 'Amor ti vieta'

73. Dusolina Giannini

74. Richard Crooks as Cavaradossi in *Tosca*

75. Marian Anderson

from *Fedora*, but then no singer could achieve much refinement to the
accompaniment of a dreadful orchestra that concludes the excerpt with
chords as from the end of a Pathé newsreel. Still, the point remains: America
has produced a good many tenors, but in his own quite comprehensive
repertoire Richard Crooks still strikes one as being the best of them.

Other tenors who did good service in these years were Paul Althouse,
Mario Chamlee, Frederick Jagel and Edward Johnson, amongst whom
Chamlee made some pleasant recordings, while Jagel earns gratitude for
much sturdy, well-projected singing in the Metropolitan broadcasts and
for keeping his voice long enough to join the cast of *Wozzeck* under
Mitropoulos, and as the Drum-Major to give one of the more accurate
performances. The baritones were headed by Lawrence Tibbett (of whom
more in the next chapter) and by John Charles Thomas, little known to
English collectors and sometimes dismissed because of the third-rate songs
which tended to occupy him in the recording studios. An early Brunswick
record of 'Eri tu' from *Un Ballo in Maschera* and 'Vision fugitive' from
Hérodiade shows a round, even-textured voice of great power and fullness;
the style, a little less of a joy, has some authority, but the portamento is
not always well-judged and the phrasing tends to lack breadth. No one
could ignore the voice and the evenness of its production, though the
Metropolitan did so until 1934: they were lucky that the forty-three year old
baritone still had plenty of good singing years left in him.

For Dusolina Giannini (born in Philadelphia of Italian parents) the call
came at an earlier age, but after still more years of qualifying experience and
success at home and abroad. Her European standing is reflected by a large
number of recordings, made in Berlin, Milan and London, and always on
the company's 'celebrity' label. In 1929 (seven years before her debut at
the Metropolitan) she was chosen as the protagonist of a high-powered
Italian recording of *Aida* and much of her singing is very good indeed.
In the long lyrical phrases of the role she keeps her finely pointed voice
perfectly steady, glowing with healthy resonance and sensitive to the
demands for quietness as well as power. Thus she is extremely fine in the
final duet, in 'O patria mia' and the quieter passages of 'Ritorna vincitor'.
In the more turbulent declamation an unsteadiness obtrudes, making a
strange, rather disturbing contrast with the steely firmness of the rest. This
is true of other records also, and so is the quality of voice that provokes the
word 'steely' as a description. There is indeed a hardness of tone that must
have deterred listeners who would otherwise count her a favourite soprano.
On this point, William Moran, writer of the *Record Collector* issue devoted
to Giannini, recalls his own experience of hearing the singer in *Aida* at
the Hollywood Bowl in 1939. Microphones were used, but spaced so that
singers would sometimes be within direct range and sometimes outside.
Mr. Moran noted that Giannini's voice was perfectly beautiful without
amplification, but as she drew near to the microphone 'the instrument
seemed incapable of receiving and transmitting the quality of the sound,

resulting in that same harshness which is found in some of the singer's records'. He goes on to suggest that just as certain voices were found difficult or impossible to record properly on the old acoustical process, so the carbon microphone in use during this period of electrical recording was inimical to certain kinds of tone. It would explain why several singers sound brilliant to the point of hardness on their early electrics, whereas the earlier process had recorded a tone that fell more kindly on the ears.

Giannini's own acoustic records comprised four Italian songs, sung with fresh, pure tone and the kind of cleanness and vigour in the way of taking upward intervals that suggests the Sembrich pupil (this is so in the early electrical recordings too, as for instance in the delightful 'Cielito lindo'). Training tells, also, in the cabaletta of 'Casta diva' *(Norma)* with its fluent, precise runs, especially some where many accomplished singers are clearly experiencing difficulty. That she could turn her lyric-dramatic voice to this and her operatic soprano to the very different world of German song suggests something of her range as an artist. It is good, too, to hear how she could lighten for Strauss' 'Ständchen', and then to go back to the operatic records for the *Carmen* excerpts where there is a transformation both of voice and character. Her 'Habanera' is not exactly seductive, but it challenges with an unexpected fierceness; the gypsy is strongly present and, without taking liberties with the rhythm, she contrives by use of light and shade to bring out the characteristic suppleness and to renew the interest of the old over-familiar tune. Hers also seems to have been the ideal voice for Santuzza in *Cavalleria Rusticana*: her recording of 'Voi lo sapete' shows a complete command of the idiom, while her duet with Gigli has refinement of nuance in company with a passionate, glowing exhibition by two magnificent voices in their prime. There is a notable gap on the shelves that have no Giannini.

She first sang at the Metropolitan in 1936, a year when the reigning singers of the Italian wing were the five who are to be discussed in the next chapter. In some (important) ways, the decades we are concerned with here were not the most healthy in the theatre's history. No doubt production and rehearsals were often inadequate, casting too, and no doubt the 'stars' were often thrown on the stage with little to interest them in any over-all conception. It is perhaps understandable that the veteran critic of *The Sun* should find this 'a day of small things, daily growing smaller'. He, W. J. Henderson, had been criticising opera at the Metropolitan since 1885, and had seen greatness in the de Reszkes, Lilli Lehmann, Melba, Caruso, Sembrich and so forth. The melancholy remark is understandable, but even so surprising when one sees that he made it after a performance of *Die Walküre* with Lauritz Melchior and Friedrich Schorr in the cast. To most of us today many of the Metropolitan casts assembled during the twenties and thirties are almost intolerably mouth-watering. It is true that the management made some bad mistakes in the artists they tried to promote and in those they neglected; but the roster remained exceptionally strong.

Some of the great performances were given by singers who have already been discussed among the artists on pre-electrical records: Chaliapin, Ruffo, de Luca, Bori, Galli-Curci, for instance. Others, such as Gigli, Schipa, Lauri-Volpi, Muzio, Lehmann, Kipnis, and the Wagnerians come in earlier chapters of the present section. Of the five great singers still to concern us, permanent members of the company in this period, one, Lawrence Tibbett, was an American singer, another, Rosa Ponselle, born in America of Italian parents. All of them sang together frequently and came to know each other's art well: one can feel this closeness in the recordings where they collaborate. Such understanding between the more musicianly and devoted artists must have done much to counteract the fragmentariness of a great deal else. So, at any rate, it seems on records; and the records, it should be said, are not merely those which appeared in the catalogues.

19. Metropolitan: Five Great Singers
Rosa Ponselle Elisabeth Rethberg
Giovanni Martinelli Lawrence Tibbett
Ezio Pinza

THE 'private' recordings mentioned throughout this section of the book become particularly important in the present chapter. Their origin is as great a mystery to me as to many others who have been excited to learn that they exist and are anxious to hear them; in any case, elucidation of the mystery does not concern us here. They date from about 1932 when the quality was good enough just about to afford recognition of the music and the voices. Throughout the thirties transcriptions were made of broadcasts usually from the Metropolitan on a Saturday afternoon, but there are also some from Covent Garden and other European opera houses. With the coming of LP and with the enthusiasm and energy of a prime exponent of private enterprise in America, the recordings began to be known about, spoken of, heard and possessed by an increasing number of collectors. The quality of the recording varies enormously, and some crazy things happen, though that of course makes life interesting. At their best they are clear and without interference; at their worst, like latter-day Maplesons, they still afford sudden and priceless glimpses of a stage that one thought had disappeared into the dark for ever. With the five singers to be discussed now, they are an invaluable extension to our knowledge. We had for years come to accept that we were to know these singers through a limited number of four or five minute stretches of singing on their studio-made 78s. Now we hear them in complete roles and on stage. There are (it has to be repeated) all sorts of limitations about these recordings, or at least about the form in which we now hear them. It is greatly to be hoped that the originals are safely in existence and that they can one day be examined afresh and made available with full historical information and with the anomalies of pitch corrected. In the meantime we must have nothing but gratitude for the fact that we have been able to have them at all, and that posterity (if it is still interested) may be able to hear famous portrayals like Ponselle's Violetta, Rethberg's Desdemona, Martinelli's Otello, Tibbett's Boccanegra and Pinza's Don Giovanni, even if at some removes from the truth.

When it comes to making judgments on the basis of what we hear, there is an obvious need for caution. We often feel a wonderful closeness to what the New York audiences were hearing and seeing on those enviable evenings, yet our remoteness is still sufficient to perplex the judgment. Which of the flatnesses in pitch are due to the vagaries of recording and which to the ageing singer? How far is the obscurity of this or that passage caused by a movement on the stage, and how much to limited power of voice? When are shrill, strident, or woolly and muffled tones the fault of the artist and when of the microphones? These are questions we have to keep constantly in mind. In loud and fast passages all is generally well, but quieter music with sustained notes normally runs into trouble. So, therefore, does the listener's ear, alternately assaulted and excited, and then abandoned to find its own way among wow and flutter, distant events on the stage or pressing reminders from the prompt box (which always seem to be recorded particularly well).

More seriously, a great singer's reputation can be harmed by the indiscriminate publishing of such records, and by ill-informed listening. Not only opera broadcasts, but also recitals and separate off-the-air numbers have been recorded in this primitive way and sometimes transferred on commercial LP discs at wrong speeds, so that the character of the voice is distorted, and without due explanation about the circumstances of the recording. Jollifications at parties, recordings made in a private home, recordings made in old age: all need to be made public only after the most thorough heart-searching, and then only with a complete accompanying statement. The listening, too, needs to be a special event: it is worse than useless to give half-attention. One has to fill in much with the imagination and also to cancel out, or sift, a lot of extraneous sound. If this is not done, the records become a liability rather than an asset, and great artists will in fact have been harmed by the enthusiasm of admirers who sought to serve them.

The studio recordings do, in any case, remain the prime source of our appreciation, if only because they catch these singers in younger days with voices at the height of their powers. This is especially so with Elisabeth Rethberg. She was once voted the world's most perfect singer, an opinion said to be shared by Toscanini. And so it surely seems to us when we play her recording of 'Morrò, ma prima in grazia' from *Un Ballo in Maschera* made in 1930. The beauty of voice and purity of style give immediate pleasure. The phrasing is broad, the shading just and sensitive, always musical, never obtrusive, and the testing high-notes are taken cleanly and without over-emphasis. Over all is the scrupulous legato that makes most other versions sound amateurish: Rethberg is the singer's singer, setting a standard of pure vocal mastery to which all but a few can only approximate. That, probably, is the impression the record leaves at first. Returning to it, one may be surprised to find what feeling there is too. This is warm singing which feels *through* the music and words, never imposing emotion on them. Comparisons may be interesting, using (say) Destinn, Callas and Nilsson to go with Rethberg. Destinn is unsubtle: in a generalised way she feels the situation, but there is hardly any shading, and, except at the glorious top of her voice, the tone is not completely steady. Nilsson, on the other hand, labours at the aria, imposing intensity sometimes by means of a soured or discoloured tone and a rather enervated style. Callas is at her best: the invididual quality of the interpreter is perfectly wedded to the music and the voice is in good condition. Compared with Rethberg, the emotion is overt, and one might expect, on going back, to find the earlier singer appearing undramatic, possibly even uninteresting. But this is not so. What Rethberg demonstrates is that the music of an aria like this, sung with true musical feeling and full command of the instrument, carries its emotion with it. Ultimately it is the Rethberg recording we retain as most valuable in our minds because it makes its expression through the purest musical beauty.

Much the same is true of her *Otello* solos. They are beautifully sung. One will have heard the final 'Ave' of the prayer sustained longer, that is true, but never, surely, with more firm-toned sweetness, or more perfectly poised evenness over the arpeggio. And again these performances are musically alive, the phrases well-moulded, the gradations of tone nicely judged. As in the *Ballo* aria, feeling speaks through the music, with nothing imposed on it beyond a slight darkening of the tone at 'nell'ora della morte'. This same combination of qualities that one wants to call 'classic' (the beauty of voice, excellence of technique, tastefulness of style) is employed in a wide range of music: Handel, Mozart, Wagner, Wolf, Puccini. Fine examples of each are: 'Rendi il sereno al ciglio', 'Deh, vieni, non tardar', 'Dich, teure Halle', 'Mühvoll komm' ich und beladen', 'Vissi d'arte'. Add to that some unexpected beauties, such as the haunting 'Adieu, mon doux rivage' from *Africana* (sung in German as 'Leb' wohl, freundlich Gestade'), a superbly lyrical version of 'La mamma morta' (*Andrea Chénier*), and a winning performance of the Londonderry Air under the discouraging title 'Would God I were the tender apple blossom'.

In all of these, vocal purity is accompanied by feeling for the music, though rarely by apparent absorption in the drama or by any very specific conception of the character whose music is being sung. Rethberg is not a Lotte Lehmann or a Callas, and sometimes her records slip from the 'classic' category into the 'standard'. Her modern counterpart in this is perhaps Renata Tebaldi, whose voice so exactly fits our idea of what a lyric-dramatic soprano should sound like that to many listeners it does not register as having a very distinctive timbre. Eccentrics are at least memorable, and Rethberg and Tebaldi are eminently centric vocalists. Consequently, it is only when the musical understanding is unusually acute that their interpretations impress themselves upon us with any great vividness; and although both were famous in the role of Aida (each was the 'standard' Aida over a period of about fifteen years) I find it harder to call to mind their singing of the music than I do, say, that of Ponselle or Leontyne Price. Rethberg's recordings in the studio include the whole of Aida's part in Act III, and the firmness and command are admirable. But in the scene with Amonasro, for instance, one is only aware in a very general sense of the changing emotions—the nostalgia of 'Rivedrò le foreste imbalsamate', the revulsion of 'Orror! che mi consigli tu' or the humility and pathos of the prayer for mercy.

The Rethberg *Aida* record that *is* classic (as opposed to standard) is the earliest version of 'O patria mia'. This is a pre-electrical recording, where the sensitive shading gives an inner feeling which the later versions do not have; and it is one of the few recorded performances where the top C is sung *dolce* as marked. It is also taken as part of a single phrase, whereas in the two performances electrically recorded Rethberg does like most sopranos, breathing before the top B flat, then taking the C loudly. In one of his lectures for the British Institute of Recorded Sound, given in 1962 and issued on the EJS label, Martinelli recalled this change in Rethberg's singing of the aria: when she first arrived from Germany to sing Aida at the Metropolitan in 1922, her phrasing and dynamics were as in the early record, but the American audience had not heard it sung that way and felt cheated of the ringing top note they expected. In later seasons Rethberg decided that if that was how they wanted it, that was how they should have it. The detail is a small one, but it suggests something about the cultural setting which was not entirely helpful to the artistic growth of a singer.

And as one listens to Rethberg recording over two decades, it is not exactly a growth that one traces. The great merits of her singing are present in the earliest records and are not notably developed in the later ones. After about 1935 it seems her singing declined, and whatever artistic direction she was under did not help to remedy the situation by choosing her roles wisely (Irving Kolodin, in his history of the Metropolitan, calls her assumption of the *Siegfried* Brünnhilde in 1942 the *reductio ad absurdum* of her career). This decline is recognisable in the private recordings, where there is not the steadiness of earlier days, and which also suggest a certain stridency about the loud singing as well as some apparent troubles over intonation. In the Air of Lia from Debussy's *L'Enfant Prodigue*, for example, the soft singing is fine, and so is her clean, bold way with the intervals. But the loud passages are almost aggressive; and to turn from this performance to an exquisite one by Ninon Vallin is to find the ears blessed in just that kindly way in which an early record of the piece by her younger self might have worked.

That younger self does appear on certain of the private recordings. From Dresden in 1934 are excerpts from a performance of *Der Freischütz* (Völker and Bohnen also in fine form); a lovely Elsa from the Metropolitan and the same year; her precise, pure tone gracing a performance of Beethoven's *Missa Solennis* in 1935 under Toscanini. And even as the thirties came to an end, there is still no mistaking the great singer in the *Otello* of 1940. Sometimes we also see her with the mind's eye acting much more vividly than the studio recordings suggest. An example is an off-the-air recording of 'Ma dall'arido stella' from *Un Ballo in Maschera*, taken presumably from a performance at the Metropolitan. The Camden recording of 1929 is more beautiful in sound, but the live performance is extremely vivid. At the exclamation 'Mezza notte! ah che veggio?' one suddenly sees a face and a figure on the stage; and the voice is clearly that of a very distinguished singer in complete command of the music. All the same, it is usually by her earlier records that Elisabeth Rethberg can be most affectionately and justly remembered.

Her great contemporary in comparable roles at the Metropolitan was Rosa Ponselle, whose voice was probably the richest soprano this century has known. Port wine, roses, pansies, velvet, cream: the search for enlightening comparisons has involved all these when people have tried to describe the voice they heard. A recipe for the voice might have suggested a foundation of Caballé crossed with de los Angeles, a dash of Milanov, another of Lemnitz, something of Flagstad for power and a drop of the Clara Butts for depth. One other name is sometimes associated with Ponselle, that of Caruso. He himself recognised an affinity, so the story goes, for when he met her as a girl of twenty-one he turned a singer's eye upon her face, bone structure and cavities, and said 'Scugnizza [little urchin], you are like me'. And Francis Robinson, assistant manager at the Metropolitan, quotes the saying of Geraldine Farrar: 'When you wish to discuss

76. Elisabeth Rethberg   77. Rosa Ponselle

singers, there are two you must put aside. One is Caruso, the other is Rosa Ponselle. Then you may begin'. Giving his own opinion, he adds: 'Those of us who came along a little too late for Caruso may console ourselves. We heard Ponselle.'

For some time it seemed that posterity would not be able to share this pleasure with much fullness, for the acoustic records, mostly Columbias, were made when Ponselle was relatively immature as an interpretative artists, and the Victors were drily recorded, the voice too enclosed, the repertoire sadly limited. Modern equipment makes it easier to hear these as exciting and satisfying mementos of her great days; and there also comes into astonishing existence a collection of songs and arias recorded as late as 1954 which greatly help us to gauge the magnificence of Ponselle in her prime; and, moreover, that prime is represented directly by private recordings of stage performances as Carmen and Violetta.

The *Traviata*, taken from a performance in 1935, shows us what we really wanted to know, that is that there was intensity, presence and imagination in her portrayals on stage. It is also exasperating to listen to (if my copy is at all representative) for the pitch varies, the sound is harsh, and Ponselle's voice records less clearly than those of her menfolk (Jagel sensitive and clear, Tibbett magnificent). There are times when she lets the emotion obtrude into the vocal line, she weeps more than one would wish, and as Alfredo denounces her before the guests it is a case of 'methinks the lady doth protest too much', for her cries continue and mount through Jagel's solo. But there is no doubt that this is a live, deeply felt, thoroughly involved characterisation; the ruthlessly set determination expressed at the start of her 'Sempre libera' being one example out of many where she makes the role thoroughly her own. And the beauties of voice are tantalisingly evident: incredibly lovely in the last Act or in the finale of Act III, and, as with Montserrat Caballé, often particularly magical in the unaccompanied phrases before an aria or solo passage. Tantalising because one would like so much to be enjoying this as a feast of sound, and that just is not possible.

Such a form of enjoyment is much more possible with the recordings made at Ponselle's home in 1954.[1] They also make us realise afresh the advantages that present-day singers have over their predecessors when they record. It is like coming face to face with a person one has often seen, but only across the road or at another table or through short-sighted unspectacled eyes. Not that these recordings are themselves anything but primitive by the standards we have come to expect since then. Two of the most vivid were done informally, with Ponselle accompanying herself— the singer, it should be added, was nearly fifty-eight and had been almost eighteen years in retirement.

---

[1] She is said to have recorded sixty songs, many of them involving several 'takes', in seven days.

Perhaps the self-accompanied aria from *Suor Angelica*, 'Senza mamma', is the greatest wonder. The sense of perspective, the power of the voice to grow and shine, then to diminish again, to darken at will, to float with apparent ease on that soft and sustained high A at the end of the aria: all of these qualities are immediately striking. So too is the genuine strength of feeling, for this is a very emotional performance and it would be intolerable if there were any suspicion of insincerity. At its most moving (the opening of the F major section, 'Ora che sei un angelo del cielo'), there is some of the indrawn quality of Claudia Muzio and, of course, a richness of sound that is entirely her own.

From time to time these late records have a suspicion of unsteadiness, an occasional creak, a reminder that this is a voice miraculously taken out of storage. But generally age has not withered. With perfect aplomb and cleanness she can sweep to a top A, as in one of Wolf-Ferrari's 'Rispetti'. The breath still supports long phrases and a thread of sound so fine that the slightest miscalculation would break it. The chest tones are continually astounding, so that even when you think you are perfectly aware of what Ponselle could do with low notes, each new playing still brings its surprises (notably the surprise that in 'Der Tod und das Mädchen' the soprano is going to take the low ending, involving the D in the middle of the bass stave). Nor has her scale work stiffened or grown clumsy: Saint-Saëns' 'Guitares et mandolines' displays the agility which was always a remarkable feature of the powerful dramatic voice. The drama and authority, too, are amply demonstrated in the opening phrases of 'Esser madre è un inferno from *L'Arlesiana*. Whether in the classic dignity of Beethoven's 'In questa tomba' or the romantic pathos of the Sicilian song 'Amurì, amurì', her technique and style are alike superbly effective.

To go back twenty or thirty years from all this to hear the singer in her prime is a moving experience. What a voice it was, after all, and what things she could do with it. The first phrases of her 'Casta diva' or of her entry in the duet 'Mira, o Norma' are so veiled and withdrawn that one seems to be as it were overhearing them, yet the tone, round and rich as it is, still has firm metal at the centre. She could make a note appear out of the air, swell it till it fills the house and control its recession into silence again. She could spin a fast and precise trill and sing scales and arpeggios without the faintest break in the even substance of her voice: the aria of Selika ('Air du sommeil') from *L'Africana* is a wonderful example of this. She could darken the tone to tense, dramatic effect as in the *Trovatore* Miserere, or float it wooingly as in her incomparable singing of 'Là tra foreste vergine' from the Nile Scene in *Aida*. There was both a voluptuous quality about her singing (as in Tosti's song 'Luna d'estate') and an almost holy stillness (as in the arias from Spontini's *La Vestale*). Yet this was the singer of whom Henderson wrote, at her Metropolitan debut in 1918: 'She has the precious gift of voice and she has real temperament . . . some day doubtless she will learn how to sing, and then she will be an artist'.

Possibly the severity of that last sentence itself testifies to what Ponselle had already achieved, for it sometimes happens that critics most doggedly refuse to be swept away when an artist arrives who patently shakes up the hierarchy, raising the question of whether there should not be a new entry recorded in the ranks of the Very Great. Ponselle seems to us to have arrived at that stage when she made her early Columbia records (witness the 'D'amor sull'ali rosee'); she certainly had when she made her first records for Victor in 1924. She had then 'learnt to sing' well enough to stand comparison with any lyric-dramatic soprano on records. We might compare versions of 'Suicidio' from Act IV of *La Gioconda*. Playing Boninsegna, Destinn, Austral, Ponselle, Milanov, Cerquetti and Callas, one hears seven exceptionally fine voices, well-suited to the role, equipped with a ringing top B and a chesty low C sharp. Only two emerge as fully satisfying, however, and one has again to acknowledge how rare great operatic singing is. All, for a start, have not the steadiness that is as necessary as the power: Callas at the top of her voice, Destinn in the middle, Milanov in both; and Boninsegna is sometimes tremulous though nowhere given to wobble. Ponselle is firm as a rock, or as Florence Austral. But this is passionate music, and Austral never suggests the *con disperazione* that the composer has written in. Ponselle does, and so indeed does Boninsegna, who, however, pulls the time around, sometimes interestingly, but surely overdoing it with an *allargando* where the directions say *stringendo*. Ponselle, like Callas and Milanov, has the right feeling for give-and-take of tempo, while the others tend to move on too relentlessly. Especially Cerquetti who, in addition to this inflexibility of rhythm, cannot or will not sing softly. One of the demands this aria makes is that there shall be a play of contrasted tones: the middle section in A major being sung softly, the F sharp major passage being marked *tranquillo, dolcissimo* and the ending marked *stentando*. Of this, Cerquetti gives the least idea and Ponselle the best, for her tone, from its loudest to its softest, spans the greatest breadth. One of the hardest requirements of the aria is an octave lift on the word 'volevan'. It should be done very softly; and here, Zinka Milanov offers a particularly beautiful note. But it is followed by a semiquaver figure which she takes awkwardly, and again one turns to Ponselle, to hear how it should be done. There are some faults in the Ponselle, it is true. The tempo is rather fast, 'domando al ciel di dormir queta' is not sung as a single phrase, and she does not observe the portamenti marked in the last bars. Callas has none of these deficiencies, and hers I take to be the other great performance among these records, for in spite of the unsteadiness (it is relatively slight) on high notes, the singing is extremely beautiful, and the interpretation creative, intense and memorable. At any rate, together, Ponselle and Callas here stand head and shoulders above the others, while for sensuous richness and range of tone-colour, Ponselle emerges as incomparable within her century.

'There were so many unforgettable hours upon the stage, during which, instead of thinking of my own role, I would be lost in the dark splendour of her voice'. The words are those of the great bass, Ezio Pinza, and when one great singer says a thing like that about another, it is probably the best of all tributes.

But if there was ever a singer to match the dark splendour of Ponselle, it was Pinza himself. As Ponselle's is the richest soprano voice on record, so Pinza's remains the richest bass. As with her voice, his sonority was round and full, yet could be diminished to a finely supported pianissimo. He too commanded wonderful evenness in scale-work over a big range, and he had a similarly sensuous and flexible way with the voice (the likeness is very clear if one compares his early version of a song by Tosti called 'L'ultima canzone' with Ponselle's record of Tosti's 'Luna d'estate'). In addition, the two singers matched each other in dignity: there was a majesty in the tone and style of both. They met in the recording studio all too infrequently (there is also a sad, sad 'private' recording of them singing together late in life presumably at a party—no explanation is given, of course—but it should never have been issued, not even 'privately'). The two records they made, however, are among the finest of all. Both are from *La Forza del Destino*: 'La Vergine degli angeli' from the monastery scene, and the final trio, in which they are joined by Martinelli.

With Pinza, as with Ponselle, it is worth listening to some of the records made in later life. By 1950, he had passed his prime, but modern recording brings him forward in close-up, and again one recognises what stuff the voice was made of: a recognition that helps to bring the old records to a more vivid life for us when we go back to them. Several of the songs recorded at this late period are both touching and impressive, particularly a lullaby, 'Dormi, amore' by da Gagliano, a composer of the early seventeenth century. In the better-known song of Caccini's, 'Amarilli', he contrasts with Gigli, singing in a style no less Italian than his (cf. p. 174), but with much better taste. He uses the half-voice exquisitely, and at times swells the tone so that we hear the sumptuous fullness of former days. The voice is worn: there is a woody sound on the surface of the softer notes. But its beauty, steadiness and smoothness are still wonderful: few basses have started their careers with anything comparable, let alone finished them in this fashion after thirty years of operatic singing.

These songs were backed by three Mozart arias, with Bruno Walter conducting, and recorded on a Columbia LP which has probably had less circulation than a Verdi and Mozart recital record made about the same time for RCA Victor. 'Madamina' (Leporello's Catalogue Song from *Don Giovanni*) and 'Se vuol ballare' *(Le Nozze di Figaro)* are common to both discs, and the two performances make an interesting comparison, for they are worlds apart. On the Victor record, both arias are dully sung, and a listener might conclude that Pinza was an opulent, noble singer who lacked lightness and humour. But the Columbia versions are different altogether. The Catalogue Song, with an intimate narrative relish, sparkles and comes to a kind of life unknown to the other recording. 'Se vuol ballare' is given with the recitative shaded expressively, the opening of the air pointed by a lively staccato style, and the rest treated with vivacity and imagination. Perhaps the singer was in a better mood, perhaps in better health; certainly he was working with a conductor for whom he had great respect and affection (Pinza was just the sort of singer most open to the influence of a great conductor. 'I'm not a great artist; I just make beautiful sounds', he used to say. He was too modest, but no doubt Toscanini and Walter greatly helped the artist in him). Whatever the reason for the difference, it is a caution against over-confident historical judgement based on a single recorded performance.

It would be a pity if a new generation of collectors were to know him only through these later records. The Verdi arias are still impressive enough to convince an unsuspecting listener that he is hearing the singer at his representative best. And indeed this is sometimes true: the aria 'O tu, Palermo' from *I Vespri Siciliani*, for example, changed remarkably little over the twenty years that separates the LP version from the 78. Yet if one does go back to that early Camden record, an additional shine on the voice and perhaps a certain ease of movement makes one know that the real Pinza is here, rather than in the more sumptuous atmosphere of the modern recording studio.

These records of the late nineteen-twenties, all too few in number, are still pre-eminent in quality. Supreme among them is the aria 'Infelice' from Verdi's *Ernani*. Pinza shades every phrase with the utmost sensitivity, while preserving a perfect legato and an incomparable wealth of tone. King Philip's great soliloquy 'Dormiro sol' from *Don Carlo*, is less distinguished. In the 78 recording and in two subsequent versions, he sings with the proper dignity and with some feeling, but we miss the private sorrow of Boris Christoff's performance in the complete opera. At least the 1927 recording corrects any idea that the slight flatness of pitch on some notes of the LP version was a regular characteristic: it came upon him only with imperfect health towards the end of his life.

Early or late, however, these recordings all show us an unmistakeably distinguished singer, and we can only thirst to hear him in something more than single items from the operas in his repertoire. Here again the 'private' recordings appear, like the *deus ex machina*, and there are also two commercial recordings of Verdi's *Requiem*, the second of them combining his vocal and artistic prime with the benefits of something like modern recording. The conductor was Serafin, and his fellow soloists were Caniglia, Stignani and Gigli. Distinguished colleagues, but so often Pinza is the one to show how it should be done. Gigli, so exciting in the very first sounds, aspirates his way through the word 'eleison' in his opening phrase; Pinza then follows with the demonstration of a master. This represents the quality of his singing throughout: alike in the superbly controlled gradations of 'Tuba mirum', the instrumental breadth of the 'Libera animas', and the subdued splendour of the 'Requiem aeternam'. Only Nicolai Ghiaurov among modern basses can compare for this mixture of tonal richness and stylistic distinction. One of Pinza's successors was Cesare Siepi, a singer with exceptional physical presence and power of voice, but it will not do to play their records side by side. If one tries it with the 'Confutatis maledictis' it can only be to regret the unsteady, spreading tone of Siepi, and perhaps to note how de Sabata's sleepy tempo, nodding off completely at the *poco rall.*, prevents a naturally impressive singer from being anything other than boring. There are modern singers, Ghiaurov and Zaccaria for example, who are more truly in the Pinza tradition of smooth, rich-toned lyricism, and of course Boris Christoff has the same quality of bringing distinction to whatever he touches. But Pinza remains the model in so many ways. Not only in the *Requiem*, but also in several stage performances we can hear this same steady superiority. The private recordings from the Metropolitan include many instances of ensemble or recitative where the weariest ears will revive as Pinza begins to sing. When the loud ladies of *Norma* are silent for a while, we recognise the ideal Oroveso; when the King of Egypt has wobbled through his phrases we are treated to a singing lesson by the Ramphis. His dashing and mellifluous Don Giovanni is there, his rich-voiced and finely acted Boris Godunov too. Finer still perhaps (if only because of its great place in a great occasion) is his singing under Toscanini in the 1935 performance of Beethoven's *Missa Solemnis* (has one ever heard the 'Agnus Dei' sung like this?). All the more moving, these achievements, when we remember that this noble, patrician singer was a man of humble origin, a self-taught musician: he mentions in his autobiography the embarrassment he felt when at meetings with Mary Martin and Bing Crosby he found that they read their music with ease straight from the score, while he had to go home and learn it up! This would never be guessed as he sings Beethoven under Toscanini at Carnegie Hall. Or as, at the Metropolitan, we hear him sing the proud Fiesco in *Simon Boccanegra* with a dignity, feeling, tonal splendour and stylistic rightness without peer.

The Boccanegra of these performances (one recorded in 1935, the other in 1939) was Lawrence Tibbett, and the role probably provided him with his crowning achievement. Two extracts were recorded in the studios, and they provide an illustration, for the authority, the resonant voice and command of legato are immediately striking. But the complete performances show him in all the stress of the live theatre giving himself to the role with the greatest intensity, yet maintaining a steady musical discipline both in fidelity to the detail of the score and in his own vocal method. The comparison with Gobbi is inevitable; but what one essentially sees here is two fine artists giving their best, Tibbett with possibly a deeper kind of resonance in the voice, Gobbi with greater subtlety in some passages. But Tibbett, like Gobbi, was a singer of marked personal character, and his interpretations also carry memorable inflections. It is not

78. Ezio Pinza as Don Giovanni   79. Lawrence Tibbett as
                                        Emperor Jones

merely a matter of 'a sturdy voice doing a competent job', though there is a
tendency, in as far as he is remembered nowadays, to write as if this were so.

He was last heard in England shortly after the war, when his voice had
deteriorated sadly. Many Americans must have heard him in the same
condition, and naturally his reputation suffered (there is an undated
private recording of Ford's Monologue in *Falstaff*, the music of his first
triumph in the theatre, that shows the disintegration mercilessly). He was
not very old (fifty in 1946) and it is sometimes said, by way of explanation,
that he gave too much (words used by Gigli of Caruso), sang too often with
full power and with an intensely dramatic pressure. However this may be,
Irving Kolodin, in his history of the Metropolitan, dates the decline
of his voice from as far back as 1940, and judgments such as 'Tibbett was
hard put to produce the vocal power the role required' become common
from then on. That particular sentence refers to a revival of *Il Tabarro*
given on 5 January 1946, when Tibbett sang Michele for the first time.
The comment is interesting because from the recording made at this
performance one would say that he was well up to the part. Except at the
fiercest climaxes, his voice would seem to be far more than merely adequate.
He has the seriousness and weight of personality for his Michele, like
Gobbi's, to be felt as a brooding presence throughout the first half of the
opera, where he has not much singing to do; and when his own music

makes its formidable demands, whether of sustained resonance in 'Resta vicino a me, la notte è bella' or in the ironical menace of 'Dove? nel mio tabarro?', Tibbett is able and impressive. On the top G at the end of the Monologue he comes down before the conductor would like, and perhaps it is this that made Kolodin remark that his vocal limitations 'laid something of a restraining hand on Sadero's conducting', for it is hard to sense any other place where singer or conductor are notably inhibited. At any rate, the two impressions, those of the critic in the theatre and the listener by his gramophone, are clearly at variance.

There is less likelihood that records and history tell different tales when it comes to the solos made at Camden in the late nineteen-twenties. They are magnificent, and make very clear the qualities which gave Tibbett his fame in America (his was, after all, a genuine opera-house success—the publicity, as Kolodin points out, came after it, not before, and so did the records). His *Pagliacci* Prologue begins ordinarily enough. Distinction arrives with the 'Un nido di memorie' section where his phrasing is quite exceptionally broad. The performance builds up steadily and lyrically to a superb climax on the high A flat, and a dramatic, declamatory style is reserved effectively for the last phrases. The Camden series also contains a brilliant 'Largo al factotum', a swaggering Toreador's Song, and an 'Eri tu' sung with all the resonance and tenderness, smoothness and feeling that the testing aria requires. Perhaps best of all is the Te Deum Scene from *Tosca*, where we hear an ideal Scarpia voice, the menace of the repeated 'Va, Tosca' eloquently effective, the phrasing exemplary, and an ability to produce that extra weight of voice and intensity of style demanded by the climax.

As time went on, he gained impressive mastery of colouring and inflection. He learnt to contrast full-blooded tones with a voice drained of colour. The control and variation of vibrato played an important part in this: singers and critics of singing can learn much from his records of 'Myself when young' and Tchaikowsky's 'None but the lonely heart'. He became one of the great actors with the voice. Sometimes the completeness of projection into the drama, the very lack of inhibition, can be almost embarrassing (the song called 'De glory road' is a *tour de force* of its possibly objectionable kind). This, more often than not, is due to the material; and when, as in *Porgy and Bess*, the material is good, the surrender of voice and body (for one feels a complete person involved) is moving and strong. A private recording enables us to see very clearly why Henderson called his Emperor Jones 'one of the striking achievements of the stage': the acting is all done with the voice but it translates visually in the mind so that one feels one has seen it. Where the vividness of this voice-acting yields most, however, is in his portrayal of Iago. In the opera house it is sometimes said to have been stagey; on records it is just right. His singing of 'Era la notte' (the narrative of Cassio's dream) is discussed in some comparisons on p. 586, but the imaginativeness working here through a close reading of

80. Giovanni Martinelli

the score is typical of his whole performance, recorded, as it is, several times.

Tibbett was playing his Iago, in these performances, to the most imaginative and intense of Otellos. This was Giovanni Martinelli. Others have had finer and more suitable voices for the role, but none has left his personal stamp quite so firmly on every phrase; and no one (unless McCracken, whom I take to be a great Otello) has seemed quite able to capture the suffering Otello as this singer does.

Yet Martinelli's records affect listeners in differing ways. With him, as with Callas, there are few who fail to recognise a distinction, but many more who find little to delight their hearing. To some, the recorded voice is rather wearing, sometimes downright unpleasant, lacking in richness and beauty, while to others it is the most exciting sound on earth. He is, then, among the most interesting singers this book has to discuss.

It may be helpful, in this instance, to check in more detail how far the division of critical opinion about his singing on record is reflected by differences of reaction to his live performances. Singers themselves differ in their estimation. Marguerite d'Alvarez wrote in her autobiography that, performing with him in 1914, she could not admire his singing, that he must have had vocal chords of steel, that he swung on the high notes like a dog worrying a bone. On the other hand, McCormack admired the fire and excitement of his singing, Farrar wrote of his 'easy vocalism', and to de Luca is attributed the testimonial that in his best years the voice was 'golden in hue and so ingratiating in its warmth that it caressed the ear'. American critics (including Henderson) seem not to have been particularly excited, but I suppose he became such an institution in America that he was taken very much for granted. Kolodin writes that by 1936 his voice 'had taken on the monotonous colouration that marred the late years of his career', yet other reports in the thirties describe him as singing 'with almost unbelievable beauty of voice'. Outside America, after his establishment at the Metropolitan, he seems to have met with no great success in Italy on his somewhat rare visits there; on the other hand, there was enthusiasm in London. Whatever the condition of his voice in later years, it is certain that when he first came before the public it was the sheer beauty of sound which won him immediate fame. 'His tone is strong and resonant above the orchestra . . . Its quality is luscious, ringing, musical, and delightful to hear . . . the natural richness of his vocal quality . . . it has a beautiful quality of its own which does not tempt comparison with any other . . . a brilliant resonance, which, without any special exertion, cuts through the mass of sound by virtue merely of its quality, not its strength'. These phrases are culled from different critiques (collected by Richard Bebb) of his appearances in London between 1912 and 1919. They should at least show that those who hear beauty in the recorded voice are not listening in some eccentric and inexplicable way.

And beauty of sound is certainly there on the records, its characteristic form being a kind of shining precision. He drew sound with the thin definition of a pencil line, but glowing brightly as if the pencil were pointed with fire. The sharpness and thrust of this could also be moderated and softened. His record of 'O soave fanciulla' *(La Bohème)* with Frances Alda shows some of the gentleness he could command; at the words 'fremon dell'anima' where most tenors find the sonority of the high E and the openness of the Italian vowels too much to resist, Martinelli covers his tone and is mindful of his partner, whose notes lie in the least effective part of the soprano voice. But it is the brilliance of his full voice that is most exciting. Pre-electrical recording dulled it, though modern reproduction and some of the LP transfers wonderfully reveal the shine under the old surfaces. Generally it is clearer on the electrical series of the late nineteen-twenties, a superb example of his impassioned style being the Improvviso, 'Un dì all'azzuro spazio', in *Andrea Chénier* (full of subtlety as one listens to detail), or of the lighter manner (that came much less readily to this most jovial of men), a gay and charming song called 'E un riso gentil' from Leoncavallo's *Zazà* recorded in 1927.

The electrical process did much also to eliminate an occasional flicker of vibrato that is present in the pre-electricals. Not that the production is always happy. When a vibrato does momentarily appear, it disturbs more than in a voice where it is a regular feature. This happens sometimes on a sustained note (the last note of the excellent 'O muto asil', for instance), and sometimes as an unevenness in the process of *diminuendo* (several examples in the Passover Scene from *La Juive*). Sometimes the sound on the high F or F sharp is too open for comfort, and the high notes themselves always seem very very high, so that one feels a tension even if the singer is not experiencing strain himself. On the other hand, this tension is certainly part of the distinctive character, and probably a condition of its particular effect.

The use of Martinelli's voice was often so strenuous that one felt even in his earliest records that the excitements of the present were to be paid for in no very great time to come. His long survival is itself something of a marvel. But survive he did, and long enough to take part in thirty consecutive seasons at the Metropolitan, to sing Samson in Saint-Saëns' opera in his sixty-fifth year, and to make his last great record (or what in the spoken introduction he refers to as 'my most recent recording') in his seventy-seventh. And it did not end even there. Nevertheless, records from the later periods of his life are to be handled with care, and listened to much more sparingly than they have been issued. I think that personally I would like to see the records made after 1940 reduced to four or five, which of course would in no time become eight or nine. The duet, 'I mulattieri', sung at the Carnegie Hall in 1948 with his old friend Giuseppe de Luca, would certainly be on the list, for the gaiety of the occasion warms the heart. Then the phrases of the old Emperor in *Turandot* recorded at Martinelli's last stage performance, at Seattle in 1967 (he was eighty-one): but why oh why was the issue of this priceless record spoilt by the interpolation of Martinelli's voice singing the Prince's responses in a studio? The sound-track of the performance presumably still exists (the scene was filmed); its release would earn some heartfelt gratitude. Solos from *Manon Lescaut* made in 1950 have the old fire and intensity; but then that is still burning in 1965 which is the date given for his recording of the song about Florence in

Gianni Schicchi. It plays a semitone down, and I just slightly suspect it may have been sung a semitone lower than that (but perhaps not); it still remains a most extraordinary testament to perpetual youth, so full of rhythmic life and energy is it and so firmly preserved the voice. His last recording of all (apart from a few notes sung in a master-class in London) was made in 1968, the year of his death, and is for preservation because of the words spoken rather than the notes sung. It is an excerpt from Puccini's *La Rondine* and concludes with two spoken, and smiled, sentences: 'Il finale mi manca. Se voi indovinate, vi ciedo la mia gloria'. It is a pleasantly enigmatic epitaph.

'My most recent recording' deserves a word to itself. It is of 'Or son sei mesi' from *La Fanciulla del West*, music that he sang first in 1911. Of course we know this is an old man singing and of course it is transposed down a semitone and recorded in a fairly resonant acoustic (though not abnormally so for these days). But the record is none the less precious both as a memento and as a performance in its own right. It is wonderful to find the artistic insight still alive, the fire still alight; and one wonders if any other tenor could make quite the effect he does at the climax, 'Ahimè, vergogna mia'. It would be daring, and probably unwise, for a young man to use so fierce a glottal attack on the high note and the open vowel. But Martinelli did it at several electrifying moments in his best days, and survived to do it again at this scarcely credible age.

His technique is continually astonishing and always serves an essentially emotional end. Instances of the kind of attack mentioned above are Don Alvaro's 'Ah, spegnasti la tua sorte' at the end of the duet from Act IV of *La Forza del Destino* ('the cry of a wounded animal' was Desmond Shawe-Taylor's vivid phrase for it), and the second 'E s'iddu muoru' in the Siciliana from *Cavalleria Rusticana*, brilliantly effective after the first singing of the line has been elided with the previous phrase and taken smoothly. Both recordings of the Siciliana contain examples of the great breath-spans, which are never employed as an athletic demonstration but to give an effect like the long curve of a violin (as in 'Ai nostri monti' from *Il Trovatore*) or because the phrase is musically one and indivisible. Although as time went on in the nineteen-thirties we hear him using aspirates, he was, in his prime, a supreme master of legato (his 'Di tu se fedele' from *Un Ballo in Maschera* is perhaps the most lyrical account on records), and he knew well how to play off the smooth lyricism of affectionately moulded phrases against the declamatory style more often associated with him (hear his handling of the recitative passage in his 1928 record of 'Di quella pira').

There are faults and limitations. He could not produce a rich, honeyed half-voice comparable to Gigli's, nor command the light bubbling gaiety of his great contemporary. 'Che gelida manina' and 'La donna è mobile' are among Gigli's best records and among Martinelli's least good. Although James Joyce called him 'tuningfork among tenors' (this was in a somewhat absurd but endearing fantasy in honour of Joyce's protegée, John O'Sullivan, who on records sounds loud and dreadful), he did inflict some flatness of intonation which along with the remorselessly penetrative tone can play like a dentist on wincing nerves.

But he still achieved a certain special greatness beyond the reach of any other operatic tenor we know on records. The peculiar power of Italian opera lies so much in its ability to give lyrically sustained utterance to suffering, tragic anger and tragic happiness. Perhaps with Muzio and Callas among women singers, Martinelli's voice and style form the most eloquent instrument the tradition has fashioned to express this. He does so not through any self-pitying indulgence in sobs, but through a kind of tension that is entirely his own. Hence the greatness of his Otello.

The best of the complete recordings from the stage is that taken on 24 February 1940. Rethberg is recognisably 'the world's greatest soprano' again here, and Tibbett is the excellent Iago. Panizza conducts with decision and flexibility, at a fantastically fast allegro in the first scene, very much school-of-Toscanini in drive and intensity, but allowing a relaxation of tempo and more room for the expression of tenderness than in Toscanini's recording. 'Esultate' and 'Abasso le spade' command attention by the tense, knife-edge cleanness, and an essential chafing in Otello is caught as the blood begins to rebel. The Love Duet draws its lines in long, smooth curves, retracts to a pianissimo that expresses this inheld emotion in which already there is the tension of fear for the future ('I do fear my soul hath her content so absolute . . .'). Martinelli is specific in his grasp of that particular phrase in the Italian, the pathos of its irony made implicit in his tone; and this is typical, for from Iago's first insinuations we are to see the suffering Otello as in some kind of X-ray of the nerves, the neurosis of unsure power, remaining aristocratic and commanding however the weakness and anguish are exposed. It would take a separate essay to comment analytically, but every phrase calls forth its own colouring and distinction, from the lurking sadness in 'Quel canto mi conquide' to the fury and loathing of 'quella vil cortigiana che è la sposa d'Otello'.

Martinelli's Otello was the last grand creation of an epoch. It marked the climax of his career and the end of an age. The other singers of that age declined or retired. The war came, and with it bad times for opera and the gramophone (some extracts from *Otello* were recorded commercially, with Martinelli, Tibbett and Helen Jepson, but the studio was so dry and the sheer loudness so oppressive that they made uneasy listening). The dearth of good new singers in the thirties made itself felt, and at the Metropolitan the closing epoch also meant the end of a generation of singers whose standards had been set or influenced above all by Toscanini. Farrar, Alda, Martinelli, de Luca, Pinza, and no doubt many others have owned his greatness not only as a conductor but as a teacher, and have acknowledged their own debt to him. Martinelli worked intensively with him (in, so it is said, over fifty rehearsals for the 1914 revival of *Il Trovatore*, for example);

and sometimes on his records it almost seems as though in such drive and incisiveness we can hear Toscanini himself singing through the tenor. With the war, this age ended, as far as the opera house was concerned. Long-established careers came to their close, and little of distinction seemed left to continue the great tradition.

But as usual in times when everyone thinks the days of great singing are over, talent soon begins to emerge. The war ended and Europe began to find its Schwarzkopf and Seefried, Welitsch and Christoff, Tebaldi and Gobbi. And we find, as we look back, that not even the war years were quite as barren as we may have supposed.

20. Survival: Wartime and Aftermath
Helen Traubel Maggie Teyte
Kathleen Ferrier Julius Patzak
Mark Reizen

The lights must never go out,
The music must always play.

THUS W. H. Auden observing the anxiety of New Yorkers on 1 September
1939. The lights went out in Europe two days later, but to a remarkable
extent the music played on and the gramophone did better public service
than ever before.

In England, good instrumental and orchestral records still appeared,
and there was singing too, but only under certain conditions. German and
Italian were no longer officially considered civilised tongues, and all
recorded singing had to be in patriotic languages, so that 'Arise, ye Russian
people' was allowed, but 'La donna è mobile' was not. French was per-
missible, and, as HMV cast around for someone in addition to John
McCormack to continue their red-label series, the happy thought occurred
that resident in England was one of the very few celebrated interpreters
of French song. So throughout the war-years we heard from Maggie
Teyte, and the catalogue was enriched by a series of records whose only
comparable issue in England had been by Teyte herself some years earlier,
available to special order only.

Those earlier records had been of songs by Debussy and were accompanied by Alfred Cortot. Cortot wrote of Maggie Teyte's ability to
convey 'imaginative resonance' and 'power of suggestion', and the highest
authorities are sufficiently unanimous on the point to make a mild disagree-
ment look much like a confession of deafness. However, listening to those
Debussy recordings, liking (and having in fact an affection for) the sound
of the voice itself, I first of all find concentration difficult. It is not the songs
themselves, for turning to Gérard Souzay I find myself held. Compare the
two singers, then, in 'En sourdine'. Souzay gives the sense of 'ce silence
profond' with a hushed tone, lightly warming it at 'laissons-nous per-
suader', diminishing to the most delicately muted pianissimo at 'voix de
notre désespoir, le rossignol chantera'. There is little corresponding to
this in Maggie Teyte's record; not does she phrase broadly enough (for

instance, the sense seems to ask for phrasing-over at 'vagues langueurs des pins et des arbousiers', but here the singer breathes after 'langueurs'). Going on to the next song, 'Fantoches', and comparing Souzay only confirms the point, so let us try again, with the 'Chansons de Bilitis' and some other singers for comparison. Teyte, Danco, Merriman, Crespin and Baker have all recorded the songs. Of these, Danco is probably the least subtle but she does present a fresh and likeable young girl, using a smiling tone for the first song. Baker also has a smile for that first song, but it is a smile on an ever-changing face: she has come from the Hyacinthia feast (it is not just any day), her syrinx is made of reeds that have been well-cut (not just anybody has cut those reeds, and she smiles approval), 'it is late' (and there is a magic in that lateness because of what has gone before), and mother will not believe her excuse (she whispers to us, confidingly). Turning to Maggie Teyte, one does not find these points, though they are present in Crespin and Merriman. It is Merriman who most effectively puts the songs into a sunnier and sultrier climate. For the second of them 'La Chevelure', she uses her rich, contralto voice for the 'he' of the poem: this is a seduction, the gorgeous sensuous quality of tone at 'par la même chevelure' translating readily into sensuality with the girl's submission 'avec un frisson' (breathing 'avec' and so catching the 'frisson'). Baker and Crespin also communicate with some intensity and much imagination. They take longer to do it than Teyte, of course: her recording lasts three minutes, Baker's 3·23, Crespin's 3·47. But longer time does not necessarily of itself mean greater intensity, and in the last song, 'Le Tombeau des Naiades', Crespin's version is slightly quicker than Teyte's (2·35 against 2·38) and hers (Crespin's) is surely the best. For one thing, Crespin picks out the voices of the dialogue (she is alone among the five singers in this). She also deepens the song, by the contrast of lightness in her staccato touch at the girl's pretty whimsical following of the satyr's tracks ('ses petits pas'), and by the darkened tone of the reply 'Les satyrs sont morts'. She also finds a way (by strong tone and *diminuendo*) of leaving the last image in our minds: the large pieces of shattered ice held skywards, and 'his' face looking through.

Teyte did of course study these songs (as well as *Pelléas*) with Debussy; her singing of them is in this sense 'authentic'. But one can only put it personally: that it is from later interpreters (who admittedly have had her records to guide them) that I learn what these songs are, and find myself able to be engaged by them. For all that, there is still something lovely and irreplaceable about Maggie Teyte's singing. One point is that she has a personal style and is instantly recognisable, though the little downward portamento, which is one of the main features of her style, becomes something of a mannerism, likeable till indulged in too often. Another point is that her interpretations are sometimes strong and vivid: the opening of Ravel's 'Shéhérazade' is strongly evocative, and her singing of 'La Spectre de la Rose' from *Nuits d'Eté* is quite different from modern versions in its lilt, catching the latent waltz rhythm, less spectrally, more substantially, and then regaining the more 'inner' quality by lingering tenderly over the epitaph of the rose in the last lines. But basically the point about Maggie Teyte is the very simple one, that her singing is so good: that is, her voice is so clear, its production so even, its emission so steady, its intonation so faultless, its movement in big upward intervals so clean and athletic, and its excellence was so well preserved for so long. In 1946, when she was fifty-seven, she recorded Chausson's *Poème de l'amour et de la mer* with most lovely tone: 'Et mon coeur s'est levé par ce matin d'été', says one line of the poem, and, as the voice places the high note at the end of the phrase, one feels how exactly the words suit the singer. This long work by Chausson ends with 'Le temps des lilacs', well-known as a song on its own, and here she sounds genuinely moved, while her singing, the lightening and moulding of exquisitely lyrical phrases, is itself moving. So it is, in deeper mood, in Duparc's 'Extase': one could never hear that song without Teyte's portamento and special tone sounding in one's head. There is tenderness, and a suggestion of frailty here, rather rare in her singing, and very lovely. And at the other end of the scale is her bold, magnetic way with the songs from Offenbach's *La Périchole*. In all of this music she is a delight; and, returning to Debussy, one feels that, while going to the recordings of others to help interpretation, a student-singer could not possibly do better than attend to Maggie Teyte's records as an incentive to master the thorough groundwork of singing in the first place.

Apart from records by Teyte, McCormack and Tauber, most wartime singing in England went onto the 'popular' labels, and it was all sung in English. The team for operatic excerpts included Joan Cross, Joan Hammond, Gwen Catley, Gladys Ripley, Heddle Nash, Webster Booth and Dennis Noble, and they did splendid work. Absolute fidelity to the score was a first principle, so Catley in *Traviata*, Hammond in the *Trovatore* arias, and Noble in *Faust* have rare features, which would please the connoisseur if he deigned to listen to such home-made stuff. The 'Celeste Aida' was contributed by Webster Booth, a tenor who did not possess such full-bodied sonority as the aria needs (after the average Italian *spinto* he sounds like a fastidiously musical choral scholar from Cambridge). But he does take the final B flat as written, and the effect is delightful. In music that suited his voice, he was always reliable and pleasing, and his Mozart arias (especially 'O wie ängstlich' from *Die Entführung*) are models of clean, able singing. His partner in a lively version of the Almaviva–Figaro duet in *Il Barbiere di Siviglia* was Dennis Noble, whose mimicry of the man 'who the wine-cup can't deny' is a nice reminder of Colonel Chinstrap, another wartime favourite. His 'Largo al factotum' is also a sparkler: nimble, humorous and resourceful as the famous barber himself. In Gwen Catley the company had a charming and accomplished Rosina: between them they could have recorded an excellent English *Barber* if conditions had permitted. But for these restrictions, too, we might have had Joan Hammond at the height of her powers, during the mid nineteen-forties, in some complete opera more appropriate than Purcell's *Dido and Aeneas*, recorded under Constant Lambert, and chiefly remarkable now for the vivid menace of Edith Coates as the Sorceress. As it is, Hammond deserved a little more recognition than has generally come her way from the critics (she had plenty from the public). Her tone was not rich but it was strong and vibrant; her style was not smooth but it was responsive. She had a live feeling for the rapt excitement of operatic music. She could also endow an aria with specific meaning at every point, so that her performance of 'La mamma morta' from *Andrea Chénier* is remarkable as an example of a complete, studied interpretation. She had also taken a careful look at the score of *Il Trovatore* to see what it has to say about the phrases at the climax of 'D'amor sull'ali rosee': very few other singers have taken the point of the emphasis marked for the note *before* the high one (first the C, then the B flat). There were many things like this that she did extraordinarily well, and to many a voice-starved ear she gave the first live evidence of the excitements a genuine operatic artist can provide.

It was to the ears of this post-war generation, longing to hear again singing that could sweep regally and soar with international authority, that the few records of Margherita Grandi were so welcome. The arias from *Macbeth* were directly in the grand tradition, noble and commanding, rich-voiced and dramatic. 'Tu che le vanità' from *Don Carlo*, valued because it was a performance of an unduly neglected aria, is less impressive, the character rather undistinctive and the tone not entirely firm. Grandi also sang Giulietta for the soundtrack of the filmed *Tales of Hoffmann* conducted by Beecham, but here a deterioration is evident. She is an example of the generation of singers who suffered most from the war. In those years she must have been at her excellent best, but no records were made.

One other rather magnificent singer was active in England, without, as it seems now, being properly appreciated. Oda Slobodskaya first came to Covent Garden in 1932 and sang in most parts of the world before and after, but in England she made her home, and sometime around her fiftieth birthday she began to be used as a recording artist. Her previous records had been few but fine, and more were to follow in her mid-sixties. Meanwhile there came a short but excellent series of Russian songs given with a pure, steady voice, a true legato and vivid characterisation. Songs by Tanelev showed the sweetness of tone and the meticulous placing; Gretchaninoff showed the control of the soft singing and the thrill (as in 'The dreary Steppe') of the loud; Rimsky-Korsakov's folk-songs show the strong spirit, as in a jolly one called 'I'm sitting on a stone' ('with my chopper in my hand'). But 'Grow old along with me, The best is yet to be'; in 1961 she recorded some more, speaking the introduction to several of them, and of course everyone reflects how marvellous to have a Russian grandma like this. 'Den dey all sit arount ant sink—Tilim-bom', she tells us in her introduction to Stravinsky's *Three Tales for Children*.

Better still, the story of The Bear (45 seconds to sing the song, 2 minutes 10 seconds to introduce it). 'Here is a bear's paw for our dinner: cook it, woman', says the old peasant in the tones of a Grand Duke. 'Wah, old man! Come, let us fight', says the bear, with his most bear-like utterances touching bass C. 'And they dragged them out from under the bed' we learn, a ruthless action which involves a mighty rolling of the 'r' and the speaking voice touching F at the top of the treble stave. As for the singing voice, it is certainly grandma's—but it is perfectly steady!

Slobodskaya was one of a generation of Russian singers that has largely got lost to view in the western world. She was born in 1895, the same year as the great bass, Mark Reizen, and one year after the soprano, Nina Koshetz. Two tenors, Kozlowsky and Lemeshev, were slightly younger, but belong to roughly the same period. There are others whose records have made their way to the west, but these few stand out to us as the main names in a period that brought war and revolution during the years which tend to be most crucial in a singer's development.

Of these, Koshetz left Russia in 1920 and appears not to have returned. She is adored by collectors, her records being few, rare and good. 'All that good?' one sometimes asks, seeing them priced high in the dealers' lists and hearing them spoken of with bated breath. But yes, we return to the best-known of them, the aria of Jaroslavna in *Prince Igor*, and there is the thrill of real distinction. It is partly in the tone, vibrant and shining, partly in the sheer power and in its contrast with the softness where this very Russian ice-princess melts, all tenderness. And it is partly in a kind of glamour, which marks also her later recordings, made in 1939, principally of songs by Rachmaninoff. The temperament seems well-suited to the material, and as she worked with the composer a good deal one can well imagine that these are performances as 'authentic' as one is likely to get (inverted commas because I am never quite sure how much of a guarantee this kind of association is—it probably is here, as with another Russian soprano settled in America, Maria Kurenko, and her close association with Gretchaninoff). I always think of Lawrence's poem, *Piano*, when I hear these records: 'So now it is vain for the singer to burst into clamour with the great black piano appassionato . . .' Koshetz clamours with a passionate Russian melancholy, then passes a veil over the voice as a deep sigh comes from the soul in the depths of mortal weariness. Just occasionally the style suggests the film-star of old, Nazimova or Theda Bara, seated at the piano and raising black eyes heavenwards: so it is in the song of that name (the celebrated 'Ochi churnya'), self-accompanied, much given to nostalgic 'tra-la-la'ing and then to a kind of declamation, which has something of lamenting speech in it, the very heart of eternal Russia in exile. But one returns to the earlier records, to the 'Estrellita', for instance, deliciously floated, and has to acknowledge the collectors' devotion as justified. There is nothing for it but to start saving up.

Meanwhile in Russia itself Sergei Lemeshev sang poetically in such parts as Lenski in *Eugen Onegin*, continuing well into the days of LP, and Ivan Kozlowsky offers the basic Italian repertoire in rather more interesting form than did many of the Italians themselves at this time. His 'Che gelida manina' has some of the freedom with tempo which marked early Italian performances but was later ironed out, and much of the charm with it. Like several tenors, he sings most imaginatively in Lohengrin's Narration: with steady tone, rather rounder than in other records, he gives a lyrical performance that has many personal touches. In an aria from *Dubrovskii* (by Napravnik) he also uses the head voice to good effect. This is a fine singer, and one can only wish that he was more readily to be heard on records over here.

Mark Reizen has become much more familiar to us. A superb recital disc was issued in London in 1959, the mere sound of the voice immediately impressive: deep, warm, firm, authoritative. He would never shout: Farlaff's Rondo in *Russlan and Ludmilla* finds him taking the patter at high speed, articulating with energy and using plenty of voice, yet making the minimum sacrifice of well-rounded tone and lyricism. He has a splendid rhythmic buoyancy and a vivid smile that lights up this as well as his singing of the Miller's Aria from *Rusalka*. Then as the smile develops into the weird laughter of madness in Act III, one sees quite vividly the bared teeth and wide eyes. He is subtle here in his colouring of the soft singing, a rounded, hollowed sound, that promotes great expectations of his Boris Godunov. These are partly fulfilled: the tenderness of family feeling is caught, the Cathedral Scene (playing to the crafty-sad Idiot of Kozlowsky) has a fine chastened dignity, and in the Death Scene there is a snarl in the voice which warns against the Boyars. The Monologue is less tormented and intense than Chaliapin's: carefully studied and varied, clearly enunciated and always musical, it wants the suggestion of neurosis and the conviction of pain. His characterisations are measured, almost as though the lesson learnt from Chaliapin was the avoidance of excess. This applies to quite different roles too: thus Varlaam is no sprawling drunkard, and Galitsky sings with refined energy rather than with the beery uproariousness of Chaliapin. But a sense of stature is always present, and, above all, the fine, instrumental usage of an extremely beautiful voice. Like some of the basses of the old school, he 'plays' his voice like a cello: we hear it finely in the slow section of the Mad Scene in *Rusalka*. The voice was also completely unified, its range well displayed in Khan Khontchak's solo from *Prince Igor*, descending with deep bass relish to the low F, and always easy in production. His was a wholesome art: another singer for students. Also one of the best of our century.

The other distinguished Russian singer whose reputation spread abroad in the years following the Second World War was the contralto, Zara Dolukhanova. A very complete singer, with a repertoire that ranged widely over continents and centuries, she had the technique to master the florid scores of Rossini and Meyerbeer; her singing of Arsace's music in *Semiramide* anticipates the revival of interest that has come about in more recent times (see p. 394). Her singing of Bach has been greatly admired, and we also find her on records in Britten and Falla: all sung with fine, well-nourished tone, and a certain boldness of presentation. The rich low notes did not form a special chest-register but were well integrated, as we hear in Ravel's 'Kaddisch', sung idiomatically and with intensity. In Russian music she is responsive to changes of mood, melancholy and personal, gay and extrovert in turn. There are limits, it is true: the operatic records, in the reprints by which I know them, are sometimes a little unsteady or matronly, and the *Seven Popular Songs* pale a little as one plays them next to Supervia (who makes, for instance, so much more contrast between the songs). But the voice is immensely impressive: its range over something like two-and-a-half octaves, its strength and richness both exceptional. One can only wish again that by a series of regular issues and personal appearances she had become a more familiar and vivid part of the musical scene over here during the years of her prime.

It is not surprising that this generation of Russian singers is relatively little known outside Russia; but one might have expected the American singers of the same period to be much more familiar to the rest of the world. Licia Albanese, Bidu Sayao, Rose Bampton and Eleanor Steber, Dorothy Maynor and Helen Traubel and Helen Jepson – these sopranos were an essential part of American musical life, and their records had wide currency in the States; but strangely enough, they did not really reach a wider audience. Even Zinka Milanov, prima donna of the Metropolitan for twenty years, fades from European view as the recordings which were almost the only contact with her begin to lose their places in the current catalogues.

Milanov does certain things to perfection; it then registers as a genuine disappointment that one can enjoy one phrase and not the next, or one part of an aria and not what follows. For example: Act I of *Aida* brings no joy until the prayer at the end of 'Ritorna vincitor', which is suddenly ideal; then the duet with Amneris in Act II has little to be said for it till 'Pietà ti prenda', which has much; and the Nile Duet is heavenly in 'Là tra foreste vergine' but something notably less in the 'fuggiamo' passage which follows. The pattern is clear by this time: where there are high notes to be floated, soft passages to be sung with a creamy tone, phrases where the solo voice can hold a long line uninterrupted by declamatory or other pressures, then all is more than well. At other times the lack of bite is felt, possibly by the singer herself, whose tone then becomes unsteady under pressure. Thus, the Aida starts badly and ends beautifully. The first trio, with its turbulent line, suggests that we are in for a squally performance; long before the final duet we have realised that there will be intermittent greatness, and all of this last scene leaves a memory of the utmost beauty. It is so with most of her recordings. The long notes and broad phrases of 'Madre, pietosa vergine' from *La Forza del Destino* are duly wrapt in the finest velvet; 'Morrò, me dall prima in grazia' from *Un Ballo in Maschera* has warmth and grandeur. In *La Gioconda* (whether in the studio recording of 1958 or the Metropolitan broadcast of 1939) some of the score clearly asks for a stronger, more Italianate cutting edge, while other parts benefit from a kind of sound rarely to be heard coming from an Italian throat—the long held high B flat in Act I ('Ah, come t'amo') is an unforgettable example. Perhaps best of all, in *Il Trovatore*, she comes into her kingdom in Act IV, with the *dolcissimo* of the recitative, and the beautifully floated phrases of 'D'amor sull'ali rosee'. It is thus that she remains a kind of archetype: where one wants soft singing, its surface suggesting velvet, its texture cream, and the whole thing set somehow magically afloat in the night-sky, well, of course one can try Ponselle, Lemnitz, Caballé, but in this particular matter it is hardly possible to do better than with Milanov.

The other soprano who claims attention for a rare kind of excellence is Traubel. Again there are limits: hers must surely be the loudest recording of Desdemona's Willow Song, the least idiomatic of Waltz Songs from *The Merry Widow*, and otherwise the most unappetising in choice of repertoire outside Wagner. Even in Wagner, her own manner and the loud, strident recording in favour at the time combine to produce a version of the *Wesendonck Lieder* without any suggestion of the dream, the hothouse, the angel, or any of the other features that usually make it an essay in relatively subtle large-scale singing (and this in spite of having Stokowski as conductor). But there is no mistaking the quality of the voice itself: one can hardly think of a more powerful, wish for a more resonant, or reasonably expect a firmer. A Brünnhilde rather than a Sieglinde, she nevertheless sings superbly in the Love Music from *Die Walküre* in a Toscanini broadcast of 1941: she does, later on in the excerpt, achieve a soft tone for certain phrases and also some innerness of feeling, but generally it is the bright-edged sword of a voice that so impresses, and the stamina to respond with unflagging energy to the tremendous demands of the conductor who secures an inspired performance from all concerned in it. In a privately recorded broadcast of *Tristan und Isolde* under Leinsdorf at the Metropolitan, we realise that she could also be an imaginative artist: good at catching the irony in Isolde's anger in the first Act, and singing the lyrical phrases of Act II most beautifully. She does not risk the two high Cs, but is clean in her way with the high notes and scrupulous about note-values. I would not say from the records that her voice has that nobility one wants from Isolde in the last Act; a certain hardness works against that. Yet the 'Liebestod', starting warmly and quietly, surges with glorious tone towards a massive climax, the voice clear and steady above the orchestra. There are impressive commercial recordings of passages from the opera, but again the private recorder serves us well, presenting a genuinely responsive and dramatic portrayal of one of the great operatic roles, quite apart from confirming a suspicion that here is one of the voices best able to do it justice throughout the whole range of recording.

81. Maggie Teyte as Mélisande in *Pelléas et Mélisande*

82. Mark Reizen

83. Julius Patzak as Florestan in *Fidelio*

84. Helen Traubel as Elisabeth in *Tannhäuser*

Maynor's was also an uncommonly full and fine voice, and with Bampton one always admires the business-like approach: she too responds to Toscanini's direction, and puts heart and soul into the Leonore of his 1944 *Fidelio*. The Marzelline of that performance is Eleanor Steber, clear-toned and capable, as in a very wide variety of recordings relatively little circulated outside America. Her singing of 'Ernani, involami' is a fair sample: there is an unfussy efficiency, extending to staccatos on the downward arpeggio from the high A, which are rarely observed, yet the aria yields none of its secrets in this reading, which conveys little feeling and no poetry. Other recordings are more imaginative: the last Act of *Madama Butterfly* and the Church Scene in *Faust*, for example, though even there the voice seems so clearly that of a young lady very well able to take care of herself that pathos is at any rate diminished. Many record collectors will be most grateful to her for introducing them to Berlioz' *Les Nuits d'Eté*: others since then have brought more warmth and intensity, but there is considerable variety in this recording, and always the pleasure of a firmly defined voice and a feeling for the rhythmic impulse of the music.

Of the mezzos, the Canadian born Jennie Tourel still gives pleasure. She could turn with a ready musicianship to Stravinsky and Hindemith, Debussy and Ravel, Mozart and Haydn. In Russian song (her parents were Russian) she brings the fullness of an opulent voice, without any over-dramatic self-indulgences (excellent, for instance, both in the attack and the dying fall wanted in Rachmaninoff's 'All things depart'). In the excerpts from operas by Rossini she was always pleasant, but rarely scintillating. In excerpts from Offenbach's *La Périchole* she surprised us all: 'Ah quel dîner' and 'Mon dieu, que les hommes sont bêtes' are as good as a glass of champagne any day. Some such quality might make a welcome difference to the records of Risë Stevens. Her Cherubino in the Glyndebourne *Le Nozze di Figaro* is greatly in need of something to quicken the pulse, to add some playfulness to 'Non so più' or some flexibility of mood to 'Voi che sapete'. The warm, womanly voice is a liability here, as it is in the *Orfeo ed Euridice* which, conducted by Monteux, ought to have been her crowning achievement on records as it probably was in live performance. It is admittedly hard to listen to the singing for the fearful fascination of the accompaniments; but the kindly voice lacks incisiveness and the portrayal remains very feminine.

Similarly with the two lyric sopranos, Sayão and Albanese, one has the feeling that there must have been something about their live performances that made all the difference, and that the records only very partially explain the high regard and affection which the public had for them. We can sense Sayão's popularity from the audience's response in the private off-the-air recordings. Yet without her charming stage presence, one can be irritated by certain mannerisms: a way she had of interposing little sounds, whether for pathos or charm or emphasis, and of leaving the note in the interests of 'character' ('Batti, batti' and the recitative before it in the Bruno Walter

Don Giovanni provides an example, though the audience can be heard chuckling, and there is enthusiastic applause). A 'Testimonial' Album issued in 1964 shows her well in Micaëla's song from *Carmen*, though here too it is hard to 'feel' the personality that was obviously vivid to the audience. Where that does become clearer is in *Manon*, the second Act of which was recorded at San Francisco in 1939 with Schipa as des Grieux. Here the tone is fresh, steady and smiling, the style is clean, the soft notes meltingly lovely, and the 'Adieu' feelingly sung.

With Albanese it is easier to sense a distinctive character in the voice, but all too often it seems fragile to the point of being insipid (recalling Bori to mind, but essentially for contrast). Her pre-war Mimì (with Gigli) has its appeal, and its irritations of vowel-sound and vibrato too; then in the LP era, with some attractive titles like the Villa-Lobos *Bachianas Brasileiras* and Tatiana's Letter Scene in *Eugen Onegin*, her voice seemed to have lost its shine and freshness. One or two post-war 78s showed her distinction better, among them the Toscanini *Traviata* with vocal assistance from the maestro. But it is in the other Toscanini recording, the *La Bohème*, that we really can enjoy her quality. From the start it sounds like a performance for enjoyment, Toscanini singing away happily, and then seeming sympathetic to Albanese's style and temperament. By Act III we are hearing a performance by Albanese as strong in emotion as it is delicate in voice, the tenderness and fragility of the character having their place in a resolutely un-sentimental reading of the score.

Toscanini's opera recordings are sometimes spoken of as though the singing is of no account. The casts were often found disappointing as reading-matter and there was a general assumption that the old man could not abide singers with minds of their own. But when Merrill sings 'Eri tu' or Albanese 'Mi chiamano Mimì' one feels that Toscanini is with them, not driving them forward; and of course some of the other individual performances are very strong. Ramon Vinay's sincere and powerful Otello is a prime example; yet it might be said that the Desdemona and Iago of that recording are prime examples of the other sort—singers without much individuality but notably reliable. The Desdemona was Herva Nelli, who came in for a lot of stick from the critics and who seemed inescapable in the Verdi works; in fact, of course, as one returns to her (in *Aida*, for example) there is a sturdy serviceable voice and a by no means insensitive style. The Iago, also Amonasro and Falstaff, was Giuseppe Valdengo, firm and resonant, especially in the middle voice, no great interpreter but matching up to the challenge of going into history as Toscanini's Falstaff principally by giving a demonstration of how the music can sound when sung by a good firm, rich voice. The *Falstaff* recording, moreover, abounds in fine performances: Teresa Stich-Randall at the start of her career with a most lovely Nannetta, Frank Guarrara an uninhibited and intense Ford, and the fruitiest and funniest of Mistress Quicklies in the opulent Cloë Elmo.

Elmo is one of a generation of Italian singers born at the wrong time. The war cut across her career in what should have been some of its best years, and by the time LP recording became established the big chances went either to Fedora Barbieri, some ten years younger, or to the veteran Stignani, whose name was so much better known. But her voice was second to none in power and richness. She was also willing to extend her repertoire, and a record of Brahms' 'Feldeinsamkeit' and Strauss' 'Ständchen' (both sung in Italian) presents a feat of slimming: the performances are unmistakeably Italian, but there is lightness and grace, the busty operatic style forsaken, the gorgeous tone still there to enrich songs which are hardly accustomed to such opulence. In full voice, and fully competitive too, she joins with Gina Cigna dueting fortissimo: the records have their comical side, but it is a marvellous sound Elmo makes in such phrases as 'L'amo come il fulgor' in *La Gioconda*.

This almost fiercely powerful style of singing was never much in favour with Stignani, though hers too was a sumptuous voice. With a more gently rounded and extremely beautiful tone, she also presents an equable personality, one that does not, for instance, turn easily to the more vindictive or voluptuous characteristics in Amneris. She sings the role in Tebaldi's first recording of *Aida*, and presents a sympathetic, essentially young character, no gorgonly matron. But despite the surviving beauty of voice, we are aware of a loosening of the vibrancy; so too in the *Norma* recorded with Callas, by whose side she sounds warm of voice but somewhat inexpressive. It is better to go back to the 78s, to the first *Aida*, the Verdi *Requiem*, and some of the solos recorded pre-war. Dalila's 'Amour, viens aider' (sung in Italian) shows the full splendour of the voice as well as the grandeur of style. The range is impressive, as is the firm edge to this sumptuous and still gentle mezzo, with its full but unaggressive chest notes.

But again one reflects that Stignani was of that generation that had grown up with the gramophone and had not yet really learnt its ways. To act, as well as sing, to the unseen audience involves a special exercise of the imagination, a specially vivid way with words. Some managed it instinctively: dal Monte in her Butterfly, Gigli always. Margherita Carosio, another singer welcomed back to the international scene after the war, showed that she could project some gaiety and charm as she did in Menotti's *Amelia al Ballo*, and a more serious, affectionate expressiveness in 'Qui la voce' from *I Puritani*. A generation later, and Gino Becchi, a baritone with a characterful, vibrant voice, would have put a smile into his face that could have charmed us through the wax as he sings his Figaro in *Il Barbiere di Siviglia*; and Paolo Silveri, whose baritone became more familiar outside Italy, a 'central' voice, beautiful in tone and even in production, would have added just that degree more of characterisation to make his Simon Boccanegra vivid in recording as Gobbi's is. But of course mention of that name reminds us not to generalise: for Gobbi was born within two years of the other baritones mentioned here, and the unseen audience is ever before him and he before them.

To Italy we look above all for tenors, and as the war ended there seemed to be only one new name to add to the roll, that of Ferruccio Tagliavini. He too had some skill in presenting character through the wax. His performance in *Un Ballo in Maschera* involves an infectious chuckle in 'E scherzo ed è follìa' and a credible death-scene. There are also moments of grace sufficiently rare at that time to be regarded as old-fashioned: a moment to hold in the memory, for instance, as he returns pianissimo to the melody of 'O qual soave' in the Love Duet of Act II. His is not an aristocratic characterisation; in many respects (in character as well as certain ways of singing) he recalls Gigli. Yet when he turns to Italian songs, he is in fact a long way from Gigli and other eminent predecessors, curiously charmless and unimaginative. On the other hand, charm is certainly exercised in his hauntingly dreamy performance of 'E la solita storia' from *L'Arlesiana*. In this and in solos like 'Parmi veder le lagrime' from *Rigoletto* he preserved the lyrical tradition. In a recording, with Lina Pagliughi, of *La Sonnambula*, he possibly extended it a little, for neither de Lucia nor Schipa include in their recordings of 'Son gelosa' the difficult run, rising in thirds up to the high C, and Tagliavini does it well. Even in these records one is aware of limitations: aspirates intruding to spoil the legato, and a too marked difference between the full and the half voice. A number of his records remain models of their kind.

Outside Italy, the post-war years brought forward a very different kind of tenor: in Germany, Julius Patzak emerging again as a major, fully mature artist, in England the name of Peter Pears becoming familiar, and from Denmark Aksel Schiøtz. Schiøtz was one of the most musical and tasteful of singers to record in the last years of the 78. His interests extended to Buxtehude, Dowland and Nielsen as well as Bach, Mozart (a particularly good record of 'Dalla sua pace') and the Lieder writers, his recording of *Dichterliebe* being typically pleasing and unostentatious. The expressive range is not great: he can sing 'Im Rhein' with sturdy determination modulating to the tender melancholy which pervades many of the songs, but his colouring is not subtle and the style is hardly intense. There may be many listeners, however, who are grateful to the singer who sings steadily with pleasing tone and good taste, and who refrains from imposing interpretation and personality upon them. By contrast, Peter Pears' art is so distinctive that one is rarely able to forget the singer and listen to the song; there even comes a point, and very quickly too, where it is hardly possible to hear the song in dissociation from the singer. In certain music this is also true of Patzak.

To many opera-goers there is no other Florestan: or rather, the sound of that music means that somewhere in the mind's eye and ear will be Patzak, inextricably associated with it. His recording on 78 of the great aria is strong enough to convey on its own the intensity of this Florestan, but his singing of the role can also be heard in two complete recordings, one of them the Salzburg *Fidelio* of 1950 conducted by Furtwängler and with

Flagstad as Leonore. In that performance, the first half of the solo gains from Furtwängler's very slow tempi and from the great intensity of his reading, while the last section ('Und spür'ich') is under some restraint: Patzak's own mastery is never in question either here or throughout the whole Act. We are lucky to have a stage performance on record; unfortunate as yet, however, in not having on record anything to represent the other role which has brought him the highest critical acclaim, that of Palestrina in Pfitzner's opera. A recording of Patzak as Palestrina does exist in the archives of West Deutsche Rundfunk, Cologne. The chances of a commercial release are, however, very slight, due to one singer's refusal to agree with any record company; EMI did think of trying to release this performance in the mid-sixties.

It is also remarkable that an artist of such seriousness can exercise so much charm and such a lightness of touch. His Eisenstein in *Die Fledermaus* has the authentic Viennese gaiety, and when he sings Richard Strauss's 'Ständchen' we feel that the maiden who withstood this serenader would be possibly wise, but she would have to be very strong-minded. The seductiveness does not lie in the quality of voice, however: in later years, as in the recording of Haydn's *Creation* under Horenstein, it sounded thin and sere, and not even in the records of 1929 and the early thirties does it sound rich. It was always firm, that was one merit, and he could soften it winningly. In the lyric tenor's repertoire he gained from the German tradition of making words count: so in 'Adieu, Mignon' he consoles, in Lenski's aria in *Eugen Onegin* he yearns, tired and saddened by the unhappy turn of events. In all of his solo records, he is inside the particular dramatic situation, and the warmth of his sympathy, with the character he is impersonating as well as the music he is singing, is always evident.

He too was one of those singers whose careers were cut in two by the war, and, though he survived with reputation enhanced as the years went by, there were many in Germany at this grim time in the country's history who either became obscured to view or who suffered as recording artists from having lost some of their best years. Thus Martha Fuchs, a strong warm-voiced Wagnerian soprano, distinguished herself in pre-war recordings of *Die Walküre* and of some Hugo Wolf songs (breathless and open-eyed in 'Storchenbotschaft', serious and noble of voice in 'Neue Liebe'); but by 1945 her career was virtually over. The lyric-coloratura soprano, Erna Berger, was one who resumed her international career, still graceful and young-sounding in her portrayal of Gilda in *Rigoletto* on LP; the sweetness and clarity of her voice in younger days can be heard in a good deal of Mozart (including an accomplished performance of 'Martern aller Arten') and, nicely defined by contrast with a very different kind of beauty, in the duet from the end of *Rosenkavalier* with Tiana Lemnitz.

Others known before the war and still prominent after it were Margarete Klose, Paul Schöffler, the accomplished Karl Schmitt-Walter, Ludwig Weber and Hans Hotter. Klose's voice was past its sumptuous best when she recorded Fricka in the Furtwängler *Walküre*, but there is tremendous authority, as there is in her singing of Schumann's 'Die Kartenlegerin'. From pre-war times we hear her very much in line with Sigrid Onegin, a true contralto, smooth in voice and even in production: Gluck's 'O del mio dolce ardor' is a fine example. There was little velvet in Schöffler's baritone, but he too became a singer of great authority. Many record collectors will have grown up with him as their Hans Sachs, though he is rough in such passages as the Cobbling Song and not really tender or mellifluous in the Fliedermonolog. Two stage performances suggest the stature and sense of presence he could command: he is a strong Pizarro in the Salzburg *Fidelio* of 1950, and as late as 1964, from the Theater an der Wien, we hear his dark voice still quite steady in Richard Strauss' *Daphne*. Darker of voice, and also commanding of presence, Ludwig Weber needed to be seen as well as heard, and by the coming of LP his voice had lost its more attractive qualities: thus his Sarastro (under Böhm) is firm and notably well-phrased, but the timbre is dry and edgy. Late 78s caught a glimpse of his Baron Ochs, and, returning to pre-war times, we can hear him as a fine black Hagen at Covent Garden, characterful, too, as Daland, playing opposite Janssen's Dutchman in the *Fliegende Holländer* of 1937.

The other bass mentioned above was Hans Hotter, who became the great Wotan of the post-war era, and who belongs to another chapter. His was an example of a career that prospered, both in the opera house and on records. But, though we have mentioned careers that in this period came to less than their full fruition, there remains a frustrater of human potential still more cruel. Death claimed Maria Cebotari at the age of thirty-nine, and allowed Kathleen Ferrier just two years longer.

Cebotari recorded before the war, though without, to my ears, suggesting the promise that she was expected to fulfil when it was over. A different matter altogether is the *La Traviata* recorded with Roswaenge and Schlusnus, and immensely full of life, especially in the vivid and complete change of expression at 'Follie' and then in the thrusting energy of 'Sempre libera'. This energy and individuality also contribute to a performance of the final scene in *Salome* that for a kind of shrewish fanaticism is probably unequalled. In her last years, Cebotari was overshadowed by the sensational success Ljuba Welitsch enjoyed in this role. When her death occurred, in 1949, nobody was likely to have guessed that in a very few more years the great and glittering voice of her rival would have been lost to us also.

Welitsch was one of the rising hopes of the new age, and Kathleen Ferrier was another. Both had great careers cut short, one by the deterioration of her voice, the other by death. In most respects they were as unlike as could be: Welitsch dazzled, Ferrier warmed; Welitsch was a creature of the opera house, Ferrier belonged to the concert hall. Both were for a time supreme in their sphere; and both were sadly missed.

The tragedy of Ferrier's death still colours our feeling for her records. This is natural and not necessarily sentimental; it is almost impossible to hear her in Mahler, for instance, and not be moved by the human situation as well as by the artistic fact. But it does encourage a distortion of memory, and a tendency to solemnize where so much was lightness and joy. It was Bruno Walter who said that she should be remembered 'in a major key', and records can certainly help in this.

A great feature of her recitals was the delight which would spread through the audience as she started her English songs. It was not because of the language or the familiarity of the music, but because of the smile. Frank Bridge's 'Go not, happy day' conveys something of this on record: the lightening of tone is delicious, and the smile vivid as though she is there before us. So too in the folk songs which were also a great promoter of smiles all round the concert hall: the restrained fun in Herbert Hughes' arrangement of 'Kitty my love', the spring in the melody which she picks up from the accompaniment in Britten's version of 'Come you not from Newcastle', and the feeling for the keen, jaunty life of the dotted rhythms in 'The Keel Row'. All these are 'essential' Ferrier, utterly remote from the phrase in a *New Statesman* critique that she herself would quote—'this goitrous singer with the contralto hoot'.

Records probably played more than their part in provoking that phrase. The reproduction of those days, with the plummy, booming bass, of which its owners were often so proud, emphasised the depth and roundness of her voice, and when the famous aria from *Orfeo ed Euridice*, translated as 'What is life', was broadcast in every other number of 'Housewives' Choice' it is not surprising that the *New Statesman* should snap. No doubt the forward drive of Stiedry's conducting when 'Che farò' arrives in the Glyndebourne *Orfeo* was partly designed as an antidote to the 'What is life' approach, more appropriate, as it may seem, to the oratorio platform. There also weighed in favour of solemnity the preponderance of slow arias in the best-known contributions of the contralto voice to oratorio. 'He was despised' reposes comfortably in E flat major for a very long time, and Ferrier's record did not even include the more turbulent middle-section. These, too, were still the days of the 'plain style' in Handel: there are no decorations, no runs, no trills in her records. Modern reproduction eliminates any question of 'hoot', but it must be admitted that the 'plain style' is very plain, and that one wishes she had varied the *adagio* with more of those *allegro* arias from the operas that have kept her successors fully exercised.

Modern reproduction has brought its disadvantages, introducing a slight occasional vibrato, which I cannot remember as part of the voice. The recording has caught it in *Orfeo*, and not quite as an integral part of the voice, as, say, with Nan Merriman in her strongly dramatic recording of Act II under Toscanini. It is there also in the earlier parts of *Das Lied von der Erde*. But this remains a great performance (Bruno Walter conducting, Patzak the tenor), especially as, in the fourth song, she has the power and the full resources of a genuine contralto to combat the orchestra in the

85. Kathleen Ferrier

'schöne Knaben' passage, as well as the unflawed legato to hold the serenity of their laughing grace reflected in the waters. In the final song, 'Der Abschied', she sings out louder at first then she needed to do in recording, but she brings a glory of tone and feeling to the performance, growing steadily so that the climaxes of the work become inseparably connected in one's mind with this recording of it.

The recording is also an eloquent testament to the artistic growth of the woman who in 1943 knew a handful of oratorios and about forty songs. To the technical training too, for the range is extensive, and as she passes over it we realise how successful had been the work which Roy Henderson describes, smoothing over any break in registers. They should run such courses in Italy! The flexibility of the voice is demonstrated in Purcell's 'Hark, the echoing air', part of a broadcast recital in Norway, which does something to preserve the warm feeling between artist and audience always present in her concerts. In a different way, 'Der Musensohn' demonstrates the soundness of technique equally impressively, for while she gives the rhythm its full lift and spring, she also preserves the legato. Then, in 'Erbarme dich, mein Gott' (sung in English as 'Have mercy, Lord, on me') from the *St Matthew Passion*, she again shows how supple-jointed the voice was and how fine the breath-control.

Of course these were means to an end, the end being something beyond beautiful singing. Ferrier is one of those in whom we feel singing to be an expression of the spirit. In the *Passion* aria the plea is set in a context of serene faith; in Brahms' *Ernste Gesänge* a compassion comforts through the bleak asperities of the text; in *Frauenliebe und Leben* it is a real woman who sings imaginatively out of a full lifetime's experience. If she had in fact lived a full lifetime (and in 1972, the year of writing, she would have been sixty) no doubt she would have extended her repertoire and deepened her interpretation still further; but a recital of her records leaves us not sighing for what might have been but rejoicing in what is.

Ferrier's recording career belongs partly to the LP period, partly to that of 78s. So with many other singers, Jussi Björling (one year older than Ferrier) being a notable example. Of the chief recording artists in the next twenty years, most appeared originally on 78s. Before 1950 we had heard the first of Renata Tebaldi, Mario del Monaco, Tito Gobbi; of the Americans, Richard Tucker, Robert Merrill, Leonard Warren. Victoria de los Angeles had a delightful and already extensive recorded repertoire to her credit, and a great Boris had clearly been found in Christoff. The distinction of Fischer-Dieskau among Lieder singers was apparent; so were the excellence of Gérard Souzay and the haunting individuality of Peter Pears. From Germany there came a new generation of admirable singers: Irmgard Seefried, Erich Kunz, Sena Jurinac, Lisa della Casa and Elisabeth Schwarzkopf. From a young man called Giuseppe di Stefano came probably the best records made by a lyric tenor within two decades. And in a version of 'Qui la voce' from *I Puritani* many a casual listener was struck by the tragic grandeur and intensity of a soprano new to him: he would then look again at the record label and accustom himself to the name of Maria Meneghini Callas.

This was a true renaissance, and happily for all these singers it virtually coincided with the new age of the gramophone. Some older singers were there to bridge the periods, and pre-eminent among these was Kirsten Flagstad, who preserved her great voice so miraculously that we can hear on LP her Isolde, the *Götterdämmerung* Brünnhilde and much else besides. She and Jussi Björling were the two singers whose arrival on the operatic scene in the nineteen-thirties did most to brighten a period of decline, and it is pleasant to think that both were able to lend their experience and authority to the performances which the new age was to record. Björling became an essential part of the opera business on LP for over a decade. And there could be no more noble torch-bearer to link the second period of the gramophone's history with its third than Flagstad, for no-one embodied more splendidly the worth of the grand tradition in operatic singing.

Part III

Renaissance
The Long-Playing Record 1950–1970

21. Wagner: Every Note, Every Word
Kirsten Flagstad   Birgit Nilsson
Wolfgang Windgassen   Hans Hotter
Gottlob Frick

THE first long-playing records were put on sale in 1948 in America, the first stereo ten years later. LP opera first appeared in 1950, and a complete opera by Wagner *(Die Meistersinger)* in 1952. The entire *Ring* became available from the Decca[1] catalogue by 1965, and the first book to chronicle a recording stage by stage and argue the aesthetic issues involved was written about this achievement, the work of seven years. And on the first page of that book is a photograph of Kirsten Flagstad.

The old and the new thus shake hands, for Flagstad was sixty-three when she recorded for Decca her last new part, the *Rheingold* Fricka. What it meant to their enterprise to have secured the co-operation of the great Brünnhilde of her age (and perhaps of any other) is made clear by John Culshaw in *Ring Resounding*, the book just now referred to; and the inclusion in the cast-list of an artist who made her debut in 1913, and her first records under the pre-electrical recording process, is a touching tribute to the past. Testimony too of the consciousness of a great tradition with which the present is to keep continuity.

So it was as well that Flagstad had preserved her voice in almost miraculously fine condition. Firm and unspreading, powerful and resonant, gorgeous in the lower half if less happy in the upper, her voice at sixty-three was still a superb, shining and noble instrument. When she sings Sieglinde's solos on a record issued in 1956, one recalls that this was the role in which she made her debut at the Metropolitan in 1935, and that the first Act of that performance is recorded. Compare the young voice and the old, and to an astonishing extent they sound the same. The long high G in 'Der Männer Sippe' has lost some of its glory, but that is all. The high A's are still cleanly and boldly taken, the breath still supports broad phrasing (no breathing before 'der Freud' in 'Du bist der Lenz', for instance, where it would have been so excusable). Right to the very last recordings she still had the control to lighten her voice, as she does heroically in the third verse of Brahms' 'Alte Liebe', though she cannot do it sufficiently to make 'Wie Melodien' the song of summery, yearning tenderness that it can be.

[1] Decca records are issued in the USA on the London Label, and HMV (EMI) on Angel.

And the *Rheingold* Fricka is sumptuous in tone, scrupulous in rhythm and enunciation, unfailingly beautiful in the grain of the voice, no vibrato, no wobble, a pure, richly glowing sound; and hearing it, one can well believe that it is gods who are entering Valhalla.

There are now two considerable *Rheingold* Frickas on record, however, the other being Josephine Veasey who sings it under Karajan (Flagstad is with Solti). Both make splendid music, and the comparison reflects credit on each, for if it is marvellous that Flagstad can sound so well by the side of a woman half her age, Veasey can take satisfaction in standing against one of the greatest voices of the century. At one point, to be sure, Flagstad has a greatness which Veasey cannot match: her 'Wotan, Gemahl! unsel'ger Mann' is awesome, and Veasey is without comparable godlike resources. But in characterisation, the comparison generally works the other way. Flagstad is by no means inexpressive (asking Wotan whether he scorns 'Liebe und Weibes Werth', for instance, she softens on 'Weibes' to match the *diminuendo* marked for the orchestra, doing it caressingly, lingering on the consonant). But she has little of Veasey's variety: the human anxiousness, the beguiling, very feminine woman who wants the gold principally so that she can wear it. Flagstad is too straightforward in her way with the seductive chromatic phrases—and this was characteristic.

Though her singing is never cold, it is rarely passionate; and though it is always alive to meaning, it is rarely vivid with local illumination. This, as much as the quality of her voice, is why she was never a true Sieglinde, or for that matter a true Lieder singer. She presented in temperament a marked contrast with Lotte Lehmann, who was both; and Flagstad's reported reaction to what she once saw of Lehmann's Sieglinde ('she behaved as a woman should do only with her husband') suggests some of the reticences which would have to be overcome by a great Isolde. Yet Flagstad was that, both in the theatre and on records. And perhaps her most enduring monument will be her recording of that most passionate of roles in an intense performance conducted by Furtwängler.

It is sometimes difficult to tell whether a great conductor makes a difference to Flagstad's performances by direct influence upon her, or whether the difference essentially lies in the impact which their combined forces have upon the listener. Flagstad made possibly her two finest recordings both with Furtwängler, and in both there is the feeling that this conductor was exactly the man to make the orchestration flame with an intensity which at once reflects in the glorious voice and makes the right warm setting for it. Among six available versions by Flagstad of Brünnhilde's Immolation in *Götterdämmerung* the recording on late 78s with the Philharmonia Orchestra under Furtwängler is the truly great one. The earliest is a Covent Garden performance of 1937, also under Furtwängler, where the voice is fresh and the enunciation deeply human ('Weiss ich nun was dir frommt? Alles, alles weiss ich' are phrases mature and vivid in expressiveness); and the last was the performance of the complete opera given on Norwegian radio and released on records by Decca, where Flagstad's singing, a little drier and tiring only very slightly at the end, is still superb. But the Furtwängler version on 78s is inspired. The dotted rhythms of the opening have weight and dignity; we see how they move towards the key-word 'fulfil' ('Vollbringt Brünnhildes Wort'); and in the singing there is a depth, localised in 'Ruhe, du Gott', where she seems to sense the mystery of the shifting harmonies, letting her own sound swell and diminish responsively.

It is sometimes said that she had an unhappy recording career (John Culshaw makes the point, adding that this was 'before she came to us'). There is something in the remark, and something to be said on the other side as well. Certainly it was not until the last years, when she was with Decca, that a wide repertoire was extensively recorded. Certainly the dry acoustic and lack of space in the wartime and pre-war 78s combined to give a limited impression of the splendid truth. Even so, it is to her 78s, to the *Tristan und Isolde*, and to certain live opera-house recordings that I would go for my own essential Flagstad. For her gaiety, and for a personal reminder of that homely vigour which was so infectious in recitals (a radiant smile, and strong arms made to wield a sturdy rolling-pin), I would choose Grieg's 'St. John's Eve' ('Og je vil ha mig en Hertenskjaer'). For the dramatic impact which her concert singing could have I would choose 'Ah, perfido', recorded with Ormandy in 1937 (tender, haunting inflections in the second section, and a tremendous, frowning authority in the opening). And for her mature art, in the Wagnerian repertoire, and combining majesty with intimacy, the *Wesendonck Lieder* with Gerald Moore accompanying. Her very earliest recordings, incidentally, do not 'add a new dimension' as one would have liked to say of them: the singing on these rare discs of 1924 and 1925 have little character and the music still less, 'Hjem, kjaere Hjem' turning out to be the celebrated English air by Sir Henry Bishop and about the best of a limp bunch. A new dimension, however, is exactly what the live opera-house recordings do provide. These are private issues, like those mentioned in earlier chapters, and as in them the quality of recording is capricious. But it is marvellous to hear her cut through the massive orchestration of the 'Sieglinde lebe' passage in Act II of *Die Walküre*, or to hear how vividly she could dramatise when genuinely moved (as in Brünnhilde's cries of 'Betrug!', or in the 'Abscheulicher' of *Fidelio* with Bruno Walter), or how in those early days the high notes came as sheer joy (glorious in the 'O heiliger Götter' finale of the duet in Act I of *Götterdämmerung*).

These make the essential 'Flagstad treasury'. Of the last phase of her recording career, the Bach, Handel, Purcell and Gluck want a sprightly touch and timbre that she was rarely able to bring, and the German songwriters generally need more specific insights (Schumann and Brahms come off best). The songs by Grieg and Sinding are more enjoyable, and best

86. Kirsten Flagstad as Dido in *Dido and Aeneas*

of all is the Sibelius record, joyously youthful in 'Den första Kyssen', and expressing a humanity which eases any itch for more studied subtleties, in the sombre 'Höstkväll'. And, of course, there is the Fricka, that bridge between old and new, made possible by a career which spanned decades with the breadth and majesty of the end of *Rheingold* itself.

But how well has a continuity of Wagnerian singing been preserved? If Flagstad, whose foundations lay in the era of Leider, Melchior and Schorr, bridges the gap between that and the age of Nilsson, Windgassen and Hotter, then what changes have occurred in that time, and to what extent have the lyricism and the fine method of that school of Wagnerians been preserved by their successors?

Certainly one of these singers has been as scrupulous a lyricist as any of the earlier generation, and that is the tenor Wolfgang Windgassen. If he has stood out well above any Heldentenor of the fifties and sixties, it is not because he had the loudest or most robust voice among his contemporaries, but because his was the most pleasing tone and the smoothest production. A late start to his career may have provided a blessing in disguise—his debut came just before the outbreak of war, and when he took up singing again, in 1945, he was thirty. In his repertoire he also had lighter, essentially lyrical roles (it is said that Wieland Wagner engaged him to sing Parsifal at Bayreuth after hearing him at Stockholm in Offenbach's *La Belle Hélène*); and no doubt these helped to keep his voice and style in trim for the ardours that lay ahead. Unfortunately the gramophone has, up to the present, preserved nothing of this side of his work, his Hoffmann, Tamino and José; for, with occasional excursions into Weber and Lortzing, his recorded repertoire has been almost exclusively Wagnerian. Two other roles are of special interest: Beethoven's Florestan and Verdi's Otello. The Otello is vivid, whether in tenderness or loathing, and there is beauty in the quieter passages. Declamation produces a thicker, more throaty tone, however, and his performance is preserved only in extracts and in German. Florestan in Furtwängler's *Fidelio* does not really find him in best voice or most imaginative spirit ('In des Lebens Frühlingstagen' is smooth but not elegant, the last section of the great aria rises well in power though not in intensity, the difficult 'O namenlose Freude' is a little sketchy).

His very delightful and considerable best is there in his Lohengrin (in the finely graded tone and broad line of the Narrative, for example) and in his Siegfried. At the opera house, my own most prized memory of him is in Siegfried's Narrative, especially the woodbird passage, in *Götterdämmerung*; and the least happy memory is of his lack of the final bite and weight needed for the *Siegfried* Forging Song. The gramophone tends to even things up, but it is still the tender, lyrical passages that most hold the attention: phrases such as 'Wo hast du nun, Minne, dein minniges Weibchen' in Act I of *Siegfried*, or the meditations in Act II about the mother, her eyes soft as the roedeer 'nur noch viel schöner'. At such points, too, the vividness of his interpretation is strongest. The realisation that his mother died at his own birth ('so starb meine Mutter an mir') is moved and compassionate. There is a warming and softening of tone as in Act II he thinks of his own loneliness: the most human and humane of Siegfrieds, this. Admittedly, in a comparison with Melchior I find a lack of excitement and exaltation in Windgassen, as well as of shine and thrust, but he is by no means a pale interpreter of the strength and joy in Siegfried; and loathing and hardness come expressively into his voice as he tells Mime how his instinct is to crush the life out of him.

In these recordings all the elements of his art have arrived at maturity, and he is at the height of his powers as a singer. The performance of *Tristan und Isolde*, recorded live from the 1966 Bayreuth Festival under Karl Böhm, has the elements less in equilibrium, for the voice has lost in steadiness and resonance. His interpretative art has risen to genuine greatness, however. Tristan is surely of all roles for tenor the one which demands the greatest stamina. He is on stage practically the whole time, has to sing his heart out in the Love Duet (while his formidable partner knows that she has a good hour's rest ahead), and then his own most strenuous solo work is still to come. At fifty-two, Windgassen gives a performance that grows steadily and ends triumphantly. His third Act still gains much from the lyrical tradition and what survives of the sweet tone. But his bold use of a full voice given unstintingly when the fever of the score requires it is intensely moving: the vivid loathing of 'Der furchtbare Trank', the heartfelt 'Ach, Isolde, Isolde, wie schön bist du', and the hectic desperation of the last pages. The whole of this Act is performed with sincere and scrupulous devotion, as well as the authority of a master.

Windgassen came upon the scene just as the hunger for a listenable Heldentenor was reaching starvation point. Old-timers like Max Lorenz had to be called out to save the day, and cries went up, such as this from the Editor of *Opera*, attending the *Ring* at Bayreuth in 1952: 'The tenors presented a sorry story. Beginning with an average Loge (Erich Witte), we had an extremely poor Siegmund (Treptow), a Siegfried (Aldenhoff) who got through his part with such a dry and unmusical voice, that I was longing for Svanholm'. Set Svanholm, certainly, was a reliable artist, incisive in his rhythmic sense, and turning out a fifty-two-year-old Siegfried who gets younger throughout his performance in the Norwegian radio *Götterdämmerung* of which Flagstad was the Brünnhilde. He and Ludwig Suthaus (an able Tristan to Flagstad's Isolde) were the best of the Wagnerian tenors before Windgassen became well known. Since then there have been Ernst Kozub, with a brilliantly powerful and individual timbre, a virile and positive Erik in Klemperer's *Fliegende Holländer*, and a Melot who one wishes could change places with the well-characterised but thin-voiced Tristan of Fritz Uhl under Solti's superb direction; Sandor Konya, a mellifluous Lohengrin, vividly voicing his dull despair at the end of the Bridal Chamber Scene, and singing throughout with precisely-placed tone and good musical sense; and Jess Thomas, whose Siegfried has found plenty of admirers, though to my ear his tone is unsteady and unsympathetic. Jon Vickers is probably the finest Siegmund of our time, but he, with James King, is discussed in another chapter. And in a special class is Gerhard Stolze.

Stolze is the Mime of both the Solti and the Karajan *Siegfried*; and (though many will remember Peters Kuen and Klein with affection) for most opera-goers of the present generation he probably *is* Mime, loud if unlovely of voice, cajoling with a bland, crooked smile that somehow finds its way on to the sound-track, full of specious self-pity, and fundamentally loathing life. In the later of the recordings (the Karajan), a more poisonous character is established immediately by the hiss and click of consonants; and in his confrontation with the Wanderer we see the resentfulness (hugging his private world and schemes), the challenge of his first question given with an impudent flick on the last syllable ('der Erde Tiefe'), and his hair standing on end with the 'Verfluchtes Licht'. His Loge and Herod, both sung with well-focused, strong voice, are similarly brilliant pieces of musical characterisation. A recording by Stolze compared with most other singers is like television after radio.

What Mime is among tenor roles, Alberich is to the bass-baritones. Three remarkably good ones appear in modern recordings. Benno Kusche (also good at the comical hypocrisy of Beckmesser) is the most vivid: snarling, malicious and ridiculous. Gustav Neidlinger is superbly dark-toned and vibrant, entirely free of Sprechgesang, and perhaps uniquely true to the letter of the score, without losing its spirit. Zoltan Kelémén, the youngest of the three, adds a plasticity, a touch of the lecher, the Viennese roué, and is more bitingly sinister than the others in the later scenes of *Das Rheingold*. The modern era has done well for itself in this department.

For its Wagnerian basso profundo, however, it has had essentially until his retirement to rely on one: Gottlob Frick, a tower of strength in the strongest cast, and one of the great basses of the century. Like Windgassen, Frick excels primarily because of excellence of voice and voice production. There have been others (Josef Greindl, Otto Edelmann and Kurt Böhme, and Covent Garden's Michael Langdon, for instance, with powerful voices invaluable in the opera house, and with plenty of character, the last three all giving vivid performances as Baron Ochs). But Frick is steady, smooth and beautiful: odd word to use about this dark, often forbidding sound, but in his time many a performance of Wagner has woken to a sense of beauty only with the arrival of its Hunding, Gurnemanz or Hagen.

Like most of the artists we think of as essentially Wagnerian, Frick has sung in quite a wide range of music. There is an interesting and rare 78 of King Philip's aria in *Don Carlo*: lyrical, inner and imaginative, the quiet tone finely supported. His Falstaff in *Die lustige Weiber von Windsor*, his Rocco in *Fidelio*, are both in their very different ways classic. The true successor to the early German basses, Wilhelm Hesch and Paul Knüpfer, he has also recorded some impressive Mozart: an ideally impregnable Commendatore, and a marvellously sonorous and spirited Osmin in Beecham's *Die Entführung*. The wholeness of his voice is on display in this role; so often if a bass loosens up on top so that the sound is free and resonant on the high notes, he finds himself foggily grunting out the low ones, but Frick is beautifully in focus throughout. His rhythmic sense is strong, and he can sing staccato without cheating his listeners of the body of the voice. In 'Ha, wie will ich triumphieren' he catches no doubt something of Beecham's gaiety; there is a caricaturist's eye in his way with the octave jumps—one can see them like the balloon swellings of a cartoon. And it is marvellous to hear how everything wakes up in the vaudeville Finale with his eruption into it.

Not everything that he does is beyond criticism. One looked forward to his Sarastro to show at last that the modern age had someone to stand by Plançon, Kipnis and Pinza from earlier recordings. But when it appeared it was in 1964, in the Klemperer recording, and Frick was by that time over fifty-five. The sound is steady and the style has authority; but the legato is not all it might have been, and elegance is not really the word. It does at least serve as a reminder that Frick's survival as a singer is itself something rather phenomenal. Basses generally last longer than tenors, but few Wagnerian basses start with Frick's steady opulent tone, and it is hard to think of any who have kept it into advanced middle age.

In the Wagner, which is his native territory, his resources seem inexhaustible. Anyone who saw Humphrey Burton's film about the making of Decca's *Ring* cycle will remember Frick repeating Hagen's Call over and over again while the experts dealt with the steerhorns. There is no forcing in his singing, and it is all firm as a rock. Whether benevolently enthusiastic as the Landgrave, or soft and intimate in Pogner's music with Eva, or voicing the dark menace of Hagen, he is king of his kind. His Gurnemanz, recorded at the astonishing age of 65 under Solti, crowns his recording career and will recall for many opera-goers the superlative performances he gave in the theatre.

We also have the Gurnemanz of Hans Hotter, in a strongly-cast, well-recorded performance under Knappertsbusch, warm in tone and feeling and with the authority of a long and triumphant career behind it. If it seems to me a second-best to Frick's version, then that is a personal judgment, based, at least, on an assumption that can be publicly shared, namely that the steady emission of tone is a highly desirable feature of singing.

Now 'wobble' is an unkind word, and more often than not critics will accept the phenomenon silently as one does an incurable disease (one knows it is there but doesn't talk about it), or they find polite circumlocutions and avoid the dreaded word. But Hotter's 'wobble' is generally admitted to exist, so one can decently discuss it. Culshaw writes in *Ring Resounding* about his conviction that Hotter should be their Wotan for the *Die Walküre* made in 1965: 'I knew that Hotter suffered from asthma, and that on a bad day he could develop a wobble in the voice that distressed some people much more than it distressed me; but it seemed essential to get his performance on record. To more than one generation, he *was* Wotan, in voice and looks and manner'. This states the balance of argument fairly (and of course there is the further question, which he puts later, of who would do it better anyway). But, although I register 'distressed' as one of those exaggerated terms commonly affected in artistic chat (we are not really 'distressed' by such a minor affliction as a singer's wobble), I also think that Culshaw's remark subtly undermines basic standards. A strong preference for a steady voice is not some fad of wincing self-styled 'connoisseurs'; and it was not just on a 'bad day' that Hotter's voice became unsteady. I cannot help recalling that I have myself heard him many times at Covent Garden and been greatly impressed too, but most of them have

87. Wolfgang Windgassen as Tannhäuser

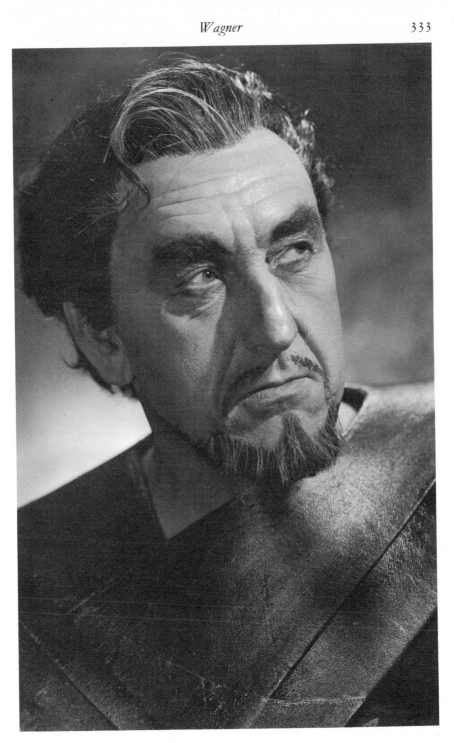

88. Gottlob Frick as Hagen in *Die Götterdämmerung*

89. Hans Hotter

been, in this sense, on 'bad days'. Some of the records made during the fifties and sixties (which were his own forties and fifties) are free from wobble, but more are not. And I think there are limitations to the success of his singing in other spheres, his Lieder singing, for instance, being often dulled not so much in interpretation as in tone. That after these objections he still registers as one of the great singers is a measure of his strengths. Melba, Bonci, Gerhardt and Gigli are others about whom, in their very different ways, similarly qualified judgments have had to be made.

The strengths could be amply demonstrated by the *Walküre* alone, in which the Farewell fully merits that adjective 'noble', inevitable, it seems, in any appraisal of Hotter's art; while the Wotan–Fricka scene becomes tense and central to the drama, instead of being the routine flyting episode it commonly is. An earlier version (1957) of the Farewell and the scene with Brünnhilde preceding it has just as much unsteadiness, but it too is deeply felt, whether in sorrow or anger; and the great phrase 'der freier als ich, der Gott' has its last words breathed into the memory.

Some of his finest Wagner singing, however, comes in the First Act of *Siegfried*, and here the 'wobble' is hardly present at all. This scene (where Wotan comes, as Anna Russell says, to play Twenty Questions with Mime) is written with special consideration for the voice: spacious, instrumental phrases placed in the easy middle of the range, and the richness of the deep timbre falling on grateful ears after the declamatory and strident music of Siegfried and Mime. One thinks of Friedrich Schorr as the ideal singer, and indeed, though all is not perfect when one turns to his record, he does have a legato and a beauty of production in such phrases as 'Mancher wähnte weise zu sein' as no one since him has matched. But in this *Siegfried*, Hotter is magnificently Schorr's successor (as he is in line from van Rooy in his boldly personal treatment of the *Walküre* phrase—'der freier als ich, der Gott'). The voice and bearing (which is almost visible in the tone) make a marvellous impression in the first bars; the phrase telling how the gods dwell in the cloudy heights is done with fine soft sonority; and then, in the Wanderer's final scene, he captures both the rapture of the prophetic music, and the sad, dignified resignation of the last phrases. The greatness of this Wotan is triumphantly demonstrated in these performances, coming in the very late afternoon of a very long career.

That career goes back as far as 1929, and his recordings date from 1935. There is a fascinating early Prologue to *Pagliacci*, a Toreador's Song, an Iago's Creed and 'Era la notte'; and at least one of the post-war 78s shows yet another unfamiliar side of his repertoire. This is Bach's 'Ich habe genug', the whole of which (not just the recitative and aria included in HMV's *Golden Voices* series) deserves preservation on LP. Often sung by contraltos and baritones, the cantata gains a Rembrandtian depth of colouring when sung by a bass. But how few would have the warmth of this voice, or the control; for after the demands upon the breath support of the aria 'Schlummert ein', there is an allegro, 'Ich freue mich', with taxing runs and difficult leaps, which Hotter does with genuine mastery and, more surprisingly, athleticism. 'As a giant to run his course', one finds oneself singing with the psalmist.

The reverse impression, unfortunately, has to be reported of the Lieder records, or most of them. There are people who find Hotter's *Winterreise* the most satisfying of all; and possibly the stronger the love (as opposed to admiration) one has for the work itself, the more one may be drawn to this performance as creating an uncompromising atmosphere of wan desolation. But if, for instance, one wishes for a temporary lightening of the heart, even if the smile merely flickers, in 'Frühlingstraum' or 'Täuschung'; or if, on the other hand, one wants passion in the desolation (anguish in the last verse of 'Wasserfluth', for example), then this will not satisfy. He is moving in 'Die greise Kopf', I think, and in 'Der Leiermann'; in both, the old, lustreless sound produces a kind of identification. But what a weary, featureless winter journey this has been, and how one comes to feel something less than gratitude for that most conscientious of Hotter's virtues, the taming of his huge voice so that its edge is dulled like footsteps padding in snow.[1] This softening marks a great deal of his Lieder singing, and it might seem to be a condition of its success, as with Kipnis. But there is a difference, for Kipnis' soft singing was done with a tone, which, however quiet, still had edge and resonance, while Hotter's tends to be breathed out almost as if tired (as if, for instance, he was yawning his goodnight in 'fein Liebchen, gute Nacht' in the first song of *Winterreise*). Sometimes the soft singing has a beauty and aptness, as in the Wanderers Nachtlied ('Uber allen Gipfeln'), but much the best part of his work in Lieder comes when he feels conscientiously able to use his full voice. Loewe's 'Meeresritt' is tremendous in his performance, and, as though having got into his stride with this in a mixed Lieder recital, he sings two other, lighter songs by the same composer with charm and a sense of humour. And we are back to Hotter as a great singer!

Contemporaries with a comparable repertoire have been few. One with a considerable reputation in Europe and America is the Canadian, George London, the Wotan of Solti's *Rheingold* and Leinsdorf's *Walküre*. His singing is not flattered by recording; it comes over as a basically impressive, strong dramatic voice, but as somewhat unsteady and constricted on certain vowels. His Golaud (Ansermet 1965) is darkly impressive and deeply felt, and the Don Giovanni and Scarpia have authority. Of the rest, Ferdinand Frantz was probably the most extensively recorded in the earlier days of LP: a sympathetic Hans Sachs, and a reliable artist. More recently the ranks have been joined by Theo Adam, some features of whose technique can be gauged from his aria in Bach's Cantata No. 59 ('Wer mich liebst, der wird mein Wort halten')—the runs aspirated, though with an apparently ample supply of breath behind them, the intervals clean, but the tone unsteady. He is also the Dutchman in Klemperer's vigorous, beautifully played performance. Far more pleasing to the ear than Hotter, London, or Adam as recorded in this role are what one might term the middle-weights, Hermann Uhde and Josef Metternich, the latter with a vibrant, rather Italianate voice, the former (very much the worthiest inheritor of Janssen's best roles) exhibiting some of the finest command of legato heard in modern times. Unfortunately neither of them gives a really vivid inter-

---

[1] Hotter recorded *Winterreise* three times. Remarks here refer to the second version, generally regarded as the best, recorded with Gerald Moore and issued in 1955.

pretation: at least, they seem unable to colour the voice to express that essential anguished yearning. The heavyweights are little better at this; and in fact all pale before the strength of Fischer-Dieskau's characterisation. Wagnerian singing has been moving, in this period, towards that kind of specificity which marks Fischer-Dieskau's performances, but in that particular respect he is still the high master.

At least there is no question who has been the grand lady of the Wagnerian scene since Flagstad. But let us first take a brief survey of the other sopranos lyric and heroic, and, like children with some especially toothsome delicacy, leave Birgit Nilsson till later.

Two who have recorded little Wagner and yet who would seem to be very well able to create an exceptionally strong impression in much of his music are Helga Pilarczyk and Inge Borkh. Pilarczyk is mentioned in a later chapter apropos of her great achievement in *Erwartung*. Borkh also has a claim to greatness, through her performance as the wife in *Die Frau ohne Schatten*. There is gloriously expansive singing in Act II, and great tenderness in Act III. She catches the edgy resentfulness of the character without losing sympathy, and the tremendous demands upon the voice are finely sustained. Her stamina is also tested in a recording of *Turandot*, and here one is aware of some unsteadiness from time to time: the authority is vivid, however, and the musical intelligence is well in advance of what this role usually encourages in its performers. The tone glows, too, and rises easily to the heights. Her recorded legacy begins to mount up, for it also includes an intense Elektra—but not, as far as I know, the Immolation and Liebestod which might also have been performances of an unusually strong character.

Among lyric sopranos who in the nineteen-fifties and sixties offered such roles as Elisabeth, Senta, Elsa and Sieglinde, my own favourite is Gré Brouwenstijn. I also think she is a more distinguished singer of Verdi than of Wagner. At the time of writing, nothing of her survives in the current catalogue except her part in Cluytens' Beethoven Ninth; and the current catalogue is notably the poorer therefore. She had not an especially powerful voice, but it was a beautiful one, and her sense of style was aristocratic. Her arias from *La Forza del Destino* and *Trovatore* all have some precious individual touches, and 'Tu che le vanità' *(Don Carlo)* is a fine memento of her intensely moving portrayal of Elisabeth de Valois: there is feeling for the grandeur as well as the human anxiety, and a strong, finely projected, economical tone with no spread or vibrato in the climaxes. In a coarse but not unenjoyable record of highlights from d'Albert's *Tiefland*, her presence brings grace and taste, and to an indifferent performance of selections from *Freischütz* she adds a similar touch of distinction. Her Wagner is well sampled in excerpts from *Tannhäuser*: radiance, though not a sufficiently impressive attack, in the Greeting; a maidenly and then a maturing tone in the Prayer. In Leinsdorf's *Walküre*, playing Sieglinde opposite Jon Vickers, she matches his enthusiastic, human and musical treatment. By no means as vivid as Lehmann, she still produces some lovely singing, and her delicacy in the soft passage 'Ein Wunder will ich gemahnen' is haunting.

Also recording in this period, and rather more prominently, were Leonie Rysanek and Elisabeth Grümmer, both of them having something of the creamy quality of Tiana Lemnitz. Rysanek does beautifully in the quiet melody of Senta's Ballad, and in the softer music of Desdemona. Her stamina is attested by her performance in the exacting role of the Empress in *Die Frau ohne Schatten*, and in such very different music as that of Tosca's 'Vissi d'arte' which provides a tender reminder of an unusually interesting and individual portrayal. Yet her tone often leaves one dissatisfied on record as it does not in the theatre: there is a lack of incisiveness or of a firm grip. And this sometimes affects Grümmer's recorded sound as well: in the opening to the Quintet of *Die Meistersinger*, for instance, the voice seems somewhat pallid, even a little breathy. Yet much of her singing records beautifully: the tender questioning of Sachs in Act II, the smiling eagerness of her Bridal Chamber music in *Lohengrin*, still young in voice even though she was well over fifty at the time of recording. There remains too a lovely performance of the soprano solo, 'Ihr nun habt Traurigkeit', in Brahms' *Requiem*, the fine broad curve of the phrases and the floating tone of an exceptionally beautiful voice amply supported by the breath.

Thus, then, some of the lyric-sopranos, always more numerous than their heroic sisters, the Brünnhildes and Isoldes. The period has, however, had three very considerable exponents of these roles, for there are Astrid Varnay and Martha Mödl as well as Birgit Nilsson. Unfortunately Varnay has not recorded with justice to herself, nor, sad to say, has her voice lasted well. The date of her birth is generally given as 1918, and when one looks up Nilsson in the reference books it is to find, somewhat incredulously, that she was born in the same year. Varnay is probably best remembered on record by a towering Ortrud in *Lohengrin*, and of course there is character to be heard in all that she does. Similarly with Mödl, only five years older: records demand more even and easy production of the sumptuous voice, though again there is no mistaking the command and authority of her performances in such roles as the *Walküre* Brünnhilde and the *Fidelio* Leonore, both recorded under Furtwängler.

And now for Nilsson. From a steady development in Stockholm during the nineteen-forties, she gained an outstanding international reputation in the fifties, so that in August 1960 the experienced correspondent from Vienna could write for *Opera*: 'On the stage Nilsson was the undisputed heroine of the evening; she was vocally magnificent, the greatest Brünnhilde of my memory. I do not think there was ever one like hers. Perhaps Flagstad's? Perhaps Mildenburg's?'.[1] Questions evidently designed to set

---

[1] Anna Bahr-Mildenburg, of whom only one record has come to light: the opening section of 'Ocean, thou mighty monster' (*Oberon*), made in 1904, and remarkable for its breadth and grandeur.

venerable heads shaking, while awed youngsters keep quiet. This might seem the ultimate in achievement, but in fact during the following decade her stature grew by as much again. So it is plainly the highest standards that we should expect of her records.

There is no lack of choice for sampling. Apart from Wagner, she has recorded a fair variety of opera complete. Two superb Turandots, ideal in the cold glitter of the tone, in the resilience, and the brilliant ring of the high notes. An aptly characterised Lady Macbeth, a great Elektra, a great Salome, Tosca and a warm-hearted Minnie, among Puccini's heroines; Aida and Amelia among Verdi's; Gioconda; Beethoven's Leonore; Donna Anna. In Scandinavian song, too, she can be attractive; like Flagstad, at her best in Sibelius, and especially in the desolate landscape painting of 'Höstkväll'.

Amidst all this, it is probably best to concentrate on two of her greatest roles, choosing Salome and Isolde. But first let us draw in the definition of her excellence a little closer. It is not, for instance, to be found in florid work. In the very earliest section of this book there was a Brünnhilde and Isolde who also gave a virtuoso's account of the scales, trills and runs required of a Violetta, Norma and Donna Anna. Now, of these roles Nilsson has sung the last, and recorded it twice, the second time (under Böhm) with more assurance than the first. What is pleasing about the performance is its humanity, warm and tender, for example, in the recitative before 'Non mi dir'. But the aria itself is satisfactory only in part, and the big and difficult run in the second half is not one of those parts: the notes are distinct enough, but there is a stiffness about it which does not encourage one to pursue the comparison.

After Lilli Lehmann, the next of the Brünnhildes discussed in detail was Johanna Gadski. She also extended her repertoire beyond Wagner, and some part of this extension she shares with Nilsson. There are arias from *Un Ballo in Maschera*, for example, imperfect but still finely sung and imaginatively treated. Play Nilsson's 'Ma dall'arido stella divulsa' after Gadski's and reactions will probably differ, but my own first one is to register a wish that the voice was steadier; on the other hand, she has a fine swell to the high C in 'deh mi reggi, m'aita, o signor', the climactic phrase whose difficulties Gadski takes care of by omission. The wish for a steadier emission recurs, however, if one turns from the complete performance of the opera (under Solti) to a recital record (Leopold Ludwig the conductor) where unsteadiness is more insistent, and where both in this and in the *Aida* extracts (sharp, for example, on some of the repeated F's in 'O patria mia') intonation is uneasy. There is, of course, an advance compared with other singers of recent times in that these performances are there to be discussed at all. Flagstad, and Nilsson's own contemporaries, did not offer such a repertoire. We are moving once again to the concept the all-round singer, whose Wagner is likely to be all the better for a mastery of the florid and lyrical work of the Italians and of Mozart: but we have not yet caught up with Lilli Lehmann.

Nilsson has, however, always been an adventurous and developing artist, and this is one of the great things about her. It is true in her own specialised field as well as in the wider repertoire. A woman who has gained such a reputation in a field where competitors are so few could easily have given one Isolde after another without ever rethinking the part. Yet Nilsson has recorded it twice (1961 under Solti, 1966 under Böhm) and the development is marked, both in overall concept and in detail. Confining comparisons to the First Act, one sees in the later version a more formidable, even sinister Isolde, a sorceress, a woman whose utterances essentially express hatred and contempt. For instance, there is a touch of spite in the places where Isolde repeats Brangäne's words in dialogue with her. Then in the confrontation with Tristan, the earlier version has a pleasant-sounding 'Wahre dein Schwert', whereas in the later one it is ice-cold with contempt, and behind the courtly manners lurks a distinctly-felt menace. The re-working of the part is revealed in tiny details: the way the phrases 'Dünkst es dich dunkel mein Gedicht? Frag' ihn denn selbst' have become twice as expressive, the question being put in disarmingly quiet conversational style, and the command given fortissimo with a vivid change of face. This is a more dynamic Isolde: there is more intensity and intimacy of story-telling in the Narrative, and a reckless total outpouring in the Curse. The recording comes from a stage performance at Bayreuth, and that may account for the extra vividness; certainly Wieland Wagner's producing hand may have had something to do with it. In the earlier performance, Nilsson was working with Solti, whose reading of the score is intensely rich in insight and new understanding; and her voice sounds more beautiful in it. But her later one shows, whatever the conditions, a richer characterisation and (as a by-product) not merely a dynamic Isolde, but a dynamic (as opposed to a static) artist in Nilsson.

A sample of achieved greatness, almost perfect in execution, is the Salome, also with Solti. At her entrance, this Salome is very young, girlish, silver-toned but yearning, unsheathing the shrewish edge to her tongue and character only with the demand to see Jokanaan. The silver in her voice is ideal, and so is the strong animal will to which it is the pretty wrapping. The final scene is done with superb breadth, and then with a chilling 'matt' voice for the 'Ach, ich habe deinen Mund geküsst', all the edge taken off, a breathed and other-worldly sound. And everywhere are marvels of pure singing, from the exciting swordblade full-voice to the most delicate fairy-like high A on 'Gewiss ist er keusch wie der Mond'. The difficult passage 'Dein Haar ist grässlich' is done with a mastery that recalls Emmy Destinn's of long ago; and for the rest there is hardly the possibility of recalling any previous performance, for this one excels. There has arrived, since then, the Salome of Montserrat Caballé, equally superb in its very different way: that two performances of such quality should appear within less than a decade (Nilsson 1962, Caballé 1969) is one sign of the genuineness of the time's renaissance.

90. Birgit Nilsson

Another is that within more recent years a new generation of singers has arisen, with its own style and distinction well marked. As the singers we have been discussing were associated very largely with the conductors Furtwängler and Solti in their recordings, so now we have a more recent *Ring* under Karajan, and most of the other Wagner operas, in which principal roles have been taken by such excellent singers as Helga Dernesch, Karl Ridderbusch and Zoltan Kelémén. Dernesch and Ridderbusch are discussed briefly in the concluding chapter of this book, for they both instance what is a very heartening characteristic—the insistence upon fine tone and steady emission. In Kelémén too we meet a character-singer whose highly personal, strong characterisations do not hide the fact of a fine voice or the ability to use it beautifully; occasionally one can even catch something of Schorr's noble tone in his singing, and his *Siegfried* Alberich is firm and resonant quite beyond anything we normally hear in this role. In some of these recent recordings he also finds himself in company with Martti Talvela, the Finnish bass, and again we recognise a distinction that promises well for the future. His dark tones, given a heavy-footed emphasis, are strikingly right for Fasolt in *Rheingold* or for Daland in *Der fliegende Holländer*. But he is more than this might suggest, for the firmness goes with a feeling for line to make an impressive Sarastro, and a live dramatic sense seconds the grandly opulent tone to make him a powerful contributor among the soloists in Verdi's *Requiem* (he might be more useful still in the Russian repertoire, a superb Dositheus, for instance, in *Khovanshchina*). A certain gruffness, which may be deliberate characterisation, marks his singing of the Inquisitor in *Don Carlo*, and detracts a little from the pleasure of his singing, especially when thrown into relief by the virtually unflawed cantabile of Ghiaurov's King Philip. But he is a big singer, with voice and style to match his huge physical presence, and will no doubt be a very positive factor in recordings, as also in live performances, for many years to come.

But along with qualifications concerning the pleasure which such modern singing gives there come others which place a further caution upon the generally optimistic tone of this survey. In general, the tendency has been, in these more recent recordings, to select singers who will produce a steady tone and give intelligent attention to the texts. Out of this policy there has still not come, as far as I can see (and indeed as far as most reviews suggest), a really satisfying Wagnerian tenor. It is true that in the LP era we have had fine performances from Windgassen, and there have been Jon Vickers' Siegmund (the Leinsdorf and Karajan versions making an interesting comparison), Sandor Konya's very likeable Lohengrin, and James King giving of his impressive best in an imaginative Parsifal under Boulez. René Kollo has sung in a recent *Tannhäuser* and *Die Meistersinger*, and one is grateful for the clearly defined voice; not, however, for the aspirates, or for the lack of legato in his Prize Song. Moreover, though the tone is bright and penetrative, it lacks the warmth and romantic ring that are also needed. With Helge Brilioth, Karajan's *Götterdämmerung* Siegfried, there is also the welcome presence of a reliably firm, well-defined tone; he catches, too, a note of gaiety and intimacy, singing beautifully in the more tender, quiet passages, very convincingly the lover and the athlete. His lightness does work against the concept of Siegfried as super-man hero, however, and there are many pages in the score where it seems a necessary one.

Nor, with all the singing-world to choose from, have the modern recordings come up with casting in other roles that might reassure a sceptical observer. If steady emission of tone is part of the policy, then surely the casting of the baritone roles should have been an easy matter in a world where operatic singing is in a healthy condition. Thomas Stewart and Theo Adam are devoted, imaginative artists, but no one could claim that their voices reproduce as reliably steady or beautiful instruments on most of their records. Adam's Hans Sachs has some fine features—the beginning of the Fliedermonolog, for instance, is quiet and sympathetic, but generally one sighs for a true evenness of production, and indeed for a different voice-character in the role. His recording of the Dutchman has fine declamatory passages, and some recordings of Bach cantatas show that he can sing the difficult intervals cleanly with breath-control to span the taxing runs: on the other hand, those runs are also very much aspirated, and one rarely feels while listening to such records that here is a singer in the line from Schwarz, Schlusnus, Janssen and Hüsch. Nor does one with Thomas Stewart, whose records of Wolf's *Harfenspielerlieder* and 'Prometheus' suggest comparisons with Janssen and Schorr that it is better not to make. Not that there is any lack of interpretative care: but steadiness, legato, depth and beauty of tone are also highly desirable in such music. Yet his records can show him to be the impressive singer that his reputation in the opera house suggests, and perhaps the best example is provided by a live performance, his Amfortas in the 1970 Bayreuth *Parsifal*. Here we have steady production, a richer voice and some fine soft singing. But all too often the studio performances create a different impression. It is perhaps curious that greater use has not been made of Covent Garden's David Ward, whose recordings (say) in Handel display an able technique, and whose singing in the close of *Rheingold* (included in the Covent Garden Anniversary Album) shows the warm tone and genuine legato that have been regular features of his work throughout a distinguished career.

The recording studios have, on the other hand, seen a good deal of another of Covent Garden's principals. Gwyneth Jones has in a very short space of time recorded an imposing repertoire of major roles, some of them too late for inclusion in this survey; but one cannot, in all truth, feel very happy about the quality of the singing in much of this recent work. Least acceptable is her Ortrud, which oddly exhibits just the sort of qualities that on the whole the modern recordings have been discouraging: that is, a sound that is big at the expense of its steadiness. Much that she has done on record has been excellent: her Medea is strongly characterised (even when compared with Callas), her 'D'amor sull' ali rosee' from *Trovatore* is an exquisite performance of a most taxing aria, and her Desdemona (recorded in the generally under-appreciated recording under Barbirolli) is most touching and deeply felt (Desdemona's suffering presence in the great Audience Chamber scene of Act III becomes more real than I have ever known it before). And the many recent recordings include an intense

Kundry, tender and tonally beautiful in the Herzeleide music. But one must only hope that the future will bring an adjustment, by which scrupulous attention goes first and foremost to the care for line and to the beauty of an evenly produced tone.

Such reservations about the modern Wagnerian scene could no doubt be taken further. There is the phenomenon, for instance, of Anja Silja: her recordings, such as *Der fliegende Holländer* under Klemperer, show, as one would expect, plenty of feeling and an equal amount of ungainly and unsatisfying singing. She could be adduced as a modern test-case, but I think it would be wrong to do so. The Editor of *Opera*, Harold Rosenthal, put the point well (*Opera*, April 1969). He tells how he, like many others who were present at the performances of *Fidelio* in the current season at Covent Garden, 'was as perturbed by this lady's vocal inequalities as (he) was excited by her personal magnetism'. But looking up Chorley's account of the great Schröder-Devrient's performance in the same role in London some 130 years earlier he found a very similar reaction—Chorley's view was that Schröder-Devrient had not learnt to sing, and she was still an incomparably fine Leonore. In other words, this is not a peculiarly modern phenomenon at all.

On balance, recent developments are in fact encouraging, as on balance the period represented by the first *Ring* recording was a good time to look back on. The general level has in many important ways been high, and greatness has come our way just about as frequently as can be reasonably expected.

It is perhaps not entirely coincidental that great singing and the gramophone seem to have been reborn at the same time. In this book we have used Wagner as the composer above others to follow developments in the recording process, and the three periods of our history have corresponded fairly naturally with changes in Wagnerian singing. In the first period the gramophone was feeling its way, and the singers were still assimilating Wagner into their systems of production. In the second, the gramophone had proved that it could serve, and the singers that they could not merely cope but could combine understanding with beauty. In the modern age the singers have deepened their understanding in detail (it is an age where we look more searchingly for specific insights within an overall rightness of conception), and the gramophone has become not merely ancillary to the musical world, but a setter of standards, and a complete musical experience in its own right. Moreover, it is now the whole work that is the object of attention, and no composer has set the gramophone a harder task in this respect than Wagner. No wonder John Culshaw saw fit to write a book about one of the great landmarks of the gramophone's history and Wagner's: 'In Vienna, on the afternoon of 24 September 1958, Decca began the first commercial recording of Richard Wagner's *Der Ring des Nibelungen*; seven years later, on the evening of 19 November 1965, every note and every word of Wagner's huge masterpiece had been recorded'. And the first commercial recording is no doubt only the first. For the singer, as for the gramophone and the composer, the future looks bright. For 'every note and every word' will not only be recorded again and again, but they will be scrutinized. And there is nothing like the consciousness of that fact for raising standards all round.

22. Trial by Mozart: Vintage Soprano
Elisabeth Schwarzkopf   Irmgard Seefried
Lisa della Casa   Hilde Güden
Ljuba Welitsch   Sena Jurinac

Nor 'Wagner' but 'Mozart' would, however, be a musician's likely answer to any question about the composer whose works most reliably test general standards of performance. Of course, 'Mozart' predictably comes as the pious answer to most aesthetic questions nowadays, but here it is sound and genuine enough. More regularly than later composers, he asks of his singers an exacting combination of flexibility and precision, and to a greater extent than his predecessors he requires that elegance should go along with dramatic force and insight into character. No age can do justice to Mozart without plenty of excellent singers to help; and by the principle of supply and demand there is probably no better guarantee than a genuine appreciation of Mozart that a full and sufficient supply of such artists will be forthcoming.

Certainly the one really significant growth-point in the performance of opera in the nineteen-thirties concerned Mozart before other composers, for the Glyndebourne experiment of assembling an international cast and working upon a production which should be a complete artistic unity revealed immediately a new (or at any rate renewed) *Figaro* and *Giovanni* and it virtually introduced *Così fan tutte*. It also worked with other festivals and resident companies to lead opera away from the star system and to-wards the modern concept of partnership, where producer, conductor and designers join a body of musicians (soloists, singers in the chorus, orchestral players) in a general collaborative enterprise. Rossini and Verdi, Beethoven and Strauss, all stood to benefit from this, but for Mozart it was essential.

And, of course, the records show that, along with the celebrated excellence of ensemble in these early Glyndebourne productions, there was much fine solo singing as well. It is interesting to take as some sort of index of standards, two recordings of live performances of *Don Giovanni*, one made in 1942, the other in 1950, and then to return to the Glyndebourne version of 1936. 7 March 1942, was the date of a performance at the Metropolitan Opera, New York, one of a famous series conducted by Bruno Walter, with Ezio Pinza as the Don. The cast included Bampton, Novotnà, Sayão, Kullman, Pinza and Kipnis. At Salzburg, 1950, Furtwängler conducted the Vienna Philharmonic in a production which offered Welitsch, Schwarzkopf, Seefried, Dermota, Gobbi and Kunz. The differences of approach, atmosphere and tempo are extreme. Furtwängler's tempi are, as one would expect, quite slow; but Walter's are very fast indeed. The Metropolitan performance is often what one might call an exhilarating scramble, the orchestra whizzing along (but sounding as though they are enjoying it, as do the audience, for there is lots of laughter), the singers hard pressed to keep up. At Salzburg, all the notes have time to sound, the phrases can all be shaped, recitatives have specific meaning instead of merely being not-boring (at the Met, Pinza and Kipnis, the two great bassos of their age, developed marvellous speed and nimbleness in their recits together, but Gobbi and Kunz point and vary them, so that one actually starts to attend to the meaning). There is admittedly only one point of serious mishap in the Metropolitan performance, where at 'Perdòn, signori miei', Leporello gets first two beats behind, then two ahead, helped out on both occasions by one of the ladies (there was an awkward moment at Salzburg too, when the Don put in his highwayman's 'Eh, eh, sei morto' several lines early, covered it up as best he could by laughing and then did it over again at the proper time). But one has a feeling of absolute security in the later performance, while Walter's unresting (yet not entirely steady) *brio* generates excitement, but some anxiety and even irritation along with it.

If anxiety and irritation enter into one's reactions on listening to the Salzburg recording (both of these live performances are on the private EJS label and the sound is only relatively agreeable), it is because of the singer who may well have been the most exciting member of the cast as far as the audience present at the live performance were concerned. Ljuba Welitsch's Donna Anna rings out strong and shining, but in detail it leaves much to be desired; in many ways Rose Bampton's less dynamic competence and authority are preferable. When it comes to the other ladies, however, there is no question. Seefried's Zerlina is warm, characterful, and scrupulously musical, where Sayão, pretty of person as of voice, has a habit of leaving the note and singing somewhere around it every so often as a contribution to the charm of the occasion. And Novotna's Elvira, accurate enough (omitting 'Mi tradì', however), pales beside the radiance, strength and intelligence of Schwarzkopf's.

In Kolodin's *Story of the Metropolitan Opera* we read that Walter's first *Don Giovanni* of that season was reckoned to be a performance 'more unified than any since Mahler's time'. By modern standards, the one we have on records is still something of a free-for-all, and returning to the Glyndebourne set one realises that *their* standards, in 1936, were much closer to ours now. The big houses and the big names took time to catch up. The 1950 Salzburg performance goes far towards the ideal, for there are the 'star' singers that this opera so particularly calls for, but formed as a company, with a generally fine discipline and a true feeling for Mozart.

Not that the standards of Salzburg in a vintage year have since become everybody's standards. But they were a sign of the times; and, indeed, of times to come, for the next twenty years were to be blessed with much very good Mozart, as records (statistical, critical and long-playing) testify.

And of course it was precisely the advent, just after the Second World War, of such singers as these in the Salzburg *Don Giovanni* that suggested a genuine renaissance in singing. In England, the suggestion was made irresistibly throughout the short season in 1947 when the Vienna Opera visited Covent Garden. Three of the five operas presented were by Mozart, and singers new to the Royal Opera House included Schwarzkopf, Seefried, Welitsch, Güden, Jurinac, Loose, Dermota and Kunz. These same singers were also becoming familiar through gramophone records in the last years of the 78, the general feeling being that the women, at least, constituted a generation comparable to that of the great German sopranos of the inter-war period. And to that number should be added Lisa della Casa, who was at Salzburg in 1947, though she did not sing at Covent Garden or the Metropolitan till 1953.

All these singers demonstrated excellence at a time when it was badly needed; but the one who has grown to greatness year by year until she has become one of the supreme singers of the century is Elisabeth Schwarzkopf. It is interesting to turn back to what was perhaps her first record issued in England, a coupling of 'Die Forelle' and 'Seligkeit', where one hears pretty singing, not very much more. Or yes, look at it with the wisdom of hindsight and there *is* more: a firm placing of the delicate tone, a nice play of legato and staccato in 'Die Forelle', and a smile that can make its way through the wax. She doesn't tell a story, doesn't arrest attention, doesn't make contact with the unseen audience. All these things were to come—to come soon, to be ever-increasing, and to last long. But the material (the intelligence, the sound technique, the fine voice) is there, evident in that unexciting little record that nevertheless sold a good many copies in the last years of the 78.

For the singer she became, one can turn to an immensely rich repertoire of recordings. A later version of 'Die Forelle', for instance, issued in 1966, shows the variety of colouring resources and the imaginative ways of communication that became hers, as well as the preservation over the twenty years of a pure bright voice to match the 'helle' of the stream. But she has also achieved a depth of expression in songs which demand the utmost intensity of feeling and mastery of the voice. Wolf's 'Kennst du das Land' is one of these, and this also will afford us opportunities for comparison. It was included in the recital given at the Festival Hall in 1967 to mark the retirement of Gerald Moore, and it is also part of a collection of Wolf's Goethe Lieder issued in 1959. This is a song where the unity of emotion is provided by its yearning, but where moods and pictures flash in rapid succession; where also the wistfulness of the young girl must be able to turn into a majestic exaltation of spirit, with a heroic supply of voice and of breath-control to support it. Schwarzkopf so evidently and amply gives all this that one can turn straight to those details in which the performances differ. The later record brings a deeper tone, and it is superbly dark and strong in the third verse with its romantic mountain mists, dragons and rocks. The earlier one is wide-eyed with the mystery of the shimmer and gleam of recollections in the second verse; the girl here is more wistful ('Kennst du es wohl?'), even allowing a little self-pity ('armes Kind'). Ever so slightly the note on the word 'zieh'n', when it is first sung, is sharp: that has disappeared in the later version, no doubt because the singer's keen, critical ears have detected it and guarded accordingly. Both readings are valid—the first emphasising the girlishness of the character, the second the maturity and strength of the music. But it is always so with Schwarzkopf, that a new performance involves new study and rewards with new insight.

The deliberations behind Schwarzkopf's work have indeed provoked some criticism. 'Can't-hear-the-music-for-the-interpretation' is a cry raised against modern singers from time to time, and sometimes justifiably so. It is, of course, the vice of a great virtue, and Schwarzkopf is not free of it. 'Anakreons Grab', discussed on p. 606, provides an example; perhaps 'Der Musensohn' and 'An Sylvia' as recorded with Edwin Fischer's accompaniment might be other instances where a more straightforward 'out-singing' manner would be welcome. But examples are not so easy to find after all, while there are many on the other side: in that same Schubert recital with Edwin Fischer the 'Lied im Grünen' is a masterly example of when to change tone and when to carry through without fussing; or in the Salzburg recital of 1953, when Furtwängler played for her, Wolf's 'Schlafendes Jesuskind' is a song which could have been affected in manner or overstudied, whereas what one hears is the most beautiful legato, the finest of lightenings, the least fussy and most sensitive of interpretations. The thought and art are so marvellously exact that one wants to call them calculated, which immediately suggests something unfeeling and insincere; yet this is self-evidently absurd, for insincerity, like sentimentality, betrays itself by inexactness and distortion. What one has in Schwarzkopf is a high degree of awareness—of colours and styles, and of the existence of *choice*.

Choice, for example, determines use of vibrato—for this singer, at any rate. When the heart is troubled, especially when the ambiance of the music is of the opera house rather than the hall or salon, then the more insistent vibrato tends to come as expressive and appropriate: in Desdemona's Willow Song, for example, where one is always aware of the underlying anxiety, or in Elvira's 'Mi tradì', which can so easily sound merely sunny and pleasant (as in fact the melody of itself is), or, to take an example from an intimate and personal song, certain phrases in Wolf's 'Verborgenheit' when the introspective joys and sorrows move towards their climax (this is also an example of how she can use her breathing—the physical

91. Elisabeth Schwarzkopf as the Marschallin in *Der Rosenkavalier*

business of breathing in and out—as an expressive instrument). Conversely, the voice can be drained of all vibrato. Thus, in Strauss's 'Ruhe, meine Seele', the dark vowel of 'Ruhe' is given on a pure 'funnel' of sound, with an other-worldly depth: but then, this is a song with a vast emotional range, a Brünnhilde in spirit, yet with a heavenly lightness for the 'lichter Sonnenschein' of the first verse. From the heroic, mature depth of phrases like 'Deine Sturme gingen wild . . . wie die Brandung' in that song, to the youthful airiness of a Gretel in the same composer's 'Freundliche Vision', or indeed to Gretel herself, where the little song she sings at the beginning of Act II is done with a child's innocence of operatic method—to move between these two extremes is surely to acknowledge the work of a singer who has explored and 'learnt' her voice as an organist knows his stops and works on his registration, the voice (involving mind and body) being so much the subtler instrument.

One result is that Schwarzkopf's performances are so reliably greater in yield, in point-by-point enlightenment, than almost anybody else's. The *Freischütz* aria and the excerpt from *Der Rosenkavalier* discussed in the Appendix illustrate this in relation mostly to singers of the past. The *Four Last Songs* of Richard Strauss measure her achievements in comparison with her very beautiful contemporary, Lisa della Casa. Della Casa's record was the first,[1] and through it a whole generation came to love the music. Her tone is springlike, and for the first song it is ideal. Schwarzkopf sings it half-a-tone lower, and is less happy with the high melisma on the word 'Wunder'. Similarly in 'Beim Schlafengehen' Della Casa goes easily up to the high note of 'tausendfach', makes lovely sounds throughout, and particularly in the 'Flugel schweben' phrase. But, these things apart, one simply registers the refinements and insights of Schwarzkopf's performance (feeling its modulations, knowing its heart, not just its sweetness and light), and notes that there is very little corresponding in the other. The nostalgic lingering of 'Der Sommer lächelt' in the second song has a sighing magic; one feels the longing in 'Um im Zauberkreis zu leben' (in 'Beim Schlafengehen'), with a sigh on the 'Nacht' and a deepening tone on the 'tief'; in 'Es dunkelt schon die Luft' ('Im Abendrot') we catch the growing stillness of darkness, and in 'Ist dies etwa der Tod' the voice responds to the deepening colours of each chord, preserving the mood and the mystery to the end. Schwarzkopf worked in a fine collaboration with Georg Szell in this and other Strauss recordings; credit for the final near-perfection goes to all those involved, with no doubt a very considerable share of it here as in so much else going to Walter Legge. But whatever the combination of forces, the result is infinitely rich, and comparison with Della Casa, lovely as she is, will only help to define the yield, as it can do, virtually phrase by phrase.

[1] Though the first performance of all, given by Flagstad with the Philharmonia Orchestra conducted by Furtwängler, at the Festival Hall in 1950, has been issued in the EJS series, a warm, glowing sound emerging through the various interference-noises, Flagstad coping well with the tessitura, and singing with fine richness in 'Im Abendrot'.

In Mozart, whom we shall take for a touchstone throughout this chapter, the distinction is similarly marked. In an early LP recital of operatic arias by Mozart, we hear a Susanna, a Countess, Cherubino, Donna Anna, and Zerlina: all are paraded vividly before us, complete in their characterisation, though no more than a few pages of their music are sung. The aristocratic indrawn 'Porgi Amor' is at one end of the scale; at the other, the breathless, uninhibited 'Non so più', with its touch of the spoilt child in the broken chromatic phrases towards the end, followed by the open-vowelled excitement of 'Parlo d'amor con me'. Just occasionally one stands back to say 'Yes, but . . .': 'Yes, but this "Vedrai carino", for all its charm, is self-regarding rather than loving'. Such complaints, or any other kind, are rare.

And, of course, wholly absent from this record are the two Mozartian characters most associated with Schwarzkopf—Donna Elvira and Fiordiligi. She has recorded *Così fan tutte* twice, first with Karajan, then with Böhm, and although the Karajan performance had a relatively short life in the catalogue it has very much to commend it: the trio, 'Soave sia il vento', is one of the most exquisite things on record (slightly slower than Böhm's, with exactly the right *mormorando* in the strings, the lightest of light tones from the Dorabella and Don Alfonso, and exactly the right balance of voices as each comes into prominence). Schwarzkopf's Fiordiligi is fine in both; and fine, also, in the two immensely testing arias. The second, 'Per pietà', can be so dull, even when the technical difficulties have been negotiated. Again, Lisa della Casa fails to make it sound as though it is *about* something; and although Sena Jurinac, in her version, sings with saddened expression, there is little bite to such phrases as 'che vergogna'. Teresa Berganza, who sings throughout with a rather fine tragic dignity, achieves an impressive grandeur here. But turning back to Schwarzkopf after these is to come suddenly face to face with a human being: there is much more warmth, humanity and meaning. Here the Böhm version is the better; she seems to be taking her Fiordiligi rather more to her heart, though in both recordings the idea is the same (the portamento and gentle pleading of the dotted rhythmic figure handling the melody affectionately, in a way heard years ago in a record by Felicie Hüni-Mihaczek, and rarely since).

As for 'Come scoglio', the first of Fiordiligi's arias, let us use this as a final test in the matter of technique. Critics have picked on this one as music which shows up her deficiencies, so one plays the records with ears cocked for fault-finding. Well, some faults there are: nearly all of them in one difficult bar, on the words 'affetto il cor', where the upward arpeggio is marked staccato and ends with a top C. Schwarzkopf does not sing staccato (as della Casa, Berganza and Leontyne Price do—but not Jurinac), and she does not take the C as easily and cleanly as the others. But there are many technical challenges apart from this: the broad intervals, for instance, in which she has the assurance and accuracy of the true virtuoso. There is also

the daunting sequence of twenty triplets. Now, in the Böhm version especially, one could wish for greater homogeneity of tone (as we are given,
together with perfect accuracy and clarity, in Teresa Berganza's record).
But the great thing is that the notes are well and truly *there*—and they are not
there in the other versions just mentioned. Jurinac on 78 is going very
fast and it is not surprising that the tiny triplet notes are not very accurately
pitched. But it may be somewhat surprising to find that, when one slows
the turntable to check, some fourteen of the twenty triplets are quite
undefined, and that, in Leontyne Price's, all, after the first group, are
virtually a matter of a rhythmic gesture around three notes of similar pitch.
Of course, critics of Schwarzkopf might persist and say that she should be
tested not by the standards of her contemporaries but by those of the golden
age; but then, 'golden-age' singers, as one often has occasion to reflect,
knew when not to try their luck too far, and of 'Come scoglio', as of much
technically exacting music, they and the recording studios remained
blissfully ignorant. Lilli Lehmann knew it, no doubt, and, had she recorded
it, Schwarzkopf would no doubt have learnt something from it (for the
records of the other Lehmann, together with those of Leider, Lemnitz,
Farrar and Seinmeyer have been, we gather, a course of study prescribed
for her by her husband); but the evidence really suggests that most of the
lessons to be learnt in singing are those for which her own mastery is the
best testimonial.

Despite the limiting force of the comparisons made with Schwarzkopf,
'mastery' is also the word for much of the work of della Casa and Jurinac,
both of whom can stand in company of however golden an age. And
although there are frequently times, as in the *Four Last Songs*, where one
wants deeper and subtler responsiveness, della Casa remains one of the
best of all sopranos in Richard Strauss. Her voice has that touch of spring
and silver that Strauss loved and wrote for; her tone will float and soar.
She is also very beautiful, very feminine, suggesting a wholly appealing
kind of fragility, tender and unmannered. A recital of Strauss songs which
appeared in 1964 shows her at her best. A great beauty in this collection is
'Der Stern': the sound is lovely in itself, and she has a way with the big
intervals—splendid, for instance, in the last line, 'Mir leuchten ins Haus'.
Then, deeper, more mature, less merely pretty in tone, 'Mein Herz ist
stumm' shows her capable of communicating and colouring as the true
Lieder singer must: she here *directs* her words in a way that is comparatively
rare with her, and she deadens the voice movingly for the last lines, 'Mein
Herz ist stumm, mein Herz ist kalt'. Humour and zest can also be hers; her
'Für fünfzehn Pfennige' is a genuine *tour de force*, never arch or overplayed, and compensating for the feeling the 'Ständchen' gave that she
lacked anything more substantial or spirited than charm, that it was all
too like a careful rehearsal.

This feeling, of something too cautious and placid, limits some of her
Mozart too. Her Elvira in *Don Giovanni* and Countess in *Nozze di Figaro*

92. Lisa della Casa as the Marschallin in *Der Rosenkavalier*

lack an element of command and dramatic projection surely needful in both; and Donna Anna's 'Non mi dir' (not helped by the pedestrian conducting of Heinrich Hollreiser) might equally well be sung by either of the characters, or, say, by Susanna in a reflective mood. Nevertheless it is certainly very *lovely* singing: heavenly, for instance, as she takes the soft high B flat on the word 'abbastanza', at the end of the recitative, and then broad, even and caressing in the melody itself. And her singing of the Countess is refined and loveable, with rather more 'presence' perhaps in the Leinsdorf version than in the earlier Kleiber: really fine in the third Act, heartfelt and eventually radiant in the aria, smiling and light as air in the Letter Duet.

But it is probably for *Arabella* that della Casa will be most widely remembered. She recorded it twice, the second time from a live performance in Munich under Keilberth with some loss in freshness and firmness of tone, but in radiant voice for the earlier version under Solti. She makes an immediate impression of beauty and graciousness with her first phrases, sings with soaring abandon as she looks forward to the appearance of Mr Right ('der Richtige'), and allows a cloud to pass over the voice as the intriguing stranger goes past her window without so much as looking up. There are limits to the success even of this performance: she doesn't really make vivid, for example, the tragic, bewildered Arabella of the denunciation. Yet the final impression is a deepening of the first: a great and gracious beauty, whose quiet, sincere singing of the 'plighting' tune to Mandryka in Act II ('Und du wirst mein Geliebter sein') will always stay in the mind warmly and blessedly.

So will the best voice and style of Sena Jurinac. One says 'best' because there is really quite a marked difference between the records made in the early fifties and those of the next decade. This comes home as one compares Ilia's solos recorded under Fritz Busch in 1951 with the versions heard in the complete *Idomeneo* of 1957 conducted by Pritchard. The 'Zeffiretti lusinghieri' is much younger, much more air-borne in the earlier version, and the solo from Act I ('Quando avràn . . . Padre germani') shows the whole instrument to have been more flexible, the soft passages more delicate, the runs more effortless. Mind, there is no doubt in any of these records that here is a distinguished artist. The Ilia of Colin Davies' recording, Margherita Rinaldi, characterises imaginatively and sometimes makes beautiful sounds; but one returns to Jurinac and to a different class of performance. The distinction is localised in the clarity and command of intervals, as in the phrase 'cagion tu sei', but it is pervasive in the greater humanity of the timbre and greater warmth in the more passionate phrases.

This voice, warm and very human, yet firm and devoid of a distinctively feminine vibrato, is ideal for the *travesti* roles in Mozart and Strauss. Her Composer in Leinsdorf's *Ariadne auf Naxos* will not do for anybody who knows Seefried's (but then, Leinsdorf's prosaic reading will not satisfy anybody who knows Karajan's). Yet she is expressive at some points (the outrage of 'Nach meine Oper', for example), and the voice is gloriously firm throughout. Her potential is better realised as Octavian in Kleiber's *Rosenkavalier*: 'Nicht Heut oder Morgen' rings out with excited conviction, 'Wie Sie befindet' vividly catches the aristocratic youth, and the Presentation of the Rose is done with ideal radiance of tone. But best of all her young men is the Cherubino who enjoyed such abundant life in the 'Non so più' recorded with Karajan in 1950. One sees the face, the eyes, the regretful pout at 'E se non ha', the smiling self-congratulation at 'parlo d'amor con me'.

Much of her Mozart is in fact a model both of style and of voice production, though little is as vital as that 'Non so più'. Two performances as Countess Almaviva are included in her comparatively restricted gramophone repertoire, the Glyndebourne 1955 recording finding her in happier voice than the 1956 version conducted by Karl Böhm. In both arias (and in both performances) one is curiously aware of the difficulty the music presents to a singer, and especially in the later recording one feels anxious for the softer singing. Yet hers is still in some ways a classic assumption of the role: a noble and sympathetic character is before us, aristocratic in the authority of such phrases as 'Lo vieto! l'onestà' in the second Act, warm in tone and feeling in such passages as lie in the middle of the voice, like the reply to the Count's plea for forgiveness in the last.

In *Don Giovanni* the technical difficulties are of another kind, for a singer's skill in florid work is severely tested in Donna Anna's part as well as Elvira's. Jurinac has made both roles her own, though the consensus of opinion generally favoured her Elvira. As Anna in a somewhat disappointing performance of the opera under Fricsay, she put some strain upon the voice, though the 'Non mi dir' is beautifully sung. As Elvira she has left an extremely fine version, a demonstration, among other things, of technical mastery achieved in our day as completely as in any other period on record. One ought not to talk of singing Mozart in terms of competitive athletics; all the same, the role of Donna Elvira must look dreadfully like a steeplechase to the singer in her dressing room as she contemplates the evening ahead. Success with the arpeggios in 'Ah, chi mi dice mai': one down, the rest of the dozen or so to come. Jurinac is superbly assured in everything, crowning the performance with a scrupulously even 'Mi tradì': she is the connoisseur's singer, after all.

Perhaps one cannot quite say that of Irmgard Seefried but perhaps there are more important things to say instead. The 'connoisseur's singer' can achieve a sort of perfection and virtuosity which Seefried hardly offers and may well not be interested in. She is not to be heard committing herself to much florid work on record (an example of real technical inadequacy is again provided by the triplets of 'Come scoglio'), and some of her best singing may have a rough edge here and there. What matters is that in her we have an artist of outstanding imaginative strength, and with that rare quality, presence; nobody but Schwarzkopf (with Schumann and Lehmann in the preceding generation) can match her vividness in a comparable repertoire, and at her best she has an exhilaration and intensity all her own.

Mention has already been made of her portrayal of the Composer in *Ariadne auf Naxos*, and we must return to it, for it is an inspired one. And of course it is an essential in this role, almost its starting-point, that the singer should be able to *sound* inspired. As the composer seizes a piece of paper and starts to write down the tune in his head, we have at once to feel the mystery of artistic creation (this is the sacred moment, Shelley's glowing coal, the fire from heaven), and we have to see the touching but comic spectacle of the youth, head aflame with his own genius and the religion of beauty, beating his luminous wings in an absurd world of social arrangements, patrons without taste, singers full of vanity and jealousy. So it is right that we should smile, and right that the singer should at once be able to see the character from outside (absurd) and feel it from inside (romantic, heroic, beautiful). Neither Jurinac nor Zylis-Gara, other Composers in recent recordings, are wearing this opera's special bi-focals. But Seefried is: hear her 'Ah!' of excitement as she catches the just-glimpsed melody, the improvising note as she sings it to herself, the very breathing of the inspired composer, and then the comic descent to a material world where even divine melodies cry for pen, paper and ink for their survival. But the part calls for so much life throughout: to capture the *innere Stimme* with a numbed, darkened, hollowed tone after the Major-domo's terrible announcement, to spit out the denunciation of an unworthy world ('Dar-über willst du nachdenken'), to sing out *mit fast trunkener Feierlichkeit*, as Strauss directs, at the credo 'Musik ist ein heilig Kunst'. All these Seefried does with incomparable vividness: it is surely one of the great performances on record.

Like her Composer, Seefried is both inner and extrovert. She has made a speciality in her recitals of songs like Moussorgsky's Nursery cycle and Bartók's Village Scenes, which ask their singer to take an uninhibited, unselfconscious risk; she must risk her child's voice, for instance, a wheedling, pouting voice for the children's excuses to the nurse, a sleepy-head voice for the lullaby to the doll, an irreverent enjoyment voice for the catalogue of aunts and uncles in the bedtime prayer. Seefried boldly projects them all, heard in the record which is perhaps her best memento, one taken from live concerts and ending with possibly the most winning of all performances of Strauss's 'Ständchen'.

For her 'inner' style, one would hope to be able to choose the *Fraunen-liebe und Leben*. Unfortunately, the ingénue sounds which she makes in some of the early songs (no doubt deliberately, to give the life-cycle its perspective) can be found irritating, and the sixth song ('Süsser Freund, du blickest mich verwundert an'), where one expects much of her, is not as tender or imaginative as one would have hoped. The best songs are those expressing the extremes of joy and sorrow—the eager, impulsive 'Ich kann's nicht fassen', and the last song, in which the non-vibrating, dead tone is ideally expressive. When her voice is drained of its vibrations, as here, it can gain a kind of wailing, or lamenting quality, marvellously employed in Schubert's four Gretchen songs, something of an equivalent in the soprano's repertoire to Wolf's 'Harfenspielerlieder' for baritone. Seefried is particularly fine in the 'Szene aus *Faust*', where Gretchen, mad and lost, hears with terror the *Dies Irae* sounding for her. A new tone is there for each new musical figure, and for the solemn hymn a strong choirboy's voice: another great performance this. But there are so many: that strong boy-voice exults, for instance, in more cheerful and extrovert music (delicious extracts from *Hänsel und Gretel* with Schwarzkopf, with whom she recorded some superb duets, or in Cornelius' pleasant short cycle of Christmas Songs, sung out with plenty of voice, yet intimate and lilting too), and it is readily adapted to a sophisticated 'folk' style in Brahms'

Deutsche Volkslieder, the charm never obscuring the sadness which underlies so many of them.

It is a knowledge of what is underlying that distinguishes her Mozart. So often the songs of Mozart register in a recital as a pretty delicacy, little more, but with Seefried one is aware of the underlying strength and warmth. Her series of Mozart songs on 78s had an exquisitely shaded 'Ridente la calma', a vividly spontaneous 'Das Veilchen', and a deepened, veiled, evening tone for 'Abendempfindung'. Best of all the Mozart, however, was a coupling, made in the same period, of two arias, Susanna's 'Deh, vieni' and Pamina's 'Ach, ich fühl's'. The first is tender and floating, with none of the fussing which marred a later version; and the great lament from *Die Zauberflöte* is given with broad phrasing, perfect placing and poise, and an absolute rightness of elegiac colouring.

The time that produced these four sopranos (for all were born within less than a decade) can well be called vintage years for them alone; yet there are two more of great fame and distinction to add, as well as several who have given much pleasure in similar music.

The two most important singers remaining are Hilde Güden and Ljuba Welitsch. Both have a glamour about their voices and personalities, and neither has had quite as happy a recording career as the sopranos already discussed.

Güden has, for one thing, been relatively unfortunate with her associates on record. Nobody now is likely to want the *Rigoletto* in which she sings an appealing Gilda to Aldo Protti's unmusical jester and del Monaco's brute of a Duke. Her sprightly, fresh-voiced Adina in *L'Elisir d'Amore* has a crude Belcore (Capecchi) and a Nemorino (di Stefano) who could have been ideal but is not. The *Zauberflöte* of which her Pamina is one of the attractions does not bear comparison as a whole with several recent versions; even her *Merry Widow* is a poor second in casting and presentation to the Schwarzkopf–Matačič recording, though it might be said that the sickly and essentially impotent *Giuditta* gets as good as it deserves, and in Güden herself something rather better.

A more worthy setting, and indeed a more interesting performance, is hers in the recording of Strauss's *Daphne* at the Theater an der Wien, opening the Vienna Festival of 1964. The best part of this, and a testimonial to her stamina among other things, is the lament after Leukippos' death, a very demanding solo to come towards the end of a big role. The soft, floated phrases are extremely lovely, in the best tradition of the Strauss soprano, and the most beautiful passage of all ('So höre, mein Leukippos') draws from her the greatest feeling. At the end of this solo comes a superbly accurate leap to the long-held high C; and at the very end of the opera, she still has the purity of voice, as it were all air, to suit the metamorphosis.

It is all the more impressive from a singer whose voice was probably at its best some few years before this: it then had the kind of youthful shining sound which characterised her Eva in the very first days of LP.

93. Sena Jurinac

94. Irmgard Seefried

95. Hilde Güden as Liù

96. Ljuba Welitsch

There was often a touch, perhaps rather appetising, of acid in her later singing, and if we are again to use Mozart as the touchstone it is not entirely to her advantage: her technique gives less than full satisfaction in pieces like 'L'amerò sarò costante' from *Il Rè Pastore* or the 'Exsultate Jubilate'. Yet she has been a considerable musician, dealing brilliantly, for example, with the role of Anne Trulove (sung in creditable English) in the first recording of Stravinsky's *Rake's Progress*. And in another of the Strauss recordings, she shows very great accomplishment in that most difficult role of Zdenka in *Arabella*: it is as though the singer of the strenuous, passionate music of the *Ariadne* composer should be required to have something like the range and agility of a Zerbinetta too. Richard for the serious and most testing side of her art, Johann for her way with lighter music (her Rosalinda has fine style, gaiety and glamour): the two Strausses between them find out the best in Güden.

They go far to do so with Welitsch as well. Her solos from *Fledermaus* and *Ziegeunerbaron* immediately present the grand manner of the genuine star (and Welitsch was emphatically that for a few golden years). It is hard to think of a voice with a brighter shine to it, or of a singer with greater energy and more sense of joy in that sheer act of producing these glorious sounds. Even here, however, one notes that subtlety is hardly in question; there is little of the lithe seductiveness which Schwarzkopf and Güden bring to the Czardas, for instance. And this limits much of her best work, even the *Salome* in which she made such an exciting impression on her audiences. One of the Metropolitan performances of 1949 has been recorded 'privately', and, fine as it is, it does not quite bring one face to face with the anticipated greatness.[1] In characterisation, we certainly see the transformation from kitten to fiend, culminating in the dehumanised tone of 'Ich fordre den Kopf des Jokanaans', low, clawing and tenacious. But quite a lot is less expressive than one would wish, and a certain amount of musical detail goes unobserved. At 'Er ist wirklich schrecklich' one does not hear or sense an inner shudder, nor is it sung pianissimo as marked. Nor is there a soft high A flat, where it really makes a difference, in the memorable phrase 'Gewiss ist er keusch wie der Mond'; nor a pianissimo, again important, at the end of the 'Dein Haar ist grässlich' passage. Still, much is magnificent, including the finale. One listens to some near-contemporaries of Welitsch in this music: Christel Goltz, clear and intelligent but unsteady on sustained notes; Inge Borkh, a true artist and an actress-singer of genuine stature, much steadier than Goltz, and often more expressive, yet sounding all too pleasant for the part; Maria Cebotari, much more in

---

[1] We have to thank one of these performances on another count, however; for it was after seeing Welitsch in *Salome* that an operatic career became the goal in life for Leontyne Price. The full excitement of her performance in the role is really better suggested by another, and earlier, record issued for the first time in 1972, after the above account was written. It is taken from a broadcast of 1944, shows the young voice at its finest, and conveys perhaps the most vivid impression of the temperament.

character, sinister and shrewish, yet inferior in sheer opulence of sound. Welitsch's dominance is very evident, and the commercial recording brings the superb quality of the voice into clearer focus.

One can draw on private and commercial recordings for her Donna Anna too. The Salzburg performance has already been mentioned. One can tell that it was a huge success at the time for the generally undemonstrative audience does not wait for the music to finish before applauding her arias. But the recording leaves one wishing she would sing softly rather more often (in the Mask Trio, for instance), that she could move a little more flexibly and gracefully, and that there was some subtler characterisation. The commercial issues have the same limitations, except that here, because of the better quality of the sound, one can luxuriate in the voice and be more content.

'Welitsch is one of the most remarkable singers of her day—I do not think there could be any doubt about that, even if she were suddenly to decide to stop singing tomorrow'. So wrote the Earl of Harewood in *Opera*, February 1953. The conditional clause was unhappily prophetic. It was just about that time that the shine and power of this exceptional voice were lost (Welitsch was forty in that year), and not long afterwards she retired. Records preserve much, and destroy perhaps a little. Salome and Donna Anna are roles that still bear the imprint of her performances, despite the limitations we hear on record. Perhaps the happiest memento of all is the one in which many listeners must have first come to know her: Tatiana's Letter Scene from *Eugen Onegin*, sung with the clearest of voices and a radiant expression.

So much radiance from the womenfolk tends to dim the male members of this company, and so much brilliance from these six stars also obscures some other very good Mozartian sopranos. Maria Stader, charming in songs like 'Das Veilchen' and Schubert's 'Nachtviolen', lacks interpretative insight in more serious music; yet she has recorded a wide range of works including at least four complete Mozart operas all with pleasing voice and style. Erika Köth's records (especially her Constanza) leave one wishing for firmer placing of notes, tone and sometimes time; better is Emmy Loose, a charming Blonda in *Die Entführung*, bringing sunshine and open-air into her Mozart songs, and performing with great verve and technical mastery in Pfitzner's 'Alte Weiser'. Among the lyric-dramatic sopranos, Hilde Zadek has style and command but is somewhat unsteady; among the coloraturas, Wilma Lipp makes little of the character of the Queen of Night but gets all her high notes in place, and is a captivating Christel ('Ich bin der Christel von der Post') in Zeller's *Der Vogelhändler* (with the Nightingale Song, whose fame was spread by Elisabeth Schumann, sung with a tremendous Viennese lilt and accent by Julius Patzak).

Patzak himself is discussed elsewhere. Chief among the Mozartian tenors, and one of the most musical tenors singing at this time, was Anton Dermota. His repertoire was wider than is often remembered, and records show him to have had an imaginative way with Italian arias, 'Ah, si ben mio' from *Il Trovatore* being a fine example, soft and inner at the start, a well-judged *diminuendo* leading to the key-change and the second half, and a pure legato such as is exhibited rarely by the Italians themselves. In Mozart we sometimes want a better legato: 'Un' aura amorosa' *(Così fan tutte)* has aspirated runs and a rather breathy tone, in both his Italian and German versions. His vowels could also sound somewhat nasal; and his technique does not do him credit in the grand test of 'Il mio tesoro' (Peter Anders, the sadly short-lived lyric tenor, elegant and personal in his interpretations, shows himself much more able in this). His 'Dalla sua pace', however, (as sung at Salzburg in 1950) is full of fine touches, with a particularly honeyed *mezza voce* at the return of the opening melody.

The Leporello of that Salzburg *Don Giovanni* was the outstanding baritone of the company and one of the great Viennese character-singers, Erich Kunz. Prominent in the list of his recordings are Viennese songs with Schrammel orchestra: songs about the Stefansdom and Grinzing, sung with an ingratiating smile, that, to someone brought up on *The Third Man*, translates mentally into a leer, and with slithery Viennese vowels to complete the snakelike attraction. If, indeed, attraction is the word, then 'Mei Mutter war a Wienerin' has the characteristic charm: it certainly shows the opera singer as popular artist on intimate terms with his public. More wholesome, perhaps, are his sturdy solos in a hearty record of German student choruses, full of 'Ju ja's and 'Hei didel-dö's. Better still, his Beckmesser in the Bayreuth *Meistersinger* of 1951, a nearly forgotten set, conducted by Karajan, with the near-ideal Eva of Elisabeth Schwarzkopf, and Otto Edelmann on best form as Sachs; Kunz gives a strong characterisation and (rarer among Beckmessers) a musical treatment of the score, as he does with his Leporello. A last splendid piece of Mozart is a 'Non più andrai', going with tremendous martial briskness, full of genial authority, the sonorous voice and the light touch being brought together in perfect combination.

'If you can sing Mozart, you can sing anything'. It isn't quite true, but most singers will say it all the same. It would be a peculiar kind of blindness, or deafness (the sort, however, collectors of old records and connoisseurs of singing are much afflicted with), that failed to recognise in such a splendid generation of Mozartians the signs of a true rebirth of singing generally. The survey made just now is not a complete one, as it centres on the Vienna Opera. Even then there are such notable omissions as Rita Streich and Teresa Stich-Randall both of whom came to Vienna early in the nineteen-fifties. Both are discussed elsewhere, as are the outstanding Mozart tenor, Léopold Simoneau, and the baritone Geraint Evans. The tradition continues, of course, but the time may well come when, in the perspective of a century, lovers of Mozart's operas will sigh for the decades 1945–1965 and say 'Those were the years'. Though, as is usually the case, it is doubtful whether the years themselves knew that they were.

23. Opera at Home: Five Great Singers
Maria Callas Victoria de los Angeles
Jussi Björling Tito Gobbi
Boris Christoff

THE years immediately after the Second World War gave rise to fears about the future of most things, and what became of the western tradition of cultivated singing was no doubt a matter of small importance in the bleak context of international affairs. Still, the subject cast its own small sighs of despondency into a world freezing with the onset of cold war; and in Britain the age of austerity invaded the re-opened opera house as well as the shops. It was felt perhaps more at this time than any other that great singing was a thing of the past: it had been in steady decline since the early years of the century, the secrets had been lost, the disciplines weakened, and people must settle down to the ungolden mean of voice-without-style or musicianship-without-voice. Admittedly, the standard of the Vienna Opera and the records their singers were making could not be ignored, which implied that mourning for a dead tradition was premature. But still their achievements did not seem to be quite central; for had not Italian opera always been the heart of the tradition, and was not the heart in singularly poor condition at that time? The San Carlo season of 1946 at Covent Garden brought reassurance to a few, the visit of the Scala in 1950 to some few more; but on the whole the suggestion was that this would not be an age of great singing, so that everybody had better accommodate themselves to the fact and hold on to their old gramophone records as nothing like them was to be heard again for many a year.

Perhaps the dialectic of history was at work even in this, the complaints helping to effect their own negation. At any rate, somewhere around mid-century events were moving, and some records being issued, to prompt a new query: whether operatic greatness was not among us again, taking often imperfect forms as has always been the case, but at least matching in many respects such records as we have of the greatness of the past. And just as the advent of the gramophone fifty years earlier had been in time to catch five great singers at the height of their powers, so the new and challenging business of recording the whole basic repertoire on LP coincided with the artistic maturing of a new generation, four of whom were pre-eminent in a remarkably fine series of performances on gramophone (the fifth of this group, Jussi Björling, whose date of birth is variously given as 1911 and 1907, was not so very much older than Gobbi 'and Christoff, and yet he already seemed something of a veteran).

In discussing the famous five of those first years we began with the bass, Pol Plançon: 'what a golden-age singer should be, he was'. In the later age too it is the bass who stands fair-and-square to proclaim greatness in our own time. From his first appearance in opera (the only performance of *Bohème*, one imagines, to have included three encores of the Coat Song) and from the issue of his first recordings, it was clear that an artist of great stature had arrived.

These first records showed him to be, for the gramophone at least, superbly Chaliapin's successor, for they brought before us a Boris Godunov who already sang with complete authority, with comparable intensity and with a voice that was at once distinctive and beautiful, powerful and schooled. In others, such as the 'Infelice' from *Ernani*, it was Pinza with whom the comparisons were made, and while Christoff's timbre was quite different, it had to be noted that there was no deficiency in his command of the legato style and that the interpretation went deeper. It is still worth turning back to these 78s to hear the beauty of Christoff's voice in his early years. At the time of writing (1971) it is still an impressive instrument, but no voice stays the same over twenty-five years of hard work, and in the Russian songs recorded in 1969 one knows that this is a voice that has lost its youth, with a very slight loosening of the vibrato and perhaps a diminution in sheer power. Without the comparison one might still call this a voice in its prime, but one would then have forgotten just how magnificent that prime actually was: never heard better than in the *Mefistofele* solos on 78s, marvellously sonorous, ringing and effortlessly sustained on the high F sharp, agile in its devilry without sacrificing the fine, resonant tone.

On the whole, passing from 78 to LP and back again, it is notable that his interpretations changed little over the years. Boris Godunov's Monologue in the complete opera conducted by Cluytens (1963) has the lyrical passage in which the Tsar thinks of his disappointed hopes for family peace, daughter's marriage and so forth, highlighted by the use of a special tone, soft, tender and private. This is simply a feature which has become more marked over the years; it was there in the generally preferable complete recording under Dobrowen (issued 1953), and in the original 78 at the very beginning of his career. This 'private' voice is used also for another great monologue, that of Philip II in *Don Carlo*, and again we can compare three versions spread over the years. Here the interpretation has deepened and the style gained in restraint, but the singer's basic conception —of a great public man solitary, indrawn and grey—remains constant. The kind of added depth comes in such detail as his introduction of the King's voice (as opposed to the sleepless private man's) at the question

'Dove son?'; all has been an inner brooding till then, then comes the awareness of time, place, rank and responsibility, and this is the right point for a change of tone. Greater restraint also strengthens the performance. In his recording on 78, the last 'Ella giammai m'amò' quivered pitifully, and the tears which threatened fell between 'per me' and 'non ha', and continued, though softly, for a while afterwards. This had all disappeared by 1964, and with no loss of emotional force.

The voice and artistry which could encompass these two roles could obviously do a very great deal, but of course there are things they could not. Bellini's cantilena does not defeat him, for he draws a firm line with appropriate gentleness in 'Vi ravviso' from *La Sonnambula* and has none of the curious interferences with legato that mark Chaliapin's recording of this. But one knows it is not an Italian singing, not merely because of the pronunciation, but because there is little of that richly honeyed sound that good Italian basses make. His tone does not bless, and so the broad melody of the 'Salva me' in Verdi's *Requiem*, or, later, what should be the veiled solemnity of 'Requiem aeternam', lacks that kind of warmth which still calls Pinza to mind. Giorgio Tozzi, the bass of Reiner's performance in slow-motion, does some effective soft singing and in general makes rather more effective use of dynamics; but the comparison brings us back to acknowledge afresh the sheer soundness of Christoff's vocalism, for his is a true legato and he is firm and precise on the note. If he is then placed in comparison with Nicolai Ghiaurov, the most impressive *basso cantante* of modern times, acknowledgement falls due to another aspect of Christoff's singing—the tremendous sense of presence. In the two current versions of Gounod's *Faust*, they, Christoff and Ghiaurov, are the Mephistopheles. The opulence of Ghiaurov's voice and the excellence of his style are such that when he sings 'Me voici' on arrival we congratulate ourselves on having the prospect of a really good bass for the performance. But with Christoff there is immediate presence, more strongly satanic and exotic, soon to be recognised as more vivid and varied. One sees his smile, shares his fun, knows exactly when he has arrived at the Kermesse—he never needs to announce 'Me voici' again.

His greatness does not lie primarily, however, in what he can do with Gounod's *Faust*; or with Verdi, or even with Boris Godunov, outstanding as all these are. His prime claim to the gratitude of musicians rests on what he has done for Russian song, and above all in that great and, one hopes, permanently enduring achievement, the recording of Moussorgsky's songs complete. It is also this album (eight long-playing sides, sixty-three songs) which shows Christoff's own artistry and resourcefulness of voice most fully.

If one thinks of the songs as pictures at an exhibition, one of the rooms is a portrait gallery. The mighty and the humble are there side by side: King Saul sings before battle with command and sturdy resonance, while Goethe's old blind harpist cries for the bitter sorrows of the poor. Calistratus contrasts the benedictions poured on him in his mother's lullabies with the reality of his present poverty; and in this, the composer's 'first attempt at comedy', Christoff catches the ecstasy of irony with a broad grin, a caricature of the mother's affectionate 'Calistratushka', a split-second break into falsetto in his bitter joking, and a fine sharp staccato style to suggest the peasant's dance. In similar style is 'The Seminarist', and in a category all their own are the children's voices in the Nursery cycle. Christoff's little-boy voice (or a sort of cracked near-adolescent for 'The Hobby Horse') might have been thought up by a Danny Kaye; his mimicry is superb (and perhaps it should be added, in view of the comparison, not embarrassing). The mother comforts in a maternal contralto cleverly suggested without falsetto; as vivid a characterisation as that of the shameless maiden gathering mushrooms (No. 24), who admittedly turns at the end into somebody sounding rather like old Varlaam from *Boris Godunov*, but whom one can almost see, spreading her skirts and dancing for mischief in the second line of her song.

In *The Songs and Dances of Death* there appears another memorable character. This is Death himself, for whom Christoff has a darkness and depth of voice and a fund of grim merriment. The first of these, 'Trepak', is the only one of Moussorgsky's songs (apart from the over-familiar 'Song of the Flea') that Chaliapin recorded, and as these two singers stand so closely in line it is a comparison that we should at some time make.

97. Boris Christoff as King Philip
    in *Don Carlo*

98. Tito Gobbi as Da Posa
    in *Don Carlo*

Here Chaliapin is marginally better in what he sings (for, presumably to get the song onto the twelve-inch 78 side, four lines are cut, most unhappily at the climax of the song). For instance, something in Chaliapin's more rhythmic way (and the quicker tempo) makes us know that Death has started up the dance before singing; the cry 'Oi moozheechok' to the peasant has a more jocular tone and therefore more terrible effect; and, most vivid of all, there is the long-drawn chilled 'Glyad' ('Look!'), with a shudder of mystery as the singer whispers 'Tak ee yest' ('There he is'). Christoff is more deliberative and literal, just slightly less vivid, though the cycle as a whole receives a magnificent performance.

Moussorgsky's songs have also depths of sorrow and compassion, and the singer must be able to rise to these demands as well. Christoff in fact expresses all the warmth and intimacy of desolate introspection that they call for, a marvellous example being the last song in the cycle *Sunless*. This is called 'On the River' and in it each phrase has its own colour. The most majestic of voices becomes the most gentle: the superb work of a golden-age singer.

What Christoff has done for Russian song, Victoria de los Angeles has done for Spanish. Nothing sunless here, either in the songs themselves or in the voice and personality of the singer. The smile and charm which have made her live recitals such happy occasions are present and infectious on records, and we find there is also charm, grace and richness in the songs of Spain from the Fifteenth Century to the present day.

The purity of voice, free, like an instrument, of operatic vibrato, goes far to protect these earliest songs from an alien vocal style. There is no reason why a courtly fifteenth century Spanish love song should be sung as the amazing Jantina Noorman of Musica Reservata sings her twelfth century Estampie, primitive and peasantlike. On the other hand, it may be argued that Schumann and Brahms are at least equally remote, and that to bring a modern cultivated tone and the delicate inflections of a Lieder singer is to introduce an anachronism. Such misgivings sometimes arise, perhaps inevitably when the singer has, as she says, deliberately tried to convert 'these lovely works . . . into living music . . . made to become palpitating and human sounds which produce in us real emotion and show us how the composers of the past felt and expressed themselves'. Fortunately, her own voice, with its chorister's purity, is an excellent defence against anything too palpitating, and in the melismatic passages of some of these early songs (such as the Sephardic song 'Una Hija tiene el rey') the eastern-sounding fioriture are done as though by nature, and the voice again asserts a purity of sound that speaks of fields and churches rather than opera house and concert hall. Emma Calvé in her autobiography tells of the saying of her father: 'Ah my daughter, it is easy to see that your forebears have economised for you. Through the long ages they have sat mutely by their firesides, spinning and weaving through the quiet hours. Your song is made of their silences'. Without knowing anything of her forebears, one is aware of Victoria de los Angeles' ancestry; it is the best, noblest and most dignified part of Spanish civilisation that has found its voice in her.

Hers is indeed an aristocratic art, possibly even a little too refined to do justice to some of the Spanish music she sings. A charming selection of solos from zarzuelas by Chapi, Gimenez and others includes some delicious melodies, matched exactly by the smiling lilt of the singer. But charm is the word, and there, on the whole, it stops. The Gypsy's Song from *La Chavala*, for instance, is delicately winning, but to play Conchita Supervia's version is to hear a different song. And one must admit that when Supervia sings at the end that she was born a gipsy ('Gitana naci') credulity is not strained, and that as she sings of the lads from Perche and Holy Trinity we believe her when she tells us how well she has known them; moreover, along with the challenge of Supervia's more earthy performance there is delicacy too, and as she remembers the valley of the Guadalquivir it is with the loveliest and lightest of wistful tones.

Yet how often the refinement of de los Angeles' singing brings just the touch that the composers themselves must have heard in their dreams only. The five Negro Songs by Montsalvatge have a charm that is also humorous; they need a sophisticated interpreter who can give a satirical smile about the time when the Cuban 'si' became the Yankee 'yes'. Above all they require the richest, creamiest, tenderest of voices for the 'Cancion de cuna', and this is a song which de los Angeles has made very much her own; in live performances it has provided one of those occasions when one has felt a whole audience hold its breath so as not to break the spell, and on records, especially in the version with orchestral accompaniment, it is equally magical. Nor is she essentially a singer of lullabies or of gentle music, for the last song of this set (the 'Canto Negro' with its 'yambambo's) finds plenty of blood and colour in the voice, just as Eduardo Toldra's 'Cabin-boy's song' ('Farewell, hills of Marseilles') finds her full of sunshine, freshness and sheer joy in singing.

It may well be that Spanish song is in fact her first and great joy; her repertoire, however, has been far-ranging, and the music of most composers and most countries has its place in it. From the days of 78s, and showing her voice in most beautiful condition, are the two songs of Respighi, 'Stornellatrice' and 'E se un giorno tornasse', the second moving in its alternation of anxiety and reassurance, the voice of the dying woman perfectly poised in its weakness, the first a flawless piece of lyricism. Among German composers, she is probably happiest with Brahms (the 'Vergebliches Ständchen' being a nice example of her humour, better in 1961 than in Gerald Moore's Farewell recital of 1967, though that too, notably the Rossini duets with Schwarzkopf, should be sampled for humour). But it is in French song that her excursions beyond the Spaniards have been most rewarding, for her elegance of touch and sensibility of nuance are invaluable here. Most herself in the charm and smile of Fauré's 'Chanson

99. Victoria de los Angeles as Manon (Massenet)

d'Amour', least in character when the nasty poem of Ravel's 'Shéhérazade' speaks of wanting to see the assassins smile as an innocent head is cut off, she brings a tasteful and fastidious touch to everything she sings.

In opera too, the French repertoire is prominent, with Carmen, Charlotte, Manon, Marguérite, Mélisande and Hoffmann's Antonia among her recorded roles. One may remember the Carmen as tame, but returning to it and putting others by its side one is soon enough grateful for the sheer musicalness and vitality—and charm. Her Manon is a fine character-study, the childlike pout at thoughts of the convent giving way to the more ruthless enunciation of 'Ah! combien ce doit être amusant de s'amuser toute une vie'. Act II brings a more mature voice, Act III a more brilliant, even brazen one (but how charmingly popping out the words 'vingt ans' in the Gavotte). The love music of the last Act, which lies low for the average coloratura who sings the part, draws on the warm heart of de los Angeles' voice, and one can rely on her taste not to make too much of the dying. Her Marguérite is particularly fine in the Prison Scene—we really do care what happens to this one. Her Jewel Song, taken at a slow tempo (Cluytens conducting) does not sparkle, however: one plays Blanche Arral as a reminder of what it can be like, with such very French vivacity and impulsiveness. Mélisande is happy in the medium-to-low tessitura of the part, while Antonia, delicate and tender, has to strive for the high notes.

These often caused anxiety to her listeners, sometimes quite needlessly. In recent years, as for example in the record of Catalonian songs issued in 1970, G has sounded as a high note, and almost daring. Yet the range upwards is there, including poor Antonia's fatal C sharp. Manon is by no means a role for a pushed-up mezzo, but the *tessitura* seems not to have presented problems. Also (if one is interested in high notes) there is that exquisitely placed, and surely most risky, high B hummed at the end of the vocalise in Villa Lobos' lovely piece for soprano and eight cellos. Still, it is hard to resist something of a feeling that the middle and lower part of her voice was so rich and full that the high notes must be there, so to speak, on loan. And it is probably true that this has limited and perhaps shortened her operatic career.

It affects her Italian opera a little, so that in an aria like 'L'altra notte' from *Mefistofele* the only conceivable criticism is that the highest notes, good as they are in themselves, are not quite unified in tone production with the rest of the voice. But this is a glorious performance, and extremely accomplished in the florid work. Her Rossini is sometimes disappointing in that respect; in characterisation too, for her Rosina doesn't really assert or enjoy herself much in 'Una voce poco fa', and in fact seems happiest in recitative. With Verdi, the *tessitura* of Violetta's music in the first Act does not cancel the beauty of much of her *Traviata*. And in Puccini she remains a movingly restrained Angelica, a most delectable Mimì and perhaps the best of Butterflys.

She recorded Butterfly twice, the second time with Santini as conductor, in 1960, the first some five years earlier with Gavazzeni. Comparison generally shows the first better at happiness, the second at tragedy. In the early performance there is an exceptional sense of togetherness: the conductor, the Butterfly and the Pinkerton (di Stefano) all with a feeling for the pulse of the music, making joy out of the first Act. About the second performance there is a slightly colder atmosphere: for example (tiny points, but typical) in the first recording the little explanation about not liking to own to your poor upbringing moves with a happier, more natural speech-rhythm, and in the Love Duet Butterfly's 'or son contenta' smiles (one can see it), whereas in the later version it is simple statement. But in the tragic music of Act II de los Angeles' portrayal has deepened over the years. As she asks the early-morning company 'che vuol da me?' it is with clearer, more terrible foreknowledge; we see the lines of the face and mouth set downwards. 'Tutto è morta per me, tutto è finita' is nearer to tears. These are small shifts of emphasis within a consistently beautiful portrayal. Whether in the youthful, affectionate phrases of 'Ieri son salita' in Act I, or the rich and now matured voice of 'Che tua madre' (the emergence here of the tragic woman), or the fine Spanish tone of lament in 'Triste madre', de los Angeles has presented in her Butterfly an example of latter-day greatness in the standard operatic repertoire: beauty of voice matched by beauty of spirit, a full heart to feel, and taste and intelligence to direct.

The Pinkerton of de los Angeles' second *Madame Butterfly* was Jussi Björling, by no means as likeable a fellow as di Stefano makes him. Björling's Pinkerton is very much the officer, abrupt with Goro, formal with Sharpless. His song about the yankee abroad enunciates doctrine rather than expressing the expansive mood of a young man with a charming Japanese house and a childbride to go with it. 'Milk Punch or whiskey?' comes as a rather grumpy interruption of the discourse. In the love music, he cheers Butterfly up quite amiably after her uncle has come and spoiled the party; but 'Bimba, dagli occhi' sounds a little military; 'Io t'ho ghermita' is suitably predatory; and though the tone is occasionally softened, it is never intimate. Now, perhaps this is deliberate characterisation, yet it is not uncharacteristic of the singer: his Rodolfo does not smile much either.

An exception to his generally rather serious, charmless portrayals is the hero of Puccini's *Manon Lescaut*. Tender and subtle (following the written directions minutely), this des Grieux is no less passionate for his essential nobility. And, although people sometimes speak of the nordic coldness of his timbre, there is no lack of southern passion in, for example, his Turiddu of *Cavalleria Rusticana*. A stage performance of 1959, with Simionato, shows him in tremendous form; fiery in the scene with Santuzza, open and free with the emotions in his farewell to Mamma Lucia (and the record also boasts what must be the world's loudest prompter).

But one goes to Björling for his singing, not for his characterisations, and it is because of the exceptional splendour of his voice and the fineness of line that he is amongst the present company of singers. Turn back to that

100. Jussi Björling as Rodolfo in *La Bohème*

record of *Cavalleria Rusticana*, and no doubt can remain that here is a tenor whose style and production are models for his kind. The Brindisi has all the energy one could want, but it is also carefully phrased, well defined, never shouted, never spreading. The 'Addio alla madre' shows an exemplary legato in phrases often broken; and particularly fine is the passage just before this, 'Io so che il torto è mio', which Björling sings perhaps more beautifully than anyone on record, relying entirely on purity of line and the beauty of unforced tone.

In that passage one recognises also, with affection, what a very individual timbre it was. In later years it became a little dry, with a certain surface-wear that can be heard on records (where often such a quality is eliminated or greatly diminished). It is true also that the 'round' ingratiating sound of Gigli's voice, like that tenor's chubby smile, is not Björling's either. Although Dorothy Caruso is quoted as saying that Björling's was the voice most like that of her late husband, one knows that that comparison does not hold too well: he made a splendidly full-voiced, Italianate recording of Tosti's song 'L'alba separa', and one thinks 'Yes, it is Caruso-like' until one returns to Caruso, and finds there a richness that is quite incomparable, overwhelming indeed in a phrase just before the climax, in amongst those unimaginable E's and F's, on the words 'il sole eterno'. But at its best, and in such a recording as that 'L'alba separa' (for it is magnificent singing in its own right), Björling's voice glowed with health. It was brilliantly resonant; there was just such a thrill to the high notes as the upper part of a tenor's voice ought to have; it was always steady; and above all it was treated as a musical instrument.

Stylistically Björling was in a class of his own among the tenors of three decades. An early record of 'Cielo e mar' from *La Gioconda* is representative of his best singing. The legato is unflawed; there is none of the aspirating that mars most Italian performances, and the flow is helped by broad phrasing. The phrases are shaped and shaded; the first verse is rounded off on the words 'o sogni d'or' with a poised soft tone that has no hint of falsetto; there is gentleness and exaltation; the high notes are generously held but not flaunted. It is true that he was not always as imaginative as on this record. There was a time, principally in the mid-forties, when records kept appearing, solidly (almost deafeningly) resonant, and stolidly uninteresting. It is also true that there were limits to what his technique and musical feeling would let him do. Although a performance of 'Il mio tesoro' at Carnegie Hall in 1955 drew much applause, it came to grief in the long run on 'tornar' (two breaths in the middle of it though it is going at a fast tempo), and there is no conception of Mozartian style. His Lieder singing varied, sometimes dull (as in 'Frühlingsglaube'), sometimes exciting ('Die böse Farbe'), sometimes curiously anachronistic (as in 'Was ist Sylvia?', taken slowly, with much *rubato* and portamento, as in Emma Eames' record of 1906).

But his singing outside the normal repertoire of operatic tenors could at one time be extremely fine. So it was on the 15 July 1939, when he recorded three songs, two by Richard Strauss, one by Beethoven. 'Cäcilie' is a predictable success, but although the balance between voice and piano in 'Morgen' is unsatisfactory, Björling's singing surprises most delightfully with its softness on high notes and the feeling for mood, evident right down to the *diminuendo* to nothing of 'stummes Schweigen' at the end of the song. His 'Adelaide' remains something of a wonder. He sang it again in the recorded Carnegie Hall recital of 1955, with all the charm and poetry gone; but in the studio those many years earlier he produced the most lovely *mezza voce*, sang with a sensitive feeling for *rubato*, and had obviously given himself, his young voice, his assured technique and his then active imagination to the song. He will be remembered of course principally in other music, and everyone with interest in such things must be grateful that the recording companies were still able to call on him to sing the basic operatic roles up to the time of his death in 1960. But why he was so valuable a singer in the first period of the long-playing record is probably best suggested by what he did in a few recordings in the late nineteen-thirties, and not least by that commercially unrewarding session of 15 July 1939.

Björling, like de los Angeles and Christoff, has the beauty and sonority of tone, the purity of line, that (arguably) begin to qualify a singer for inclusion in the ranks of the great: one feels, at least, that it would be a very crabby and narrow golden-ager who would refuse to admit any of these three. About the others remaining to be discussed in this section one can appreciate that there may be some argument; on the other hand, the narrowness which excluded them would be a still more disabling kind.

Gobbi and Callas are very central figures among the singers of their time, but to stress their modernity may do an injustice both to them and their age. Both are great actors with the voice; both (though in different degrees and ways) are imperfect vocalists. This might lead one to say, 'Yes, and here indeed we have the representative distinction of modern times: a greatness of concept maybe, but a notable failure of method'. The implications would be wrong, in the first place because 'modern times' have also produced a Schwarzkopf, a Jurinac, a Christoff, a Marilyn Horne, a Janet Baker, to go no further with what could be a long list of demonstrably sound vocalists; also because a regularly insistent feature of the history of singing has been the generally admitted greatness of certain imperfect vocalists. What is significantly modern is the success these two singers have had on gramophone records: they have mastered the art of invisible acting, and, with them pre-eminently to show the way, a new generation has grown up to whom it is an essential part of singing.

It is obviously a great boon to the invisible actor if his voice is individual enough to be more or less instantly recognisable; and so it certainly is with Tito Gobbi. We know him by the distinctive vibrancy of his tone, by certain features of his pronunciation, and by a concentration of utterance that compels attention. Like Christoff, he has presence, and, again like that singer, one never needs to ask whether he has arrived. Scarpia's entry in Act I of *Tosca* always makes an effect in the theatre; on record, the actor's stride, gesture, frown and command, all have to be implied by the voice. Gobbi immediately establishes a hateful, strong and subtle authority, alternately snarling and suave, courtly and bestial. After the angry interrogation of Cavaradossi in Act II, he turns to Tosca ('Ed or fra noi') with lyrical smoothness, as though fastidiously drawing on silk gloves, changing the tone again with ugly menace ('Or sù parlate') and uncovering the barbarism of that off-stage torture-chamber with vivid ferocity. Every Scarpia has to attempt all this, but none has achieved it on record as Gobbi has done: that is, with such vivid acting skills as well as ample resources of colourful Italian resonance in the voice, and indeed a very considerable beauty of tone to convey the charm which masks the ugliness.

For Gobbi's has been a voice of intrinsically great beauty. Its characteristic sound is essentially Italian, with a quick vibrato present as part of its health and richness; and its rare sensuous appeal combines with the power of personality and of ability as an actor to provide many supremely precious experiences in the opera house. On the gramophone, a roughness of singing style sometimes obtrudes. Aspirates affect the flow of such melodies as 'Urna fatale' *(La Forza del Destino)* and 'Per me giunto' *(Don Carlo)*. Some of his quieter singing has one aware that 'crooning' would be the word of a more severe critic: in 'Di Provenza' *(La Traviata)* and 'Piangi, fanciulla' *(Rigoletto)*, for example, the listener is disappointed of the even, well-nourished sound of the baritone voice that these melodies seem to want, while the style and timbre are so intimate as to doubly (and unnecessarily) underline the pathos. With age, too, has come a tendency to hammer notes from above, sometimes to force the volume of high notes which have lost part of their former resonance. He recorded Verdi's *Nabucco* at the age of fifty-one, offering a fine characterisation and many individual touches which proclaim, as ever, the irreplaceable artist; but the limitations of the singer (as opposed to the artist) are apparent, and highlighted if one compares the solos recorded by Riccardo Stracciari at about the same age. In 'Dio di Giuda' Stracciari's legato is scrupulous when Gobbi's is broken; there is a grace in the fioriture and triplets, missing in the other; and in the second-act aria ('Chi mi toglie') Stracciari provides an object-lesson in accurate placing, and in expressiveness that makes minimal interference with beauty of line and tone.

Sometimes Gobbi will himself provide just such an object-lesson. One does not think of Rigoletto's 'Pari siamo', Iago's Creed, or the Prologue to *Pagliacci* as demonstration pieces for the art of *bel canto*, but Gobbi's versions on 78s are shining examples of genuine lyric drama, the two elements in perfect balance. The 'Pari siamo' is surely a masterpiece, not least in the sheer beauty of sound. But interpretation and voice work perfectly together here: 'il retaggio', sweet-toned and lingering, 'Ma in altr'uom' healing gently as the touch of a good nurse upon a still open hurt.

But he does nothing without bringing distinction. One is never more aware of Amonasro as a dominant figure in *Aida* than when Gobbi sings the part. He does not announce himself ('sua padre') in the stentorian tones that sometimes in Italian opera houses stop the show and secure a round of applause all to themselves; but he establishes the character as a tough man, of exceptional authority, which he exercises in a way that is all his own by a magical change of tone-colour for the prayer in which Amonasro leads his captive people. Then in the Nile Scene, where the mood is always changing, he draws on his rich store of colours and voice-faces, from the stern national leader intent on business, through the evocative tones of nostalgic appeal, the insinuations of the diplomat and the spy, to the terrifying cry 'dei pharaoni tu sei la schiava', the last word projected with such concentration of will and patriarchal command as to be overwhelmingly vivid.

In Gobbi's 'full-length' Verdian roles, Rigoletto, Boccanegra, Falstaff, the strength of overall presentation will still prove itself in the care and understanding of local detail. Play, for example, Falstaff's Honour Monologue in a succession of recordings (Scotti, Ruffo, Stabile, Fischer-Dieskau, Gobbi) and Gobbi's is quite markedly the most satisfying, partly because he attends to what Verdi has written and sees the point of it. The phrase 'voi coi vostri cenci' is marked with a crescendo on the first word, followed by three staccato syllables. Scotti takes no notice, Ruffo and Stabile take little; Fischer-Dieskau observes the markings, as ever, but it is Gobbi who sees the pictorial force, the crescendo carrying a comical menace and the staccatos punching or flapping at the despised company as with a broom handle. Similarly when it comes to the play of contrasts between the *voce grossa* for which Verdi asks and the suave, light voice needed for the bland satire, we find that Scotti does nothing, Ruffo makes good basic contrasts though without much subtlety, Stabile does more, stroking the suave phrases effectively and in fact showing the way, but neither he nor Fischer-Dieskau has Gobbi's variety of colours. Nor have they his beauty of voice: for if Gobbi is no Ruffo in sheer opulence, he is notably richer of tone than any of the others.

Still, Gobbi's voice, chameleonlike as its owner is in his impersonations, lends itself more readily to pathos and seriousness than to comedy, and of all the roles he has undertaken none suits him better than Simon Boccanegra. This calls to mind one final comparison, involving on the one hand himself and two other singers of the five now under discussion, and on the other four of the five great singers of Verdi at the Metropolitan in the inter-war years. Gobbi, de los Angeles and Christoff with Giuseppe Campora as the tenor recorded the opera in 1958, and imperfect but serviceable private recordings exist of Tibbett, Rethberg, Pinza and Martinelli in live performances in 1935 and 1939. These are singers of comparable status in their time, and again the historical questions arise: change of what sort? deterioration? improvement? Overall, the modern performance will probably strike the listener as milder, easier listening, but less exciting. This is partly due to the conditions of studio as against theatre, more to the difference between conductors (Santini reflective, Panizza urgent in the Toscanini tradition), and also to the mere pleasantness of Campora's Gabriele Adorno as against Martinelli's exceptional intensity. De los Angeles is a gentler, younger sounding Amelia; Christoff sometimes achieves a stronger, more formidable characterisation as Fiesco. But generally the honours are even: certainly the modern singers witness to no decline in the sheer accomplishment of singing, while any idea that performances 'in the old days' were grossly inaccurate or undisciplined finds no support either. There is the difference of intensity and excitement; there is also the difference which, eventually, Gobbi himself comes to represent most markedly, that is the growth in the art of acting with the voice. The two Simons seem to be equally fine (Tibbett sings with magnificent tone, authority and expressiveness); but in the last half of the role, after the great Council Chamber scene, Gobbi's performance attains to a kind of humanity that is outside any normal range of operatic characterisation. Its sadness and sickness, the strength of will and purpose mustered for the final confrontation with Fiesco: for these one turns to Gobbi. He impresses like a single Rembrandt in a room of fine portraits: if the rest are paintings, another word seems to be needed to say what this is.

The fifth singer of that inter-war group was Rosa Ponselle, and perhaps discussion of Maria Callas, the remaining artist of the present five, might begin with a comparison between records of these two great sopranos. Two arias from Spontini's *La Vestale* were recorded by both, the music suiting them well and the recording sessions finding them in good form. Expectation would probably suggest that Ponselle draws a purer line but that Callas is more expressive; actually, this is not so. Callas sings with a good, if not faultless, legato, and Ponselle treats the music dramatically and imaginatively. The very great difference, especially apparent in the aria 'O nume tutellar', lies in the richer beauty of Ponselle's voice and the more complete control that she has over it. She can modulate from the loveliest, utterly firm but veiled pianissimo to an astonishingly full forte without any sign that the voice is under pressure, without any shrillness or unsteadiness, but every assurance that further power remains in reserve. Turn then to Norma's 'Casta diva' and that basic point of comparison is confirmed. The ending of the recitative ('e il sacro vischio io mieto') finds Ponselle marvellously poised in the soft high passage where Callas spreads, and this is so again at the end of the aria where Ponselle's note is sustained quietly, beautifully and firmly above the chorus, while Callas' develops a beat that affects the beauty of the sound and the accuracy of intonation.

There is more to say about her 'Casta diva' than that, of course, but for the moment let us try once more a sequence of performances to help 'place' Callas critically and historically. Playing three recordings by Callas, then one of Joan Sutherland, and back in time through Ponselle, Vallin,

Boninsegna, Sembrich to Patti, it simply is not true that a pattern emerges whereby one could say that a student-singer should go back to the early years of recording to find how a true legato sounds. Indeed among these great singers there is only one really sound model in this respect, and that is Ponselle. Nor does the florid singing fall conveniently into line. In some bars of the cabaletta, Sembrich momentarily makes one feel that all the others are amateurs; but of course they are not, for Callas sings everything that is written with great mastery and Sutherland does so too as well as providing some dazzling embellishments for the second verse. For the others, one observes much beauty and asks a number of questions. Why did Ponselle take to that rather hectic way of treating the semiquavers on the words 'il diedi' when she managed them perfectly well only a year or so earlier on the Columbia record? Why did the accomplished Boninsegna get out of doing the descending chromatic scale, substituting something easier, duller and less idiomatic? Why did Vallin record two more or less un-differentiated verses when it meant using such a quick, matter-of-fact, poetry-killing tempo? Why did Patti record it at all? (But perhaps the question is harsh, for there are a few lovely touches to carry a suggestion of what must once have been).

Callas' distinction in this company is easy to define. Reverting to the simile of the portrait gallery, hers is simply the most interesting and most fully human face there. Hers is the most aptly expressive treatment of the music: she is rapt but not sleepy, dignified but not statuesque. She sings with what can best be called love; that is, with care, understanding and sudden personal insights, such as a way of dropping the descending chroma-tic figures from their high note with a gentle tone and a soothing suggestion of *glissando* to make an effect like the shining path of moonlight on water. And if this is true of 'Casta diva', it applies still more to the tragic Norma of later scenes. The softly lamenting 'Teneri figli', the baleful sound of the chest voice in 'In mia man alfin tu sei', the tragic shading of the last solo, 'Deh non volerli': these are a few places in which the sound of the music and of Callas' voice in it become inseparable to one who knows them both.

Norma also provides an opportunity to see how Callas developed during the years of her greatness, and to see how studio recording corresponds to what was heard when she was acting in a live performance. The Covent Garden performance of 8 November 1952, is on a 'private' issue, and two commercial recordings were made, the first in mono, 1954, the other in stereo, 1960. Any conception of Callas as an impulsive, wilful, unpredict-able artist is certainly discouraged by the comparisons; it is, if anything, a little disappointing to find how consistent the interpretations are. In a very very few places the live performance dramatises more strongly, the one really notable example being, as one would expect, the point of resolv-ing to kill the children, and the revulsion against it. Even there the analys-able differences are small: an additional crack (or a kind of chesty, emotional underlining) in the voice during the phrase 'i figli uccido' and a sharp,

audible indrawing of the breath after it, and then a wilder note in the cry of
'Ah no! son miei figli'. In those same phrases very little has changed over
the years. In the 1960 version, 'i figli uccido' gains power by a quiet start
and a *sforzando* on the middle, stabbing syllable of 'uccido'; this is effective,
yet a wrenching sense of agonising self-violation is conveyed by the possibly more instinctive handling of it on the Covent Garden stage. This kind
of rehandling or reinterpretation is fairly unusual, however, while what
has notably changed is the state of the voice, which by 1960 had developed
its unsteadiness to an uncomfortable degree. In the Covent Garden performance, as recorded (somewhat toplessly, it must be said), the beat is
noticeable only on a few high notes, and the same is true of the first studio
performance. But by 1960 the upper-middle notes were also affected, so
that the two sustained F's at the end of 'Casta diva' (before and after the
cadenza) spread badly: at their most extreme the vibrations spread over a
whole tone if played at 16 r.p.m., so that at the correct speed and pitch it
would be about a semitone. Much of the singing is still very good, and of
course as a whole the performance is still a great one; but development
during Callas' years of supremacy appears, if this is representative, to
have been a matter of the deterioration of voice rather than the further
deepening of an already profound interpretation.

But just how profound her interpretations were is instanced in about
twenty complete operas on record, and many more excerpts. The highly
individual and instantly recognisable voice is capable of character changes
just as an actor's characterful face will sometimes prove unexpectedly
adaptable in the make-up room. Her Gilda, Amina, Leonora, Medea, all
have different voice-characters. The Puccini heroines are particularly
distinct human beings, made so not just by the normal expressiveness of
the singing but by something akin to make-up or costuming in the choice
of voice colours. Thus the Tosca calls on a deeper, more mature and vibrant
tone than the Mimì or Butterfly, and both of these are distinct individuals
even with their common features of youthful frailty, tenderness and sadness. It is remarkable that she can do this so readily at will without having
to work into the role in a performance of the complete opera: her recital
record of Puccini arias (the excerpts not being drawn from complete sets)
is a marvellous collection of people—Butterfly, Mimì, Angelica, Lauretta,
Liù—who in almost any similar recital by her predecessors would have
been practically indistinguishable. Can one think of any earlier soprano on
record (even Muzio, even Lotte Lehmann) whose voice could characterise
with such completeness as this? Nowadays, to be sure, most singers are
aware of such possibilities, but only, it seems, since Callas has shown the
way.

She also provides that more intense and concentrated pleasure that we
associate with the great moments of opera. She will seize the moment, say,
of noble or tragic decision, summoning all the dramatic force of what has
gone before, evoking our knowledge of what the consequences are to be,

101. Maria Callas as Leonora in *Il Trovatore*

and focusing precisely upon the moment on which all depends. Such moments often depend upon an exact and intuitive sense of timing (as with the B flat which is held at once wistfully and resolutely before the crucial decision of 'Dite alla giovine' in *La Traviata*); or it may depend on a way of opening out on the single note towards the generous resolution ('Ah si, fa core e abbracciami' or 'Ah si mi lascia' in *Norma*); or on the power to make the voice as hard and even harsh as the will which is to be asserted (as in Carmen's last scene). The surprising experience which accompanies this is that when one returns to moments which have been especially vivid, as these are, it is to find that, so far from imposing an expansive, emphatic individuality upon the text, Callas has worked within an intense but moderating discipline. The chest voice which one remembers as so strong and distinctive bites into phrases like Norma's 'è troppo tormentoso, troppo orrendo è un tal dubbio' and stamps them on the memory; but return to these phrases, and this fine etching is seen to have been achieved economically, even with restraint. Nor does she fuss the line of an air like 'Qui la voce' in *I Puritani* half as much as most (from Boronat onward) who have seen it as expressive and not just a pretty tune. There is pathos without self-pity, and shaping without distortion: that is, essentially a nobility achieved within the tradition. And Callas has been essentially the great exponent and advocate of the tradition, in spite of the inperfections which seem to defy it: she has been the singer best equipped to reveal and recommend the grand operatic mainstream as a refreshing and fertilising part of modern musical life.

So, with Callas and the others discussed here, with the Wagnerians and Mozartians, and with the many who are still to be considered, 'modern musical life' has not done at all badly in its provision of singers. The age of austerity lasted just about as long as it did in the shops, and if we had to wait some years before plenty followed peace, the prophets of perpetual dearth were eventually confounded. The end of the 78, with the limitations that now seem so primitive, coincided with the arrival of this generously endowed generation, while the coming of LP itself acted as a stimulus to new musical endeavour. It also set more self-critical standards among artists whose records were to be ever more closely scrutinised in reviews and whose reputations now depended upon recordings as upon performances in theatre and concert hall. The presentation of complete operas rather than excerpts, with great conductors to give a unified reading, and with increasingly musical staffing on the side of the record companies to promote study-preparation of the recordings as for a festival performance, coincided also with the growing respect for opera as an art-form and as a collaborative enterprise; and at last brought the audible part of this most complex and expensive entertainment into the home.

Opera at Home was in fact the title of a series of books published by *His Master's Voice* between 1920 and 1928, giving details of plots, dates and records available, illustrated with photographs of singers, and still sought after by nostalgic collectors. The cover of the early paperback edition showed a dignified gentleman listening thoughtfully as his single-sided pre-electricals sizzled away on the horn gramophone: he was probably playing Faust's Cavatina, recordings of which were in abundant supply (Caruso, Gigli, Martinelli, McCormack, Schipa) or perhaps Marguérite's Jewel Song (Patti, Melba, Sembrich, Eames, Farrar). What a lot he could *not* have been playing, and what a lot he could not have been hearing even of what he played. Still, magic names! The nostalgic and romantic may even now find it hard to acknowledge what good sense and critical listening still have to assert: that is, that opera is 'at home' at last, and that its singers are at least worthily in line with the great ones of the past.

24. Let the Florid Music Praise: Rococo Revival
*Joan Sutherland   Beverly Sills
Anna Moffo   Teresa Berganza
Marilyn Horne*

IT might have to be admitted that, by somewhere around 1955, Mozart and Wagner, Verdi and Puccini, even Bellini and Donizetti were being reasonably well served by their singers. But there was still another, and very nearly last, ditch for the detractors of modern singing to fall back upon. 'Ah yes,' they could say, 'but in historical terms this is still *playing* at singing. The real golden age was, of course, more remote from us than any of these composers; you have only to look at the music which Giacomelli, Riccardo Broschi and others wrote for Farinelli and his contemporaries to know what virtuoso singing really means and how far from its achievements we with our present-day singers really are. The scores of Handel's operas pay abundant testimony to the standard of those times, and we know of course that what was written was nothing to what would actually be performed, for the singers would embellish freely and with a brilliance unknown to us today'.

The argument could be advanced with less conviction in 1965 than in 1955, however, for between those dates Joan Sutherland had arrived on the international scene, and with her her husband Richard Bonynge. 'She has put back my work by a hundred years', Callas is reported to have said, adding that it was not Sutherland herself ('she sings beautifully') who was responsible for the enormity, but Mr Bonynge. Credit must be given where it is due, and while there is little to suggest that Callas' work has suffered because of Mr Bonynge's activities, there is every reason to believe that Handel's, Mozart's, Rossini's, Meyerbeer's and Donizetti's (to name but a few, as they say) have benefited considerably.

Sutherland's first performance as Lucia di Lammermoor, in Zeffirelli's production, took place at Covent Garden in February 1959, and very shortly afterwards records appeared to show the rest of the world why it had been such an exciting event. It is a pity that the companies could not have been enterprising enough to record at least excerpts from Tippett's *Midsummer Marriage* when it came out in 1955: for in Sutherland's singing of Jennifer's music there was enough to show everyone that here was a quite exceptionally beautiful voice, a mastery of difficult florid music, and a musician withal. As it was, the enterprising record-collector had his best chance of foreseeing the singer's eventual triumph if he bought in 1958 an inconspicuous extended-play record issued by a company called Belcantodisc which otherwise concerned itself with reissues of rare records from the early part of the century. On this, Sutherland sang three pieces: a long and demanding solo from Donizetti's *Emilia di Liverpool* in which the scale-work was dazzling, the aria by Spohr which we know as 'Rose softly blooming' where the voice floated deliciously and which also made it clear how much body there was in the middle range where coloratura sopranos are often uninteresting or plain inadequate, and a pleasant song by Rossini sung with gaiety and point, ending on a full and easy high E flat, and arriving there by way of some brilliant scale passages. The piano accompaniments were played with unusual sense of style and presence by Richard Bonynge whose tastes and interests as well as the singer's own the record no doubt reflected, though few people can have been aware of that at the time.

These interests were to lead to the opening of many long-closed doors and shut-down apartments in the house of music. The whole tradition of great singing was consciously sought out: titles of some of Sutherland's two-record sets, such as 'The Art of the Prima Donna' and 'The Age of Bel Canto', emerge from the search. The study of scores, memoirs and reviews inevitably drew attention to the accomplishments of 18th and 19th century singers in terms of sheer range and fluency; and about these aspects of Sutherland's singing there can be little argument. In record after record she has exercised marvellous virtuosity as well as an ease and full-bodied beauty of tone in the upper register that, in combination, are virtually beyond compare. The second part of Queen Marguérite's great solo in *Les Huguenots* has such perfect evenness of scale-work and brilliantly rapid ascending staccati in the cadenza that the legendary Melba cylinder or the record by Margarethe Siems simply cannot be pointed to any longer as representing a virtuosity unknown to modern singing. If one then makes comparisons between Sutherland and the excellent Frieda Hempel in the duet which follows, it is to find Sutherland technically superior in all the most difficult passages: however good, Hempel still appears in the comparison sketchier in the triplet sequences, less scrupulous in placing each of the notes there. Or take the many passages in which Sutherland sings a decorated version at the repeat of the melody: the whole thing is done with more sheer professionalism, daring and thoroughness than by most of the earlier singers. Tetrazzini in 'Vien, diletto' *(Puritani)*, for instance, will occasionally offer an embellishment with delicious effect, but the relatively uneven production, the carelessness over observing directions, and sometimes again the sketchy partial fulfilment of technical challenges — all are contrasts to place Sutherland as the 'golden-age' singer, superbly accurate, for example, in the chromatic descending figures, and crowning

102. Joan Sutherland as Alcina   103. Marilyn Horne

the brilliant solo with a fine full-voiced high E flat. With her own contemporaries, her ascendency in this particular field is equally complete: surpassing Callas because of her steadiness and beauty of tone, Sills because of the greater fullness and power, Caballé because of her greater excellence in the trill and her greater ease on high.

But mention of Caballé brings to mind those features of Sutherland's singing which are justly open to criticism. She has a way, as the great Spanish soprano has not, of often leaving unsatisfied that most basic of requirements, the need for an even, instrumental tone in the unembellished melodic line. Examples would be 'Dite alla giovine' in *La Traviata*, or 'Ah non credea' *(La Sonnambula)* where one wishes for the sort of firm outline which Toti dal Monte would give; or the songs sung by so many prima donnas of old in their unbending moments, 'Home sweet home' and 'The Last Rose of Summer', in both of which Sutherland misses an essential simplicity. It is partly that she apparently feels the need to give each phrase and each part of each phrase its own mouldings, and this is certainly a sign of non-superficiality: but whatever the gain, there is a loss in one of the basic pleasures òf singing, in the sheer flow of sound. And no doubt it is a matter of taste, but it will certainly seem to many that the music does not ask for this treatment: 'let well alone', it often seems to cry. As part of the moulding-treatment, but also sometimes simply as a mannerism, will come the lifts and droops. In nearly every phrase of Micaëla's song in

Carmen there is a lift to the high note; and Gilda's 'Tutte le feste' in *Rigoletto* is overlaid with the pathos of a drooping portamento, so that one is conscious of a design to intensify the melody beyond the character Verdi has given it. In any case, the droops and lifts generally have a relaxing effect, especially when seconded by the sameness of vowel-sound which so often has dulled her enunciation. All the vowels are shaded towards an 'ah' sound, which distorts pronunciation and (more seriously for the effect of the music) reduces the vitality of language. The characteristic became marked quite soon after the start of her international career. Thus, the complete *Lucia di Lammermoor* of 1961 under John Pritchard shows her to have changed appreciably from the first recital record issued in 1959, the year of her great success at Covent Garden. In the Fountain Scene, for instance, the vowels of such a phrase as 'l'ombra mostrarsi a me' are open in the recital, and shaded towards a rounded and dulled uniformity in the complete performance of the opera. This is typical; and once it has registered with the listener as an irritant it has defeated its own purpose, which was presumably to facilitate a loveliness of sound in which one could bathe blissfully undisturbed.

Fortunately, much of the music in Sutherland's repertoire prohibits languor and promotes brilliance. Fortunately too, there is more in her own character: hence the verve and humour of her *Fille du Régiment*. The energy and ring of 'Ocean, thou mighty monster', with a genuine dramatic soprano's voice at the opening, remind us of the very different career that once seemed to be mapped out for her, where her Eva might have led to a Sieglinde and that to an Isolde. There is plenty of stature in this singing, and it is good to hear her ring out full and strong without inhibitions in the last section. Then, of course, there are the explorations into relatively unfamiliar territory: the operas of Handel and his contemporaries, full of sprightly allegro arias, where any singer is under such bracing command that the style has to be athletic if it is to stand the pace at all. The aria from Piccinni's *La Buona Figliuola*, which opens the recital called 'The Age of Bel Canto', is a fine example of rapid, accurate and thoroughly *alert* singing. The virtuosity of the aria 'Tornami a vagheggiar' in Handel's *Alcina* involves passing at high speed over the whole range of the voice in a way that tests every link in the chain: if there is any unevenness or division of registers, it becomes a ludicrous kind of yodelling piece. Sutherland is superb, and the decorated *da capo* section is brilliant even beyond the standards we have come to expect of her in such music.

No wonder if the term *la stupenda* has followed her around Italy as the popular papers say. At least three of her performances at La Scala, Milan, survive on 'private' recordings *(Semiramide, Les Huguenots* and *Beatrice di Tenda)* and bequeath to the future a valuable assurance that the effect of her singing in the opera house was by no means flattered by her studio recordings. She rides the ensemble, seems tireless in sustaining these extremely arduous roles, and hardly smudges so much as a semiquaver. Moreover, one senses the ample, generous size of this voice—and there is no mistaking what the audience thinks about it!

In the Scala *Semiramide* (12 December 1962) Sutherland played opposite Simionato and was conducted by Santini. The studio performance has Marilyn Horne as Arsace and Bonynge as its conductor, and it benefits from both in any comparison. The duet 'Giorno d'orrore' from Act II is a great test-piece in several respects, and one notices the greater buoyancy of rhythm in the Bonynge version, the nicely judged *diminuendo* to piano for the repeat, the greater variety and life throughout, as well as the brilliance of its embellishments and the extended cadenza demanding that virtuosity from both singers which belong to the supposedly forgotten art of the past. And the interesting thing now is that, exceptional as is Sutherland's brilliance in such music, a singer has been found, within the decade, to match it.

The partnership of Horne and Sutherland is probably the most brilliant on record: the beauty of the voices, breadth of range, evenness of scale work, agility and discipline, make their achievement, especially in *Semiramide*, the fulfilment of a tradition, not a latter-day apology. There is musicianship and a musical delight too, not the mere warblings of trained songbirds. Let us take the comparison between stage and studio performances a little further. Simionato is a magnificent artist, but Horne here sings with a great deal more imagination. See, for instance, in the recitative before the duet 'Serbarmi ognor si fido' from Act I, how the excitement of 'Ah, dunque lo conosci' is caught, or how she lightens her part in the 'Alle più calde', so that the music gains a serenity, and a magic in reprise, hardly to be guessed at from the other version. Simionato has warmth and authority, and magnificent depth to the chest voice—and it says something for Italian singing in the post-war period that it could produce a mezzo able to deal as well as she does (and at the age of fifty-two) with such technical problems as this music poses. But connoisseurs of the it-isn't-what-it-was school would have no trouble in pointing out the limitations: the unequalised tone with its sharply differentiated registers, the use of aspirates in runs, the loss of firmness above the chest voice. Horne passes all such tests with flying colours, and one can reach back into the remotest past of the gramophone, deep into the collector's treasury, for the record of Arsace's 'Ah, qual giorno' by Guerrina Fabbri (1903) without any embarrassment to the modern singer. Rather the contrary, for though Fabbri's runs are exemplary in smoothness and rapidity, her placing is not always steady, she is relatively unventuresome in upward range, and the final impression of her interpretation is not gracious. One reaches for the reference books to look up her dates, for she sounds like a great singer getting on in years, but no: born 1866, and, with that thorough training which we are always hearing about, surely then in her prime. Horne is firm, accurate in placing, sings with a pure legato, makes sense of the sentiments, rises easily to the high B, holds it, goes straight (and clean) down a couple of octaves, and treats the reprise of the second part of the solo with both brilliance and delicacy. Among the mezzo-sopranos on record she is, in these respects, supreme.

Saying this, is not to forget or to slight the names of Schumann-Heink and Sigrid Onegin, two great and comparable technicians among the contraltos of the century; nor is it to imply that their records are superseded, for they were artists, irreplaceably individual. But in several testing solos, the comparison is inevitable, and as far as voice and technique are concerned, Horne emerges best. 'O prêtres de Baal' from *Le Prophète* brings the three singers together, and three marvellous records they made of it. Where Horne provides a special satisfaction is in the richness of her voice compared with Schumann-Heink, and her ability and willingness to expand and ring out on the high notes, which Onegin will so rarely do. Horne's voice is very like Onegin's (often sounding like Rosa Ponselle's too: there is a similar velvety richness and depth). So when we listen to the same three contraltos in 'La Gitana', Arditi's gay and charming song which was such a favourite with Schumann-Heink, it is to note many similarities between the two more modern singers. Both have marvellous high notes, Onegin taking hers with fastidiously exact placing, Horne commanding a greater vivacity. Schumann-Heink hasn't their sensuous quality of tone; but what command, variety, spirit and personality!

It is in some such terms that we begin to note what Marilyn Horne, thus far in her career, does not so indisputably have to offer. Again, standards are made by comparisons. Except at the highest level, it would be absurd to say of Horne that there is a lack of any of these things—'command, variety, spirit and personality'. Yet at this highest level of artistry, there is a limitation. Let, say, Schumann-Heink or Janet Baker set the standard, or, among sopranos, Lilli or Lotte Lehmann, Callas or Schwarzkopf: and there appears in many of Horne's recordings what one can only vaguely gesture towards as a lack of inner tension. For example, she has recorded 'Abscheulicher' from *Fidelio*; glorious in its sound, vivid and determined in the powerful opening, tender and spirited in turn. Yet 'Komm, Hoffnung' does not beseech, the climax does not exult. One characteristic is the absence of an expressive rubato; and this may be deliberate policy on the part of the conductor, Henry Lewis (who is Marilyn Horne's husband). But in this music, and still more in the Bach and Handel which they have recorded together, the policy will seem to many listeners to want sensitivity. Certainly, 'Schlafe, mein Liebster' from the *Christmas Oratorio*, avoids any dangers of sentimentalisation taken at this easy jog; and if one does not shape the phrases, then at least one is not fussing them with imposed romantic warmth. But surely there should be tenderness, and in the tenderness a tension or concentration, which is virtually impossible in such a matter-of-fact reading. Again, to return to the operatic repertoire, and to Schumann-Heink and Onegin for comparison: Fidès' 'Ah, mon fils' in *Le Prophète* lacks the note of lament that both of the earlier singers brought to it (for though there is a little weeping sound at one point, it is, as it were, interpolated, rather than emerging from the basic expression of the voice—as in 'Una voce poco fa' her laugh seems interpolated).

Yet, by any normal standard, it would be ridiculous to suggest that Horne is inexpressive or narrow in the range of her musicianship. The gramophone has not done full justice to the singer who at an early age caught the attention of Stravinsky and Robert Craft; who was first heard in England in a first performance of some difficult modern compositions; and whose debut at Covent Garden was in *Wozzeck*. She has, however, recorded a sensitive performance of Mahler's *Kindertotenlieder*, and her operatic repertoire takes her back to Handel (superb solos from *Rodelinda*, for example), to lesser-known composers like Lampugnoni (a virtuoso solo from *Meraspe*, all arpeggios and runs, over a two-octave range), and to Gluck (a warmly human Orfeo, hauntingly tender in the phrase 'Euridice non è più, ed io vivo ancora', hushed and serene in 'Che puro ciel'). And the potential expressiveness and strength of personality cannot be gauged better than by going to the centre of the mezzo-soprano's repertoire, her Carmen. This is not yet on record in its entirety,[1] but some excerpts already put her among the most vivid exponents of the role. The touchstone is her solo in the Card Scene. A sharp intake of breath as the prophet of death stares up at her; a most beautiful, very quiet and inner start to the meditation, 'En vain pour éviter'; a steady growth of feeling and voice, eventually giving all with the phrase 'la carte impitoyable répétera la mort', with its open, fearlessly projected vowels. There is genuine intensity here; some of it surely inherited from Carmen Jones' 'dat ole boy', the part which Horne sang for the sound-track to Dorothy Dandridge's acting in the film back in the early nineteen-fifties. There is certainly one of the great singers of the century here, and it is significant that, with her strength lying in so many fields, she should still be so closely associated with the Sutherland–Bonynge revival of forgotten music and an almost forgotten art.

Associated with Sutherland and Bonynge have in fact been many whose careers have become spectacularly international, and several others with less widely celebrated reputations still have technical skills rarely met with on records between the earliest years of the century and the present time. There has been a succession of highly accomplished tenors like Pierre Duval, John Alexander, Anastasios Vrenios and Richard Conrad. The last of these singers has runs with a flexibility unheard on records since de Lucia. One can make a direct comparison in the 'Ecco ridente' from *Il Barbiere di Siviglia*, among of the classics of the gramophone in de Lucia's versions, and included by Conrad in the album called *The Age of Bel Canto*, in which he makes a third with Sutherland and Horne. Tonally, it must be said, there is little comparison, for de Lucia's voice has an unchallenged ring and capacity to open out, reminding one, even in this music, that he

[1] Her performance under Bernstein has now appeared (*Gramophone*, June 1973).

was also a Lohengrin. But the runs and decorations are astounding in Conrad's performance as in de Lucia's; in some ways, rather more so, for one of his runs carries him up to high C and down with perfect evenness to comfortable bass G, while the trills are a delightful embellishment that de Lucia did not offer, and the triplets of the often abbreviated final passage are all scrupulously in place. He shares with de Lucia the characteristic of a quick vibrato, not much in favour these days; and in a simple air like Handel's 'Care selve', for all Conrad's accomplishment, one misses the firm, well-placed tone of a McCormack. But then, moving on to one of Handel's florid arias, Sesto's 'Sperai ne m'ingannai' from *Giulio Cesare*, we have again to marvel at the virtuosity of scale-work in the da capo section, and to ask whether any tenor has recorded Handel with this kind of skill before him.

Of the other tenors, the Australian John Serge and the Californian-born Vrenios have joined Sutherland in roles for which their suitability has been thought questionable. Serge is the Idreno in *Semiramide*, rather pallid in tone perhaps, and with less body and ring to the voice than Gianni Raimondi, the tenor in the Milan performance. But then, he does sing the complete role, including some passages of great difficulty, the problems of which the Italian performance solved by simple omission. Idreno's scene in Act II is sung on the basic assumption that the music calls for elegance; it gets it, along with thorough mastery of arpeggios, scales, diminuendos, a wide range up to C sharp, and a technique to meet the requirements of elaborate embellishment in the return of the already florid melody 'Si, sperar voglio contento'. Vrenios, the other tenor mentioned here, light and lyrical, an Almaviva or Ernesto by nature and training, appears in *Les Huguenots*—as Raoul, no less. Jean de Reszke, Caruso, Zenatello and recently Corelli are the illustrious, full-throated predecessors of this tenorino, who arrives on the scene 'Sous ce beau ciel de Tourraine', slight as a pageboy, a nimble, unheroic youngster. But then, of course, one may be like the present writer who realised, rather gradually, that he was actually enjoying that first aria, 'Plus blanche', and that come to think of it, he could not recall having genuinely done so before.[1] Instead of the effortful, charmless sound left in the mind as the sum-total impression from many other records, we hear in this performance a pleasant lyricism, clever in florid work, and eventually floating to a high E flat with suitable airiness into the 'beau ciel'. There is a loss, certainly, when Raoul has to cry 'Aux armes' in Act V, and so there is in some other passages expressing heroic resolution. The surprising thing is that so much of the music very positively gains from being sung by this kind of voice; and his opening of the duet with Sutherland ('Beauté divine') with its sympathetic intertwining of

---

[1] There are some fine versions on early records, nevertheless, outstanding among them being the performance by Dmitri Smirnoff, which was included among the specially repressed 78s issued under a subscription scheme in 1972 by the British Institute of Recorded Sound.

voices later on makes very agreeable listening indeed.

The tenors of the *Norma* and *Puritani* recordings are John Alexander and Pierre Duval respectively; the former, firm, fervent and accurate in the often omitted or slurred semiquaver passages, part of a generally ungrateful role, the latter (a Canadian) singing the *gruppetti* with real virtuosity and ringing out the high notes, up to a full-voiced high D, excitingly and musically. Others, like Werner Krenn, Renato Cioni, Bergonzi and Pavarotti, are discussed elsewhere, and, apart from Krenn, are less remarkable for sheer flexibility; but the list of able lyric tenors does not end with them.

In fact it is, for present purposes, an uncomfortably long one. Alva, Benelli, Kraus, Monti, Valletti . . . these are among the names that come to mind as singers who in more recent times have admirably filled roles for which there was little competition between the two wars. In those years, Tito Schipa stood as an artist well above any Italian rivals (Dino Borgioli probably the best of them), and in memory he remains a name to conjure with, a singer of an altogether more starry status than the modern tenors listed above. Ultimately, this is right, though only because of the hard, unpalatable truth that a certain quality X, elusive of analysis but inescapable of recognition, sets the stars in the sky and keeps the rest of us earthbound. At best, there is a poise, magnetism and individuality about Schipa's singing that the others cannot match. But in some other, more mundane and factual respects. they have already excelled beyond him.

Valletti was a pupil of Schipa, and no doubt learnt some of the graces of production and interpretation from the master. At any rate, whoever he learnt it from, he can sing 'Il mio tesoro' (see p. 171). And whoever taught him the style and the repertoire, he does well in Schubert and Schumann, Fauré and Debussy (cf. p. 170). His achievement in French song is doubly remarkable, perhaps unique, in that he is an Italian tenor: Fauré's 'Dans les ruines d'une abbaye' shows a way with rhythm and a feeling for French intimacy and charm that recalls Edmond Clément rather than any of his own compatriots. He is also an artist who changes tone and 'face' with sensitivity (from the spirited, firm seriousness of Duparc's 'Le Manoir de Rosemunde', for example, to the honeyed ease of Hahn's 'Si mes vers avaient des ailes'—and how very creditable that he can sustain so much elegance and refinement while the pianist in this recording clonks along, robotlike and armour-plated). In Schipa's own operatic repertoire, Valletti is also an expressive Werther; and, some little way outside it, he is a Pinkerton who has a Lieder singer's skill with words (especially in 'Amor o grillo') as well as an Italian's free-throated, characterful fervour in the love music.

It is in that music, especially in certain vowels (the open 'Vieni' on the high A, or the phrase 'tenue farfalla') that one can hear something of Schipa in Valletti's singing. One hears something of him, too, in Alfredo Kraus, born in the Spanish Canary Islands and coming to international notice during the 'sixties. He exceeds Schipa in his upward range, taking the high notes of arias from *I Puritani* and *La Favorita* with ease (the Englishman known professionally as Benvenuto Finelli has also made a speciality of coping with the extended range required by the scores of such operas, doing so at the expense of colour and richness, yet singing warmly, as well as providing a mere top C sharp, in 'Una vergine' from *La Favorita*). Kraus has not an ingratiating voice; he is unmelting and charmless, for example, in 'Un' aura amorosa' from *Così fan tutte*. But there is a personality there, and at his best, as in parts of *Lucrezia Borgia* (with Caballé), he has an incisive, commanding style, and a useful, penetrative tone in ensemble: in the trio towards the end of Act I, his broad, gentle line, the crescendo to its climax, and the poised soft passages following are exemplary.

The three remaining lyric tenors just mentioned are all notably and hearteningly in the tradition, and, as far as the gramophone is concerned, all extend its application. Nicolai Monti and Luigi Alva, for instance, both appear in *Il Rè Pastore*, bringing an Italian glow to the performance of Mozart, and a Mozartian elegance into Italian singing. Monti's voice sounds a little warmer than Alva's, perhaps less bright in projection; he is rather more interesting in his treatment of the melodic line, but it is Alva who has the most fearsome technical difficulties to contend with. Monti will probably be best remembered for his Elvino in both Callas' and Sutherland's *Sonnambula*, sometimes breaking the flow with an aspirate, and rather less likeable when singing loudly, but always shading sensitively and giving a well-poised, graceful account of his part in 'Prendi, l'annel ti dono' and 'D'un pensiero'. In the sweetness of his tone he resembles the third of these tenors, Ugo Benelli, whose voice is uniformly attractive and whose style is unspoilt by the use of aspirates or of any of the devices of less fastidious singers. In Schipa's basic repertoire, he provides a splendid Ernesto and Almaviva, and, as an extension into the kind of virtuosity that Schipa never committed himself to, on records at least, he gives an immaculate performance of the florid aria 'Si, ritrovarla io giuro' in *La Cenerentola*. The runs, arpeggios, and high B's and C's are taken with every grace, and behind all this dazzlement is the intelligent musician with the sound legato. His recording of Almaviva's music in *Il Barbiere di Siviglia* includes the scene, normally omitted, towards the end of the opera, in which the Count has a solo of extreme difficulty where every kind of skill is called for: grace in *cantabile* (actually, Benelli's legato is less reliable in this recording, and in 'Se il mio nome' his intonation is uncharacteristically at fault), flexibility and breath control in some long runs, an extended range, and a tone which will both ring and caress. Benelli's accomplishments are well worthy of his great predecessors (who so rarely risked anything as demanding on record). His timbre sometimes reminds one of the young McCormack, and his melodic line (in 'Cercherò lontana terra' from *Don Pasquale* for instance) stands comparison with Bonci and Schipa at their best.

Luigi Alva, the remaining tenor, brings us back to Sutherland and Bonynge and the revival of interest in the baroque. He was one of the many brilliant singers assembled for their recording of Handel's *Alcina*. He sings the part of Oronte, using plenty of voice in the difficult runs (compare de Lucia's tendency to sing his runs in a lighter voice than he normally uses), and always impressing with the well-defined, economical use of his tone. He too shows his virtuosity in a testing Rossini role (that of Lindoro in *L'Italiana in Algeri*) and, though Bonynge, Henry Lewis or Roland Gagnon would no doubt have fixed him up with some less timid embellishments than Varviso's recording allows him, he still has plenty to exercise him—a superbly taken semiquaver run, for example, in the Cavatina from Act II. Most admirable of all is his Don Ottavio in Giulini's *Don Giovanni*. The 'Dalla sua pace' is aristocratic, the 'Il mio tesoro' (see p. 561) a model of technical mastery and artistic rightness.

Turning to the lower voices, the baritones and basses, one cannot write so happily. If de Lucia's virtuosity is approached and Schipa's in some ways surpassed by a respectable number of lyric tenors, there is no baritone to offer the panache of Battistini or quite to match the lyrical smoothness of de Luca. When Sutherland recorded *I Puritani* her baritone was Renato Capecchi, who makes a human character out of Sir Richard Forth, but is the absolute antithesis of Battistini, singing it as such placid music, relaxed in style, furry in tone, everything aspirated except the cadenzas— which shows that he could have sung differently had he the training and the inclination. One of the best in the early nineteenth century repertoire, especially in Rossini, is Sesto Bruscantini, who sings a tasteful Figaro (good at his runs in 'Dunque io son') while the nearest successor to de Luca as a pure lyricist is not an Italian at all, but the American Robert Merrill, who has his place in the next chapter. In florid Handelian music, probably no one is more successful than John Shirley-Quirk (see p. 505) who sings in the tradition of Peter Dawson, and thus ultimately of his master Sir Charles Santley. On the other hand, when Bonynge recorded his elaborately ornamented version of *Messiah* he turned to the Finnish baritone Tom Krause for the bass part. His is an exceptionally fine voice, with a good range, an even production, and a breath control that deals effectively with the long runs (he is also a stylish opera singer and recitalist, better at working the ruthlessness of Pizarro into his tone than the fun of Dr. Malatesta, and showing his feeling for words in a recital of songs by Sibelius). The runs are not absolutely bound in firm legato, however; the triplets of 'Why do the Nations?', for instance, are made distinct by the use of light aspirates, perhaps inevitable at this speed, but it is not the way Peter Dawson used to do them. Of course it is true that the first and essential requirement in these fast semiquaver runs is to make the notes clearly heard, and to this end it may be thought necessary, especially for a baritone or bass with a big voice, to use a style which taps out each note *marcato* in the way that choristers are regularly taught to do nowadays, and which is particularly habitual with Germans. Fischer-Dieskau does it in many of his runs in Handel's *Giulio Cesare*. The American bass, Norman Treigle, singing the part in a version which omits some difficult numbers, does not do this; and while it is good to hear such a deep strong voice maintaining a genuine legato, it also has to be admitted that the music and the dramatic character do not some to life as in Fischer-Dieskau's singing (and Karl Richter's conducting). In general, modern singing has made do, rather than come up with specialists in the bass clef to match the virtuosi in the other voice parts.

Back to the ladies, then, and a more general look at the whole field. It is a large one, in a thriving way of business, that is the first observation; and its boundaries are indistinct. A few artfully selected passages of music, dates and artists could probably make it seem more extensive still. For instance, Russophiles might like to take whatever credit the revival merits (alternatively, it could be condemned as backward-looking, artistically bankrupt bourgeois homage to the aristocracy of an age thankfully gone for ever). It is true, at any rate, that the first post-war singer to set the runs and arpeggios of *Semiramide* flowering in the recording studios was the Russian, Zara Dolukhanova. Arsace's 'Ah, quel giorno' and the duet 'Serbami ognor' (the soprano is Sakhavora) were recorded, and, though the acoustic is boxy and the voices are uncomfortably close to the microphone, these are notable performances, standing up better than one might first think to comparison and repeated listening. In the duet, both singers are incisive and fluent, and the solo, warm-toned and affectionate, is concluded with an impressive cadenza. The wide range, with bold descents below the stave and frequent excursions above it, is certainly a feature which we are now coming to expect from our mezzos; but Dolukhanova was ahead of her contemporaries and provided something of a revelation in those days.

And of course much of the interest for which Sutherland and Bonynge were to provide a focal point had been in the air for some years. It was not merely that Callas, as another significant individual, had made florid singing respectable again; it was not merely that a relatively small but insistent number of critics and record collectors kept before the public the ideal of an accomplishment in singers beyond that to which we had grown accustomed. But there was also the growing interest among music lovers in exploring back beyond Beethoven, into the lesser-known parts of Mozart and of Handel, their contemporaries, and their predecessors, back further still, to Purcell, Monteverdi, and to the Middle Ages. 'A more adventurous repertoire' was one call from the public to the singers, and inevitably with it came the call for more skill. The operas and oratorios of Handel could, after all, be looked upon as central musical fare, and gradually throughout the post-war years performances became more frequent. If young singers in England wanted engagements for the Handel Opera Society's summer season, they would have to polish up their scales, look after their lungs, and generally see that the voice was in good working order. Thus, in the summer of 1959, while Covent Garden was hearing Callas' Medea and Jurinac's Butterfly, visitors to Sadlers Wells could find Joan Sutherland, fresh from her Lucia, singing an equally outstanding Rodelinda. *Semele* was the other opera given that month, and the casts also included such able singers among the women as Heather Harper, Janet Baker, Helen Watts, Margreta Elkins, Patricia Kern and Monica Sinclair.

The last named of these is an interesting 'case' (as well as being a joy to find in any cast-list). She is a mezzo with a strong contralto depth and weight to the voice; and a generation or two ago she would have been a stalwart of the inter-war English Wagner productions, spending much of her year singing in *Messiah* and *Elijah* all round the country, with *The Dream of Gerontius* at Worcester or the Albert Hall. In her own time she might very well have been known to us on records essentially for her series of full-scale predators in Gilbert and Sullivan (the biggest and best since Bertha Lewis), and for her creation of the flouncy-bouncy Madame Popova in Walton's Chekhov opera, *The Bear*. Without the baroque revival, we might not have known that we had in our midst a quite astonishing virtuoso, whose runs would act as a pace-setter for any featherweight 'coloratura'. In Bononcini's *Griselda*, her Gualtiero makes a huge impression as the strong timbre jigs along in a jolly aria called 'Affetto, gioia e riso', whose first section ends with a flourish that takes the singer up to the high A and down two-and-a-half octaves to a bottom E. Another one, 'Le fere a risvegliar', is if anything more brilliant still, for the aptly masculine voice also produces a good trill and a top C. In Handel (again in association with Sutherland and Bonynge), she is superbly equal to the fast tempi and elaborate embellishments of these recordings: her Ptolemy in *Giulio Cesare* completes the extension of range to its full three octaves (C to C), and in the all-star *Alcina*, already mentioned, her aria 'E gelosia' is outstanding — amongst the most accomplished of contralto solos on record, and certainly the most dazzling performance recorded by any English contralto or mezzo up to that time.

The *Alcina* recording recruited the talents of another remarkable mezzo, Teresa Berganza, born and trained (obviously with great thoroughness) in Madrid. She sings with due brilliance in the allegro aria 'Va cercando', and complements this with the long, cool, unfussed phrases of 'Verdi prati', very beautifully and evenly sung. Her accomplishment in fioriture is in fact the distinguishing feature by which she rises from the crowded ranks of the pleasant but un-unforgettable. Not that she is a superficial interpreter; but it is when one hears this clean, business-like singer moving through a sequence of rapid triplets as though difficulties did not exist that one also comes to recognise a distinctive character in the performances. Hers is one of the very few technically unflawed recordings of 'Come scoglio' from *Così fan tutte*; her roulades in Rosina's 'Una voce poco fa' are scrupulously neat; her strong, precise voicing of Sesto's part in *La Clemenza di Tito* is the work of a singer who has completely mastered her craft. The distinctive character, in fact, is that of the able, confident virtuoso; not at all showy, but on the contrary rather dignified and even impersonal in manner. There is nothing like the knowledge of thorough technical control to lend a stylishness and sense of status; and the repertoire itself has helped, sufficiently individual to promote interest, sufficiently near-centre not to repel it.

It is curious perhaps that an attempt to define the contribution of such a good singer should find itself halted at this point. Another anomaly may explain it. 'Charming' is the word on everybody's tongue when Berganza makes a personal appearance; at an unusually well-cast concert performance, under Giulini, of *Le Nozze di Figaro*, for instance, Berganza's Cherubino won the warmest applause from the London audience, for not only was it well sung, but the pretty, compact little Spaniard had a presence and a charm. Yet charm, personality and 'face' are precisely what the records for the most part do not have. The three solos mentioned above for their technical efficiency will serve as examples because the arias in question all lend themselves so well to the personal touch which often is what makes a performance memorable and the recording of it precious: Schwarzkopf frowning her 'Come scoglio', Galli-Curci running her tongue in playful determination round 'mi lascia reggere, mi fo guidar', Schumann-Heink hushed and haunting at the unaccompanied 'Guardami's of Sesto's air in *La Clemenza di Tito*. Berganza's 'Una voce' is sung for the most part with a sort of matronly firmness, unsmiling and essentially uncharming. And further comparisons tend only to underline the basic point; if one shifts the ground, for instance, to Dorabella's 'E amore un ladroncello' *(Così fan tutte)*, where Berganza is certainly quite pleasing and by no means pedestrian, it is to find Christa Ludwig (not so readily thought of as a 'charming' singer) much more vivacious and impulsive, more characterful, more charming.

Yet if the requirement is a mezzo who will be sure to sing the notes, all of them, a singer with a firm pure voice, no spread, no breaks of register, but resonant and healthy; one who will also give a scrupulously musical performance and look beautiful while doing it—then Berganza will come as a very pleasing answer to the impresario's prayer. And if given a chance to sing some Spanish songs, she might throw in other treats as well. Granados' *Tonadillos*, especially 'El tra la la', bring the long-awaited smile. Here she confides, lightens, lilts and captivates; and in 'La Maja Dolorosa' she shades and sighs ('enamorabar'), is sensitive in her use of *rubato* and *portamento*, sings, in fact, with a true personal insight. Comparisons with de los Angeles and Supervia (or the specialist in Granados, Conchita Badia) show her in this part of her repertoire to be as individual as they are. She is less pretty than Supervia in the Granados songs, but perhaps surprisingly can match her in that fierce, chesty, challenging sound that Supervia makes at the end of Falla's 'Jota', and which Berganza produces in the phrase 'siendo nuestras cuerpos dos' concluding an exciting recording of Turina's 'Farruca'. In Guridi's 'Jota' ('Come quiere'), one of the songs popularised by Victoria de los Angeles, she has her own way, cool and rhythmic, unsmiling but not entirely unplayful. And in another of Guridi's songs, a real beauty called 'Mañanita de San Juan', she provides singing that might be used for a whole course of lessons if the soft spell of a summer's day did not exercise its magic, leaving us with the loveliest of pianissimos for the words 'en lo profundo del mar', and prohibiting anything other than mere (and sheer) joy.

If the prayerful impresario were then to coax from the singer a Rossinian showpiece for an encore, he might be treated to the final solo in *L'Italiana in Algeri*, and we would have another example both of her own brilliance and of the standards to which this modern revival has attained. She is superb in the exacting florid work: another jewel in the crown which modern singing is now surely worthy to wear.

For modern achievements in fioriture there is, after all, a relatively modern test in the solo written for Zerbinetta in Strauss' *Ariadne auf Naxos*. There was trouble with this from the start, for the original version as (we understand) sung by Frieda Hempel apparently had to be modified for Margarethe Siems and Selma Kurz, neither of whom was exactly a novice. In those early days it was recorded by Hermine Bosetti and Hedwig Francillo-Kaufmann (see p. 194) and when Ivogün recorded it electrically it was reckoned one of the wonders of the world, though later records on 78 by Erna Sack and Adele Kern excited relatively little comment. In England since the war, the music has been sung so as to receive the acclaim of critics, by Ilse Hollweg (in the original key), Gianna d'Angelo, Reri Grist, Mattiwilda Dobbs, Rita Streich, Mimi Engela-Coertse, June Bronhill, Marion Studholme, and Sylvia Geszty. The list is not inconsiderable and it makes no pretensions to completeness. Recordings add Erna Berger, Alda Noni and Roberta Peters, and testify to the excellence of three of the others, Streich, Geszty and Grist. This music makes great demands on the upper register of the voice, on its flexibility, and its capacity to take a clean, sudden leap; moreover, the singer has a fully written-out score to follow, not a choice of embellishments to suit her own tastes and abilities. Hempel, Siems and Kurz recorded nothing from the opera, so we cannot know exactly what they sang and did not sing, and how it would sound to our ears now. Ivogün's record is often delightful and brilliant, and perhaps purer and prettier in tone than its successors. She is less than fully satisfactory on other counts, however, for she has a way of wisking some of the notes, of singing the highest notes without resonance, and of characterising in only the most general way. Streich, by contrast, addresses the aria tenderly to her Ariadne, and is expressive in denouncing the menfolk ('treulos sie sind's'). Peters too has the words constantly in mind, while Geszty gives perhaps the most warm, varied and humane performance of all. And in all three there is a technical mastery which, in meeting such demands, passes the last grade in tests.

Other tests might find out a weaker side, but these would involve questions of feeling and interpretation rather than of sheer technical efficiency. It is always difficult for a soprano with a light, high voice to convey depth or warmth. Later in this chapter we shall discuss Beverly Sills, one of whose great distinctions it is that in spite of the lightness of her voice, with even a certain shallowness in its tone, she manages to express such strength of feeling that her performances will sometimes achieve a genuine grandeur. This is not as yet true of the other sopranos mentioned above. Although Roberta Peters sings an intelligent Zerbinetta and a characterful Susanna (giving a lovely performance of 'Deh vieni, non tardar' after a somewhat arch portrayal in the first Act), her Lucia di Lammermoor achieves pathos but not full tragic stature. Her weightiest moment is well-chosen—the phrase 'La mia condanna ho scritta' in the marriage ceremony; her trills, staccati and ornamentation in general are neat, and the legato is satisfying (at times very beautiful, as in the opening of 'Verrano a te'). Nobility, stature, subtlety: these are not so readily found. Nor should we with much confidence go for them to Rita Streich, though her imagination and feelings do catch fire in the *Ariadne*. One feels her to be touched by the Composer's ardour in the Prologue (but then it is Seefried's Composer, so this is not so surprising): 'Ein Augenblick ist wenig' she sings, with a tender humanity, and she enters eagerly into the fun of the thing. The characterisation has range just as the voice part has. Her Susanna in *Le Nozze di Figaro*, too, is charming, vivid and not arch; her Aennchen in *Der Freischütz* has some of the live freshness of Elisabeth Schumann. But the limits soon become apparent. What poker-faced children she and the matronly-sounding Gisella Litz make of their Hansel and Gretel; what expressionless story-telling she gives in songs like 'Die Forelle' and 'Heidenröslein'; and what little difference she makes between the verses of songs such as 'Auf dem Wasser zu singen' and 'Seligkeit', both of which suit her very well in other respects. Her value is still considerable. There is a sameness about all her phrases in Milhaud's 'Chansons de Ronsard', for instance, but the virtuosity is quite marvellous. On the same recital record, in Nicolai's Variations on a lullaby by Weber, we have a pure legato, a gentle firmness of tone in the florid work, still preserving the caressing mood of the Wiegenlied, and an exhibition of a technique in the tradition of Siems, Kurz and her own teachers, Maria Ivogün and Erna Berger. And where these sometimes floated themselves sharp in pitch, she never does. She is a very fine singer, but only occasionally does the 'face' change, the heart cry out, or anything disturb the placid loveliness of her art.

Rather similarly, a song recital by Mattiwilda Dobbs offers the pleasure of listening easily to a conscientious, refined artist in some delicately tuneful music: so perhaps it is ungrateful to grumble. But here (unlike Streich and Reri Grist) the basic tone is not really firm, is sometimes rather breathy, and in bloom only on the high notes; in some (such as 'Nacht und Träume') there is even some trouble with intonation. Turning then to her Constanza in the English recording of *Die Entführung aus dem Serail* (under Menuhin), it is to hear her as more properly a Blonda (sung here by the firmer-sounding Jennifer Eddy), for Constanze wants heroic reserves and more dramatic warmth. On the other hand, the runs are fine: again modern singing passes this particular test, when a chance comparison with the stronger, better-projecting Frieda Hempel finds that accomplished Mozartian sometimes breaking the runs for a breath, and occasionally inaccurate in them too. Reri Grist, mentioned just now for her accomplished Zerbinetta, is another who is capable of keeping up with the early coloraturas in much of her florid work (her singing lesson in *Der Schauspieldirektor* is the real thing, displaying a fine breath-span, clean, bold intervals, an impressive high E flat, and, in the trio following, brilliant scale-work up to high F). Some of her runs are not so exemplary, however: her singing of Iphis in Handel's *Jephtha* has virtually all of them taken as a series of separate notes (the aria 'Tune the soft melodious lute', for example, demands a genuine legato in its runs, and does not begin to get it). And, like the others, she finds it difficult to warm or intensify the bright, high-toned voice. On records she has so far done it most effectively in Mozart: her Zerlina sings tenderly in 'Batti, batti', her Susanna is brisk and bright without pertness, and her Aminta in *Il Rè Pastore* sings the famous 'L'amerò sarò costante' gently, sometimes with an affectionate tone where the upper harmonics and the edge of the voice are filtered. But generally she does little to vary the tone: her 'Caro nome' in *Rigoletto* suffers from this, though everything is finely placed. And one reflects, in the *Rè Pastore* recording, where she is joined by the well-matching Lucia Popp, how hard it is for sopranos of this kind to modify the colour or temperature of the clear stream their voices so refreshingly provide. Lucia Popp is perhaps most refreshing of all, for her tone has something of an oboe's sharpness of flavour in with the sweetness (a characteristic which also distinguishes her Sophie in *Der Rosenkavalier*). Her legato is normally true, her runs are fluent and distinct, and a lively rhythmic sense makes her an ideally wholesome springday singer of Handel and Mozart. A heavenly sound her voice makes when first heard in *Xerxes*, supposedly and aptly coming from the summer-house. The pointed elfin tone can also shine with a frosted glint to suit the Queen of Night: superbly accurate and spirited, she is probably the best exponent of this role on records.

But as we have said, not all the so-called 'coloratura' sopranos stop short at this kind of emotional range. Of course, one of the great achievements of Callas was that depth and intensity could now be heard by everybody, in music in which up to her time during this century only a relative few had suspected its existence. Sutherland also brought feeling and warmth to her portrayals, as have certain of the Italians, notably Scotto and Zeani, discussed in a later chapter. The two sopranos who remain for present consideration are both Americans, and both have succeeded in increasing the expressive possibilities of light voices.

Anna Moffo is one of those rare singers whose facility in the highest soprano register emerges naturally, but in a way surprisingly, out of a voice that one would otherwise place (on its recordings, that is) as lyric, even sometimes lyric-dramatic. She sings Aida's 'O patria mia' and 'Morrò, ma prima in grazia' from *Un Ballo in Maschera* with apparently ample resources: not so much a matter of volume as of timbre, and effective largely because she is skilful in the gradation of sound. Many louder voices give less effect of power. Hearing the *Ballo* aria on its own, one would not predict that this same Verdi recital would contain a performance of 'Ernani, involami' in which the already extensive range is increased to include a high E flat in the cadenza. Nor would one readily think at first that here was a Lucia, a Rosina and Anina, the usual parts for the 'coloratura' specialist.

Some of her best recordings are in fact of lyric roles such as Butterfly and Mimì. She sings feelingly, never leaving the impression of a light-weight performance. Though her Butterfly is a young girl, not a prima donna, she rises to full tragic status with mature dignity. 'Che tua madre' is warmly maternal, and again one is aware how effectively she grades the sound, observing the crescendo markings scrupulously, so that her full voice is heard only at the final climax. Many individual phrases stay in the memory: her tender recollection of Pinkerton's bidding her farewell, her mimicry of the 'bravo giudice' and the shifty 'marito' up in front of him, the childlike pained surprise at the very idea, in the Letter Duet, that she could have forgotten ('Non mi rammenta più'). Once or twice something is missed—the full happiness and abandon of 'Trionfa il mio amor', for instance. But generally this is the performance of a sensitive, devoted artist; and the voice, for all its youthful clarity, has warmth and depth.

It is all the more remarkable that her singing is genuinely creative yet so unmarked by mannerisms. Her habit of opening each note out, swelling it slightly, is musical in feeling, but it is true that one could sometimes wish for a simpler and more even line: an otherwise captivating performance of 'Sul fil d'un soffio etesio' in *Falstaff*, floating and lingering exquisitely, suffers a little from this. More noticeable is a tendency to take notes from below: her duets from *Manon* with di Stefano find both singers 'lifting' in this way rather too often. But these are not insistent features of her singing. What one notices most repeatedly and gratefully is the skill with which she handles a naturally beautiful instrument. She is not one of those singers with such a distinctive voice-character that the first hearing is unforgettable, while subsequent recognition brings that brief but priceless thrill of excitement. Yet it has character and strength, so that one feels (say) Lucia's distresses, as well as having every confidence that the technical difficulties of the music will be met. And when she sails up so easily above the stave, in the Mad Scene, it is with no sense of a soubrette's facile lightness, because when singing in the middle register, as throughout so much of Act II, her voice has had body, and even something of a mezzo quality about it.

104. Teresa Berganza

That is not something that can be said of Beverly Sills. She achieves profundity perhaps more genuinely than any other singer discussed in this section, but it is in spite of her timbre rather than because of it. The voice is light, and, in itself, shallow; it is beautiful only on high, the middle register being thin and the upper notes on the stave becoming slightly tremulous under pressure. Her technique is often superb, and her high florid singing is delightful to the ear. But the interesting thing, finally, is that she is so satisfying, not as a sweet-sounding, highly-trained nightingale, but as a singer of remarkable intellectual and emotional strength.

Her Lucia di Lammermoor presents the most detailed psychological study of the part so far on record. The Mad Scene is its climax not because it contains the longest stretch of brilliant singing, but because it is the culmination of a clearly realised series of pressures put upon a tender, anxious

105. Anna Moffo

106. Beverly Sills

human being. Stage by stage we come closer to the madness which is
latent even in the first aria, 'Regnava nel silenzio', normally sung so
complacently that nobody bothers about its meaning at all. Perhaps even
the news that it tells a ghost story may come as a surprise to many of its
listeners, though in most performances, in a generalised sort of way, one is
made to realise that much. That the ghost is heard before it is seen; that it
appears with hair-raising suddenness; that it equally suddenly vanishes;
and that the water of the fountain turns blood-red: these points emerge,
not just nominally, but with vivid illumination from Sills' performance.
The first two points, for example, the moan and the sudden appearance:
the word 'gemito' on its descending notes, themselves suggestive of the
moan, is given a pallid, ghostly colouring, while the apparition is brought
before us startlingly as with a quick turn of the head by spotlighting the
word 'ecco' in 'ecco su quel margine'. She makes us hear this thing, then
she makes us see it: so that when the runs and high notes come, they register

not as the conventional decorative way of rounding off the verse of a song, but as a cry from nerves shivering at the chill of the supernatural. The effect is both simple and profound. But the specific insight which sees the need and finds the means is not to be discovered when looked for in a whole series of eminent predecessors: Tetrazzini, dal Monte, Sutherland, Moffo, even Callas, all, by comparison, are singing an aria, rather than something which is more essentially a ballad.

The point made is not some gratuitous gothic nightshriek. If the blood-red water shocks us, and if Lucia's own shock is expressed in a spiky, feverish kind of fioritura, we are moved because we know of the blood which will before long stain the white marriage garments, and we recognise in Lucia's fascination for the unpleasant story a dim but fearful acknowledgment of the forces already pressing upon her own mind. When she then sings of Edgardo 'egli è luce ai giorni miei' we see the face light up and realise, again more specifically than in her predecessors (it is worth comparing Sutherland here—the 'voice-face' hardly changes), how dependent this vulnerable creature is upon her lover. When Act II comes and the lover is so cruelly represented as undependable, insanity comes closer. In the score and libretto, the words 'oh ciel! oh ciel!' look as conventionally operatic as it is possible to be, but with Sills they are touchingly unstagey, an almost involuntary cry from a perplexed, anxious girl. At the marriage ceremony and the sentence 'la mia condanna ho scritta' the words highlighted are the last two, and again something specific is added to the drama: the horror which a person of habitual integrity feels at putting their name to an evil (like Faustus signing his soul away, or John Proctor his reputation). Madness takes a further step; soon it will be in alternately serene and febrile possession, and the trills, runs and high notes of the Mad Scene will also be newly heard as expressive.

These features of 'coloratura' signing often serve merely to decorate an elegant musical score, but they can also be apt expressions of some heightened emotional state. The trill is a kind of shake, and one shakes with fear, horror, joy, expectation—a variety of emotions, all keenly felt. There is also something exalted, non-pedestrian, even crazy, about the high notes of the soprano voice (so far above the pitch of the woman's normal speaking voice), especially when taken in context with fast, brilliant passage-work. No 'coloratura' seems quite to have sensed this as Sills has done. Her singing of Queen Elizabeth in Donizetti's *Roberto Devereux* provides many examples. The first aria 'L'amor suo mi fe beata', touching as an utterance from the heart and not from the throne, has trills which tell how the pulse quickens with the private hopes that can never publicly be declared. Then in the cabaletta following, the second verse is decorated with an excess of energy: the Queen prepares to give political battle to support her private hopes. When in Act II the phrase 'Il tradimento è orribile' is launched with an E in alt, the high note is there not to be shown off, but to express outrage.

In these and many other ways her Elizabeth is a very imaginatively characterised performance. It raises a quite different point, however, and that is whether it was a suitable assumption for this delicate, girlish voice. Remarkably, she can make of it a dramatic instrument, but not a rich or regal one; so a rather shrewish kind of edge comes into the tone, at one point springing rhythmically, bristling with jealousy, or later, in the scene of the death-warrant, dominating the ensemble by energy and thrust rather than by natural opulence. That the voice itself has suffered somewhat in consequence is certainly suggested as one compares records made over only a relatively brief space of time. Thus the complete *Lucia di Lammermoor* just now under discussion appeared in 1971, less than three years after a Bellini–Donizetti recital which included Lucia's first solos. In the later performance the tone is edgier and thinner, less attractive generally, more inclined to become tremulous under pressure. It is a great pity, for it obviously limits her success in such a part as Massenet's Manon for which she was in many ways so well suited. 'Elle est charmante' they say on Manon's arrival, and so she is as far as the rather stringy sound will let her be. Similarly in the St. Sulpice scene, the heart is there, but a telling, well-nourished middle register is not.

Yet heartfelt is the word for this Manon. There is lovely shading and phrasing in the St. Sulpice scene; just as with the *Lucia* there are countless individual insights, and the music is always warmly felt. It is so with nearly all her work. Suppose, for instance, her solo 'Robert, toi que j'aime' from Meyerbeer's *Robert le Diable* leads one to try Hempel and Lilli Lehmann for comparison, it is to gain new respect for both these artists of the past (Hempel's finely placed voice, Lehmann's aristocratic style), but Sills certainly makes it mean more: she never loses sight of the specific dramatic and musical meaning. And it also has to be said that in terms of sheer mastery of florid technique she gives us fuller value, including the climax omitted on 78 and a brilliant cadenza. One has to salute, in her, warmth and intelligence certainly, but it is finally the technical brilliance at which one returns to marvel.

Going back to her recording of Cleopatra in Handel's *Giulio Cesare*, the role in which she first won renown in 1966, and to the last solo there, 'Da tempeste il legno infronto', one finds the most beautiful scale-work, brilliant semiquaver runs, the most accurate and compact of trills, and an absolutely dazzling display in the *da capo* section. There is no question about the quality of the modern revival when it produces singing like this.

It may be that at any time earlier in the century, Handelian singing of this mastery was to be had for the asking; certainly the record companies never asked for it, in that case. The 'coloraturas' of the pre-electrical era are impressive both in number and in accomplishment. But in this most testing field of eighteenth century baroque they are rarely to be found. And on their own ground, in early nineteenth century music, they tend to work within what by the standards of Sutherland, Sills, Horne and so many more are cautious boundaries. A particularly lovely record of Galli-Curci's, for example, is 'Come per me sereno' from *La Sonnambula*. To go back to it after playing Beverly Sills' version is to fall in love again with Galli's style and voice, so firmly placed and sweet in tone. But how tame her cadenza is by comparison. Not that Sills is showy; it is simply a satisfyingly affectionate and brilliant piece of decorative work gracing the conclusion of her solo. Taste and technique have developed fast in these recent years. The long-closed doors have been opened; the whorl and filigree of baroque glisten all around; and in these elegant chambers the artists are still at work.

25. America: The Seal Goes West
Leontyne Price Martina Arroyo
Shirley Verrett Grace Bumbry
Jon Vickers James McCracken
Richard Tucker Robert Merrill

OF the five singers written about at most length in the last chapter, three were American; so was a high proportion of the others; and so it looks like being in any discussion of singers or singing in the second half of the twentieth century. 'The keeper of the seal of Italian melody' was the title Verdi is said to have conferred on Puccini, as his successor; but singers as well as composers are needful guardians of that historic possession. In the nineteen-twenties it left its native land for a time, won by the more fluent and lyrical Germans and Austrians. In the sixties, like a good many European treasures, it appears to have crossed the Atlantic.

'A new Anglo-Saxon hegemony', one might like to say, claiming Britain's share of the credit, for British singers have certainly been doing much better on the international front than formerly. Anglo-Saxon is hardly the word, however, when one reflects that a very considerable part in the American achievement has been played by Negroes. The four women whose names now come forward most inevitably are all coloured: Price, Arroyo, Bumbry and Verrett. All have won high esteem in the opera houses of the world, and all are in urgent demand among the record companies. And of Leontyne Price·it might well be proposed that records show her as the best singer of Verdi among the sopranos of this century.

Yet, oddly, Price's most brilliant performance on records is probably not of any of Verdi's heroines, but of Bizet's anti-heroine. Carmen is a gift of a part for breaking the sound-barrier and giving the gramophone a built-in stage or screen. With a few other roles, like Otello, Boris, Grimes, Salome, Tosca perhaps, it is physical enough to prevent any singer from treating the recording studio as an oratorio platform. But the vividness depends on just how specific the singer is, and Price, more than anybody else in complete recorded performances of *Carmen* (though not perhaps more than Supervia and Horne in extracts) is always a particular woman singing a particular phrase at a particular moment. A contrast to this is the highly praised performance of Grace Bumbry; even Callas, when one comes to a point-by-point comparison, relies comparatively on a general strength of temperament leading up to a hair-raising death-scene, rather than on sharply focused insight and detail throughout. Victoria de los Angeles is always alive to detail, as well as being genuinely attractive and individual (not the vamp of the early films, a type nowadays extant only on the operatic stage and in this role); but it is hard to think of her drawing a knife on a fellow worker in the cigarette factory (she is too ladylike to work there in the first place), and the mixture of sultry moodiness and steely determination is not in her. It is exactly what is there in the Carmen of Leontyne Price.

Never was a surer, subtler, sexual expert than this one. At her entrance, paradoxically, the town-square wakes up from its sleepy midday routine, only to sink into a languor more intense (Karajan's slow tempi make the opening of the Act more cotton-nosed than usual, but the enervation is full of purpose). The Habanera is smoky, languid, exact, cool; the warning 'prends garde à toi' trembles sensually, and indeed the whole piece is an exercise in sexual control. Stronger still, the Séguédille. Again the quiet start, the smiling 'j'irai danser', the slight quiver of excitement which is a form of sympathetic magic: Carmen acts it that José may feel it. The confidence broadens into laughter: 'J'emmènerai mon amoureux', a fever to him, an amusement to her, and the laughter carries through into the next phrase. Best of all, the passage after José's Flower Song, where conductor and singer effect between them a particularly cruel enchantment. Using the last note of José's 'Je t'aime' for her own purposes, this Carmen moves in, catlike, towards her prey (something stealthy in the accompaniment well caught in the playing helps to enforce the effect): the reiteration of the single note is hypnotic and dangerous, and we see what she is up to as she slides, lithe and casual, into 'Là-bas dans la montagne'.

Like Schwarzkopf's recorded Marschallin (also under Karajan), this is a modern performance that is immensely rich in yield: at every point it has a life of its own, where the broad feeling for the character and music as a whole has led to a new, thorough and imaginative apprehension of its parts. Perhaps Karajan helped; perhaps, for Price, there was also something in the role that associated with the kind of realistic detailed life on the stage which she had known in *Porgy and Bess*, one of her early successes, and the opera in which London first heard her in 1952 (knowing that it was hearing something good though not quite foreseeing that she would turn up so superbly at Covent Garden six years later as Aida). The *Porgy and Bess* recordings are deeply felt and strongly characterised. And yet, curiously, in a fair number of Price's recordings, it is a certain absence of flexibility in characterisation that one notes. For example, we might have expected that the singer of whose Carmen Shakespeare might have said something about custom not staling its infinite variety, would have caught that quality in Cleopatra. Two scenes are recorded from Samuel Barber's *Antony and Cleopatra* (the work with which the new Metropolitan opened in September, 1966), and both are in many ways magnificently sung: the bold intervals, the sustaining power, the ring and vibrancy. But Cleopatra's 'Give me some music' wants so many changes of face and mood. Critics (and possibly Shakespeare from the cellarage) might inwardly add 'some other music', for the score cannot be said to express the text at all fully; but there must surely be some sense of sport and fun, some kind of smile, however nostalgic, however predatory, at 'Ah, ho! you're caught'. But the Carmen who smiles so tauntingly at her 'bel officier' does not characterise very vividly here. Or again, in a recording of the Final Scene from *Salome*, although there are vivid flashes (and the tone of mockery is certainly eloquent in this) much passes without effect. 'Ich hab'es gesagt', for instance, has little of the girl's hateful will in it. And when one turns the record to play the Awakening Scene from *Die Aegyptische Helene*, it is to admire a radiant soprano (of just the sort that Strauss loved and wrote for), but to hear very largely the same character singing.

Even so, the very existence of such recordings reminds us of the breadth of this singer's repertoire. So far, records have found her only occasionally outside opera, but there is a Schumann recital, with a tender *Frauenliebe und Leben* (but contrast the range of expression and the detail which Janet Baker brings to the last three songs); and a performance of that strange, difficult song 'Heiss mich nicht reden' wholly suggests the serious, idiomatic lieder singer she might become. Some Mozart concert arias, also, seem well enough until one makes comparisons: her K.505, 'Ch'io mi scordi di te', was unfortunate in being issued about the same time as a version by Schwarzkopf, who with Szell and Brendel to help, makes a much more meaningful thing of it. Price's runs tend to blur every now and again, and so her Mozart, always enjoyable, fails to give the final degree of satisfaction. Her Fiordiligi in *Così fan tutte*, for example, has many fine things about it: at its best probably in the duet 'Fra gli amplessi', and always alive, human and humorous throughout the recitatives. But the arias are a mixture of excellence and imperfection, and quite apart from the variable precision and evenness of the runs, her tone itself causes some misgivings. 'Come scoglio', sings Fiordiligi—'like a rock'. But not with that vibrato, one might object. 'Per pietà', she pleads, abasing herself in the lower half of the soprano range; but the smoky tone which has done good service for Carmen and Aida seems less well-suited to the clear lines and cool air of the eighteenth century.

Both of these features are part of the essential character of the voice, and one could not wish them to be otherwise without destroying the character: it is simply that they are more appropriate to some kinds of music than to others. It is also true that recording exaggerates their share in the voice-personality. At a recital in the Albert Hall in 1968, the programme included 'Io son l'umile ancilla' from *Adriana Lecouvreur* and the encores included a second performance of the aria, for it was exquisitely sung. But her recording, issued in 1967, has a somewhat breathy tone at the start, and although the singing is extremely beautiful, the vibrato attracts attention

107. Leontyne Price as Aida

108. Martina Arroyo

in a way that it never did in the live performance. This vibrato is of the quick kind, distinct from wobble, and not affecting pitch; it is the kind which in fact does much to give a healthy voice its dramatic quality, a sort of glamour, as it did with, say, Meta Seinemeyer and Hina Spani. But it suits our ideas of some roles and not of others: Verdi's Leonoras, for instance, but not his Violetta; Puccini's Tosca, but not Butterfly. Price is a *towering* Butterfly: the last section of 'Un bel dì' is an immense statement of faith, the soaring music of the death scene a cry of almost classical nobility. She has some wonderfully tender moments in the love music, but when she remembers her fifteen years and affects a pretty childish tone it is too remote from her own voice-character to convince, and when we hear her coming up the hill in Act I we expect to see Aida.

109. Shirley Verrett

And indeed the crowning glory of Price's singing is her Verdi, and especially her Aida. The *Trovatore* Leonora, culminating in the aria 'D'amor sull' ali rosee', is another of her great roles, and as it has been recorded twice over a span of eight years (1962–1970), it is useful for seeing how she has developed in this period of international fame. The Act IV aria just mentioned is sung with the same basic conception, but with a surer art in the later version, more refinement of phrasing, and a greater depth of feeling. Whether the engineers have caught her voice more faithfully, whether it has settled down over the years, or whether conscious control has made the difference, the tone is certainly deeper and finer, the vibrato less edgy. Certain technical points have been improved: she is smoother in the group of notes on the word 'memorie', and is exact in the first notes of the cadenza which were only approximate before. She has rethought the phrasing at its most important point: the obvious, symmetrical phrasing of the passage with the high C is loosened and made more interesting by the phrasing over in the second recording. She has also introduced a join to the word 'ma' which leads into this passage. Finally, time has brought a deepening of feeling: in the recitative, the words 'tu non sai' have an imaginative depth (she thinks of her imprisoned lover unaware that she is so near him), the 'pietosa' lingers more exquisitely, and in the aria itself there is more affection in the great phrases of 'le pene'. The signs are of an artist in love with her music.

But if ever music made love to its performer, it is Aida's to Leontyne Price. The shine of her voice and its smokiness have something exotic and distinctive to the right degree; her ability to ring out clearly above a great mass of sound is complemented by the control which enables her to float high notes softly and sweetly. One could pick individual moments: the solo bar in the Triumphal Scene where Aida's voice is heard unaccompanied (the sound now recognisably that of a Negress, making, as she does of the cadenzas in *Un Ballo in Maschera*, unusually expressive cries of affliction); the beautifully broad phrase at the climax of 'O patria mia' with its soft top C; the dark seductiveness and floating tones of 'Là tra foreste vergine'; the monotoned pleading to Amonasro.[1] Here and there in Price's Aida is something less than the ideal; the possibility of anything nearer to it seems remote.

If the Aida of Martina Arroyo is ever recorded, however, it also ought to approach the ideal; for at the time of writing she appears to be the other great lyric-dramatic soprano before the public, and she too has made a notable impression in that opera. 'Ought to' but possibly might not, because as with Price, recording catches a vibrato, a slightly slower one, and the gramophone has not yet properly captured the intensely dramatic feeling which this voice creates in the theatre. Even so, if she were to record nothing more than she has done up to the present, she would still have earned an honourable place among her contemporaries.

Or indeed, among the century's singers. Her Leonora in *La Forza del Destino* will help to place her. Most comparable singers have recorded the aria 'Pace, pace, mio dio' from Act IV, and it is interesting to play a

---

[1] References here are to Price's first recorded Aida, issued 1962, conducted by Solti. Her second (Leinsdorf, 1971) is not better sung though the dramatisation has gained in vividness.

selection of them, going back from Arroyo as the most recent, through Price, Tebaldi and Callas, to Rethberg, Ponselle, Giannini and Muzio, Raisa and Boninsegna. The first impression is that it is one of those arias in which everybody sings well. Rethberg's is a very routine performance, pleasing neither as sound nor as an interpretation (it is one of the broadcast items privately recorded), but all the others are remarkable in one way or another. Yet of course there are differences of quality even among such distinguished singers as these. The differences begin with the first note. The word 'pace' is written with crescendo and decrescendo marks on the first syllable. Some of these singers do nothing: Raisa, Muzio and Giannini simply hold the note; Rethberg does next to nothing; Boninsegna does a little (this is the HMV recording); Tebaldi makes little of the crescendo but then softens effectively. That leaves four who do more or less as they should; one is Arroyo, the others are Price, Callas, Ponselle. What then has to be said is that Ponselle is very much the best at it: not only is her range of sound the greatest and the most effective, but the process of growth and diminution is absolutely gradual and firm-toned. With Price one can hear it, as it were, in stages while Arroyo is really effective only on the crescendo and Callas is unsteady in tone. This shading and shaping of the first note points to the nature of the solo; it has many expression marks in the score, and it wants a supple-toned performance. Three of the nine singers do not do this: Rethberg, Raisa and Giannini (but the last two sing with great beauty of tone in their contrasted ways). One point where the marked *diminuendo* can make magic is on the G flat on the word 'duol'. Of the nine singers only Leontyne Price makes magic by following the score; Ponselle, Tebaldi and Callas do it by inserting an 'Ah'; the others more or less pass it by. The greatest single challenge of the aria is no doubt the octave leap to the soft high B flat in 'Invan la pace', and all of these sopranos manage it: Callas is the least successful, for she does not take the note cleanly or very softly and it soon develops an unpleasant beat; Rethberg and Muzio come down from it rather soon; Ponselle and Price are not as soft as one had hoped they would be; Arroyo, Tebaldi and Giannini take the note softly and then crescendo on it; Raisa and Boninsegna have a pure, steady, genuine pianissimo note, and are very much the best. There is also a fortissimo high B flat and a lot of tense drama in the solo. Callas' incomparable tragic intensity throughout, and Muzio's personal touch in the cries of 'fatalità', Giannini's rhythmic drive in the *agitatissimo* bar, Ponselle's strong accentuation of the 'maledizion's, Boninsegna's unique distinction of actually singing what is written in the last bars: all of these stay in the memory, though probably none more than Arroyo's saddened tone at 'profondo il mio sospir' and her vividly acted change of mood at the start of the final section. In all respects—beauty of voice, technical control, musical and dramatic feeling—she belongs to the tradition; though (final detail) it is *not* in the tradition to aspirate little groups of notes as in 'l'immagin sua saprò'.

Distinguishing her among all these singers is a nobility of timbre, rather deeper toned than Price, stronger in the lower middle register, and the sheer opulence of it. The great solo starting 'Son giunta' and going on to the aria 'Madre, pietosa vergine' has the breadth and intensity of true Verdi singing. The final trio (with ineffaceable memories of Ponselle) has them also, and a beautifully floated *dolcissimo* at 'io ti prometto'. All of which should bode well for the *Requiem* and especially the 'Libera me'. This is urgent singing, and in every way it makes a strong contrast with Caballé's performance, which is often preferable, the tone smooth, rich and even as cream, the mood more serene. Yet Arroyo is fine, catching a note of lamentation in the 'Requiem Aeternam' (helped by a chorus which does more than provide a cushion for the soloist), and remaining in full control through the various technical crises of the work.

The technique is severely tested in two other major recordings: a *Don Giovanni* in which she sings Donna Elvira, and the Sutherland–Bonynge *Les Huguenots*, where Arroyo is the Valentine. The Meyerbeer finds her in superb voice, glorious in the great span of melody in the duet with Raoul, and in the sustained high C's of the duet with Marcel. Her aria 'Parmi les pleurs' is tenderly sung, and excels in the clarity of its triplets and the florid work of the second part. In the Mozart, some parts of the Masks Trio and of 'Mi tradì' want polish, but one is always grateful for the warm, strong, shining sound. Her solo in the finale, darkly shaded and dignified, leaves us with the awareness of a distinguished artist and a voice of rare beauty.

When Arroyo arrived at the finalists' auditions for the Metropolitan in 1958 she found herself in company with a remarkable mezzo-soprano, who was also an exact contemporary. Grace Bumbry, born in 1937, was to gain an international reputation very quickly, for her performances as Venus in the 1961 Bayreuth *Tannhäuser* were a triumph. Arroyo's first triumph in one of the great opera houses was at the Metropolitan in 1965, and it may not have been at all a bad thing that she had to wait those few years longer. The *Tannhäuser* of the following season, 1962, was recorded from the stage at Bayreuth, and there is no mistaking the opulence, power and energy of the Venus. But there are also some features that become disquieting in view of the singer's youth—notably that, though gloriously firm when singing very loudly (which is most of the time), she becomes somewhat unsteady at a mezzo forte. Again, no doubt recording exaggerates; it is doubtful if anything of that kind was troublesome 'in the flesh'. And indeed there is plenty to enjoy on the record: not only the ample, resonant tone, but also the velvet of the seductive 'Geliebter komm'; not only the athletic cleanness of the intervals, but also the enthusiasm and drive of the young singer. But what a part for a girl in her early twenties; and if it comes to that, what a part for a mezzo of whatever age.

But a high *tessitura* has never appeared to alarm Grace Bumbry. At her best as Amneris in *Aida* (every bit the proud 'figlia de' Faraoni'), sailing up, as one hears on the records, to luxuriate in the high Gs, A's and B flats, she has more recently added Salome to her stage repertoire and has even recorded a recital of soprano arias, complete with 'Casta diva'. In these, the fioriture are clear and well-practised, and the high-notes full-bodied and unforced. Among the excerpts is an account of Lady Macbeth's invocation in Act I, magnificent in power, grandeur and stamina.

Unfortunately, records also suggest penalties: at any rate, the glorious voice does not always give the satisfaction it should. Even in the early *Messiah* recording under Boult there was a certain want of firmness and focus (compare, for instance, Sinclair under Beecham). But the excerpts from Gluck's *Orfeo ed Euridice*, made only seven years later, are really quite spoilt by the unsteadiness of tone. It is a great pity, for Bumbry might have been an ideal Orfeo. Reviewing *Orfeo* (with another singer) at Covent Garden, Philip Hope-Wallace remarked that the role needed so much more than a pleasant voice and a tasteful musicianship—it wanted 'a contralto Boris'. Bumbry might well have been in the line of Clara Butt and Kathleen Ferrier to give the part its due stature. A point in the score where she does provide exactly this grandeur of voice and character is the cry 'Barbari numi' and the passage following. Feeling and dramatic vividness are also there, though in a rather generalised form. But it is in only a few passages that the unsteadiness does not intrude to spoil the pleasure of listening.

Her special study of German song might have led to an interpretative strength which would be sufficient compensation, but only occasionally do records show this to be so. An early recital contained two of the most demanding of Schubert's Lieder, 'Die junge Nonne' and 'Der Doppelgänger', the former without its necessary urgency of narrative or darkening at 'Und finster die Brust, wie das Grab' or contrast of outer turbulence and inner peace, the latter well-controlled but without any suggestion of a shudder or a sense of anguish as the scene is set, or of pain in the great climaxes. Perhaps it is too much to ask of a young singer that she should do this, and so one turns to other kinds of song in a later recital. Brahms' 'An eine Äolsharfe' finds her lightening her voice, and there is also a darker tone of lament lying in reserve. But remembering that there exists a record of this by Elisabeth Schumann, one looks it out, and oh what a difference: the 'luftgebornen Muse' takes possession, the breeze, the scent of the rose, the nostalgia and the secrecy enter the song, the sadly affectionate exclamation in 'Ach! von der Knaben', the dying away ('hinsterbend wieder'), all become real. Brahms' little folk-song 'Trennung' ('Dort unten im Tale'), which brings out some affection and vividness in Bumbry, only confirms the judgment. Again, one senses that there is more in the song than she is giving us, pleasantly as she sings; and of course there on the shelf is a record by Irmgard Seefried who, taking a faster tempo and apparently being more casual about it at first, leaves one in real possession of the song because she is imaginatively *addressing* it to someone, and with

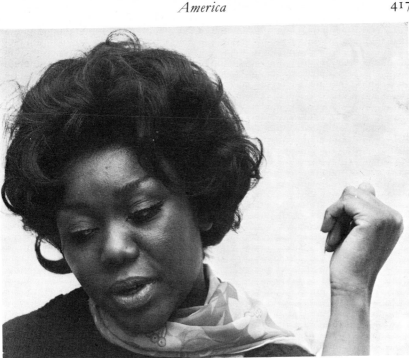

110. Grace Bumbry

the simplest but rightest of touches can make her listener quite unexpectedly find himself moist about the eyes and unwilling to let the song go without a repetition.

In a third recital record, issued in 1967, something of this sense of touch has entered Bumbry's singing, notably in an utterly charming performance of Schumann's 'Der Sandmann'. She is clearly aware of the possibilities of colouring the voice, for here it is essentially the lightest of soprano tones that she is using. Not only is the sound delightful but the song is vividly characterised. Maybe the future will bring a satisfying development here.

Up to the present, her most enduring contribution[1] to the record library is probably her singing of the Princess Eboli in Solti's *Don Carlo*. Others would probably give pride of place to her Carmen; but though there is some gorgeous tone in the Card Scene and some drama in the Finale, her characterisation has little zest, danger, sex, charm at so many vital points in the opera, and the singing itself (sketchy semiquavers in the Gypsy Song for instance) can hardly, one would think, satisfy the normally rather fastidious standards of some of the critics who have spoken warmly of it. Her Eboli, on the other hand, does capture something of the distinction

---

[1] At the end of 1971 there also appeared a new *Aida*, with Bumbry's Amneris newly impressive, particularly fine in the Trial Scene, on the breathless interjections and the broad lamenting phrases of its climax.

which is hers on the stage. Sumptuous in voice, the richness, size and range of it ideally suited to the great solo 'O don fatale', she establishes herself as a real character in the Moorish song, and is inspired to give of her very best in the Garden Scene. The impulsive, emotional confession to the Queen is warm in spirit and superb in voice: eloquent testimony to the rich satisfaction which this singer has given to so many audiences in these early years of an already spectacular career.

Happier in her recording career, however, has been the fourth of these singers, Shirley Verrett. Her voice and its production contrast with Bumbry in ways that certainly favour the recording studios. Less rich, it is precise and firm; less opulent in volume, it is directed with a sharp sense of dramatic immediacy and intensity, so that it draws the listener towards it and establishes power of a different kind. She also offers a wide range of musical interests, a scrupulous attention to detail, and a virtuoso's brilliance of execution. She is to quite a remarkable extent the complete singer, and her work for the gramophone has kept pace with her attainments in the opera house and concert hall.

It is in a live concert that she has been caught most completely for the gramophone. The recital she gave at Carnegie Hall on 30 January 1965, has been recorded and is valuable and delightful as it shows the singer communicating. Schubert's 'An die Musik', which opens the programme, is especially interesting because its style comes so much closer to the Gerhardt-Nikisch record of 1911 than would have seemed possible nowadays: the affectionate moulding of phrases involves both *portamento* and *rubato*, the two features which have so largely diminished in Lieder singing as the century has progressed. The effect may surprise modern listeners, but it is entirely musical; and one feels (though in the absence of a studio performance of more or less the same date it is impossible to prove) that the freedom of a live performance may have contributed, and more especially the fact of an audience there to be made responsive, to be drawn into the music. Whatever the truth about that, it is quite clear that the audience is held, and that by the second half of the programme, made up of traditional songs and spirituals, it is one with the singer as audiences used to be in the recitals of Marian Anderson. Verrett's rhythmic sense, the uninhibited projection (always singing *to* people), the fun (as in the spiritual called 'Witness', asking for every trick in the book, including a big Samson-voice, and all to come as if by nature), the ability to convey sad and tender emotions without sentimentality (as in 'He's goin' away'—magical, this one, in its loving, time-taking treatment of a simple tune): these are all needed to work the particular spell, and the needs are wonderfully well met.

Without this recital, a listener to gramophone records might not guess that Verrett can be such a warm singer. She is resolutely unsentimental and her voice is not lush. Dalila's 'Mon coeur s'ouvre à ta voix' has probably never been recorded with less suggestion of port wine and red velvet;

and, with the absence of yodeling, lifting, drooping and embosoming, it has probably never been more enjoyable as a piece of music. Sometimes this brings its limitations. In another grandly and rather beautifully old-style piece of French opera, 'O ma lyre immortelle' from Gounod's *Sapho*, it is the enveloping warmth of Mother Schumann-Heink that one remembers in lines like 'Seul le trépas peut finir ma douleur' or 'Je vais dormir pour toujours dans la mer' rather than Verrett's milder tastefulness. Just as, in a very different field, Montsalvatge's lullaby ('Cancion de cuna para dormir a un negrito') still wants the richer, more maternal voice of Victoria de los Angeles, in spite of the beautifully poised pianissimo and the shaping of the melody which Verrett generously provides.

But this relative austerity of tone and taste has its advantages too. In Spanish songs it brings a folk-like purity, sufficiently remote from suggestions of the cultivated *Liederabend*; in Russian music it has the kind of shine and definition which enable it to capture melancholy without mawkishness. More important perhaps, it has a classical straightness which helps her to sound something like the ideal Orfeo in Gluck's opera: not 'a contralto Boris', true, but firmly masculine, making so much more emotional effect than her contemporaries in the role because of the absolute first-principle avoidance of 'spread', and because of a strong intellect and personality, the one understanding every change of mood, the other working for a vivid, and sometimes electrifying, projection of the emotions.

This vividness is beginning to add a final distinction to her performances in Italian opera. Comparing her recording of Eboli's part in *Don Carlo* with Grace Bumbry's, one finds a more specific reading, and (fine as Bumbry is in this) ultimately a more memorable one. In the many impressive versions of 'O don fatale', from Fremstad to Callas, hers is the first I have found to fix on 'Un dì mi resta' as a key-phrase, leading from the agitation of 'O ciel, è Carlo' to the exaltation of the final section. This, and many other moments in the role, leap out of the canvas into real life through Verrett's treatment. Not that comparisons always work in her favour like this: for example, in the *Semiramide* duet, Marilyn Horne is stronger in tone, rhythm and sense of direction than Verrett is in her recording with Caballé. But that music serves also to illustrate Verrett's virtuosity—even, brilliant scale-work, and a wide range, all in prime condition. Occasionally she forces her lower notes (the Carnegie Hall recital shows a certain recklessness in this, and consequently a tone which is not properly homogeneous, in Schubert's 'Die Allmacht'). But in general, technique matches musical feeling, and both are delightfully and intelligently directed.

Verrett, Bumbry, Arroyo, Price, Sills, Moffo, Horne: it has been a remarkable decade that has produced such an array of women singers. The list could be increased. Felicia Weathers (another Negress, sensitive in such operatic music as the Aida solos and in some of the lesser-known songs of Richard Strauss, like 'Wie sollten wir geheim sie halten' and 'Ich trage meine Minne'), Lucine Amara (wanting depth and spirituality in Verdi's *Requiem* and in *Lohengrin*, but a splendid Musetta in Beecham's *La Bohème*), Claire Watson (a musical Donna Anna in Klemperer's *Don Giovanni* and a sympathetic Ellen Orford in *Peter Grimes*), Evelyn Lear (an outstandingly able musician whose performances are discussed in chap. 29), Rosalind Elias (a firm and beautiful voice, heard at its best in a recording of *Werther*, or as a Cherubino without quite that extra touch of charm that one would like in Leinsdorf's *Le Nozze di Figaro*): these are some of the others, all of them considerable artists.

Then there is the remarkable Teresa Stich-Randall, now thought of as a European singer by adoption, but born in West Hartford, USA, and known first to the record-buying public as the exquisite Nannetta of Toscanini's *Falstaff*. Her flute-like tones are heard, pure and well-nourished in the manner of Lemnitz (and with flute obbligato to match), in one of Bach's Italian cantatas ('Non sa che sia dolore', number 209); and with it is an air of authority, an aristocratic style, and a kind of glamour, that sometimes suggest an artist of the stature of a Schwarzkopf. In company with Schwarzkopf and Christa Ludwig, she contributes to Karajan's great *Rosenkavalier* recording: a Sophie the sound of whom makes us see with Octavian's eyes, a dream of radiance and young beauty. One thinks of Schwarzkopf in connection with Stich-Randall also because of the sophistication of her art. This has brought its disadvantages too, especially for recording. Draining the voice of its harmonics and expressiveness will sometimes produce a sense of flattening and a strangely hollow tone. It can be heard in her singing of the Oechalian princess Iole in Handel's *Hercules*; and also inescapable in that recording is the habit of aspirating the runs and separating the notes with a little growth or push on them. But the performance has presence: the individuality of character and the loveliness of sound make each reappearance welcome. Her feeling for characterisation is also strong, making hers the most vivid of Euridices. 'Non m'abbracci? non parli?' she asks, with the prettiest femininity; and her appeal, growing from a winsome kind of pouting to the full-bodied reproach of 'senza un addio', is very properly irresistible.

The Orfeo of this recording is the excellent Canadian contralto, Maureen Forrester. Somewhere between the strong, masculine interpretation of Shirley Verrett and the rich, bosomy singing of Marilyn Horne, she creates a noble, sympathetic Orfeo, classical in that it never runs into extremes (there is no desperation in the misery, no ecstasy in the joy), yet alive in feeling and always pleasing to the ear. This is a humane, beneficent voice, and the spirit seems to match, so that Mahler's 'Urlicht' finds in her a most beautiful interpreter. She catches the solemn mood of the opening, sings to perfection the long phrase 'Je lieber möcht' ich im Himmel sein', and also conveys some passion in the melting beauty of the tone. Passion and other extreme emotions do not come readily within her emotional range; that is probably her major limitation. Never inexpressive (she is, for instance, a great deal more vivid as Cornelia in *Giulio Cesare* than her counterpart, the gifted Julia Hamari, in Karl Richter's version), she is nevertheless somewhat bound by decorum. Her singing of Dejanira in *Hercules* is marred only by this: the taunting aria 'Resign thy club and lion's spoils' is too mild, and the great final scene is really too ladylike, not bitter or intense, though dramatised well enough in a general way. Otherwise her performance is a genuine *tour de force*, coping well with the fearsome runs and displaying a *whole* voice, no breaks in its evenness, a good, strong, well-rounded sound.

'What more can one ask?' is a question that also arises while listening to the recordings of Eileen Farrell. That there *is* something else, some mysterious quality of voice or character, becomes apparent in a comparison of her singing of Cherubini's Medea with Callas'. Callas' enunciation of 'Numi, venite a me', her way of breathing emotion in 'Oh cari figli', her vivid change of face at 'Si, vostra padre' (and so the list could continue indefinitely): all are superb, and few find a comparable quality in Farrell. Yet she still gives a splendid performance: by no means pedestrian in style, and powerful in voice. In certain records she even achieves a Callas-like intensity. Two come to mind: Magda's desperate solo in Act II of *The Consul* where Farrell makes the voice act with an intensity that becomes immense, and Turandot's 'In questa reggia', where the usual gorgon is displaced by a much more interesting mystic—she is in love with that martyred Principessa Luo-Ling, 'dolce e serena', and her voice catches the mood suggested by the timeless movement of parallel chords in the orchestra. She is a genuine artist, and one who in her Puccini recital (like Callas in hers) has a new face and feeling for each character. The generous size of the voice is apparent in her recording of Brünnhilde's Immolation Scene, as is her ability to soften and sweeten it. The touch of greatness in Farrell is sufficient to make one wonder why the evident goodness was not more extensively recorded and still more widely acclaimed.

With Farrell, a dozen or so years older than the singers previously discussed, we are on the way back to look at American singing in the forties and fifties. Coming up for debut at the Metropolitan were such artists as Steber, Kirsten, Stevens, Thebom, Resnik and Merriman, with Tucker, Peerce, Warren, Merrill, Harrell and Hines among the men. The first four of these appear in the last chapter of Part Two, though they continued to make records well after the demise of the 78. Nan Merriman and Regina Resnik have both had careers which have taken them further into 'the age of LP' and which have concerned some important recordings. Merriman sang, for example, in two versions of Mahler's *Das Lied von der Erde*, gave rich and idiomatic performances in French and Spanish song (brilliantly effective in a song by Turina called 'La Giralda'), and has a particular association for most English listeners with the role of Dorabella in *Così fan tutte*, where the vibrato may be too noticeable for some ears but where the buoyancy and freshness are as charming as in her stage appearances.

Resnik too has strong associations with certain roles through her stage appearances: she was the best Ulrica in this writer's memory (the 1971 recording came several years too late to do justice to the memory) and for long was the most genial of Mistress Quicklies (well preserved in the Bernstein recording). Her Carmen appeared in 1963, richly creamy in tone, a committed contralto sound, a little matronly perhaps, though helping to give tragic weight in the later scenes. She is probably most memorable in Act II ('Au quartier? pour l'appel?'): exceptionally strong here, though aurally very much the old she-dragon, making one wonder more than usual what Don José liked so much about her. We are also aware of the voice registers beginning to split apart, and of a tendency to spread unsteadily, as she does rather badly in Brangäne's Warning early in Act II of *Tristan und Isolde*. This is a fine voice, all the same, and an ever-reliable singer, who could turn to Britten (she was the Metropolitan's first Ellen Orford), to Johann Strauss (Rosalinda in a generally intolerable American *Fledermaus*), Wagner, Verdi, Richard Strauss (a strong Klytemnestra to Nilsson's Elektra) and most of the standard operatic repertoire. No doubt the early exploitation of such natural richness has something to answer for. She began her career as a soprano, and we read in Kolodin's *Story of the Metropolitan Opera* how the Leonora of *Trovatore* was followed by that of *Fidelio* in 1945, and how the 'large and luminous voice' acquired 'a quaver rarely absent thereafter' (p. 529).

But this was not a good time for American singing if we are to believe either Kolodin or the evidence of our own ears. Youngsters were rushed into great roles (Donna Anna for the debut of Florence Kirk), and reliable singers were mercilessly overused (Norman Cordon singing Varlaam, Colline, Hunding, Pogner, King Henry, Basilio, Lothario, the Bonze, Angelotti, Sparafucile and Monterone among other parts in one season). Such overuse did no good, either, to the major talents of Jerome Hines and Leonard Warren. Kolodin writes (p. 557) that 'a good technique and a strong back preserved Hines from permanent damage'. But records tell another tale, for the fine voice heard as late as 1959 in Leinsdorf's *Macbeth* had deteriorated by mid-sixties into the sound heard in the same conductor's *Lohengrin*. Nor are gramophone records likely to inspire quite the same enthusiasm for Leonard Warren as Kolodin (and a very large public) had for this artist in his lifetime. There is certainly much to admire, and it is quite clear why he should have been such an asset to the company, with an exceptionally ample, powerful voice, resonant and penetrating, and rejoicing in the high *tessitura* of the great baritone roles in Verdi. He can tone it down, and in lyrical passages his legato is often exemplary: 'Alla vita' in *Un Ballo in Maschera* and 'Urna fatale' in *La Forza del Destino* are both excellent pieces of singing. But that last solo is followed by an excited recitative, where the voice loses focus, and, as the scene continues with the very demanding 'Egli è salvo', we feel the other limitation, that no tension or inner excitement communicates itself. Both of these feelings are evoked

by his Macbeth, which should have been a great recording. At his best in
the last scene, he is generally unsteady, and though he finds a suitable voice
for the 'sights', his vocal-acting is rarely imaginative. The nature of his
career in recording might very largely have been foretold from what were
probably his first (if unofficial) records. In the Metropolitan performance
of *Simon Boccanegra* recorded privately in 1939 and discussed in earlier
sections, he played Paolo Albani. The other men were Martinelli, Tibbett
and Pinza, none of them light-weights, yet Warren appears to have had
quite the most powerful voice among them. But no one listening to the
records and comparing the lower voices would be likely to think that this
was a young man in his twenties at the start of his career, in company with
two much older men well on towards the end of theirs. For their notes are
sharply focused and the vibration of their voices is even: with Warren the
impression is not so.

The recording angel, like time itself, has been kinder to Robert Merrill.
Some eight years younger than Warren, Merrill shared much the same
repertoire, and after Warren's tragic death on stage at the Metropolitan in
1960, he became more or less indisputably America's principal baritone
and perhaps the best lyricist since de Luca. The easy and even production
of a beautifully well-rounded tone is not common, especially when the
voice is also a powerful one; yet this is, after all, the basis of operatic
singing, and Merrill's records will always commend themselves in these
terms. On the other hand, the repertoire and the interpretations are as
'central' as the voice itself. His records are not stamped with the sort of
individuality that lodges immediately in a listener's memory; they are
simply the work of a very good opera singer and a source of unfailing
pleasure to the ear.

Let us take him first at a point some way off-centre. The dark tones,
snarling manner and thrusting edge that generally go with heavy operatic
villains are not his by nature or easy adoption, nor is the declamatory
style appropriate to 'O monumento' from *La Gioconda* where Barnaba is
found in cynical soliloquy. Even so, as one lines up the comparisons, he
emerges well. Taking five other baritones (Cappuccilli and Warren as two
who have recorded the complete opera, Carlo Morelli from a live Metropolitan performance of 1939, Ruffo and de Luca from earlier times), we
find only Ruffo to be a consistently more intense and dramatic interpreter.
Cappuccilli, in his early years and in good voice, sings with little expression;
Morelli, also sounding well, is unsubtle in declamation; so is de Luca,
whose scrupulous placing and virile tone are still superb. Warren is unsteady, but enunciates effectively and produces a genuine piano for the words
'la spia' as well as a big voice for the great phrase 'sovra la Signoria'.
Merrill's tone is powerful, steady and resonant, and he characterises well,
brooding over the corrupt city of Venice with some bitterness and fine
open vowels. Ruffo is better at seizing on the 'Signoria' phrase as the
moment of inspiration and maintaining greater intensity through the last

section. But, of course, in all this, one hears so clearly in one's head another voice pouring its scorn on that old skeleton, the Doge: search in the catalogues, however, fails to discover any recording by Tito Gobbi.

So often, through the fifties and sixties, as operatic sets were published with one or the other of these two as the principal baritone, it seemed to be assumed that some sort of antithesis prevailed—'Merrill for singing, Gobbi for character'. Put like that, the formula is unjust to both. Gobbi's voice was one of the most beautiful in memory, and Merrill sings with feeling and expression. He can snarl Iago's 'vile son nato' with the nastiest of them, and his way with the end of the credo is particularly effective (in the 1963 recording)—drawing out the question 'e poi?' long and soft, almost lovingly, and then quietly dropping the answer 'nulla', deadly and final, like the insertion of the stiletto's point. He can rap out his scorn of the 'cortigiani schernitori' in *Rigoletto*, and can command pathos in the way that de Luca could, without being abject, in 'Ebben, io piango'. He can make an appealing and convincingly tormented Michele in *Il Tabarro*. But there the unfair formula comes back in sight, for one knows that this Michele is not the one which has lodged in the mind, just as, coming back to Rigoletto and his monologue, one knows that, though scorn for the courtiers is caught, much else is missed, including that kind of haunted, oppressed tone that must colour the repeated phrase 'Quel vecchio maledivami', essential to the feeling of the opera as a whole.

Basically we go to Merrill to hear in this later age a reliably beautiful baritone. To hear, for example, as in the baritones of old, a performance of 'Vision fugitive' from Massenet's *Hérodiade* where all notes from the very soft to the very loud are produced without the spread of laxity or pressure, where the phrases are well-bound and the second verse is joined beautifully in the tradition of Renaud, de Gogorza and the others who used to make a lovely thing of it. Or to hear 'Eri tu' with a genuine legato, the continuation in our time of an art recognisably related to that of de Luca. It is remarkable also how consistent his singing seems to have been. Recordings from the stage of the Metropolitan (such as some extracts from the *Don Carlo* of 1950, with Björling at his most inspired) suggest that he may have resorted to a slightly more dramatic and declamatory style in the theatre, but the difference is very slight. Recordings made over a span of twenty years show the voice and style changing little. Only rarely do we come upon points like that in *Rigoletto* where in one recording (under Perlea in 1958) he leads excitingly into 'Sì, vendetta' from the previous phrase, while in a later one (Solti, 1965) it is separated and less dramatic. If we compare him in three complete recordings of *La Traviata*, the first made under Toscanini on 78s, the next with the outstanding Violetta of Anna Moffo in 1961, and then two years later with Sutherland, we find little alteration. The voice is that bit fresher in the first recording, that is all: and we notice how both in this and in *Un Ballo in Maschera* Toscanini seems unusually willing to allow this firm young singer the

111. Robert Merrill

freedom he needs to shape his phrases (in the 'Eri tu' he even allows Merrill to pull back slightly on the tempo, as he obviously wants to—Toscanini is for once genuinely accompanying). Probably, on balance, the best *Traviata* is the second, the one with Moffo, where there is just a shade more feeling, grace and ease. But in all of them we have the nearest thing to *bel canto* in baritones that the post-war world has yet produced.

At one time it looked as though this is a distinction Merrill might have shared with Cornell MacNeil. He too sings a lyrical, warm-toned 'Eri tu', and excels in some of Verdi's father-and-daughter duets, notably in the third Act of *Luisa Miller* with Anna Moffo again on top form. But turning to the most famous of these combinations, in *Rigoletto*, we become aware of a less sturdy singer than he had once seemed to be. He has recorded two performances, one with Sutherland, issued in 1962, the other, in 1968, with Reri Grist. Between the two has come a deterioration of voice, show-ing itself for example in the duets of the second scene. In the first version his 'Deh, non parlar' was quiet and smooth, a good piece of singing; in the second it has lost its poise and the voice has gained a beat. One feels aware of the high *tessitura* of the role, and the sense of discomfort grows during 'Ah, veglia o donna'. To some extent the singing fits the characterisation, which is of a tired Rigoletto, weighed with a sense of suffering pre-ordained. Yet there is not really enough character in the voice itself to leave a strong dramatic impression. Going back ten years, to *La Fanciulla del West*, the recording in which many will have heard him first, an excellent, full-bodied voice and an effective interpreter are to be saluted: for a time, when

he, Warren and Merrill were all singing and recording the principal baritone roles in Italian opera, America seemed to have cornered the major
part of a traditionally Italian market.

Not until the sixties was there a serious take-over-bid for the tenor area,
though the post-war years brought a prominent position to four: the
Canadian Léopold Simoneau (see pp. 435–6), Eugene Conley (an alternately ringing and throaty Faust, and the strong but rather stiff protagonist
in the first recording of *The Rake's Progress*), Jan Peerce, and his brother-in-
law Richard Tucker. Peerce sings in several of Toscanini's opera recordings,
perhaps most happily in *La Bohème*, where the maestro seems to have been
in a good mood, singing Colline's entrance music and the bars before
'Che gelida manina', giving a fine old bellow in the 'castelli in aria', and
another some octaves below during the high C (which is a good one).
In *Fidelio*, Peerce and Bampton cope well and at top speed with 'O namenlose
Freude'; in *La Traviata* everybody seems to have relaxed sufficiently to
give a moving performance only in the very last pages; in *Un Ballo in
Maschera* we spend most of our time listening to the orchestra and marvelling at the energy and precision. In all these, Peerce gives intense, devoted
performances, but on the whole the records are unloveable marvels. In
other, more run-of-the-mill, opera recordings, he is musical, well
focused, a little nasal, a little lacking in variety. He has the distinction of
making Bacchus' music in *Ariadne auf Naxos* sound reasonably graceful
and unforced; and he survived impressively, as we hear in a recital issued
when he was well into the fifties and which contains a creditably fervent
account of Lenski's aria in *Eugen Onegin*—in Russian.

Tucker also sang in one of the Toscanini operas. This is the *Aida*,
broadcast in 1949, and from the start there is no mistaking the authority
of its Radamès. The fine voice and legato become doubly effective when
there is such strong feeling for time and rhythm. The dotted notes of the
recitative introducing 'Celeste Aida' show the warrior-hero keen for
action, just as in *Madama Butterfly* he gives his Pinkerton a brag-and-bounce
jauntiness by emphasising the dotted rhythm of his explanation about
marrying 'in the Japanese fashion'. The Toscanini *Aida* also shows him as
a tenor who can sing softly when he wants to, and one who has a way of
making you listen to him. A later *Aida*, with Callas and conducted by
Serafin, is similar except in its beginning and ending. Toscanini used what
he said were Verdi's directions for singing the last phrase of 'Celeste Aida'
if a soft B flat, as marked in the score, were not available; the tenor was to
take the high B flat loudly if he had to, and then come down an octave,
repeating the last words quietly on the middle B flat. Tucker does this to
pleasant effect, but in the later recording gives vent to the customary
fortissimo. The last scene of the later recording, by contrast, contains some
particularly fine soft singing. In the solo 'Morir, si pura e bella' he uses a
head-voice, rare with him, and, within the context of a true legato, he
observes all the markings, giving a finely studied performance.

112. Richard Tucker

More of the kind would be welcome. Tucker's singing is passionate, commanding, alive, intelligent, firm, resonant and rhythmical, but it is not often charming or tender. Perhaps some would say the same of Caruso and Martinelli: but no, for if one puts Tucker's singing of 'Ah, sì ben mio, 'Apri la tua finestra' and 'Donna non vidi mai' (they occur consecutively in a recital record) against theirs, one finds something almost fierce and unyielding in his style that makes it less engaging. On the same record he sings 'Un dì all'azzurro spazio' from *Andrea Chénier*, and again the Italians come to mind. Tucker's performance has all the virtues listed above, yet even here something limits his success. Caruso, Gigli and more recently di Stefano give wonderfully lyrical performances where Martinelli's is fiery and intense, but Tucker gives out so much *sforzando* or *marcato* that the manner ceases to be effective. Turn from this to his singing of the duets in *La Traviata* ('Un dì felice' and 'Parigi, o cara') and one again finds much to admire, including a genuine legato and an observance of expression marks, yet some final gift or art of elegance is lacking, if one has a Schipa or McCormack in mind. The quieter, lyrical passages of the repertoire want poise, while the loud passionate singing wants the tension induced by restraint.

That he himself may have been critically aware of the last point is suggested by a comparison between his two recordings of *La Forza del Destino*. The Callas *Forza* of 1955, made in Milan, finds him in excellent vocal form and perhaps determined to show that the Mediterranean races do not have a monopoly of temperament, passion and tears. At any rate, he is unusually lacrymose. Ten years later (Leontyne Price the new Leonora), he has reduced the sobs in 'O tu che in seno' and banished them almost entirely from 'Solenne in quest'ora'. This is an achievement, for in the first version virtually every phrase had its sob, and the 'Addio's were heavy with tears and aspirates. Now both have gone.

And the voice has stayed. If a listener were told that the two recordings were made within a fortnight of each other he might doubt on the grounds that the style of singing and the quality of recording were different, but against this he would set the fact that the voice was virtually unchanged. Yet at the time of that second recording Tucker was in his fifties, an age when few heroic tenors sound quite their young selves. His fiftieth year probably found him in his prime, vocally and artistically. The *Madama Butterfly* of 1963 certainly suggests as much. The love music (Price as Ciò-Ciò-San) has a certain throaty sexuality, settling down seductively with 'Vieni la sera'; but it is directed by the brain and by artistic feeling too, graceful in 'un po'di vero è ce', for example, so as to set off the excited, rapacious forward movement of the next phrase, and leading to the climax not of the expected top C but of the more pointed alternative ending, with Pinkerton's voice heard in separation from Butterfly's. 'Vieni, sei mia' he sings again, fervently as ever: a man momentarily possessed no doubt, but essentially the possessor.

Another of Lt. B. F. Pinkerton's favourite maxims was that the Yankee goes all over the place ('dovunque al mondo'). It is not a sentiment that Richard Tucker put into practice quite as much as might have been expected, for though his appearances abroad were highly successful they were relatively uncommon. More recently American tenors have become a regular feature of operatic performances almost as much as their Italian counterparts. And nowhere have they been more in demand than at Bayreuth.

The Canadian, Jon Vickers, is the one on whom discussion will centre, famous for his Parsifal and Siegmund as for Otello, Aeneas and Grimes. There are also Jess Thomas and James King, who have enjoyed a very considerable reputation in Europe as well as at home and who have recorded extensively. Thomas' voice is another of those valuable in the theatre but little joy on records, for the tone is too often unsteady to be a pleasure in itself. It is good to hear him singing very softly, as in Siegfried's phrase 'In Schlafe liegt eine Frau', and the fortissimo ending of the first Act of *Siegfried* is impressive too. Very fine indeed is his singing in the second Act of *Die Frau ohne Schatten*: this is interesting because the usual unsteadiness is present in the other acts, while this very strenuous solo scene could hardly be better. King also sings a good deal of Richard Strauss, who generally has a way of making the tenor voice sound unlovely, as King himself does in *Ariadne auf Naxos*.[1] In spite of conscientious efforts at lightening and relaxing his voice, his Bacchus is effortful and unromantic ('very youthful, in tender tones', wrote Strauss hopefully at one point in the score). Better in some of the Strauss songs, and excellent in 'Heimliche Aufforderung', he can also rise impressively to the grander kind of Schubert song, such as 'Der Atlas' or 'Die Allmacht' with its fine lyrical line and magnificent climax.

But there are singers who make one listen to them and others whom one hears. Thus, in a session spent on the respective Siegmunds of King and Vickers, the first impression is that Vickers (listening to him in his earlier recording, under Leinsdorf) is far more alert and responsive than King. Careful point-by-point checking shows that often it is simply that one has been more alert and responsive oneself. In Siegmund's narrative ('Friedmund darf ich nicht heissen') Vickers certainly makes expressive the lines telling of the mother's death; but if one goes back to King, having played him first, one finds that he has given the words a deliberately emotional inflection too, if anything a little more obviously than Vickers. Why then had it passed unnoticed? Another example comes soon after. For the last line of the solo, 'Nun weisst du, fragende Frau, warum ich Friedmund nicht heissen', Vickers sings very softly, making a beautiful sound and a strong impression. Again memory suggested that King had done nothing. But on the contrary he had done much more. On the first three words he had swelled to a near-forte and back again, making a crescendo on 'Frau' to a full forte, giving an emotional, very slightly tearful suggestion to the first syllable of 'Friedmund', isolating 'heissen' deliberately and giving it a marked attack and *diminuendo*. All Vickers had done was to sing very softly, delaying any crescendo till the second syllable of 'warum', then making it slight, giving a slight emphasis to the syllable 'Fried' and a final *diminuendo* at the end. So why does that version register as expressive, and the other (conscientious, intelligent and no doubt sincere) fail to impress one way or the other? Or is it simply the accident of time, place and person?

My own beliefs are that it is not accidental, that to a certain point it is capable of analysis, and that, beyond that, analysis might still be possible but so complex as almost bound to go astray. Some of the reasons are no doubt that at his first appearance Vickers had sung more beautifully, that his anxious, sensitive Sieglinde (Brouwenstijn) had done more to create genuine drama than the other (Crespin, to whom Siegmund's arrival seems something of an everyday occurrence), and that by various imaginative touches on the way (the tenderness of his 'Zwillingsschwester', the vividness of his story-telling when he comes to the point about returning

[1] Very fine, however, is his singing of Apollo in Strauss' *Daphne*, recorded live in 1964; he sings with tenderness and imagination, and, as ever, the sheer sturdiness deserves gratitude.

113. Jon Vickers

to find the house burnt down) he holds the attention. Beyond that it is a matter of voice and personality; and it will have to do to say the obvious, that in both respects Vickers is quite exceptionally strong.

Perhaps it is only the very strong who can be quite so quiet and gentle as Vickers often is. We can hear Chaliapin singing so softly in a Covent Garden performance that we wonder how so quiet a sound could carry through the house. Similarly when Vickers begins 'Winterstürme' (in the Karajan recording of *Die Walküre*) so intimately, as if no one further away than Sieglinde is meant to hear, we may wonder whether this is not 'microphone singing', useless at the back or the top of a great opera house. But of course several thousand people have by now sat in just those places and heard him perfectly. Vickers' voice production has set many a connoisseurish head shaking since he first showed himself a considerable and possibly a very great operatic artist, but one of the usual tests in such matters is precisely the kind of thing just mentioned. Another is the development of an unsteadiness which in turn is to become downright wobble. By the age of forty-five, with some fifteen-to-twenty years of strenuous singing to look back on, such a development might well have begun to show, but neither records nor live performances have as yet suggested it.

On the other hand, forty-five is the age when a heroic tenor must begin to look around and ask himself what he has not yet done that he ought to have done. There are one or two things left for Vickers to do for the gramophone, wide as his recorded repertoire has been. One is to add Peter Grimes to the list of great portrayals in the record catalogue, and another is to replace his Otello. The Otello is a fine performance in many ways but it was issued when Vickers was only thirty-four, and he had not at that time sung the part on the stage. It is always worthwhile to have a second recording from Vickers anyway, for his art has not stopped growing. The intimacy of the 'Winterstürme' mentioned just now was not a feature of the earlier *Walküre*; and his second Florestan strengthened an already mightily intense performance.

Like every highly individual artist, the sort whose singing will always stamp itself on the music (Callas, Supervia, Martinelli, Gobbi, for instance), there are faults and idiosyncracies which may be found tiresome: his high notes are not of the kind called effortless, his vowels (especially in French) tend to be rather extreme, and he sometimes has a way of producing power without ring and shine. Unique among heroic tenors in this respect, he may even leave one wishing for less restraint, for more unabashed opening-up and letting-fly. In Verdi's *Requiem* it is as though he would prefer not to be singing tenor at all. In the 'Quid sum miser' with the two women soloists he makes his voice blend to sound almost like a second alto, and in the 'Lux Aeterna' he merges as a good chorister will, using a half-voice gently placed between the bass and the contralto, not adding an assertive sharp-edged presence as is usually the case. Perhaps this is part of the conductor's scheme, for Vickers is singing in Barbirolli's particularly etherial version: it all happens in heaven, with Montserrat Caballé's soprano luminous like a halo above the mass of sanctity. Just occasionally one wishes for the usual mortal competitiveness, as in Bernstein's recording, where Placido Domingo sings to the glory of God with heartfelt thankfulness that He made him a tenor.

But of course Vickers is not 'a tenor' any more than Caruso was. Both are voices unlike any other, and simply share their range and repertoire with the world's tenors. 'A tenor' cannot sing Aeneas' scene with Hector's ghost in *The Trojans* as Vickers does: Guy Chauvet is 'a tenor', and a good strong one too, but his work in the role is not the same thing at all. This is not meant to imply that Vickers is a pushed-up baritone: his upper notes ring superbly in this with a fine high C to crown them. But the kind of sound he will make around the F at the top of the stave is something other tenors cannot do (just as, though in a different way, Caruso had a quality around that part of the voice quite unlike anybody else); and it is also astonishing that after he has been singing with apparently full voice, as in the passage starting 'En un dernier naufrage' in *The Trojans*, he still has reserves for a towering climax, as in the last phrase 'par un tel désespoir'. More than that, and what finally makes him something that cannot be suggested by the term 'a tenor', he sings with such full soul—as in Aeneas' 'obéissant aux dieux, je pars et je vous aime'—that one senses an exaltation which might very well be called religious.

At a more mundane level, let us list some of the things he can do. He can take those famous soft high B flats in *Aida* and *Carmen* softly (the one at the end of 'Celeste Aida' is swelled to a mezzo forte, but it is approached and taken softly, and the phrase in Don José's Flower Song is floated tenderly and very beautifully). He can sing Handelian runs in 'Every valley' with all the semiquavers in place, no aspirates, and a panache to match the conductor's. This is Beecham, who gets great fun out of his *Messiah* and assures us in his written introduction that Handel would be vastly in favour. So the cymbals clash in 'Thou shalt break them', while Vickers, athletic in his runs and sonorous in tone, enters into the spirit of the thing enunciating with good Old Testament ruthlessness and relish. He can also sing a 'stock' Italian aria with great beauty of voice. 'Cielo e mar' *(La Gioconda)* is a good example, where the long-held 'o sogni d'or' ending the first verse is finely supported, while the last section is sung with full authentic ring and passion. Moreover, the air is 'built': it progresses with the care that a Lieder singer gives to the preparation of a song of Schubert or Wolf, so that the development from the hushed feeling of the first phrase to the exaltation of the end is a journey, an experience of some length and intensity. It is the work of a *big* singer: voice, technique and spirit all proportionate.

Such ingredients should surely make up the ideal Otello. Oddly, having waited so long for this ideal to materialise, the gramophone and stage have now been presented with another, for Vickers' recording, as suggested on the previous page, was probably premature. Instead, it is James McCracken, an American of almost exactly the same age as Vickers, who has brought Verdi's Otello most completely before the public, coming near to capturing, as Martinelli did, the suffering Otello, and having, in addition to what his precursor could offer, the body and freshness of voice that the part also needs.

Records do not show McCracken as a comparably great singer in other music, except possibly in *Fidelio*. The cry 'Gott, welch Dunkel hier' is vividly anguished; 'In des Lebens Frühlingstagen' has its sweetness; and the strain of the last section is emotional, not vocal. Maazel's conducting does not strike one as helpful, and under the circumstances McCracken emerges well, with an intensity matching that of Vickers and Patzak. But he overplays embarrassingly in *Pagliacci*, and arias from *Faust* and *Il Trovatore* are lacking in grace. Suffering is the thing he is best at, and so it comes as no surprise that the scene from Act II of *Carmen*, recorded with

Sandra Warfield, his wife in real life and a characterful mezzo, succeeds well, with José as more pathetic than usual and Carmen harder and more calculating. But it is on his Otello that McCracken's reputation ultimately rests.

A starting-point for his distinction among singers of this role is that he does not try to present Otello as a normal person. There is no need to psychoanalyse the libretto or to look into Shakespeare to find out about Verdi's Otello, for the music tells all that is needed. The solo voice must somehow dominate those twelve bars starting with 'Esultate' as the combined forces of chorus and orchestra have been doing; and in some way Otello must in retrospect seem to dominate those forces too, for his arrival comes as their climax. This is not a normal man; and the music goes on to tell us that he is not merely an outsize version of some other operatic hero, Radamès perhaps, or Manrico. In his lecture on Verdi, Martinelli noted how in the Love Duet the lyricism of the four opening phrases contrasts with the more declamatory nature of the fifth ('Tuoni la guerra'); and we might go on to note that even by the end of the first Act, Otello's music, so broad and solid in his 'Esultate' (corresponding to the language of Shakespeare's Othello in his Act I), has disintegrated into the fragmentary, exclamatory tones of 'quel gioia m'innonda . . . sì, fieramente . . . mi giacio'. The man of Verdi's music like the man of Shakespeare's lines is something other than the noble hero of convention. With McCracken this is clear and with Vickers it is not. McCracken's 'Esultate' establishes Otello as an emotional man, abnormally excited and emotional about his own good news (it is right, and we transfer it to our feeling for his situation with Desdemona); Vickers very firmly and simply gives the islanders and his followers some gratifying information with impressive dignity. At his second appearance, Otello is brought on the scene by the uproar of quarrelling voices and clashing swords. Again McCracken presents something more than normal feeling, in this case anger; and as Desdemona enters he changes tone, in a way that is again characteristic and right. Vickers, cleanly and strongly, sings with the soldier's authority and gives the rioters a straight-forward dressing-down. But there is nothing straightforward about this situation: it is a matter of emotional, if not physical, coitus interruptus, and the sensitivity towards Desdemona's appearance *has* to be registered by a change of tone (which it is not). And so one could go on through the role and the recordings. Vickers is never to be caught out in anything shoddy; on the contrary, he sings most beautifully and very scrupulously. McCracken does not always do that, but on the whole he gives us Otello. 'On the whole' and not entirely; for there are still many points where Martinelli is incomparable. For example, in Act III Otello resumes the terrible irony of the start of his duet with Desdemona, only to ask her forgiveness for mistaking her for 'that vile courtesan who is the wife of Otello'. Over the last words, 'la sposa d'Otello', the score directs a *voce soffocata*. Vickers does very little here; McCracken is sorrowful and still relatively mild; with Martinelli it is a terrifying recrimination. Then, later in the Act, the ambassador from Venice arrives and Otello kisses the seal of the message he brings from the Doge: 'Io bacio il segno della Sovrana Maiestà'. From Martinelli's tone (but not from the others) we know that some terrible thing has happened to this man who must now turn from the tragedy of his private life to the public duties so sacred and once so joyful to him. Again the examples could be multiplied.

Still, McCracken's Otello is a great achievement, and, with a great recording by Vickers still a possibility (as surely it must be), we can feel that American operatic singing has reached a certain point of grandeur and maturity. But it is not, perhaps, the place where we should leave this survey, or at which we should leave the American tenor. A great Otello has to do

114. James McCracken

much more than sing, and, while fulfilling these functions, he may some-times also do rather *less* than sing. A better test of the essential skills is to be found once again in Mozart, and we will turn briefly to two tenors who pass the test well.

An interesting and valuable arrival on the recording scene in the later nineteen-sixties was George Shirley. A negro from Indianapolis, he sings with character and musicianship. There is a fine sonority to his tone, as when he gives out 'Clarissimus Oedipus, pollikeor divinabo' with regal authority in Stravinsky's *Oedipus Rex*, and there is urgency and pathos in his charac-terisation here. The live urgency also serves well to make him a very suitable Pelléas to counteract, as Boulez puts it, the image of the 'refined page-boy'. He sings with plenty of body, with a certain sensuality in the love music, and then with a vivid and full-blooded portrayal of a tormented spirit ('Je ferais mieux de m'en aller sans la revoir'). It is in this last scene for Pelléas that the excellent Camille Mauranne gives less satisfaction. Where Shirley is a real man in torment, Mauranne (especially in his first recording, under Fournet) is still merely graceful, like a prince in a story-book. In his second version (under Ansermet) there is more intensity, largely because of the more perceptive conducting. For instance, in the phrase starting 'Je vais fuir en criant de joie et de douleur', it is the orchestra rather than the singer that makes the music fully expressive, whereas Shirley's Pelléas takes upon himself the pain of the chromaticism. At certain points, it is true, one misses the lightness and elegance of Mauranne's performance: he is extremely delicate and graceful in the love music of the Castle Tower scene, especially in his first version with Fournet where they get the balance with the solo violin (in the G flat passage) exactly right, catching the growth of animation and the 'doucement expressif' of the score's directions better than Boulez and Shirley. Shirley is, in fact, less 'charming', but he is more real and more interesting. This is true also of his singing in Mozart. His Ferrando in *Così fan tutte* is a flesh-and-blood creation, with a sense of fun, but also with some passion and nobility, both of them a strong pres-ence in the duet 'Fra gli amplessi'. There are limitations: 'Un' aura amorosa', for instance, gives a feeling of some tightness on the high notes, and he sometimes uses a rather curiously non-resonating tone. In *Idomeneo* we also come upon technical problems that are not quite completely solved: the runs and the trill in 'Fuor del mar' are highly impressive till one brings out old Hermann Jadlowker, in whose record the notes in the runs are marvellously distinct and where the trill is an object lesson in itself. Yet by the standards that we have come to know in the intervening years, Shirley's is a virtuoso performance. It is also a strong, imaginative and individual reading of the part. He remains one of the most interesting and useful artists to have emerged on the international scene in the last ten years.

But the most elegant of Mozart tenors—one was about to say since the Second World War, but possibly since McCormack—was also born in the

North American continent and trained there too. This is Léopold Simoneau, the French-Canadian; a singer whose recording career has been a short one, he has nevertheless made records which still set the best standard in our time. We think of him nowadays almost exclusively in Mozart, but several other parts of the lyric tenor's repertoire have been graced by his performances in them. In *Pêcheurs de Perles* we become immediately aware of a tenor singing in the tradition of Edmond Clément. That is, his tone is absolutely clear and precise in focus, and he draws a fastidiously clean, even line. One anomaly forces itself upon the attention even here; it is surprising that so careful and tasteful a singer should have allowed the habit of lifting upwards towards a high note to become so noticeable a feature of his style. Sometimes he will take the note with the precision one would expect of him ('Une femme apparait' for example, in the duet 'Au fond du temple saint') but sooner or later he will resort again to an upward portamento (as we shall find later in that same duet). But this is still fine singing, remarkable in modern times for its poise. His, for instance, is surely the most even and finely poised modern recording of 'Una furtiva lagrima' from *L'Elisir d'Amore*, and the most elegant, well-mannered performance of 'Dei miei bollenti spiriti' from *La Traviata* (and, hearing him, one remembers that 'Alfredo' was a Frenchman). In these and in arias from *Manon* and *Mignon* we can hear a tenor who like Clément and Muratore in the earlier generation kept the voice trim and slender, their style graceful without becoming insipid.

In Mozart these were priceless qualities. The clarity and sweetness of tone, unmuddied by any throatiness, fitted the temperate brightness of a Mozartian score, and his excellent technique could take the severe demands put upon it without sign of strain. In the concert aria 'Misero! o sogno' he can float the long melodic phrases of the earlier sections and keep the tone perfectly in focus throughout the agitated allegro. His wife, the soprano Pierrette Alarie, would often join him in these records, both in duets and in solo work, and here too there was much delicious singing, with delicate tone and the sort of fluency in runs that connoisseurs would rave over if they had been recorded about forty years earlier on 78s. It is Simoneau too who best survives the comparison with McCormack in 'Il mio tesoro', the famous test-piece in *Don Giovanni*. All is distinct and the legato is unbroken. In the other aria, 'Dalla sua pace', there is great pleasure in his well-supported soft singing and in the elegance of his phrasing-over. Comparisons also show how characterful a singer he could be: trying himself, Ernst Häfliger and Stuart Burrows in Tamino's arias from *Die Zauberflöte*, all of them singing well, it is Simoneau who most interestingly shapes his phrases and yet still preserves the most finely drawn evenness of tone. Similarly he can transmit a smile through the microphone as he sings 'Un' aura amorosa' in *Così fan tutte*, the soft singing finely supported without a trace of falsetto tone. And as Idamante in *Idomeneo* we hear again something like the ideal combination of virility and refinement: warm and sympathetic in feeling, shading the music most sensitively, and never smudging the perfect definition of tone.

Such accomplishment as this would seem to provide a fit point for closing what in historical fact we must hope not to be by any means a closed chapter.

American singing has prospered splendidly in these last decades, and there is good reason to hope that it may long continue to do so. No doubt much is not as it should be in the use of what must be an enormous potential. But a great deal has happened since the early part of the century outlined in Part I of this book. At least now, the young American singer stands a fair chance of getting decent training at home, and of being able to work and gain experience at an appropriate level before being brought forward in the great national opera house. At least now, racial opposition does not prevent a coloured artist from singing in that national opera house, and at least an American is not regarded as inherently inferior to a singer from Europe unless he happens to have made an unassailable European reputation first. Much has been done; and, though it may be an exaggeration to say that the seal of Italian melody in song has passed out of its native land, at least it seems that there is now, in the new world, a reasonably good facsimile.

26. Italy: A Tale of Two Tableaux
Renata Tebaldi   Mirella Freni
Giulietta Simionato   Fiorenza Cossotto
Franco Corelli   Carlo Bergonzi
Giuseppe di Stefano   Luciano Pavarotti

WHATEVER the progress in American singing, and however distinguished the company in Vienna or the German houses, Italy is still the country to have contributed the largest number of important opera singers in the post-war era as well as in earlier times. The period has, however, seen a notable change both in the pattern of the recording of Italian singers and in the quality of the performances recorded. For several years after the coming of LP a substantial part of the operatic repertoire was available with all-Italian casts on the Cetra label; and until recently the EMI companies, Decca, and Deutsche Grammophon have also gone to Milan, Rome or Naples, and, with a foreign artist or two in some star-roles, more or less simply recorded Italian performances. Thus from 1950 on into the sixties there was a regular formula for the casting of a large number of operatic recordings: Tebaldi or Stella, Simionato or Barbieri, del Monaco or di Stefano, Bastianini or Taddei. At the same time there appeared the genuinely international casts involving Callas, Nilsson, de los Angeles, Björling and Christoff, and these were generally of a higher standard. In them the Italian wing was represented by Tito Gobbi, as an artist in a class apart. During the sixties the pattern began to change. For one thing, the Americans came further into prominence, with Leontyne Price as the soprano most in demand for Verdi and Puccini (Sutherland and Caballé being other major sopranos in the Italian repertoire). For another thing, the Italians themselves were producing a number of singers more fastidious in style than almost any to have appeared there for a long time. Pre-eminent among them was the tenor Carlo Bergonzi; others were Mirella Freni, Renata Scotto and Luciano Pavarotti. Hence, the earlier division of recordings into two classes (the interesting-international and the straight-forward-Italian) began to disappear. Interesting, if very different, test-cases are Tebaldi and Franco Corelli, who belong to the scene as set in the fifties and as it changed in the sixties. Both are singers with great natural gifts, neither of them exactly subtle artists (though Tebaldi was always distinguished by a certain sensitivity and refinement); but we see both of them develop in their recordings, responding to the demands of the time, and ensuring their position in the two tableaux which Italian singing basically presents during this period.

The period is one which has seen Renata Tebaldi enthroned as prima donna for a quarter of a century. Her first records were made on 78s in 1950, and at the time of writing her most recent recording is a performance of *Un Ballo in Maschera* published in 1971. From first to last she has been at the centre, not only in reputation and repertoire but in style and timbre. As far as there can be such a thing, this is a voice without idiosyncracies: standard in range (though the top has not been easy for some years now), standard in power (the Tosca she sang at Covent Garden in 1955 stays in the memory as less powerful in sheer volume than that of Amy Shuard, Marie Collier and Gwyneth Jones, though it was quite loud enough), without vibrato, shrillness or (until very recently) a detectable division of registers. This, in itself, represents something of an idiosyncracy if she is placed among Italian sopranos of the past, and of course a great deal to be thankful for. But it is rather the same tale as with Robert Merrill among baritones. Just as the very sound of Gobbi commands a kind of attention that Merrill does not, so the very centrality of Tebaldi's timbre means that attention and interest have to be gained by a special insight or intensity in the interpretations. Now Tebaldi is a sympathetic and careful interpretative artist—and, as one checks, always more sensitive than memory had recalled. But that itself is interesting, for it means that the interpretations were not imprinted there: that some flash of individuality, some sudden illumination of the score, has not appeared to stay as a vivid and enduring part of the listener's mind. Yet sensitivity, beauty, dignity and warmth are there in plenty; and that is much.

Dignity and warmth are distinguishing qualities of her Tosca. Her second recording, issued in 1960, gives a finely developed dramatic portrayal, and her voice is in prime condition. A brash convention of self-regarding grandeur tempts so many singers of this role to coarsen the lines of their performance, but in the eight years between this and her first recording of the opera Tebaldi has moved consistently towards delicacy and restraint. The light, neat singing of the difficult phrase in the Love Duet, 'le voce delle cose' has always been a memorable feature, but very impressive too is the emotion of the 'Vissi d'arte', achieved through pure singing (no sobs or exaggerations, but a careful reading and firmly-judged dynamics). Her murder of Scarpia has unusual composure, and the obituary ('E avanti a lui tremava tutta Roma') is intoned as written, and not declaimed as it generally is. The directions to poor dead Mario are also sung, scrupulously voicing the written notes, and this too is rare; while the last phrase of all is no hysterical yell, but a noble utterance, patrician in its strength and control. With this goes a tenderness that one misses in many more temperamental performances. 'Gli occhi ti chiuderò con mille baci', she sings in the last Act: the future is deemed to afford such opportunities

115. Renata Tebaldi

for affection, and Tebaldi brings such womanly gentleness and feeling to the phrase that the sad irony makes its mark—the eyes are shortly to close not in sleep but in death, and there will be no time in the subsequent scrambling pressure of events for even one of the thousand kisses.

Her range of expression of course covers more than these gentler, nobler emotions. A memorable phrase in the *Tosca* tells (with the help of a superbly solid top C) how she knifed the tyrant baron ('Io quella lama gli piantai nel cuor'), and a toughness in the tone proclaims over the fearless two-octave stretch that she is exactly the woman to have done it. Similarly as Santuzza she hurls a deadly Easter curse, and as Minnie (of the Golden West) cheats gloriously at cards, confronting nasty Jack Rance with the winning hand

and a triumph that is all-Italian. Yet there are limitations. It is not so much that the more unpleasant side of humanity does not come easily to her (most operatic heroines are good girls anyway), but her dramatising is often thoroughly professional but nominal. In *Un Ballo in Maschera*, for example, she puts Amelia through her paces with the sure skill of a seasoned trouper, but nothing suggests a new realisation. And comparing her Gioconda with Callas', we find two extremely fine performances, only one of which stands out in bold relief while the other settles pleasingly and undisturbingly down within its frame. One notes the reappearance after the scene with Laura in Act III as a good example of Tebaldi's generous tone and sympathetic expression ('I have saved her for him'), but Callas is thrilling: 'salva per *lui*' she sings, with that sudden thrust of emotion and that feeling for an inspired moment.

Perhaps one would expect to be able to say 'Yes, but the balance inclines back to Tebaldi if one also requires sheer beauty of sound and excellence of technique'. There is some truth in this: Tebaldi rides the concerted finale to Act III of *La Gioconda* with full, even tone where Callas is unsteady and rather thin, and there are the usual flaps on high notes with Callas where Tebaldi is generally firm. But there are also times when pressure on the middle voice makes one wish for greater steadiness in Tebaldi and where one actually finds it in Callas. Then, as soon as there is even an incidental need for the technique to deal with a florid passage, it has to be admitted that Tebaldi sounds like something other than the first lady of Italian opera. In *La Gioconda* the need is only momentary; in *Trovatore* it is more important; and in *Traviata* it is essential. In this, the scale work may satisfy, but the cadenzas do not. The aspirating is blatant; as it is, to a disqualifying degree, when she turns to eighteenth century music. It mars solos by Handel, Sarti and Scarlatti, and, nearer home, destroys any true legato in such a lyrical air as 'Selva opaca' from Rossini's *William Tell*. The years have also brought their problems. As early as 1957 a recording made live from a concert in Chicago includes a prosaic performance of Tatiana's Letter Scene from *Eugen Onegin*: Solti conducts as though he hates the music, and Tebaldi sounds not only charmless but rather hard and fierce (like some of Rethberg's late recordings), and the high B flat lacks life and resonance. A two-record album issued in 1970 skilfully obscures the losses in ease, steadiness and range (and imaginative interpretations might have completed the disguise, but by and large Tebaldi is at her most pedestrian). The 1971 *Ballo in Maschera* contains much to admire, but many notes, phrases and even entire passages (such as the Gilbert-and-Sullivan-like trio in Act II) are negotiated with little suggestion of enjoyment.

Despite this, Tebaldi's management of her voice in these later years has been one of the remarkable features of her career. A 'new' Tebaldi voice was heard in an operatic recital published in 1964. Perhaps it was because of the centrality, the normality of the voice-face, but previously it had seemed a little as though here was the-girl-next-door-who-made-a-marvellous-success-of-it-and-yet-was-just-the-same. Now came a new depth of tone, a stronger and richer chest voice, a more commanding style and presence. In a series of taxing arias (including Turandot's 'In questa reggia', fearless and imaginative), she sang as from the throne: Maria Callas was on her way out and Leontyne Price on the way in, but in the meantime there was Renata Tebaldi. The programme was also prophetic in that it contained excerpts from three operas which she was still to record in complete performances: *La Gioconda*, *Don Carlo* and *Un Ballo in Maschera*. All of these are warm yet careful, human yet authoritative. No question of the-girl-next-door now: they belong to the aristocracy of operatic singing, and not least when her voice is most taxed by the demands of the music.

For this very 'central' singer, however, it is to the middle-period of her career that we return with the greatest pleasure. That is, for the records issued around 1960 when she herself was in the late thirties: for example, the *Tosca* discussed earlier, the gentle, clean-sung *Bohème*, the sensitive, deeply felt *Aida*, both of 1959, and perhaps above all the *Otello* of 1961. In this her voice is at its most beautiful, and the whole art and personality seem matched to the role. From the first phrases of the Love Duet (rising beautifully to the soft sustained A flat) to the last dying words (sung pianissimo, but sung and not croaked) we are blessed with a Desdemona whose music heals where the rest wounds, who catches the sadness overlaying the Willow Song and has the reserves of dignity and strength which will make her a positive and not merely a passive figure in Act III. It is exactly through such performances as this that the tradition survives, and standards for the future are set.

As with several performances in which distinguished singers excel themselves, the conductor of this *Otello* is Karajan, whose presence may also have helped to draw out the best in its protagonist, Mario del Monaco.

Del Monaco was heavily criticised throughout his recording career (by the more exacting critics, at any rate), and as one opera succeeded another, punctuated only by an occasional recital in which the unremitting sound poured forth without the presence of other singers to bring relief, it seemed that if this was the indispensable heroic tenor of our days, then our days had better learn a little stoicism or keep a hand on the volume-control. But this *Otello* deserved a different reception. Of course there were limitations: it was not subtle, it broke into anger a stage or so too early in Act II, and addressed Desdemona in the intimacy of her bed-chamber with much the same stentorian volume as had been appropriate for the entire court in Act III. Nevertheless it was an Otello to command respect and some gratitude. Firm and resonant, the tone has massive solidity proportionate to the appearance (and part-reality) of the character; more than that, del Monaco has here conscientiously and successfully managed to moderate it. The opening of the Love Duet is gentle, its *diminuendo* markings are observed, and such phrases as 'mi colga nell' estasi' and

'Amen risponda la celeste schiera' are quite movingly softened. When it comes to the great solo in the third Act, 'Dio, mi potevi scagliar', and to the Death Scene ('Niun mi tema'), he sings nobly: there are no cheap histrionics, but a conviction of genuine feeling and an artistic conscience at work in the attention to Verdi's markings. He proves himself in this recording, and in it he has a very decent, and one would think enduring, monument.

It prompts a rehearing and possibly a revaluation of his other recordings. In most of the opera sets there are passages where he sounds magnificent, though in *Rigoletto* and *Norma* they are elusive; it also cannot be denied that some of his singing is unpleasant, much of it insensitive, and perhaps most of it unimaginative. Unpleasant, for example, is Don José's Flower Song in the complete *Carmen*: that puts it mildly. Insensitive is 'Come un bel dì di maggio' from *Andrea Chénier*: graceless and ineffective because of its unyielding loudness. Unimaginative is 'Celeste Aida', which he must have sung hundreds of times, yet it is stiff in tone, rhythm and phrasing, belted out and hurried towards its final immense B flat, stolid and charmless. His rare excursions outside the basic repertoire were occasionally successful: from *Walküre* he sang a firm, vigorous 'Siegmund heiss ich' (along with three other Wagnerian solos in which the sleeve note claims defiantly that he employs 'a remarkable variety of tone'), and from *La Juive* he sang, on 78, a version of 'Rachel, quand du Seigneur' with a sense of drama, a marvellous body of tone, quite well moderated, and a good legato.

That, the soundness of legato, was generally a virtue to be depended upon in his singing. It provided one of the basic guarantees for acceptable Verdi, and certainly much that he did was more than merely acceptable. The Temple Scene in *Aida*, the quiet lyrical solo 'Morir, si pura e bella', the solo from the last Act of *Un Ballo in Maschera*, almost the entire role of Don Alvaro in *La Forza del Destino*: these are parts of the repertoire in which one could be thankful for his good, straightforward production of even tone, and in which he was by no means without feeling. If all that was left of del Monaco was the legend of his fame in the world's opera houses and a single record, the version of 'O tu che in seno' from *La Forza del Destino* made on a 78, he would be a name to conjure with. It is not subtle and the phrasing is conventional, but there is tenderness as well as strength, a reasonably soft start to the aria, a good instrumental evenness in the turns and in the broad span of the melody, and of course a magnificent voice. The reading on LP (1955) has changed very little and so has the sound, for the dryness of tone which was to increase (as with Zenatello and Martinelli) has not yet begun to make its appearance. There is more to be said for del Monaco than might meet the ear in a good many of his records.

The other mainstays among Italian tenors during this period were Giuseppe di Stefano and Franco Corelli. Like del Monaco, if to a lesser extent, they have met with a critical opinion unwilling to hold them in marked esteem even while admitting great natural gifts and a well-deserved popularity. Again, retrospect confirms the criticisms; but it also brings its pleasures and ends in recognition of genuine worth.

Let us look at di Stefano on top form in a recital issued in 1959. The Italian arias *(Tosca, Turandot, Andrea Chénier)* tempt investigation less than the second side of the record, devoted to French opera. This may come as something of a revelation from the start, opening with a broadly phrased, gently lyrical version of Ossian's Song, 'Pourquoi me réveiller' from *Werther*. The end of the first verse ('souffle du printemps') is superbly in the tradition of de Lucia and Schipa, held as something delicate and lovely in itself, a fine thread of sound poised on a strong sustaining breath and dying away to nothing. The Flower Song from *Carmen* and 'Salut, demeure' from *Faust* are also distinguished by intelligent building, phrasing, and treatment of words as well as fine tone. Better still, des Grieux's Dream in *Manon*, sung very quietly with magical use of the head voice, and, like the others, in relatively good French. Turning now to the Italian side of the record, one might wonder if it is to return to routine performances, but the first item is a version of Andrea Chénier's Improvisation ('Un dì all'azzurro spazio'), scrupulously lyrical, except for a well-marked passage where anger against a corrupt Church and aristocracy is allowed declamatory bitterness, all the more effective in the context of pure, continent singing. Feeling for mood is consistently sensitive in this recital, so the affection in 'Non piangere, Liù' is rendered with all due Italianate luxury of sadness, as well as an exemplary legato (rare in this). And absolutely classic is the most famous of all, 'E lucevan le stelle', the so-familiar melody outlined, just touching the notes, with the inspiration of a first performance, the word 'scioglea' drawn out softly with fine control, and the climax built with emotional restraint and unforced power.

A few comparisons now suggest themselves. The Dream in *Manon* was sung also in some extracts from the opera, recorded with Anna Moffo (1964). Here the effect is less happy for he is singing in two voices: a very soft, somewhat crooning head voice, and a basic tone which is too loud in relation to the other. In the recital record five years earlier he had the balance and homogeneity of tone exactly right. With 'E lucevan le stelle' three other performances are available for comparison. The first two, one on 78, the other in the Callas *Tosca*, are fine, very like the 1959 recital, the 78 being rather more luscious in tone, the complete-opera version rather drier. But a later recording (Price and Karajan in 1963) has lost much: the voice has lost its bloom, the phrases their shape, the 'scioglea' its magic, and the climax its effectiveness.

It is often said that di Stefano was a lyric tenor, unwise in the extension of his repertoire to include dramatic roles like Radamès, Manrico and Canio. This may be true, but then he was hardly satisfactory in many of his recordings of what should in that case have been his proper repertoire. His Bellini, as exemplified in the complete *Puritani* recording with Callas, lacks grace and charm: 'A te, o cara' is sung without affection, and with some of the habits that made his appearances less than welcome among discerning critics—the way of lifting towards a note rather than taking it cleanly, and an openness of vowel sounds that could nag remorselessly. In *L'Elisir d'Amore* he characterises with resource, but aspirates often ('ca-hara', 'sposa-harlo', 'anco-hora' etc.,), and takes no apparent pride in the finish or polish of his style. On the basis of this sort of thing he is sometimes held up as an awful example of bad modern ways and wastage. There is something in it. Those 78s made at the outset of his career show the most marvellous voice, and quite a promising style—if it is a beginning that is to be developed and refined. The *Mignon* arias, the *Arlesiana*, the haunting Sicilian song 'Cantu a timuni': all are splendid records and suggest a rich vein for years to come. Implying that the vein was misused and wasted, senior collectors of old records will say that he is one of the reasons why they pursue their hobby and stick to their period.

But the judgement is indiscriminate. There is plenty of good di Stefano as well as plenty of wastage and faulty style in the artists of the collectors' own period. Meanwhile, here is a splendid Pinkerton, Cavaradossi (in the Callas version) and Rodolfo (interesting to compare his liveliness with Björling's conventionality); a man who can spring a surprise (who would imagine him to do well in the Love Duet from *Otello*? yet with Rosanna Carteri pleasing in the soprano part, he gives a broadly-phrased, well-shaped performance); a characterful singer with one of the best tenor voices of the century.

Another of those best voices is certainly Corelli's. It is perhaps the most distinctive and exciting of its type since Lauri-Volpi, whom he resembles in several respects. The repertoire is similar, and more notable in the recordings is a likeness of timbre and vibrancy. Corelli was unusual among modern singers in having a quick vibrato, less prominent in later years (as with Lauri-Volpi, Bonci and de Lucia) but quite marked in his first records and adding a rare, dramatic flavour: it was a voice that in the opera house one would drink and want more of, in spite of the attendant shortcomings. Those included a tendency to lose the conductor (as when towards the end of Act II of *Roméo et Juliette* he wants to move forward in a rather beautiful passage marked *andante*, and does actually get ahead in one bar), and to lift to notes (as with di Stefano, but somewhat more persistently, examples occurring more or less wherever one likes to look for them, whether in the early *Aida* or the late *Roméo et Juliette* just mentioned).

This *Roméo*, issued in 1969, also shows that Corelli had come a fair way towards meeting the tastes of Anglo-Saxon record critics who must seem unfathomably to think the more of a tenor the less they can hear of him. He is still too loud, of course, but he has definitely made an effort. In *Il Trovatore* (1965) we can compare him with his earlier self, for some extracts were recorded in a recital for Cetra in the late nineteen-fifties. 'Ah si, ben mio' is the test-piece, buoyant and keenly felt in the earlier version, but

116. Mario del Monaco   117. Giuseppe di Stefano

118. Franco Corelli as Calaf   119. Carlo Bergonzi in
     in *Turandot*   *La Forza del Destino*

badly aspirated, grossly inelegant in the cadenza, and with little variety of volume. The later performance remedies most of the faults: there is still some aspirating, but it is not gross, a well-controlled *diminuendo* gives point to the bridge between the first and second half (on the word 'trafitto'), and another rounds off the aria with such finesse that it looks like a flagrant appeal to the orchestra stalls.

All the same, his appeal is basically that of the warm south. For some reason you have to be born within easy distance of the Mediterranean to sing like this, and we ought to thank our stars that in a world of pop-grinding and film-making a man like Corelli chooses opera. His, too, is the voice to hear in those Italian songs which used to be a pleasure until they were spoilt by inflated orchestrations, alien harmonies and a general aura of exploitation for the middle-brow tourist. In spite of these things, there is still the old thrill in hearing a great and distinctively Italian voice raised in a fine flow of melody; sad songs, the best of them, like 'Senza nisciuno', 'Tu, ca nun chiagne' and 'Fenesta che lucive'. The first two were sung by Caruso with a consuming passion that did not make comfortable listening; Corelli captures the longing, the passion too, and if his accompaniments could be obliterated the listening would be fine (of course the songs are good examples of Italian bad taste, but as E. M. Forster says of Italian bad taste 'it attains to beauty's confidence'). 'Fenesta che lucive' is another matter: a sad melody in the style of Bellini, to whom it used to be attributed, finely sung by Caruso and, with exquisite shading and at a slow tempo, by de Lucia. Corelli sings with less conscious art, but with just the fineness of line, the feeling and the timbre to preserve this part of the tradition. It is not a totally unimportant part either, for a century of Italian opera and operatic singing has developed alongside these popular songs: a youngster brought up on the songs could turn easily to the operas, and the composers of opera often (and often without knowing it) turned to the songs. So some of the essentially Italian character of Corelli's opera singing registers as the taming by art of something which has its roots in folk-song. In an aria like 'L'anima ho stanca' from *L'Amico Fritz* one is gratefully aware of the national 'folk' character and of the art, and in many of Corelli's important recordings *(Pagliacci, Turandot, Andrea Chénier)* there is a similarly satisfying blend. It is on this kind of blend that the peculiar contribution of Italy to singing has so largely depended.

Just how invaluable that contribution can still be is shown by the fourth tenor of this generation, Carlo Bergonzi. More than any other Italian tenor on record, he combines power, beauty, intensity and elegance. Not as powerful as Caruso, not as beautiful as Gigli, less intense than Martinelli, less elegant than Schipa, he nevertheless presents a balance of these attributes that puts him well into the illustrious company; and in case other names from the past are adduced, it might be added that his intonation is reliable, he sings accurately and does not exaggerate. Wild horses might drag him from the straight and narrow of his vocal line, but not even the temptation of three exclamation marks and the directions *con un grido* and *con trasporto di giubilo* (as in Act III of *Ernani*) can make him leave the written note and shout something instead.

In his earlier recordings he too, like Corelli, had a quick, very fine-grained vibrato; with him too it added to the character of his singing, and, as with the other tenor, it has lessened over the years. Gabriele Adorno's scene and aria in *Simon Boccanegra* illustrates the vibrato and also the way in which he would spoil his legato by the use of aspirates. But Bergonzi has obviously applied himself in the closest detail to all that he has sung, and one result is a tenor with fewer faults per hundred grooves than any of the others.

There are also an inner fire and outgoing command in this early *Simon Boccanegra*. The attention to markings and meaning is apparent even here, the section starting 'Sento avvampar' having a baleful, menacing tone at first, then taking the words 'io piango' softly, ringing out in 'il tuo pietà, gran dio', and rounding the passage off with a fine *diminuendo* on 'del mio martire'. In terms of interpretation and feeling he has probably not developed all that much; generally a comparison of first and second recordings shows little change (the last scene of *Lucia di Lammermoor*, for example, is almost identical in both versions). This is, in fact, the chief of his limitations, the other probably being that the characters in all these operas sound very alike. Yet the people he impersonates respond like human beings to any given circumstance, and the response is full-blooded. Thus, Rodolfo, in *La Bohème*, asks his spoken question at the end of the opera in a way that is more natural and more powerful than usual. 'Che vuol dire quel' andare e venire, quel guardarmi così?' (or in the standard English translation, 'What's the meaning of these goings and comings, these glances so strange?'): Bergonzi leaves the realisation of what the answer must be to the last three words, with the first part spoken conversationally, the heart-stopping suspicion appearing, and the fact pleading for denial in the last word. Above all, whatever he does is musical, so that the most famous tenor solo of all, 'Che gelida manina' in the same recording of *La Bohème*, is treated with a musical sensitivity that also works to strengthen the set-piece as integral music-drama. Thus a finely drawn diminuendo on the first high note (the high B flat), carrying over into the next phrase, makes good musical sense and better delineation of character than the normal solid double-forte-breathe-and-start-again (the words are 'Chi son, e cosa faccio'—'who I am and what I do'—normally given in a style which imputes to Rodolfo the tenor's own egotistic relish). As a musical construction, the piece is a related collection of lyrical and declamatory fragments till towards the end, when it introduces a broad melody which is to become the main love-theme of the opera ('Talor al mio forziere'): Bergonzi's performance gains effect by interpreting as the construction suggests, making a series of tentative approaches, each with its own mood, till, with the start of the theme, he knows where he stands, what essentially it is he has to say, and can sail on confidently to the top C to make the statement of his life. The marvellous, hackneyed pages are made new again by the simplest of processes: following the suggestions of the score.

To effect the musical process, Bergonzi has been exceptionally disciplined in the preservation of his voice as a musical instrument. In the emotional scores of Mascagni, Leoncavallo and so forth, he gives generously at the climaxes, but judges them well and for the rest he spares his voice and spends his energy. 'Ventitre ore' and 'Un tal gioco' in *Pagliacci* achieve their effect by rhythmic pointedness rather than brute strength, and always the voice is perfectly defined on the note. Remembering how in an earlier period, with Aureliano Pertile as the prime example, tenors would set their voices quivering with passion, wide of the tonal centre and often to an effect that was musically crude and dramatically hysterical, we can see that in Bergonzi Italian singing has touched the opposite pole. The scene is set for the second tableau.

In this, singers born in the thirties rather than the teens and twenties of the century, and making their names on record in the sixties rather than the fifties, begin to take their places. In the foreground: Freni, Scotto, Cossotto and Pavarotti. Their style: close kin to that of Bergonzi, who is essentially part of this scene rather than the other. Background figures: misty.

The sopranos named here share two important qualities with each other and with Bergonzi: their style is tasteful and their tone perfectly defined. Neither of them can be seen as successor to Tebaldi, and though it may be that this successor is already in the making she seems not to have made herself known in the studios.[1] Perhaps the nearest is Gabriella Tucci, a vibrant Nedda in a *Pagliacci* with del Monaco, and a really good Leonora in Corelli's *Trovatore*, where she sings 'Di tale amor' with staccatos, trills and semiquavers in place, and 'D'amor sull'ali rosee' with fine tone and musical sensibility. But then, there was no-one who really came within hailing distance of Tebaldi in her own generation. Anita Cerquetti made a brilliant impression on audiences in the opera house, but recordings show her as a somewhat erratic singer and her career was short-lived, while Antonietta Stella, big and warm of voice (very good, for instance, in 'Laggiù nel Soledad' from *La Fanciulla del West*), never acquired the distinction of style that makes an interpretation memorable. The Roumanian-born Virginia Zeani shared such roles as Mimì and Violetta with Tebaldi, and sings with a seriousness and boldness that do imprint the memory. She could also be good in Donizetti and Bellini, an interesting,

[1] Two very promising sopranos made their debut on records in 1972, both of them sounding persuasively as successors to Tebaldi in several respects. Maria Chiara displays a fine variety of tone colour in her *Aida* arias, and she also includes in her recital record a fine and imaginative performance of 'Qui la voce' from *I Puritani*. Katia Ricciarelli similarly extends the range of expectations we associate with Tebaldi, in a Verdi recital remarkable, among other things, for fluency in fioritura.

rather intense Lucia, and sometimes singing in a characterful way that would call Olympia Boronat to mind. No really first-class lyric-dramatic soprano has emerged, however, and Freni and Scotto have wisely restricted themselves to the lighter roles for which nature intendéd them.

Not that 'light' is the word for Violetta and Lucia as roles or for Renata Scotto as a singer. She has the art of colouring the voice, of thickening and darkening the bright, thin-edged tones of the Italian lyric and coloratura soprano into an instrument that will express sorrow and heroism. No doubt she has learnt something from Callas, as more 'dramatic' singers like Elena Souliotis and Leyla Gencer have done, but she has never picked up Callas' mannerisms, or allowed into her own singing any of the more disruptive features of the expressive school—the register-divisions, the unsteadiness of tone under pressure, the overelaboration of plain phrases and so forth.

She is a strong interpreter. Whether it is youthful charm ('O mio babbino caro'), minxish determination ('Una voce poco fa'), tenderness, devotion, vision ('Un bel dì') or tragic tension ('L'altra notte'), she creates a mood and sustains it. Those four arias are all included in a recital record made fairly early in her career, showing considerable mastery in the lyric part of the repertoire. This is not quite matched by distinction in the florid part, though much here is also very admirable. Although the high notes are all there (high E flats duly in place at the end of Lucia's Mad Scene), they do not seem to come all that easily. As with Toti dal Monte, they often have a rather hard, sometimes pinched quality, and one is glad when she is back on the stave again. Her trill is genuine, her scales are fluent, and the long crescendo and decrescendo on a held note are well controlled. All these features can be heard in the 'Caro nome' of her complete *Rigoletto*, yet, accepting that she is probably the best of modern Italian representatives, one also reflects that Italian sopranos have not played any notable part in the 'coloratura' revival of recent years.

The 'Caro nome' is remarkable not for any fireworks, but for the reasons that normally distinguish Scotto's singing: firm, characterful tone and sensitivity to mood, in this instance meditative and tender. In the later Acts, she presents a more mature, noble Gilda than we generally hear, one who might credibly brave the storm and the assassin's knife if she had made up her mind to it. Nor are her Butterfly and Violetta carbon copies: both are individual characterisations, the Butterfly growing from a smiling, charming, very young girl to a woman who embraces her tragedy almost fiercely. Her Violetta cries out against the tragic destiny at three memorable points: one is the phrase 'l'uomo implacabile' ('God may forgive the fallen woman, man never will') in Act II, then in the same hard tone 'E tardi' ('Good news comes too late') in the last Act, and the strong final protest leading into 'Gran dio, morir si giovane'. The whole conception appears to centre on this: the woman always inwardly aware of an unhappy destiny, her whole being crying out passionately against it. Hence the hard-toned determination of the repeated 'gioir' ('I'll live to enjoy myself') and the almost grim expression accompanying the repeat of 'Sempre libera' in the great solo at the end of Act I. This is a beautifully sung, finely wrought characterisation: the notion comes as a slight surprise, but Scotto's recorded Violetta is very probably the most generally satisfying of all.

It is also a slight surpise at this date to recall that at one time it was common experience for opera goers and record collectors in this country to get mixed up about those four sopranos, all fairly light and lyric, all disyllabic of surname, and all coming into international prominence around 1960. They were Scotto and Moffo, Freni and Sciutti, and they are all really very different after all. Graziella Sciutti has been a charming Zerlina in *Don Giovanni*, a bright clear-toned Susanna in *Le Nozze di Figaro*, singing a beautiful 'Deh, vieni non tardar' (rather more beautiful in recital than in complete performance), and a pretty little minx of a Giulia in *La Scala di Seta*. But as one listens to her singing of that role, or of Nannetta in *Falstaff*, some lack of stamina, of firmness on top, intervenes to limit the pleasure. Nor does she project well; often it is as though she is singing to herself. A delicate trill, some precise scale work, a pretty voice with just that touch of something astringent to make it interesting; yet there is still a need of some stronger direction, both technically and interpretatively, to fulfil the promise of this talent.

Freni also came upon us as a young talent, most delightfully cast as Nannetta in the Covent Garden *Falstaff* of 1961. Her voice was refreshing, cool, pure and sweet as a fine white wine, her style was musical, her personality charming. It seemed too good to be true, or at any rate to last. That its goodness was true is attested by a record issued about that time by the World Record Club; that it has lasted unaffected by ten years singing is certainly suggested by the most recent of her records as well as by a reappearance ten years later at Covent Garden as Micaëla, the part with which she is probably most associated and which she has already recorded twice.

The essential and consistent beauty of her records is undoubtedly this purity of tone, steady, even and in fresh bloom. Though the waltz song ('Je veux vivre') from *Roméo et Juliette* takes her up to a high D, she does not dwell in the topmost regions of the range longer than she has to, choosing the lower-pitched runs in the first solo where alternatives are offered. And although the runs are perfectly competent, she does not show a great deal of interest in florid singing. She has a good trill, but does not use it on the high A in 'Je veux vivre' where a trill is marked. On the other hand, she is scrupulous about note-values and about such details as a careful, strict execution of the appoggiaturas in this waltz song, generally interpreted as simply giving license from the composer for the kind of smudged attack from below which the singer would otherwise have done without permission. More important, Freni generally maintains a true legato, the line being well bound, unfussed, unaspirated and firm. So some quite simple melodies (like 'Ange adorable' in *Roméo* or 'Le roi de Thulé' in *Faust*) are particularly enjoyable when she sings them, and her solo, 'Tra speme e timore', in Handel's *Alcina* (after dazzling displays of super-virtuosity by Sutherland, Berganza and Sinclair) also registers as an exemplary piece of modern singing in its clean style and beautifully produced tone.

While she has not yet found the ability to impress her interpretations vividly upon the memory, she is not at all an inexpressive singer. Her solos from *Adriana Lecouvreur* compare very well with a whole range of earlier singers (Krusceniski, Muzio, Ponselle, Hammond, Tebaldi, all of whom sing with much feeling), and it is interesting to see the modern Italian expressing emotion by purely musical means. For example, the last words of 'Poveri fiori' ('Tutto è finito') are often taken with a sob, a sigh or a gulp; in Freni's singing the tears are implied in the voice-colour and the music responds to the confidence placed in it. Her singing of Mimì's Death Scene also shows her ability to act with the voice, singing out for all she is worth in 'Sì, rinasce' and eventually, for the last phrases of all, taking the edge off the voice, its power dying away for the last words. But this is a glowing Mimì, radiantly pure and youthful in tone, warming when the music calls for ardour, letting anxiety and illness tell their tale through the expression of her singing, and always maintaining a fine, firm musical line.

Firm, musical and scrupulous are also words for Fiorenza Cossotto, the best Italian mezzo of this generation. Closer in tone quality to Minghini-Cattaneo, the mezzo of the twenties and early thirties, than to her immediate predecessors, Stignani, Barbieri and Simionato, she has up to the present avoided troubles that have beset most of her kind. She has, for instance, developed a very wide working range without apparent register-divisions. The high *tessitura* of Adalgisa's music in *Norma* holds no terrors, and in the duets, with their 'anything-you-can-do' sequences, she is continually setting her colleagues a good example. The Norma of this recording is Souliotis, and the contrast shows Cossotto as a thoroughly tutored singer, to whose style the rough production of the soprano is quite alien. Then in *Trovatore*, where Azucena's music tests both extremes of the range, she takes the written cadenza in Act II fearlessly up to the high C (not, however, in her earlier recording on Deutsche Grammophon), having just given equally firm utterance to the deep sustained contralto notes two octaves and more below. More important than the extremes, the middle part of the range is also absolutely firm. In the inevitable comparison with Simionato, one finds that she too is fine on the top C and low A, but relatively unsteady in the middle register. Simionato was forty-five when she made this first *Trovatore*, while Cossotto was only thirty-five at her second (1970). The years have still to show how her voice will stand up to time and hard usage, but the signs are all favourable.

The signs include the evident awareness which is brought to bear on her singing, whether in the details of the score or in the use of her own voice. The voice is bright-toned and strong to the point of hardness, and her records show repeatedly how she will lighten and sweeten it as need arises. A fine example of her soft singing occurs in Act I of *Norma*, with the unaccompanied phrase 'un altro cielo in lui' beautifully floated; and in Verdi's *Requiem* (both recordings, but more especially the later one under Barbirolli) we find her using a specially rounded, 'spiritual' voice for her solos in 'Lux aeterna'. For Cherubino's songs in Giulini's recording of *Le Nozze di Figaro* she lightens quite remarkably to produce something like the boyish tone which English choirmasters know as 'continental'. Without the charm and vividness of Supervia's singing of these, she has nevertheless produced varied, spry performances such as one cannot imagine the Verdian mezzos of old being able to give (at any rate none of them has done so on records). She also knows the value of restraint, so that in *Cavalleria Rusticana* she begins 'Voi lo sapete' with a poised, indrawn quietness, and in the duet with Alfio reserves her full voice for the broad-spanning phrases of lamentation, and so gains much in effectiveness.

The other remarkable thing about Cossotto and her place in the tradition is the care with which she studies the score. None of the examples I have in mind is exactly a matter of minutiae, yet in the long tradition of lax attention to the composer's markings they may seem niggling. In Verdi's *Requiem* the mezzo's first phrases in the 'Liber scriptus' have a diminuendo to pianissimo marked over 'proferetur' and 'continetur'. These occur as the voice rises a fifth and they cannot be easy: Cossotto does them (especially well in the Serafin version), where many do nothing at all, and most make only a token effort. Or in Princess Eboli's Moorish song in *Don Carlo*, a difficult pianissimo is marked on alternating high notes, and earlier in the verse there is a tricky sequence of twelve semiquavers, with the eleventh (A sharp) marked for emphasis. These too are dynamics which Cossotto observes, while neither Bumbry nor Barbieri bothers about the last point at all.

Let us take one further example, as it leads us to the most eminent of the mezzos who have their place as Cossotto's predecessors in Tableau One. Giulietta Simionato's two recordings of *Il Trovatore* have many virtues, but so, it must be said, have Verdi's expression marks. 'Condotta all'era in ceppi' (Act II) is full of them, all effective in creating the tension which the principal figure in the accompaniment suggests but (the rhythm being reassuringly regular) is unable of itself to enforce. One realises this as Cossotto sings it because she observes the markings; Simionato does not. She is no worse than her predecessors (random checks included Boninsegna, Offers, Branzell, Minghini-Cattaneo), but it is in the light of this sort of thing that one looks askance at the kind of comment that appeared in print after one of Cossotto's London appearances, to the effect that she might possibly become the Barbieri of our time, but never the Simionato. On records she is already better than either.

120. Giulietta Simionato

Innumerable testimonies to Simionato's excellence in the opera house make her place in the history of singing quite secure, but records support this reputation only up to a certain point. They suggest the authority of her manner: her Amneris bears down forcibly upon Aïda in the Act II duet, and sighs forth her love-longing in the earlier high phrases with pure tone and fine control.[1] They show her as a mezzo with a contralto's richness and a soprano's range upwards. They include a fair proportion of that enterprising part of her work that took her into the scales and roulades of Rossini's writing for mezzo. And they leave a clear impression of the size of this voice which could sound so ample beside whatever company she sang with at La Scala. The mere date of the records also tell their tale: her *Cenerentola*, for example, was issued in 1964 and Simionato was then fifty-four.

This is all impressive, yet that does not make it enjoyable. For a Cinderella

---

[1] But note she does not observe any of the 'arrow' markings in the score; and though the voice is pure and steady, it is not sensual. Compare Rita Gorr's singing, under Solti, of these phrases, where the three repetitions are all different, and where there is much more passion and sense of luxuriating, like Shakespeare's Cleopatra feeding herself with 'most delicious poison' while Antony is away.

with half-a-century's experience she manages not to sound too matronly, but it is not an appropriate tone that she brings to the role, nor has she the way of characterising with her voice that might make a livelier effect, whether as the day-dreaming girl of the opening, or the sad neglected Cinders of later events, or the sparkling queen of hearts of the finale. It is also said that the aspirating of her runs was less noticeable 'in the flesh' than on record (though I have not found this to be so with other singers); it is certainly very noticeable here, and in fact spoils most of her recorded Rossini. A steadier tone and/or a more vivid and/or scrupulous reading of the score is really needed to give pleasure in any modern recording of the great Verdi roles. Very probably, for enjoyment of Simionato's singing one does better to look outside this central part of her repertoire to the Zia Principessa of *Suor Angelica* sung with dignity and richness, or to the Leonora of *La Favorita*, at her expressive best in the last Act, or to her Santuzza in *Cavalleria Rusticana*, pleading warmly and cursing like a fish-wife. For a touch of the greatness that she could undoubtedly achieve in Verdi, perhaps one might then go back to that veteran Azucena of the 1965 *Il Trovatore*, where a flash of pride and a cry of desperation bring the capture-scene of Act III to life, and so to add its testimony to that of so many who have admired her performances in the house.

On the whole, Fedora Barbieri, the other distinguished mezzo of the fifties, fares better on records. Her Azucena is tense and imaginative, and particularly strong in its grasp of the rhythmic character of the old gipsy's music. Her Amneris rises grandly to the great lamenting phrases of the last Act, and in the recording with Callas (she also sang with the less effective Milanov) she is the soprano's equal in the duet of Act II: some really admirable singing and characterisation here. She had a good sense of fun, too, making a splendid Mistress Quickly, not just going through the fruity-voiced routine, but giving a freshly studied performance. The strong chest-voice makes a great impression in this as in other roles, but the penalty so often is that the voice breaks up into registers, and Barbieri did not escape. Nor did she keep the firmness of voice which was a superb feature of her earliest recordings. She sings the part of Ulrica, the sorceress in *Un Ballo in Maschera*, both in a performance with Gigli on 78s, and with Callas and di Stefano fourteen years later, in 1957. By that time she had come to be aware of a few more markings in the score and to achieve a rather more subtle effect. But the voice is steadier and more opulent in the early version—recorded when she was no more than twenty-three years old. Her career did not span the decades as extensively as Simionato's, but in the years of her prime she gave good value. All in all, Italy produced two considerable mezzos for Tableau One of the LP era. Cossotto is a great credit to Tableau Two, but there is still only one of her.

When we look at the baritones, the number of Italians who have interested the record companies in recent years has dwindled alarmingly. Nor can it be said that in this instance quality makes up for quantity.

Mario Sereni is certainly valuable to the community, lyrical and pleasant, and, as Gérard in *Andrea Chénier*, singing with force and without forcing. Piero Cappuccilli, on the other hand, makes an ungainly, unattractive Enrico in Beverly Sills' *Lucia di Lammermoor*, a role he recorded more impressively a decade earlier with Maria Callas. Others do not readily come to mind, though of course it is possible that Gobbi's successor is about to emerge along with Tebaldi's.

In the immediate pre-war scene Gobbi, Silveri, Bechi, Valdengo and Tagliabue were prominent, and with the coming of LP we began to hear from Taddei, Bastianini, Guelfi, Panerai, Bruscantini and Aldo Protti. If this was not a generation to match the vintage years of the nineteen-hundreds, they nevertheless made a more impressive array than appeared in the interwar years. Giangiacomo Guelfi had the kind of voice that stops the show after Amonasro's first words in *Aida*, but it lacks the definition and focus to make a strong impression on records: graceless in the Torea-dor's Song, frowning terribly in Alfio's 'what a jolly life, boys' ('Il cavallo scalpito' in *Cavalleria Rusticana*), probably at his best in the duet 'Invano, Alvaro' from *La Forza del Destino* sung with Corelli (who is splendidly characterful by comparison). Giuseppe Taddei is a stronger interpreter and a much more adaptable singer, with a useful turn for comedy, making him an excellent Gianni Schicchi, and a lively Figaro and Leporello in the Mozart operas. By 1965, when his *Macbeth* was issued, he was approaching fifty, and the voice, though still powerful, had loosened and lost some resonance. But only two years before that came his second recorded Scarpia with its fine play of tones (smooth, courtly and even mellifluous in dialogue with Tosca, loathsome when the velvet gloves are off), combining with Karajan and the technical staff to make an incomparably atmospheric recording of the Te Deum scene.

Of the other baritones, Ettore Bastianini and Rolando Panerai were rather lighter of voice and more precisely focused than Taddei and Guelfi. Bastianini surely ought to have been one of the best Verdi baritones of the century, for he had an exceptionally attractive middle register, a clear definition of tone, and an easy way with the high tessitura. He was unfortunately one of those singers apparently incapable of singing any single syllable on more than one note without inserting an aspirate, and the habit destroys smoothness of line. He was also one of those who would rarely rise above an average, routine interpretative standard. Some of his best singing of Verdi is done in *La Forza del Destino* where his voice is in its finest condition, and another pleasing performance is his Marcel in *La Bohème*.

Apart from Gobbi, the most satisfying of this generation's baritones on record is Panerai. Their voices sound rather alike, and it is curious to hear them together, with Gobbi singing Falstaff but sounding awfully like a miscast Ford, which Panerai is singing with dark, vibrant tones and plenty of dramatic insight. His voice, with its fast vibrato, seems to be in line with Amato and Franci, though it was probably less powerful than theirs; and, with a good sense of humour and an agile technique, his repertoire has included a fair amount of comic opera (a nimble Taddeo, for example, in *L'Italiana in Algeri*). This able technique helps to make him a better Sir Richard Forth in *I Puritani* than we have much reason to expect these days; his natural panache does the rest. And if we want a restorative to faith in the continuation of the best tradition of the Italian baritone we cannot do better than listen to his singing of Silvio's music in *I Pagliacci*, ardent, fresh-voiced and stylish.

For the basses, one, Ruggero Raimondi, has emerged with distinction in recent years, though others like Ivo Vinco and Giovanni Foiani have done much good work. Raimondi created something of a record (of the other kind) when he made Monterone the true hero of *Rigoletto* (this in the MacNeil recording of 1968). His powerful tones were then promptly engaged for two versions of Verdi's *Requiem*; and very fine they are too, except that every now and again while listening to them (and more often than that towards the end) one wishes for a little more suavity, a little more of the traditional Italian richness. His Philip II in *Don Carlo* (1971) has some finesse, and there is plenty of time for development. One thing, he is at present firm as a rock, which his most famous immediate predecessor, Cesare Siepi, never was in his recordings. Siepi had an enormous voice and was a good actor: facial expressions are a lively implicit accompaniment to his singing of Mozart's Figaro and the Mephistopheles of both Gounod and Boito. But even on 78s he sounded unsteady, and in the cantabile style of an aria like 'O tu, Palermo' *(I Vespri Siciliani)* he is graceless. An unsteady line and aspirated, sketchy runs also spoil the work of Fernando Corena, while Nicola Rossi-Lemeni, after singing well on 78s (smooth and opulent, for instance, in the monologue 'They guess the truth' from *Ivan Susanin*) seemed to lose edge and resonance, giving a performance of Rossini's Moses patriarchal enough to suggest long beards in stained-glass windows but otherwise lacking power. The most pleasing of Italian basses since the war is in fact Nicolas Zaccaria, a rich and firm basso cantante recognisably in the Pinza tradition. Accurate in his reading (observing the staccatos of Ferrando's narration in *Il Trovatore*, and singing them neatly), he is equally careful to preserve a good legato, as in 'Ah, del tebro' in *Norma* (a notable contrast to Carlo Cava, the woolly Orovesco of the Varviso-Suliotis *Norma*). As recorded, his voice does not suggest overwhelming volume, though the authority of his style lends weight to it; probably he could do with some of Raimondi's great power, while Raimondi could be the better for some of the older singer's richness and grace.

Among the younger tenors are Renato Cioni (not yet recorded in his best roles, but capable of intensity, and sometimes admirably stylish as in the Quartet from *Rigoletto* with Sutherland), Eugenio Fernandi (an interesting timbre, a little like Merli or Cortis, perhaps, in the Callas *Turandot*, and good at observing the dolcissimo markings of Verdi's

Requiem), Bruno Prevedi (a spinto with some fire in him, ringing out brilliantly over the chorus of Levites in *Nabucco*), Carlo del Monte (lighter, but spirited and rhythmical, especially effective as an ardent Rinuccio in *Gianni Schicchi*), and Franco Tagliavini (a good strong voice not flattered by recording, as we hear in excerpts from Boito's *Mefistofele*). None has quite the star quality of del Monaco, di Stefano, Corelli, Feruccio Tagliavini or Bergonzi. And the recital of these names reminds us that there were others in the earlier period ('Tableau One') who sang well enough to deserve a place in the story: Flaviano Labò (at his best, as in much of the Deutsche Grammophon *Don Carlo*, a powerful and exciting singer), Gianni Raimondi (a clean-cut Alfredo to Scotto's Violetta), Giuseppe Campora (a convincingly romantic Rodolfo and a reliable Gabriele Adorno), and Mario Filippeschi (ruler of the high Cs but a less satisfying Don Carlo than Labò). Out of the modern successors to these well-stocked ranks one is outstanding, and fortunately he is also the Italian tenor whose work seems most likely to carry on that of Bergonzi. A comparable definition of tone and avoidance of the unmusical, together with the most brilliant young voice heard for many a year, make Luciano Pavarotti a hope for the future as well as a distinct pleasure in the present.

The present pleasures date from Sutherland's *Fille du Régiment* (1968). One of the best performances by any tenor on record, his Tonio has the character and polish of a much older singer, while his voice is that of a young man and in absolutely prime condition. The solo 'Ah, mes amis, quel jour de fête' is the kind of *tour de force* which, recorded sixty years earlier, would be the classic collector's piece; perhaps Escalaïs compares in combining such brilliance of high notes and energy along with a musical imagination. The leaps to high C are tireless, and are not there as a great show-off but as part of the fun of the fête, expressions of joy and energy like a youngster doing cartwheels or standing on his head, and none the less artistic for that. The voice is firm and true, brightly placed yet not a naggingly brilliant sound, and one that he can soften and round. Beautifully quiet and gentle in the passage following—'mais c'est un rêve affreux'—and matching Sutherland with considerable grace in the cadenza of the duet which has gone before, he also establishes a character (a nice sprightliness and some natural chuckling in recitative, for instance.) The air from Act II, 'Pour me rapprocher de Marie', suggests comparison with McCormack who sings it in Italian as 'Per viver vicino'. With the utmost grace and beauty of tone, McCormack sets the highest possible standard, rounding off the song with a perfectly poised head voice. But Pavarotti has his own excellence; as in the charm of his second verse, the fine ring and diminuendo, the superb descending scale from high B.

That he can turn to a serious work and give a sensitive performance is clear from his part in Verdi's *Requiem* under Solti. Singing out in the Kyrie with a fine legato (none of Gigli's aspirates here), he provides a genuine pianissimo when it is asked for ('parce Deus', 'spem dedisti' and so forth

121. Mirella Freni

122. Fiorenza Cossotto in *Favorita*

123. Luciano Pavarotti

in the 'Ingemisco'), and in the 'Hostias' his tone is a finely poised *mezza voce*, not a falsetto and not an unsupported crooning sound. Moreover, there is a kind of tension in his singing which, for one thing, focuses interest (his voice will cleave through a mass of sound by virtue of its tense tone), and, more important, enforces the urgency of the music and the conviction that this is not just a performance, but *the* performance.

It would be marvellous if we have here an artist who will maintain throughout his career standards as high as this in works that are so different. Two recordings suggest misgivings, and, at the time of writing, both are among his latest. One is his complete recording of *Un Ballo in Maschera*, which is superb in many ways but does not show growth as an interpreter. Not that he fails to act—he is, on the contrary, quite vivid,—but he has not created a character who impresses by his nobility (as Vickers does preeminently on the stage, and as Bergonzi is at least relatively able to do in recording). The kind of serious devotion that marked his singing of the *Requiem* is not here: though everything else is. The other misgiving arises from the aria 'A te, o cara' *(I Puritani)*, included in a recital of arias also issued in 1971. His style in this is almost fiercely uningratiating; almost as though he had heard Bonci's old record, disliked it, and decided to do the opposite. So all is loud, except the rounding of the first verse; the phrases are solid and charmless; and the 'runs' (or words with several notes on certain syllables) are comparatively awkward. This aria and 'Com'è gentil', the Serenade from *Don Pasquale*, are disappointing patches in an excellent recital; but it is a pity that the 'bad patch' should cover the two arias that are of the older, 'bel canto' school. A magnificent excerpt from *Il Trovatore* and another from *William Tell* suggest the direction in which Pavarotti may be moving, for his voice (sounding slender, perhaps, because of his pin-point definition) is strong and penetrating. There is certainly a heroic tenor in potential. What we want (and have actually had once or twice for a very few years in a very few individuals this century) is a heroic tenor who has cultivated the arts of the lyric tenor and retained the lyric graces.

In Pavarotti, then, is an interesting test-case. Modern singing, that much decried institution, and most especially where tenors are concerned, has produced him. In him, as in Scotto, Freni, Cossotto (and with Bergonzi as something of a pioneer), modern Italy has produced a singer who sounds properly schooled: to know that an unspreading, continent tone and a proper legato are the first essentials of acceptable singing, and that a sensitive, expressive line is the next. Recording has surely played a large part as teacher in this schooling process. Size without focus, passion without subtlety, may win applause in the arena and even in the great opera houses, but they are no use on record. In the not-so-very-long-run the lessons apply to success in live performances too. It is true that loud, unsubtle singers may win applause, but it is also noticeable that, generally speaking, a pure steady voice and a refined art win more. Since the war, Italian singing has moved towards some such recognition: the best of Italian singing, that is. Cultural conditions are, of course, changing rapidly, and it could be that only a more sophisticated, or well-educated type of person will now go in for operatic singing; in which case no doubt the well-schooled, tasteful and sensitive style will develop among them and perhaps become pervasive. And perhaps then Italian singing will be no more important than English or Swedish or French; and then we shall remember the fable of the goose that laid golden eggs. In the meantime, the increased contribution to musical pleasure can only be welcomed.

27. European Notes: Moscow to Madrid
Régine Crespin   Rita Gorr
Irene Arkhipova   Nicolai Gedda
Geraint Evans

STUDENTS of international affairs sometimes set themselves exercises in reorientation, looking out on the world as from poor beleaguered Moscow to correct any conditioned assumption that the universe must be centred somewhere in Washington or Westminster. Perhaps record collectors should do the same. Operatic cosmography marks Milan, Vienna and New York in its largest letters, and the greatest number of internationally famous singers certainly have come from Italy, Germany and Austria, and America. But there have been plenty of good ones elsewhere; and the map may reflect the limited knowledge of its makers rather than the facts of existence.

As far as Russia and the other communist countries are concerned, there might be some difficulty about its doing otherwise, for the records that find a place in our catalogues, or even arrive as special imports, are relatively few. Inscrutable Russia has always challenged exploration, and among collectors of early gramophone records are those who guard their St. Petersburg 1903s as they might the Romanov Crown Jewels. They may then hold that the great tenor of those days was not Enrico Caruso but Ivan Erschov, and that while Chaliapin was a wonder to the West, a mightier than he stayed behind in Russia, where he was known as the great Sibiriakov. Caruso's successor (or Erschov's) then becomes not one of the names that spring most readily to mind, but Ivan Koslovsky, and the only bass worth speaking of in that period is Mark Reizen. Sometimes the argument is merely partisan, as in a conversation whose pattern I remember being slow to perceive. In its early stages the greatness of Shostakovitch had somehow seemed to preclude that of William Walton, and later on a German pianist was dismissed as a fit subject for discussion, to be replaced smartly by the Russian Gilels. Light dawned only when a chance remark provoked mention of Zara Dolukhanova as Russia's answer to Kathleen Ferrier. On the other hand, it must be said that only the ignorant will be quick to scoff, for Erschov, Sibiriakov, Koslovsky, Reizen and Dolukhanova were quite exceptionally fine singers. And there is no reason to suppose that the modern Russians will have let things slip.

Still, sampling does not create an overwhelming appetite. Until very recently, for example, it seemed to me that the last Russian soprano with a voice that could properly be called steady was Oda Slobodskaya, born in 1895 and still free of wobble in 1961. Tamara Milashkina brings some reassurance on this point, and is one of those who make one want to hear more: a clear-cut voice and a style that is not mass-produced, all evident in Aida's 'Ritorna vincitor', as good a test of expressive resources as any. Yet the most famous of sopranos to us in the West, Galina Vishnevskaya, tends rather to confirm such preconceptions. Her reputation is well-founded, but not on the richness or steadiness of her voice. English listeners know this particularly well, for they go to concert performances of Britten's *War Requiem* in which Heather Harper has made the soprano part sound beautiful, and return to their records where the word for Vishnevskaya has to be something like 'impressive'. In *The Poet's Echo*, which Britten wrote for her, she is rather more than impressive, colouring subtly in 'The Nightingale and the Rose', cutting with deep-edged irony in the 'Epigram', and draining the voice to express the flat desolation of the last song, the 'Lines written during a sleepless night'. But there is always character in her singing, the voice itself commanding attention, sometimes by a kind of slim, aristocratic grandeur, sometimes by the great beauty of its softer tones. Both are heard in a song of Rachmaninoff's called 'I wait for thee', while the intensity of feeling that can accompany her soft singing is clear in the aria from Shostakovitch's *Katerina Ismailova* which follows on the same recital record: the unexpectedly rich lower register and the murmuring pianissimos contribute to a haunting performance. Her distinction often makes itself felt in just such passages: during the high, softly hummed melody of Villa-Lobos' 'Bachianas Brasileiras', or at a particular moment, as when she takes the high note in Lisa's third Act aria in *The Queen of Spades* very cleanly and softly, swelling it gradually, and with an effect unmatched by any of the sopranos tried in comparisons—Xenia Belmas, Joan Hammond, Ljuba Welitsch. The last two singers have also recorded the Letter Scene from *Eugen Onegin*, which is probably Vishnevskaya's most famous role, both of them in better voice than the Russian singer at the time of the complete recording of the opera. There are moments to remember in this, especially in the last Act, and in particular the long sigh 'Ah, happiness was so close at hand'. But the echoes answer with their own sigh; for though dignity and nobility do mark Vishnevskaya's records with a certain greatness, it is only so very intermittently.

The recording of *Eugen Onegin*, issued in 1970, gives probably the best available picture of the Bolshoi at work in this period. As usual with performances from the communist countries, the ensemble and chorus impress as both disciplined and energetic, giving a sense of genuine enjoyment and pride in team work. The supporting characters range from the very good (the Nurse, Larissa Avdeyeva) to the provincial or even parochial. The Olga, Tamara Sinyavskaya, is firm and strong, if somewhat solemn. Prince Gremin is sung by Alexander Ognivtsev who had previously earned gratitude by introducing a firm voice into Shaporin's *The Decembrists*: he plays the Tsar in this, a fine piece of undoctrinal casting, for the hero-conspirators are a wobbly collection. In the last Act of *Eugen Onegin*, Gremin has a tuneful song affectionately known to lovers of opera in English as 'Onegin, I should not be human if I did not adore that woman'. Comparisons show Ognivtsev shaping the melody more than Sibiriakov, though he is less impressive in voice, especially at the extremes. He is a good deal less imaginative than the Yugoslav, Miro Changalovich, who makes it sound like a love song, where Sibiriakov's is a sepulchral ditty sung by old Father Time, and Ognivtsev makes a series of formal statements rather as though princely protocol did not allow anything more personal. Changalovich sings well in every respect except that he is not steady; he also has a conductor who will allow a certain amount of *rubato*, which is all to the good. But the song probably profits from more still, as the old recording by Vladimir Kastorsky suggests. This is in a different class, not only because the voice has an extra distinction, but because of the shading, giving the line grace and meaning, and adding various rather charming touches that are possible only with a greater rhythmic freedom than modern taste generally allows. All the same, Mark Reizen's recording lets us know that they are not imperative, for he commands the delicacy of shading without taking the liberties: with his superbly even, beautifully rounded voice, he gives quite the best performance among all these singers. Ognivtsev, who sounds well among his contemporaries, does not really join ranks with his distinguished predecessors.

The other principal singers are Yuri Mazurok and Vladimir Atlantov. Mazurok seems to have a curious attitude to the character of Onegin ('I feel he expresses the sentiments of our time', he is quoted as saying), but he certainly sings him very well. The firm, clearly defined voice, with its ringing high notes (heard also aptly in Valentine's air from *Faust*) would be an asset in any company, and he makes a convincingly romantic, young-sounding Onegin when so many sound like Lenski's father. The Lenski, Vladimir Atlantov, also gives a positive characterisation: not the mild, dreamy poet often heard, but an ardent, big, rather simple fellow, his voice strong and with a touch of the baritone about it, unusual in Russian tenors. He is sometimes ungainly: his record of 'No, Pagliaccio non son' is vivid, strenuous in the use of the voice and ultimately coarse in effect, and in the finale of the second Act of *Eugen Onegin* he has the grief at command but not the grace. The poetic, lingering elegance of a Smirnov is not his, nor is the lyrical gentleness of his own predecessor in the role, Serge Lemeshev, or his Yugoslav counterpart Drago Starc. But it is a remarkable voice, and there is temperament behind it.

The male singer whose records have been best known here in regular additions to the catalogues over several years is the bass, Ivan Petrov. His singing always has authority, and his evident command makes him able to venture a little more independently than most of his colleagues, producing a fine *mezza voce* for the phrase after the thunder has clapped (but feebly) in *Russlan and Ludmilla*, or for the attractive song about what the translation gives as 'endless versts of virgin snow' in Act One of *The Decembrists*. He displays the range of his voice in Khan Khontchak's solo in *Prince Igor*; an indication of his expressive range too (languorous and energetic in the right places, with a fine toothy laugh of manly knowingness). But of course, the role that gives the fullest opportunities is Boris Godunov, where his recording suggests the power rather than the weakness of the man, the sober strength of purpose rather than the stricken body and the haunted soul. Memorable, therefore, are the cries of 'Aha, Shuisky' as the crafty Boyar (a characterful performance by Gyorgy Shulpin) is announced, 'Tsarevitch' as he commands his son to leave, and the final, formidable 'Ya Tsar yeshcho' ('I still am Tsar'). Agony and tenderness in the Monologue, physical debility in the Death Scene, grief in the Prayer: these are harder to find, though there is a sense of age (heightened in the meeting with Pimen by Mark Reshetin's relatively young-sounding voice and slightly prosaic manner—he doesn't sound like an old man who has come a long way to say the things to which his life has led). Possibly Petrov's acting may supply what the recording lacks; in the meantime its great feature is the extent to which the music is sung as written. He is not an impeccable singer: not always steady, and inclined, especially in the Coronation Scene, to approach notes from below. But he has the distinction, among Borises on record, of singing the notes that are written for the Clock Scene and very little but the notes, and still carrying conviction as drama.

Dramatic considerations are probably less to the fore in the notion that the best of Russia's singers in the nineteen-sixties has been the mezzo, Irina Arkhipova. Certainly her voice and its production suggest that she deserves that title. A splendidly rich sound that is bright-toned and yet has some grandeur, her voice rings out strong and clear, without divisions of register and with complete freedom from throaty constrictions in any part of the range.

As with Petrov, there are certain kinds of mood, emotion and colouring that seem to be missing. The Séguédille from *Carmen* does not seduce; Lel's songs from *The Snow-Maiden* do not dance or smile; and Fairy Spring from the same opera sings with much the same voice, a voice that is rather too mature and regal, either for the shepherd or the fairy. In Arensky's cantata, *The Fountain of Bakhchisarai*, Zarema sings of her loss of love and of native land, yet there is no frailty of tone in Arkhipova's voice to suggest pathos and no subtler colouring to suggest nostalgia. 'Ya plachu' ('I weep') she sings at one point; but the voice doesn't.

On the other hand, there is an urgency about the performance, and, at the climax of Zarema's appeal to her rival, a genuine intensity; dark and powerful in character in the last lines, in which she tells that she knows how to use a dagger if she has to—and we believe her. Also about midway through this long aria there comes a point of tenderness (she absolves the rival of any intention to harm her), and it becomes clear during the course of Arkhipova's recital that she has the ability to produce these softer, gentler tones, and therefore possibly to introduce a greater variety of colouring as her art matures. Marfa's sentence, 'We shall burn together like some holy candles' (*Khovanshchina*, Act III) becomes memorable, as she takes the edge out of her voice. Best of all, the very fine solo from Prokoviev's *Alexander Nevsky*, where a young bride tells how after the battle she will go over the field of the slain and kiss those who have died for Russia. This is sung with depth and humanity; she gives herself with genuine devotion to the sad melody, and ends the song with an extremely beautiful edgeless gentleness.

Still, Arkhipova's prime musical offering is her voice, and the attraction of her records lies primarily in this gloriously healthy sound. We hear it excitingly in the passionate lyrical phrases telling of a time of 'unbroken ecstasy' in the Arensky cantata just mentioned. And another superb example is the earliest of these records, the solo from Tchaikowsky's *Joan of Arc*, most familiar to us by its French title, 'Adieu, forêts'. The heroic acceptance of the time's challenge ('Da chas nastal'—'The hour has come') has a magnificent ring: it is a performance that presents Joan the soldier,

124. Irina Arkhipova

125. Nicolai Gedda

and the last note is held high, steady and proud. If it still rings out like that in the Bolshoi, it almost makes of itself sufficient reason for travelling east; and no doubt there are numerous accompanying splendours of which this record-sampling gives little more than a glimpse.

If from Moscow we were now to travel to the west, staying in communist Europe for a while, we may still find that the Western record catalogues have afforded an inadequate introduction to the singing there. Going south and working northwards, no doubt there would be singing worth hearing in Sofia, but the chief Bulgarian exports since the war have been three of the world's best basses, Boris Christoff, Nicolai Ghiaurov and Raphael Arié, all mentioned elsewhere. Bucharest would present cast-lists of unknown names. Budapest very largely too, though the tenor Robert Ilosfalvy and the contralto Erzsebet Komlossy are no strangers to us (Ilosfalvy somewhat disappointingly tight-sounding on records, Komlossy smooth and dramatic but not always well-focused, both of them heard representatively in Dvořák's *Requiem Mass*). Belgrade is a different matter. From the early years of LP there has been a series of recordings, mostly of Russian works, made by the National Opera, and we have become well acquainted with the name of Melanie Bugarinovich, and the rich, authoritative sound of her voice. She sings Marfa in the *Khovanshchina*, hoisting herself up to the high notes, but making with Miro Changalovich, as Dositheus, an impressive pair of Old Believers. Changalovich has the besetting sin of so many of these singers, a failure to keep the tone firm and steady; he is a genuine artist all the same, a patriarchal and human Ivan Susanin, and a convincingly tormented Boris Godunov. Among the deeper basses, Drago Bernadic is outstanding: an easy, resonant, homogeneous sound, creating an effect much greater than the role itself in his appearance as the Viking Guest in *Sadko*. Sadko himself is an able tenor, Drago Starc, managing well in the breathless bars of eleven-four time, and singing his Dance Song energetically; rather better, in fact, than the gentler song in scene 2, about the dark, pathless forests, where he is not really smooth or subtle enough. The cast also contains a good high soprano in Maria Glavasevic, the Sea-Princess. She is neat in the melisma with which this role and that of Antonida in *Ivan Susanin* open, though she generally aspirates it; sometimes (for instance, as Princess Swanhilda in *Tsar Sultan*) she sounds a little hard in the higher part of the voice, but generally the effect is pretty, fresh and precise.

Probably more than by the individual roles, one leaves the Belgrade recordings impressed by excellence of ensemble and frequently of chorus work (the Chorus of the Yugoslav Army giving full-bodied extra strength in *Ivan Susanin*), and the same is true of most that we hear from Prague. Naturally, the main contribution of the Czech company has been in the works of Dvořák, Smetana and Janáček. Two recordings of Dvořák's *Rusalka* have come from Prague in ten years, the second, of 1963, having an exquisite heroine in Milada Subrtova. Her predecessor, Ludmilla

Cervinkova, had a clean, well-modulated tone and gave a good performance, but Subrtova has a very feminine delicacy of sound, even a frailty, that has a strong dramatic quality about it, shading her famous song to the moon beautifully, and pleading in winning fashion to her aunt-witch. Here the earlier recording did better, boasting that super-rarity, a witch without a wobble. This is Marta Krasova who casts her spells in fine style, the emphatic refrain 'Cury mury fuk' being Czech, we find, for abracadabra. The 1953 version has also a vastly preferable Prince, Beno Blachut, one of the best Czech tenors of the century. Tender and warm in his singing of this role, he was always a singer with good, natural production. The voice had hardened by 1962 when he sings in Dvořák's horror-cantata, *The Spectre's Bride*, and probably he could sound rather more fiendish in his advice to dispense with prayer-book, rosary and cross; but the style is unfailingly musical, the reading intelligent, and the voice pleasing and steady. More remarkable, he could sound graceful in Janáček's difficult writing for the tenor voice: coping with the difficult intervals of *The Macropoulos Affair* and giving a performance of exceptional sensitivity in *The Diary of a Young Man who Disappeared*. His successor in Rusalka is Ivo Zidek, harsher of voice and less graceful of style. He, however, comes into his own in *Jenůfa*, where he sings the irresponsible Steva convincingly, with Vilem Pribyl, another strong-voiced, rather unsubtle tenor, as Laca. The Kostelnička of this 1970 recording is Nezevda Kniplova, a widely travelled heroic soprano who (appropriately here) sounds every bit of her less than forty years. But it is ungrateful to criticise a fine Kostelnička for not tickling the ears, and Kniplova captures the strong hard note of hate and resentfulness in her voice, giving full feeling to the terrible line 'He was born in sin' as the wretched woman takes the unwanted baby out 'to God'. Her Jenůfa, Libuse Domaninska, contrasts well, with a girlish tone that was more beautiful some years earlier when she recorded the Prayer (Act II) for Supraphon. But how difficult Janáček makes it for singers to remember that singing is their business. We find the Prague Katya Kabanová, Drahomira Tikalova, sensitive to the beauties of what is often a remarkably tender score, yet having to spend much of her time pecking at high semiquavers following 'the melodic curves of speech'. There are obviously many fine singers in Czechoslovakia (many, like the excellent baritone, the late Ladislav Mraz, so far unmentioned); but it is a pity that the great national composer of opera did not write with more consideration for the voice.

What Janáček asks of the voice is nothing, however, to the demands which Penderecki makes of his singers. *The St. Luke Passion* and the *Auschwitz Oratorio* both set fearsome problems for the choir, which must pick the pitch of the chordal clusters apparently out of thin air, move accurately in the angular voice parts, each of them no help to the others, achieve unanimity in the *a capella* movements where the sounds may appear to the listener to be somewhat random until a difference of opinion among, say, the altos makes it clear that there is one right and many wrongs in this just as in the *Messiah*. The Cracow Philharmonia give tremendous performances, and along with the protesting, muttering, shrieking, hissing, whispering, mocking and wailing that they have to do, they also sing with much beauty of tone. The soloists work often in painfully clamorous, jagged phrases, and in the circumstances it seems almost frivolous to note that the soprano, Stefania Woytowicz, is unsteady and that the baritone Andrazej Hiolski sings with pale tone. Wiestaw Ochman, the tenor, enters effectively into the final 'Apotheosis' section of the *Auschwitz Oratorio*, firm and strong; while the bass is one of the best-known of Polish singers since the war, Bernard Ladysz. In the west we have known him previously as a sonorous chaplain in Callas' *Lucia di Lammermoor*, and also through a recital record of 1959 which proves less satisfying on repeated listening, with some faulty legato and inconsistent tone. Even so, there are some impressive things in it, such as a warm, gentle account of the Prayer ('Tu sul labbro') from *Nabucco*, and an expressive, rather more brilliant and baritonal performance of King René's solo in Tchaikowsky's *Iolanta*. In Penderecki, the depth of his voice adds a further sombre colour to the grim tonal picture; and his accurate reading, like that of all taking part, pays testimony to the thorough musicianship that Polish singers are expected to acquire.

The record collector's catalogue-guided, whistle-stop tour through the communist countries has yielded a fair amount, after all, and it is not quite over. For travelling north from Poland towards Scandinavia we take in Estonia, where one of the best of the Bolshoi's singers was born. Georg Ots has impressed as a firm, pleasant (possibly even too likeable) Eugen Onegin to Vishnevskaya's Tatiana in her 1963 recording of the final scene. But his excellence extends to a wide range of music; to Italian opera, for instance, where his recording of 'Eri tu' from *Un Ballo in Maschera* is exceptionally idiomatic, smooth, brilliant-voiced, and strongly dramatised. The only hindrance to enjoyment is the fierce vowel sound on 'e' (as in 'terra'), which is perhaps a national characteristic as it reappears when he sings Iago's Creed with some blood-curdling inflections in his own language. His accomplishments also include a mastery of Handelian runs, as shown in the clearly articulated, even-voiced performance of a taxing allegro aria in *Julius Caesar*. It is well to leave these countries with his singing in mind. Material is not plentiful enough to enforce the comparison with much finality, but Georg Ots is probably a good example of the need for reorientation that we were speaking of at the start; he may well be at any rate the equal of such baritones as Robert Merrill and Sherrill Milnes, and when material for a complete assessment of these singers on record becomes available, this son of Talinn may well be one of those who help to change the collectors' map.

In Scandinavia we hear two recitals. Kim Borg, the Finnish bass, made an auspicious early appearance on records in Christoff's first recording of

Boris Godunov, where the uninitiated would be more likely than usual to say 'This is him' when in fact it is only Secretary Shchelkaloff, but sung with remarkable sonority and style. His subsequent career has been substantial if not quite as grand as it might have been. In the opera house his voice was not always incisive enough, and the characterisations were not always satisfying. But he has made good records, many non-operatic. The depth of feeling and of tone match beautifully in a recital of 'dark' Lieder. The Michelangelo songs were the last Wolf wrote and they are material for a mature singer: Borg rises to the climax of the first, 'Wohl denk' ich oft', with a strong assertive ring, and in the second, 'Alles endet was entstehet' he shows what an expressive interpreter he can be, colouring imaginatively, as well as singing with exceptionally beautiful tone. In the *Vier ernste Gesänge* of Brahms, as in other Lieder, the beauty of tone is in fact the chief pleasure of his performance. Not that he is uninteresting, but (like Shirley-Quirk in this, as opposed to Fischer-Dieskau) we listen comfortably to a beautiful voice finely produced (like Shirley-Quirk, bringing a smooth, well-supported *mezza voce* to St. Paul's phrase about seeing through a glass darkly), but we do not learn the music anew. Yet he does carry a revelation or two in his repertoire, as in the bass solo, 'Pro peccatis' in Rossini's *Stabat Mater* which responds to some exquisite touches. Like the Finnish baritone Tom Krause and the bass Martti Talvela, he has brought a distinctive character and a fine voice to the international scene, Finland, like Bulgaria, giving more than its fair share of power to the bass clef.

Sweden has a long established tradition as a supplier of good sopranos. Elisabeth Söderström reminds us just how long in her recital of music sung by Jenny Lind. Cosy indoor music or wholesome fresh-air songs these are; all too pretty and complacent to give more than casual pleasure (though they could become favourites as a sort of musical escapism), and they impose narrow limits on the modern singer. Söderström is much too interesting a singer to have quite the virginal purity and simplicity that the Swedish songs seem to want, though just occasionally (as in the long-drawn pianissimo murmurs of one called 'Herdegossen') she works that spell which has an audience holding its breath, drawn in to the singer and the short-lived loveliness of the song. In her own character she is a gracious and sympathetic Countess in *Le Nozze di Figaro*, a light vibrato sometimes obscuring the clear lines of the arias, but especially delightful in the Letter Duet with Reri Grist as the lively and bright-voiced Susanna; somewhat out of it, she is cast as Octavian in some excerpts from *Rosenkavalier*, a fine youthful glow on the voice, but very feminine. The femininity, a grace that is a thing both of nature and of sophistication, makes her a clear choice for Debussy's Mélisande, and in Boulez' famous recording she sings with vivid presence—not easy in the part of 'un petit être, si tranquille, si timide, et si silencieux'; but then, her reactions as Golaud's ring falls into the water suggest that this is not the whole story.

Söderström is one of several singers from the Stockholm opera who have gained a sturdy international reputation. Others are Ingvar Wixwell (the baritone whose warmly rounded voice and even production made an unusually sympathetic effect as Count Almaviva in Colin Davis' *Nozze di Figaro*), Margareta Hallin-Boström (a light soprano with a good technique and a way of focusing attention, as we hear in her 'Una voce poco fa'), the mezzo Kerstin Meyer, the sumptuous contralto Bette Björling, Aase Nordmo-Lövborg, and, of course, Birgit Nilsson, whose international fame has grown so that her many years with the Stockholm company tend almost to be forgotten.

The complete international is another Swede, Nicolai Gedda. Born in Stockholm of a Swedish mother, Gedda was brought up in musical matters by a Russian father who directed a choir in Leipzig, and since then he has become very much a citizen of the world. One feature of his work that has no doubt followed on his relatively cosmopolitan youth is his proficiency in languages, so that on records he sings in English and Spanish as well as the singer's basic trinity of French-German-Italian, and his own native Swedish and Russian. With this linguistic mastery has also grown a feeling for a wide range of styles: few singers are so readily at home with the whole body of European music, up to—though on records not including—modern times.

He has recorded some Bach, the 'Benedictus' of the *B Minor Mass*, beneficent in tone and in the even flow of sound, being a fine example. In Mozart he sings a fervent Don Ottavio and a graceful Tamino. Beethoven is represented by a deeply felt performance of Florestan's taxing solo in *Fidelio*, and by a collection of tender and high-spirited songs. Italian opera and French are there in abundance; Gluck, Weber, Lortzing, even Wagner, with a lyrical, imaginative reading of solos from *Lohengrin*, are represented. Oratorio and operetta, songs of Richard Strauss (a marvellous performance of 'Heimliche Aufforderung', for example, which follows all the quickly changing moods), Fauré, Rachmaninoff, Respighi, Turina . . . The list could be doubled, and then again.

If anything, Gedda has been over-exposed. No one can record as much as he has done without at one time finding himself better than at another, or without finding himself suffering from comparisons with his predecessors (his Hoffmann seeming strangely charmless when compared with the solos which Tauber recorded, his solo 'Bannis la crainte' from Gluck's *Alceste* sounding effortful and insecure compared with George Thill). He is not a routine artist: a performance has to catch alight. Whether because of the state of the voice, the feeling of the audience or the other participators, or the character of the conductor, one does not know, but the standard of achievement certainly varies from one recording session to another. 'Dies Bildnis ist bezaubernd schön' from *Die Zauberflöte*, for instance, comes off much better in a recital record of 1967, where the conductor is Heinrich Bender, than it does in the complete set under Klemperer

(1964). The later recording has a smile, a poise, and a graceful echo effect in the repetition of 'Die Liebe'; the Klemperer record goes more stiffly, is more solemn, and has little smile. It may be due to the conductor (Gedda's other Mozart with Klemperer, in *Don Giovanni*, is also less graceful than most of his singing), but the actual condition of the voice as well as the presentation seems better in the recital: sweeter-toned and firmer too. A comparison of the Flower Song from *Carmen* in the two complete performances he recorded also shows how he responds to different conditions, and in this case the best comes out under the great conductor and in the earlier recording. In the Prêtre–Callas recording (1964) the solo starts with a somewhat unfocused sound, and the emphatic treatment of later phrases (for instance, 'te revoir, Carmen') shakes him off the precise centre of the note. The earlier performance under Beecham (1960) is taken more slowly, *con amore* as the score says, and it is different from the start, the soft opening being poised and defined, and in the development everything is dramatised afresh. The ending is less satisfactory, for the B flat phrase is quite loud whereas the later recording has it done softly with the last note of all in better focus. But over all there is a world of difference, in that the one is a piece of conventional singing, and the other is a 'lived', re-created experience.

So is the best of his work in both opera and song. As Rodolfo and Pinkerton in the Puccini operas, he creates real people and clearly has his own personal insight into the dramatic and musical character of the roles. In *La Bohème* he makes us see Rodolfo in a different light, passionate and genuine enough though more superficial in nature than Mimì, always bouncing away in compound time, until the bubble collapses (as in Act III—'Mimì è tanta malata') and a sadly helpless anxiety takes its place. In *Madama Butterfly* he presents a much more sympathetic Pinkerton than most, a man with the charm, as well as the thoughtlessness, of youth, a tender lover, whose reappearance in the last scene becomes moving, as in hardly any other performance, because we see the likeable person of the first Act now craven and reduced, and can believe that his remorse comes from the heart. He acts vividly with his voice, so that we even seem to see him smell the flowers as he enters the sad house amid the 'bitter fragrance' of these blossoms that have been spread for his welcoming.

He is one of those surprisingly rare singers, one whose voice can smile. He smiles his Love Duet in *Faust* and his meeting with Marguérite at the Kermesse. He has a broad, enthusiastic smile for Act II of *La Bohème*, and a keen humorous relish for the situation which develops after Musetta's song. Or he can produce a tiny little voice and use it with great fun as in the scene with Abul Hassan (Oscar Czerwenka) in *Der Barbier von Bagdad*. In Italian song he can catch the lilt and gaiety, as in a charmer called 'Stornelli capricciosi'. And he is the ideal man to bring out the lightness of heart in the Beethoven songs. 'Der Kuss' is a straight-forward joke-song, and he sings it with enjoyment; but more difficult is such a song as 'Mit einem gemalten Bande' where any heaviness or stiffness of voice and style would be fatal, and where Gedda's feeling for rhythm, for the play of staccato and legato, and his nimbleness of movement capture the mood perfectly and represent a triumph of the Lieder singer's art. *An die ferne Geliebte*, which is a relatively sustained test of sensitivity, also goes beautifully: like Ernst Häfliger he gives a performance that has charm and delicacy of nuance, and, perhaps rather more than the Swiss tenor, he get just the right balance between serenity and excitement, happiness and longing.

It is true that he is sometimes over-emphatic. In Flotow's *Martha*, the beginning of the duet 'Solo, profugo' finds him at his least gracious, giving a lumpy treatment of the melody (compare Tauber, who phrases so much more broadly and charmingly), and cultivating a thumping way with the rhythm. At other times he can sound over-studied and precious; his solos in *Elijah* are an example here (tenors of the older school, like Walter Widdop, would have a rare time imitating this fancy style). But the excellence of so much more remains as a delight both to the intelligence and to the ear. We might leave him with the most famous test-piece of Italian *bel canto* in our ears, 'Una furtiva lagrima' from *L'Elisir d'Amore*. The smoothness, the sweet tone, the phrasing and shading, the faithfully observed pianissimo, the fluent cadenza: all are features of a performance which is well at the centre of the tradition.

Cross the North Sea and, as a visitor, look for the tradition in the British Isles, and what does one find? Looking for it now, not (as we shall do later) in the school of singing that has formed round Benjamin Britten and other living composers for the voice, nor among those who have helped the work of scholars to bear fruit, delving into the lesser-known music of Bach and Handel and Purcell, and back beyond them, nor even among those who (like Janet Baker and John Shirley-Quirk) have recorded more as from the concert platform than the operatic stage: looking, rather, as the tourist might, at the opera houses and the traditional centre of their repertoire. Looking, as a starting point, for a tenor to sing 'Una furtiva lagrima' as well as Gedda did.

Well, that (on records, at least) we shall probably not find. Perhaps Heddle Nash has a successor in Stuart Burrows, but records have still to show it in this 'central' operatic part of the tenor repertoire (if comparison with Gedda is in question, he would also have to learn the Geddan art of smiling with the voice, which at present, even in the most charming, happy music, is noticeably missing). The aria in question has been recorded fairly recently by a British tenor, Charles Craig, and he is certainly the tenor whose records are most likely to come the way of our hypothetical tourist, and impress him favourably. In 'Una furtiva lagrima' he lifts his voice to the first note, and again at the beginning of the second phrase; this is a fairly common characteristic, and it is a pity because he sings the aria with some poise, and with a clean, unostentatious musical style. That is particularly creditable as he is generally thought of as a *spinto*, a Radamès (he has also sung an admired Otello) rather than a Nemorino (though, after all, it was a role that Caruso kept in his repertoire to the very end). In the more heroic music, he has recorded 'Celeste Aida' in a way that represents him fairly: there are no miracles of phrasing, and there is little to establish a distinctive personality in the memory, but the performance is blest with a genuine legato, with a good, clear-cut, ringing voice, and with a character that is effectively contrasted with that of the hero of *La Bohème* whose 'Che gelida manina' he has just sung. At least there is no doubt about the tradition to which Craig belongs in that music; the honeyed *mezza voce*, the portamento, even something of a little pout of affection, all suggest (as does the *Faust* solo later on) that like most of his generation he was brought up on DB.1532, Gigli's performance of these arias on a best-selling 78. But he is a very good Puccini tenor in his own right, singing attractively in the *Tosca* duets with Joan Hammond, and in some excerpts from *Madama Butterfly* with Marie Collier: having always a fine definition and a natural ring, and opening the Love Duet with a tenderness which the master himself might have envied.

The *Butterfly* record is one of a series made in the early nineteen-sixties with highlights from well-known operas sung in English and adding up to give a good picture of the Sadlers Wells Company at this time. Craig himself was by then singing regularly at Covent Garden, as was Collier, an Australian soprano with a powerful and exciting voice which did not take easily to recording. The distinctive vibrato that could add to the dramatic effect of her singing in the theatre combined with a certain shallowness in the lower part of the voice to place her as a 'non-phonogenic' soprano: yet her singing of Chrysothemis to Nilsson's Elektra is compelling in its intensity, and there are many phrases (such as 'niemand kommt, kein Bruder, kein Bote' . . . 'Viel lieber tot, als leben und nicht leben') that will recall, all too tragically, the thrill of that unique voice taken from us by her lamentable death in 1971. But the Sadlers Wells Company was strong enough anyway to need no assistance in such records from the Covent Garden stars. Among their tenors, for instance, was another Australian, Donald Smith, whose Duke of Mantua in the *Rigoletto* excerpts glows with health of voice, and is graced by a genuine sense of style in the lyrical 'E il sol dell'anima'. Their resident Butterfly was Ava June, at her best, warm and ample, in Majenka's aria from *The Bartered Bride*. In Elizabeth Fretwell they had another lyric-dramatic soprano, under-represented on records (what a pity they did not record *The Girl of the Golden West*, one of the company's best productions around this time, in which she and Donald Smith were for the time being the equal of any Italians who came to England). She sounds well in the broad phrases of the Finale of Act II of *Il Trovatore*, and shows how well she kept this dramatic voice in trim in the duets from the last Act with the baritone.

This was Peter Glossop, who was subsequently to have a career centred on Covent Garden and flourishing all over the world. As one goes back to them, these Sadlers Wells records are newly impressive, and one wonders why the record companies did not take more notice. A decade has gone by, probably with the voice at its best, in which he has certainly appeared in some important recordings, yet not in as many as one might have expected and not quite establishing himself as, say, Merrill and Milnes have done. His work in *Roberto Devereux* reveals the warmth and resonance of his voice, and his singing of Billy Budd's ballad, unaffectedly touching, shows him as a good, sensitive musician. Yet if I personally[1] want to recapture the sound of the Peter Glossop that I remember with most enjoyment, it would be through the opera-in-English series: the *Rigoletto* record perhaps, not quite intense, yet idiomatic and so much the right voice for the part, but probably even more so the *Trovatore*, where 'Il balen', with its smoothness and easy high notes, gives such promise of a remarkable operatic baritone, and a natural in Verdi.

Several singers from Sadlers Wells, like Glossop, have gone on to sing at Covent Garden and/or abroad. The Gilda of his *Rigoletto* record, Elizabeth Harwood, is one, and the Azucena of the *Trovatore*, Patricia Johnson, another. Harwood, precise, light and high of voice, makes an appealing Gilda, all her trills in place and no hardness of tone or disposition (a successor, perhaps, to Gwen Catley in this), and she went on to sing a particularly engaging Bella in *Midsummer Marriage*, her pretty ways not being arch of self-regarding, and a warmth coming into her voice for the tender music of Act II. Patricia Johnson, a mezzo who later made a solid reputation in Germany, also excels in modern music. Probably the greatest credit of all these records to Sadlers Wells was the *Oedipus Rex* of Stravinsky in which she sang a still unbettered Jocasta: urgent, vivid, and absolutely firm. Since then she has sung on records mostly with German casts: showing her turn for comedy in Henze's *Der Junge Lord*, rather stiff and awkward in the extremely difficult vocal line of the alto aria in Bach's *Easter Oratorio*, accurate and accomplished, however, in *Lulu* where she sings the Countess. But what a Carmen she was, and how the sheer nerve of it comes across in that Sadlers Wells recording. Another souvenir of England's place in the tradition for the traveller to take away with him.

He ought, of course, to have some more up-to-date souvenirs. Sadlers Wells have revived Wagner-in-English with great success in recent years, but if the visitor wants to hear their Wotan and Hans Sachs (Norman Bailey) he will have to search catalogues and records diligently and judge from various bits and pieces. Others have fared better: their Hunding, the excellent Clifford Grant, can be heard as a fine, firm Basilio in *Le Nozze di Figaro*, and their Heldentenor (Alberto Remedios) is Mark in *Midsummer*

---

[1] I remember a principal tenor of Sadlers Wells at this time telling me how he would leave the stage during *Pagliacci*, passing through the chorus and always hearing a voice that would raise goose-pimples on his skin as he heard it. The voice was Glossop's, very soon to emerge from the chorus to sing a fine Silvio, following the soprano (when I heard him) up to a high A natural in the imitative bars of the Love Duet.

Marriage (strong, surprisingly mellifluous, and good at catching the ecstasy of 'the summer morning dances in my blood'). Yet their Brünnhilde (Rita Hunter), an exceptionally fine one too, is the waiting woman, Ines, in *Il Trovatore* and the mother in *Hansel and Gretel*. It is time for a new series.[1]

The *Midsummer Marriage* recording, already twice mentioned, brings us to Covent Garden and to several other fine singers to be heard there. Of course, the very fact that such a recording exists and that it is so fine as a complete performance, suggests much about the standard of music-making at the Royal Opera House. An opera chorus who can cope so confidently with such music is a prize possession in itself. The youthful sound of the soloists who can bring assurance and a secure technique to this unnerving score is again reassuring. Elizabeth Bainbridge and Stafford Dean are Ancients who suggest antiquity by their authority rather than their wobbles. Helen Watts, the Sosostris (giving also a deeply felt and richly sung performance as the mother in *Riders to the Sea*) sustains the long notes and the long solo with firmness matching her dignity. Even King Fisher, a fine part for loud, unlovely baritones, is sung with definition and warm tone by Raimund Herincx, another recruit from the Sadlers Wells of the early sixties. In the soprano lead (the role of Jennifer, first sung by Joan Sutherland), we hear Joan Carlyle singing with quite exceptional beauty of tone. Ever reliable, Carlyle has had a very fair share of major roles at the opera house, while important recordings have been infrequent. The voice is not rich or voluptuous; nor on the other hand is it notably pure or bell-like in sound. Neither her Nedda in *Pagliacci* (recorded under Karajan) nor her 'Dove sono' from *Le Nozze di Figaro* registers quite as beautiful or exciting singing, though it would be very hard to find any specific fault. The Jennifer is something more, however: fresh-sounding as the young girl she is representing, floating her high notes coolly and beautifully into the midsummer air, determined and strong as such a character should be, dancing like a virtuoso to this most joyously rhythmic music, apparently forgetful of its difficulties.

Yet it could well be that the unsensuous, energetic efficiency of this soprano might keep its place in the traveller's mind as an emblem of British operatic singing, its limitations as well as its achievements. Where is the soprano to sing with richness and passion (and steadiness), where the tenor with fire in his voice, or the baritone with that kind of dark vibrancy which can infuse this comfortable, middle-of-the-road voice with character and drama? Perhaps the mezzos would help to send the traveller away better satisfied in this respect. Leaving aside Janet Baker, who is quite exceptional in her ability to intensify the effect of a voice that is by nature medium in most things, including power, the British opera season is likely to offer at least two remarkable mezzos in Josephine Veasey and

---

[1] August 1972 brought a record of excerpts from *Götterdämmerung* with Hunter and Remedios singing (in German) with incisive tone and impressive authority.

Yvonne Minton. Veasey, like Gwyneth Jones and David Ward among Covent Garden's Wagnerians, has been mentioned in chapter 21, in a creditable comparison with Kirsten Flagstad. She is a singer of real stature, as records confirm, even though they bring out a well-mannered Englishness of timbre that ever so slightly restricts intensity. It is there appropriately enough in *Beatrice di Tenda*, where she sings Agnese, whose offstage Romance sounds gentle and almost angelic, the high notes beautifully poised. Berlioz' Dido needs a great deal more, and almost all of what it needs she gives: the sonority and energy which must mark her entry (going at top speed under Colin Davis), the sheer beauty of tone for the love music (though one would like both of the singers to take advantage of recording conditions and sing really softly), the authority for sending Aeneas about his business in the parting scene, and then the spirit, the noble resolution, the 'gémissant' of the dying cries, in the final scene. Yvonne Minton has as yet to record anything which gives quite the opportunities of this great role, but her Octavian in *Der Rosenkavalier* under Solti shows how characterful her singing can be. Handling the text with intelligence, thrusting manfully, giving a manful female impersonation too, she sings with a gloriously firm resonance; and indeed, in another role in the opera, that of Annina, she impresses, in the Covent Garden Anniversary record, as having just about the best voice in the company.

Her Ochs in that excerpt is Michael Langdon, idiomatic in pronunciation as in style, and notable on records for his effectively dour, heavy-gaited characterisation of the Master-at-Arms in *Billy Budd*. The other principal basses in the company so far unmentioned are Joseph Rouleau (ample and reflective in the Coronation Scene from *Boris Godunov*) and Forbes Robinson, who also has recorded Claggart's Monologue in *Billy Budd*, and with greater subtlety. No doubt Solti's conducting has something to do with this. Britten himself conducts in the complete recording, but in this extract Solti brings out with greater effect the chatter of devils going *pizzicato* in the brain or prodding fiendishly through the woodwind. The voice begins broodingly, shades off the notes on the word 'born', opens up on the word 'hell', returns to his theme of the painfulness of beauty with an inner tone and a genuine pianissimo, poisons his voice in the words 'if love can escape', cools the blood with an other-worldly pallor in the resolution 'I, John Claggart . . .', crushes the life out of 'beauty, handsomeness, goodness' in the final assertion ('. . . have you in my power and I will destroy you'). It is one of the most vivid of recorded exercises in evil.

Let us return to our visitor. He will hear these singers, and some of their names will have been already familiar, for several of them are well-known abroad. Two others might justly be called famous, and the traveller will look for their records too. With the soprano, Amy Shuard, he will have to search around, for this powerful singer, indispensable in the opera houses for two decades, is not to be heard in any major recording. Tatiana's Letter Scene in *Eugen Onegin*, included in a programme otherwise orchestral, shows that the voice sounds well on records, though it can sometimes seem a rather hard instrument in the theatre. The main trouble with her singing here is that it is out of character: instead of the affectionate, impulsive girl, she gives us a mature and formidable woman, making such urgent demands upon her correspondent that it is no wonder he declined the honour. But when the character is Turandot or Elektra, that is a different story. In Turandot's 'In questa reggia' she takes the reins firmly and soars aloft in the tradition of her teacher, Eva Turner. In Elektra's great Monologue (entrance music, like Turandot's, and in its way equally taxing) she challenges comparison with Nilsson, and emerges unscathed. Less silveredged than Nilsson, she has the same brilliant way with broad upward intervals, and gives a comparable impression of power. If anything, there is a greater sense of perspective in Shuard's performance, more inwardness and love along with the bitterness and revulsion. One phrase in particular ('die Stunde, wo sie dich geschachtet haben') has the stamp of greatness: the tender, sickened memory is itself made memorable, and in it the singer has her own worthy memorial.

No doubts, at any rate, as to the identity or the memorial of the remaining British singer: Sir Geraint Evans—*Falstaff immenso*. A recorded *Falstaff* has to be seen by the mind's eye (of all operas, it is the one that demands most action on the listener's mental stage). But the protagonist usually makes this difficult in one respect, and it is here that Evans scores: he *sounds* fat. Stabile, Gobbi, Fischer-Dieskau (or back into earlier times and the excerpts in which we hear Scotti, Ruffo and the first of them all, Victor Maurel): they may carry a ton of padding round the midriff, but as for the voice—it is very much as the Bible says, you can't add the cubits by thinking about them. Evans is much more of a bass-baritone than the others, and this helps. The bass quality in his voice supports, for instance, the rotund dignity of his 'Va, vecchio John' as he prepares to go a-wooing; or the matter-of-fact complacency with which he accepts Mistress Quickly's compliments about his prowess as a seducer of women. He is also helped, it must be said, by having an exceptionally good cast to play up to him; so that the first scene, with Covent Garden's John Lanigan as Dr. Caius, Giovanni Foiani as Pistol, and the prince of comprimarios, Piero de Palma, as a very funny Bardolph, goes with marvellous style and spirit. Then, as Alice, he has Ilva Ligabue in gorgeous voice, leading him on with wide-eyed, breathlessly affected admiration. He responds with a splendidly vivid characterisation, whether in his indignation at the inn-keeper's bill, or his fleshy relish at the prospects of cuckoldry, or in the awed *sotto voce* which recalls that it is death to look at the fairies in Windsor Forest.

One also realises what one ungratefully tends to forget—that he has a fine voice. Its warmth and resonance enrich such passages as that in the last scene where he consoles himself in his present predicament by thinking what Jove did for the love of Europa. On the other hand, one sometimes wishes for a sharper focus, even in this opera, and certainly when he turns

126. Geraint Evans as Falstaff

to other roles, such as Mozart's Figaro. This he sings in the recording conducted at a steady *adagio con moto* by Klemperer, in which his strong sense of rhythm does good and necessary service. But if one compares, say, the Figaro of Sesto Bruscantini, it is always to find an increased pleasure in the Italian's well-defined tone, open-throated and evenly produced. In Handel, where voice and style are exposed in a colder light, one feels the lines drawn thick with a workman's hand; so that 'Si tra i ceppi' from *Berenice* goes with sturdy tone and plenty of energy, but with a way of hitting notes over the head and without quite the control that makes the voice run like a thoroughbred over even ground and within strictly parallel fences. Not that there is anything slapdash or makeshift about his singing: no aspirating of the runs to make them easier, and no nicking of phrases to facilitate the breathing. But finally it is for character-singing— with the emphasis on the first word—that we remember Geraint Evans.

The range of the character-singing is wider than one at first supposes. Of course there is the tribe of lesser Falstaffs: the strenuously articulate Fra Melitone of *La Forza del Destino*, and Don Pasquale capering with amorous expectation in jubilant waltz-time. And there is Bully Bottom, clear and vivid in the single recorded extract (the dream that 'hath no bottom'), yet not as funny or as touching as Owen Brannigan makes it in the complete performance. There are also the villains: Iago, open-vowelled and derisive in his Creed, Don Pizarro stern and formidable in 'Ach, welch' ein Augenblick', Beckmesser mean and vivid throughout. There is a real change of voice-character for these, and in fact they are rather more successful than some of the funny-men he has recorded: the patter-comics of Gilbert and Sullivan, for example, make heavy going in his hands (he sings in a series of recordings in which 'serious' opera singers took the parts which were being recorded with more expertise by the D'Oyly Carte Company, whose male principals, Thomas Round, Kenneth Sandford, Peter Pratt and Donald Adams, were at that time particularly strong). Yet it is still to musical comedy (in the literal sense) that one returns to find Geraint Evans truly on home ground. The ground covers song as well as opera, so that he bring a fine story-telling style and a sense of ironic fun to Mahler's song about the intellectual contest between nightingale and cuckoo ('Lob des hohen Verstandes' from *Des Knaben Wunderhorn*). This is sung too with a suggestion of his whimsical Papageno voice—a still better voice lying in reserve for Leporello, whose Catalogue Song has just enough of nudging insinuation and is all well and truly sung rather than clowned. Best of all, of course, is the Falstaff with which we started. 'Questo è il mio regno: lo ingrandirò', as Sir John sings. Long may he reign, we add piously; and long live Sir Geraint to impersonate him.

It seems appropriate to take leave of England with a reference to this Italian opera which is nearest to being English (even if the chief singer is Welsh, and no doubt half the chorus with him). If we travelled to France by way of the Low Countries, we would rejoice in Gré Brouwenstijn (p. 337), salute a musical and distinctive tenor in Frans Vroons, and a kindly sounding, musicianly contralto in Aafje Heynis (sensitive and affectionate, if sometimes a little breathy, in Bach, really excellent in a most satisfying performance of Brahms' Alto Rhapsody). We could also recall that, if it might be some exaggeration to say that Belgium is to French opera as Wales is to English, nevertheless quite a number of the best 'French' singers this century have been Belgian, and that a recent, and shining, example has been the mezzo-soprano, Rita Gorr.

Her voice is powerful and penetrating, of the kind one feels great opera houses are built to accommodate. It is of the kind too that Wagner must surely have had in mind when he made such demands upon the stamina of his Ortrud and Fricka. Gorr sings with dauntless vigour and attack in Ortrud's Curse (*Lohengrin* Act II), and her Fricka also projects her denunciations with a bright, edgy tone, cleaving the orchestral mass as she does, still more remarkably, in Isolde's Liebestod. The Liebestod impresses not merely because one knows that this is a mezzo singing a soprano's music, but because it brings out a tenderness and sensitivity in the singer that is not always apparent. How welcome a little more suppleness and sweetness would be, for instance, in her singing of Saint-Saëns' Dalila. It is true that between the issue of this recital record and that of the complete *Samson et Dalila* in 1963, she had come to observe the *dolce* and *diminuendo* markings in the first solo, 'Printemps qui commence'. But she still has little conception of the music's ability to woo and to charm: a few comparisons make it very clear, Rosa Ponselle (in retirement) taking the song much more slowly and persuasively, Schumann-Heink catching its restrained excitement, Kirkby Lunn lightening her beautifully rounded tones and creating sheer loveliness. Where Gorr normally comes into her own is where the score calls for grandeur: in the majestic phrases (the quiet passages too) in Gluck's 'Divinités du Styx', or in the fury and pleading of Massenet's *Hérodiade*. It is as Amneris, however, that dramatic power seconds the strength of the voice most effectively, and in which the imagination is also most in evidence, giving the effect of a long-drawn sigh on the repeated cries at the opening of Act II, and assuming and discarding the mask of benevolence vividly in the duet with Aida which follows. The voice will not please all listeners, for even here, at its best, it records with a vibrancy that will sound in some ears as an edgy, if dramatic, quick vibrato. But no one could miss the magnificence of her singing in the last Act. Breadth of phrase, depth of feeling (so that we feel *for* Amneris at last), brilliance of voice: the recording shows well why, when she was on top form, Rita Gorr could be the most exciting mezzo-soprano to be heard in such roles since the war.

When the record collector looks at his panorama of Paris for a general view of French operatic singing since 1945, he finds much that sinks into the obscurity of a low-roofed skyline. One feature is a fair showing of tenors: Guy Chauvet and Albert Lance among the more heroic, Henri Legay and Alain Vanzo among the lyric. Legay is des Grieux to Victoria de los Angeles' Manon, engaging and stylish, singing the Dream Song with poise and due sadness, and phrasing over into 'Nous vivrons à Paris' with a long *diminuendo* and a magical pianissimo in the duet of Act I. Vanzo will be known to English collectors chiefly through his part in Joan Sutherland's *Lakmé*, but he has recorded extensively on French records that have had some currency elsewhere as special imports. The excellence of his technique can be gauged from his performance of 'Ecco ridente' (sung as 'Des rayons de l'aurore') from *Il Barbiere di Siviglia*. The runs are fluent, smooth and defined, and he includes his very able account of some difficult bars towards the end of the aria that are frequently omitted. He ends the first half with well-poised soft high notes, and the second with a sturdy top C. A fine legato, matched but hardly surpassed by the very best French tenors of this century, marks his recording of 'Je crois entendre' in *Pêcheurs de Perles*, using the original key and sung out with a bright lyrical tone (no crooning head-voice). And his Gerald in *Lakmé* will stand comparisons with Schipa and McCormack, and therefore, one can assume, with anybody else. It is worth listening to a few versions of the song 'Fantaisie aux divins mensonges' in the first Act; a young tenor can learn much about grace, poise, lilt and variety. Not, however, from David Devries, who certainly ought to have things to teach the younger generation: he is stiff in his phrasing, missing the grace notes, surprisingly charmless in fact. José Mojica is much better, singing with pleasing tone and finding some of the poetry in the music. Schipa is finer still, but if he is analysably better than Vanzo it is only in the extra rhythmic buoyancy he achieves; his recording is magical in its phrasing and its contrasts of the urgent and the idyllic, but in all of that, Vanzo is his equal. Comparison with McCormack is possible in the aria from Act III ('Viens, dans ce forêt profond', which McCormack sings in Italian). The Irish tenor gives a superb demonstration of what should be meant by a legato style, and his tone is at its most beautiful. Even so, Vanzo can be heard side-by-side; and in the lead-in to the aria (with its *diminuendo* on 'Revivait sous ton souffle') he is in fact more imaginative and stylish. Comparison with McCormack can be deadly; Vanzo survives—with distinction.

His records, as we said, are not well known outside France. Yet there must be many who, like the present writer, have gone to the opera in Paris, and found their visit justified by his singing and rather little else. Another of my own most vivid memories of nights at the opera also concerns him, and goes back to one of his rare appearances at Covent Garden, where he sang a splendid Edgardo to Sutherland's Lucia. It was one of those occasions when enjoyment was almost a tangible presence in the house, on both sides of the curtain (one sign of it was the encoring of the Sextet, a rare event indeed at Covent Garden). The baritone of that performance was Louis Quilico, a French-Canadian, who since then has sung for several years at the Paris Opéra, and who fully shared the honours of the evening. Quilico is an excellent singer and, like Vanzo, far too little known on records (Handel's *Hercules* shows the firm, warm voice, the dramatic sense, and fair proficiency in florid passages, but it is not the music in which he should be remembered). It is a curious commentary on the gramophone as historian, that of the three singers who together provided a quite exceptional evening in the opera house, one should be a household name while the others have scarcely an entry to their name in the catalogues.

Not Quilico, but Gabriel Bacquier and Michael Roux are the baritones who have recorded most conspicuously in the French operatic repertoire. A stylish Mozartian, Bacquier also makes a more than usually attractive Count Almaviva in Klemperer's *Nozze di Figaro*. Other French baritones in recent years have been pleasant rather than striking: Robert Massard, Ernest Blanc, Michel Dens. Gérard Souzay is in a category of his own, and belongs to another chapter.

Among the sopranos are Janine Micheau (first lady of the Opéra for many years, her most sensitive self to the fore in Debussy's *La Damoiselle Elue*) and Marthe Angelici (pleasing in some early French songs, like 'Jeunes fillettes', on 78s, and a pretty Leila to Legay's elegant Nadir in a complete recording of *Les Pêcheurs de Perles*). Suzanne Danco has been a prolific recording artist, also from the later days of the 78, where her limpid tone and fluent scale-work are charmingly heard in a little song by Bononcini called 'Deh, più a me non v'ascondete' (the record became something of a best-seller, principally because of the tunefulness of Caccini's 'Amarilli' on the other side, but on the whole the Bononcini is a better piece of singing). On LP she turns up more or less wherever one likes to look, whether in something very French like *Les Enfants et les Sortilèges* (a graciously smiling Princess and a lusciously waltzing squirrel) or in German song (one of the few women to sing a successful *Dichterliebe*) or in operatic composers as diverse as Verdi, Purcell, Gluck, Massenet and Mozart (a spirited Cherubino, a somewhat formally efficient Donna Anna). And somewhere a few octaves above all these voices we should hear the bell-like tones of the lamented Mado Robin, who died at the age of forty-two and at the height of her powers. She sang some of the highest notes to have been recorded by the human voice; more worthy of her memory is the firmness and technical accomplishment of her Lakmé, which has a virginal charm and some finesse of style.

But, as the voice of Mado Robin soars in pitch above this consort of French singers, so that of Régine Crespin rises pre-eminent among them for the quality of her art. This is one of the great singers on record, and as with perhaps four or five others discussed in this book, her singing is an acquired taste that becomes addictive. She cannot be heard casually. The voice itself (strong as it is, and beautiful at a pianissimo) is unlikely to register as particularly rich or pure or even as 'original'. And though one can hardly remain indifferent to her use of it for very long, the critical faculty may well be provoked to make some strenuous objections, as, for instance, a flattened or a soured note twinges like toothache. Of course, the listening which will flinch so sensitively can hardly be called casual, but when we say 'flattened' or 'soured' we imply something purposive, and it can happen that an unengaged listener will be jerked into critical alertness by a sound that suddenly jars against expectation, and yet has its place in the interpretation.

Such, at any rate, was my own experience, and of all Crespin's recordings it applied most to the one which I now think of as her best, the *Nuits d'Eté*. Reasons for belated appreciation are not hard to find: a combination of flat notes and rave notices, earlier acquaintance with the more straight-forward performance by Eleanor Steber and later with the incomparably beautiful one by Janet Baker, a relatively casual (and later fragmentary) hearing of the record. The sort of passage which repelled by its flattened intonation was the last repetition of 'La fleur de ma vie est fermée' in the fourth song, 'L'Absence'. Yet this is the song in which Crespin now seems to me to be most inspired. It begins with the words 'Reviens, reviens, ma bien aimée', a call to the beloved, living somewhere far-off, separated from the lover by miles of countryside ('D'ici là-bas que des campagnes'). Crespin *calls*; and she shades the notes so pictorially that we feel the voice going out into the distance and hear its echo return over the desolate fields. The first 'reviens' is shaded down to make the echo; the last syllable of 'aimée' grows as a call sent out into a valley. Other versions at hand

127. Rita Gorr   128. Régine Crespin

are those by Janet Baker, Sheila Armstrong and Leontyne Price: all (in different degrees) do as the score directs, but none of them addresses the song, as a call, and none gives a comparable sense of a loving heart in a desolate void. The refrain, 'La fleur de ma vie est fermée', is no great pleasure to the ears as Crespin sings it in the third verse, weighted as it were against the upward movement of the music, and leaden in tone-colour; but then, it was not meant to be. The song is being taken as though it means what it says, and when one has followed her through it, the shading seems just and the effect is moving. And so it is throughout most of the cycle. Perhaps the first song, 'Villanelle', could do with a lighter touch (Baker is enchanting here, and the tenor Frank Patterson also brings much of the required grace and charm to it). But after that Crespin is inexhaustibly rich in specific insights. The second, the 'Spectre de la Rose', floats sleepy and spellbound: the dreaminess caught by lightening the upward curve of the melody (as Baker does and Price does not) and by using more portamento than the others allow. A ghostliness enters the tone at one point; at another, the glitter of last night's ball ('parmi la fête étoilée') evokes not just louder singing but a newly brilliant tone-colour. Or in the Lament, 'Sur les lagunes' (a man's song, and movingly recorded by John Shirley-Quirk), she finds a strong, darkly coloured, masculine tone, dropping expressively to the low E of 'linceul', embittering the last repetition of the refrain ('Ah, sans amour s'en aller sur la mer'). And then the opening of the last song, 'L'Ile inconnue', following the grey tones of 'Au cimetière', has a complete change of face, radiantly lit, and using a portamento to catch the capricious charm of the singer's invitation to travel wherever whim directs. The whole record is a masterly demonstration of insight and its translation into sound.

Her art does not always triumph as completely as this. The *Wesendonck Lieder* of Wagner surely require more sheer opulence of tone than they receive here; and they surely ask less for her special kind of tone-colouring than the Berlioz does. Much is fine, especially the hushed 'Im Treibhaus', and at the other end of the dynamic range, the shining, pointed forte of 'Schmerzen'. But her interpretations tend here not so much towards new insights as to a sort of underlining, and the voice lacks freshness or sensuous beauty at a basic mezzo forte. This too may limit one's enjoyment of her singing as the Marschallin in *Der Rosenkavalier*. A highly praised and often exquisite performance, it lacks the bloom that Strauss' characteristic writing for soprano craves. The opening of the trio ('Hab' mir's gelobt') sounds worn, and the 'Heut' oder Morgen' in Act I wants the fullness of voice to sound out warmly over the orchestra playing at fortissimo. Then as to characterisation, while there is tenderness and dignity, the recording misses those touches that 'round' the Marschallin into a less simply noble, but more interestingly human woman. The contempt for Ochs' boorishness, the ironical distaste for commercial marriages, the satirical imitation of gossiping voices: Elisabeth Schwarzkopf catches all this, but there is little of it in Crespin. More (or perhaps most) fundamentally, one must feel within the Marschallin a will that struggles against fate and time; and this too is vivid in Schwarzkopf's reading of the part, where Crespin presents merely a wistful serenity. Even the cry 'And I didn't kiss him even once' brings from her little of the impulsiveness with which Schwarzkopf lets us know how Oscar Wilde's paradox (the tragedy of age is not that we are old but that we are young) applies so painfully to this woman just over the threshold into middle-age.

Yet there is much in Crespin's Marschallin to remember with gratitude. Nobody can have concluded Act I making a more beautiful impression in the last phrase ('da drinn ist die silberne Ros'n'). Few can have found so happily the right tone of tender playfulness at the beginning of the opera, or the rueful observation to the maid—'You've made me look an old woman'. But one would certainly expect no less of her Marschallin, having heard so many of her other operatic records and knowing her skill in song recitals too. The chattering wench of Wolf's 'Ich hab' in Penna' is all energy and appetite; the Mary Stuart of Schumann's five songs is all sobriety and sombreness. The dark colouring may lighten in mid-song, as in Wolf's 'In der Frühe' where the troubled night-thoughts have her characteristically leaning towards the flat side of the note, then as comfort comes with the sound of morning bells so emphasis in the voice shifts to the upper frequencies, and the tone becomes all sweetness and light. Poulenc's 'Fêtes galantes' goes at high speed, fleet and flippant; Ravel's 'Shéhérazade' swoons languorously, the voice a faithful echo of the music's mood. Apply such intelligence and sensitivity to Italian opera and the performances are likely to be unusually interesting. In Desdemona's Willow Song and Ave Maria we always know, through the subtlest of nuance, that this is a woman under the shadow of death. In Lady Macbeth's Sleepwalking Scene we can actually believe (and this is surprisingly rare) that she is asleep: a haunted, other-worldly voice sighs, lingers and pleads. One feels that she is too fond of slow speeds, and sometimes that she is trying too hard. Yet there are also times when she will sing a melody with no less (as well as no more) simplicity than it demands. Thus in 'Morrò, ma prima in grazia' from *Un Ballo in Maschera* she registers as the true successor to Elisabeth Rethberg: letting the music speak through a beautifully drawn vocal line. It is the final sign of grace in a subtle artist.

It is good to be able to leave the French operatic scene with such a singer as its representative. On the final lap of our European journey, we could certainly treat ourselves to a taste of similar excellence in Spain. Victoria de los Angeles and Teresa Berganza have, however, been encountered in earlier chapters, and we have to reserve Montserrat Caballé for a later one.

This leaves a few singers, such as the lyric tenor Juan Oncina and the baritone Manuel Ausensi, for honourable mention (Oncina showing the valuable asset of a sense of comedy in the Glyndebourne *Comte Ory*). The contralto Oralia Dominguez, sumptuous of voice in Wagner as in Rossini, also shines in one of the Glyndebourne productions: as the nurse Arnalta in *L'Incoronazione di Poppea* she sustains with rich tone the long phrases of 'Oblivion soave' and makes a fine effect with low notes and hockets in the comic scene which comes later. More prominent still as an international artist and a singer on records is the soprano Pilar Lorengar. Her great opportunity in the recording studio came in Lorin Maazel's *La Traviata*, with Fischer-Dieskau as the father. Her Alfredo is another Spaniard, Giacomo Aragall, secure and attractive in voice if not always in pitch, and they sing their music together with feeling and a sense of style. It is in the scene with the elder Germont, however, that Lorengar is most memorable; extremely fine, for example, in the restrained bitterness and rhythmic strength of 'Morrò, la mia memoria'. Definition of tone is affected somewhat by a vibrato which recording tends to exaggerate, and the emotional appeal of the voice is limited by its lack of richness in passages where an expansive warmth is wanted. And it is hard to remember that she is Spanish—even when she is singing Spanish songs. The decorum of her art has no place for Supervia's challenging play of personality; nor has her voice the southern glow of Victoria de los Angeles'. The fun and excitement of *Los Reyas de la bareja* ('The Kings in the Cards') is exceptional in a collection of songs, sung to guitar accompaniment, and all with, if anything, rather too much refinement.

Yet it is another sign of the times, that such a complaint could be made about a Spanish singer: it might even be thought of as something of a triumph.

28. Singer and Song:
An Exhibition of Artists
Janet Baker   Christa Ludwig
Peter Pears   Dietrich Fischer-Dieskau
Gérard Souzay

THE European tour of the last chapter (and indeed the American one before it) involved more time spent in the opera house than the concert hall. We come now to a group of distinguished recitalists. All have had considerable operatic experience, but they are still primarily associated with song rather than aria, and, as we listen to them, we are more than usually aware of a distinctive sensibility, of emotional maturity and intellectual strength.

That does not mean that they compensate in artistry for what they lack in voice. The first of them, Gérard Souzay, has in fact one of the most beautiful baritone voices on record. The beauty of tone and excellence of technique are certainly among the great pleasures that his singing affords, and for some listeners his records will be preferable to those of the second singer, Dietrich Fischer-Dieskau, because of this: for, whatever the interpretative issues involved, they will know that in a record by Souzay there will be some exceptionally beautiful singing to be heard, and no lack of musical sensitivity either. They will find in him the successor to Herbert Janssen; a singer sufficiently imaginative to bring the song to life, and, above all, one whose finely produced voice would delight the ear, whether by its resonance at full ring or by the velvety richness of its softer tones. He reminds one of Janssen often, especially in his earlier records of German song: in Schumann's *Liederkreis* op. 24, for instance, where the second song ('Es treibt mich hin') has that gentle power which never batters at the loud notes, and where the melody of 'Schöne Wiege' is caressed with a yearning sweetness and sadness, all the gradations of tone and passion finely judged and perfectly controlled.

Then, if he is Janssen's successor in German song, he is Panzéra's in the French repertoire. A similarly natural, warm and well-focused tone, matched by an elegance of style, makes him the only really comparable singer in modern times; and when one comes to make direct comparisons they generally show Souzay as the more interesting interpreter. So it is, for example, in Duparc's setting of Baudelaire's 'La Vie Antérieure'.

Slightly faster, slightly more prosaic, Panzéra's opening of the song ('J'ai longtemps habité sous de vastes portiques') is not in the tone of a man who is going to tell of palms, azure skies, 'des splendeurs et des esclaves nus'. But in this poem all leads towards the last line, 'le secret douloureux qui me faisait languir'. Duparc marks it with a change of key, but the sensitive interpreter will be responsive to this and show it. Souzay does so by slightly lengthening the syllables of the word 'approfondir' which leads into this phrase. The poet tells us, enigmatically, that this is the 'unique care' of these palm-waving slaves: to deepen the unhappy secret on account of which he is languishing. Panzéra's business-like manner at the opening suggests little flair for guessing the dolorous secret; Souzay, more relaxed and evocative, is responsive to the subdued urgency of the conclusion just as he has been sensitive to mood from the start.

Of all singers, the specialist in French song needs imagination, clarity and character: otherwise he will be mildly, tastefully, noncommittally boring. The heart sinks as one glances over the translations and reads 'Fastidiously as it were, in an undertone and bit by bit the rain falls on the fresh and dormant garden'. This is 'Le jardin mouillé' by Roussel, which not even Souzay can succeed in imprinting 'as it were' on the memory. But his Debussy, Duparc and Fauré we remember, and not simply because of the beautiful sounds. Fauré's miniature song-cycle 'L'Horizon Chimérique' was recorded twice, the second time when his voice had lost that velvety richness that was present in the recording on 78. But the performance is still fine, gaining a vivid suggestion of wave-motion in the first song, otherwise changing little. The expressive resources which give life and strength to these gentle songs can be seen clearly in the more characterised songs of Poulenc. The 'Chansons Gaillardes' find a boozy, bass-toned energy; the collection called 'Tel jour telle nuit' brings out a vivid narrative power, almost Chaliapin-like in the 'Figure de force brûlante et farouche'. And a subtler kind of humour marks the difficult song 'A son page' by Laguerney, charming in the 'hms' and 'brms' of its throw-away ending.

It is surprising that a singer with so much character should not have made more operatic recordings. He sings a severe, though not a fierce or saturnine, Golaud in *Pelléas et Mélisande* (Donald McIntyre is probably rather more interesting and human, but also rather more unsteady and inclined to speech-sing). The kind of operatic music in which he is particularly good is Zurga's air from *Les Pêcheurs de Perles*, elegant in style, bright-toned and resonant, and finely judged in its 'building'. In Mercutio's Queen Mab solo from *Roméo et Juliette* he moves nimbly and 'brushes' the legato phrases lightly as with a feather duster. Such excerpts from opera, and a few Bach cantatas (the energy and definition of the long runs in number 56, *Ich will dem Kreuzstab gerne tragen*, demonstrating his ability in florid work) mark the principal limits of his excursions on record outside the realms of French and German song. The quality of performance is fine, but it is a smaller output than one would wish.

In German song too there are limitations. He sings Richard Strauss, for example, but is rather too well-mannered about it. 'Heimliche Aufforderung', has little feeling of expansive festivity at the beginning, and its invitation to come into the garden is hardly seductive. Fundamentally, there is no real longing behind it (one remembers Tauber's jaunty lift to the dotted rhythms, and his change to an almost indecently honeyed tone as the music becomes more romantic). Then, in 'Ruhe, meine Seele' which might be a more congenial song, he also misses quite a lot. Like most of the moderns he takes it a good deal more slowly than the composer's own recording on 78 (3·35 minutes to 2·50 in the Schlusnus–Strauss recording on Polydor). That makes less difference than one might think; what does matter is that his performance lacks the perspective that singers as diverse as Elisabeth Schwarzkopf and Tom Krause reveal in it. It really needs something grandly Wagnerian as an utter contrast to the introspective mood. Souzay gives a rather muted, miniaturised performance. On the other hand, he has recorded much Schumann, Wolf, and (above all) Schubert, virtually to perfection. Among the Schubert songs, one would expect to find him ideal in the gentle and delicate 'Nachtviolen', or in 'An die Leier' or 'Du bist die Ruh'. So he is, singing with all the charm, warmth and vocal control that the songs demand. But he is also fine in the darker, more dramatic songs, grinning with a gnomish possessiveness in the Erlking's utterances, finding a deep, sturdy tone for 'Gruppe aus dem Tartarus', and a carefully graded intensity for 'Der Doppelgänger'.

It is Schubert, of course, who in *Der Winterreise*, confronts a Lieder singer with what is generally regarded as the greatest challenge of all. Souzay has recorded the cycle twice, one issued in 1959 by HMV, and the other in 1963 by Philips. Comparing the two, we note a slight loss in beauty of tone (it is more evident in recordings from about 1965 onwards). Tonally, he has also done something to release the voice from a certain evening-dress formality which would sometimes intrude when he was singing in German (in the very first song, for example). But the main change in interpretation has been a tightening-up: a greater rhythmic tautness, and an austerity of mood gained by the omission of touches that made the first version essentially *pleasant* listening. 'Erstarrung' (number 4), 'Rückblick' (9) and 'Frühlingstraum' (11) provide examples. In the Philips recording of 'Erstarrung' the words 'vergebens' in the first verse and 'erstorben' at the corresponding place in the last, are urgently and intimately breathed; the concert-resonance has gone and we are a step nearer emotional reality. But also gone are points of tenderness and pathos, made attractive in the first version by a honeyed tone and a portamento. 'Rückblick' has also become more rugged. The poet makes his way through ice and snow out of the stony city, and Souzay brings now a harder-hitting *martellato* style to the opening and to the last verse. The HMV version indulged (very delightfully) a touch of Viennese charm in the reference to the two girlish eyes ('zwei Mädchenaugen') which had glowed in happier

129. Gérard Souzay

130. Dietrich Fischer-Dieskau as
Mandryka in *Arabella*

times. The changes are all a matter of fine degree, but again he has hardened
his interpretation just enough for this to register as a bitter-sweet recollection rather than simply a moment of ingratiating charm. Then in 'Frühlingstraum', the later version sharpens its contrasts, enforces the buffeting
rhythms of its harshest bars, and quickens the tempo throughout. I think
that I personally still enjoy the first version more, but it increases one's
respect for a favourite artist to find that his development has been a movement from the ingratiating to the astringent.

How, then, does he compare, in this later stage of development, with
Fischer-Dieskau? In much of *Winterreise*, including the songs mentioned
above, there is not a great deal of difference in the quality of insight, the
interest or the energy of the singing. Where a difference does come to be
felt is in such songs as numbers 14 to 16, 'Der greise Kopf', 'Die Krähe'
and 'Letzte Hoffnung', a grey, anxious group, subtly plaintive, unsure and
chilled. Here Fischer-Dieskau's mastery of voice-colour makes a profound
effect. Control of vibrato is probably the principal technical means: if the
vibrancy of the voice is reduced it makes for a note that is tonally flat,
and may even give the impression of being slightly flat in pitch because of
the reduction of upper harmonics. Thus, the vision of a dreary world, of
greying heads, ill-omened birds, and falling leaves, is rendered in the pallid
tone of the voice at certain points, culminating in the weeping tone at the
end of 'Letzte Hoffnung'. Souzay sings feelingly, but a listener with no
German and no translation could well miss the essential lamenting quality

of that last line: 'Wein auf meiner Hoffnung Grab' ('weep on the grave of my hope'). The feeling and care of Souzay's treatment could express, say, affection, a caress. With Fischer-Dieskau there is no doubt about it. Partly by this kind of colouring, partly by an emotion which can be sensed even in the breathing, partly by a habit of specific reading (telling, for instance, that the 'poisoned', deathly centre of the last musical phrase is the second, flattened note on 'Hoffnung'), he *realises* the phrase. And this is typical of Fischer-Dieskau's work over a huge range of music.

Strange to say, it does not please everybody. Or (to put it more fairly): there are people with a strong interest in singing who would be reluctant to name Fischer-Dieskau among the truly great singers. Few will deny his power as an interpreter (though some will, and vociferously too); the general complaint will be about voice-production, lack of legato and so forth, with the names of Schwarz, Schlusnus, Hüsch and Janssen brought forward (by those who remember them) to suggest what singing really is.

It is impossible to do justice to Fischer-Dieskau's recordings in a few pages, but we might keep the objections in mind while taking a representative selection of his records. The colouring of the word 'wein' in 'Letzte Hoffnung' might recall a Bach aria, 'Achzen und erbarmlich Weinen' (from Cantata No. 13, *Meine Seufzer, meine Thränen*) in which the verb 'weinen' is similarly drained of resonance and shaded towards the flat side of the note. It reminds us too that he has recorded a good deal of Bach, and that Bach is notoriously a severe tester of a singer's technique. In this aria, as in much else, it is clear for a start that Fischer-Dieskau's Bach will not be sung on the assumption that the human voice is essentially just another instrument. There are times that one looks at a Bach score and feels that the bass part (say) might just as well be a cello or bassoon solo. One almost wishes that the words could be 'thought' rather than articulated: a perfectly even voice-instrument singing 'ah' would do very nicely. This is just what Fischer-Dieskau does not believe, so that in this aria, 'Achzen und erbarmlich weinen', he is eloquent with the text and exploits a full range of expressive dynamics. Sforzandos, marcatos, slurs, a kind of sighing-tone: all are used. Then, throughout a series of arias from the cantatas he will produce a 'voice-face' to match a great range of moods and emotions, each as vividly different as a collection of operatic solos by Falstaff, Iago, Don Giovanni, Wotan and Wozzeck.

But arias by Bach also contain runs of inordinate length, many of them performed at high speed, often spanning a wide range and jumping over broad and difficult intervals. It is quite possible that Schwarz, Schlusnus, Hüsch and Janssen could have shown us how these things should be done, but they left no records either of these arias or of anything comparably difficult, so we have to judge Fischer-Dieskau without the help of comparisons. There are plenty of recordings to choose from in his case, but let us take the one following the 'Achzen und weinen' aria: 'Ja, ja, ich halte Jesum feste' (from No. 157, *Ich lasse dich nicht*). All is distinct, sustained and even. Using more voice in 'Doch weichet, ihr tollen' (No. 8, *Liebster Gott, wann werd ich sterben*), he still sings the difficult florid passages with great accomplishment, and with a forthright, virile tone: quite straightforward and uncomplicated when this is what the aria seems to him to want. Sometimes, as in the fast arias in Handel's *Giulio Cesare*, he will achieve distinctness, not by aspirating, but by giving each note its separate emphasis: rather like the technique of a pianist playing semi-staccato. But there is no breathiness, and in fact the supply of breath is so ample that he will sometimes crescendo at the end of a long run when many singers would be on the point of 'fading'. These composers also call quite frequently for a trill. Telemann does so in his *Canary Cantata*, and again Fischer-Dieskau's technique stands the test: the whole cantata is a splendid example of his skill in comedy, but the 'goodnight' song towards the end shows him singing smooth, sweet and ornate as any baroque virtuoso.

'Il trillo invade il mondo', says Falstaff, who himself is not given to trilling. But Iago is, although very few baritones who sing the role sing that particular part of it. Five trills are marked, all of them important except perhaps in the Drinking Song where it is only incidental and is covered by the orchestra: at other points it seems to be associated with the flourishing of evil (culminating in 'Ecco il leone'). Fischer-Dieskau is one of the few with the technique and/or artistic conscience to include them. He is also a very good Iago on other counts. After the Creed in Act II, Iago first observes Otello from a distance, then joins him and begins his work of insinuation. Fischer-Dieskau, taking his cue from the staccato markings in the orchestral parts, makes his voice either dance maliciously with them or else plays against them a lithe snakelike legato. When one looks, it is all there, written out or implied, in the score; but it is quite typical of Fischer-Dieskau that he should be the one to make clear what it means and translate it into a supremely vivid performance. Typical too that we should be able to pick a relatively inconspicuous page of the score and find him exercising the same care and creativeness as he would over the great solos.

But the great solos of other operas call upon other skills. *Rigoletto, Don Carlo, La Traviata*: what happens when Fischer-Dieskau undertakes the lyrical passages in these operas, where what we want to hear is a beautiful, well-rounded tone and a finely poised smoothness of line? A test-case in *Rigoletto* is the last part of the outburst 'Cortigiani, vil razza', starting 'Miei signori', and no, he is not good. There are aspirates, the line is lumpy, the tone lacks richness. In *Don Carlo* the test is 'Per me giunto' (Act IV), and the result much better: the trill on 'fedel', the soft high F are individual points, and he also succeeds in moulding the phrases broadly and smoothly, and producing a pleasing, steady tone. In *La Traviata*, we try 'Di Provenza' and its rarely sung cabaletta, 'No, non udrai', and in these again he satisfies at certain specific points by which we commonly judge the 'bel canto' baritone: he rounds off the first verse with a beautiful and well-controlled *mezza voce*, and in the cabaletta he joins up the reprise of the opening line with a natural feeling for the ways of Italian melody. Still, the satisfaction is not really complete, for a slight beat develops under pressure and his voice seems not to have among its resources the firm Italian richness that the music requires. As against this, one could advance any number of interpretative insights, fine things which all these performances illuminate or deepen in our minds. But the point remains that certain basic qualities and habits of lyrical singing are not to be regularly counted on in his recordings. An unlikely further illustration comes with *Wozzeck*, where his contemporary Walter Berry shows how much more 'bound' and 'sung' the singing phrases can be.

Another (and probably allied) characteristic has been a tendency towards a particularly emphatic style, working sometimes through extremes of volume, or sometimes by hitting the note hard, over the head as it were. His Don Giovanni is harsh, emphatic and hectoring. The unsentimental portrayal of arrogance might be its defence, but hardly its justification for too much musical pleasure is lost. His Elijah also punches hard at some of the fortissimo passages; and again the harshness and occasional loss of focus are not cancelled out by the reflection that he is presenting, deliberately and interestingly, a powerful, passionate Old Testament prophet, who jeers and snarls as often as he prays and blesses, and orders a massacre as cheerfully as resting in the Lord. But of course, there it is: he is always interesting. Has he ever sung anything, one wonders, without shedding some new light on it? And, if the light has sometimes glared rather than glowed through his singing, records also suggest that in this respect he is his own best critic. The remarkable thing about his re-recordings is that, while they generally preserve and develop the earlier insights, they also tend to reduce emphasis, increase the smoothness and beauty of singing, and thus absorb the individual points into the body of the music. The two recordings of *Der Winterreise* provide many instances: such as in 'Wasserfluth', with its reduction of tonal contrasts, its refinement of crescendo, and removal of some *marcato* effects, or 'Auf dem Flusse' with its smoother line, its quiet anxiety that is now so toned into the rest of the singing that it needs no underlining.

It is necessary to face up to the criticisms that Fischer-Dieskau provokes because he is so important and influential a singer. But of course the essential critical reaction to this wealth of recording is about as simple as Dryden's cry of admiration for *The Canterbury Tales*: 'Here is God's plenty'. The Schubert songs alone are virtually inexhaustible: 408 of them, many recorded more than once. Haydn, Beethoven, Schumann, Brahms, Wolf, Strauss, Mahler: all have found in him their busiest recorder and (among the men) their most understanding interpreter. Operatic roles as diverse as Papageno and Wotan, Scarpia and Barak, Pizarro and Falstaff, have all sprung to life at his touch. His fame is great enough for him to leave the appallingly difficult scores of twentieth-century composers alone if he wished; but he sings many of them, including Berg's *Wozzeck* and *Lulu*, and takes the trouble to pitch accurately and not approximately.

We could dip into this store of recordings more or less at random, put the stylus down on the record at almost any point, and immediately learn something about both the singer and the song. Let us leave him by way of some such near-random selection: a *Liederabend*, drawing from various recordings, not offered as 'The Best of Fischer-Dieskau', but choosing each for its own particular interest. The concert opens with two songs by Schubert. He recorded 'Am Meer' on a 78, and it is a beautiful example of his youthful maturity: a fine, easy legato, and an intensely emotional performance, the pain growing little by little till it fills the voice. Detractors might object: 'Yes, and so "easy" is that soft opening that it is near to crooning; it lacks poise, support, and would probably not carry in a large hall'. Anyone who has heard Fischer-Dieskau from far-away seats in large halls knows that it does carry, but for our second Schubert song let us have him singing 'live' and see what impression recording gives of his voice under these circumstances. From the Schubert group in the programme given in honour of Gerald Moore at the Festival Hall in 1967, let us take the first song, 'Der Einsame'. The first point is surely the warmth and full-bodied character of the tone. I have often thought the voice more likeable 'in the flesh' than as recorded in the studios, and this record gives a faithful impression of what an audience hears. The other point is the wide dynamic range and perspective of his singing, from double forte to pianissimo, and (as had not always used to be the case) all of the fine gradations between. Our programme continues with two songs by Brahms and two by Strauss. Brahms' 'Mainacht' shows him *not* imposing on the music: he takes a moderate tempo and achieves a just balance between the sadness and exaltation in the song. It is rarer than one might think. 'Wie bist du, meine Königin' allows comparison with Herbert Janssen: Fischer-Dieskau emerging as the more poetic interpreter (the last verse actually in love with its concept of a love-death) and as better and broader in his phrasing. The Strauss songs are 'Traum durch die Dämmerung' and 'Ständchen', included because they are familiar, and one might suppose there is nothing new to be said about them. In the first he catches a haunted quality in the twilight yearning, that is there in the music (rather than the words) of the middle section; and in the second he shows us a song that *grows* (from a sprightly, elfin beginning, through the deepening sense of mystery, to a full-blooded, passionate climax).

As an encore to this first part of our programme, we will have Wolf's 'Ganymede'. This is a selection made partly for the writer's own pleasure (I know the transposition annoys some listeners), and also to supplement some remarks about John McCormack's recording on p. 59. McCormack's in an unforgettable performance, but there is so much more in the song that Fischer-Dieskau finds. He catches a lightness in the first part (the 'liebliches Morgenwind' can be felt); a boyishness, too, that is right for the character.

He senses the swing-motion of the alternating notes at 'Du kühlst den brennenden Durst meines Busens', lingers slightly over the modulation at the word 'schmachte', observes the pianissimo marking in the accompaniment at 'Warme' and matches his voice to it ... So much is learnt about the music, and it must also be said that the sheer beauty of sound is increased: there is a greater delicacy, something of the open air, something of the classical (as opposed to the nineteenth-century) Ganymede.

For the second half, a song-cycle: *Dichterliebe*. And no time to discuss it, for we have been with this singer longer than with any other. But here too is insight and newness. More than with other recordings, we see the cycle as neurotic. It is still beautiful, tender and smiling at times; but he lays bare the unstable alternation of moods, especially in the middle section, presenting something akin to the neurotic patchwork of poems in Tennyson's *Maud*. How, for instance, in 'Das ist ein Flöten und Geigen', he sets his face bitterly against the tripping dance-measure in the piano part. Of how in 'Ein Jüngling liebt eine Mädchen' the rhythmic spring exactly matching the piano part gives a feeling of forced gaiety, pointing forward to the bitter ending of what is on the surface a merely pretty song.

But Fischer-Dieskau's concern has never been limited to what is on the surface. The depth of insight and the strength of personality behind it have made him not merely a singer much heard by the public, but also one who influences the course of singing and the practice of his own contemporaries. Just as it has been difficult for English tenors singing in song and oratorio over the last twenty years not to find themselves influenced by Peter Pears, so the German baritone singing comparable music is likely to be seen as closely associated with Fischer-Dieskau. Eberhard Wächter and Hermann Prey are cases in point. It may well be not so much a matter of influence as the fact that all three were brought up at the same time, and that it was a feeling in the air, for anyone to catch on to, that the art of a Lieder singer should now develop in expressiveness, depth and detail rather than in the generalised sensitivity and undisturbed tonal beauty of their predecessors. Anyway, there is little doubt that to record collectors, Wächter's singing of Wolfram's solos in *Tannhäuser* (say) will register as essentially 'school of Fischer-Dieskau' as surely as will much of Prey's Schubert and Brahms.

Still, each is a singer in his own right, and both have recorded with distinction. Wächter has a natural gaiety that he turns to good account in *Die Fledermaus*, and his voice can sound mellow, even mellifluous, as it does in Don Giovanni's Serenade. Yet more often the voice takes on a hard, thrusting sound, and the mood seems excessively disagreeable. The Count in *Le Nozze di Figaro* snarls and storms with plenty of character but without providing much pleasure for the ears; Kurwenal in *Tristan und Isolde* sings his song frowningly; the poet of *Dichterliebe* is not a charmer and it is hard to feel sorry for him either. Wächter at his best is strong, resilient and authoritative: qualities well represented by his singing of Jokanaan in the Solti–Nilsson *Salome*.

With an exceptionally fine voice and a strong artistic conscience, Prey has recorded extensively, as a Lieder singer for the most part, rather than in major operatic roles. In some relatively minor ones he made a strong impression early in his career: the sound of his Arlecchino in Karajan's *Ariadne auf Naxos* must have sent many a listener turning back to the cast-list to make a mental note of the new name. And often it is the more operatic kind of song that impresses in his Lieder recitals: in Schumann's 'Der Spielmann' he tells Hans Andersen's eerie tale with dramatic intensity and a good body of deep tone, while Schubert's Erlking is a tenory seducer played against the stolid bass of the father. The quieter songs are less satisfying on the whole. He has a way of sounding tired, of suggesting a facial expression in which all the lines are downwards. Schubert's 'Im Abendrot' is an example here, and Beethoven's *An die ferne Geliebte* shows how he will also overload music with expression marks that are alternately enervating and over-emphatic. Yet he can sing with a good legato. In a comparison with Hüsch and Schorr, his singing of 'Sonnst spielt' ich' from Lortzing's *Zar und Zimmermann* emerges as superior to Hüsch both in smoothness and expressiveness, and though his tone does not match Schorr's it is notable that he phrases with much more breadth (taking the last phrase in a single breath where Schorr breathes three times). But in Lieder he is best when not taking himself too seriously. Perhaps Richard Strauss frees him a little more than Schubert and Brahms from the high seriousness of the 'heilige Kunst', so that it is in a Strauss song recital that we find him in really top form: the swashbuckling mood of 'Bruder Liederlich' finds a glowing resonance and energy, and he caresses the warm phrases of 'Zueignung', glorying in the broad span of the climax.

An eminent baritone who remains to be discussed and who is clearly not 'school of Fischer-Dieskau' is Walter Berry, mentioned some pages back for his Wozzeck. This he sings in the recording conducted by Boulez, and 'sings' is, for once, the word. Not that Fischer-Dieskau is given to speech-sing more than the score marks; and his total conception is of a gentler, more imaginative and introverted character where Berry is simpler and more peasant-like. But where the score is marked *molto cantabile* (as it is quite frequently), then in Berry's performance one hears a true legato and well-rounded beauty of tone (the first example is the 'suffer little children' passage in the first scene, and it is followed by a very low-pitched phrase in which unlike Fischer-Dieskau he has the necessary downward range to sing what is written).[1] The difference in emphasis and method is clearer still in his Bach. He sings the bass arias in the *St. Matthew Passion* under Klemperer (Fischer-Dieskau a strong, very human Christus), and offers probably the most pure 'instrumental' singing in the whole, unsurpassed performance. The runs are distinct without 'separation' (no aspirating or

[1] Since then he has added Baron Ochs to his recorded repertoire, dealing impressively with a part essentially written for the bass voice.

marcato devices), and the tone is beautifully round and firm: 'Am Abend, da es kühle war' ('Twas in the cool of eventide') is particularly lovely, and even the long *da capo* of the final aria is almost welcome (and even at this slow tempo). Yet he too begins to sound like the others when it comes to songs like the *Harfenspielerlieder* of Hugo Wolf: his voice has an unusual pallor and little of its customary beauty. Gains in expressiveness have to be considerable to balance loss of tonal beauty, and it may even come as something of a disappointment (as it did to me) to find that he had conformed to modern ways in this. He might, of course, have recorded it quite differently another day, for his performances vary a good deal. As Leporello under Klemperer, for example, he is unsmiling, snarling, aggressive, even sinister, while under Moralt he is much more the conventional humourist. As Papageno, he sings the first song smoothly in the Klemperer recording, but without the sense of fun he showed some years earlier under Böhm; while the second solo ('Ein Mädchen oder Weibchen') has been refined without losing spontaneity. It is interesting, too, to compare the two versions of *Des Knaben Wunderhorn*, in one of which Bernstein conducts and in the other plays the piano: 'Der Tamboursg'sell' especially comes to a different sort of life in each, though the great moment of both performances arrives with the donkey-judge in 'Lob des hohen Verstandes' and his verdict ('Aber Kuckuck singst du gut Chorale')—Bernstein 'takes it away' with sheer joy in the oompah accompaniment. There is plenty of joy to be found in the singing too, of course. Firm, musicianly, unaffected and kind to the ears: Walter Berry earns our gratitude by being essentially a singer who puts the traditional virtues first.

In *Des Knaben Wunderhorn*, as in several other recordings, he shares honours with the mezzo-soprano, Christa Ludwig. The orchestral version finds her displaying a smoother, more opulent tone, while in the concert performance with piano accompaniment she achieves greater intimacy and more vivid characterisation. Schumann's *Liederkreis* Op. 39 is similarly divided between the two singers, Ludwig catching both the excitement and the melancholy of the songs, and contributing a particularly beautiful performance of 'Mondnacht'. She also plays Judith to Berry's Bluebeard in the Bartók opera, singing in Hungarian and placing the notes with firm accuracy as well as gorgeous tone. Antithetical and equally impressive are the pianissimo whispered urgency of the demand to see what is behind the last door, and the fortissimo top C sounding over full orchestra and organ as the fifth door is opened. The two singers come together again in several Mozart recordings (Ludwig as Dorabella and Cherubino, using her full voice with its contralto richness, and yet lightening gracefully too), in the *St. Matthew Passion*, *Der Rosenkavalier* and in *Fidelio*, where in an inspired piece of casting she sings a radiant Leonore.

The working range of her voice, then, is as ample as the variety of her repertoire. For the voice, it encompasses other soprano roles, such as that of Elvira in the Klemperer *Don Giovanni*, her technique matching up finely to the runs and arpeggios, though in the grand test of 'Mi tradì', her tone sometimes takes on a slightly tremulous quality, which suggests a discomfort of some sort. For the repertoire, it extends well beyond the scope outlined above. It takes her into Italian opera (an expressive, highly accomplished Adalgisa to Callas' Norma); and though little has been recorded so far, the majesty of tone and manner that she can bring to the Verdi operas can be gauged from her part in the *Requiem*. The Wagnerian repertoire includes a magnificent Ortrud and a Fricka whose great scene in *Die Walküre* avoids the shrewish and achieves an ever more formidable strong-willed majesty. And how many singers of those roles can then turn to Schubert, to 'Der Hirt auf dem Felsen', and sing it in the original key? And then couple this, on the same record, with songs by Rachmaninoff sung in Russian, and with an idiomatic account of the Three Madagascan Songs of Ravel?

Let us compare her singing of the Ravel with Janet Baker's. Points immediately striking are: Ludwig's richness of tone and reserves of power; Baker's absolute steadiness, and the vividness, in her singing, of an expressive face. Both are extremely fine performances, always alive and always beautiful in sheer sound. In one respect at least, Ludwig is more effective, for her fortissimo has that extra volume which makes the contrast between the first song and the second very dramatic indeed. Also, in the first song, Ludwig's more voluptuous, languorous tone may be thought preferable to Baker's fresher, brighter-coloured sound. Yet it is in Baker's performance that the specific sense of music and words finds most illumination. In the first ('Nahandoue') she introduces a playfulness ('le lit de feuilles est préparée'), excited semi-staccatos ('j'ai reconnu la respiration'), delicious pianissimos for the gentle love-making. In the second ('Aoua!') a baleful, darkened voice warns of the trickery of white men and of the grim consequences. She spits out the words 'obéissance et esclavage' with disgust. In the third ('Il est doux') she floats the soft high notes in a way that Ludwig does not, and her singing of the last line ('Allez, et préparez le repas') is beautifully judged, preserving the dreaminess, almost visibly stretching, lazily, in the full heat of the day. The performance has a sense of direction: a greater purposiveness, working, for example, to a more intense climax in the middle song, and then making the last cries of 'Aoua' sound exhausted after the outburst and thankful after the victory.

On the whole, this ultimate fineness of detail and imaginativeness of overall conception are narrowly missed in Ludwig's singing. Trying one or two more comparisons, this time with singers of the past, we find the point holds. A Brahms recital contains 'Von ewiger Liebe' and 'Immer leise', coupled long ago on a record by Elena Gerhardt. Both are good, and the performances of 'Immer leise' are very similar; yet one feels sorrow has been absorbed into Gerhardt's tone, and in the other song there is more tenderness in Gerhardt's little lightenings and rubatos. Ludwig imparts no inner affection for the splendid girl in the song; Gerhardt obviously warms

131. Christa Ludwig as Dorabella in *Così fan tutte*

to her. In 'Feldeinsamkeit' we might compare that other early Lieder singer of great distinction, Julia Culp. Ludwig certainly phrases better; she also sings with a fine legato and great beauty of tone. But Culp survives more vividly in the memory for two reasons: one is the magic of a particular moment (the effect of quietening and holding back a little on the word 'wundersam') and the other is a general rightness of feel, a way of caressing the melody so as to spread the balm which the peaceful dreams of the poem bring with them.

This said, one simply has to sit and enjoy, and there is a wealth of material for enjoyment. She is superb in the more dramatic kind of song, such as Schubert's 'Die Allmacht', or in Wolf's settings of the Mignon lyrics (including 'Kennst du das Land?'). Sometimes (perhaps not often enough) she will smile in song, but if one misses some of the humour and gaiety of a born Lieder singer, there is compensation in an unlikely quarter—her Orlofsky in *Die Fledermaus* is a marvellous creation, speaking the languid lines with a phoney accent, throaty and guttural, affecting the heavy eyelids of aristocratic boredom, and then giving a great burst of bold, busty energy to her song. Humour and charm also characterise her Octavian in the Karajan-Schwarzkopf *Rosenkavalier*; but one also is aware of depth, and in the last Act a strong emotional response to the Marschallin's magnanimity. Perhaps best of all, we can hear her in Mahler, notably in Klemperer's great recording of *Das Lied von der Erde*, with Fritz Wunderlich incomparably fine in the tenor part. Her own performance is marked by breadth of phrase, intelligent handling of words, and a special beauty of the soft singing. And a fine appendage is 'Ich bin der Welt abhanden gekommen', the voice here glowing with its richness: surely among the most beautiful of our time.

The one mezzo really comparable in this triple role of Lieder singer, opera star and general musician is Janet Baker. She too has done wonderfully well in the Mahler–Rückert songs, with 'Ich bin der Welt abhanden gekommen' recorded twice, both times with Barbirolli. The mixture of strength and tenderness also marks her singing of the great solo song-cycles. In *Kindertotenlieder* her embittered biting edge in the storm music of the last song plays affectingly against an anxious, deeply human tone, and the gentlest, loveliest pianissimo possible in the last lines; and in the *Lieder eines fahrenden Gesellen* she lets the sunshine in with the second song, and challenges a newly braced response in the third, bold in the clarity of her enunciation and in a kind of thrust given to the final cry.

But this is the distinguishing mark of Janet Baker's achieved greatness. She has the natural and the technical equipment for challenging an audience to a new and more intense response, and, marvellously, she also has the spirit for it. She is not a cushion for day-dreams; she offers nothing that is merely *gemütlich*, cosy or *joli*. Her art is insistent: bold in the ways one fondly hopes Gerhardt was, to take the song to her heart and communicate it to her never-forgotten listeners.

The beauty of her voice impressed in her very first records, but so did a subtlety and an emotional strength in the use of it. Her first Lieder recital (not her first record) came out on a cheap label in 1966, and it included performances which it would be hard to improve upon throughout the whole range of recording. Schubert's 'Der Musensohn' goes at a spanking pace, but it is difficult to accept it at a slower one after hearing this: the sprightly rhythm and radiant tone combine in a reading that lets the music take its own joyful way without fuss or fidget. Then Brahms' 'Von ewiger Liebe' has just that feeling of warmth and affection that were found in Gerhardt, and it is also built to achieve a finely controlled grandeur. These are both favourite end-of-recital songs, and perhaps the essential intimacy and miniature vividness of the great Lieder singer were still to come. The record also contains *Frauenliebe und Leben*, beautifully done, yet coming somewhere short of the enthusiasms, the impulsiveness and eventually the full tragedy of loss. Performances of this most heartfelt cycle differ remarkably in depth. There is Maria Stader, pretty and quite placid; Helen Watts, scrupulous in production, but duller than one would have thought so fine a singer could be; then Lotte Lehmann, full of spirit, whether exultant or tragic; and Kathleen Ferrier, whose performance grows with each hearing, always real, vivid in its happiness, supremely beautiful in sheer qualities of voice. As surely as Baker's 1966 recording belongs to the last two rather than the first, so there is some fine degree of sympathy or communication that separates it from them. And this she was surely to encompass within a very short time. The Lieder recital published in 1968 showed a mastery that was fully mature, whether in the radiant full-bloom of Schubert's 'Auflösung', the strong, agonized voice of the questioner and the beatific replies in Wolf's 'Herr, was trägt der Boden hier', or the delicacy of Strauss's 'Wiegenlied', its tempo so slow and yet its performance so right that one seems to be hearing it for the first time.

With so much feeling for the character of a song and with so much character projected by the singer herself, one would hope for great things from her in opera too. There might be some doubt as to the power of the voice: Amneris, Ortrud, Brangäne . . . the possibilities would seem remote and risky. But 'power' is such a curious concept. Everyone knows the 'big' voice that remains confined to the wrong side of the footlights, and the 'small' one that seems to be placed somewhere in mid-air and quite close. Baker's first great success in *The Trojans* at Covent Garden (taking over at short notice from Josephine Veasey) showed that the confidence inspired by the operatic records is no deception of the recording studios (and of course reports of her singing with the Scottish Opera have glowed and tantalised for some years now). Her recording from the last Act of *The Trojans* projects character, emotion and voice with such a sense of engagement that one goes out to meet it; and no doubt it would be so in the theatre. The Lieder singer's art is useful to her: the trained sensitivity to small changes of mood, the knowledge of when to focus attention upon a particular phrase or word. By comparison, Régine Crespin, often an exceptionally imaginative artist, is generalised and unsubtle; and Josephine Veasey, possibly more vibrant, has not really the varied range of expression (the serenity of 'Adieu, fière cité, the pallid, sighing tone at her start of the last scene, *en songe* as the score directs).

Her dramatisation of the death of Dido is worthy of any Italian expert in death-scenes. And the great demonstration of Baker's dramatic power does in fact come in Italian opera: not in Verdi, however, but in Monteverdi. From *L'Incoronazione di Poppea* she sings superbly Ottavia's solos, the lament from Act I and the farewell, 'Addio, Roma' from Act III. The grandeur of style—an uninhibited yet aristocratic outpouring of emotion—places the performance in the grandest, almost legendary line of operatic singing: Lilli Lehmann's Donna Anna, Fremstad's *Don Carlo* solo, Callas' Norma perhaps. The curse upon Nero, with the downwards scales invoking thunderbolts, is attacked with towering regality; and as she revokes her own words ('ce me ne pento') self-reproach brings a new colouring, bitterly darkened, the vibrancy deadened. This essentially operatic intensity she brings also to her most familiar roles out of English opera, to Purcell's Dido and Britten's Lucretia. We must hope that before too long others from the German and Italian repertoire are added: the Composer in *Ariadne*, for instance, Gluck's *Orfeo*, just possibly the *Fidelio* Leonore. And, back to Britten, what a superb Gloriana she might make.

The same dramatic quality is present when she sings Bach and Handel. A Handel cantata (like the *Armida abbandonata*) is seen, rightly, as compressed opera; and its mood ranges from the tenderness of the first aria (some especially lovely singing in this) to the vigorous denunciations of the recitative that follows. Then in Bach, she will find a character to match music and text: after the joyful Sinfonia introducing number 169 *(Gott soll allein mein Herze haben)*, for instance, she takes the first solo simply, almost like a folk-song—a housewife singing for the joy in her heart as she sweeps the room or puts the washing out on a fine spring morning! But these records also draw attention to the technical accomplishments of her singing. The Handel cantata, *Ah crudel, nel pianto mio*, ends with all the rewarding difficulties of the Handelian allegro: elaborate runs, long phrases, demands for a wide and even working-range. The flexibility and control allow her to enjoy the trial: she sings spryly, with a smiling sense of fun. Bach, often so much more angular and so less considerate of the singer, is also met with a technical equipment that can make it sound almost easy. In *Vergnügte Ruh'* (another of the solo cantatas, no. 170), the aria 'Wie jammern' is just the kind that can sound so academic and unvocal, but here it goes beautifully, the runs perfect, the whole aria a delight.

This technical control is a needful quality too in the part of the repertoire most native to her. She is, after all, an English singer, and quite apart from the tradition that English contraltos sing *Messiah* and *Elijah* world without end (and she sings both of them with great distinction on record), there are Purcell and Britten to encounter, and both demand much. One remembers that she is also, in a way, a successor to Dame Clara Butt. She herself reminds us of it, inadvertently maybe, by a quality that at certain times appears in her voice. It has nothing to do with the meaty man-voice that kept the Empire in order and reduced old generals to tears. Instead it echoes a warm and very personal sound that the great contralto would produce in quieter passages; something solemn, full-hearted, and yet restrained in emotion. It is a special tone, and she sometimes uses it in passages remote from any recollections of Dame Clara (in the death-scene of Berlioz' Dido, for instance, at the words 'Je sens . . . rentrer . . . le calme . . . dans mon coeur'). But, not surprisingly, Elgar's *Sea Pictures* (Clara Butt sang the first performance in 1899) evokes it most: 'and though this sabbath comes to me', in the third song, is an example. The *Sea Pictures* also have examples of another characteristic, something of a mannerism in fact: a way of 'lifting' to a higher note, not by the slow curve of a portamento but by a kind of vertical take-off which has the previous note as its spring-board. Again, the latter half of the third song (Elizabeth Barrett-Browning's 'Sabbath morning at sea') has examples, including the last phrase, 'the full Godhead's burning'—and is it fancy, or does she really sing 'Godhead's b-burning'? But of course what really has to be said about *Sea Pictures* (and especially about that song, and that part of it) is that it is just about the most glorious piece of full-blooded and completely English singing on record. The songs come freshly to most people nowadays, whereas they were once the inevitable offering for contralto and orchestra. Butt's recording of 'Where corals lie', the fourth song, is surprisingly delicate and restrained, and Gladys Ripley's (on a late 78) falls pleasantly on the ear. But Baker is so very supple in rhythm and phrasing and so beautiful in voice that the piece and the whole cycle become moving in a quite unexpected and (emotionally) almost alarming way.

Still, if that part of the Edwardian contralto's song-book proves worthy of revival, one cannot imagine that all those 'ballads' are due to be salvaged as well. In fact, the term 'successor to Clara Butt' is in another way absurd, for the music involved in the two careers is so different, reflecting, no doubt, changes of musical interest in the country at large. Baker, like most of our singers nowadays, goes back to the Elizabethans and to Purcell. One great distinction she has among her contemporaries is that she sings these early composers so powerfully. So much singing of Elizabethan music has a quality that is refined to the point of being precious, and one can hardly believe that the Elizabethans themselves can have sounded nearly so bloodless. On the other hand, when a full-bodied voice trained in the grand operatic tradition tries to sing them, we generally hear the nineteenth century intruding. With Baker there is a 'straight', pure voice without operatic vibrato, but there are also strength and passion. So Dowland's 'Come again' or Purcell's 'Lord, what is man?' are sung as direct, urgent utterances, always *addressed*. And, again like most British

132. Janet Baker

singers (though not like all the great international stars discussed in this book), she has involved herself in the music of her own time, and particularly in that of Benjamin Britten, in whose work English song and opera have grown most abundantly. It is good to find, for instance, that she can characterise unpleasantness, as with Kate in *Owen Wingrave* ('What you would do and what you think has ceased to interest us', she sings, coldly, and as it were between clenched teeth). Good too to hear her as a Lucretia in whom virtue is a shining affirmation, and not just an absence of vice. But then, she brings something positive, with characteristic strength and beauty, to whatever she sings.

The dominance of Benjamin Britten in the modern part of a singer's repertoire is evident not only in Janet Baker, but in most of her English contemporaries too. It is so with John Shirley-Quirk, for example; a singer who, like Baker, turns everything to beauty, including the kind of speech-sing which in modern music seems almost inevitably to induce an unlyrical, unsteady lumpiness in a singer's production. He is Colatinus to Janet Baker's Lucretia, his warm, firm voice appropriate to the sympathetic character of the man. As Coyle in *Owen Wingrave* he again gives a fine demonstration of how it is possible to sing such music with the firm, full-bodied sound that some sturdy (and improbable) singer from the past (Peter Dawson?) might have brought to it. He too is a Lieder singer; and no doubt more is going to come from him than the not entirely satisfying Beethoven and Brahms of his 1970 recital record. The *Vier ernste Gesänge* benefit from the kindly tone and the broad phrasing, but his singing here is not magnetic: play Fischer-Dieskau alongside this and one is always realising new things (the Hardyesque life-abnegation of the second song, for example, with its weariness of tone as the singer views the oppression and suffering of an afflicted planet). *An die ferne Geliebte*, similarly, is pleasant, smooth and well-nourished: but here a chance comparison with Ernst Häfliger shows how much more vivid and meaningful the cycle can be (how the voice can dance with the piano part in 'Es kehret der Maien', giving more point to the rhythm, smiling and narrating, giving a hushed and poetic feeling to the picture of the declining day in the last song). Yet he will sometimes sing with great intensity (as in 'Sur les lagunes' from *Nuits d'Eté*), and he always earns our gratitude for the sheer excellence of production and beauty of tone. His version of Bach's solo cantata *Ich habe genug* is most beautifully even in its legato and accomplished in its runs. In English songs, such as Vaughan Williams' *Songs of Travel*, again one sometimes wishes he would *tell* us more. 'Bright is the ring of words' says the lyric, and brighter, one feels, should be the face of the singer; on the other hand, what easy breadth of phrasing and what warmth of voice. So too (to return to Benjamin Britten) in his dramatic work. Perhaps the Ferryman of *Curlew River* might introduce into his voice something corresponding to the weird weeping voices of the players; yet he is splendidly incisive at the opening and always effective in enunciation. And in *The Prodigal Son* the part of the father suits him wonderfully well: the voice capturing the warmth and goodness of the character, and, more essentially, a kind of serenity and stillness that is so important a part of this work.

One of the Ferryman's lines in *Curlew River* is 'Did you see who it is that is singing?'. But there are no prizes for the answer: it was Peter Pears, and there would be no need to look. The voice is one of the most distinctive of all the century's singers, and (like Tauber) the only reason why it can hardly be called inimitable is that it has found so many imitators. And of course Britten's music has played such a large part in his career (and he in its) that it is almost impossible to think of the one without the other.

He has recorded a good deal else, however: Schubert and Bach, notably, and a wide range of British composers from John Dowland to Richard Rodney Bennett, with *The Dream of Gerontius* as a still surprising climax to this part of his work. Even here, Britten is part of the inspiration, conducting with the freshening qualities that also mark his piano accompaniments. Their recording of *Der Winterreise* consistently impresses as the fruits of a fresh study, voice and piano as one in mutual understanding. The journey-ing-music is realised almost pictorially: the recurrent quavers of the first song given a sharper articulation, emphatic as a march-rhythm in the third verse, a suggestion taken up again in the third song ('Gefrorne Tränen'), reappearing in 'Rückblick' and 'Der Wegweiser'. If it is the pianist who keeps the singer walking, step by step, the effects of the journey, physical and mental, are the singer's business. Pears conveys the exhaustion wonder-fully well: in 'Das Wirtshaus' the grey voice-colour tells of the effort of taking up the staff again to move on from the full graveyard (no room or rest even at this inn). The 'happier' songs, 'Frühlingstraum', 'Die Post' and 'Täuschung', tuneful, with major key and buoyant six-eight rhythms, take their place in this process of exhaustion. The natural characteristics of the melody are allowed full play (the lilt and charm of 'Täuschung', the sweet lyricism of 'Frühlingstraum'), but something in the tone is always there to enforce the ambivalence (in 'Täuschung' something taut or brittle to point the irony, in 'Frühlingstraum' the delusive sweetness of the dream overlaid with the suggestion of a limp delirium). Insanity threatens more vividly in this version than in others. It lurks in the mists of the penultimate song, 'Die Nebensonnen', its tone tinted with falsetto, or in the weirdly affectionate singing of 'Die Krähe', or in Pears' sensitivity to the chilling modulations of 'Auf dem Flusse'. If a *Great Recordings of the Twentieth Century* series is compiled in the Twenty-first, this will surely have its place among the first issues.

Objections may arise, as they do with Fischer-Dieskau. They might vary from some grim admonition like 'That's all right as long as you don't call it singing' to a milder but still rueful complaint about unsteadiness and lack of richness. The second comment might indeed be the chief rational cause of the first (prejudice often enters into it too), and the objectors might prefer to turn from *Der Winterreise* to the other Schubert cycle which Pears and Britten have recorded, *Die schöne Müllerin.* They might play the beginning of 'Danksagung an den Bach' or 'Pause'; and if they have a gift for mimicry they might attempt an imitation with some success (Dudley Moore shows the way in *Beyond the Fringe*). Returning then to serious criticism, they might continue with 'Die liebe Farbe' as an example of the kind of song Pears interprets particularly well, and then compare Ernst Häfliger: draining his voice of vibrancy, Häfliger sings with completely firm tone, with much variety and depth, and indeed with great distinction. 'There,' they might say, 'is singing for you'. They might even argue that it is not entirely a one-way matter even as far as interpretation goes: in 'Der Jäger', for instance, Fischer-Dieskau and Gerald Moore find much more fun, and Häfliger, going at top speed, conveys the energy of the song by completely musical means, placing the notes of the hectic last lines accurately, and losing none of the excitement. But fundamentally the complaints would remain, mainly directed against the sheer sound of Pears' voice: wanting body, they would say, and steadiness.

Much can be said about this. One point is recognised by the singer himself. In an interview with Edward Greenfield (*Guardian,* June 1970) Pears talked about his recordings and said how he disliked the process, especially the play-back, 'an enormous presence' with every consonant exaggerated. There is, with Pears, an unusual disparity between the overall impression created by the records and by the voice as heard in live performances. My own pleasure in his records has nearly always been affected (though never cancelled) by an unsteadiness which has never struck me as a marked characteristic in the flesh. One recording where he appears to be distanced a little further than usual from the microphone is that of the *St. Matthew Passion* under Klemperer; here there is very little unsteadiness, whereas the performance under Münchinger issued three years later, in 1965, has him more forward in recording, a shade more unsteady and a shade less like the voice one hears in the concert hall. And another point is that 'the voice one hears' has been quite remarkably consistent over a period of about thirty years. After the first performances of *Peter Grimes* a critic said that at this rate the voice would not last beyond the present run. Prophecies of early doom have dried up recently as they so evidently are not going to be fulfilled. The *Gerontius* recording shows him at sixty, singing with a voice that in some ways seems stronger than ever, for it has acquired a deeper sonority. If one wants to hear how his voice sounded at various stages in his career, there are the three recordings of Britten's *Serenade for Tenor, Horn and Strings,* the first issued on 78s, then the first LP version (with Dennis Brain and conducted by Goossens) in 1954, and a second (Barry Tuckwell and Britten) in 1964. The first was a classic example of creative, utterly original singing; the second added little except a moderation of certain characteristic effects (notably the portamento on 'lulling' in the Keats Sonnet); the third lost a touch of stiffness that had made its way into the second, and came very near to the ideal in sensitivity and balance. The voice is steadier in the last recording than in the second, and has changed relatively little over the whole period. It is also, from first to last, a remarkable instrument, responsive, it seems, to everything that a subtle artistic mind requires of it, whether in colouring or in a special effect like the octave glissandos of the Dirge ('This ae night') or in the runs and staccatos of Ben Jonson's 'Hymn to Diana'. A steadier sound would be welcome in the first song, possibly a more ringing tone in the second (the Tennyson); but there has never been more characterful singing on record, or better musicianship to be saluted in a singer.

These two factors (personality and musicianship) have made him a

133. Peter Pears (right) and Benjamin Britten

singer of exceptional value to modern composers. Sometimes one feels that the voice itself inspired the writing, as in Priaulx Rainier's *Cycle for Declamation*, written for Pears in 1954. The intensity of the first song, the ghost-voice of the second (masterly voice-painting in the phrase 'away with dust with every wind'), the distinctive low register repeating the Latin text in the last: all must so wonderfully repay a composer's cares. In the song-cycles of Britten himself, Pears' rightness is almost a liability. How can we ever hear another voice in 'The Choirmaster's Burial' *(Winter Words)*, 'Since she whom I loved' *(The Holy Sonnets of John Donne)* or the passage from Wordsworth's *Prelude* in the *Nocturne*. In the Michelangelo Sonnets, too, we feel it will always be his voice we hear, whether in the brighter, thinner tone of his recording on 78s (with its slyly flirtatious touch in Sonnet 38, and its Italianate, impetuous singing of the 31st), or in the darker, more mature sound of the LP (better in the last song, Sonnet 24).

The voice that can colour and characterise so subtly and strongly can also act. For so individual a voice, it is also remarkably adaptable. The prissy Pandarus voice (only a few bars of that role preserved on record) modulates readily into the Nebuchadnezzar of *The Burning Fiery Furnace*: weak, wide-eyed and slightly silly. The malignant melisma of Peter Quint's invocation *(Turn of the Screw)*, the old General rapping out his summoning 'Sirrah' and weeping *(Owen Wingrave)*, the aristocratic self-searching of Captain Edward Fairfax Vere *(Billy Budd)*: all lodge firmly in the mind. In *Midsummer Night's Dream* he sings Lysander, instead of his stage-part of Flute the bellows-mender. Flute is well-sung by Kenneth Macdonald, and is a vivid memento of an artist whose untimely death brought a sad loss to Covent Garden; but we miss in this an example of Pears' flair for comedy (represented otherwise by *Albert Herring*). Sometimes his voice will grimace, shudder, raise its eyebrows: an ironical head-wagging accompanies 'Colatinus is politically astute to choose a virtuous wife', just as the face hardens into resentful meanness as 'Colatinus is lucky, very lucky' is sung as though between clenched teeth (phrases sung by the Male Chorus in *The Rape of Lucretia*—the last of them particularly good in the early recording on 78s). He has always been good at madness (the slow smile in Rodney Bennett's 'Tom o'Bedlams Song', as the crazed singer is drawn to the moon like a moth to the light). So the weirdly lamenting portamentos of the woman in *Curlew River* are part of a characterisation touching in its suppressed emotion and fearful expectancy. As Peter Grimes he can command plenty of truculence and toughness, but it is the tender, neurotic and eventually mad soul that comes to life most irreplaceably in his singing. Phrases like 'Alone, alone with a childish death', 'What harbour shelters peace', 'Turn the skies back and begin again' are impossible to dissociate from his voice.

Above all, he is a spiritual singer. In the *War Requiem*, as the soloists repeat again and again 'Let us sleep now' at the end of 'Strange Meeting', their tones matching exactly, one feels how Britten has managed to express 'the tenderness of silent minds', and how, even if, say, a violin or clarinet were playing the singers' phrases it would still be making the sound of Peter Pears—the voice is there in the music and all that it expresses. It is interesting too that, if he has a greatness as a dramatic singer beyond even his achievement in the Britten operas, it is as the Evangelist in Bach's Passions. In the passages concerning Peter's denial and the crucifixion itself he is especially memorable, but the whole reading has strength and imaginativeness quite out of the common; and (particularly in the *St. Matthew Passion* with Klemperer) a rare grace, vocal and spiritual.

Pears, then, takes his place with these few singers who in the depth and completeness of their work are so emphatically artists. Of course, all the chapters of this book, in all three periods of gramophone history, have been concerned with singers who are artists. But modern times have seen a distinct increase in subtlety: an understanding of the music localised in its closer, more imaginative attention to detail. We have also seen an extension of the singer, represented most by the last few singers discussed here, and perhaps most of all by Peter Pears. The repertoire is no longer centred on the Nineteenth Century: the very exacting demands of earlier and later ages have to be met. The singer has always had to do more than sing; but for the extensions to the old repertoire he has to be a widely educated musician. In the next chapter we shall be looking at that great number of singers, fully involved in this tough workaday profession and often without attaining the status of an international 'star', who in recent years have become exactly that.

29. Ancient and Modern: The Singer as Musician

'THE singer has always had to do more than sing.'

Singing has nevertheless been the basic function, though for the avant-garde, the logic of such a state of affairs is not self-evident. There are compositions where the singer may, every now and again, sing; but the interest tends to lie in other activities.

Thus Peter Maxwell Davies, writing the sleeve-note on his 'Revelation and Fall', describes the solo soprano as ranging 'from normal singing, through *Sprechgesang*, to screaming through a loud-hailer'. Mary Thomas performs the part in the recording (1968): imaginative in the quiet opening, screaming nightmare animal cries, conveying a shivering horror in the insane melisma of 'O bittere Tod'. The spiky, shuddering phrases for 'normal singing' are done with what one would 'normally' call rather breathy, shallow tone, but this may be irrelevant. It is possible that the piece might be less effective if given with richer tone. It may be that richer tone is hardly possible if the voice is to wisk and shiver over such a jagged, feverish vocal line. A piece making similar demands upon the male voice is his *Eight Songs for a Mad King*, recorded by Julius Eastman. Here the voice is to move from treble high C to bass low G sharp on one syllable, to produce a chord of F minor, to scream and shout—all of which it does to chilling effect. The high-master of the 'extended voice', however, is Roy Hart who makes sounds over eight octaves in Henze's fierce setting of an arrogantly oblique text in *Versuch über Schweine*. Henze also uses the singer for anything but singing in *El Cimarrón*. This is his setting for baritone, flute, guitar and percussion of the narrative of a negro in Cuba, 104 years old, and born into slavery. The soloist again ranges wide in pitch—from deep bass to falsetto—and in dynamics—from whisper to scream. William Pearson, an American Negro with a considerable reputation in Germany, gives a great performance, tireless and immensely resourceful (intoning in the nose for satire on the bloodless clergy, sometimes sounding the voice of the old, old man, squeaking the voice of the Headless Horseman in the section called 'The Spirits', giving a marvellous impression of feverish, breathless running in the flight). He carries complete emotional conviction, and his voice in its natural state is rich and resonant. One wonders whether it can remain so after many performance of *El Cimarrón*, but a well-produced speaking voice will stand up to years of hard use on a military parade-ground, and Mr. Pearson sounds resilient enough to take the strain.

And certainly not all the non-singing devices of modern music are necessarily a strain upon the singer. To the twelve soloists in Messiaen's 'Cinq Réchants' (superbly recorded by the John Alldis Choir and by the soloists of the Rédiffusion Français), the 'tk,tk' noises and so forth must come as something of a relief from the ardours of song. The six vocalists in Stockhausen's *Stimmung* are also required to shout and laugh, recite and repeat the 'Magic Names', as well as (the composer points out) learning a new way of singing. The Collegium Vocale of Cologne performs 73 minutes of *Stimmung*, a work which, says the composer, 'will reduce even bellowing wolves to silence' (though apparently it could not quite silence the Provos of Amsterdam). 'Over several months the singers learnt a completely new vocal technique; the vocal notes must be sung rather quietly, with specific overtones (indicated by a series of numbers from 2 to 24, a series of vowels drawn from the phonetic alphabet) as dominant as possible; without vibrato; resonating only in the forehead and the other cranial cavities; with long, gentle, even breaths'. The six young performers do it very well. But one rather hopes that the new technique can be un-learnt at will, and that not too many new techniques will be required of young students 'over several months' in which they might be trying to master the traditional ones.

It might be argued that such extensions of the tradition are by this time themselves traditional. Certainly the *Sprechstimme* (a cross between speech and song) had a good half-century's history before it came to be used by Henze and Maxwell Davies. Most notable for its part in the work of Schönberg, it is still probably most famous as the mode in which he voiced the poems of *Pierrot Lunaire* (the score written in 1912). In spite of the half-spoken character of the utterance, the part is still normally given to a singer, and, although the market is still fairly limited, sopranos have gradually accustomed themselves to the idea that they might one day be balancing the claims of 'sprech' and 'gesang', and be chastised by the critics for either inexpressiveness or for intrusion of personality. 'Wherever it seems important to the author to render, by tone-painting, the events and sentiments of the text, this is done by the music itself. Wherever this does not seem satisfactory to the performer, he should not attempt to give something which the author did not want.' Thus Schönberg in his preface to the score. And again a new technique for the singer, who having learnt to be expressive, communicative and personal, now has to leave all that to 'the music itself'. Ethel Semser (with Leibowitz) and Alice Howland (with Zippler) obey what one imagines to be the force of the instructions; Ilona Steingruber (with Golschmann) sings much more than most and the piece loses part of its character; Bethany Beardslee (with Craft) performs with much expression and personality, drawing on a wide range, making strong contrasts, and using a sort of shivering portamento that seems appropriate to the character. There are other recordings, each with its own individuality, but these are representative.

When Schönberg does want his singer to sing, his demands are often cruelly exacting and in their own time must have seemed impossible. In March 1913, the *Musical Times* amused itself and its readers by transcribing fifteen bars of music for soprano under the heading 'The Vocalist of the Future . . .?' 'The following delightful passage', the critic wrote, 'concluding a recent song, *Herzgewächse*, by the irresistible Arnold Schönberg may, if his theories be correct, afford a perfunctory peep into the vocalisation of the future. The idea is obviously in its infancy. Earlier in the composition the low G sharp appears in the score. Schönberg's soprano, then, is evidently expected to possess a compass of nearly three octaves. The F in alt.,pppp, is a touch of inspiration.' The fearsome bars follow after a few urbane observations about the composition itself. Looking at them, one is quite prepared to laugh with the *Musical Times*. Listening to Rita Tritter's recording, however, one stops laughing: she sings accurately and (it seems) effortlessly, and the effect is most beautiful. The *MT* might have added that as a further challenge to the singer, Schönberg sets the long 'F in alt.,pppp' to the first syllable of 'mystischer'; Miss Tritter does not risk the squeak (and probable physical dislocation) which this invites, and she contents herself with a single 'p' rather than four. But she does a marvellous job. It is a pity the critic of 1913 could not hear her.

He would also have been surprised to find that 'the vocalist of the future . . .?' has become that of the present at least in so far as there are now singers who will perform these works and sound well in them. In *Moses und Aron*, Helmut Krebs sings Aaron's music with a lyrical style that might even be called ingratiating. He is a singer-musician who has been involved in many important recordings, such as the first LP version of Monteverdi's *Orfeo* (1955) where again he sings well though in slightly nasal, German-sounding Italian; that, together with the *Moses* (recorded from a broadcast made in 1954) suggests something of the pattern of activity for such singers —a strenuous one in terms of the musical mastery required. It is also notable that the chorus in this recording manages to cope with its formidable assignment and also to produce sounds (spoilt a little by some wobbly sopranos) that often have a rich sensuous beauty. Sheer beauty of sound is also a feature of the *Erwartung* as sung by Dorothy Dow (Mitropoulos conducting): the tone is sweet and firm, and firm too is her placing of the difficult intervals. One limitation is that the pitch is not always accurate; another (and a more surprising one) is that the singer makes so little impression dramatically in so very dramatic a work. The development from anxiety to agonies of desperation, and then to the lamenting stillness of the last part finds no response in her. And this is relatively common in the singing of Schönberg. The *Four Orchestral Songs* are designed as music which will do 'justice to the subtlest nuance of the text' (Schönberg's note); yet there is little nuance or even expression in Regina Sarfaty's recording of them—again perhaps it is supposed to be 'done by the music itself'. At least Helga Pilarczyk takes the full business of expression upon herself in her recording of *Erwartung*. She has mastered the problems of pitch as far, I imagine, as is humanly possible; very occasionally she will pitch slightly high; but this is a magnificent and compelling performance of the haunted, traumatic 'Isolde (who) has had a nervous breakdown', as Robert Craft puts it. Pilarczyk is a singer with a powerful, dramatic voice and a strong sense of presentation, and her *Erwartung* is certainly one of the great achievements on record: a testimonial too to the number of times (it was nearly a hundred when the record was made, in 1962) on which she has been through those concentrated twenty-five minutes of nightmare on the stage.

In some respects, the avant-garde (and despite the passage of time, for most of the public Schönberg, Berg and Webern still come within that category) encourages good vocal habits. Nobody, for instance, is likely to be asked twice to wobble her way through Berg's *Five Orchestral Songs* (the Altenberg Lieder). Bethany Beardslee sings them with exactly the instrumental firmness and definition they require. She is efficient over the whole wide compass, placing the notes in alt with clean accuracy and pure tone. There is a little group of fioriture on the word 'schöner' in number 2, and again this is very elegantly sung. She has not quite the sonority needed for the last song—it wants the tone and temperament of a Lotte Lehmann—but one cannot have everything, not even in 'the vocalist of the future'. And what of the vocalists of the past? How sad the gramophone is so silent. The Great left these things alone for the most part (we don't, as far as I know, find Hempel or Kurz or Ivogün turning their very suitable talents to Schönberg's *Herzgewächse*, for instance). But I can hardly think of a more valuable record-that-never-was than that of the first two of these songs by Berg as they were performed in 1913 in Vienna under Schönberg.

The operas of Berg seem, on the other hand, to encourage some bad qualities in their singers, and (for the singer) some disastrous assumptions in composers who are influenced by them. One of these is a view of the singer's function in which beauty of tone is expendable and perhaps even intrinsically undesirable. In *Wozzeck*, the Captain, Doctor and Drum-Major have a great many phrases to learn, and in not one of them is it required that they should sing beautifully. Nor do they. There is a lot to admire about the performances of Gerhard Stolze, Helmuth Melchert, Karl Kohn (for example) in these roles, and part of the admiration lies in a more than half-sad appreciation of their willingness to sacrifice themselves as singers to fulfil a post as operatic artist—but it is a strange situation in which these functions should come to be mutually exclusive. Berg's writing for the tenor voice is surely vindictive. Donald Grobe sounds much better as Alwa in *Lulu* than does the unsteady Hans Liebert, and both

Waldemar Kmentt and Loren Driscoll do well as the painter, but the murderous writing ensures that pleasure in their singing shall be minimal. The demands made upon Lulu herself are also so great that one feels any criticism made about the quality of voice is ungrateful or even flippant. Neither Ilona Steingruber not Evelyn Lear can be said to invest the part with any great tonal beauty, but they cope with the florid work and the cruel tessitura, and they have the energy and vocal stamina to survive. Evelyn Lear does in fact have a voice that can in some records sound quite rich and beautiful. She is the Marina of Christoff's second *Boris Godunov*; and she brings imagination and an urgent sense of drama to a Hugo Wolf recital shared with her husband, Thomas Stewart. In *Wozzeck* her Marie is a strong and attractive performance, pitching the *Sprechgesang* much nearer the written notes than Isobel Strauss (who sings the part feelingly under Boulez), probably somewhat at fault in singing the Bible reading at all (though by doing so she brings out an otherwise hidden melody, and some like myself will no doubt be grateful to her for doing so). She is also accurate in pitching Marie's music, though in *Lulu* (generally by pitching too high) she is sometimes out.

Following records of these works with a score and a piano, one spends half the time in wonderment that anybody gets anything right, and the other half amazed to find that they can get away with so much that is wrong. Few of the singers under Boulez in *Wozzeck*, for example, are thoroughly accurate, and the Doctor (Karl Doench) sings quite regularly a whole fourth or fifth above though following the 'melodic' outline reasonable closely. Comparing Eileen Farrell's Marie (recorded in a broadcast performance of *Wozzeck* under Mitropoulos) with the score on one's knee, one would assume her to be working from a different edition, the pitching is so approximate. In this performance, the Captain (Joseph Mordino) performs most of his part in a kind of *Sprechgesang* generally about a fourth above (perhaps strangely, it is much more common to find singers above the written notes than below them—no doubt many must have surprised themselves as perhaps Farrell did, landing a magnificent high C sharp where the score asks for a mere high B). The Wozzeck, Mack Harrell, sings and characterises well (better than he does as Nick Shadow in *The Rake's Progress*), and he pitches what might be called the 'essential' notes correctly while not being too particular about the ones between. This of course was in the early years of LP, and it is unlikely that such a performance would be issued on records now unless it was thought to have some quite exceptional quality in other respects. Walter Berry's finely sung Wozzeck has shown how parts of the score require and can receive a genuinely *cantabile* treatment. Just possibly similar revelations lie ahead about the more cruelly written roles in these operas; but it is to be feared that they have already too much to answer for in the recent history of the voice and its abuse in modern music.

Of course nobody expects modern composers to write like Bellini;

we simply have to be grateful when a lyrical and considerate passage shows that they could write well for the singing voice if they really wanted to. Henze has done so in his time, as in his *Elegy for Young Lovers* and in *Der junge Lord*, where Luise has a long solo in the last scene, allowing Edith Mathis, in the recording, to sing feelingly and with her customary freshness of tone (delightfully heard, spry and smiling, in Bach's Cantata no. 78, *Jesu der du meine Seele*). Britten, too, is not always the most lyrical of composers, and his operas do not stop very often for singers to pour out their hearts and voices in a 'Vissi d'arte' or 'Vesti la giubba'. But he does write for voices and not against them, and the recordings of his work contain much excellent singing. Some of it we remember principally for character: Sylvia Fisher's Lady Billows and Miss Wingrave, Denis Dowling's Junius, Owen Brannigan's Swallow, Gregory Dempsey's Red Whiskers. Quite often a particular singer's voice is caught in the very phrases that Britten writes. Pears is the obvious and essential example; but Joan Cross too, so closely associated with the earlier operas. She was one of the best of English operatic sopranos in the nineteen-thirties and forties, and her records of solos from *Madama Butterfly*, *Bohème*, *Otello* and some Mozart operas must have helped to start many an opera lover and record collector on his way. It is still hard to dissociate Ellen Orford in *Peter Grimes*, the Female Chorus in *The Rape of Lucretia* and Mrs. Grose in *Turn of the Screw* from her voice and style as we knew them in these roles (but no records, alas, of the crowning achievement of her stage-career, Queen Elizabeth in *Gloriana*). The sound of Jenifer Vyvyan as the Governess in *Turn of the Screw* is another that becomes virtually inseparable from the score. A certain bite, even an acidity, in the tone made Vyvyan a bracing singer, and her technique and general musicianship made her a reliable soloist in many recordings of Handel and Purcell (there was also a charming record of two Duet Cantatas by Scarlatti with accomplished singing by herself and Elsie Morison). But it will always be in phrases like 'Who is it, who?', 'Lost in my labyrinth', and perhaps most of all the Governess' ride to Bly that Jenifer Vyvyan will be most remembered by most listeners (unless perhaps in another of Britten's less frequently performed works, the *Cantata Academica*, where she very beautifully floats her solo over the student song hummed by the chorus). The writing and the voice are a perfect match—as they are also in the music that Britten wrote for that exquisite light soprano, Margaret Ritchie. Her part in *Albert Herring* (Miss Wordsworth) is sung in the recording by April Cantelo, but we can hear her as Lucia in the first *Rape of Lucretia* records, unforgettably lovely in her duet with Flora Nielsen (admirable singer herself, pupil of Gerhardt and heard all too rarely on records). Ritchie—also a pupil of a distinguished teacher, Agnes Nichols—had a small, fresh voice which she used with authority and style. Her scalework was always excellent, and her trill an especial delight, so genuine and unostentatious in use. Her record of Schubert's *Der Hirt auf dem Felsen* is still very probably the best; and

Britten remembered all her qualities in writing the parts she was to sing.

Just possibly, Stravinsky also may have had particular singers' voices in mind as he wrote *The Rake's Progress.* Chester Kallman tells how his collaborators left behind them for the composer's attention records of Steber, Stignani, Björling and Domgraf-Fassbänder as voice-types for the leading roles. Whatever the cause, the vocal writing is both considerate and effective, as though the composer sang in his head, with his singers, while writing (as surely any good writer for the voice must do as by second-nature). The first recording of the opera (Güden, Conley, Harrell, Thebom), only partly successful, was followed by another, issued in 1965, also conducted by the composer and with a less star-studded but more uniformly satisfying cast. Some were American: Judith Raskin, affectionate, young-sounding and accomplished as Anne; John Reardon, a steady and positive Nick Shadow. Others (including the Sadlers Wells chorus) were from England: Don Garrard, warm and resonant in his singing of Truelove; Kevin Miller, projecting a vivid characterisation as the Auctioneer; and, above all, Alexander Young as Tom. Always gratefully heard (for example, in a pleasant recital of songs by Arne, ever so slightly spoilt by runs lightly aspirated, or in Handel's *Hercules* where he takes the runs and the decorations added for a *da capo* with ease and great efficiency), Young emerges from *The Rake's Progress* as a singer of real distinction. The sweet, lyrical voice of the first scene has hardened when we hear it in the second (the 'progress' has begun). In Act II it has gained a ruthlessness in enunciation and is bright-edged and further hardened with the decision to marry Baba. The miserable, frightened Tom of the 'card scene' is caught with diminished voice, and the onset of madness at the end of that same scene is marked by a drained, other-worldly tone. In the Bedlam scene, his address to Venus ('at last') carries its pathos, and his part ends with a most lovely *mezza voce* in the last phrase ('weep for Adonis whom Venus loved'). Throughout the opera, the natural sweetness of his voice will return at thoughts of Anne, and the Cavatina ('Love, too frequently betrayed') is a model of lyrical singing.

But then, that solo is perhaps the nearest that a modern composer ever comes to writing for the voice like Bellini. Stravinsky's admiration for that composer is well-known (preferable to Beethoven was his judgment at one time), so it should not be entirely surprising that his opera is singable. Even so, one does not first think of him as a singer's composer. *The Nightingale*, completed in 1914, certainly contains rewarding material for a high soprano (recorded with clear bright tone and great proficiency by Reri Grist). But Stravinsky was not particularly fond of this work later on, and the percussive style of so much of his writing is not good for the voice. Thus soloists and chorus batter away remorselessly at the rhythmic iterations in *Les Noces*; and though the effect is exciting for the listener, the voices take their punishment. Nor can we properly enjoy our listening if the punishment has been inflicted on those particular voices too often already. Like one of the gods of old, hungry for sacrifice, none but the best will satisfy. When a Häfliger is among the soloists (as he is in a performance recorded live at the Holland Festival of 1954), the fact is gratefully acknowledged as in a piece of Mozart; when, in *Threni*, the bass soloist is the incompletely focused Robert Oliver (hard-worked but unlovely soloist too in Schönberg's *Die glückliche Hand*), only the fact that so many hard things are required of him stops our grumbling. Such clean-lined serial music as the *Three Songs from William Shakespeare* (1953) need exactly the kind of instrumental, non-sensuous, firm singing they have from Grace-Lynne Martin: a bright, even needly voice, like a particularly penetrative oboe added to the instrumental ensemble. Marni Nixon, an intelligent and characterful singer, with a curiously innocent piping voice, has just the girlish purity wanted for the *Three Japanese Lyrics* of 1913 (also sung imaginatively by Evelyn Lear) or the *Four Russian Songs* of 1918 (still more remarkable in a marvellous collection of songs by Charles Ives). *In Memoriam Dylan Thomas* (1954) finds its right precision of tone and diction, as well as that kind of classical detachment which is far from dispassionate, in the singing of the tenor Richard Robinson. He sounds a little like an American Ronald Dowd, that very musicianly and devoted Australian singer, whose own most notable work on records is in Stravinsky. This is the *Oedipus Rex* where, firmer than Pears in the role, more varied than George Shirley, he gives a wholly admirable performance: not least because he feels for the *dolce* in among all this angular notation and declamatory urgency. Stravinsky benefits, too, from being sung by a singer of character. Dowd has a very individual voice; still more so, Hugues Cuénod, whose singing of the *Cantata* (1952) supplies a highly personal, memorable vocal tone to match the haunting quality of the music.

Cuénod specially deserves our attention in this chapter. That unmistakeable voice has had a long career, and its work has taken him pre-eminently into those two areas, ancient and modern, in which the singer-musician has found himself occupied beyond the average experience of his predecessors. The Stravinsky *Cantata* may represent him in modern music (though his repertoire is extensive, ranging, as the sleeve-note of one of his records says, from Noel Coward's *Bitter Sweet* sung in London and New York, to *Wozzeck* at La Scala). His contribution in early music has been more notable still. As one of Nadia Boulanger's singers, he was involved at the start of the great Monteverdi revival that (for record collectors) dates from the publication of the famous album of 'Selected Works' in 1937. Some of the most delightful items in this are his duets with Paul Derenne, the other tenor of the group. Their voices matched well at that time, both of them characterised by a light flicker-vibrato and by an easy flexibility (Derenne turns up again years later as a mellifluous serenader of Suzanne Danco in *L'Heure Espagnol*). Cuénod's voice (he always says that he has none and that he is engaged because of the strangeness of his repertoire) became drier over the years; or perhaps the crackly brittleness of firewood suggests its tone. The spark of good humour is present too: as in the drunkards' duet in *L'Incoronazione di Poppea* or in Cavalli's *L'Ormindo*, where he plays the old nurse Erice, good at meditating on her amorous youth (better still on the stage, when one sees those long arms reaching out to illustrate the point), conjuring the spirits and resenting interruptions. Still further into the past, his records of mediaeval and renaissance songs filled a wide gap in the catalogues. Just occasionally in these records something seems to be pulling the pitch downwards; the flicker of sound and the light aspirating of runs may also disturb the flow from time to time. Yet his voice can sound quite sweet-toned (he uses a honeyed tone for the Italian troubadour songs), and there is abundant grace and vitality. As for the repertoire—English, Italian and Spanish lute songs, troubadour songs from Italy and France, mediaeval songs from Germany—it offers a virtually inexhaustible source of pleasure, and points the way to still more.

For example, among the mediaeval French songs is one by Guillaume de Machaut: it might well open the door to a great wealth of 'new' music in the work of this composer. If a chance listener to Cuénod's old record were to turn up his catalogue in the early 1970s, he would find a record of music by Machaut which included along with some choral works nine songs sung by another tenor, Ernst Häfliger. He has been mentioned several times in the last twenty pages or so; and it is worth drawing attention to the nature of his achievements among his contemporaries and predecessors. He is, for instance, an opera singer with a voice that will ring generously in a Verdi aria, taking its high notes without yelling or skimping in (for instance) Rossini's *Stabat Mater*, and riding the old war-horses gracefully. He will also bring grace to Wagner: how often the Steersman in *Der fliegende Holländer* sounds constricted and unsteady, but with him we hear firm, lyrical and delightful singing. He is fine, too, in *Das Lied von der Erde* (recorded twice, once with the musicianly, somewhat cold-sounding Mildred Miller, under Walter, and again with Nan Merriman, more personal and magnetic, under van Beinum). Häfliger has sufficient power to match the fearsome orchestration of the first song, and also the delicacy for the third, 'Von der Jugend'. He is a dramatic tenor who is also modestly stylish in Mozart (a fine Tamino and Belmonte—firm and unforced, with breath for the long phrases and precision in the runs). He is an opera singer who is also sensitive and refined (not excessively discreet either) in Lieder (his beautiful vocalisation well heard in Schubert's 'Stimme der Liebe' and his feeling for mood in Brahms' 'O liebliche Wangen'). He is a singer of nineteenth century music who has extended himself into the twentieth (not, on record, to the avant garde, but to the Stravinsky already mentioned, and such works as Janáček's *Diary of a Young Man who Disappeared*). Finally, he is a modern musician who has explored back through C. P. E. Bach (an incisive, firm and—by the year of this recording—fifty-year-old Aaron in *Israel in Egypt*), J. S. Bach (as in the vigorous, difficult solos in the Cantata *O Ewigkeit, du Donnerwort*, a standard of achievement that he also brings to the major works), and back into the middle ages themselves, for this recital of ballades and so forth by Machaut. The most striking of these songs is the Virelai with Drehleier accompaniment called 'Dame, votre doulz visaire', with its elaborately winding melisma superbly sung. It is wonderful to hear a really good voice in these, and marvellous to hear Häfliger sustaining the long, high-pitched songs, avoiding anachronistic or sentimental inflections, yet giving strong expression to them as well. He deserves gratitude for the enterprise; still more for the standard of performance.

Machaut, and mediaeval music in general, are still relatively specialist concerns, for both listeners and performers. The day is still some way off when tenors learn 'Dame, votre doulz visaire' as if it were 'La donna è mobile'. On the other hand, the work of research scholars and editors, the interest in universities, the presentations on radio and in recorded histories of music have all widened and opened up the field. When a singer like Häfliger extends his repertoire to the Fourteenth Century, something quite important in the history of singing has happened. He does it, too, without finding a 'special' voice for the work. So does Ian Partridge, one of the best young English tenors now recording. His extremely beautiful voice, unforced in its production and stylish in its usage, is heard in two of Machaut's songs, both of them delightful pieces. What is interesting for present consideration is that his singing of these solos is part of a record including Machaut's *Messe de Notre Dame* sung by the Purcell Choir, whose artistic director in this record writes as follows: 'Much mediaeval music demands and contemporary professional singing techniques certainly included methods of rhythmic articulation and dynamic control which few singers trained by modern methods possess'. If the singing of the choir is anything to go by, a 'pure', unvibrating tone is also required. Now, again it looks as if the extension to the singer's repertoire is likely to have some salutary effects upon singing-method. Just as the vocal lines of Stravinsky's songs or of Schönberg's *Herzgewächse* forbid a spreading, unsteady tone (the notes have to be placed purely and accurately as by an instrument), so a mediaeval ballade or virelai (or a vocal-line in a choral work or part-song) imposes a discipline. Where there is any unsteadiness, there intrudes something which sounds immediately anachronistic; and since melisma, elaborate and often strenuously rhythmical, is also a prominent feature, then the singer is compelled to dispense with aspirates—their habitual use, always regrettable, would be grotesque in this music. The notable thing here, however, is that good singers like Häfliger and Partridge do not appear to change their method or to have cause to do so.

On the whole, the solo voices one hears in this music are less opulent or sweet-toned than those two singers. Austin Miskell, an American tenor, has made a special study of mediaeval song, and with a somewhat thin tone nevertheless sings pleasantly, using his head-voice to good effect and always keeping clear definition. An extreme example of a voice 'created' for the performance of mediaeval music and hardly acceptable in anything much later is that of Jantina Noorman, who sings with Musica Reservata. One should really speak of 'voices', for she has two (maybe many more). One is a dulcet, piping sound, quite gentle and entirely without vibration; and when singing in this way she achieves exceptional precision in rapid ornamentation. That voice can be heard in Emilio de' Cavalieri's 'Godi turba mortal'. Then, in the same record, called *Florentine Festival*, she sings in some trios where one would not recognise the voice, which is itself revealed more fully in some anonymous dance songs, notably the frisky fifth called 'Bussa la porta'. Here is the voice of a peasant, and the technique of a virtuoso: an uninhibited primitivism of tone, with the sophistication of modern musicianship. For sampling in a properly mediaeval context, the twelfth century Estampie called 'Kalenda maya' should be heard: once heard, rarely forgotten.

With time, ears will no doubt grow accustomed to such strange sounds, just as over the last twenty years or so they have learnt to accept the voice of the counter-tenor as a regular part of the musical fare. The growth of interest in early music required the reappearance of the counter-tenor; and Alfred Deller's great gifts were luckily at hand at just the right time to give a lead, inspire new interest and virtually to found a school. His repertoire centred not so much on the middle ages as on Elizabethan and Restoration music; and in his first records, on 78s, he gave some incomparable performances of songs by Dowland and Purcell. Of its kind his voice was unusually full-bodied and vibrant. He could float it very beautifully, but many altos and falsettists can do this. Where (as far as I know) he is still unique is in his strong resonance; also, of course, in the style, which though often imitated was entirely his own. Ornate in its fondness for crescendos, sudden pianos, emphases, and in its knowledge of voice-colouring, his style was perhaps most at home in Purcell: the erotic languor of 'Sweeter than roses', the gentle mystical swing of Alleluias in the Evening Hymn, the minor-keyed, languishing chromatic comforts of 'Music for a while'. When the poets spoke of making delicious moan and so forth, they must have had singing something like Deller's in mind. He could catch Elizabethan melancholy as well as the more exotic Purcellian kind; and in Dowland's 'In darkness let me dwell', we hear something essentially stronger than melancholy. In Campion's pretty piece of wantonry, 'It fell on a summer's day', he sings with charm and without the embarrassing nudging that the song sometimes provokes. He was a quite exceptional artist, who (for the music-makers and the public of his generation) brought volumes of old music to the light of imaginative performance: the songs of Byrd (his resonant voice matching the sonority of the viols in the Elegy on the death of Thomas Tallis), old folk songs (vivid and tender as he tells the tale of Barbara Allen), and a whole wealth of music from tavern songs to Monteverdi with his Consort, a fine body of singers, and strongly directed. Benjamin Britten paid his tribute with Oberon's music in

Midsummer Night's Dream, which Deller recorded, using his full voice for this often aggressive part, and luxuriating in the Purcellian solo 'I know a bank'. There have been plenty of counter-tenors during these years: John Whitworth, Grayston Burgess, James Bowman and many others in England; Russell Oberlin, firm, fresh and free of the throat, notable among the Americans (well heard in Noah Greenberg's version of the mediaeval *Play of Daniel*, in songs by Purcell, or in Bernstein's *Messiah*); and a few who have recorded well from the Continent. They should all from time to time join in a fanfare for counter-tenors in praise of Alfred the Great, the first of a steadily prospering line.[1]

In England, the Elizabethan–Purcell revival of the post-war years was helped greatly by the creation of the BBC Third Programme. Every week, almost every night, there would be some discovery to be made in music that had never before reached a wide public; and almost as regularly we would hear musicianly, reliable singers doing their jobs well. There were the two Margarets, Ritchie and Field-Hyde, Deller himself, tenors like René Soames, Eric Greene and Wilfrid Brown, with William Parsons, Henry Cummings, Gordon Clinton, Trevor Anthony among baritones and basses. Records do something to preserve their good work. Some can be heard in ensemble in the Golden Age Singers (under Margaret Field-Hyde's direction); separately they appear in such post-war recordings as the *St. Matthew Passion* under Reginald Jacques (Ferrier the contralto, Eric Greene the deeply spiritual Evangelist, music with which he was very closely identified during this period), or in the Purcell recordings made when the LP industry developed in enterprise and scholarship during the later nineteen-fifties. Purcell's *King Arthur* may serve as an example of standards here. Recorded in 1959, under Anthony Lewis, it presented the delightful score with enthusiasm and style. Its chorus, the St. Anthony Singers, were tidy and rhythmical, if slightly tremulous in the soprano line. General impression of the soloists is that some of them also could be firmer in tone, but they are without exception good on their runs and well-schooled in all matters of intonation, rhythm and diction. A case in point is Elsie Morison, who sings some of the soprano solos (though not 'Fairest Isle', which was given to the young Heather Harper who sings it very gently, almost apologetically). Morison's tone was clear and lovely, but a slightly tremulous quality is picked up by the microphone. She also sings the very beautiful soprano part in Tippett's *Child of our Time*, and makes one realise what a very English voice it is, and how the music

[1] Deller was the first counter-tenor, so far as I know, to record a serious repertoire of solo songs and to re-engage interest in the musical possibilities of the voice. The male alto is to be heard in many choral records of earlier years, and the very first years of the gramophone were also the last of the castrati. Alessandro Moreschi (1858–1921) a castrato-soprano of the Sistine Chapel Choir made some records in 1902–3 (nine are listed in Bauer). I have heard only one, Tosti's 'Ideale', where the voice is direly afflicted, the style gusty and the total effect sadly comical.

calls for a negress. The song 'How can I cherish my man in these days' or the notes floating over the chorus in 'By and by' want several additional qualities. Yet she is always business-like: good in Handel's runs, trilling well when a decoration is called for in Purcell, stylish in her feeling for the effective alternation of staccato and legato markings to support the sprightly rhythm of such a solo as 'Thou doting fool' in *King Arthur*.

And of course, in spite of the extensions into earlier times, Handel (and his *Messiah*) continued to play a large part in the life of most English singers. Styles and ways of performing *Messiah* have changed: the modern tendency has been towards smaller choruses, faster tempi, more authentic instrumentation, and the re-introduction of florid ornaments invented by or for the soloists. The last point has been mentioned earlier on (chapter 24); we might here make a brief and rather more basic comparison in style. If we listen to the opening tenor solos, 'Comfort ye' and 'Every valley', with Walter Widdop's recording (c. 1930) as an example from pre-war times, and Wilfrid Brown (1960) from more recent times, we shall have to note first that of course these are two very different types of tenor: Widdop with a big heroic voice, Brown very much a chamber singer. But the records are still representative of their periods, and while the fact that Widdop's voice is altogether more sonorous and Brown's slighter has its representative place in the comparison it is not of prime importance. The basic difference is one which, slightly magnified, looks like this: to a man of Widdop's generation (say, a tenor in the Huddersfield Choral Society), the modern performance would sound mincing and ladylike, while to modern ears the old record is likely to sound unsubtle and undisciplined. A good deal in both no doubt deserves mutual respect: not only Widdop's fine voice but his clean and fluent runs, and the vigour of his style, while the hypothetical Huddersfield tenor would admire Brown's breath-control and musical feeling. But in his performance, all these echo-effects, all this variety within the runs, this tripping, fairy-like rhythm . . . he would surely smile and think it 'fancy' and precious. Widdop's vigorous relish communicates more excitement, and yet, by modern standards, there is a lack of discipline which limits enjoyment. Why, for example, break the phrase 'Speak ye comfortably to Jerusalem' for a breath both times it is sung? And could not singer or conductor keep a check on the tendency to hurry forward during the runs?

Here, of course, is another point. Widdop *had* a conductor (the record label says 'cond.Barbirolli'), but one would hardly know it. Brown's conductor is Walter Süsskind, and there is no doubt about his presence. Possibly more important still is the quality of the playing: Widdop's tempo is faster than Brown's, but the orchestra plods, the basses stolidly un-rhythmical, so that the singer has no incentive to be anything other than straightforwardly vigorous himself. Singers of Handel profit immensely nowadays from the greater feeling that instrumentalists and conductors have for the vitality and spring in Handel. Thus we listen to two records of solos by Handel made in the mid-nineteen-sixties by Bernadette Greevy and Forbes Robinson. The singers are fine in both, but how they are helped by the playing of Neville Marriner's Academy of St. Martin-in-the-Fields, and by the direction and colourful harsichord playing of Philip Ledger and Raymond Leppard. Greevy, firm-voiced and able as she is, might, I suspect, sound a little dull without them; while Forbes Robinson, with his operatic training and feeling for drama (hear the first of his solos 'Revenge, Timotheus cries'), exactly matches the panache and technical skill of the players.

The tenor whose singing of Handel and practically everything else has been most central to the English musical scene in the post-war years is Richard Lewis; and since his Handel has been cited (to me) by golden-age connoisseurs as an example of how not to do it, we might look at that first. Listening to his recital for faults, one might pick on the aspirated vowels in 'War, he sung, is toil and trouble' *(Alexander's Feast)*. It does not matter as much in this jaunty kind of music as it would in other solos; still, one would not advance it as a model performance. In 'Sound an alarm', too, he gains precision in the runs somewhat at the expense of smoothness, and the tone is still that of a lyric tenor without quite the desirable full-bodied ring. But then turn to the famous solo from *Jephtha* and it is hard to resist the notion that here is one of the best Handelians on record. The gentle, soft-grained voice is capable of firm, strong resonance, and the repeat of 'Waft her, angels' is sung at a genuine pianissimo, with a voice that is both beautiful and distinctive. The dramatic life of the recitative reminds us too that he has been for a large part of his career an operatic artist, one whose interpretations have always had presence. His mastery of a difficult modern score is proverbial in the profession, and rather under-represented on record: perhaps best gauged from his singing of Achilles' song to guitar accompaniment in Tippett's *King Priam*. In romantic opera one wants a more opulent and Italianate tone (the grand love duets in Puccini are recorded with Lenora Lafayette, but it is a record with continual good touches and an overall lack of rightness in idiom and voice-quality). His Mozart is better known, especially the Idomeneo (the virtuosity of 'Fuor del mar' tame, however, in comparison with George Shirley or Hermann Jadlowker, from present and past times). More characterful is his Nerone in *L'Incoronazione di Poppea* (singing with Magda Laszlo, a remarkable artist who with a very feminine manner can still command sufficient grandeur of style to give her slender voice weight). Best of all, probably, are two intensely dramatic roles from outside opera. His second recorded Gerontius (issued 1965) is carefully studied and deeply felt, while the first (1955) has firmer tone and a simpler, perhaps stronger, impulse. And in Bach's *St. John Passion*, he sings superbly, both as the Evangelist and in the arias. He is good with words (biting on 'krähete der Hahn'), and has a breath-span to deal firmly with the pictorial, florid runs and the long-sustained notes of the arias. 'Golden age' connoisseurs may still profess dissatisfaction, but one imagines that the singers they favour would have no doubts about the enviable merits of such a performance.

Looking outside England to the post-war revival and extension of the musical scene, we see similar developments, especially in Germany. A German singer of outstanding musicianship and versatility, who most surely wins at least a perfunctory salute by the golden-agers, is Heinz Rehfuss. Some quality of tone or style recalls Friedrich Schorr, or at other times Herbert Janssen. He was the son of a professional singer, and one feels him to have been brought up in the lyrical tradition of Schwarz and Schlusnus, and to have taken it to heart. He too has done possibly his finest work in Bach (singing, very finely, for instance, with Lewis in the *St. John Passion* mentioned above). But he has recorded a great variety of music. He deals lyrically with the rather ungrateful vocal line of Milhaud's *Les Choéphores*; he gives distinction to the short roles of King Mark in Frank Martin's curious Tristan and Isolde oratorio, *Le Vin Herbé*; he sings with fine operatic resonance and a lightening of voice-personality in *L'Heure Espagnol*. He brings sonority and dignity to Moussorgsky's *Songs and Dances of Death* (without catching the sinister-grotesque, however); he treats Hugo Wolf to a purity of legato that rarely comes his way (exemplary in 'Gesang Weylas') . . . and so one could continue. There are limits to the voice itself. He is taxed by the high notes of *Des Knaben Wunderhorn* for example. Expressive though not newly illuminating, his interpretation does not make us feel the chill of death in 'Der Tambourg'sell'. But he is always a pleasure to listen to, and in Bach the warmth of timbre and the instrumental use of the voice are ever-welcome. His recitatives are an object-lesson, intelligently enunciated, beautifully rounded. In a quiet arioso like 'Betrachte, meine Seele' *(St. John Passion)* or in a strong bright D major aria like 'Grosser Herr' *(Christmas Oratorio)* he firmly upholds the tradition. This is what singing essentially is, it seems to say: a beautiful voice trained to sing beautifully, and a brain and heart to guide it—but the beauty comes first.

It would be nice if this were the general rule in the Bach industry. The output of cantatas, especially on German recordings, has been prolific, but a great deal of the solo work has been undistinguished, some of it abysmal. When the Dutch soprano, Elly Ameling, is singing, all is well: a dull day suddenly becomes sunny (her Handel and Mozart are a pleasure too, with fresh, pure tone and even, unaspirated runs). Agnes Giebel and Theo Altmeyer have done much good work, but the contralto, Marga Hoffgen, an internationally famous and valued artist, does not really sound well: Cantata no. 54 (*Widerstehe doch der Sünde*) may be taken as an example, the depth of voice impressive, but not the snatched breathing in recitative, or the rather plodding, emphatic style (rebuking Wotan in Act II of *Die Walküre* she is much more impressive). A tenor who creates an extremely favourable impression in Bach is the Viennese, Werner Krenn. The aria 'Sanfte soll mein Todeskummer' from the *Easter Oratorio* suits this very sweet-toned voice particularly well. He produces naturally and easily over a wide range and gives unfailing pleasure. His technical skill is clear also from his singing of the tenor solos in Richard Bonynge's elaborately decorated recording of *Messiah*. The runs are exemplary in smoothness and facility, and he contributes an athletic, unforced version of 'Thou shalt break them', taking a final flourish up to the high C, and not skimping (as many do) the high A's on the word 'dash'. His youth (debut, 1966) is suggested not only by the freshness of voice but also by some interpretative limitations. In *La Clemenza di Tito*, after a most sympathetic and able performance of the rest, he wants some extra weight of maturity in the last scene. And in his recording of 1971 coupling songs by Schubert and Schumann he rarely draws attention to specific meaning (but what liquid, gentle singing—something like a tenor version of Tiana Lemnitz, something of a miracle in itself). He remains an exceptionally pleasing and accomplished singer, and one who at the time of writing is still in the early phases of his career.

Among younger English tenors, Krenn compares with Ian Partridge and contrasts with Robert Tear. Partridge, mentioned earlier in the chapter for his fluent singing of Machaut, has a similarly sweet tone and gentle, smooth production. These can be heard in his brief appearance in *The Trojans*, singing Iopas' song with grace and charm befitting this particularly beautiful passage in the opera. More can be heard in his performance of *On Wenlock Edge* and Vaughan Williams' Blake Songs. He brings depth of feeling as well as fine tone; and when he drains his voice for the ghost-friend of 'Is my team ploughing?' and for the end of the second song he does it by eliminating all vibrato without any hint of colouring by flattened pitch. He has much of Pears' sensitivity and yet seems to have avoided the influence of his idiosyncrasies. Tear, on the other hand, could often be mistaken on records for a younger Pears: vowels and consonants, a certain allowance of unsteadiness (showing up in a record called *The Art of Bel Canto*), a way with runs whereby the notes are very distinct but only by a kind of separation (another contrast with Krenn in this)—all these recall Pears. In *The Prodigal Son* the likeness is put to happy effect. Pears sings the Tempter, Tear the Son. The affinity is made explicit in the libretto, where the Tempter says 'I am your inner voice, your very self'; the likeness of the singing voices enforces the Morality. Tear's value in the contemporary scene lies of course entirely in himself. His versatility and feeling for style make him invaluable in the whole range of music, ancient and modern; well heard on records in a recital of music by Handel, Arne and Boyce, spirited and nimble, rhythmically pointed and lively in characterisation.

Like most of the singers discussed in this section, Tear and Partridge have been much occupied by the Purcell and Monteverdi revivals. They are part of a more recent group of musicians taking the place of the first post-war generation, with Heather Harper and April Cantelo leading its sopranos, Helen Watts and Pamela Bowden among the contraltos, Shirley-

Quirk distinguished among the lower voices with former choral scholars like Richard Standen, John Carol Case and Christopher Keyte. All of them have recorded a vast amount. Somewhere or other in the whole output there might be a quaver or two out of place, but one would have to look for it. Cantelo, for example, is always bringing new music into the catalogues: a delightful collection of eighteenth-century Shakespearean songs is a typical record, neat in style, highly accomplished in the runs, shakes and triplets as well as the basic purity of phrase. Harper has one of the loveliest voices of her generation, and a still wider repertoire (some enterprising private recorder must surely have taped her very beautiful Violetta on television, and perhaps somebody has the Elsa which she sang with great success at Bayreuth). Her standing is no doubt high enough to enable her to withdraw from the kind of group-activity in which these singers share, but she still belongs. She sings, for example, in the complete set of Monteverdi madrigals issued in 1971 under Leppard's direction (a strong, expressive Venus to the sonorous Pluto of Stafford Dean in *Il Ballo delle Ingrate*). She has also faced up to the challenge confronting 'the vocalist of the future', singing Berg's *Four Songs* and Webern's *Cantata* no. 1 with most beautiful tone, undeterred by the difficulties.

These singers and various contemporaries must have worked together so often that they express and form a national culture in singing. Where they themselves have acquired a large part of their musical culture, and where others in turn take it up from them, has been in the group-work involved in the increasingly specialised and professional small choirs that have come into existence in recent years. The nucleus of these comes in turn from the larger choirs, and particularly from the colleges of Cambridge and Oxford. It is notable that of the male singers mentioned in the last paragraph, five were choral scholars, four of them from King's, Cambridge (Ian Partridge is from New College, Oxford). Many of these small choirs have been led by university men, again many of them from King's (John Alldis, Grayston Burgess, Louis Halsey, John Whitworth, for example). Their recordings have been among the most valuable in the catalogues, and in their influence, achievements and newness they have an important place in the history of recorded singing.

The 'newness' perhaps should be qualified. There have always been groups, amateur or semi-professional, singing madrigals and part-songs. In pre-war times, the St. George's Singers, directed by E. H. Fellowes, recorded some Weelkes, Gibbons and so forth; and there were a few (but not many) others. But the first-ancestor of the modern groups just now in question was very probably the ensemble formed by Nadia Boulanger in the thirties, and heard in the famous Monteverdi recordings. Playing these alongside three more recent groups in a similar repertoire, one still finds the old enchantment. Even Madame Boulanger's piano (no-one would record nowadays without a harpsichord) is acceptable: perhaps especially so, for it is a source of some of the inspiration these records had—they presented civilised people making music of a rare beauty in a drawing-room, and there was the sense that they were only at the surface of an untold wealth still to be discovered. The growth of the phrases, and the shaping of cadences in 'Hor che'l ciel e la terra', the feeling for the legato/staccato alternations in 'Ecco mormorar l'onde': such details reflect the care and freshness they brought to the work. Marie-Blanche de Polignac sings the *Lamento della Ninfa*, 'Amor', with great charm and at a tempo which allows the music a sway and lilt which it sadly lacks in most other performances. Perhaps scholarship says that the tempo should be slower, the notation being in breves, but generally the charm flies; and when done as by Annalies Monkevitz (with a group under Gunter Kehr) with literal note-values and emphatic style, desperation may make the nymph's lament more urgent, but its elegance and beauty are fled with the charm.

The three English groups, singing on LP, can be compared in their performances of the *Lamento d'Arianna*, a sequence of four madrigals of which the Boulanger singers recorded only the first, 'Lasciatemi morire'. The Golden Age Singers, founded by Margaret Field-Hyde in 1950, sing well but with less character than the Deller Consort (recording issued in 1970) or the singers with Raymond Leppard (1967). Of these, the Deller group remember always that this is Italian music: they give plenty of voice, singing with full resonance, and so making particularly effective the softer passages. What the Leppard singers keep before themselves as the guiding principle is that the work is a lament; they are more tender and have a greater variety of dynamics than either of the other groups. But then, they are in very expert hands—those of another Cambridge musician. Again, music in the university has had an influence well outside it.

This is clear again as one turns to the record catalogues to list others of the smaller groups. The Purcell Consort of Voices (directed by Grayston Burgess), the Ambrosian Consort (Denis Stevens) and the Elizabethan Singers (Louis Halsey) have all set themselves, and everybody else, the highest possible standards. Perhaps there is too much gentility. The Ambrosians singing the Penguin Book of Madrigals are fresh-toned and trim, pretty and sometimes prissy: for instance, the daintiness of Farmer's 'A little, pretty bonny lass' is caught very well, but playing against it (along with the cross-rhythms of 'I swore I would' that get the local madrigal society in a tangle) there surely needs some reminder that the 'I' is a man, something masculine and boldly humorous. Similarly, when the Purcell Consort sing Morley's 'I love alas' the pretty soprano line tells of nineteenth- and twentieth-century drawing-rooms, so refined are they. It seems hard to praise singers for refinement and then criticise them for it. And perhaps there is nothing to be done anyway. Madrigal singing has long been an educated and basically upper-class preserve, and though it is unlikely that the upper-class accent of the present day bears much resemblance to that of the Elizabethans, one cannot expect people to change their normal pronunciation for the silver swans, Suffolk owls, and honey-sucking bees. At least the Purcell Consort coarsen themselves suitably for Weelkes' *Cries of London*, and 'fling the pisspot' in Deering's *Country Cries* with rustic accents and enjoyment all round. The performers' enjoyment is in fact one of the great features of these records, and many are the gems of perfect concerted singing tucked away in these period-anthologies that have been so resourcefully concocted: in the entertainment for Henry VIII, for example, there is the three-part piece by Cornish, 'Ah Robin, gentle Robin', while Queen Victoria's musical evening ends with 'The long day closes', TTBB, beautifully balanced and shaded. In the basic Elizabethan repertoire, they achieve all those felicities of rhythm, subordination and clarity of parts, that amateur societies all over the country strive for. There are other groups with a comparable standard, of course; the Wilbye Consort, which recorded under Peter Pears' direction, is an example. But mention of Wilbye means, to most madrigal singers, 'Draw on, sweet night'; and that, of all madrigals, means the Cambridge Madrigal Society, which used to go floating down the river to its sweet strains, and which began setting the post-war standard with their set of recordings (including that madrigal) on 78s. Again the debt to Cambridge music is inescapable.

At the centre of Cambridge music is the choir of King's College. About twenty years ago, in mid-century, the standards there were incomparably the best in England. They are just as high now, but the rest of the country has learnt from them and is beginning to catch up. Records support this view very fully. In the last years of the 78 there appeared a series of recordings, to which the best choirs in the country at that time contributed. King's were recorded dully, and they did not get most praise from the reviewers. When the records are played on modern equipment they can be heard for what they are—models of their kind, and unmistakeably better than anything else to be heard at that time. Gibbons' 'Hosanna to the Son of David' illustrates the fine balance of vigour and refinement which was such a great quality. The rhythms dance, easing and lightening at the cadences; a new energy comes into play with the words 'And glory in the highest heaven'; and the entries in the final 'Hosanna' section go up like a series of gently luminous fireworks. In the performance issued on LP in 1956 something of this is lost. The tempo is slower (timing is 3·20 as against the 78's 2·50) and the rhythmic vigour has weakened. The final bass lead has weakened too, and this was exciting, like a strong announcement of coda, in the 78. Both of these records were made under Boris Ord, the first during one of the best periods in the choir's history. Since then, under David Willcocks, there has been a very regular provision of recordings, involving an ever widening repertoire: the great choral works of Bach, the Haydn masses, Fauré's *Requiem* (exquisitely sung), Vaughan Williams (the G Minor Mass massively impressive in the great slabs of double-choir antiphony, as well as having a play of energy and serenity that reveals it afresh as a work of great emotional and structural strength), and many more (there is even a record of operatic choruses). Sometimes one wishes for a less etherial treble tone, especially when the absence of 'continental' bite goes with a breathy quality. Comparing performances under the two choirmasters can be interesting. Byrd's 'Haec dies' was recorded under Boris Ord (issued 1958) with brighter trebles than Willcocks has in his recording (1965); the later recording compensates by marking certain melodic figures and rhythmic changes more insistently. They have quite different ways with the triple-time passage ('exultemur et letemur'): stroking it into a gentle dance in the first, breaking into a friskier dance altogether in the second. The brighter trebles of the first outline their dotted-note rhythms on the 'in ea' more clearly and effectively than their successors, but then David Willcocks brings that section to a stronger, more exciting rhythmical climax. The honours are even: the real point is that here is a choir whose tradition is essentially continuous, but which can respond so sensitively to what are in most cases minutiae of direction. At their very best, perhaps, in the 1962 record of Taverner's *Western Wind* Mass, they bring such uninterrupted beauty before us, that one often wonders why one spends so long listening to melodramatic operas and self-pitying Lieder; at such times one feels this is the only music, and for such a feeling the choir deserves its share of credit.

The influence of King's was prepotent in improving the performance of church music throughout the fifties, and during the sixties better standards were evident in most choirs of any position. The standard of performance in earlier times may be misrepresented by records, and yet on the whole they tell a consistent tale. Presumably the choir of St. George's Chapel, Windsor, was reckoned to be better than the average choir in the period around 1930, when it made what for those times was a lot of records. It was under the direction of E. H. Fellowes, whose St. George's Singers recorded madrigals with a sense of style. The chapel choir singing 'Oh Saviour of the World' (Goss) and 'God is a spirit' (Sterndale Bennett), two pot-boilers from the parish church list of anthems, really does not show how they should be done. The basses, who appeared such tremendous fellows when we did not particularly want to be aware of them, shrink to half size when it comes to their solo phrase, yet giving an extra and involuntary push on the low G when they get there. The tenors make the most (meaning too much) of their imitative phrases in the Goss; the altos chaunt owl-like in the phrase above the trebles in Sterndale Bennett. The trebles sound reasonably well, but there it is: this is a choir of individual parts and not a homogeneous body of voices. St. George's Windsor seem to have been the Columbia recording company's answer to HMV's Temple Church, London, which was the choir most successfully recording for them. This was probably the best choir in the country at that time and their records still sound well. The chorus from Brahms' *Requiem*, or the unaccompanied anthem of Walford Davies, 'Lord, it belongs not to my care', show them as a finely trained choir (Thalben-Ball the choirmaster), singing out strongly and capable of subtlety. But they were exceptional, as records made by most other choirs show, right on into the nineteen-fifties. St. Paul's, for example, recording on LP in 1954 and 1955, were still singing with something of the old lay-clerk tone among the men, and with a very indifferent sense of style: Charles Wood's 'Hail, gladdening light' badly balanced and untidy, Howells' 'A spotless rose' sung as a series of chords instead of shaped phrases (but with a good soloist in Maurice Bevan). Cathedral acoustics place obstacles in the way of balance, sensitivity and even intelligence (difficult to sing the psalms to anything like speech-rhythm in buildings where normal speech is largely unintelligible). King's brought intelligence to bear on whatever they touched (the psalms were a test-case, as again there are recordings to show). They also created a new kind of sound which made for unity and freed the choir from that bottom-heavy dullness which marked most others. With youth to help, the bass line was shaded upwards towards tenor, the tenor to alto, the alto to treble: the sound became airborne.

A new set of English Church Music records issued in mid-sixties shows a notable raising of standards. Not that the really distinguished singing is necessarily to be heard in the places where they might be most expected: in Cathedral choirs you have to shop around. An excellent recording of music by Batten and Deering comes from Peterborough Cathedral (1962) under Stanley Vann, who even persuades his trebles to smile their Alleluias in 'Factum est silentium' (unlike Westminster Abbey's boys, who sound worried). On the whole, apart from the two Cambridge colleges, the church choirs which appear to me to have done the best work on records are Westminster Cathedral (George Malcolm), Chichester Cathedral (John Birch) and Magdalen College, Oxford (Bernard Rose): this, it must be said, among a wealth of good material. Chichester contributes the Twentieth Century volume to the Treasury of Church Music, and they are superb in the setting of the Magnificat and Nunc Dimittis which Herbert Howells wrote for King's *(Collegium Regale)*. Leonard Bernstein's composition of the *Chichester Psalms* (1965) is a tribute to the musical standards there, though the recording of it was made by an American choir, the Camerata Singers. Magdalen and New College, among Oxford colleges, have both recorded well, Magdalen singing their Elizabethan polyphony with a stroking style, the notes and phrasing growing and receding most beautifully. They and several other choirs (Ely, for instance) force upon our notice a modern menace: the influence of King's may again be the cause, or perhaps hi-fi recording is responsible. There are times when a Kyrie Eleison or David's lament for 'Absalom, my son' is like a most beautiful twining of patterned strands in mid-air while somebody continually cracks eggshells or takes the whistler on and off a boiling kettle—these are the explosive 'k's and the forward sibilants (gone the days when one of the tests of a strong choirmaster was whether he could make his boys lisp). None of this affects the singing of Westminster Cathedral, which has its own style and character, and is always invigorating. The bright-edged tone of the boys is refreshing in itself after the mild, comfortably rounded treble sound that is the general rule in England: completely appropriate, for instance, in Britten's *Missa Brevis*. Their performance of Victoria's *Responsories for Tenebrae* is also surely one of the great choral records: strongly dramatic, controlled and very distinctive.[1]

The brighter-boys movement is also felt as policy behind the choir of St. John's, Cambridge. Under George Guest, John's have come to share with King's the distinction of being the church choir most in demand for recordings. In some years, some ways, and some works, they are even preferable. For example it may be that King's record of Haydn's *Missa in tempore belli* (the *Paukenmesse*) is preferable to John's in some respects: the soloists are rather better, the soft passages are more etherial, and there is some intense jubilation. John's (with the Academy of St. Martin-in-the-Fields) are certainly better in the electrifying change with the kettle-drum beats from the 'Agnus Dei' to the trumpets of 'Dona nobis pacem': it is intense like the trumpet-call in *Fidelio*. But the choral singing too has extra impact through the greater clarity, particularly of the boys' voices, which call out with tremendous spirit in the 'miserere nobis': their extra brightness can make 'et vitam venturi' spring up in the 'Credo' in a way that the King's performance does not. This more aggressive sound with the voices helps also when they sing European music: their Palestrina, Victoria and Monteverdi have been particularly exciting. They have also had a special interest in nineteenth century music, though the principal recital record (issued in 1964) was not made in one of the choir's best periods (good, though, to hear Walmisley in D minor sung so well). Modern works too, written for the choir and recorded by them, have shown how well-trained youngsters can make sense of music that would have seemed an impossible task for a church choir only a generation ago. Tippett's Evening Service (1962) is an example here: the singing is firm and well-pointed, the trebles undeterred either by the dominant flourishes of the organ's trumpet stop in the Magnificat or by the discords the rest of the choir are very correctly making in the Nunc Dimittis.

What youth can do with music that ranges from the tricky to the impossible is shown in recordings of various school choirs. The choir of Downside School, Purley (director Derek Herdman) gives a neat, confident performance of Britten's *Friday Afternoons*, with the composer there to conduct them. Without the composer in person, the semichorus (a mere sixty voices) of Wandsworth School Boys' Choir sing Britten's 'Hymn to St. Peter' with enthusiasm and fine finish, its exceptional vitality saluted by

[1] The very bright-edged treble on this record must be Michael Ronayne, and he is good enough to earn a place in the story, as indeed does this tribe of transient voices. Ernest Lough (Temple Church soloist in Mendelssohn's 'Hear my prayer', most famous of all church records) is still the Caruso of choirboys. John Bonner was another pioneer, for he lived to record 'Somewhere a voice is calling' as a duet with himself as bass-baritone, both on 78. Simon Woolf is one for whom the angularities of Stravinsky and Prokoviev hold no terrors. And Robert Chilcott, King's soloist in Fauré's *Requiem*, puts many mighty madames from their seat, singing with a flutelike tone, precise in placing, beautiful in quality.

Britten himself who recorded *The Golden Vanity* with them. The conductor here is Russell Burgess, whose full choir numbers two-hundred. Another boys' choir, that of Ealing Grammar School, with the West London Youth Choir (director, John Railton) made a delightful recording of pieces by Phyllis Tate, requiring neatness and imagination, and above all enthusiasm. A girls choir doing well is the Orpington Junior Singers (Sheila Mossman) who are quite up to the considerable demands of Bliss's 'Prayer to the Infant Jesus'. An example of children involved in modern opera is the Finchley Children's Music Group (John Andrewes) who take part in Malcolm Williamson's *Julius Caesar Jones*. Most remarkable of all is probably the success Peter Maxwell Davies achieved in his four years at Cirencester Grammar School. The recording of his 'O magnum misterium' shows the children doing far more than merely coping with difficulties. There are no blurred harmonies; there is no fuzzy diction; the angular melodies and irregular rhythms are apparently completely understood, and with every sign of enjoyment.

Perhaps such records should make slightly less surprising the achievements of the professional choirs. But as one hears the John Alldis Choir singing Schönberg and Messiaen surprise quickens into something more like awe in the presence of the uncanny. Schönberg's 'Friede auf Erden' and Messiaen's 'Cinq Réchants' are fiendish scores, though they sound easy enough here. Not least impressive in the Messiaen are the rhythmical unison phrases, or the placing of the last note of all, separated from the previous note by a wide interval and twenty-five seconds of 'tk' sounds. Their performance of 'A Latter-day Athenian speaks' by John Gardner contains in the final passage a superb example of a long controlled crescendo, and throughout Elisabeth Lutyens' Motet to words by Wittgenstein (they include the dubious proposition 'Logic fills the world') one never ceases to wonder how in such music the individual parts can sound in perfect unity as a single voice. The Louis Halsey Singers have similar qualities (they may indeed be partly the same people—I understand many of the singers are shared by several groups). They make magic out of some part-songs of Delius: gorgeous in richness of sound and precise and subtle when the chromatic progressions might merely promote a sort of slithery lushness. Mixed choirs singing Church music have also done some notable work. The Carmelite Priory of London (John McCarthy) convinces us that they recorded Victoria's 'Lauda Sion Salvatorum' for sheer joy in singing and in syncopation (it is rare, incidentally, for a choir to sound smiling, and one of the many good features of George McPhee's Choir of Paisley Abbey, is that they can give a neat and smiling account of holy jollity, as in Poulenc's 'Hodie Christus natus est'). The Carmelites bring many imaginative touches to bear, as in the 'Jerusalem' passage from Tallis' *Lamentations*. This is dramatically shaded in a way that sounds natural and right; unlike (it must be said) the Renaissance Singers (Michael Howard) who make a *tour de force* of the passage, treating every note *sforzando* to give the effect of a funeral march. The Renaissance Singers can be somewhat mannered in other matters, such as their pronunciation of Latin: it may accord with the best authorities, but the thin 'ee' sounds, in the Byrd four-part Mass for example, are over-insistent. They nevertheless sing Byrd and Palestrina with much character and beauty, managing to make their ladies sound as boyish and innocent of vibrato as possible. This elimination of vibrato is more and more the concern of choirmasters in the larger choirs too. The BBC Chorus (Alan G. Melville) excellent in Vaughan Williams' G Minor Mass, the Chorus of the London Symphony Orchestra (Arthur Oldham) particularly inspired in the Verdi *Requiem* under Bernstein, and the Philharmonia (Wilhelm Pitz), a choir of exceptionally beautiful tone and responsiveness, at their best in the Giulini *Requiem* or in Verdi's *Four Sacred Pieces* under the same conductor, with the Amens of the 'Ave Maria' down to the most subdued yet perfectly defined choral murmur: all of these have excellent soprano lines, free from any jagged and disturbing vibrato. They are probably the best among many who are maintaining and developing a distinctively British tradition.

European and American choirs would need a chapter of their own to treat with any fullness, and it could not be written adequately on the basis of records in normal circulation in England. The American choir best known to collectors outside America is still the Robert Shaw Chorale, and that principally during the period of its association with Toscanini. The voices are firm and strong, and their energy plays its important part in making the 1953 recording of Beethoven's *Missa Solemnis* such an overwhelming one. It is hard to dissociate the choir from the conducting, but only a very remarkable body of singers could carry out the maestro's intentions so well as when (for example) 'sepultus est' dies to a murmur to leap up suddenly in 'Et resurrexit', and then to achieve such clarity and speed in 'et in vitam venturi', giving then a melting lyrical warmth to the first Amens at the end of the movement. Vitality is one of the great features of American choral singing. It is there in the Gregg Smith Singers, who with the Texas Boys' Choir, E. Power Biggs on the organ, and some splendid brass players, went all the way to Venice to record Gabrieli *in situ*: they have plenty of the expected colour, and, more remarkably, they secure sprightliness as well as splendour in these massive two and three-choir works which might so easily become ponderous. A precise, cool energy is also present in the recording of *Carmina Burana* in which the New England Conservatory Chorus sing.

The European choir which has most emphatically matched this new-world vitality is the Berlin Motet Choir. Its recordings of unaccompanied Bach have tremendous life as well as great accomplishment: unforgettable, for instance, in the fifth section ('Trotz dem alten Drachen') of 'Jesu, meine Freude' (the King's performance seems sleepy by comparison). Another Berlin choir, that of St. Hedwig's Cathedral, again provide an antidote to the more retiring kind of choral singing, their full-bodied performance of Palestrina's *Missa Papae Marcelli* lacking repose but maintaining massive intensity. The Stuttgart Choral Ensemble under Marcel Couraud also achieve virtuoso-standard in the fast-driven 'Fecit potentiam' of Bach's *Magnificat*. Everything else is so well disciplined there that one wonders the sopranos have not been drilled into greater steadiness. In Austria the Vienna Academy Choir has recorded stylishly in a wide repertoire, and the famous boys' choir maintains its standards in a more specialised one. East of Vienna it seems one would be lucky to find a steady soprano line anywhere: in the Budapest Choir perhaps, certainly as it was when Kodaly conducted them in his *Missa Brevis* for the recording issued in 1959. No wobbly sopranos in the Red Army Choir, but deep basses and high tenors all singing with lusty tone and an impressive combination of discipline and high spirits. Probably nothing matches this in western Europe. Franco's army does not seem to have organised a counterblast, but the Chorus of Spanish Radio has given a good demonstration of Spanish musicianship in a recording of 1964 under Markevitch singing music from Victoria to modern times. An example of French choral work is the recording of Josquin's 'Miserere' and other works by the singers of Saint-Eustache: not a homogeneous sound, but creative and passionate. The soloists of the Radio Choir have recorded Messiaen's 'Cinq Réchants': I have not been able to hear this, but if it is anything like their performance at the Queen Elizabeth Hall it will show a superb standard of achievement. The Netherlands and Switzerland have also contributed. The Hilversum NCRV Vocal Ensemble (1969) have mastered the sombre harmonies of Gesualdo, with their unnerving modulations and sudden disturbances of mood. And the Schola Cantorum Basiliensis sings a finely edged, accomplished performance of Machaut's *Messe de Nostre Dame*; different in several ways from that of the Purcell Choir which, while more austere in sound, is livelier in rhythm and rather more fluent in style.

Notably absent from this necessarily brief survey is any Italian choir. There may be some fine records, but they have not come my way. What one is gratefully aware of is the improvement that is generally apparent in Italian opera recordings when the RCA Italiana Opera Chorus is used rather than a chorus from one of the opera houses. The RCA Chorus sounds hand-picked, but before this many important recordings were weakened because a chorus that may be impressive in the theatre has its rough edges shown up on recording. This is not just an Italian trouble: the RIAS Kammerchor, for example, providing the chorus for Kempe's recording of *The Bartered Bride*, is lively and forthright, but the sopranos are often unsteady and sometimes shrill. Where special choirs have been called in, such as the Ambrosian Singers (excellent for example in Barbirolli's *Otello*), they raise a sigh of relief all round. Well-justified national pride makes me add that where the Covent Garden Chorus is available, as in *The Trojans* or Solti's *Don Carlo*, no substitutes are required.

Sheer convenience rather than national pride has been the reason for concentrating attention principally upon British singing in this chapter. The developments it notes are no doubt common to many countries, and could be followed in similar detail. But as Britain has been the centre of interest, we may as well end with a look at the most 'British' work of all, Handel's *Messiah*. A recording which sums up many of the features and includes several of the artists discussed in the previous pages is the performance of *Messiah* conducted by Colin Davis. Its soloists are a quartet very much at the centre of musical events in this generation: Heather Harper, Helen Watts, John Wakefield and John Shirley-Quirk. Each of them sings finely throughout, and each has some particular distinction: Harper simple and forthright, decorating well and without ostentation, in 'I know that my Redeemer liveth', Watts with unflawed legato in 'He shall feed his flock' and with power and virtuosity in 'For he is like a refiner's fire', Shirley-Quirk articulating the triplets of 'Why do the nations?' with perfect clarity, evenness and rapidity, and singing the runs throughout his solos on an apparently limitless supply of breath. John Wakefield, the tenor, calls for a separate mention. Possibly the best of lyric tenors since Heddle Nash, he shows his value to the opera company in excerpts from *La Traviata*, while he too has been part of the modern extension, singing the leading role in Cavalli's *L'Ormindo*. In this *Messiah* he combines much of the best in both the Widdop and Brown records contrasted some pages back, and shares the limitations of neither. The real heroes of a good performance of *Messiah*, however, are the chorus, and in this recording the LSO Chorus (now under John Alldis) surpass themselves. Some of the fast choruses, 'And he shall purify' and 'His yoke is easy', are miracles of lightness and clarity: the runs in the first are rapid and absolutely distinct in each voice-part, and in the second the singers have a rhythmic vitality one might associate with coloured races who have dancing in their blood, and which here sounds as the celebration of Christian souls dancing in the service of perfect freedom—and then with a marvellous surging depth to the newly powerful solidity of the last page. This is, as a note in the accompanying leaflet says, 'scraping off the barnacles'. The choir consists of forty voices in this recording, a far cry from the 4,000 voices (216 choirs) which used to be advertised in the pre-war Columbia catalogue singing the Halleluia Chorus at the Crystal Palace. Numbers are down, but quality is up; and the numbers are still there in much enthusiastic and successful singing all over the country, as the modern record catalogues show.

Music-making has increased and improved markedly during these years, and the singer as discussed in this chapter is a music-maker who has taken a full part in the development of his time. Few of them when confronted by the formidable 'extensions' we have been talking about, whether ancient or modern, would be likely to say that this particular yoke is easy. But on the whole, they learn their scores, keep their technique in trim, and move busily and efficiently from concert to broadcast to recording studio; and perhaps for the singer who is a true musician the burden is light after all.

30. 1971: Present and Prospective
Montserrat Caballé   Gundula Janowitz
Placido Domingo   Sherrill Milnes
Nicolai Ghiaurov

IT would be unfortunate if the last chapter suggested that there is anything new about the concept of 'singer-as-musician'. Singers have certainly been extended by the requirements of the present time, but essentially the role is traditional and the concept based on a truism. When we speak of 'the *grand* tradition', however, there is no doubt that we do have something else in mind. For better or worse, music has always had its 'celebrities', and the opera house has always had its stars. But that can be said in at least three different tones of voice. One of them is factual and neutral; another is mordent or just regretful (implying 'the more's the pity'); the other puts a sad emphasis upon the tense of the verb. 'The stars *were* brightly shining', it says, 'but lo, it is 1971, and the heavens are bare'. The present chapter looks at singers on record in the first eleven months of 1971, judging the present by the standards of the past, and casting an enquiring eye into the future. As a starting point, we might challenge the sad tones of the man who sees an unlit sky, coupling a toast to the eternal stars with the name of Montserrat Caballé.

Records tell of four supremely great operatic sopranos who with voices for the lyric-dramatic repertoire had also outstanding facility in florid music and could rise to tragic nobility. Lilli Lehmann, Ponselle, Callas and Caballé, for all their differences, have in common grandeur and brilliance. Such qualities in combination rise high and shine bright; and in 1971 Caballé's star has clearly been in the ascendant. Happily too for those who prize sheer beauty of voice and production, it is Ponselle whom Caballé most often calls to mind among singers of the past: the rich texture, cream or velvet according to taste, and the smooth ease of movement are of the kind that make us still revert to Ponselle as a classic for love and study. Like most of the singers we shall be discussing in this chapter, Caballé is reconstituting the singer's order of priorities. Without putting the processes of the last half-century into reverse, she has in her singing reasserted what many forces have been conjoining to suppress: that the singer is an artist who makes beautiful sounds, and that the essentials of the whole art are fine tone, true legato and ease of movement. I think that the group of singers to be discussed here is the first to practise consistently according to such principles since the group very near the beginning of our survey—the group which included Melba, Battistini and Plançon. The qualities and achievements of the two groups differ in many respects; but in as far as a tendency towards these priorities is in evidence, it surely bodes well for the future of singing.

Evidence is plentiful in the recordings, and most especially in those of Caballé herself. The beauty of her voice is clear as a virtually unflawed presence in everything she has done up to now. If one wants an example of sheer loveliness of sound there is the 'Requiem Aeternam' of Verdi's *Requiem*. The soloist sings quietly above the chorus in long, linked phrases. From a single forte to a quadruple piano, the voice is to float without orchestral accompaniment, to comfort the senses, and to leave the listener with some presentiment of the joys of paradise in a final sustained high B flat, sung as softly as possible. It is beautifully written for the voice yet its success is precarious and rarely complete. Here Caballé is (and how often has it been possible to say this in these pages?) perfect. The supported soft tone, rounded and warm, carries through the broadly phrased lines, swelling on a long sustained note to be joined pianissimo to the phrase 'et lux perpetua', allowing the voice to bloom, and finally to crown the whole passage with the B flat taken from an octave below without lifting or break

134. Montserrat Caballé

of filament, held firmly, very softly, and very beautifully. There is, of course, more than beauty of voice in all this, but again if one wishes for more evidence of her fine legato in the classic, older Italian repertoire, there is much to choose from. The opening of 'Casta diva' would be an unfortunate example, for she uses a light aspirate, inflects the line rather too much for one to be able to speak of classic purity, and she is not a model of grace and elegance on the group of notes making up a turn at the beginning of each verse. Almost anything else will show her as a very complete mistress of *bel canto*: her solo in the duet 'Mira, o Norma', for example, poised, even, and finely phrased. And if one then asks for a show-piece in which the gentle glow of this mellow voice will shine with point and brilliance, there is an embarrassment of riches: the aria from Act IV of Verdi's *I Lombardi* is one of many records that show her as graceful and delicate, yet willing to give herself with spirit and energy to this highly demanding music.

Another aria from early Verdi suggests one technical limitation. I have not seen a score of *Un Giorno di Regno*, and do not know whether there are trills marked in the aria 'Grave a core innamorato'; but one feels the need of them, and they are not forthcoming. In places where they certainly are marked, as in the Jewel Song from *Faust*, they are generally unimpressive (the last one in the Jewel Song is all right, but on the long introductory note it is little more than a flutter at a single pitch). It is strange that so brilliant a technician should apparently not have acquired this accomplishment. One of her finest solos is the scene and aria from the Prologue to Donizetti's *Lucrezia Borgia*, recorded years ago on an early electrical 78 by Giannina Arangi-Lombardi. In most ways, Caballé is preferable (Arangi-Lombardi sings well, her voice in fine flower, but provides less to store in the memory); but the earlier singer can round off her performance with a precisely voiced trill, and it makes more difference than one might think.

In other respects there are no more impressive combinations of beauty and brilliance on records than those to be found in Caballé's collections of Italian rarities. In Rossini's *La Donna del Lago* there are runs over two octaves, and some deliciously soft chromatic scales; in an aria from *Armida* there is a marvellously rapid triplet sequence, an amazing virtuoso-piece, this one. Above all, there is the ability to float a phrase on high with most exquisite gentleness and beauty: these are the sounds that one takes away with one most unforgettably from Caballé's singing, both in live performance and on record. That long, long note held above the whole ensemble towards the end of the Prologue in *Lucrezia Borgia* is a prime example. Often the most heavenly phrase of a whole opera will be the last one of a recitative leading into the aria: 'Deh! tu, innocente, tu per me l'implora' sings the heroine of Bellini's *Il Pirata* at just such a point in the score, and though the notes look uninteresting enough on paper, Caballé's singing holds the phrase in suspension, while the moment takes its lodging in the memory, and its emotion touches the heart.

For the heart is always involved in Caballé's singing. Elisabeth de Valois is one of the most moving of Verdi's heroines, and Caballé, in the recording of *Don Carlo* under Giulini, presents a mature woman of refinement and deep feeling. She comforts her banished waiting-woman with a compassion that is expressed in the shading of phrases and the gently soothing use of portamento. She achieves intensity in that touching passage where Elisabeth remains on stage alone ('Ah! Iddio su noi vegli') for a few moments of supplication in Act II. And her cries of 'Giustizia' have dignity as well as urgency and distress.

On the other hand, records do not range her among the chameleons. All these heroines of Donizetti and early Verdi sound more or less indistinguishable as characters (perhaps they are) and not dissimilar from the Puccini heroines; in a recital of French arias, her Micaëla, Thaïs and Marguérite are much the same people too. The playful, girlish excitement which might accompany Marguérite's discovery of the jewel casket is not communicated, nor, on the whole, in her recording of Strauss' opera, is the kittenish, or even the lustful and horrible side of Salome. She is by no means inexpressive: the recklessness and forward drive of 'Dein Haar ist grässlich', and the hard menace of 'Ich fordre den Kopf des Jokanaan' are vivid and convincing. Yet it hardly amounts to a character-creation: to the daughter of Sodom and the girl who says she would shriek aloud if anyone came to kill her. Another way of looking at it, however, is to begin with the fact that her Salome is like nobody else's, and that this by itself is characterisation enough. The individuality of this Salome is established essentially by voice: the magic (as exercised over Narraboth for instance) is made real by the magic of this highly individual voice, and that in itself is a major contribution towards any lifetime's accumulated experience of the opera.

Her recording of Salome brings us to a final point about her. The very fact that she has this role in her repertoire reminds us how widely ranging an artist she is. Not only the operas of Richard Strauss but also his songs are in her province, not completely happy in a recorded recital and yet marvellous in certain of them, such as 'Befreit' and 'Die Nacht'. She sings Brahms' *Requiem* as beautifully as Verdi's: sometimes so softly that it seems the filament must break, yet in fact there is never a flaw. It is a far cry from this to the Spanish zarzuela, but here again, whether in solos or duets with her husband, the tenor Bernabé Marti, she sings with boldness and a feeling for the idiom. Zarzuela music generally seems to me to be curiously frustrating: it is always leading up to a marvellous tune that never comes. Sometimes, as in the song from Chapí's *El Barquillero*, the music eventually commits itself, and Caballé is fully responsive to its several changes of manner. She herself is always committed: she knows, for instance, how to make her voice smile, and in such music as Montsalvatge's *Songs for Children* she reminds us (by charm and voice alike) that she is a country-woman of Victoria de los Angeles. It is Italian opera that allows us to hear

Caballé at her most impressive, yet hers is a kind of voice and art that Italy seems not to produce; and no doubt the suppleness of Spanish song and the subtlety of German have been influences contributing to the distinction of her essays in the traditional Italian *bel canto*.

The new master of this tradition among tenors is another Spaniard, Placido Domingo. His voice too, despite its Mediterranean warmth, is in some way un-Italian: when the ghost of another voice comes into one's mind while listening to his records, it is perhaps that of Renato Zanelli, or Cortis or Fleta, and just very occasionally two unlikely Richards, Tucker and Tauber. There is a slightly baritonal suggestion, contrasting with such a very Italian voice as Pavarotti's. The high notes are in fine form (a long solid top C held over the chorus at the end of Act III in *Il Trovatore*), and his tone will ring out strong and resonant, coming clearly through a great mass of sound (as in the Kyrie of Verdi's *Requiem*). Yet the distinction of his singing lies in less primitive attributes than these, some of them connecting him with singers of a rather earlier generation than those mentioned above.

It is unusual, for instance, to find that the tenor who belts out a lusty top C (unwritten) in *Il Trovatore* is just as good at coping with the written demands of 'Il mio tesoro' from *Don Giovanni*. Domingo sings the longest of the runs in this famous test-piece with plenty of voice, in a single breath, even managing exactly the right amount of *rallentando* towards the end, and making each of the notes clear without the use of any aspirating or *sforzando* techniques. Perhaps there should be more contrast between styles (the lyrical and the martial), but the voice is beautiful and the technique excellent. It is also unusual for the protagonist of *Il Trovatore* to have a trill, in spite of the fact that his main aria asks for one, twice. Domingo trills extremely well in the complete recording of the opera, as he does in Don Carlo's aria at the opening of the Fontainebleau scene. He also phrases with remarkable breadth, both in this aria and in the last Act of *Trovatore*, where all the sentences ('Riposa, o madre . . .') are taken on a single breath, instead of the customary two or three, so that the music flows and the singer's sustaining power conveys the character's power to sustain, which just at that time is what is in question.

These particular passages, chosen to illustrate the quality of Domingo's technique, have each of them provided a kind of *locus classicus* as recorded in the early years of the gramophone. Thus it used to be said of 'Il mio tesoro', and especially its long run, 'Ah, only McCormack can sing that'. For the trill in 'Ah sì, ben mio' you went to Dalmorès or Jadlowker; for the long phrasing in the *Trovatore* duet, to Martinelli. It is another sign of grace in modern singing that the latest in the line of 'central' operatic tenors should be one who has such a technique and who bothers about such refinements of style.

Mention of Martinelli brings us to another matter, and something more difficult to pinpoint. Domingo's performance in *Il Trovatore* is exceptionally scrupulous, but it is not (in my own experience) of the kind that sometime later is there, irreplaceably, in one's head. There is character, certainly: it is an affectionate Manrico that we have here, and that is rare enough as a point of character-emphasis. But ultimately one wants an intensity, which, for example, can transform the unremarkable-looking phrase starting 'Il presagio funesto' (Act III). Domingo's tone is so much more rounded and 'pleasant' than Martinelli's that it is harder for him to convey the tension of foreboding, or of anger, bitterness, suffering, as Martinelli could do. Yet it is something like this that one feels, ungratefully and almost unreasonably, while listening to the *Trovatore* and (still more) to a recital of duets, so very nearly classic, with Sherrill Milnes. All the old favourites are there *(Bohème, Forza, Pêcheurs de Perles, Gioconda . . .)*; all ringing with associations from the past (Caruso and Scotti, Gigli and Ruffo, Martinelli and de Luca, McCormack and Sammarco). A point-by-point comparison would do credit to the Domingo–Milnes combination time and time again: we would find their legato more reliable than most of the Italians, they are tasteful and disciplined, they phrase broadly, they sing with expression, they have fine voices. But they do not generate much excitement; there is little tension. 'Ah, that the slave had forty thousand lives' cries Otello: but there has to be bitterness as well as determination. 'Infamia', cries Enzo Grimaldo, and when Martinelli sang a word like that you knew that he meant it; but the scalp does not tingle in response to the equally sturdy tones of Domingo. Milnes insults and insinuates with suitably villainous inflections, but there is still something at once too relaxed and too well-behaved. One almost wishes they would shout.

But the criticism is probably perverse. Domingo's recorded output contains plenty of excitements, and there is the regular satisfaction of refined musicianship in association with virile tone. There are surprises too: Lohengrin's Narration, warm-toned, Tauber-soft and lingering, strong and vigorous in the conclusion; Lenski's aria especially imaginative in the ending, and sung in Russian; an aria from Handel's *Giulio Cesare*, smooth in the air, bold in the cadenza. All of these were in his first recital record to be released. But his great qualities are normally those shown in the central Italian repertoire: the knowledge of how to work a personal kind of magic with a soft phrase leading back into the opening melody of the aria (a fine example in 'Angelo casto' from Donizetti's *Duca d' Alba*), or the holding of reserves, that can be drawn on for a final, doubly effective climax. An example here is the last section of the aria 'Ma se m'è forza perderti' from *Un Ballo in Maschera*; but this is perhaps his finest record of all, show-ing, as it does, that there *is* an intensity of feeling in this singer (the suffering face is vivid), and that it never leads him away from the scrupulous observ-ance of the first principle—that 'the singer is an artist who makes beautiful sounds'.

Sherrill Milnes, Domingo's associate in several recordings, is certainly such an artist, for a more generously rounded and full-bodied baritone

135. Placido Domingo as Manrico in *Il Trovatore*

136. Sherrill Milnes

voice has not been heard in the Verdi operas for many a year. Not only Verdi and Italian opera, but a fair variety of other music has already brought him before record collectors, and the companies have been quick to realise his value. Excursions outside opera include the taxing baritone part in *Carmina Burana* (singing with Evelyn Mandac, beautifully clear-voiced in the soprano solos). He has the ring for the high *tessitura* of 'Estuans interius' and the resonance for 'Ego sum abbas', though not perhaps the big-bellied, bacchic brag. Nor, in the very different world of Brahms' *Vier ernste Gesänge* does he show the kind of spiritual depth which might send the mediaeval reprobate back to his prayers. Leinsdorf plays the piano accompaniments in a performance that jollies Ecclesiastes along and fairly lets rip with St. Paul on charity. It might be thought a refreshing corrective to the private, sober and subdued meditations normally presented, all performed here on a grand scale, with 'Glaube, Hoffnung, Liebe' fit to set the chandeliers rattling in any opera house in the world. Perhaps, after all, the right kind of music for that setting is opera itself, and, up to the present, it is in the operatic repertoire that Milnes is genuinely distinguished.

From St. Paul to John the Baptist may not seem a very far cry, but between the idioms of the Brahms songs and the Strauss opera there is a great gulf fixed, and Milnes is much more aptly heard in the latter. Indeed it is very gratefully that the voice of him that crieth in the cistern is recognised actually to be a steady one and not that of a German incapable of disguise. Youthful and potent, this prophet: Salome's interest in him becomes more credible than usual. He himself is credible as a lover (baritones are not always) in a style far removed from Strauss's biblical drama, the Guglielmo of Leinsdorf's *Così fan tutte*. He has many good, perhaps unexpectedly light touches, including the flexible management of a neat cadenza inserted in 'Non siate ritrosi'. He can also use his big voice with that kind of gracefulness which is needed in French opera: the famous piece from *Pêcheurs de Perles* is one of the best of his duets with Domingo, and one of its best moments is the elegant way in which Milnes leads from his solo passage into the Grand Tune for both voices.

But it is essentially in Verdi that he has made his mark. In a notable line of American baritones (Tibbett, Thomas, Warren, Merrill, MacNeil) he has the range and the resonance; to a remarkable extent, too, these have been singers with a genuine care for legato, and Milnes is no exception in this respect either. The second Act of *Il Trovatore* shows him to good advantage, smooth and unforced in 'Il balen', accurate on the groups, taking the high F ('infonde') *dolcissimo* as marked, phrasing broadly, and then going into the second solo, 'Per me ora fatale', with well-nourished tone and no loss of definition in this full-bodied, passionate music. If any misgivings need be voiced about definition, it is in the quieter singing. His is not a sharp-edged voice; and whereas, when de Luca sang softly (also with a rounded rather than an edged voice) one is aware of a very clear, firm centre to the note, with Milnes there is the very slight suggestion of a yawning sound (as with some of the soft singing of Hans Hotter). The suggestion is there in Roderigo's Death Scene in *Don Carlo*, in the recitative 'Convien qui dirci' and the aria 'Per me giunto'. This scene also shows him as a singing-actor achieving vividness up to a certain degree. Fischer-Dieskau helps one to understand this scene (in detail), Gobbi to feel it, and both of them provide experience of a greater intensity than Milnes. Examples: Fischer-Dieskau sings the aria in a very personal, affectionate and intimate style, then changes to a more sonorous and business-like tone to give the instructions which follow, and then, when he is shot, we know it, because of another change in the voice, a change which gives additional force to the pianissimo marking at 'così serbar' (and not many of them observe that at all). Gobbi is harder to analyse, but he presents a man who has made a sacrifice of religious intensity, the sacrificial altar being that of friendship. Milnes acts well and puts a good deal of feeling into the last pages, but he does not make a comparable impact. One admires the voice, however, the ability to sing softly as Verdi marks, and the due inclusion of the trill (not there in Gobbi). At his best, Milnes is, in fact, a mightily impressive singer. That best is heard in the Library Scene from *Un Ballo in Maschera*: in the recitative (vengefully determined in the cries of 'Vendicator'), the aria (smooth and accurate, and superb on the high G), in the conspiracy music and in joy that the election falls upon him. It is good to know, too, from his appearances in this opera at Covent Garden, that his voice sounds in the theatre exactly as on records; while his impressive stage presence adds to the vividness of characterisation.

Caballé, Domingo, Milnes: these are three singers on whom the record-ing of Italian opera is most dependent at the time of writing. With the other obvious names (limiting the list to singers who have had records issued here in 1971—Price, Sutherland, Sills, Verrett, Horne, Bumbry, Bergonzi, Pavarotti, Ghiaurov) they make a company whose approach to singing must be reassuring because it reasserts the values which certainly seemed to be in danger: beauty of sound, steady tone, well-bound phrases, fluent passage-work.

In the normal course of nature, there would have been one other name to add to this list of singers whose art adds grace to the present age. Fritz Wunderlich died in 1966 at the age of thirty-five; in the year of writing he would have been in his full prime, and no doubt the record-year which we are just about to survey would have been an important one for him and he for it. However, he recorded widely and with much distinction.

Using Mozart as a first touchstone, we hear a singer with poise and elegance. He phrases 'Dalla sua pace' *(Don Giovanni)* with breadth and imagination, preserves a good legato and returns to the melody with a pleasantly softened tone that is still well-defined. There is nothing precious about his Mozart: 'Dies Bildnis ist bezaubernd schön' *(Die Zauberflöte)* is sung out as a love-song in which the ardour grows to the broad climax of those last phrases which often (but not here) are found so taxing. As Belmonte in *Die Entführung aus dem Serail* we can compare him with Simon-eau, probably the best Mozart tenor of post-war times, and it is true that there is in Simoneau (singing in Beecham's recording) an added grace; but Wunderlich also include two extremely difficult arias ('Ich baue ganz' is the first) that are omitted in the Beecham–Simoneau recording, and the runs, which are fearsome enough to make 'Il mio tesoro' look plain-sailing, are superbly done.

He was a singer of strong personality, not least in the gaiety he could bring to his singing. His sense of fun and vividness of character-portrayal are clear in the recording of *The Bartered Bride*, especially in his duet with Kecal (Gottlob Frick), repeating the various enticements with suitably bucolic relish. He was also one of those singers, rare in our day, who could bridge the cultures: he could sing to a popular audience and (one can tell it in the records) establish real communication. There was no cheapening involved in the process, and, although he took over much of the earlier tenor's repertoire, he is completely out from under the shadow of Richard Tauber. He has his own kind of intimacy, his own use of the head-voice, his own feeling for shaping a song. Even where the music is of no great merit (as in a Mario Lanza type of song called 'Be my love', sung in English) the singer's own enjoyment is infectious, and the outcome is attractive. He was also without apparent inhibitions in this lighter kind of music: he sings the shameless 'gypsy' tune of *Countess Maritza* with the confident presentation of a man thoroughly and happily at the heart of show-business: and without any vulgarities or showiness on high notes.

Yet his finest contributions to music-making were in fields remote from these. In Haydn's *Creation*, for instance, he sings not only with wonderfully wholesome resonance and evenness, but also with a sense of drama, fully responsive to that of his conductor, Karajan. As Leukippos, in Strauss' *Daphne*, we can hear him in a live performance from the Theater an der Wien in 1964, and it is a rare occasion indeed for here is a tenor to whom it is actually a pleasure to listen in Strauss' music (so much of his writing seems to bring out the worst in the voice). Best of all is his part in *Das Lied von der Erde* in the great recording under Klemperer. His finely differentiated tones on the three repetitions of the words 'Dunkel ist das Leben, ist der Tod', the softness of his voice as he listens to the 'Vogel im Baum', the great beauty of tone at all points in the difficult score: like Kathleen Ferrier's recording of the contralto part a generation or so earlier, his singing here makes a fine and no doubt enduring monument.

For the rest of this chapter, however, let us take a look at one year's records, or, more accurately, eleven months (up to November 1971), collecting a few singers still to be discussed, and noting the general tendencies represented. I am following now the monthly review-list in *The Gramophone*, and mentioning (with occasional references to reviews) only what appear to be the records most important as examples of present-day solo singing.

The year began predictably enough with a major offering from Fischer-Dieskau: the complete Beethoven songs, issued first in 1967 and now given new currency as part of the Beethoven Centenary collection. Fischer-Dieskau also sang, with Rita Streich, in music by Cornelius and Rheinberger, while another soprano-baritone association was that of Elly Ameling and Hermann Prey in Bach cantatas. Leontyne Price's recital, exceptionally varied in programme, was critically reviewed by Andrew Porter, who, rather to his surprise, found himself enjoying the duets by Caballé and Verrett. Stephen Plaistow doubted whether Dessau's *Puntila* would win many friends in spite of a 'lively cast'; but excerpts from *Carmen*, an opera never short of friends, brought Marilyn Horne 'to your fireside with a vengeance' (Alan Blyth) in the glory of Phase Four.

For February's Fischer-Dieskery we had 'Haydn and Mozart Rarities' and the Speaker in *Zauberflöte*, given 'a refreshing new look' (Edward Greenfield). Beverly Sills in *Lucia di Lammermoor* and Caballé in Puccini arias showed the prima donna still enthroned. Ian Partridge's Vaughan Williams record and Nigel Rogers in Morley's *First Book of Ayres* were also warmly welcomed. The *Zauberflöte* (under Solti, with Lorengar, Prey and Talvela also in the cast) brought another British tenor a good deal of praise, this being Stuart Burrows, the Tamino. Burrows was also to be heard later in the year singing with warm tone and a lively sense of rhythm in *Midsummer Marriage*, and then in a solo recital, which received reserved praise from John Warrack. As the reviewer said, he gives probably his best performance in Fauré's 'Prison', while elsewhere, especially in the

Schubert group, there is something wrong with the expression. In this record, he sings softly but without edge, and, regularly, it seems to the present writer, without charm. The long phrasing and the varied dynamics are welcome, but there is no smile or sense of audience-contact in 'Le violette', or 'Heidenröslein', or 'Sylvie'. His Tamino in *Die Zauberflöte* has much more character, though in 'Dies Bildnis ist bezaubernd schön' he tends to give emphasis at the expense of instrumental purity. An enthusiastic summary is contained in Edward Greenfield's review: 'Generally this is a thrilling performance, from a voice of heroic size, but with beautiful quality, and with an intelligence and musicianship rare among today's tenors'.

One other singer in this new *Zauberflöte* must detain us here: this is Christina Deutokom, the Queen of Night. She also was to bring out solo recitals later in the year, and again admiration has to be tempered with some misgivings. Her voice is bright and clear, and her range extensive. Her flexibility is exceptional, but so is at least one of her ways of achieving it. She separates the notes of a scale-passage by what Edward Greenfield hears as an 'intrusive w', and which sometimes seems to run through half the letters of the alphabet as well (in the *Armida* aria I have it noted as an l and sometimes as a d! but no doubt it is really subtler than that). Such bright voices are always hard to modulate, to soften or to colour. To some extent she does so in turning, on her Mozart recital record, from the Queen of Night to Constanze of *Die Entführung* and then to a more authoritative and noble tone for Donna Anna's 'Or sai chi l'onore'. But she sings 'Ah! fors' è lui' *(La Traviata)* in as prosaic a manner as one would think possible: the exact opposite of Magda Olivero, whose ever-responsive, deeply tragic interpretation, recorded in 1940, has also come to more peoples' attention this year through a private LP. Deutokom is still a remarkable singer, doing marvellous and lovely things, not least as the Queen of Night. The bright, deadly accurate staccatos glitter and peck: a predatory night-bird with a curiously sinister suggestion of clockwork. In some respects, it is the Queen of Night one has always wanted to hear.

As though to leave time for digestion after one rich month and to create appetite for another, March brought no operatic fare (beyond *Jesus Christ—Superstar*). The third volume of the Elisabeth Schwarzkopf song-book made up for this, and Heather Harper and Robert Tear were praised by John Warrack for their performance of Britten's *Les Illuminations* and *Serenade for Tenor, Horn and Strings*. Ameling, Watts and Krenn were praised by Trevor Harvey for their work in the *Mass in B Minor*; and 'altogether superb singing and artistry' is the phrase for Tom Krause.

No Fischer-Dieskau in March, and only a minor part ('conjuring wonders', says William Mann) in April. That was as the Music Master in *Ariadne auf Naxos*, conducted by Böhm and boasting a highly accomplished Zerbinetta in Reri Grist. The Ariadne and Bacchus (Hildegard Hillebrecht and Jess Thomas) seem to me well-matched and no joy at all, but the Dancing Master, Gerhard Unger, and the Composer, Tatiana Troyanos, help to produce a distinguished Prologue. Troyanos is of course a distinguished singer: a mezzo with the richness of a contralto and the upward range of a dramatic soprano. Indeed, a soprano role that she sings on records, the Cleopatra of Handel's *Giulio Cesare*, is sung on another recording not by a dramatic soprano but by Beverly Sills (and there is no transposition). Not everything in Troyanos' performance is ideal: the *tessitura* of Cleopatra's arias does give some trouble, for although she sings the high notes fearlessly the volume or the quality of tone is sometimes out of proportion with the rest, and a slight flutter-vibrato sometimes intrudes. An extremely beautiful piece of singing is the recitative 'Che sento!' and the aria 'Se pietà di me non senti' in Act II. Here she drains the voice of vibrato and achieves a fine sound of lamentation, with breadth of phrasing and depth of feeling. She is better in this mood than in the light playfulness of Dorabella in *Così fan tutte*: turning from her performance of the song in Act II ('E amore un ladroncello') to Christa Ludwig's, one values the lighter Viennese touch, the intimacy and the delicacy of contrasts. Similarly with the Composer in *Ariadne*. Going back to the old Karajan recording, one finds greater tenderness as well as more inspiration in Seefried's Composer. But Troyanos still impresses. The solemn mystery of the Death-god, the holiness of the art of music, they are passionately apprehended by this Composer. And the voice soars aloft, strong-winged and regal.

So does that of Helga Dernesch in the *Fidelio*, conducted by Karajan and reviewed that month, with Vickers, Kelémén and Ridderbusch also in the cast. Tebaldi, Pavarotti, Milnes, Resnik and Donath were a curiously assorted company to make a homogeneous *Un Ballo in Maschera*; and the nearest Andrew Porter could come to enthusiasm was to promise that 'it is not without its rewards'. More could be said for Pavarotti's solo recital and for Ameling in Handel, though hardly for the effect of boy-trebles and counter-tenors in the solo parts of the *St. Matthew Passion* usually sung by women, or for Werner Hollweg's recital of tenor arias by Mozart. The rewards of this, and of another, of concert arias, are an opportunity to note how modern singers can accomplish what used to be thought of as miracles of breath control. Hollweg not only sings the longest of the runs in 'Il mio tesoro' in one breath but carries on to include the first phrase of the melody following. Then, to give us something else to write home about, he turns a whole sequence into another long run, also on the word 'tornar'. Most of the arias contain something remarkable in this way, but charm, elegance, variety, poetry, softness, depth, are at any rate elusive. The aria 'Konstanze' from *Die Entführung* is an honourable exception: much more expressive, and much the most enjoyable, despite the technical accomplishments of much else.

But the recital of the month (if not of several years) was made by Margaret Price. Presenting a programme of great difficulty and proportionate interest, it exceeded any reasonable expectation of success. Her recordings also included a brief appearance, as Barbarina, in Klemperer's *Nozze di Figaro*, long enough, nevertheless, to jerk any wandering attention into wakefulness. More rewarding, the soprano part in Boult's warmly conducted performance of Elgar's *The Kingdom*, with the main aria, 'The sun goeth down', sung with a stream of clear, beautifully sustained tone. To come later in the year were a *Messiah* (vivid in the Christmas Eve narrative, sensitive to the eschatological mysteries of 'I know that my Redeemer liveth') and a Schubert recital. That was something of a disappointment, for, in spite of the care and beauty of so much, there was a relative lack of magnetism. Something of the authority and fresh purity of her singing brings Margaret Ritchie to mind, but a comparison of the two sopranos in 'Der Hirt auf dem Felsen' finds more life, more smile and more heart in the earlier recording. Similarly a chance comparison of Price's 'La Pastorella' with an old recording in German by the contralto Sigrid Onegin shows a magic and many-shadedness in Onegin, as well as some light, rapid and perfectly smooth fioriture which are not matched by the soprano. But this earlier recital record is superb by any standards. The Nursery Songs of Moussorgsky are sung in Russian, with vivid and unexaggerated characterisation. Liszt's Petrarch Sonnets, expressive and uniformly beautiful, involve her in that athletic cleanness of stride in upward intervals that recalls Sembrich or Farrar. And in the cantata, 'Die ihr des unermesslichen Weltalls', we hear some of the best Mozart singing on record: a command of manner and technique, absolute firmness, some beautifully smooth soft singing, and a vivid radiance in the final section. A few more recordings of this calibre and there will be no question that here is not just a very good singer, but a great one.

May brought further credit to English singing with the issue of Tippett's *Midsummer Marriage*, the Figaro of Sir Geraint Evans in Klemperer's *Nozze*, and the Brahms and Beethoven of John Shirley-Quirk. Troyanos, Zylis-Gara, Prey and Adam were heard in *La Representazione di Anima e di Corpo*; Sills, Gedda and Souzay in *Manon*. June was principally notable for two operas of Britten, *The Rape of Lucretia* and *Owen Wingrave*, both with Pears and Janet Baker among the singers. Baker also sang in Beethoven's *Mass in C*, while the only song recital that month was the Schubert–Schumann collection sung by Werner Krenn.

July saw the return of Fischer-Dieskau after four full months' absence, but there were two records so the output began to average up. Loewe's Lieder and Ballads ('Fischer-Dieskau can also summon the technique to put many a so-called bel-cantist to shame', said John Warrack, trailing his coat more provocatively than usual) show one side of his art; duets with Janet Baker another (a live recording, with the audience heard laughing in one of the pieces, listed by JW among the drawbacks). Prey in Telemann, Frank Patterson delightful in Beethoven's Irish songs, Simon Woolf (boy soprano) in Stravinsky and Prokoviev were other recitalists. Operatic duets were sung by Domingo and Milnes, who also combined forces in

Don Carlo, with Caballé, Verrett and Raimondi. A recital by Stars of the Bolshoi, and a first recording of *Riders to the Sea* were other single discs reviewed in a well-endowed month.

August yielded less, though there were two records of Caballé: one of operatic duets with Marti, taken apart by Andrew Porter who also had fun with the soprano's French pronunciation in her solo recital, issued in Spain some years ago. Deutokom's Mozart, and the two Prices, Leontyne in Schumann, Margaret in Schubert, made up the rest of the harvest, which became more abundant in September.

More from Caballé and Deutokom, and the first appearance in this year's lists of another famous soprano, Elena Souliotis. Her Lady Macbeth is played opposite Fischer-Dieskau, at his most Germanic and unlovely; between them they seem an ill-favoured pair. We know that Verdi did not want his Lady Macbeth to sing beautifully, and it is true that Souliotis catches something of the music's rhythmic energy and the character's murky depths. But her voice is in bad condition: the first aria is painful to hear. That same aria was recorded by her in a recital record issued in 1967. It was then impressive: there was a grandeur and fearlessness about it, and a voice that had a steely quality which could still be softened. Even then one knew that the singer was risking a lot: used as strenuously as this, the voice must surely spread, and with the register divisions so marked (a marvellously exciting chest voice, but an awkward passage just above it), it must surely be under some potentially damaging pressure. An ordinary listener was likely to feel this, and to some extent it affected one's pleasure even then. But there certainly was something else about her singing that at its best was breathtaking. It was impossible not to attend. In that recital, for example, the Final Scene from *Anna Bolena* comprised an amazing variety of moods and tones. Then, among the complete operas she recorded, there is an inspired and thrilling performance in the fearfully demanding role of Abigaille in *Nabucco*: some of the fioriture were careless, but much was sung with skill and panache (the two-octave drop from the high C on the words 'O fatal sdegno', for example). Often a full-heartedness would communicate itself and a really imaginative treatment such as she gives to the duet with Alfio in *Cavalleria Rusticana*. One warms to her at such times. The *Norma*, too, very much 'after Callas', has moments of greatness, but also much that is simply below standard. Ominous biographical details are given in the leaflet accompanying her complete recording of *Anna Bolena*, where her first aria is sad and bad in virtually all respects. At the age of twenty-four, we learn, she had already sung the leading roles in *Aida*, *Il Trovatore*, *Nabucco*, *Forza*, *Ballo*, *Luisa Miller*, *Otello*, *Anna Bolena*, *Norma*, *Gioconda*, *Mefistofele* and *Cavalleria Rusticana*. It is a great achievement; but the old heads must have been shaking as they read. We know that old heads tend to shake unnecessarily; but they are not always wrong, and the *Macbeth* recording suggests that they may be all too regrettably right.

Caballé in *Il Pirata* gave a more heartening demonstration of the modern singer's work in nineteenth century opera, and in the cast of *Macbeth* were also Pavarotti and Ghiaurov to help restore faith. William Pearson, superb in *El Cimarrón*, nevertheless made one newly aware of the pressures modern composers put upon the voice; and Pilarczyk in *Pierrot Lunaire*, under Boulez, gave another reminder of how singing is only one function of the singer in twentieth century music. Prey in Mahler, Fischer-Dieskau, in C. P. E. Bach will not reassure everybody about the beauties of modern singing, but Janet Baker in Schubert surely will. *The Gramophone's* veteran reviewer, Alec Robertson (he heard them all, Destinn, Melba, Gerhardt . . .) felt himself compelled to be 'lavish with superlatives' about what he called 'a magnificent event'. A new *Dido and Aeneas* (Veasey, Donath, Shirley-Quirk, Bainbridge) represented more general high standards in Britain, though for Jeremy Noble it is the Texan-born Helen Donath, as Belinda, who 'steals the show'.

Donath, a delightful Sophie in Solti's *Rosenkavalier*, further enhanced her reputation with a 'neat, pure and true' Eva in *Die Meistersinger* (Andrew Porter's adjectives—he also said of her 'I like her performance so far as it goes, but I want more'). I want more out of the Sachs, Theo Adam, though Andrew Porter finds the part 'very beautifully sung'. René Kollo, (the Walther), Ridderbusch, Evans, Kelémén, Schreier, also contribute to a strong cast. This is one of a clutch of Wagner recordings issued within a few months of each other. November's *Gramophone* contained Alec Robertson's review of the Boulez *Parsifal*: praise for James King, Franz Crass and Donald McIntyre, qualified admiration for Gwyneth Jones as Kundry. Jones has been having a busy time, for the same month her *Salome* was released, a live performance from the Hamburg Opera. William Mann wished 'that she had waited three or four years before recording what is obviously going to be one of her best roles'. Others might wonder what will be the condition of her voice in three or four years time if she continues to sing such heavy roles in the way she seems to be doing at present. Her Ortrud in Kubelik's *Lohengrin* does not augur well at all. That recording has not at the time of writing been reviewed in *The Gramophone*, but I shall break my self-imposed rule and mention it now, as it contains a superlative performance by another soprano who must have a place in this book, Gundula Janowitz.

Her Elsa is one of the most beautifully sung Wagnerian roles on record. The Dream-narrative, taken at a slow tempo, is absolutely firm and pure in tone, and maintains (uniquely, as far as I can recall) a trance-like quality, living the mystery of her vision and eventually radiant with her faith in it. Most of her singing in the opera is gentle and tender, but her voice can shine out like a blade, and she can use it (as in the later part of the love music) with dramatic intensity. I have heard that it was Walter Legge who singled her out in the early sixties and drew her to the attention of Karajan, with whom she has made many of her best records. One can well believe this,

137. Gundula Janowitz

for it is a voice of a certain class and that a high one: she will sometimes make a pure 'tube' of sound that will recall Schwarzkopf and (a singer high in Mr. Legge's estimation) Meta Seinemeyer. He would have seen too that she could come to sing with the authority and style of greatness, as indeed she does in the recording that introduced her to most listeners, the *Zauberflöte* under Klemperer's direction, issued in 1964. Her singing of the aria 'Ach, ich fühl's' exemplifies this 'tube' of sound, and all here is beautifully felt and placed. Her excellence in the duet 'Bei Männern' reminds us how rare is complete success in this easy-looking music. Comparing performances in different periods, from Kurz and Demuth, Eames and de Gogorza, Bettendorf and Hüsch, Lemnitz and Hüsch, Güden and

Berry, Stader and Fischer-Dieskau, one finds little that is completely satisfying. All sorts of things go wrong. Either the Papageno cannot keep the line of his melody even and steady (Demuth cannot), or the Pamina indulges in too much portamento (as Kurz does). Sometimes it loses lightness and charm (the Eames and de Gogorza version has some lovely singing in it, but it does not smile or lift the heart to those realms of light and clarity which this music properly inhabits). Or too brisk and sprightly a manner (Stader and Fischer-Dieskau under Fricsay) can lose the poetry and become merely pretty. Many singers trying to invest Pamina's music with character fall into archness (as rather surprisingly Lemnitz seems to do here) or affect an 'innocence' that is not a natural possession. How difficult too appears to be the meeting of technical difficulties (Güden finds the scale passages awkward and the difficult downward runs at the end). Of all these performances only the Bettendorf-Hüsch comes near to fulfilment—but it is surely there in this recording of Janowitz and Berry. The legato of both solos, unfussy and characterful, the firm beauty of tone (without Lemnitz' rather tremulous sound), the delicious effect of forte and piano alternating in the 'Mann und Weib' section (Kurz and Demuth hardly bother with this at all), the runs clear and smooth, the high B flats cleanly, joyfully taken. Here is genuine distinction.

As Pamina, Janowitz has not the strong projection of character she was later to acquire, but this was no bad thing in that particular role. Her part in *The Creation* has a similar ingenuous freshness, but there is also a greater sense of presence. Her singing of 'On mighty pens' also makes an interesting study, taking two contemporaries for comparison. As against Stich-Randall's cooing girlishness, Janowitz draws an entirely firm line; and as against the edgier sound of Mimi Coertse she is smooth and crystal clear. But both the other sopranos do sing the trills as marked in most scores, and Janowitz uses no decorations at all. There are other points in the performance of the work where her note-by-note distinctness in the runs is just faintly clouded over, but there is no doubt about the sunbright clarity of most.

Sunlight again seems to stream from her singing in the last part of *Ariadne auf Naxos*. 'Und ging in Licht' she sings at the beginning of her role, and throughout the opera a certain glow illuminates even the most elegiac passages. But in the final duet all is radiant: a fine crescendo on 'Ich grüsse dich', and later the conviction of a woman made youthful by new love. It is an exquisite performance by a singer for whom we must hope a long and ever-developing artistic life.

Still, here it is the continuing life of singing in general that we are concerned with; or rather with the continuation of the Grand Tradition. October's review list also included one of those albums, now so typical of the gramophone and its association with singing, but not so long ago an unthinkable luxury: the madrigals of Monteverdi on five records, costing £11.50 when the 'special offer' period is over. 'Riches indeed', says Jeremy

Noble, who nevertheless is not always too delighted with the singing of tenors Tear and Alva; Heather Harper and Sheila Armstrong are more to his liking. One thing is quite clear from this sort of reception accorded to a once unthinkable issue: the presence of high standards of criticism and discrimination, and this itself says something for present conditions and future prospects.

So we come to the last month, the last section, and the last great singer of our survey. Records reviewed in November included no less than eight complete operas. There were also Bach cantatas (Mathis, Häfliger, Fischer-Dieskau), rarities like C. P. E. Bach's *Israel in Egypt* (Geszty, Gayer, Häfliger, Prey), modern works by Boulez, Schönberg (another *Pierrot Lunaire*), Webern (Erika Skiklay), and choral music from the Crusades to Handel (a *Messiah* with Price, Minton, Young and Diaz—Justino Diaz, a bass of sumptuous voice, previously heard, firm and sonorous, even and good on runs, as in the nineteen-year-old Beethoven's *Cantata on the Death of Emperor Joseph II*, and greatly admired by the reviewer, Trevor Harvey, for his performance in this new recording). Handel is also represented by an *Acis and Galatea* (directed by Alfred Deller), and British singing by Tear, Bainbridge and others in Janáček's *Diary of a Young Man who disappeared*. And, of course, there is some Fischer-Dieskau: Brahms' *Die schöne Magelone*, 'the fruit of long affection' on the singer's part, as John Warrack notes, and no doubt stimulated afresh by association with his accompanist, Sviatoslav Richter.

The eight operas were: *L'Elisir d'Amore* (Sutherland, Pavarotti), Handel's *Orlando* (Stefan, Sciutti, Greevy), *Nozze di Figaro* (Jessye Norman, Ingvar Wixwell, Wladimiro Ganzarolli, Freni, Minton), *The Love of Three Oranges* (Russian cast), *Salome* (Jones, Fischer-Dieskau, Richard Cassilly), *Aida* (Price, Bumbry, Domingo, Milnes, Raimondi), the *Parsifal* already mentioned, and a *Boris Godunov* with Ghiaurov in the name part (Talvela, Vishnevskaya, Ludovico Spiess also in the cast). Notable perhaps that the artists named here tend to be young, and that Fischer-Dieskau alone began his recording career on 78s: it may seem aeons ago, but twenty years or so is not really a very long time. LP has already passed through its first generation of singers. Does it mean that careers are getting shorter, voices not lasting so well, incompletely trained and prematurely squandered? They are questions to which we must revert. In the meantime there is Nicolai Ghiaurov.

As one would expect, his Boris Godunov is exceptionally lyrical; the strength of dramatic impression is primarily enforced by sheer qualities of voice, sonorous and unflawed, a kingly instrument in itself. We have come to know him well in recordings over the previous seven or eight years, and to recognize his voice as that of one of the very few great lyric basses of the century. He had been singing at the Scala since 1959, but became known to record collectors principally through the superb performance of Verdi's *Requiem* conducted by Giulini and issued in 1964. Less round and honeyed

138. Nicolai Ghiaurov as Boris Godunov

than Pinza's voice, it was magnificent in its firmness, resonance and power. Very occasionally, as in the Hostias, would come something less than perfection: an aspirate, or a discoloured tone (artistically motivated, in the modern manner). But wherever else one tried him, there was a magnificence that placed him quite clearly as the great lyric bass of post-years: both the full voice enunciating 'Confutatis maledictis', and the quiet, smooth lines of the same solo, 'voca me cum benedictis'. Dramatic authority was there too in the 'Mors stupebit', and, in the Kyrie, that kind of excellence which is most emphatically needed if a 'central' voice like this (for it is not marked, as Christoff's is, by an immediate individuality of tone and manner) is to stand out with full effect in a great ensemble.

The absence of idiosyncrasy and the determination to sing beautifully whatever the odds tend make it harder for a singer to establish character: to give the personal stamp to his singing that can make it unmistakeable and unforgetable. There is a difference between Ghiaurov and Christoff here; not that Christoff sacrifices anything in the interests of expressiveness, but his voice is utterly unlike any other and he has developed a very personal style. Ghiaurov makes less impression, on record, in a role like the Gounod Mephistopheles, though the opulence of voice and the grace of its usage are distinguished enough. There is also the point that, while the low notes are perfectly sound, his voice registers essentially as a bass-baritone, and in passages like the Duel Trio there is need of an unequivocally bass tone to stand distinct from the baritone. Sometimes too the feeling and imagination seem limited; Ivan Susanin's monologue, for example, is less hauntingly emotional than Chaliapin's singing of it, even though Ghiaurov gives a more varied and studied reading. On the other hand, in Khan Khontchak's solo in *Prince Igor* he matches up to Chaliapin better than Christoff does, with plenty of character in the masculine, joking roughness and in the smiling insinuations of the later part.

Until the issue of the *Boris Godunov* recording, however, it was not for his singing in the Russian repertoire or for interpretative skills that Ghiaurov was most notable. Rather, it was for what one can quite properly call *bel canto*. His Don Giovanni is well characterised, but the real distinction is that it is most beautifully sung. We know from the start of this performance that here is a Don who will take every opportunity to sing legato (superb in the trio with Leporello and the Commendatore) and who will give all the notes their full value. It is a clever performance, too, managing to make the character vocally beautiful and psychologically ugly (as in the mock-wooing of Elvira in Act II); and in the trio quoted above he can sound both beautiful and satirical, observing the dying Commendatore with crocodile tears. But we have had perceptive and characterful Dons before; never one (even including Pinza, as far as the private records allow one to judge) who sings so well. In the nineteenth-century Italian repertoire we can savour the voice more fully still. Fiesco's solo in the Prologue to *Simon Boccangra* shows him again as Pinza's successor: everything beautifully placed, the final arpeggio over an octave and a fifth down to the low F sharp taken smoothly and in a single breath. His King Philip in *Don Carlo* is again a fine example of the natural marriage between dramatic effectiveness and a scrupulous singing style (thrown into relief in the scene with Roderigo, where Fischer-Dieskau sounds rough by comparison). In *Anna Bolena* it is not so much Pinza as Plançon who comes to mind, for there is something of that instrumental evenness about Ghiaurov's singing, and especially in the first Act, that recalls the old style and once more gives assurance of the continuing tradition.

Turning finally to the *Boris Godunov*, we have probably to acknowledge that others have better communicated the agony of mind. Neither the Coronation solo nor the Monologue seems to have the full underlay of sombreness or torment, and the cry of protest at unkindly death has not the bitterness one remembers in other performances. And yet this is a genuine characterisation. He catches the awe of superstition, for example, as, after dismissing Shuisky, he tells him to stay, and the voice is already chilled with the horror of the question filling his mind—'do dead children rise from graves to question tsars?' But above all else this is a beautifully *sung* performance. Several passages become newly moving because of the new lyrical beauty: the words sung to the Tsarevitch after the parrot song, the summoning of Pimen to calm the secret gnawing of conscience, the instructions to Feodor to guard the faith and care for his sister. And though we miss some intensity in the alternations of hope and despair, the Monologue remains one of the finest of bass solos on record.

To meet with such a singer and such a recording at journey's end is pleasant and reassuring. The year's recordings, too, leave one impressed by an art that is flourishing. It is dangerous practice to cry 'a golden age', whether about the past or present. As to the art of singing, let us say that a lot of artists are providing a lot of pleasure, and leave it at that for the moment. For the association between voice and gramophone, it has surely never been happier and closer than at present. In that respect at least we are living in an age that earlier times might well call golden. We must hope that the future will have just as good reason to think it something less.

Conclusion

The Grand Tradition

PLOTTED as a progress-chart and reduced to simplest form, the graph of seventy years recorded singing is v-shaped. So, at least, I read it, even though behind that firm outline there are peaks and troughs that make no regular pattern at all and a whole complex of intersecting lines that run in contrary directions.

We began by overhearing what we could of the nineteenth century, finding singers who in their declining years had a still recognisable greatness, highly impressive in certain features of technique and in strength of personality. Character was also vivid in the command exercised by the five chosen to represent singing at its best around the turn of the century, smoothness, flexibility and fine tone being their other prize possessions. But a different order of priorities was beginning to establish itself. Following the demands of composers and the public, singers concerned themselves more with power of voice, drama and emotion, though the lyric traditions were being sustained by certain notable artists and skill in fioritura was still cultivated by many to a high degree of excellence in these early years of the century. In the concept of music-drama and in the growing importance of the orchestra we saw forces which would work against these traditional skills, especially when seconded by an increase in concern for realistic acting on the operatic stage. In a series of regional surveys, we found Russia and France then at their richest for provision of singers, while the Americans were only just beginning to find opportunities and recognition. In Italy, where the tradition still produced the most abundant harvest of voices, the cult of emotionalism and volume was becoming more disruptive and did not bode well for the future there in the period after the First World War.

It was in this interwar period that we saw the decline most marked. The essential skills of smooth production and flexible movement were relatively neglected; in the musical world, and in the gramophone itself, interests declined; and greatness in singing became ever more rare. In Italy there was a notable generation of tenors, but the traditional skills were less well cultivated than before, and as the twenties gave way to the thirties the decline continued. In Germany the picture was brighter. Fioritura, legato, 'bel canto': the traditional virtues were being fostered there by a generation of singers that flourished most impressively in the 1920s. This period marked the rise too of a fine school of Lieder singers and Wagnerians. In England, interest and confidence were increasing; in France there was not the distinction of old. Both countries had relatively few representatives in America, which especially in the twenties drew many of the best European singers. The age of the American singer was still to come, but at the Metropolitan persisting more or less to the outbreak of war was a distinguished company, five of whom we saw as among the greatest the century has known. The war itself brought a fragmented musical life: there was still much worth hearing, but during the forties, after the war as well as during it, people became accustomed to the idea that theirs was not an age of great singing.

The gramophone played its part in the revival. For one thing, recordings on a scale not envisaged before became possible with the coming of LP. A new generation of singers was needed in the recording of Wagner, for example, and this provided a valuable stimulus. But the opera houses and concert halls knew of better times first through the excellence of a new school of singers centred on the Vienna Opera, and soon it became possible to form international casts in which greatness again could be recognised. When there followed on this a renewed interest and excellence in florid singing, one could begin to speak of a renaissance. During the sixties the American singer came into his (her) own; and Italian singing, a sturdy if not particularly sensitive growth during the fifties, began to gain in its best representatives a finesse which it had not known for a long time. All around Europe, on both sides of the Iron Curtain, there was a good deal of devoted music-making, the singers playing their part, and among those whose interest lay in song at least as much as in opera we saw five who had brought their art to an exceptionally high level. But a wider musicianship was being more insistently asked of singers, for they were to cope with the difficulty of modern writing for the voice and with the opening up of areas belonging to the remoter past. The general raising of musical levels was also reflected in groups and choirs, and the future soloist would often gain experience and breadth of musicianship from working in these. This brought us to the present day, and to the survey of one year's singing on record. Again five singers were seen as outstanding, and the nature of their excellence marked a return to the old priorities: smoothness, flexibility and fine tone. They and their records were individual parts of a flourishing art and a thriving industry: the line in the progress-chart still moves upwards.

That then is the basic outline of our findings. They do not support any notion that the greatness of the past is a myth; or that today's singing is a poor thing compared with what it was 'in Caruso's time'.

We have not been concerned with proof of a thesis or with disproof of anybody else's. On the other hand, it does seem to me that certain of the more dogmatic and generalised claims of 'golden-agers' are discredited. I read, for instance, on the sleeve of a record called *The Old School of Singing*, a note which announces a series of reprints from 'what has come to be known as *The Golden Age of Opera*'. The series offers 'some of the finest examples recorded of the art of *bel canto*—beautiful singing', and there follows a definition of this in unexceptionable terms. But we also read '*Bel canto* is an art almost totally lost today. Its few remaining exponents, though following the proper traditions and training, still fall short of the many achievements in great singing preserved here'. The first singer represented in the catalogue that follows is Luisa Tetrazzini, and of course one casts an eye back over the definition: 'preserving the same characteristic sound at all volume intensities as it progresses through the scale, with a seemless join where one register passes into another . . .'? Then comes Claudia Muzio, then Caruso ('effortlessly . . .'?). The first singer to have two records to himself is Giovanni Zenatello ('Bel canto . . . beautiful singing . . . an art almost totally lost today'). This is a handout on a record sleeve and of anonymous authorship, but it represents an attitude which, for all its sincere enthusiasm, can do much harm to its cause. Tetrazzini was splendid in many ways and her records are delightful in certain respects, but there are dozens of modern singers who satisfy the given definition of *bel canto* better than she does. Zenatello, too, made some fine records, though they need to be sifted out: but as an exponent of 'bel canto' ('adept at accurate fioritura, even movement through the scale, rapid or slow, precise rhythmic control, and an honest trill between two fixed notes . . .'), he is a non-starter, for the records give no suggestion that he had any marked abilities of this nature at all (where several modern tenors on record demonstrably have). Of course the note does not say that every singer on the lists had every one of these abilities, but it does say that they had them to an extent that modern singers do not; and this is a widespread belief among people who are at all interested in old records. Now in these particular instances (and many others) it is demonstrably untrue. What reflection, then, must arise in the mind of some reasonably critical and musical listener who tests these generalisations and in such repeated instances finds they will not hold? He will, I should fancy, not want to hear much more about 'The Golden Age of Opera', and the notion that it was all a myth will have advanced a stage further. The preservation and use of our heritage of records is likely *only* if standards of discrimination are increased; but I fear that in many cases there is no field of serious musical concern in which the presentation has been so undiscriminating.

It has also to be faced that for many musicians, this heritage is hardly a serious musical concern in the first place. The sceptical amusement of *The Observer's* music critic, Peter Heyworth, is probably shared by many. Introducing a review in which he praised in the highest terms some reissued recordings by Elisabeth Schumann and Lotte Lehmann, he referred to the folk who won't hear good of any singing unless it was recorded in their grandmother's time and wouldn't enjoy it even then unless it could be seen whizzing around at the maniac rate of 78 rpm. It was an attitude and activity that evidently remained a mystery. And of course the activity does need some defence, or explanation at least, as a musical pursuit: anybody can see it may be an absorbing hobby and an interesting historical study, but for musical pleasure . . .? I certainly hope that this survey has also suggested that there is musical pleasure in abundance, but let us suppose the objection persists. Suppose the objector says: 'Yes, but if I'm to put up with all the limitations of primitive recording then I want to know for certain that there is something of genuine musical importance which one of these early singers did better than any of today's people to whom I can listen in comfort'. This man will not be interested in Calvé's 'fourth voice' in music of no 'importance', and he won't want to listen to de Lucia in Neapolitan songs, or even in Rossini. Take him on his own terms, wanting something of 'musical importance' (Bach, Beethoven, Monteverdi, Mozart . . .) How will the golden age respond to this?

It could not do very much better than to put out as a hostage John McCormack singing 'Il mio tesoro' from *Don Giovanni*. It is one of the most famous of pre-electrical records and one of the most universally praised. The objector must acquiesce; he must agree that the singing is excellent. But 'excellent' means that it excels: whom does it excel, then, and how? Well, it excels Björling, Crooks, de Lucia, Dermota, Devries, Gigli, Jadlowker, Kullmann, Nash, von Pataky, Schiøtz, Schipa, Senius and Tauber, for a start. But our objector is not interested in them, for they are 'old' (pre-stereo) also. In any case, *how* does it excel, or surpass, these performances? An obvious answer, and happily irrefutable, is that the breathing is better; McCormack has the breath-control to sustain the long phrases without breaking them for breath, and, apart from Heddle Nash, he is the only one among these to sing the longest of the runs without interruption. But on LP the following all do that: Alva, Anders, Domingo, Hollweg, Krenn, Valletti and Wunderlich. Anders does it without a preliminary breath before 'tornar' and with a continuation into the next phrase. Hollweg also continues the run, a little longer, and later he has an extra one thrown in for some possibly defensible reason. More easily defensible and enjoyable is the decoration to the melody on its re-appearance in Werner Krenn's performance (we remember that knowledge of ornamentation and skill in fioritura was among the features of the artist in *bel canto*, 'an art almost totally lost today'). More important in the performance of the aria is that there should be an effective contrast of style corresponding to the two main melodies (the 'Il mio tesoro' smooth and affectionate, the 'Ditele che i suoi torti' determined and martial). Here our hostage is in some peril for he makes very little of this. Léopold Simoneau does, and he, I think, would be the modern champion in terms of stylistic elegance and cleanness of tone (he breathes once in mid-run but is thus able to make a broader rallentando at the end of it and so lead back more gracefully into the melody). Yet set all these records side by side and McCormack's is still the virtuoso performance: it is still the voice best practised in rapid movement, still the most closely 'bound' in runs, the notes perfectly distinct and the tone perfectly even and continuous. His is also the tone that most freely grows to a healthy full-bodied resonance, its texture most even and unflawed, its beauty most distinctive. There are faults even here, but as soon as one starts to list them they seem niggling and (as one returns to the record itself) quite disproportionate. Looking at it one way it might seem that the margin by which the record still 'excels' is narrow and itself a kind of niggle; looked at another, it is by the most important matters of all in singing, those on which the whole tradition is based and by which standards for its continuing life are set.

If we still have to answer the question about musical pleasure, the answer surely does lie, paradoxically enough, in quality of sound. The excellence of sound we hear in the singing compensates for other inadequacies and makes the listening a joy. As for the sizzling surface, it concentrates the mind wonderfully: you listen through it and focus intently in the process. It lasts about four minutes, and during that time listening is a more active business than usual.

Our musical objector is not yet satisfied; but perhaps he is never likely to be. He may have time for a superlatively sung aria by Mozart, but could still object that we had to hunt around to find it and that it is not representative either of the standard of those times or the repertoire. He would be right on the first count in as far as that particular aria is concerned (Jadlowker does it well, but otherwise records made in the last ten years tell of a very general raising of standards); and the second point is certainly true, for it is a frustrating feature of the early catalogues that much of the most testing music for these virtuoso singers was not recorded or (in some cases) recorded but never issued. But we might ourselves raise some objections now. The sceptical musician, we said, would not want to hear Calvé and her 'fourth voice' in music of 'no importance', or de Lucia in Neapolitan songs. But what a pity! Calvé, for example, is to be heard in a short and extremely 'insignificant' song called 'Ma Lisette': there is some miraculous singing but the music is 'of no importance'. Yet its melody has a clear, simple outline and in this record retains a certain folk-character: it pleases and stays agreeably in the mind. Singing and melody combine to make a rather rare musical pleasure, and one that it seems a pity to be without. So with the Neapolitan songs. Perhaps they are not a 'serious musical concern', but perhaps musical concerns do not always have to be serious.

Where it does come to 'serious' interpretative questions, however, is it not true that modern singers have advanced in subtlety and thoroughness well beyond their predecessors?

The question is formulated like one of those in the Latin grammar book expecting the answer 'yes'. But the examples provided in this survey give rise to no simple generalisation, except in one certain respect. That, I think, is in what one might call literary-music. It applies to German and French song, especially to such composers as Wolf and Debussy, and also to the operas of Wagner and Strauss. Where text-and-music are inseparable (the very nature of the music making full sense only in relation to its text) then modern singers generally do a better job than their predecessors. Several examples are given in the sections on Lieder in the present book, and the general result of the more detailed comparisons in the Appendix strengthen the notion.

Let us make another comparison now, and one that seems to me representative. We can compare Herbert Janssen and Fischer-Dieskau in Wolf's *Harfenspielerlieder*, Janssen's performance being included in the Hugo Wolf Society's second album (1932) and Fischer-Dieskau's in a recital of Wolf's *Goethe Lieder* (1961). The opening of the first song is typical. 'The man who gives himself to solitude soon enough finds himself alone in the world' is the paraphrased sense (not a literal translation). This can be said or sung in two ways. The first way is to recite it as a generalisation, the sort of statement that might come from the Book of Proverbs. The second has it as an essentially personal reflection arising out of bitter experience. To the first we say 'Yes, no doubt, poor fellow'; to the second, 'Ah, you've found that, have you? Tell me more'. The first way is Janssen's, the second Goethe's and Fischer-Dieskau's. The difference is great. It makes itself felt partly through the sighed 'ach', partly through the bite of consonant and the slight emphasis on 'der' in 'ach, der ist bald allein'. Or, to take another example, in the third song the blind harpist sings that the man who has not known bitterness and sorrow 'does not know you, ye heavenly powers'. Janssen is authoritative and powerful, but Fischer-Dieskau is more than this: he injects venom into the words 'ihr himmlischen Mächte' so that here we are also made to feel the weight of personal experience that has prompted this attack—and it *is* an attack, on God, after all, which again one would not gather from Janssen's more generalised interpretation.

Much of this greater depth in the modern performance is due no doubt to factors other than the difference between the two singers. The change of status enjoyed by the accompanist in the modern musical world is one of these. Fischer-Dieskau's work with Gerald Moore bears the print of a real creative collaboration. Again and again the singer takes his hint from something in the piano part, and always to fine effect. We see evidence of this greater thoughtfulness in the tempo chosen for the second song. *Langsam aber nicht zu schleppend* (i.e. not dragging) is Wolf's direction, and the emphasis of the caution is in clear distinction to the marking for the other songs. Fischer-Dieskau and Moore take it accordingly a little faster than the others, whereas Janssen has it at much the same pace: he has not really noted the *nicht zu schleppend*. One result is that his accompanist, Conraad von Bos, cannot (or at any rate does not) shape the principal motif in the piano part; the very slow speed obscures its lamenting rise and fall. Another result is that the total effect of the Harfenspieler songs as a *work* is weakened. Two short songs of exceptional bitterness and intensity have in between them a shorter song in the same emotional key but of a milder sorrowfulness. In the later performance one is aware that the artists have thought how the miniature song-cycle is shaped, and the gain is considerable.

Now this is representative, and it marks real progress. It does seem that on balance Lieder singing today is better than it has been at any time this century. Its strengths lie in the greater application of intelligence, in greater care, precision and imaginativeness in the interpretation. This will apply to songs of other nationalities and to certain kinds of opera as well as to Lieder. The modern trend, welcome as it is, also brings its dangers, however.

Intelligence can become a sort of intellectualism that deadens the emotions. Care can overburden what should be a joyful art. Precision can restrict spontaneity. Imaginativeness, too, has its abuses and dangers, inducing a singer to search, as an end in itself, for some original way of presenting a song, and leading to all sorts of excesses and oddities because of this. Among the examples included in the Lieder comparisons in Appendix A is a record of Brahms' 'Mainacht' by Hermann Prey. It is extremely careful, expressive and individual; it has all the virtues just mentioned but they have led the singer into what registers, in the comparisons, as a vast, and disqualifying, excess. The slowness, over-solemnization and over-conscious artistry found there are not untypical, and another example is close at hand. Christa Ludwig also sings 'Die Mainacht' and very finely too, but on the same record is a performance of Schubert's 'Fischerweise', which again is taken very slowly and, as it were, significantly. She certainly brings to our attention the fact that in the song 'peace hangs all around' and that words like 'sorrow' and 'suffering' occur in the poem. But this care not to be superficial and conventional seems to have resulted in the virtual loss of the song itself; whereas, if we listen to singers of an earlier generation, to Schumann or Gerhardt, we find a much freer, more enjoyable essential rightness. Elisabeth Schumann is all sunshine and happiness: with her, the song catches early-morning freshness, free from any stickiness of romance. There is the shepherdess on the bridge, vivid and pretty as a picture, determined that no angler is going to catch her ('schlauer Wicht'). With Gerhardt, we hear the strong, vigorous will, but with a marvellous lightening of the rather matronly voice, and an effective pointing of staccato and legato contrasts. Both have faults of vocalism that Ludwig does not have, but both command a rightness of feeling for the song that Ludwig with all her care and thoughtfulness has not achieved. Going with such features of modern singing as these illustrate can also be a tendency to overlay the music with fussy pointing and stressing, and indeed to lose the ability to present a phrase of music as a unit. Each note receives its special attention, and the pure, instrumental flow of the phrase is lost. And clearly this affects the singing of opera even more than that of Lieder.

So let us return to our sceptical objector and to the comparison with which we started. The objector, we will suppose, has agreed with the main force of the Janssen/Fischer-Dieskau comparison as supporting his own view that a musician's interests are likely to be better satisfied by today's singers than by those on early recordings. He may have agreed also with the cautionary comments that followed, since these were advanced to qualify but not to contradict that basic view of things. But there is a little more to say about the Janssen/Fischer-Dieskau comparison, for though I think that the total effect of Fischer-Dieskau's record is the stronger, both in meaning and musical beauty, I have to set against that the fact that Janssen's is to me the better voice in these records, and that if I put the stylus down at any random point in Fischer-Dieskau's record the tone is likely to seem inferior to the other singer's. Janssen's voice seems richer, more exciting and sympathetic in timbre, and for most of the time more steady. There is an oddly unfocused note or two at the beginning, but otherwise the sound is, to my ears, one of great beauty. Fischer-Dieskau's is not exactly that: it is good and strong, but not rich, and in the louder passages a beat which is unlikely to have been noticeable in the flesh is picked up by the microphone. Now the objector may say that this proves his point very happily: the very fact that one can say Fischer-Dieskau's performance is the stronger 'both in meaning and in musical beauty' shows that rich tone, instrumental evenness, so-called 'bel canto' for short, are secondary to artistic imagination and interpretative thoroughness in a singer. But for the present writer the anomaly does not ring happily at all.

The individual instance matters little on its own. The history of singing is full of examples much more extreme than this one: after all, Herbert Janssen was a fine interpreter, and Fischer-Dieskau has a fine voice. The misgivings point in another direction, towards the composers. We do not think of Wolf as a modern composer, and we do think of him on the whole as writing sympathetically for the voice. But his songs are still of the kind, literary-musical-dramatic, that insist upon interpretative skill first and foremost. A listener with no German and no translation is less likely to enjoy a song by Wolf than one by Brahms or Schumann; a singer with little talent for interpretation is more likely to give enjoyment in Brahms and Schumann than in Wolf. A change of emphasis has come into play, affecting the singer. Wolf died in 1903, and since that time the change has continued and intensified. The music which we think of as modern asks much from its singers: great skill in reading and memorising, a high degree of rhythmic accuracy and vitality, clear articulation, effective acting, an intellectual and emotional grasp of the composer's purposes, a wide working range, strength of voice, physical stamina. The list does not contain any mention of beautiful tone. Perhaps it is taken for granted, but on the whole I think it is reckoned to be not so very important. And of course it is of very secondary relevance in the concept of opera which has gained most ground during the century. Perhaps to talk of a single concept is to over-simplify (obviously there are great differences between Berg, Henze, Britten, Tippett and so forth). But let us put it this way: singers of twentieth-century opera spend a relatively high proportion of their time on the stage talking to one another. The talk is pitched on notes to be sung; but essentially it is talk because essentially the opera is drama (and drama of the kind where people spend a lot of time talking to one another). Everything works to support this: the emphasis of critical reviews, for example, in which perhaps three-quarters of the space is devoted to comment on the production, the remaining space going largely to a discussion of the conductor's work, the review ending with a list of the singers who took part (perhaps an adjective for each). If the elements that constitute an opera are ranged in this order of importance ('opera is a form of drama, therefore the first essential is production—but it is music-drama, therefore the conducting is vital—but it is music-drama that is sung, therefore singing actors are needed'), then the voice of a Caruso, a Ponselle, a Caballé, becomes a luxury and even an embarrassment. The modern composer does not write his voice-parts with that sort of sound inside his head; essentially that sort of sound is an anachronism.

The tradition whose recent history we have been following in these pages has had its changes of fortune. Even within the period of the gramophone we have seen it fall on relatively hard times, and it has revived. But an anachronism has to battle for survival. For one thing its standards need jealous preservation so that if a time comes when composers start to write for the tradition again it will be there at hand ready with singers to represent it and teachers to perpetuate it. Hence, it would be a pleasure to see critical judgment favouring the singer who most nearly represents the traditional virtues: but that is not always possible.

Perhaps consignment to the museum is the inevitable fate both of grand opera and the tradition of singing associated with it. Perhaps for the majority of people, the average television-viewer, the fate has already overtaken; an evening's opera on the television, or the appearance of some celebrated (in other words, unheard-of) opera singer is an obvious occasion for switching over to the other channel. More powerful than the modern composer is modern pop-culture, and that has now taken hold long enough for 'singing' to mean something quite different. To the average youngster, the sound of the operatic soprano voice on records or television is now quite actively unpleasant: it sounds unnatural, being so high above the speaking voice, it sounds assertive, unfriendly and uncomfortably loud in its power, and its quality carries a mental image that is somewhat comical. The male operatic voice is easier to take, and most will see, in a theoretical kind of way, that there is 'something in it'. But 'singing' means something else: it may be deafeningly loud coming over the amplifiers, or it may be the merest breathing into the microphone, but its purpose is to express a lifestyle which is in utter opposition to all that grand opera and its traditions seem to them to stand for. Grandeur is implied in the whole nature of opera: its theatres, its formalities, the size and complexity of its resources, its social history, its principal subjects, its kind of singing. There is nothing more remote from the pop-world, and this utter remoteness from popular culture is something new. Only thirty or forty years ago, popular singing had something in common with operatic singing. The Forces' Sweetheart, the Whispering Baritone, the Street-Singer, Our Gracie, they were all recognisably 'singing'; a crooner like Bing Crosby still made a sound that was a 'pleasant' singing-tone. There was also the world of musical-comedy, where a Binnie Hale or Harry Welchman *sang*; and this was not far from operetta which might not so long ago involve exquisite artists like Yvonne Printemps or Fritzi Massary. But these links with the singing-style of grand opera have largely disappeared. Sometimes a pop-singer will show that he has a voice: he will sing high A's and B flats without apparent difficulty and the sound could obviously be trained to good effect. There may be a strong personality, and some musical feeling: a generation or two ago this pop-star would have found his voice, would have warbled 'Because' or 'Santa Lucia' until he heard a record of Caruso, would decide that that was the life for him and would set out on a career which in those days could have a glamour beyond that of rival attractions. The tradition has in fact depended very much on recruitment from unsophisticated people, whose voices were an asset they learnt to try out in fields, churches, private and public houses, and who would bring both respect and vitality to the art they were to serve. And what they took up, though involving formidable disciplines, was not absolutely foreign to what they already knew. 'Two lovely black eyes' or 'La paloma' or 'Old folks at home' were fairly and squarely diatonic and regular in rhythm; so were the Toreador's Song or any of the roles in *Il Trovatore*. But to move from the world of T. Rex to *The Knot Garden* involves the sort of interplanetary travel that the wonders of our age can do little to facilitate. The grand tradition is caught up in a complex of cultural change.

And there may be other and more technical forces at work. Those who believe on the whole that the decline has not been arrested and that it has continued fairly steadily from the early days of the gramophone generally argue on the basis of singing-method: on the existence in the past of certain singing schools (associated with famous teachers) and on unsatisfactory alternative methods employed in the present. A writer to do so with great cogency is John Stratton, whose paper 'Operatic singing style and the gramophone'[1] has a similar object to that of the present book—'to try to

---

[1] *Recorded Sound*, The Journal of the British Institute of Recorded Sound, April–July 1966.

make a beginning at sorting out our legacy of phonographic recordings and putting them to work'. He believes that we can already trace 'the rise and . . . the fall of the sort of singing that brought opera into existence'. His diagnosis of 'the fall' runs against my own relatively optimistic findings; but I would be willing to admit the limitations (as well as defending the advantages) of the probably more empirical means by which I have reached them. It may indeed be that the improvement we have witnessed over the last twenty years is a temporary one; and that the technical factors which Mr. Stratton examines, seconded by the social and cultural forces mentioned here, are working overwhelmingly against survival.

I said at the outset of this chapter that though the progress-chart was shaped like a v, there were still lines on the graph that ran in contrary directions. Such misgivings as those just now voiced form the line which goes from left to right and points downwards.

But there is another line which would show a steady upwards movement and which gives good hope for the future. One opinion represented by this line would be that of G. B. Shaw as quoted on p. 18: 'We sing much better than our grandfathers'. Writing in the nineteen-thirties, he said it was no use talking to him about the golden-age singers: he heard them, and he would prefer Mr. Heddle Nash any day. He was ready to admit that the old school could sing their roulades and that generally speaking the moderns could not; but he still thought that the voice production as well as the sheer musical utility of modern singers made them preferable. This was in the trough of the v. Following this opinion, one could see the regression as a matter, perhaps, of *reculer pour mieux sauter*. The singer may not have been required to produce the pure legato of former days, or the florid brilliance or even the beauty of tone. But this did mean that the art could become less self-regarding, and that with a temporary fall in status and stardom there would also be the opportunity to drop those traditions which were certainly bad for music (when Jean de Reszke could habitually omit 'Celeste Aida' when he sang Radamès, because he was not properly warmed up, or when Lilian Nordica could walk about on the concert platform during the introduction to a song, or when Frieda Hempel could ask—and evidently expect—her pianist to omit the postlude of Wolf's 'Ich hab' in Penna' because it made a better effect for her without it). The traditional arts were never dead, and when the time came for their more general revival it could proceed with all the advantages of an additional scrupulousness in such respects as these.

The gramophone can itself claim to have played a part. It has worked in several helpful ways. It has contributed to the general improvement of intonation: instrumentalists will testify to this (Menuhin, for instance, has ascribed the better intonation of violinists very largely to the fact that with the gramophone they have been able to hear themselves and have acquired the habit of listening and checking intently and critically). It has increased our awareness of vibrato and unsteadiness: both are highlighted by recording, and while tastes will differ on the question of a quick vibrato, there can be no argument about the undesirability of a wobble. It can also restrain the demand for power at the expense of quality.

A good illustration of several of these points is provided by the recent recordings of the operas of Wagner, many of them conducted by Karajan. Among the singers have been some whose vocal method has not shown up well, and on the whole they have met with a critical reception in reviews. But a widely observed feature has been the tendency to aim for a pure, steady quality of voice and for a lyrical singing style. Recordings of Wagner have been used in each section of this book to point particular developments in the history of singing and its relationship with the gramophone. Perhaps at this late stage we may do so again, noting two singers prominent in these recent records: even offering them as hostages for a declared belief in the future of operatic singing.

Among the men, Karl Ridderbusch distinguishes himself in the most practical of tests. One listens to a new *Rheingold* and hears an unknown Fafner: the sound first pleases and later impresses. One notes the name and forgets it. Then a broadcast of *Götterdämmerung* plays on the car radio starting at some point half way through the second Act. One listens to the end to catch the name of the Hagen. A little later there is a new *Meistersinger* to hear on records. Without the score, attention can lapse during Act I, but there is a voice among those numerous basses and baritones, the voice of the Pogner, and consulting the cast-list one finds again the name of Ridderbusch. Pogner's 'Das schöne Fest' is a taxing solo, and his performance is remarkable if only for its ease; but it is also remarkably smooth (yet catching the spring in the rhythm) and strong-voiced (yet completely without unsteadiness). There is great warmth of character too, and with the baritonal tinge to the bass he will surely become a fine Hans Sachs. It is a Sachs-like character that we hear, somewhat incongruously, in his Hagen; and curiously, this forthright, manly tone brings out something akin to *Meistersinger* tunes in Hagen's music. But this is no lightweight voice: the power is there, and it rings out with fine dramatic conviction.

As does that of the soprano, Helga Dernesch. She was first heard as the *Siegfried* Brünnhilde, radiantly effortless, glowing with health, and only very slightly less meaningful and intense than a more experienced singer might be. With the *Götterdämmerung* recording she had developed in depth, both of voice and feeling. In the final scene, the strength of the lower register combines with the firm control to achieve a perfect stillness in the phrase 'Ruhe, du Gott'. But long before this supremely testing solo, we have realised that here is an artist who has the stature to meet its challenge. The noble, quiet response to Waltraute's appeal, and the nightmarish perplexity when confronted with Siegfried's apparent betrayal have registered as the work of a genuinely imaginative singer. When she came then to record her *Fidelio* Leonore in a great performance under Karajan she seemed to have grown a stage further. There is a more consistent intensity here, and an art which conceals the great technical difficulties of the role much more successfully than most. Above all, she is absolutely steady; her voice is well-produced and even throughout its range; and it is a voice of great beauty. As Ridderbusch is surely in a line with Friedrich Schorr, so Dernesch inherits from Leider: again an essential part of the tradition is maintained.

These represent the kind of singer whom the gramophone most encourages. But public taste does so too. Another of the prophetic books crying woe is *The Crisis of the Art of Singing*[1] and in it the author lays blame upon indiscriminate and mechanical applause in opera houses and concert halls; and no doubt a performance has to be pretty bad before it forfeits the normal applause which is an expression of pleasure (not necessarily critical) in what has been heard. But my own experience suggests that there is discrimination. At Covent Garden on the whole the audience knows a good singer when it hears one, and makes that clear. Beauty of timbre and control of emission are recognised. Of course other factors are involved too, but these are still primary as far as the audience is concerned (though they receive little attention in the accounts of the evening that appear in the papers next day). In live performances as well as on the gramophone record there are at least sufficient signs of a discriminating influence to help the line across the graph paper to continue moving in the right direction.

Perhaps, having looked in as balanced a way as he can, an author should at this stage declare himself. Ultimately one may see a great many arguments on all sides of a question and know perfectly well where one's heart is. Mine is with the old recordings. I make, shall we say, a virtually random selection of 78s (a Sembrich, an Eames, a Calvé, an Alda, an Amato, Martinelli, Renaud) and hear singing to which the heart responds much more fully than it would to a similar programme sung by artists of recent times. Very likely it is something other than the quality of the singing that explains the difference of response. But I *feel* that the quality of singing is the prime influence. Then I am fortified in this feeling if I play an anthology of collectors' rarities recently compiled in memory of a greatly respected collector.[2] The items include two solos by Fernando de Lucia, a marvellous record by Olimpia Boronat, a charming one by Angelina Pandolfini, the first Adriana Lecouvreur. Then there is a high-spirited, infectiously gay duet by Demuth and Hesch (you can feel their enjoyment), and David Bispham singing with a twinkle and a feeling for presentation. There are also names formerly unknown to me: a soprano, Cathérine Mastio, pure of voice and delightful in style, and another, Luise Perard-Petzl, exquisite in the delicacy and sensitivity of her singing. There surely is something here

---

[1] *Die Krise der Gesangskunst*, by Wolf Rosenberg, Karlsruhe, 1968.
[2] Rubini, *In Memoriam: Recordings from the Collection of Dr. Dick Alexander. 1924–1968.*

that can be objectively adduced in defence of what is no doubt a very subjective emotion.

But the gramophone was wedded to singing as its first bride in its very earliest days, something like three-score years and ten back in the past; and it took it then for better or for worse. Which of the comparatives we judge to be operative matters less than the fact of the union. And the union matters because of its fertility. It has begotten an innumerable progeny, inexhaustible in variety, pleasure and interest, and (if treated with reasonable care) indestructible. Through them we come to know a voice and an art as we would a human being, one that, in this instance, brings the further delight of the music itself. Some of them do so with that degree of excellence in which we see a kind of human and artistic greatness; and it is these whose work pre-eminently forms a tradition whose grandeur is not so very remote from the historical centre of western civilisation.

Appendix: Essays in Comparison

Twelve arias and eight Lieder are discussed in the studies which follow.[1] In each of them, six records are used and the commentary is generally limited to these. They represent twenty sessions with the gramophone, playing the records in several different orders, sometimes through continuously, sometimes stopping to compare particular points of detail, always with the musical score at hand. The six records are chosen to represent the first six decades of this century, and also to afford a fair critical range in terms of merit: they are not selected as being the best recordings of the music, though each of them contains at least one record that would come within that category.

Part I: From Patti to Callas Twelve Arias

1. *JOSHUA—Oh, Had I Jubal's Lyre.*

   (The records: Lilli Lehmann from OD.50392 on ELP O-463; Hempel DA 676; Schumann D 1632; Baillie 9697; Catley B 9138; de los Angeles ALP 1838).

There is no more joyous sound than the Handelian allegro with its clean harmonies and bold intervals. All six sopranos capture the sprightly energy of this aria, though only three of them take it at a genuine allegro. The others jog along amiably, the most satisfactory of them being Gwen Catley whose clear tone and excellent technique are seconded by the cool rhythmic buoyancy of her accompaniment. In this she has an advantage over Isobel Baillie. The freshness of Baillie's voice however (she was then Bella Baillie), and her easy accuracy in the runs make this also a very attractive performance. Both these English sopranos have a happy, square-the-shoulders-for-business approach to Handel, with no nonsense in it; and this may be part of the national inheritance. They may not project personalities as vividly as their European counterparts, but that isn't all loss to them. In Elisabeth Schumann's recording, for instance, there is a good deal of personality and this may be thought to compensate for a technique that really isn't up to it. But greatly as I love Schumann's art, I cannot hide from myself that Handel reveals its limitations with uncomfortable clarity. There is an unfortunate breath in the first long run and the second obviously causes her difficulty. The repeated alternations between the fifth and sixth of the scale are insecure and none of the florid work has that facility which is found in the English performances mentioned above let alone the German ones below. Of course there is the Schumann character, and the shine of her voice is certainly delightful. But the mannerisms are not happily employed here—the scoop on the second note of the song, for instance, or the too spirited assault on the last

[1] From articles originally published in *The Record Collector*, XV (5, 6) and XVI (11, 12).

phrase. Records lay all bare and no doubt in a Schumann recital one would be quite won over by the charm of the voice and the woman, just as in our day a Victoria de los Angeles recital takes all hearts and leaves the critical faculty stingless. But here too the record is not entirely satisfying. This is partly Gerald Moore's fault. It is rare to have any occasion to criticise the most famous of accompanists, but surely his playing here is out of character—that odd jerkiness combined with an unpointed (and unwonted) heaviness of style and touch are certainly very remote from any Handel playing that I want to hear. De los Angeles herself, like Schumann, is not really heard at her best. She too takes breaths in the long runs, even though the aria is now moving at a spanking pace. The second of these breaths is obtrusive and though all the notes are distinct and accurate the runs do not have the fluidity of the singers whose performances remain to be heard, the grace and facility of Hempel or the sonority and fleetness of Lilli Lehmann. Both these old records have their drawbacks. With Lehmann there are two: however marvellous the preservation of the voice, the lower part of it is clearly in ruins, and however impressive the grand manner is in other contexts, such authoritative, almost martial, grandeur seems a little out of place here, especially when combined with that rather prima donna-ish way of 'whisking' some of the notes along. With Hempel there is a very slight tendency to hurry the runs, and then (one gets used to this and accepts it after a bit) considerable freedom with the time in the last page. But nothing of this can destroy the pleasure of hearing how beautiful and exciting such florid work can sound when performed by singers who have really learnt to do it. For the aria itself, perhaps most of us would often choose the Catley, but for glory in the precious art of singing one would always cherish Hempel and Lehmann.

2. *ZAUBERFLÖTE (Act II)—In diesen heil'gen Hallen.*

(The records: Plançon 052117; Andresen E 10574; Kipnis DB 1551; Strienz DB 3476; Greindl DGM 18268; Böhme LXT 5086).

Interest here focuses largely on the famous recording by Plançon, but let us come to it by stages. If our knowledge of the aria had to be gained through one performance only, and that one Kipnis', we should be doing pretty well. He produces his sumptuous tone with marvellous evenness over the range of nearly two octaves phrasing broadly and singing with exactly the proper dignity and authority. If, on the other hand, our single performance had to be chosen from one of the sets on LP we should have a legitimate grouse, and so would Mozart. There are three generally available Sarastros—Wilhelm Strienz, Josef Greindl and Kurt Böhme—and they are all sadly deficient.[1] All, to begin with, sing unsteadily. Greindl has a

---

[1] These essays were written in 1963. Remarks on records currently available refer to the catalogues of that year.

difficulty in controlling the voice around the upper B, but Böhme's wobble[1] afflicts him throughout (listen to him, for instance, on the words 'Mauern', 'Mensch', 'erfreu'n' and on the last bottom G sharp). Strienz is somewhat better, but compared with any of the three earlier singers, he is still uneven. He seems too not really happy on the low notes, although like Kipnis' his recording is in F and not E, as written. Böhme is worse: which is a pity for he has an enormous voice and can put up a wonderful performance as Ochs or Hagen. It is a commentary on the times, however, that this should have been thought to make a Sarastro. The plodding gracelessness may be partly the conductor's fault, but the outcome is at odds with both the lyrical music and the dignified character; almost as if the High Priest of Osiris were really only jolly old Osmin from the local seraglio. But this at least has some character even if a wrong one, and in that respect it is preferable to Greindl's enervated, throw-away version. With a restricted range of volume and colour the performance seems stripped of imagination: at one point the singer himself seems tired of it and the phrase 'kann kein Verräter lauern' emerges with a kind of yawning tone. Again the conductor may be partly responsible, which is not likely to be true of Strienz who had Beecham. Yet Strienz, in an effort to introduce variety, uses a heavy marcato style for the second verse and the smooth line is of course destroyed. None of these faults occurs in Ivar Andresen's single verse. He begins tenderly, makes a warm, steady crescendo, and uses his fine voice like a sensitive instrument, shading with imagination and preserving a good legato. It is, in fact, a performance very close to Plançon's, the main difference being that the French bass had a more supple, lyrical voice and was surer in his intonation. But both of these singers make very free with the time, and it is in this respect that Plançon himself is far from being 'beyond the pale of criticism'. I use this phrase because it occurs in Mr. Hevingham-Root's remarks on the record ('Record Collector' VIII, p. 179) and because I have rather reluctantly to disagree with it. 'Plançon uses a rather slower tempo than we usually hear,' says the writer, 'but that does not detract one whit from the beauty of Mozart's music.' That much is no doubt true; but what Mr. Hevingham-Root does not mention is that Plançon also employs far more rubato than we usually hear—and this, in the judgment, probably, of most modern listeners, does detract quite a lot from the music. I say this with regretful certainty, having recently used the aria and these recordings amongst the illustrations for a talk to a society of young musical people. They agreed about the excellences of all the early records in the programme, except the 'Qui sdegno' of Plançon. I played the record again and this time the merits of tone and smoothness were recognised but what constantly made these attentive and generous listeners screw up

---

[1] Wobble; the term is used in these studies to denote the wide, slow vibrato, or unsteadiness, and distinguish it from the quick, regular vibrato of which Supervia's recordings give an extreme example.

their noses and shake their heads was the rubato. It is coupled too with much portamento, and together these characteristics of style weigh the music down. It gets slower and slower, and of course the tempo was quite slow enough in the first place—particularly for an aria in the second half of this opera which is always in danger of going to sleep because, unlike the other Mozart operas, it has no sustained allegro passages to balance the slow music.

Mr. Hevingham-Root adds: 'Of great interest to students is the fact that the singer keeps to the written score, and does not try to "improve" Mozart, as so many singers see fit to do.' Well, none of these other five singers 'improves' Mozart (except that Kipnis takes the end of the second verse down instead of up, which seems a very natural and rather satisfying progression when done without fuss and ostentation). But, of course, Plançon does *not* 'keep to the written score', because the score says nothing about these perpetual rallentandi, or about the slow portamenti with which he moulds his phrases. By what authority does he impose them? The authority of tradition, perhaps; but in 1906 this meant essentially nineteenth-century tradition, and, as in most things, the spirit of the nineteenth-century was far removed from that of the eighteenth. It seemed to them that Mozart needed this kind of handling to bring out the warmth in him: but he himself gives no such directions, and in 1963 most people seem to agree that he has enough warmth without this nursing—or 'improving'. So to many, it would seem that there are not three unsatisfactory performances here but five—one of these also being a very distinguished piece of singing by a very great master. These listeners (and I should be amongst them) would then turn back with renewed gratitude to Kipnis.

3. *FREISCHÜTZ (Act II)—Wie nahte mir der Schlummer.*

(The records: Austral D 775; Seinemeyer E 10484; Lehmann PXO 1016; Jeritza DB 982; Schwarzkopf SAX 2300; Nilsson SAX 2284).

These six Agathes arrange themselves nicely in pairs. There are, for a start, two Brünnhildes amongst them, providing the excitements of their shining heroic power in the second half, and moderating their big voices for the first. But (tell it not in Bayreuth, publish it not in the halls of EMI) Madame Nilsson could learn a thing or two from Miss Austral. There is, for example, the art of keeping dead centre in pitch when singing softly, and that of holding the tone absolutely steady. And how accomplished Austral is in the big tune, all those awkward quavers scrupulously in place, distinct and yet flowing. With Nilsson fair distinctness is achieved but then only at the expense of the flow (this becomes clear when comparing), and in many of the phrases she is clearly having difficulty. Mind, nobody can teach Nilsson anything about hitting the high notes, and her top B is a stunner.

The second pair heard in this aria are Sieglindes, warm and ample but practising a more intimate art and achieving greater expressiveness. The lovely voice of Seinemeyer is at its best, while her phrasing in the prayer and her smoothness and accuracy in the vivace are a joy. Especially fine moments in this include the lightening on the F sharp of 'gebet zur Himmelshalle', the romance of 'O süsse Hoffnung', the breadth of 'Himmel, nimm des Dankes Zähren'. In addition this is a performance with some poetry in it: and a prosaic *Freischütz* is as pointless an entertainment as one could devise. Much of the poetry resides in the recits; or rather it is the vividness of the singer's realisation of these that illuminates the aria as a dramatic whole. If they are unimaginative then you have a concert aria; the girl at a starlit balcony is nowhere to be seen, the forest murmurs are out of hearing. Austral sings a version in which much is cut so she can hardly be judged, but Nilsson's is very much the concert performance. In any case, in giving just this kind of imaginative life Lotte Lehmann is nearly always supreme. When she sings 'O wie hell die gold'nen Sterne' we look out with her and see them; when the clouds thicken over the forest, darkness closes in on the tone and we see that too. Then there is the excitement, the radiance, the restrained joyfulness so movingly expressed in 'will sich morgen treu bewähren'. Also the beauty of voice and the smile, for Lehmann can smile through wax as clearly as through glass. And who that knows the record can ever hear 'nur die Nachtigall und Grille scheint der Nachtluft sich zu freu'n' without seeing Lehmann's smile behind it?

But possibly this warmth and womanliness are all too mature for Agathe. If so, our third pair of singers, sounding more like Evas than Sieglindes, will provide the maidenly innocence requisite. Jeritza seems excessively girlish perhaps, but this is not her fault for the record is one of those early electricals which at 78 play annoyingly a semitone above proper pitch. Anyway, no amount of turntable adjusting will turn this into a good performance. The phrasing is uninteresting, the adagio is matter-of-fact (nobody would gather this to be a prayer), information about the nightingales and crickets is as prosaic as possible, 'Alles pflegt' (marked pp) goes at a sturdy forte, and a good handful of quavers drops by the wayside in the vivace. For the firmness and clarity of the voice one is grateful but it is hard to believe that much thought or care was given to the aria. By contrast, the care that has gone into Schwarzkopf's record is almost infinite for it includes that scrupulousness of style and technique that is habitual with her. Nothing in the score has gone unheeded and, much more than that, the absolute fidelity combines with an imaginative grasp so that one feels the scene has never been quite so completely realised before. The phrasing is broad and the inflections are all beautifully right; the voice is extraordinarily lovely with its finely poised tone and its plentiful reserves. Indeed although this may possibly be the least powerful voice among six singers (it is hard to estimate this sort of thing), she gives more *effect* of strength than any of the others. Every gradation has point, so that the unrestrained 'Er ist's' rings in the memory far more vividly than the same phrase as given by the louder ladies in this comparison. But there are so many fine things here: the understanding of the directed 'pp' at 'Alles pflegt' with its delicious effect of lulling restfully against an inner excitement, the glorious happiness that later bursts open and the buoyant floating of the 'grand tune'. There is a lot wrong with modern singing, we know; but a few performances of this calibre may suggest that there is something right with it too.

4. *SONNAMBULA (Act III) — Ah, non credea mirarti.*

(The records: Patti 03083 on ORL 212; Tetrazzini DB 533; dal Monte DB 1317; Carosio DB 6388; Callas CXS 1471; Freni CM 19).

Singers divide rather interestingly in their dealings with this aria. For some it seems to require subtle, ever-changing colours, the phrases having an emphatic point within them, after which they must fade to a pianissimo, and so forth. For other sopranos, the music seems largely to 'sing itself': or rather, the singer has to provide beautiful tone and a pure legato, but the melody will generally look after its own expressiveness. In the first group are Patti, Bori, Muzio, Callas and Sutherland. In the second are Galli-Curci, dal Monte, Pagliughi, Carosio and perhaps Mirella Freni; and Tetrazzini should really be added to that list for though decorating a good deal she sings with a basically non-inflected tone. The score itself (at least the Ricordi one in front of me) might seem to support the 'plain-singers', for it gives only one marking for a crescendo and back again, and only one verbal direction ('abbandonandosi' towards the end). But of course it may just be that Bellini thought he would leave his singers to it. Certainly a written-out version of Muzio's performance would present a very different appearance. Most phrases would be marked with subito pianos and sforzandos; add to that the shadings and decorations of Patti's record and it would become a complicated document indeed.

The most richly varied of the performances now being compared is Patti's. She colours with more emphasis than Callas, who as one would expect gives a performance of some intensity and also of some vocal insecurity. Indeed these two records align themselves for two reasons — they are strong in imagination and faulty in execution. The elderly lady singing into the old horn gives one some uneasy moments: a sudden forte in one phrase, a loose bit of timing in another, and some hard-toned scurrying in the cadenza. But Callas in her prime and with all EMI at her service gives more. Hear for example, the pianissimo of 'o fiore' loosen; and that is just a beginning, the first appearance of an almost unvarying characteristic. The high G of 'pianto' is treated to a diminuendo, but it isn't a steady process — there is a point where the *kind* of tone changes, and spreads. It does so even more in the final bars, sometimes even affecting the pitch; and it might well be found surprising that the last notes of the solo should be the carefully and critically recorded sounds of the most famous singer of her time. There is also beauty and insight in this record, but on the whole I prefer Patti, who in addition to an intimate feeling for the music has retained some accomplishments—the swift turns, the trill with its fantastically fine texture and lightness—that few of the others have ever really acquired. The decorations too I find quite lovely, unobtrusive and graceful. Tetrazzini's additions are not quite that, but they are immensely exciting. The phrase 'potria novel vigore' provides an instance; after taking a fair-size breath she interpolates a stunning top C and a descending scale from it. This is not as inartistic as one might think, because the music shifts momentarily from minor to major, the words speak of new life, and the decoration is an appropriately bold, joyous expression of the feeling. Other marvels are performed in the course of the aria, and though she sounds too sturdily in command for the gentle Anina I have often found this record a joy simply because it is so healthy, so clearly not wilting and drooping like the frailer somnambulists such as Bori and Sutherland.

Similarly I must confess to finding the 'plain song' school more satisfying in this aria than its more creative sisters. At Covent Garden Joan Sutherland has sung it with the utmost wealth of 'expression' as well as lovely tone and superb ornamentation, and all the time I have had in mind as something infinitely desirable the plainer singing of Toti dal Monte—who is not usually a favourite of mine. But in dal Monte's record you have a firm line, which though not insensitive is kept at fairly even volume. The melody emerges with more continuity, and the flow and balance of phrases carry the beauty without any persuasion of colouring or inflection. Dal Monte's voice is at its best in the middle register to which this aria is largely confined, and here it projects with sweetness and definition. A hardness appears above G, and in that respect Mirella Freni is preferable. This young singer has some of the same Italianate point to the tone and her voice is still in its first bloom. She also conveys some of the aria's elegiac wistfulness. If a warmer quality is wanted, however, it is supplied by the remaining singer among the present six—Margharita Carosio. This is a touching performance, though still quite 'plain'; and for many her rounder, gentler tone may seem just the instrument through which the warmth of the music should speak. Nevertheless, repeating the comparisons, with dal Monte so to speak sandwiched, her greater firmness makes Carosio seem just a trifle woolly and fluttery, and her greater directness makes Freni seem fussy. For, to return to the original point, Freni veers towards the 'expressive' school. Her singing is perhaps too careful, and her comings and goings, though most delicate and musical, still fuss the melody about. Once one has acquired the taste for a pure, uninflected line in 'Ah non credea', even this much cosseting of the lyric oversweetens and cloys. It is perhaps odd to find dal Monte appeal in so austere a fashion, yet it is to her gentle, unfussy firmness that I personally return for this music.

5. *TRAVIATA (Act I)—Ah! fors' è lui.*

(The records: Melba 03017 + 03026 on ORL 208; Tetrazzini DB 531; Galli-Curci DB 257 and DA 216; Catley C 3358; Sutherland LXT 5617; de los Angeles ALP 1780).

This is, of course, one of the greatest soliloquies in Italian opera and the performances chosen here are some of the finest and most famous of all vocal recordings. To discuss either the music or the records at all fully would not be within the scope of a short critique, and in fact I am including them in this series for only one reason. Of the sopranos involved, five are among the greatest singers of the century and are household names all over the world. The sixth is little known outside her own country, and there liked well enough but not regarded as being among 'the great of all time' or anything of that sort: and her *recording* is, in my judgment, *marginally* the best. I use the italics because this is a claim that may look cranky or perverse, and I certainly wouldn't want to overstate it. I never heard Miss Catley in the flesh and am quite ready to believe that on the stage of Covent Garden the other singers might sound incomparably more impressive. Moreover, I am not denying for a moment the various outstanding merits of the other performances: but can only repeat the judgment that if I had to choose a *recording* that did full justice to the score, this is the one I should go for.

Let us listen to the records in chronological order. Melba's 1904 version is beautifully vocalised: the heavenly clarity and definition, the superb precision of the scales and that exciting projection of voice leave little to be desired. Just occasionally an untidy interval upsets the perfection, just occasionally she neglects to give the composer what he wanted ('godea sovente', for instance, should have the same kind of rests as the opening phrase), and, more important, the emotions—the hopefulness and growing happiness of 'Ah! fors' è lui'—are only barely suggested. Tetrazzini, on the other hand, is surprisingly dramatic: 'e nuova febbre accese' really speaks of a fever, 'gioire' has superb determination. And, of course, much of the singing is very brilliant. But it's far and away the most faulty of these records. She is unaccountably slipshod over details in the early phrases; again when Verdi marks ppp for 'destando mi' he means *some* notice to be taken. Her 'Sempre libera' is breathlessly fast, and it is impossible to get everything in. She is also choppy in her breathing towards the end—though we don't get anything like the deficiencies mentioned by W. J. Henderson in his famous critique of her Manhattan debut. Galli-Curci is far more scrupulous and sings with unfailing beauty of tone. There are many individual beauties (her diminuendo on the first 'croce' for instance, and some of her echo effects). Her florid work is splendid and so is the high E flat at the end, held absolutely steadily for nearly ten seconds. She isn't able, however, to suggest the depth and subtlety of these quickly changing emotions, and the 'E strano' recit is relatively inexpressive.

Now we come to Gwen Catley's war-time plum label—in English. The first impression is of a rather small tone but it is so finely modulated as to sound ample and effective at a forte. The intelligence is immediately apparent, and the tenderness and rather desperate unhappiness of the character are convincing and vivid. She employs a most beautiful soft tone for the opening of the aria, and those difficult high A flats are exquisitely floated. There is plenty of authority, and the semi-staccatos of 'misterioso' are exactly right. Firmness and warmth in the 'Ah quell'amor' and a perfect performance of the tricky cadenza as written are further distinctions. In the next recit, there is sensitive word-shading ('lonely, by all abandoned') which also seconds the rhythmic impetus of the music. And the coloratura is brilliant—every semiquaver in place with no slowing down to accommodate, and a lovely dolce in the difficult place marked (including a pianissimo top D flat). 'Sempre Libera' is taken at a sane pace, so that all the triplets and trills can register. She leads in to the melody with effective emphasis and in the last pages gets everything in exactly as written. No other singer in my knowledge has done this. Readers will remember the rising scales which take the singer from the low E flat to the high A flat and later up to the high C. Now each of these notes is marked staccato, and Catley is the only singer I know who observes this. The effect is delightful, each note as precise and firm as an evenly spaced row of little pin-pricks. Often it is such points of detail and accomplishment that distinguish the great singer from the good; but here it is the good singer who distinguishes herself among the great.

And there is no doubt in my mind that Sutherland is of that company. In many ways her singing is heavenly, as when I have heard it in the opera house. All the same, coming after Catley and before los Angeles, her tone sounds surprisingly less well-defined. Perhaps the infirm sounds of some of the earlier part are meant to characterise her Violetta; certainly there is enough genuine pathos without this rather frail colouring. At least the high florid work that follows has nothing infirm about it, and there is a glorious shine and warmth to the voice. With greater richness and a firmer line, de los Angeles completes the series giving a wonderful performance not only in a passage like 'Ah quell' amor' where one would expect it, but in the runs and high notes of 'Sempre libera' where perhaps one would not. Occasionally the high tessitura worries (those difficult A flats, for example, early on in 'Ah!fors' è lui') and she cannot command a dolce on the 'gioir's. But generally it is an outstanding performance even among the records of this most well-loved singer of the present time.

So let us pay grateful homage to all these great ladies of the lyric stage: not forgetting also to have a look in the second-hand shop for that war-time plum label which will, I believe, give us just slightly better Verdi than any of them.

6. *TRAVIATA (Act II)—Dei miei bollenti spiriti.*

(The records: de Lucia 052129 on T314; Zenatello 92206 EB 50; McCormack DB 631; Gigli DB 1222; Crooks EJS-170; di Stefano 33CX 1370).

I suppose most collectors could readily make a list of favourite un-recorded or unexperienced records; my own would include the 'Dei miei bollenti' by Schipa. It is that sort of grace and personal charm that the aria requires, a cross between the vocal elegance of McCormack's record and the pliant liveliness of Gigli's. Certainly it is a far cry from that imagined perfection to the all too solid reality of di Stefano and Zenatello. Zenatello has always been something of a mystery to me: the usefulness of a good, strong tenor in the opera house is obvious enough, but how people can cherish such performances as this on record is a puzzle, for the tone is so often coarse-grained and the interpretations rarely seem to afford insight or musical pleasure. In this aria he is admittedly not entirely on home ground, but he recorded it twice and in the Fonotipia with some little responsive-ness. Occasionally he moderates the tone, but the singing is charmless and cast in an inappropriately heroic mould. The very open vowels nag too, as I find they do with di Stefano. The modern tenor does at least convey some eagerness, and he is alive rhythmically. But the lack of refinement is again fatal to success here. Listen to the recit, for instance: the ungainly 'lifts' to the higher notes, the unevenness of 'qui presso a lei', the loud assault on the phrase, the aspirates, the sketchy turn in 'passato'. From these versions it is a pleasure to turn to Richard Crooks, recorded at the Metropolitan in 1939. Here is a round, warm tone instead of the aggressive thrusting sound both Italians produce, and how much more graceful and firm he is at the 'passato'. In the air he sings with liveliness, only to mar it with one detail—his distortion of vowel sound on the high A flats. He opens them to produce a rounder and more secure tone but the sound is so unlike the pronunciation of the same word ('vivo') which we hear several times pronounced normally that it attracts attention to itself and spoils the climax of the aria. A feeling for that climax is one of the distinctions of the de Lucia, but this is in any case a marvellous piece of singing and brings our listening on to a different plane. Here we have someone who can do wonderful things with the voice—things that I suppose he would never be allowed to do today. Yet this art, free as it is in its handling of the score, does in fact *serve* the music, so that although Verdi has given no such directions, de Lucia's fine spinning-out of the climax sustains the moment as a magical, precious thing—holding it out to us as vividly and tenuously as the young man holds up his new-found happiness before his own eyes. This is no mere vocal exhibitionism, for de Lucia's style is actually more 'inner' than any of the others: I mean that at the opening of the solo we feel ourselves listening to a soliloquy, sung here with rapt tenderness that takes one close to the singer as a dramatic character. There are innumerable places where we could catch de Lucia out if we believe in absolute fidelity to the score: but this record seems to provide a good example of those rare instances of inspired deviation which in fact *add* a delight. Still, for a more conventional yet masterly performance, there is McCormack. And what a blessing *his* evenness and elegance are to ears pummelled by the Zenatellos et al. The voice is at its most beautiful and the interpretation is not without some urgency and ardour. But there is still something in the aria that remains uncaptured and which is present, I think, in the Gigli. Again there *are* vocal short-comings, some aspirates for instance. But the voice is almost incredibly lovely and the whole immersion of the man in the music and situation is rare and delightful. Gigli seems brimful of Alfredo's enthusiasm and wonder: 'vedea schiava ciascun di sua bellezza' is done almost with an appreciative chuckle, and the aria has a kind of smiling glow cast over it. More than this he captures the rhythmic *buoyancy* of the music, the lightness of spirit that Verdi's markings are clearly meant to suggest. He is superbly in the spirit of the thing, for instance, at the second 'dal dì che disse' floating joyously in the new life he is describing. Gigli's buoyancy and McCormack's purity: if they could be combined. Sir Compton Mackenzie tells how he sat with McCormack at Covent Garden during a performance of *Traviata* with Gigli as Alfredo. When it came to this aria, McCormack, dissatisfied with the way things were going, sang very lightly to his neighbour and the people began to shush. So one man, at least, has heard the desired combination: o lui felice.

7. *TRAVIATA (Act II) — Di Provenza.*

(The records: Battistini DB 201; Danise 50007; de Luca DB 1340; Gobbi 33 CX 1370; Merrill RB 16029; Sereni ALP 1781).

This *is* a fine aria, and yet . . . And yet, for example, it takes more than Giuseppe Danise's sturdy singing to convince one of it. The rich, even tones gladden the ear, until ungratefully the ear finds itself responding only dully, for so much evenness lies heavy on the music. The song settles too cosily into the restful key from which it scarcely modulates, the accompaniment doodles along and the facile harmonies of the introduction seem to sum up the whole stodgy idiom. Let us listen to it again, with Robert Merrill to show the way. He too has a fine, warm voice, a natural, unforced production and a good legato. He also introduces some variety (e.g., a pleasant soft tone on the fourth phrase and again on the eighth). Just occasionally he reminds us that this is not a song without words; 'ch'ivi gioja a te brillò' suggests joy, and 'se in me speme non falli' a quiet, unsure hope. But if we now look at the score it quickly becomes apparent that Verdi had in mind a performance very unlike that by Danise, while the more expressive Merrill still does not produce anything like the variety of tone and manner for which he asked. The Germont of the recent HMV set does do this. He is Mario Sereni, a baritone with some character and style, not perhaps all that powerful and yet making an effect by the well-judged gradation of volume. He has a gentle, more persuasive way with the music, which does not, however, put it to sleep, for Verdi has often marked one phrase 'dolce' with the next 'marcato' and Sereni generally speaking obeys his suggestions. But for one flaw his legato is fine; Merrill, by comparison, is rather more choppy in his treatment of the words. The flaw is a serious one, unfortunately, for he aspirates the grace-notes and thus spoils half his phrases. He forces the last note too: and indeed he is not yet a master-singer. So we play de Luca. What a world of difference there is after all. It is true that not every direction is observed and obeyed, and it is also noticeable that the singer, then in the fifties, had not the steadiness of earlier days. But the tone, beautifully round and gentle at the opening, glows into a resonant vitality warming the verses into a kind of life they have not known in the performances thus far. De Luca's rounding off of the first verse is justly famous, but there are many individual beauties and over all a wonderful feeling not only for the phrases but for the shape of the verse: the unity over all the variety. Nor is the performance undramatic, for the gentle portamenti of the second verse carry a pathos that is always dignified and restrained, speaking through the music but never disturbing it. Yet, appreciating all this in de Luca, I still find Gobbi's performance so vivid as almost to make me think that nobody had really entered into this music before him. Like Sereni, he is very tender; but with much greater eloquence the aria makes its impression as an *appeal*. He is less dignified and patrician than de Luca, but his colouring belongs more to the frank sentiment of the words: 'il tuo vecchio genitor tu non sai quanto soffri'. He can even make one realise there is some horror in 'il suo tetto si coprì di squalore, di squalor' and that the easy-going D flat major tune has reserves of deep feeling within it. He is not, it is true, a perfect vocalist: like Sereni he aspirates the grace-notes, and unlike him he makes a rather dry, unresonant, even slightly coarse sound on high notes. But the voice has a character and beauty of its own and the dramatic imagination is incomparable. Or almost. The challenge to that word 'incomparable' comes from a possibly unexpected quarter. Battistini and Gobbi might seem to be poles apart, as in many ways they are, but Battistini is the other singer in these comparisons who really devotes an imaginative interpretative art to this piece. He too appears to have observed that Verdi was at pains in his directions to work against a pure 'bel canto'. We generally think of the aria as a good example of music which requires just that smooth, even, instrumental warmth that de Luca so pre-eminently had. Yet the score is full of staccato dots and sforzandos. It demands a big dynamic range from pp to forte 'con forza', and it is constantly alternating the directions 'dolce' and 'marcato'. Battistini's performance is quite unlike de Luca's in this respect, achieving a supple and subtle expressiveness; and of course it is more accomplished than Gobbi in vocal grace (the grace-notes themselves, for instance, are exquisitely of the old school). He has deficiencies too: the woolly low notes and the forcing of an additional high note. And perhaps also that grandiloquent flourish that is often so exciting a feature becomes slightly out of place here. But anyway singing is a very personal thing and when all is listened to and discussed I have to admit to allegiances which are not radically disturbed. For I know that personally I still regard both Gobbi and Battistini as *excursions*, exciting, illuminating and on no account to be missed; but home-ground is elsewhere, and it's de Luca for me.

8.   *WALKÜRE (Act III)—Wotan's Farewell.*

(The records: Van Rooy 2-2685 on private dubbing; Kipnis D.1225; Schorr D 1332—3; Edelmann LXT 5390; Frantz ALP 1161; London LDS 6706).

It is probably in this comparison that the division into two periods is most clear-cut: the three early singers heard here are firm and even, the three modern ones unsteady and often ungainly. If we added Hans Hotter, the most repected of post-war Wagnerians, I doubt whether the picture would be much changed, for though Hotter has magnificent presence in a stage performance and a deep feeling for the music, his big rich voice has also a wide slow beat which recording does nothing to diminish. The modern Wotans of the present comparison are Edelmann, Frantz and London, their conductors being, respectively, Solti, Furtwängler and Leinsdorf. All these singers lack the firm tone of their predecessors; in fact so general is this affliction in Wagnerian performances that we come to expect it as part of the show (did the reviewers in 'The Gramophone' find it unusual enough to comment on, I wonder?). But a few bars of Schorr or Kipnis are all that is needed to show just what inferior sounds we are accepting. If anybody's ears don't register the difference he might try a few notes of each singer at a reduced turntable speed. Play Schorr (transferred to LP) at 16 r.p.m. and one hears a very clear and surprisingly large vibrato; surprising, that is, until one plays Edelmann whose fluctuation is enormous by comparison. Moreover Schorr's is quite even, while with each of the modern singers the variation is irregular, often growing to a desperately wide flap as the note goes on. Return to 33, and you hear Schorr's vibration as the natural resonance of a healthy voice, and recognise afresh the unsteadiness in the others which makes the comparison so striking. This is only a beginning, however. Let us hear the moderns in the tender middle section of the farewell: 'Der Augen leuchtendes Paar'. That opening phrase can be a wonderful moment in the opera, but how disappointingly distorted its beauty is in the oddly unsteady production of George London, the vowels emerging as it were sideways and a kind of flattened tone being used. Edelmann lightens his massive voice but only to produce something of a charmless croon: he eases himself into notes and only occasionally achieves the evenness of a genuine legato. Then Frantz, whose tone is full enough to remind one a little of Kipnis; but what a contrast when one comes to play them side by side. Kipnis is so firm and smooth and so elegant. There are two beautifully turned grace-notes, for instance, which Frantz simply leaves out (Frantz is also very loose in his time in the opening phrases). After this it seems almost unfair to play Schorr again, for the beauty of his voice, the velvety evenness, the controlled resonant softness of it, are like a singing lesson. Moreover, so fine is the sheer production that one tends to overlook the suppleness and imagination of his reading— and indeed it is not of the kind that draws attention to itself by the modern singer's devices of flattening to colour darkly or banging unmusically on a consonant to secure emphasis. All the tender sadness and pride of the passage is expressed *through* the music and nothing is felt to be overlaid *on* it. One would, it is true, like broader phrasing, more as Kipnis and some of the moderns have to offer. But generally this is a superb performance, from the gentle farewell to the powerful invocation of Loge. Schorr has also a dignity of timbre and style that contrast with the all too human Wotans of LP. Edelmann particularly is far too plebeian (despite his name): one can hear Leporello perhaps or Rocco in his tones, and, if this is not unkind, the sound would not come amiss from within the Dragon (listen, for instance, to what he does with 'Noch Meth beim Mahl mir reichen' and then compare Schorr's aristocratic yet warm style in the same phrase). Again, none of these modern singers manages to provide those moments of illumination which the memory can retain and cherish. Let us be fair, Frantz does capture the loving exaltation of the first section, and his almost whispered 'So küsst er die Gottheit von dir' remains in the mind after the record has stopped playing. But who can match the fine relish of Kipnis in 'der lachende Lust meines Auges' or the generous warmth of Schorr in 'Dem glänze sein Stern'. Or, to mention the remaining record at last, can any of them, perhaps even Schorr and Kipnis included, come up to the vigour and sonority of van Rooy, or give us anything as boldly beautiful as his last phrase, that memorably softened and spread-out 'der freier als ich, der Gott'? To that phrase we can trace back a grand tradition of lyricism and finesse in Wagnerian singing; let us hope it will not lapse for much longer.

9. *OTELLO (Act III)—Era la Notte.*

(The records: Maurel 2-32814 on AJK 105 or 39042 on ORE 202; Sammarco on ELP 0-470; Franci DB 1154; Tibbett DB 5790; Protti LXT 5010; Gobbi LDS 6155).

Should the singer take his score seriously? That sounds like one of those silly Latin non-questions expecting the answer yes, but it is prompted by the fact that the general *practice* seems to imply an answer something like 'Well, he's got to get the notes right of course, but he shouldn't be too score-bound'. Where the score in question is *Otello* this seems something of a presumption.

'Era la Notte' is, of course, a great piece for the singer-actor, the sort of baritone its creator, Maurel, appears to have been or, in our day, Tito Gobbi. It was in fact one of the artistic triumphs of Maurel's career: Henderson has left a vivid account of its impact in the theatre, and Gatti-Casazza also paid it special tribute. But the records (played here on Bel-cantodisc and Olympus transfers, and not differing much in style) offer curious commentary on this, for it is difficult to hear Iago in them. Someone to whom the record and the aria were new might hear a dignified gentleman with a pleasing voice singing a rather indeterminate song with some soft bits on one note in it. The same listener confronted with Gobbi or Tibbett would certainly know that the singer was up to something nasty. Now possibly this is a subtlety of Maurel's art, that the listener should quite see how plausible Iago was and how understandable it is Otello should have been taken in by him. But such an explanation doesn't really accord with the impression of the *kind* of performance left by Henderson, any more than the record itself does. Henderson tells of 'the shimmering variety of vocal colour and the far reaching eloquence of his interpretation', the narrative being 'whispered sotto voce into the ear of the writhing Otello'. No, it is more likely that by 1903 (or 1905) it had, for Maurel, become a concert piece and that the recording room was too remote from the opera house for him to feel himself into the drama. What we have on record is a good piece of singing, the piano passages being particularly fine; but it isn't the Iago we understand Maurel to have been. There is no sense of a whispering intimacy, and the directions explicitly ask for it. Nor is there any real sensitivity to the flow of the music. The first sentence, for instance, is chopped into three: the score marks it as a single phrase and in spite of Maurel's age I'm sure he didn't need the two breaths. If a singer does this at all noticeably, the dream-like sway of the 6-8 is lost and you have a rather dull and square effect. But then, as I have said, hardly any singer really goes on the assumption that the markings in the score mean what they say.

German and English musicians have no doubt often raised their eye-brows at the row of six ps (pppppp) at 'seguia più vago', but Verdi would have needed six more to impress many of his compatriots. Sammarco, for instance, in a generally well-sung performance, produces a pretty solid mezzo-forte here, and so does Franci. Sammarco goes to some trouble (drawing a prefatory breath that the veteran Maurel didn't require) to elide 'vegliamo' and 'l'estasi del ciel' as the score marks. But Franci doesn't do that either. Nor does the unsteady and ungainly Aldo Protti whose conductor, Karajan, might have persuaded him into trying it. It is interesting—and to a collector of old records rather a satisfaction—to observe that here the modern singers (with their famous conductors) are no more scrupulous about the score than their predecessors. Protti, for instance, does not even attempt a sotto voce at 'il rio destino'—nor, somewhat to one's surprise, does Gobbi.

If these were all isolated cases it would be niggling criticism to bring them up, but in fact the criticisms have only picked a few instances out of many possible ones where the singer has not concerned himself closely enough with Verdi. Let us look at it another way and see what becomes of the music when somebody *does* take the score markings seriously, as more often than not Tibbett does. We have, for a start, a real sense of a whispered confidence, something which corresponds vocally to the direction 'avvicin-andosi molto ad Otello e sotto voce'. When it comes to Cassio's words they are vividly the drowsy uncanny sounds of a man talking in sleep—and this by obeying not merely the 'sotto voce' but also the instruction 'parlate'. At 'ei disse poscia' we have the sense of Iago timing the body-blow he will deliver with the next sentence—and this too is done by *obeying an instruction* ('parlando'). But there is much more to Tibbett's performance than this— much more, that is, to Verdi's music. Several notes are marked in the score with emphatic arrows, some pointing one way, some another (I don't know what the difference is intended to be). Two occur in the first sentence 'Era la notTE Cassio dormiA'. When these are observed there is a quite special effect—we begin to hear the music as a kind of heavy, sleepy breathing, opening and closing from the repose of the common chord, sagging heavily in its return to that repose. And then again as the dream is over, Verdi has placed arrows over the weak beats of the bar: 'E ALlorA IL sogno'. The effect is, for one thing, to make much more interesting music. Instead of a regular 6-8, the rhythm now goes: 121121123123 etc., (counting 1 as a strong beat, and counting the two full bars with those words in them). It is also very subtly pictorial—the effect of the slump on those beats is a return to the sagging sleepiness of the opening. Now all of this Tibbett has realised; or at least he conveys it. It is done essentially by taking the score seriously and it is not conveyed by any other singer I have heard. Gobbi doesn't do it, though he is far nearer than the others to achieving 'that shimmering variety of tone colour' that Henderson heard in Maurel. Apart from Tibbett, that is, whose record seems to me a very fine one indeed. I know his stage performances in this part were considered to be rather theatrical and perhaps some listeners may find the insinuating character overplayed even on the record. His Italian pronunciation too has been found wanting, but that rather nasal quality of vowels is not inappro-priate to Iago. Personally I find the vividness incomparable and the sheer singing also wonderful (that sustained high E, for instance, beautifully floated and the phrase taken all in one—also the tone range, from the mezza voce of the narrative to the resonant fullness of 'in cieco letargo sì muto'). Nor is he 'score-bound'; indeed he is far more imaginative than the others (e.g. the poison of his 'che al Moro tì donò'). But this score is so fully marked that a singing-machine which obeyed all Verdi's instruc-tions would stand a better chance of bringing the aria to its full life than a singer who contents himself, as most do, with 'the notes' and a few sotto voces here and there.

10. *PAGLIACCI*—*No, Pagliaccio non son.*

(The records: Paoli DB 469 on private dubbing; Caruso DB 111; Martinelli DB 1139; Gigli DB 2307; Hislop DA 1062; Corelli SAX 2400).

Few and far between, but distinct highlights in one's musical experience, are those records that establish themselves as literally incomparable performances. The singer has so worked himself into the song, the pianist into the sonata, that for one listener at least, he has virtually *become* it. That listener may then preserve the utmost honesty and responsiveness when he hears other performances of the work, but it is unlikely he will be moved by the most excellent of them into a reaction that goes further than 'yes . . . but . . .' So it is, I find, with Martinelli's 'No Pagliaccio' of 1927. Partly this is due to the very individual quality of voice—its firm incisiveness and tension, perhaps, which make it a fitting vehicle. Partly also the famous breath control, which can take that first long phrase of the cantabile section not merely in one (several singers do that) but at a very slow speed and with astonishingly fine effect. More than that, it is some quality of sensibility, an imagination peculiarly responsive to the music and situation, able indeed to raise it to heights of tragic dignity that of itself it rarely attains. The passage before the aria proper is particularly vivid: 'vo il nome' coloured with the distortion of ferocity yet perfectly vocalised, the menacing sway of the music brought to its climax in 'o turpe donna' where the singer's bitter denunciation towers over the woman who tries to restrain him. Restraint is a key word here, for Canio's appeal is partly an exercise of restraint and to do it justice the singer must realise this. It is in this moment, rather than in the self-pitying 'Ridi Pagliaccio', that the sufferer achieves his tragic status. So Martinelli indulges in no gulps, sobs or shouts. The aria itself is given with firm fidelity to the score, letting the orchestra express the tempest of the soul with its turbulent dotted rhythms and menacing intervals. If the singer is feeling all this deeply and sensitively, the tension of restraint will emerge through the *colouring* of the voice and here again Martinelli is incomparable—the thinning of tone at the second 'No Pagliaccio' for instance, and the tensing for the just-contained misery of 'ed un amor ch'era febbre e follia'. That phrase brings to an end the first half of the aria, and with a sense of climax that is exactly right Martinelli pulls back the time here, as at the first climax of the piece he achieves such intensity as to make the 'maladetta' an overwhelming recrimination. In the second half Leoncavallo has introduced what is at first a complete change of mood. He marks it 'cantabile espressivo' and his metronome speed is *half* that of the previous section. 'Legato molto' he writes for the orchestra and Martinelli's delivery of the long phrase is certainly a miracle of breadth and smoothness. Moreover, the expressive intensity never lapses, so that we have the same towering authority, as the high note of 'e fidente credeva' is joined to the next phrase. He is sensitive also to the development of the music back towards the more declamatory manner of the opening, and broadening for the 'va, non merti il mio duol' he brings the performance to its fine climax, achieving a massive authority in the last phrase.

There is more one could say—I think it is a musically analysable point, for example, that the small departures from the letter of the score in the opening of the record are in fact deeply in the spirit of it. But enough has been said to illustrate the richness of this performance. With the others it is largely a matter of noting that they have very little that corresponds to it. Caruso's record is of course magnificent because he is Caruso: the voice is splendid beyond words and the style is both dignified and passionate. But the sensibility is an altogether simpler thing here—or rather, it is less *complete*. The emotion is a generalised one, not located in the ever-changing responsiveness that makes Martinelli's performance so richly varied in its range. Gigli makes a good object lesson in comparison (this is the recording from the complete opera), for he breaks phrases and secures emphasis largely by shouts and sobs. Again the voice is magnificent and in one phrase—'ma il vizio alberga sol'—there is some vividly scornful colouring. Hislop too has fine moments, spitting out 'o turpe donna' with conviction. But generally the drama is crudely enacted and the voice has not the bite which the music needs. About Paoli it is hard to say anything good at all, so wobbly and barn-storming is he. The modern singer Franco Corelli is, however, a different matter. Here is a superb voice and, in this recording at least, a live passionate temperament and conscientious musicianship. It is a very satisfying performance. Or it would be if the best did not tend to eclipse the good.

11. *TOSCA (Act II)—Vissi d'arte.*

(The records: Destinn 2-053053; Rethberg Bruns 50065 on A115; Jeritza DA 972; Muzio LB 40; Stella ALP 1428; Price SB 6505).

It would be hard to miss the beauty of Rethberg's recording but easy to overlook its distinction. It has that kind of rightness, musically at any rate, that draws no attention to itself. How, one feels, could it go otherwise? But it can and usually does, as the playing of twenty performances was, I found, quite sufficient to demonstrate. The preservation of a pure line, free also from vibrato, wobble or flutter, seems to be as rare in this music as the preservation of Puccini's phrasing—and Rethberg is the only one of my twenty sopranos to achieve both. A more typical performance is Antonietta Stella's. It is by no means ineffective, but the natural endowment of a warm, strong voice, and a feeling for the 'grande sentimento' of the piece need a stronger discipline than any shown here: the tone spreads and the phrases are broken again and again. This is not a malady peculiar to our own times. Play Jeritza, the most famous of inter-war Toscas, and there is hardly more to admire. Her tone may be steadier but it has an unfocused region in the lower half of the stave, which is important in this music. Again, she may be less strident in the first high passage ('quante miserie'), but she is neither as firm (and there are marcato marks) nor as clean. She concerns herself not at all with the several grace-notes, breathes where she thinks she will, and is as inexpressive as it is possible to be in the climax and last bars (the only one of these singers to make no real diminuendo on the notes following the high B flat). The 'Tosca prostrata' won a great following with her stage performances but this little record is a dull memento of those enchanted evenings, for the lack of musical merit is not compensated by any distinctive character or dramatic insight. This, of course, is just what does happen in the Muzio. The aria again springs to life and now brings before us vividly a passionate and distressed soul. Whatever the defects of Muzio's singing the record remains precious, because of her involvement, and because her voice and style in their maturity came to express such words of feeling. We realise, with Muzio, how this ought to be 'inner', a soliloquy, or, in the opera, a point where the tense world of public men and women, battles, causes, intrigues and celebrations, stops for a moment to admit the internal, personal world which is so grievously caught up in it all. Few performances have this 'inner' quality. I do not think, for instance, that Farrar possessed it. The pathos of her admittedly glorious singing lies in her habit of adding little sobs to the line—there are more than a dozen of them—and a true tragic depth finds a more noble means of expression than this. Apart from Muzio, I have a distant memory of the Fremstad record and a closer one of Callas, whose rapt intensity nearly makes one forget the unsteadiness. But no singer has everything, and this aria really asks for a Muzio and a Rethberg in one.

There are, of course, several sopranos who, without the pure lyricism of the one singer or the emotional creativeness of the other, have given fine performances. In inter-war years Seinemeyer, Giannini and Turner made splendid records, and their standard is carried into our own day by Leontyne Price. Here we have the grand sweep of the music, the Tosca whose soul is bold in extremity and even before God. Occasionally her vibrato becomes obtrusive, but generally it is a performance in the great tradition and for this kind of authority one has to look further back in the century to Destinn. Destinn's record is a continually astonishing one. Only a very great artist could take the music with such bold hands and not distort it: she is complete mistress of it, and the life of the music glows at such strong, independent treatment She takes it more slowly than most, spreading the phrase 'diedi fiori agli altar' to make a kind of half-way climax—as, of course, it roughly is, for the form of the solo (a, b¹, b²) places this at the end of b¹ as the great climax occurs at the end of b². When this comes, Destinn again produces a wonderfully strong effect, making a long and dramatic diminuendo on the A flat and repeating the note on the same breath before joining it to the G pianissimo. She holds the three notes a good long time, which is what Puccini wanted: he had an argument about it with Emma Eames who told him he was wrong and was asking for three climaxes instead of one. These bars are amongst the lyric-dramatic soprano's great challenges, and there are many ways of singing them (Giannini, for example, takes all three high notes in one breath). Few, however, have the boldness or the technical ability of Destinn, and few achieve quite such an effect. But what, to return to the opening bars, can one say of those portamenti, sagging heavily between the second and third notes of each phrase? This, perhaps: that she would never be allowed by conductor, critic or public to do such things if she were singing today— and neither, very probably, would she be allowed the freedom which otherwise goes to make her performance such a glorious one.

12. *ROSENKAVALIER (Act I)—Marschallin's Monologue.*

(The records: Siems 043179 on R 20; Bettendorf E 10341; Ohms CA 8108; Lehmann DB 2063; Reining LW 5336; Schwarzkopf SAX 2423).

The heat generally rises quickly beneath opera-going collars when Marschallins are being discussed. Everybody has his favourite and it seems inconceivable that some people should actually prefer another. No doubt this is because the Marschallin is a character 'in the round', which is rare in opera, and also because her nature is warm, her predicament moving and her action noble. Not every soprano with a good voice can encompass so much humanity. That, indeed, is a lesson which our times seem to be in danger of learning the wrong way round: the Marschallin with a good voice is regarded suspiciously and absence of voice points persuasively to 'intelligent artistry'. In a great Marschallin of course these things will go together: there will be intelligence, authority, warmth of feeling, beauty of voice. So it was in Lehmann; so, to my mind, it is in Schwarzkopf. But there the heat of controversy begins to glow: 'Not to be mentioned in the same breath,' 'Not right in the part at all', 'But then, you didn't *see* Lotte', 'I prefer Reining'—I have even heard *that* said. Perhaps it is time we listened to the records.

Two fine singers of contrasted vocal character are Emmy Bettendorf and Elisabeth Ohms. Bettendorf's gentle tone brings before us a woman of warmth and tenderness, while Ohms with that sumptuous, intensely dramatic voice suggests a tragic nobility. With both, however, the face behind the record is unchanging. Where Bettendorf quite nimbly voices the notes and words of the Marschallin's little imitation ('Do you see? There goes the old Princess Resi'), it is without altering the face; or when at 'die gleiche bin', Strauss marks 'heiter bewegt' Ohms doesn't really cheer up with any vividness. Mobility, or a responsiveness always alive and develop-ing, is one of the essential attributes here.

The creator, Siems, had it. Her reminiscence is charming and cheerful. 'Frisch aus dem Kloster' she came to an arranged marriage and Siems' own lightness suggests what a charmer and an innocent she must have been. As she approaches the deep waters of the mystery, a seriousness comes into the tone, in turn to be lightened so that 'da liegt der ganze Unterschied' floats reflectively and without any bitterness in the clear 18th century air. So there is no lack of characterisation in Siems' record, and certainly none of vocal finesse (how beautifully, for example, the 'kleine Resi' is held up before our charmed eyes). Two little faults prevent one saying 'perfect': she is sometimes choppy with words in the phrases, and sometimes doesn't allow a note its full value.

It is a pity that we do not have Siems in what is virtually the second part of the monologue, the passage starting 'Oh sei Er gut, Quinquin' and continuing into 'Die Zeit, die ist ein sonderbar Ding' (or what one of the old catalogues used to call 'The March of Time'). These are the pages that take us into the Marschallin's soul—more deeply, I think, than in the wistful, lightly shrugged-off musings of the earlier solo. In them Ohms comes much more into her own with some compelling, richly dramatic singing. And here is another characteristic of the great Marschallin, an authority, and nobility of feeling that must express itself in the timbre. It is something that, to my ears, never begins to be heard in Maria Reining's recording. In 'Die Zeit' she has only a sort of girlish clarity; I can feel no depth, imagination or warmth, and without these things there is no Marschallin, only a Sophie without the high tessitura.

One passage may serve to illustrate: 'Manchmal steh ich auf mitten in der Nacht und lass die Uhren alle, alle stehn'. Ohms is beautifully hushed, Lehmann allows a profound stillness to settle at 'alle stehn', Schwarzkopf tells the confidence with the deep feeling of a woman and some of the pathos of the girl locked away inside her. Reining does nothing. However, it is a performance that has been much admired, the shallow and unsteady tone being apparently compensated for by a certain unmannered rightness. When the term 'unmannered' is introduced in this context it is usually an oblique way of passing adverse comment on Schwarzkopf. For everyone knows that though Schwarzkopf (as far as this is true of anyone) never sings out of tune, is never inaccurate, has a lovely voice and a virtually flawless technique, has a large repertoire and is a conscientious and imaginative interpreter, is also a beautiful woman and presents a vivid personality— nevertheless it is generally reckoned a safe critical comment to say 'Oh she's so mannered' or 'She's not so mannered as she was' according to whim. The glory of this criticism is that it can never be checked because the dividing line between a personal style and a mannered one is very thin and depends very much on intuition; and if people decide that that is the way they feel it to be, then all the subtleties and beauties of a performance are somehow effectively negatived by that one word. The beauties of Schwarzkopf's Marschallin are innumerable: on every page something is brought to a life we have not known of before. 'Da geht er hin, der aufgeblasne, schlechte Kerl': Ernest Newman wrote an article on the untranslatableness of the line. With Schwarzkopf there is no need for a translation, so vividly does she characterise. 'Und kriegt des hübsche, jünge Ding und einen Pinkel Geld dazu': the satirical sharpness is caught in the slightly staccato style. 'Das alles ist geheim, so viel geheim': the whispered mystery is then shrugged-off with a regretful stoicism and the passage rounded off with a light sigh. 'Alles zergeht wie Dunst und Traum': the transitoriness of life is sung of with the serene purity of Brahms' Requiem. 'Wie man nichts packen kann': for once the earnestness is tragic and unrestrained. 'Oh, Quinquin': the warmth is of a loving woman speaking with heart and soul. And so one could go on. As yet, the performance has not generally been placed by critics and others amongst the great of the century: with Lehmann's, for instance, or with Chaliapin's Boris, or Gobbi's Boccanegra. But 'die Zeit, die ist ein sonderbar Ding', and perhaps it will tell.

Part II: From Gerhardt to Fischer-Dieskau   Eight Lieder

13. *SCHUBERT—Gretchen am Spinnrade*

> The records: Eames and unnamed pianist 88367 on R 29; Gadski and Frank La Forge 88111; Giannini and Michael Raucheisen DB 1265; Ferrier and Phyllis Spurr K 1632; Schwarzkopf and Edwin Fischer CX 1040; Della Casa and Karl Hudez LXT 5258.

By one of time's little ironies, the chalk-and-cheese of a past age becomes the two-peas-in-a-pod of the present. Or (to translate these homely mysteries), an Emma Eames and a Johanna Gadski can now sound remarkably alike. Their differences, plain as could be to their contemporaries, are now less apparent than their affinities, and a listener unpractised in distinguishing one pre-electrical soprano from another, might even think that these two Gretchens were one. He would note a more impetuous quality in Gadski's recording and, as recorded, a more evenly produced voice in Eames', but what might impress him most is the common depth and frankness of emotion and the common assumption that a principal means of conveying this is the use of a bold and free downward portamento. Nowhere in the other records do you hear a portamento at all: this is the feature of style in singing which has changed most over the years since recording began.

In the present records by Eames and Gadski its use is effective and readily justifiable. The words 'finde' and 'nimmer' in the refrain are given a heavily tragic inflection by these means. It is rather like the throb in an actor's voice as he recites Shakespeare or Racine: this too can be pure 'ham', and like the singer's portamento it is now unfashionable. But it may also be natural and genuinely expressive within that world of heightened emotions which the work of art inhabits. I think this is true of these early Gretchens: they are feeling the song, and the emotion they display is neither excessive nor inappropriate in kind. An example of bad portamento in Lieder singing will be given in the section on *Ich grolle nicht*: the stoical words and the decisive movement of the music alike forbid. *Gretchen am Spinnrade* is quite different, and Eames in particular achieves a haunting eloquence of lamentation which is not present in any of the later versions.

In two of these, the emotional expression is not really eloquent enough. Kathleen Ferrier's voice is at its most beautiful, and for the first half of the song that is sufficient. Sadness is present in tone-colour and in a kind of stillness that seems to attend it. But as the feeling mounts, and the girl, to her own distress, is betrayed by the passionate obsessiveness of her thoughts (which *will* keep turning towards this man), so the singer must abandon stillness and restraints. Ferrier does not project herself: the singing remains beautiful but the fiercer emotional intensity of the song is lacking. She is possibly restricted a little by the low key (A minor) which she uses. The song is really for sopranos: Gerhardt, strong though her projection was, does not sound right for it. Nor do all sopranos. Dusolina Giannini, for instance, is not a very apt Gretchen, either in style or vocal timbre: a Santuzza rather, though the two women at any rate have something in common. Giannini is good in the verse where Faust's 'noble gait' and 'fine stature' are recalled. The enthusiasm is almost too vivid. At 'seines Augen Gewalt' it is as though the spinning-wheel is bearing her away in imagination as, for a moment, the six-eight takes wings and the little quaver-figure of the left hand becomes the clop-clop of a high-spirited Pegasus. Not all of the performance is as imaginative as this, but what principally limits the record's success is the unsuitability of so vigorous a style and so commanding a voice. One feels she is quite able to look after herself, and sympathy is accordingly restricted.

As if in answer to this, we find Lisa Della Casa, most beautiful and appealing, singing with what is surely just the voice of Goethe's and Schubert's Gretchen. Her tone is young and sweet, yet firmly defined and perfectly true in its placing. The pace of her performance is rather slower than the others, and its shading is always very delicate. More effectively and gradually than the others she builds up to the first climax, of 'sein Kuss' (she has noted the 'pianissimo' marking in the piano score at 'sein hoher Gang', and applied it to her own part). Everything is done very simply, and this is again part of the truthfulness of her performance. Where it does not quite meet the demands is in the final climax. Like Ferrier, she sings within definite emotional restrictions, and where the music becomes feverish the singer remains cool. It is Schwarzkopf who, perhaps with Emma Eames, comes nearest to completion in this song. As always, she has brought a strong imagination to bear, and we hear the song afresh through her. The refrain deepens as a piece of appalled, secret self-knowledge. The girl is possessed by her vision, and the words 'sein Kuss', which come as the first climax have something of the terror of this ecstatic possession. Then as she surrenders her spirit, giving full vent to the desires she knows and fights, we recognise a growing fear in the self-abandon.

There is subtlety and richness here, and with it a radiant voice. Should one, I wonder, be aware that some great secret of voice-production has been lost as one goes back to the two golden-agers: that in Schwarzkopf and Della Casa true legato has been replaced by some inferior way of singing? I must say I do not find it so. When there is a vocal unsureness it is generally in the earlier records. Gadski changes pitch during the held note on 'Kuss', for example; Eames allows the emotion to upset her tone in the voicing of the last word, 'schwer'. Moreover (but this is a different point), having sung the climax magnificently, she makes her pianist play a bar twice over before coming in for the last phrase. The conditions of pre-electrical recording did not favour perfection and both performances are generally very fine. But the two modern singers are quite as good: upholding and sometimes refining the great tradition, for all their differences of approach. These differences too, chalk and cheese to us, will pretty certainly seem small enough in a hundred years time or so, and someone digging out this book and listening to the records in his local institute of recorded sound will say 'Oh, but they are alike as six peas in a pod'.

14. *SCHUBERT—Wohin? (Die schöne Müllerin No. 2)*

The records: Sembrich and unnamed pianist from IRCC 129 on R 23; Gerhardt and unnamed accompanist DA 706; Gerhardt and Cönraad von Bos DA 1219; Schumann and Karl Alwin D 1411; Fischer-Dieskau and Gerald Moore ALP 1913; Pears and Benjamin Britten LXT 5574.

The use of portamento, illustrated by *Gretchen am Spinnrade*, is one of the main features in which style has changed over the last sixty years. Freedom in matters of tempo is another, and of this *Wohin* provides an example. Schubert wrote 'moderato' at the top of his score and that is all. The accompaniment, in a state of perpetual motion, depicts a stream which, like Tennyson's brook, goes on forever; and this, in turn, suggests that the 'moderato' should be both unchecked and unhurried. Among the present singers, both Sembrich and Fischer-Dieskau, ancient and modern in recording, allow themselves to ease the tempo at certain points. With Fischer-Dieskau, however, it is twice and very slightly, with Sembrich it is seven times and quite markedly. Dieskau's bars are 40 and 53; Sembrich's are 13, 29–30, 33, 40, 48, 52 and 71. This is fairly representative of the extent to which style has changed in this matter. Sembrich also alters several note-values: for example, the word 'immer' (bars 27 and 31) becomes dotted quaver and semi-quaver, so that the singer stays longer on the upper note. There may be a case for the use of rubato, but inaccuracies of this other sort are indefensible. The rubato itself is also more than suspect, for while Dieskau's two bars are suggested by good sense, musical and verbal, Sembrich's seven notably include those parts of the song which are most difficult to sing. *Wohin* is a difficult song, and none of these singers quite has the legato that ideally one would like to hear. But Sembrich makes particularly hard work of it, labouring the up-and-down movement of 'immer heller der Bach' (bar 33), and spreading the semi-quavers at bar 71 so as to give a pause on the high note. It is not easy to sing that bar in strict or near-strict time: to take the interval of a seventh cleanly, to sing the highest note of the song lightly and then pass on smoothly to the rest of the phrase. Fischer-Dieskau and Pears do it without fuss and the earlier singers do not. There is no question where the technical superiority lies in this instance. Sembrich's performance is not entirely unlikeable: there are moments when one hears the tone and style of a great singer. But it is a continual astonishment to me, in listening to these old singers, how they could combine the most dazzling feats of vocalism with the clumsiness or carelessness of an amateur. There are times when Sembrich seems the most brilliant soprano on records. But nobody can say she made a good record of *Wohin*.[1]

Perhaps that is why it was unissued. Sentimentally, I wish it had remained so, and that Gerhardt's early version and Schumann's had stayed in the vaults also. Schumann is a great disappointment in this: too fast, with rather a fierce edge on the tone, somewhat inaccurate and with a poor legato. Gerhardt's pre-electrical is also regrettable. But it makes an interesting comparison with the later, electrical recording which is splendid. At 78, the pre-electrical plays in A flat; slow it to G and it is certainly better, a saner pace and a sound more like Gerhardt. But there is still a tendency to hurry (bars 25 and 64, for instance), and the voice is still wobbly. Many of the dynamics are the same as in the electrical recording, but that really is a different affair altogether. It is marvellously delicate and obviously the work of a very great Lieder singer. She lightens her voice most beautifully and yet catches the deeper undertones of the song. If one wants a specific moment to point the contrast between the two records there is the difficult up-and-down of bar 33: competent but heavy in the pre-electrical, magically light in the later performance. Admirable too is her use of semi-staccato in certain phrases contrasting with the smooth flow of others. There are many examples, and for a singer the whole record is worth studying in detail. If Fischer-Dieskau seems to me to be better even than this, it is partly, I suppose, because of the younger voice and partly because of his easy, unemphatic way with the high note towards the end and the phrase in which it occurs. But it is also, and most essentially, because of a way that he has of going to the heart of a song, not simply with the general rightness of touch that Gerhardt so often had, but also with an insight which manifests itself in illuminating detail. In this song he follows the changing moods with incomparable vividness: an almost visible shrug of the shoulders at 'ich weiss nicht wie mir wurde', a little more intentness of story-telling at

[1] It may not be playing at proper speed and pitch in this transfer. Several other items in this Rococo disc are too high and too fast. A flat seems an unlikely key, and it sounds better slowed.

'hinunter und immer weiter', the frown disappearing with the return of the major key and, as it were, the return of sunlight to the fresh, clear stream. Then we come to the delicate nerve-centre of the lyric:

> Du hast mit deinem Rauschen
> Mir ganz berauscht den Sinn.
> Was sag ich denn vom Rauschen?
> Das kann kein Rauschen sein;
> Es singen wohl die Nixen
> Dort unten ihren Reih'n.

One of those faint misgivings, an apprehensiveness no heavier than a shadow and just as unsettling, comes and passes: the shadow lifts and of course there was nothing there to be troubled by after all. It was not the quietly malignant goblins, youth's intimations of mortality; it was only the water-nymphs, and the sun is out again, the mill-wheel is turning and the stream is clear as ever. Very, very lightly, with the most delicate changes of tonality and colours, composer, poet and singer create this for us. Dieskau's part in the creation involves, for instance, the 'inner' tone of 'ist das denn meine Strasse', the slightly darkened colour of 'mir ganz berauscht den Sinn', and that very slight easing of tempo at 'das kann kein Rauschen sein', which is the point where the shadow lifts and the stream flows happily in major key again. This is the kind of thing which makes Fischer-Dieskau surely the greatest of Lieder singers on records. The interpretative points are no longer too heavily underlined as they sometimes used to be. In these records of his maturity there is no 'applied' interpretation; only a very full emotional and intellectual entering of the song.

There are other modern singers who from time to time achieve this kind of completeness too. Peter Pears is often among them. But in this he does not really present any comparable distinction: there is an occasional touch of the Pears–Britten magic (the repeat of 'du hast mit deinem Rauschen' for instance), and, of course, the stream, though flowing fast, is at its clearest and brightest in Britten's playing. But Pears' tone is rather pale and unsteady, the cost of his distinctness in the quick passages is some very noticeable aspirating, and the song registers as little more than a pretty thing. Mistress and master here are Gerhardt and Fischer-Dieskau.

15. *SCHUBERT—Nacht und Träume*

The records: Culp from Od. 64009; Bettendorf with unnamed accompanist E 10399; Erb and Bruno Seidler-Winkler EG 3611; Schumann and Gerald Moore DB 3184; Seefried and Gerald Moore LB 106; Souzay and Jacqueline Bonneau LX 3154.

This is a song for dreams, after all. The mind's ear hears it clearly, perfectly, as it seems; but one turns on the gramophone, and fled is that music.

The song is generally known as one of the most difficult of all in performance; and so it must be, for none of the six apt and excellent singers in these records really do it justice. 'A perfectly calm and steady flow of beautiful tone is wanted in *Nacht und Träume*', writes Richard Capell (*Schubert's Songs* p. 209); 'not a moment's agitation or constriction, nor a misshapen syllable, can be forgiven'. Stern words. He also says, 'It cannot be too slowly sung'; and Gerald Moore, while not quite agreeing with that, for he suggests a performing time of three minutes fifteen seconds, proposes as a further condition that 'the voice does not rise above m.p. during the entire song' *(Famous Songs)*. Schubert himself left no instructions so we are at liberty to think for ourselves. As to speed, the extremes are suggested by Elisabeth Schumann, who takes less than three minutes over it, fitting *Seligkeit* in on the same side, and Gérard Souzay, whose performance lasts nearly four minutes. No doubt at all that the tranquillity, the sense of a secure motion, a kindly depth ('such a tide as moving seems asleep'), is better conveyed by the slower tempo. But Souzay, thinking for himself, has also decided that the song is in two parts, the first peaceful, the second disturbed. Perhaps that puts his conception too crudely; for his singing of the second page begins and ends with the same softness as the first. But at 'Rufen, wenn der Tag erwacht' he swells to a mezzo forte; again at 'Kehre wieder, heil'ge Nacht'; and to a fairly solid forte in the next phrase, 'O holde Nacht'. His reasons for doing so are probably that in these lines the repose and confidence of the poem are disturbed, and that so too are Schubert's harmonies. But the basic mode of the music is preserved (the lulling motion continues), and I think it follows that the basic tone of voice should also be unchanged. Souzay imposes on the song a greater dynamic range than the music requires. A subtler modulation in tone, matching but not exceeding the harmonic disturbances, can be heard in Karl Erb's recording. Here another imposition on the music arises, however. Half-way through, the speed is suddenly increased. The pianist, Bruno Seidler-Winkler, initiates this at bar 15 and the singer follows at 'Die belauschen sie mit Lust'. The interpreters have perhaps argued that the eagerness expressed here warrants a change of tempo; perhaps they felt that it was a boring bar (it certainly looks it) and that the music needed enlivening. Yet it is just at this point that the most delightful modulation (B to G major) occurs, and that a new melodic pattern is introduced. Try to underline this by pressing the pace, and the spell is broken as surely as it is by Souzay's loudness. Mr. Capell and Mr. Moore between them are reliable guides, after all.

Interpretative matters apart, the song makes fearsome demands upon the singer's technique. The long, soft phrases need perfect support and control. Julia Culp breaks the two phrases, 'Die belauschen sie mit Lust', and Souzay breathes rather obtrusively twice in 'Durch die Menschen stille, stille Brust'. Seefried manages long spans of breath and sustains the mood tenderly, but only, it seems, at the expense of her tone. Very oddly, she produces an effect of amateurishness, for the softness is infirm. The difficult first note is an example, and so again is the 'durch die Menschen' phrase quoted above. As recorded, Erb's tone is better: his firmness and definition in no way interfere with its softness. Better still is Souzay's soft singing (his is, to my ears, one of the most beautiful voices on record, and it is well suited to the song). Above all, perhaps, Bettendorf's tone comes near to the ideal. Schumann's voice by comparison is a daylight sound; or twinkling starlight maybe. Bettendorf's rounder tone has the warm glow of moonlight; her musical personality too is comfortable and easy-going, while Schumann's is full of wide-awake energy.

But Bettendorf's is not a good record, and this brings us to a further demand that the music makes—that the singer shall be accurate. And these early singers are not accurate at all. If Leo Slezak's very pleasant Polydor record had been included, it would only have reinforced this point. Meanwhile, in the present records we have Julia Culp and her accompanist who between them manage a mysterious effect of mis-timing on two occasions. Culp also gets the note-values wrong on 'die belauschen', and on the syllable 'er' of 'erwacht' she sings D sharp instead of D natural (possibly early editions of the music were defective, but I doubt it). Bettendorf misses an entire beat (bar 22) and, perhaps suspecting the mistake, comes in too loudly, so spoiling her otherwise quite lovely record. Even Schumann does not always hold the notes for their full length, though out of all this I think she probably emerges most creditably. She nourishes her phrases, feels with the words, and lifts up the heart with the shining, very personal sound of her voice: in the circumstances it seems churlish to ask for more.

Has it ever been perfectly sung? I cherish the memory of three live performances: two by Elisabeth Schumann in concerts after the war when her soft singing was still exquisite, its tone (and her art) mellower than in the thirties when the record was made; and one by Elisabeth Schwarzkopf, unbelievably in her fiftieth year, opening the programme with this most exacting of songs. These are (perhaps blessedly) unrecorded; so they have now only the reality of dreams, sharing at least a security that is hymned by the song itself.

16. *SCHUMANN—Ich grolle nicht (Dichterliebe No. 7)*

The records: Gerhardt and Arthur Nikisch 043199 on TQD 3024; Gerville-Réache and orchestra on R 14; Schorr and unnamed pianist from EW 86; Panzéra and Alfred Cortot DB 4987; Souzay and Dalton Baldwin ABL 3369; Wächter and Alfred Brendel LXT 5675.

All sorts of exotic and unlikely folk, strangers otherwise to the poet's love songs, venture forth to tackle this one. Stars of the opera house find it almost as rewarding as *Softly awakes my Heart* or Valentine's air from *Faust*. Even public school boys open their hearts to it; for I am told that late in the decadent 'twenties it flourished as a house-song at Rugby. But then, it is a fine stoical piece, combining the virtues of the stiff-upper-lip with the satisfactions of a richly romantic emotional indulgence. Of course, twentieth-century taste has frowned on the emotionalism which, generally speaking, the nineteenth century made no bones about liking. Choice of tempo is revealing here. Schumann wrote the direction 'Nicht zu schnell', meaning, I suppose, that he did not want the hard-driven relentlessness which his quaver-grouped two-in-the-bar might seem to invite. But if we play these recordings in chronological order, we see it getting schneller and schneller. It is in fact a very good illustration of the point that a direction which says 'Not-too' something-or-other is a singularly futile one; for everyone says to it, 'Why, of course not, I quite agree' and sings the song just as he wants to. The chronological process also shows the century increasingly unsentimental (on the face of it), and determined not to wallow.

Both of the pre-electrical performances here are slow. The style of one of them, by the standards which modern recordings imply, is deplorable; and that of the other—Gerhardt's—is at least dubious. Gerville-Réache sings with the voice of Saint-Saëns' Delilah, tinged by the tragic tone of a Bernhardt. Her voice is gloriously sumptuous: a full, rich, plush, port-wine contralto. Her emphatic way with the German language, particularly the final consonants, is odd, but somehow suggests a tragic emotion, perhaps old-style, silent-screen or maybe Garbo, but still, within its own terms, eloquent. I wish she had taken the high note more cleanly and that she had sustained the word 'längst' properly. On the other hand, I like her marcato treatment of 'Ich sah, mein Lieb' and the diminuendo on the first note of 'elend'. What really is rather terrible is the downward portamento to the last note. Plunket Greene warns against this (*Interpretation in Song* p. 177 f): 'Would any master of style,' he asks, '. . . dare to slur down the last "Ich grolle nicht".' Question expecting the answer 'No'. Worse still is the nonsense that the accompanying orchestra makes of the last bars. Slower and sleepier and drearier and sillier they become, and one can only think what bad music this is—which one does not when it is in competent hands.

The Gerhardt-Nikisch performance would, I should think, command more respect from modernists, yet it has more in common with Gerville-Réache than it has with either Souzay or Wächter. The mood is elegiac, the pace slow. The singer caresses and lingers when she wants to—and she wants to often. The pianist rarely makes two consecutive quavers sound the same length. All of this makes the record an extremely interesting 'document'. I do not think we can lay it down as a principle that such treatment is right or wrong. It would be wrong with a modern composer who wrote instructions for every nuance and change of tempo; wrong also for an earlier composer on whose music an alien romantic freedom was being imposed. What is demonstrably wrong, for instance, is the fact that Nikisch does not detach the three last chords, as is clearly directed; and the fact that it would not have fitted his conception of the song to have done so might tentatively suggest that his conception was not the composer's. Even so, for this tender, melancholy performance, imaginative and deeply felt, there is much to be said. All questions of value apart, the sheer difference of its assumptions from those of the present day make it a fascinating piece of musical history.

Moving on in time, we find the tempo increased and the emotion less committed. Friedrich Schorr's noble voice makes his record worth listening to, but we learn little more about the song from his performance. One sign of the times is that the pianist uses very little rubato: four quavers means four quavers here, and very dull the result is. It even involves the singer in a dully syllabic iteration of 'und sah die Schlang' die dir'. More imaginative, but still quicker, and still more remote from the old 'warm' emotions, are Panzéra and Cortot. I am fond of their *Dichterliebe*: it is always alive and interesting, however wayward some of the playing seems to be. But this song is not representative of their best, and they make a particularly ineffective job of the climax. Perhaps it is a crude thing, but I must confess to being disappointed when the singer takes the low notes, instead of the optional high ones at the end of this song. Wächter, like Fischer-Dieskau and Hermann Prey in their recordings, produces a stunner of a top A, and, elementary thrill though it may be, I still find it is one. Souzay and Panzéra both sing the alternative version and the climax is less powerful. With Souzay there still is an effect of climax for he has observed an all-important 'piano' marking a few bars back, and so has something to work a climax from. Panzéra has not bothered about this and the effect is greatly weakened. Elsewhere in the song there is plenty of drive, some real Sturm and Drang particularly in the playing—how Cortot relishes and makes good strong sense out of the left hand in the 'wie du auch strahlst' bars. But it is a determinedly unsentimental performance: they allow no rallentando for the singer's last phrases and Cortot even accelerates in the remaining bars, pounding out the insistent common chords in a manner that is the opposite of Nikisch's or of the somnambulists in Gerville-Réache's orchestra.

Cortot's pounding, however, is nothing to Alfred Brendel's, the pianist with Eberhardt Wächter. Wächter's is the angry *Dichterliebe*. He greets the lovely month of May with frowns, and even the rose, the lily, the dove and the sun seem to annoy him. Naturally, when he comes to singing that he isn't going to grumble, he still sounds fairly cross about it. He treats the quaver-sequence as a punching-bag, and when he has done, the pianist pummels his little postlude in, as parents say of their spirited children, 'a regular paddy'. Nothing sentimental here. Nor, indeed, in the performance of Gérard Souzay, generally, in this cycle, Wächter's opposite. Souzay's tone is honeyed where Wächter's is craggy; his manner is charming where Wächter's is fierce. But his tempo in *Ich grolle nicht* is the fastest of all (even quicker than Pears and Britten, who also do a no-sentimental-nonsense version); and again a new way of looking at the song is before us. This time the mood is impulsive, vigorous, serious. And there is a lot to be said for this one too. So almost any sort of mood, it seems, is possible in modern interpretations—except the moods which seemed appropriate only fifty or sixty years ago!

17. BRAHMS—*Die Mainacht*

> The records: Demuth and unnamed accompanist E 328; McCormack and piano DA 628; Ginster and unnamed accompanist DB 1877; Teyte and Rita Mackay LXT 6126; Ludwig and Gerald Moore CX 1552; Prey and Karl Engel LXT 6037.

Looking back, I realise that it has always been a pleasure to see *Die Mainacht* down on the evening's programme, and that this pleasure has had nothing at all to do with the words. One rather vaguely registers the song as being about the moon, nightingales and lonely tears; but this seems all a marginal concern when settling down to enjoy the rich harmonies, the long melodic lines, and the splendours of voice which one hopes will be forthcoming. The song is very well written for the voice; it extends the singer but gives a proportionate reward. Listening to the records, however, I find enjoyment rather less general; rather more dependent, moreover, on the mood and on other interpretative matters. Leopold Demuth's prosaic power suggests a first qualification: the ability, or the willingness, to sing softly for at least part of the time. Maggie Teyte's business-like clarity suggests another: the need to convey a feeling of 'innerness' and to use some imagination in colouring the voice. A listener who understood nothing of the words would be unlikely to form any idea of the song's mood from Demuth's performance, and would gain little more from Maggie Teyte's. Her characteristic and rather endearing downward portamento conveys tenderness, and on the last word, 'herab', a half-sob in the voice expresses, somewhat suddenly, the self-pity which is certainly a marked feature of the poem. For the rest, this sounds like a healthy English girl singing a pleasantly non-committal German song. But, of course, the song is heavily committed; to passion, for one thing, and this, at any rate, is caught in John McCormack's record. McCormack is splendidly warm and alive to the hungry emotion of the song: the play of repose against urgency, of the completeness in nature against the unfulfilled human heart. So it is a much more interesting and compelling song that he presents, beginning coolly enough then letting his tone fill out and ripen as it so wonderfully does in the second half of Wolf's *Ganymed* (or in *Kathleen Mavourneen* for that matter). Also with McCormack we have real care and art in the managing of phrases. Where both of the previous singers have not scrupled to breathe between adjective and noun in 'einsame Träne', McCormack carries the long sweeping phrase in one. At several other points he again gives pleasure by phrasing-over, paying attention to the sense of the words and to the demands of the music for a smooth, broad flow. What McCormack does not give, I think, is the indrawn romanticism of the earlier parts. The poet wanders about among the bushes looking at the moonlight and hearing the nightingales; but when he tells us this, it is not, as it were, a public statement, and it is not as objective natural description that these details are offered. We are not so much hearing as over-hearing him, and the facts about what he sees are really oblique statements about how he feels. So it is a private world that we are entering, and for this it seems we have to look to the singers of more recent times.

In Christa Ludwig's recording, for example, we feel that this is a lyrical soliloquy and not a concert-piece. Having all McCormack's beauties of phrasing, yet going rather more slowly, Ludwig shows great technical skill; this skill has also reached the point of not attracting attention to itself or distracting the performer's own attention from the feelings of the song. I do not hear it as an absolutely steady voice, though it is certainly an exceptionally good one; nor is her legato all it might be, for the habit of slightly swelling and retracting on individual notes works against the 'binding' effect of a true legato. Even so, the song itself 'binds' more convincingly in her treatment of it than in that of any of the others heard here. Her version brings us to an interpretative crux, however, for she sings it as though it were written in a minor key. Now there is some warrant for this. 'I wander sadly from bush to bush', sings the poor poet, '. . . and the tears of loneliness tremble hotly down my cheeks.' Then, if we read Lotte Lehmann on the subject (*More than Singing* p. 55), we find this advice to the singer: 'You are a lonely and miserable soul, disgusted and disillusioned by life and love. You begin to sing, under the shadow of your unhappy experience. Your voice must be dark and veiled.' Ludwig's singing answers exactly. But the curious thing is that this notion of the song is quite at odds with the music, and, when one looks at it, with at least half of the poem. The music is *not* in a minor key; the harmonies are beneficent, the melody soothes. No disgust or disillusionment is expressed by the music, and one sees that for Brahms it was not a song of despair but rather of hope. 'Wann, o lächelndes Bild, welches wie Morgenrot, durch die Seele mir strahlt, find' ich auf Erden dich?' This could have been treated as a despairing cry: a question with the implied answer 'Never'. But Brahms has used the comforting, secure music of the opening, only quickening the pulse a little by the accompanying triplets. There is restrained excitement, an expectancy that in its musical mood is hopeful. This underlines the whole song. The sense of beauty in the may night, with its turtle-doves and so forth, is quite real, not disillusioned or disgusted. A yearning sadness observes this beauty (the plaintive little motif in the right hand of the piano part at bars 15 and 16 suggests it); but the face is not, after all, downcast and despairing. The evidence is in the music and it speaks quite plainly. Therefore, in some ways, I feel that the right tone is not so much the sombre one of Ludwig's record, as its opposite, the lighter, even radiant, tone of

Ria Ginster. Ginster's performance is not perfect, but it is sensitive and interesting, and very lovely in sheer sound. I personally find a virtual perfection in the record by Fischer-Dieskau (ALP 1584), where exactly the right balance is struck between melancholy and a tender kind of happiness. But that record is not included in this set of comparisons.

A tail-piece for the performance that remains to be discussed. It is Hermann Prey's, the most recent of these records, and a very individual account indeed. It lasts six minutes (Dieskau's is about 4.20 and most of the others are slightly faster). It ranges from a whispered pianissimo to a double-forte that seems even louder in context. There is much feeling, much skill in phrasing, much beauty of tone (though I find the soft singing sometimes has a kind of yawning sound). Every care has been lavished on its preparation. Far too much, in fact. The poet wanders sadly, yes, but here we watch him in slow motion, and we feel sure that he is watching himself very carefully too. We have now eight beats to the bar instead of the customary four, and by about half-way through we find ourselves thinking of the irreverencies which the *German Requiem* provoked in G. B. Shaw. No other of our six performers has done that.

18. BRAHMS— Von ewiger Liebe

The records: Jadlowker and unnamed accompanist B 22432; Lehmann and orchestral accompaniment R 20013; Kipnis and Gerald Moore DB 2994; Ponselle and Igor Chicagov LM 1889; Fischer-Dieskau and Karl Engel ALP 1584.

Three fine performances here, and three interesting ones. Extremely beautiful in tone and style is Victoria de los Angeles. Her voice is full, warm and steady; a rich feast for which heaven make us thankful. A pure style and a generous heart almost complete the demands of the song, and los Angeles has both these. She sets the mood well, lightens a little to tell the story in the second verse, sings the boy's words at a strong forte, and then begins to work her own particular kind of magic at the change of key and the words 'spricht das Mägdelein'. She loves this maiden: we know it by the warm smile which is one of the things for which we in turn love this singer. With generous fervour at 'wer wandelt sie um' she comes to the climax of the song, giving to it all the energy and power at her command. In general, this is probably the most satisfying of the six records.

Ponselle and Kipnis are also in great form, and their records have features that are more exciting than the all-round excellence of los Angeles. Ponselle at fifty-seven sings with a voice that still compares with de los Angeles in beauty and bloom, though there are certain peculiarities of vowel-sounds (not a matter of her German pronunciation) and changes of register that are not entirely pleasing. She also takes some notes from below. Nevertheless, this is a fine performance, hauntingly beautiful in the second half of the song. The soft sound of 'spricht das Mägdelein' is perfectly poised: 'sie trennet nicht' with its grace notes is smooth as can be. More breathtaking still are the indrawn quietness of 'Eisen und Stahl' and the very gradual growth of power towards the climax. With Kipnis, still more than with Ponselle, the initial thrill of an incomparable voice practically silences criticisms. And indeed the criticism that eventually refuses to be silenced has nothing to do with his actual singing. It is simply that the balance with the piano is so bad; a fault that was probably not that of the engineers but of the singer himself. Gerald Moore, who greatly admired his singing, remarks in *Am I too Loud?* (p. 96) on Kipnis' quite unnecessary anxiety about being 'drowned': 'Grishka', he says, 'gave the impression that he would have preferred giving his recitals *a capella* if he possibly could.' In *Von ewiger Liebe* the pianist should be a full partner, and one can sense Moore's frustration in this record, as he refrains from seizing the rich fistfuls of notes that Brahms puts within his grasp. Still, the singing is magnificent. Not only is the voice great and glorious, with its power and its gentleness, its great range and sonority; but the interpretation is sensitive and intelligent, careful not to anticipate the final climax by giving too much earlier on, yet conceiving the whole song on a large scale. As Gerald Moore says, '*Von ewiger Liebe* is a big song and it must be performed in a big way' (*Singer and Accompanist* p. 24). If, by one of these wonders of the modern world, Kipnis's singing could be re-recorded with Gerald Moore rendering a new and uninhibited accompaniment, we should hear it 'performed in a big way' indeed.

Mr. Moore, speaking of this 'bigness', concludes that 'the miniaturist should fight shy of this song'. I have never thought of Fischer-Dieskau as a miniaturist, yet it is almost what he appears to be in his dealings with this. He treats it as a nineteenth century pastoral, passionate in places, but not so as to call to mind at any point the broad and bosomy end-of-recital piece that we often hear. His pace is quicker than most, his manner altogether less portentous. The story-telling is light-weight, almost throw-away, except that certain colourings of tone add subtlety and suggestiveness. This is precisely the art of the miniaturist. 'Redet so viel' and 'Lerche sie schweiget' are amongst the phrases for which this coloured tone is used; or possibly 'uncoloured' would be a better term, for it has that kind of slightly sour, unresonant quality which Fischer-Dieskau generally uses sparingly and effectively, but which sounds out of place here. More-over, by comparison with the glory of voice (Gerald Moore's phrase again) that the song so clearly wants, Dieskau's tone in this record is spare and lack-lustre. One thing he does extremely well is the impetuous verse of the young man, singing the paired quavers marcato. But the performance is still essentially in the category of the 'interesting'.

The two remaining records are also 'interesting', but on historical rather than musical grounds. Jadlowker introduces several rallentandos in the old-fashioned style from which we have (arguably) progressed. They all seem fairly pointless, especially the longest of them at 'man schmiedet sie um': very odd. But Jadlowker was a peculiar singer: a mixture of bull and china-shop, singing trills and triplets like an angel, and then making very unenchanting beefily Germanic noises when there is a call for lyrical grace. The present record is one of his few electricals, and he was over fifty when they were made: still, one would not have thought otherwise.

As for the sixth record, its claim to historical interest is one shared by many others. It is a sample of the presumed taste of the record-buying public in mid-twenties and early thirties who (so the theory seems to have run) would not think they were getting their money's worth unless 'full orchestral accompaniment' were offered. A terrible orchestra, it seems, was considered better than none, and many were the records spoiled thereby. I am sure that under the right conditions Lotte Lehmann's *Von ewiger Liebe* would rank with the best. But here she sounds interested principally in getting the thing over, and it is hard to blame her.

19. *WOLF—Anakreons Grab*

The records: McCormack and Edwin Schneider DA 1170; Janssen and Cönraad v. Bos DB 1826; Lehmann and Erno Balogh DA 1470; Schumann and George Reeves ALL 746; Fischer-Dieskau and Gerald Moore ALP 1853; Schwarzkopf and Gerald Moore 33CX 1657.

We take up McCormack's Lieder records with eagerness partly because they are few and we wish they were many; partly because we know that he 'had it in him' and that the gramophone sometimes brought it out of him; partly because it is a fascinating extension of the artist, that a man who could do so well by Handel and Mozart, Donizetti and Herbert Hughes, should also encompass Brahms and Hugo Wolf. Sad, therefore, to tell that in this song he has little to offer. In spite of one's determination not to let it matter, the very open vowel sounds do nag, grindingly on a word like 'Reben'; and the hard tone, rather unremitting and none too steady, suits this tender, reflective song not at all. One distinction he has: the long phrase 'das alle Götter mit Leben schön bepflanzt' is taken in a single breath. So it should be, though as Gerald Moore says (*Singer and Accompanist* p. 201) the 'recommendation is a tall order' (the only other singer to do it in these records is Schwarzkopf). Otherwise McCormack is not really very satisfying. He is free with note-values, defensibly perhaps as giving a natural speech-rhythm to 'Frühling, Sommer und Herbst', but no more than carelessly when he brings the second syllable of 'endlich' down on the first beat of the bar where it has no business to be. More simply and seriously: he sings too loudly. 'Anakreons Ruh' and the word 'geziert' come out at a good mezzo-forte though marked pianissimo, and the general level of volume is several degrees too high for the peacefulness and intimacy of the song to have their effect. Where also is the charm that the song needs and that McCormack possessed? Although it concerns a grave, the poem is a thing of light and beauty, tranquil and smiling in mood. Wolf's setting is similarly serene, comfortably and unequivocally (in spite on the chromaticism) in D major, the twelve-eight rocking and lulling gently. But McCormack doesn't smile; nor does Herbert Janssen.

Janssen might have been the ideal singer here, but like McCormack's his record is disappointing. It suffers from poor piano-playing: there is some untidiness of the old left-hand-before-right school, and a jumble in the chromatic 'alle Götter mit Leben' bar. The pace, too, is hardly 'sehr langsam'. Janssen himself does certain things beautifully: at 'Anakreons Ruh' his voice softens to secure the feeling of a hushed sanctity, and its velvet quality makes admirably tender the last phrase, 'Vor dem Winter hat ihn endlich der Hügel geschützt'. Yet his interpretation remains studiobound. We see a concert-singer and a big black piano, not a man singing his thoughts; certainly not an open space, a rose tree, crickets and turtledoves. With the rather plummy sound of the opening Janssen gives no feeling of air and light, and the lines of the face seem to be all downward. So we turn to Lotte Lehmann. No disappointment here in respect of smiles. Without archness, with warmth and simplicity, Lehmann tells how the seasons blessed the poet and how nature finds a blessedness around his grave. She enunciates affectionately, warms the tone at 'welch ein Grab ist hier', and hushes it, taking off the edge, at 'Es ist Anakreons Ruh'. Nevertheless, there is a kind of stillness that the song has and Lehmann has not. She sings out, with too full a voice in the opening, arriving at a very substantial forte with 'alle Götter mit Leben'. Again Gerald Moore is surely right in his note on the song when he says that the long-held 'Leben' must be no louder than mezzo-forte or the reflective mood will be lost.

But little by little we come in sight of home. Lehmann takes us a long way, Elisabeth Schumann perhaps a little further. Tenderness and serenity were not lacking in Lehmann, but Schumann could add to those characteristics a quietness and an airy quality of voice and spirit that are more evocative and appropriate here. Her limitation is that the quietness is preserved with very little variety: the tone hardly changes, and so, though the basic rightness remains, a good many local points are lost. But when a right general feeling is combined with a fineness of individual insights, then we are home and should ask no more this side of paradise—except a good voice, a healthy tone and a sound technique, perhaps. Fischer-Dieskau has all these. Taking the song a little more slowly than the others, yet never over-solemnising or putting it to sleep, he achieves by far the greatest concentration and unbroken beauty of all our singers. A warm, gentle, yet well-defined tone pleases the ear; a serene, yet faintly elegiac mood set at the opening engages the feelings. As the harmonies stir and darken at 'Welch ein Grab ist hier', so the voice senses a mystery; as the harmonies come to rest at 'Anakreons Ruh', so the singer relaxes, lingers a little and allows a perfect stillness to settle. For the first time in these comparisons we hear the special effect Wolf had in mind when he wrote pianissimo for the second syllable of 'geziert'. We also find in Fischer-Dieskau a sign of musical grace that may be common enough in singers yet has not been generally apparent in their recordings: he looks at the accompaniments. Wolf was very sparing of marks written into the voice part, but liberal with his directions to the pianist. More often than not these are relevant to the singer as well. Thus, 'sehr zart', written into the piano part at the words 'wo das Turtelchen lockt', is also a suggestion to the singer. Fischer-Dieskau notes it gratefully, and makes magic out of it. Out of the song itself, he and his accompanist have made something Wordsworthian. In the poem, a beneficence ranges between man, God and nature; a 'blessed mood' and even 'the burthen of the mystery' are captured in what is virtually a perfect collaboration between poet, composer and performers. One can go no further than this, and the remaining record shows what happens when a supremely imaginative artist tries to do so: to give something beyond what the music requires. A great admirer of Elisabeth Schwarzkopf, I think the criticism that she lacks simplicity and sings with too much art is sometimes true. *Anakreons Grab* is given here with every care, every subtlety of inflection, fine phrasing, a rapt, indrawn expression, as though breathing the song purely from the mind. But, after all, it won't do. The 'breathing' affects the tone, which is often breathy: intentionally so, but that isn't necessarily a justification. At several points the tone is drained of all colour whatsoever; it becomes like a recorder, or a child's voice, or a kind of spirit-voice. 'I swear I use no art at all,' the highly sophisticated simplicity seems to be saying; but we are not deceived and find ourselves listening far more to the singer than to the song. The art is marvellous: but that does not necessarily justify it either, for the song does not need so much. I have heard it offered as a definition of love (in a sermon, I may say) that it is 'the accurate assessment and fulfilment of another's needs'. Mutatis mutandis, this is true of the interpreter in music. Fischer-Dieskau is the true lover here. Too much is a more interesting form of untruth than too little, but it is one nevertheless.

At so much high-seriousness, however, the real Anacreon would probably turn in his celebrated grave. He was a bibulous old man who met his death—a likely story, but so the books say—choked by a grape-stone.

20. *WOLF—Nun wandre, Maria (Spanisches Liederbuch 3)*

The records: Marchesi and Agnes Balford from JG 41; Gerhardt and Cönraad von Bos DB 1617 on COLH 142; Erb and Bruno Seidler-Winkler EG 3498; Schumann and George Reeves ALL 746; Raphael and Gerald Moore C 3591; Fischer-Dieskau and Gerald Moore ALP 1750.

A song for age, I think. All but one of the singers here had passed fifty when their recordings were made, and in that one, great singer as he is, some quality, hard to define yet readily sensed, is lacking. It is a song of the rarest tenderness: of the kind that involves both senses of the word. We express tenderness when we gently support and give help to a person for whom we have affection; and we say that an injured place is tender when it is sore and any exercise of it is painful. So Joseph comforts Mary, feeling (the closely-bound thirds of the piano's right hand express it) that sympathy and that desire to take the pain upon himself which makes his situation and Wolf's song so moving. A young voice in full bloom is if anything a disadvantage here, and half-a-century's experience is likely to be a great help.

For once, then, Fischer-Dieskau presents a starting and not a finishing point in these comparisons. His is certainly the most pleasant record: the most readily listenable. It is beautifully sung, and, as always, certain aspects of the song suddenly become more vivid than ever before. Here it is in the plangent, almost desperate tones of 'kann deine Schmerzen, ach, kaum verwinden'. These and the two preceding phrases are the bars where the harmonies, still comfortable in their undisturbed thirds, are most contorted and painful; and the tenderness is that of the blistered heel, the tired body and pitiful spirit. This is the passage which gives the song its shape. It is like a picture in which a long road winds wearyingly through flat country, becomes a track over a harsh, craggy landscape, and then continues its desolate way till out of sight. This picturing exists in Wolf's music, but it is Fischer-Dieskau among the performers who in the proper sense of the word interprets to us. He does it by the difference of tone, the frankness of sorrow, which elsewhere is restrained. This and many other fine things distinguish his performance. Yet I am still left at the end of it feeling that something in the spirit of the song has not been caught; and, as I say, the something tends to elude definition.

The elusive quality does seem to be present in the other recordings, however. With Elisabeth Schumann, it is a tenderness felt in her enunciation and in the infinitely gentle, warm tone of her voice. With Gerhardt, it takes a very different form but is there none the less. There is a turbulence and impulsiveness in this performance, but also a strong intentness of anxiety and affection. With Marchesi, there is the hauntingly peculiar sound of her still-beautiful seventy-five year old voice; also an eloquent compassion making itself felt through the old-fashioned portamenti at 'Wohl seh'ich, Herrin' and the following bars—not just a local access of feeling, this, but something which pervades the whole performance. With Mark Raphael, there is perhaps a stranger beauty still: for his voice is dry and sere, only just taking the strain at the high 'schon kräh'n die Hähne' bars, and devoid of any conventional beauty of sound at all. Yet the effect is one of beauty: it comes, I suppose, of the spirit, by way of a devoted fidelity to the score. With Karl Erb, there is this 'inner' beauty of Mark Raphael's together with a silvery, other-worldly quality of voice that seems to me to achieve something like perfect expression in this song.

Perhaps its most touching moment comes at the words 'Wär erst bestanden dein Stündlein, Marie'; something of the essence of all Joseph's affections and anxieties is felt in these bars, and it is Erb who seems to be most at the heart of the song here.

There are, of course, faults in all these records. Not bad ones: a note shortened, a marking not observed, an unsteadiness here and a dryness there. All these singers were, as we say, 'getting on'. When Peter Pears comes to sing it (he too is beginning to get on), his record may sound less conventionally beautiful than any of these and it may be the best. In the meantime it is pleasant to find a song in which all six artists perform worthily. Pleasant too to think that, in it, singers have something to keep in reserve till the days of advanced maturity and the onset of old age.

Select Bibliography

THE essential references in this book are to the records themselves, all of which were issued with matrix and catalogue numbers. Where there is a likely query about which recording of an artist's performance has been used, then it is usually identified in the text; and of course the great majority of the records are unobtainable in their original form (except from second-hand dealers), while transfers and repressings are constantly arriving in the catalogue and disappearing again. So it seems best to direct the reader's attention to the most helpful sources of information existing in specialist publications.

For readers who want to know what is currently available in Great Britain there is *The Gramophone* Classical Record Catalogue issued quarterly and available from any dealer. In all the principal record-buying countries there are magazines which keep the reader up to date with reviews and new issues; of these *The Gramophone* was the first and remains a model of its kind.

The most comprehensive catalogue of records issued up to and just beyond mid-century is *The World's Encyclopedia of Recorded Music* (Clough and Cuming), last published, with its third supplement, in 1957. For the earliest period of recording the main authority is Robert Bauer's *Historical Records 1898–1908/9*, first published in 1947, re-printed 1970.

Important parts of the '78' catalogues are made available in a series called *Voices of the Past* published in Great Britain by the Oakwood Press. Details are as follows:

Vol. 1. The English Catalogue (J. R. Bennett)
Vol. 2. The Italian Catalogue, with supplement
Vol. 3. Dischi Fonotipia, with supplement & addenda
Vol. 4. HMV DB series (Bennett and Hughes)
Vol. 5. HMV D & E series (Michael Smith)
Vol. 6. HMV DA series, plus DJ-DQ etc. (Bennett & Hughes)
Vol. 7. The 1898–1925 German Catalogue
Vol. 8. Columbia English Celebrity Issues
Vol. 9. HMV French Catalogue 1899–1925

Vertical Cut Cylinders and Discs (Girard and Barnes) covers another part of
the field. The British Institute of Recorded Sound issues a monthly
magazine, *Recorded Sound*, which also includes much useful catalogue
material and critical discussion.

Most important for readers interested in old records is *The Record
Collector*, editor James Dennis, 17, St. Nicholas St., Ipswich. Now in its
twentieth volume, the magazine, started in 1947, has provided invaluable
material in its series of discographies. The magazine also lists currently
available books on singers and records.

For the records themselves readers will find advertisements by second-
hand dealers in *The Gramophone* or in *The Record Collector*.

Among articles on singers and records published in other places, two
very useful series have been run in the *Opera* magazine: one called *Opera on
the Gramophone*, which takes a single opera and discusses the recordings
(from all periods), and *A Gallery of Great Singers* by Desmond Shawe-Taylor.

Books which deal exclusively with this as their subject are very few.
Despite certain inaccuracies, *Le Grande Voci* (Celletti) published in 1964 is
probably the most important, containing a biographical note on many of
the most celebrated opera singers, a short critical discussion and a list of
their operatic records. *The Golden Age Recorded* by P. G. Hurst discusses the
recordings of many of the early singers and also lists some of their records.

A survey of western singing from the seventeenth century onwards is
provided by Henry Pleasants' book called *The Great Singers* (London, 1967),
but this is not concerned with records. Readers of the present book will
find a most useful, perhaps essential, complementary work in the encyclopedia of singers on records compiled by Kutsch and Riemens, first
published in German under the title *Unvergangliche Stimmen* and now (1972)
translated into English as the *Concise Biographical Dictionary of Singers*.
Another valuable reference book is the *Concise Oxford Dictionary of Opera*
(Rosenthal and Warrack), London, 1964.

Many singers have written their memoirs. Kutsch and Riemens give
details, and there is a handy bibliography in *The Singing Voice* by Robert
Rushmore (London, 1971).

The one individual singer to have had books published about his
recordings is Caruso: *Caruso on Records* by Aida Favia-Artsay includes also
texts of the songs and arias, and further discussion is included in *Enrico
Caruso. The Recorded Legacy* (Freestone & Drummond, 1960).

On the gramophone itself, the prime authority is *The Fabulous Phonograph*,
Roland Gelatt, New York, 1954.

Composers Index

SONGS

General Index

Figures in brackets are the page numbers of photographs; figures in bold type indicate the fullest discussion of a singer.

$25.00

Many years before the gramophone
could do justice to an orchestra, a
string quartet, or even a solo instrument, it was able to reproduce with
comparative fidelity the sound of the
human voice. Patti in old age, Melba
in her prime, Caruso and Chaliapin at
the start of their international careers:
these singers and many more were recorded in the earliest years of the century, and the records, however primitive they may be, are a part of musical
history. What do these records tell us,
and how do the performances we hear
on them compare with those of later
times and of our own day? Is it true
that here was a 'golden age of singing',
or does a critical examination explode
this theory as a myth?

John Steane charts a way through the
great mass of singing on record, and
follows the fortunes of 'the grand tradition' over the first seventy years of
the gramophone's history. The 'tradition' involves song, including choral
singing, as well as opera. Mr. Steane
is concerned above all with the recognition and preservation of a tradition:
the discriminating enjoyment of singing on record.

A selection of photographs accompany
the text, some of which are reproduced
here for the first time.